Other Titles by LtCol Jon T. Hoffman, USMCR

Once a Legend: "Red Mike" Edson of the Marine Raiders

CHESTY

CHESTY

The Story of Lieutenant General Lewis B. Puller, USMC

LtCol Jon T. Hoffman, USMCR

Random House
New York

Library of Congress Cataloging-in-Publication Data

Hoffman, Jon T.
    Chesty: the story of Lieutenant General Lewis B. Puller, USMC / Jon T. Hoffman.—1st ed.
        p. cm.
    Includes bibliographical references and index.
    ISBN 0-679-44732-6
        1. Puller, Chesty, 1898–1971.   2. United States Marine Corps—Officers—Biography.
    3. Generals—United States—Biography.   I. Title.

    VE25.P85 H64 2001
    359.9′6′092—dc21
    [B]   00-068352

Random House website address: www.atrandom.com

Printed in the United States of America on acid-free paper

9 8 7 6 5 4 3 2

First Edition

Book Design by Mercedes Everett

To my parents, Thomas and Doris Hoffman

Preface

Lieutenant General Lewis Burwell "Chesty" Puller requires no introduction to an audience of Marines. Army partisans may quibble whether the greatest soldier was George Washington, Ulysses Grant, Robert E. Lee, Stonewall Jackson, John Pershing, Douglas MacArthur, George Marshall, George Patton, Audie Murphy, or any of a host of other possible candidates. Navy and Air Force enthusiasts would face the same dilemma in identifying a preeminent leader. But there is absolutely no doubt that Puller is *the* mythological hero of the Corps—the very icon of the entire institution. His larger-than-life image is etched indelibly in every Marine almost from the first day at boot camp or officer candidate school. His stern, leathery, square-jawed visage stares down from the bulkhead in every building throughout the Corps. Countless times every day his name is invoked, like a magical incantation, by officers and noncommissioned officers (NCOs) in every conceivable setting and for every purpose under the sun. His pithy words, daring deeds, and colorful mannerisms are ingrained into the culture of the organization.

I thus thought more than twice when I approached the idea of a biography of Chesty. There was, first and foremost, the daunting challenge of trying objectively to examine the deeds of an institutional idol. Anything less than hero worship might be viewed as heresy by some Leathernecks, while others might sneer at anything short of a revisionist reappraisal full of warts as a mere whitewash.

A second deterrent was the paltry prospect of turning up new and revealing sources of information on a man who once boasted that his pockets constituted his entire filing system. In a career that spanned nearly four decades, Puller had a well-deserved reputation for writing little and saving even less. Documentation of his personal life, especially for his early years, was likely to be even more elusive a quarry.

Finally, and perhaps most compelling, there already was strong competition in the form of Burke Davis's lively and widely read account of Puller published in 1962. *Marine!* is and always will remain a classic of Leatherneck literature.

The better part of valor in such a case would be to move on to an easier subject. A number of factors outweighed those considerations, though, and persuaded me that Chesty would make an excellent subject for a new biography. A major reason was the nature of Davis's existing work. In 1961, official records of the Korean War were classified and the author did not have access to those important documents. Due to time constraints, he made little use of similar records for earlier wars and campaigns. He also created the biography as a joint venture with his subject, under a contract that gave Puller the right to control the content. Davis realized the potential shortcomings of his work and took pains to point them out in a special author's note: "This book is as much a memoir as a biography. . . . General Puller's prodigious memory is often relied upon, and in matters large and small his point of view is taken; controversial points are not examined from every side, and thus this does not pretend to be an objective history of the many campaigns in which he fought."[1]

Marine! remains a valuable contribution to military history because it recorded for posterity how Puller felt about things in 1960. Davis also successfully captured a partial image of the man. Due to his book, everyone knows that Chesty was the epitome of the old Corps— hard as the frontal armor of a tank, tenacious as a bulldog, courageous to a fault, and scornful of anyone or anything that did not wear the eagle, globe, and anchor insignia. The biography portrayed the loving family man, too. Puller was all that, but he was a much more complex character than he was willing to reveal to Davis or the public.

Part of the cloak shrouding Chesty's life stemmed from the fact that he was a living legend long before he retired from the Corps. Puller's exploits and idiosyncrasies were a staple of barracks and barroom conversations. Given the Marine penchant for sea stories—small threads of fact woven into tall tales—it is no surprise that myth soon mixed with reality. The general, raised on the romanticized recollections of Confederate veterans, was himself an inveterate storyteller. Colonel Robert D. Heinl, the premier historian of the Old Corps and a former subordinate of Puller, believed that Chesty was "one of the greatest raconteurs that ever wore the Globe and Anchor." There is evidence that Puller, like his distant cousin Patton, also felt compelled to live up to a public persona. One officer who served under the Marine general recalled his superior's advice that it was wise to "adopt the personality that your cohorts, especially those junior to you, seem to expect of you." Thus Chesty was inclined by his nature and beliefs to live his public life, and remember it as well, in a manner that fit everyone's preconceived notions of the Puller legend. As a result, myth has enshrouded and encrusted the facts, which are remarkable enough on their own merits.[2]

Another difficulty in ferreting out the real Puller stems from his occasional changes in attitude during the course of more than thirty-seven years as a Marine. The modifications were significant, but none were reflected in the interviews he gave to Davis in 1961. Those shifting opinions show a leader who adjusted and adapted much more than anyone has given him credit for doing.

In a career that spanned two world wars, two small wars, and an incongruously titled police action, Puller also found himself at the heart of a number of controversial events in U.S. military history. With the passage of time, historians and memoirists writing about some of these campaigns increasingly have criticized Chesty's performance. He has drawn particularly scathing condemnation for Peleliu. The gap between the larger-than-life myth and the searing revisionism is a yawning chasm.

Was Puller the compassionate leader who put his men first, or was he a cold-blooded commander who measured a unit's effectiveness in direct proportion to the length of its casualty list? Did he fail in some way at Peleliu and needlessly destroy his regiment, or was he the scapegoat for the mistakes of others? Was he a great troop leader, but unable to grasp the importance of good staff work? Was he a superb small unit tactician who rose above his level of competence at higher command? Did he really base his plans on the simple proposition that the shortest distance between two points was a straight line? Which of these portraits is accurate? Or, as is often the case, does the truth lie somewhere in between?

The list of such questions is endless precisely because there has been no thorough, objective study of Puller's life and career. Nearly everything written about him has been based either on *Marine!* or on an interview with Chesty taped in 1961. Subsequent commentaries consequently have suffered from the same shortcomings that Davis himself came to lament about his own work. Puller's story thus cried out for a fresh, balanced, detailed treatment.

Chesty left behind only a small collection of personal papers, but I was able to turn up a wide array of valuable sources, many of them not available in the early 1960s. Just a few years after Burke Davis's book appeared in print, the Marine Corps History and Museums Division initiated its oral history program, which recorded the recollections of Leatherneck leaders, often as not Puller contemporaries or subordinates. I was able to supplement the memories of these senior officers with my own interviews of some of the thousands of enlisted men and junior officers who served with the general. These sources presented a wider viewpoint than the narrow circle of Puller's friends and admirers who participated in the making of *Marine!* The statements of all three groups must be used gingerly given the understandable vagaries of memory years after the fact, but, mixed with other evidence, they provided reliable clues and occasional answers. The History and Museums Division also has amassed an extensive collection of personal papers, which include many documents created at the time events occurred. The National Archives and the service history offices possess all the official records of campaigns, as well as much of the paperwork typically associated with the bureaucratic workings of large organizations. A thorough combing of these voluminous holdings produced a substantial quantity of material written by or about Chesty, to include a complete collection of his Nicaraguan patrol reports. The archives of other institutions, such as the Virginia Military Institute, yielded additional details. Finally, Puller's personnel and medical records, plus his own small collection of personal papers, provided more than just a glimpse into his life.

I employed all these sources in an attempt to re-create the real Chesty Puller, insofar as that is possible. Brigadier General Edwin H. Simmons, emeritus head of the Marine history program, once pithily observed: "Truth stalks naked across the battlefield at midnight, but with the coming of dawn, assumes the uniform of a field marshal." The portrait of Puller that follows probably does not capture him entirely in the flesh—no one could claim to know that much about another person or about events several decades in the past. But it is an honest attempt to strip away many of the layers that have long encumbered the reality of Chesty. In some cases, it provides surprising support for the general against his critics. In other instances, it punctures long-cherished myths. There are those who believe such a reexamination of a military icon does a disservice to the institution because it removes some of the luster from the burnished image held up as an example to be emulated. There is a definite and vital benefit in recalling the shining moments when an organization and its members were at their best. But it is equally important to highlight those occasions when things went wrong, for failure, more often than not, is the breeding ground for lessons that can improve future performance.[3]

Puller certainly deserves to be one of the great historical figures of the Corps, but if current and future warriors and students of warfare are to be nurtured on his legend, it should come as close as possible to the pandemonium, carnage, and unbridled emotion of midnight, rather than the polished bronze statue of dawn.[4]

Acknowledgments

This project benefited from the assistance of many people. General Puller's daughters—Virginia Dabney and Martha Downs—gave me unfettered access to his personal papers, provided recollections of their father, and pointed me toward others who knew him. They and their husbands, Col William H. Dabney and BGen Michael P. Downs, also read and critiqued the draft manuscript.

The invaluable collections of the Marine Corps Historical Center were made available by the expert staff: the chief historian, Chuck Melson; historians Rich Smith and Dave Crist; reference historians Danny Crawford, Bob Aquilina, Anne Ferrante, Lena Kaljot, and Sheila Gramblin; archivists Fred Graboske, Judy Petsch, and Christine Laba; and librarian Evy Englander. Ben Frank, the former chief historian, Dick Long, the former oral historian, and Amy Cantin, a former archivist, pointed me toward many sources before their retirements. All the Marines and civilians working in the supporting elements of the center keep the entire show running: LtCol Leon Craig, Maj John Vanden Berghe, 1stLt Katrina Patillo, GySgt Michael Cousins, Sgt Joslyn Benjamin, Sgt Gordan Gipson, Cpl Cassius Cardio, Cpl Ryan Ohnstad, LCpl Adrian Baldwin, LCpl Joe Echenique, LCpl Lukiya Walker, Jack Dyer, Jim Fairfax, Gordon Heim, Steve Hill, Cathy Kerns, Wanda Renfrow, Kris Reed, and Bob Struder. Dr. Tim Nenninger of the National Archives performed his usual sterling service in unearthing boxes of records that otherwise seemed buried forever. Richard Boylan worked similar miracles at the Records Center in Suitland. Kerry Strong and Mike Miller at the Marine Corps Research Center provided ready access to their archives. Robert K. Krick and his son Robert E. L. Krick, both with the National Park Service, went far beyond the call of duty in digging out important information on Puller's nineteenth-century ancestors. Diane Jacob turned up many useful documents in the archives of the Virginia Military Institute. Barry Thoerig helped unveil information in the Marine Corps Military Awards Branch. William Harrison, Diane Harper, and Michelle Carr of the Manpower Division made available personnel and medical records. Joe Sunseri and Sally Wooten provided important material on Mrs. Puller's time as a student at Saint Mary's College.

BGen Edwin H. Simmons, Dr. Allan R. Millett, Col Joe Alexander, and Mr. Aubrey Buser each read the entire manuscript and provided their valuable thoughts on ways to improve it. Many others, including a large number of retired Marines, either read and critiqued one or more chapters or otherwise furnished key assistance: Darrell B. Albers, Col John Apergis, Gen Robert H. Barrow, John R. Beck, Lt Edward G. Bourne, USNR(Ret), LtGen Alpha L. Bowser, Harry Brandt, W. H. Brockinton, Dave Brooks, Homer W. Buck, Maj Jack Buck, Col Richard D. Camp, Jr., the Hon. R. Lawrence Coughlin, Gen Raymond G. Davis, Col John S. Day, Maj Mayhlon L. Degernes, Jr., LTC Carlo D'Este, USA(Ret), SgtMaj W. X. Durkee, Capt William Eisenhower, Robert M. Evans, Maj Ashley W. Fisher, Col Robert A. Foyle, Richard B. Frank, Cokey H. Godfrey, Col John Greenwood, Col Jack Hawkins, BGen F. P. Henderson, Judy Hession, Kevin Hession, Col J. Wright Horton, Col Sanford B. Hunt, Stanley C. Jersey, Col Bernard T. Kelly, LtCol William F. Koehnlein, BGen James F. Lawrence, George MacGillivray, MajGen Marc A. Moore, Rev. Paul Moore, Jr., MSgt Charles H. Owens, Col Preston S. Parish, William T. Pierce, MajGen Jonas M. Platt, Maj Everett P. Pope, Dr. Mark Reardon, Rev. James M. Rogers, J. Nicholas Russo, MSgt Everett H. Shults, Col Carl L. Sitter, James Smith, LtCol Gary Solis, Dr. W. A. Stelck, Carl Stevenson, Matthew Stevenson, Col Nikolai S. Stevenson, LtCol Victor H. Streit, Col Gerald C. Thomas, Jr., Capt John Todd, Ralph Tulloch, Gen Merrill B. Twining, Capt R. Bruce Watkins, Col Waite W. Worden, and Col Robert P. Wray.

A large number of Marine veterans or others who knew General Puller took the time to write letters or give interviews describing their memories of him or their service with him. They are too numerous to mention here, but most of them appear in the source notes. Without their input, this biography would not be as complete or personal.

Bob Loomis of Random House faithfully stuck by the project as it dragged out over the years. His experienced editorial eye also helped guide the text to its final form.

My wife, Mary Craddock Hoffman, endured many lost evenings, weekends, and vacations and learned more than she ever wanted to know about General Puller. She also placed her own imprint on the book with her well-designed maps.

Contents

List of Maps

CHESTY

1

"Making a Man and a Soldier"

Genesis of a Marine

1898–1919

The 231 handpicked enlisted men marched into the gymnasium at the Marine Corps base in Quantico, Virginia, for their last muster as a unit. It was June 16, 1919, graduation day for the 3d Officers' Training Camp (OTC). After five months of strenuous effort, each man had earned a commission as a second lieutenant in the Marine Corps Reserve. The post band opened the ceremonies with a medley of martial tunes capped by John Philip Sousa's march "Semper Fidelis." The music turned out to be the most stirring portion of the program, which otherwise consisted of short speeches and the presentation of commissions. A reporter noted that the "striking feature of the proceedings" was their solemnity and simplicity in comparison with graduations at West Point and Annapolis. Although the writer ascribed this difference to "that precision and lack of fuss so characteristic of the doings of Marines," in truth there was little to celebrate at the moment. Seven months earlier there had been rejoicing when an armistice ended the "war to end all wars." Now the United States was rapidly demobilizing its forces. The Commandant of the Marine Corps, Major General George Barnett, pointedly noted in his speech that this placed the class "in a peculiar position." This commissioning ceremony would not launch the lieutenants on a grand and glorious new career; rather, for most of them it marked the end of their service as Marines.

With the exception of a few prewar NCOs, the vast majority of the men had joined the Corps with patriotic fervor to fight the Germans. Few of these wartime volunteers had seen action and they now had to return to civilian pursuits with the exhortations of the speakers as their only reward. Barnett told them: "Whatever after this you do in life your service will have left its traces in your hearts . . . once a Marine, always a Marine." Major General Littleton W. T. Waller echoed that theme: "You have come in and absorbed our traditions and beliefs and I tell you you can't go wrong if you live up to their principles."[1]

One of those men faced with an imminent return to the civilian world was Lewis Burwell Puller, a Marine private with less than a year in the Corps. At five feet, eight inches and 144 pounds, he was not a physically impressive figure, except for his pronounced barrel chest, serious square-blocked face, and outthrust jaw. His voice was his most distinctive trademark. One listener described it as a "Virginia drawl combined with an individual Brooklynese." Young Puller spoke slowly, with more than a touch of Southern accent, underpinning his own unique pronunciations with a deep-throated, gravelly intonation. He was not normally loud, but when the situation warranted it, he could "bark like a howitzer" or "shout commands with all the vigor and carrying power of an angry bull." He did not possess any special athletic ability or a superior intellect. His final standing in OTC, just below the middle of his class, did not indicate any outstanding military aptitude. He might have accepted his fate and gone quietly into the military obscurity that awaited all of his companions, but his reaction demonstrated what may have been his greatest strength. He had his mind set on a military career and would persevere with relentless resolution in pursuit of his dream. He would not only find a way to remain in the Corps, but would excel as a combat leader. Decades later, he would be the most legendary Marine of all and his deeds and words would do much to establish the traditions, beliefs, and principles that continue to mold succeeding generations of Marines.[2]

☆   ☆   ☆

Lewis Puller was the product of a distinguished line of Virginia gentry on his maternal side. His mother could trace her roots back to Lewis Burwell, who had come over from England in the mid-1600s as a leader in a company of military settlers. Four generations later, another Lewis Burwell fought as a colonel in command of Virginia militia during the

American Revolution, owned a 3,400-acre plantation, and served in the state House of Delegates. His daughter, Alice Grymes Burwell, married William Clayton Williams, a lawyer and also a delegate in the Virginia legislature. Their son, Lewis Burwell Williams, became an attorney and followed in the political footsteps of his father and grandfather. His daughter, Mary Blair Williams, gave birth to Martha Richardson Leigh, Lewis Puller's mother.[3]

Lewis Puller's distant paternal ancestors apparently were not so illustrious. Samuel and Mary W. Puller were the first to leave a permanent record, but little survives about them beyond the fact that they had five children and lived in Gloucester County, Virginia. This small district occupied part of the peninsula formed by the Rappahannock and York rivers, in the eastern region of the state known as the Tidewater. Mary gave birth in 1833 to John William, her second child and first boy. Apparently Samuel died before 1850. By that time, seventeen-year-old John already was working as a blacksmith to help the family. At the age of twenty-two, now a farmer, he married Emily Simcoe. Their first child, born in 1858, was Matthew Miller, Lewis Puller's father.

John Puller clearly had ambition and ability. He aspired to something more than manual labor and soon opened a hotel with his younger brother Sam. His neighbors obviously put some faith in his potential. In 1859 they elected him to a captaincy in the local militia, a cavalry unit known as the Gloucester Light Dragoons. The honor was all the more notable given that he was only twenty-six, far younger than the norm for such a position of responsibility in those years. Sam joined him in this endeavor, too, enlisting as a private. Outsiders with a financial background were not so certain of the capabilities of the two brothers. A credit-rating bureau placed a hesitant appraisal in its books in the fall of 1860: "Shd [should] not sell them largely on cr. [credit] not much means & quite extravagant notions. May be good. Wd. [would] advise caution." January 1861 brought a harsher assessment: "Fast men, advise cash sales."[4]

If "fast" could be construed as aggressive or freewheeling, John W. Puller appears to have fit that description, though he had no immediate opportunity to demonstrate it. In May 1861, less than a month after the first shots of the Civil War were fired at Fort Sumter, the seventy-eight men of his militia unit reelected him as their captain. The cavalrymen remained close to home for the next ten months, however, outposting the entrance to the York River at Gloucester Point. In March 1862, during the Peninsula Campaign, they saw their first fighting. A few weeks later, they merged into the newly formed 5th Virginia Cavalry Regiment. Thereafter, action was plentiful. The Tidewater horsemen participated in the Seven Days' Battles in June, the cavalry raid on Catlett's Station and the Second Battle of Manassas in August, the Battle of Sharpsburg in September, Major General J.E.B. Stuart's ride through Pennsylvania and Maryland in October, and clashes in the Shenandoah Valley in early November. In the last action, Sam Puller was captured by the Yankees, but was exchanged for Union prisoners days later.[5]

The regiment was winning a high reputation in the Army of Northern Virginia. Following another raid in late December, Major General Fitzhugh Lee, the brigade commander, praised the 5th's attack across a difficult river ford as "one of the most admirable performances of cavalry I have ever witnessed." Jeb Stuart, commander of the cavalry division, had cried out during a tight spot in one battle: "Go bring the Fifth here, I know that will charge, that never goes back on me." Although John Puller was never mentioned in dispatches for bravery, he had performed well enough to rise to the rank of major in December 1862. He also had developed a stoic attitude toward the increasingly bloody conflict. He frequently told his men: "There was but one way [out of the war] and that was to be killed out."[6]

In November, a Tidewater sheriff had asked Stuart to allow the local horsemen to come home for the winter: "The citizens of Gloucester would be delighted to have our much-beloved Capt. Puller & his men with us." With a Union army in northern Virginia and threatening Richmond, that was not possible. Lee's brigade bivouacked in the field, with the mission of guarding the left flank of the Confederate position along the Rappahannock River. It was a hard winter, made more so by the lack of good shelter and provisions. One soldier wrote home: "The horses are starving, they get only a little hay every other day and we don't get much ourselves we get a quarter pound of bacon a day." Morale also was hurt by a feud between the regiment's commanding and executive officers, with each lodging formal charges against the other.[7]

On the morning of March 17, 1863, word came that strong Union forces had crossed the river at Kelly's Ford, ten miles to the east. The rebel brigade had just eight hundred men available that day, but they saddled up and trotted out to meet the enemy. Puller took on the challenge with a light heart. One of his men recalled the major's words as the company formed up: "Boys, be prepared to bite the dust today." A fellow officer remembered Puller's jovial shout as he passed by: "Harry, leave me your haversack if you get killed!" Later that day, the 5th tried to outflank the main Union cavalry force, but ran into two mounted brigades and simultaneously came under fire from sharpshooters posted along a stone fence. The twin threats and the heavy fire created confusion in the Southern ranks. The regimental commander called for Puller to assist in rallying the men, only to hear the reply: "Colonel, I'm killed." A musket ball had passed through John's chest; moments later, he fell out of his saddle and died.[8]

Before the day was over, the outnumbered Confederates had driven the Yankees back across the river. A few days later, Fitzhugh Lee heaped plaudits upon his men and pointed to a lesson in the outcome: "You have repeatedly charged an enemy sheltered by stone fences and impassable ditches, in the face of his artillery and volleys from thousands of his carbines. . . . Rebel cavalry have been taught that a determined rush upon the foe is the part of sound policy as it is the part of true courage." Stuart commended "the determined bravery of [Lee's] men for this signal victory, which, when the odds are considered, was one of the most brilliant achievements of the war." The cost had not been cheap. Among the 133 Southern casualties was Major John Pelham, an exceptional young officer who already had thrilled the Confederacy with the audacious exploits of his horse artillery. Puller's death was not lost in the outpouring of grief for Pelham. Fitzhugh Lee praised the Gloucester leader as a "gallant and highly efficient officer." Stuart mentioned "the brave Puller" in his dispatch on the battle. An officer in another regiment lamented his passing: "Courteous, good, and brave. He was a great loss to us."[9]

Sam Puller escorted John's body back to Gloucester County in the midst of a snowstorm. A Confederate chaplain on leave conducted the funeral service at the Puller house, where he was surprised by the "very large collection of citizens and soldiers." He preached from the Second Book of Samuel: "How are the valiant fallen in battle? Jonathan slain in the high places? I grieve for thee, my brother Jonathan." Emily Puller, left with four-year-old Matthew and his two-year-old brother, "was very much distressed."[10]

Lewis Puller's maternal ancestors also fought with distinction in the war. The brothers of Mary Blair Williams were among those who rushed to the colors. Lewis B. Williams, Jr., a lawyer and VMI professor, quickly earned the rank of colonel and command of the 1st Virginia Infantry Regiment. He was severely wounded while leading a charge during the Peninsula Campaign, but recovered and rejoined the Army of Northern Virginia for the 1863 invasion of Pennsylvania. At that time, he and several fellow officers were disgraced following their court-martial for imbibing too much alcohol during the army's march through Richmond. Restored to his command on the eve of Gettysburg, Williams led it in the glorious and ghastly frontal attack that went down in history as Pickett's Charge. Of the 155 men in the 1st Virginia, 120 were killed or wounded, including their colonel. One of the few survivors recalled that "foolishly and insanely he rode cooly and deliberately in front of the regiment, mounted on his horse." Williams was shot through the spine and spent several days in agony before finally succumbing. Colonel Waller Tazewell Patton, a distant relative and fellow regimental commander in Pickett's division, was mortally wounded in the same desperate gamble. Two other Williams brothers fought for the South in the three-day battle. A fourth, Robert, probably was also present, but on the opposite side of the lines. A graduate of the Military Academy at West Point, he had stayed with the North when war broke out. He served at the time of Gettysburg as a major in the staff corps.[11]

☆   ☆   ☆

The Civil War left the Puller family with a heroic legacy and little else. According to family lore, Union forces subsequently burned Emily Puller's home to the ground on the pretext that John's spurs and sword hanging on the wall constituted possession of military equipment. It was winter and the widow and two youngsters walked ten miles in blowing sleet to Gloucester Courthouse to find shelter. She died soon after of pneumonia. Another Confederate officer took in the orphans and raised them for a time. Sam Puller survived the war and tried to establish himself as a merchant, but never prospered and led a bachelor's life in a hotel. A sister, Sara, eked out an existence as a live-in house-keeper. These were difficult times, especially in a "burnt county" such as Gloucester, which had suffered considerable physical destruction. John's proud tradition at least lived on; the local Confederate soldiers named their veterans organization after him.[12]

When Matthew M. Puller grew up and struck out on his own, he settled in the Tidewater village of West Point. He had a taste for business like his father and uncle before him, and became a modestly successful salesman for a wholesale grocer. He was a dapper dresser, habitually sporting long, double-breasted frock coats, custom shoes, and a cane. Despite his minimal education and modest upbringing, he exhibited a refined, gentlemanly air. He married Martha Richardson Leigh, known as Pattie to family and friends. Lewis Burwell Puller, their third child, was born June 26, 1898. He and his two older sisters, Emily and Pattie, were joined later by a younger brother, Samuel. The family lived comfortably in a two-story, white-frame house, with a stable, a carriage, two horses, three servants, and a view of the York River. It was a happy and loving home. Lewis later would remember only one time when his father ever was angry with Martha. She had taken the children to Richmond for a visit but failed to show them the state fair: "He seemed to think it was pretty awful that we did not see the prize horses and cattle. Next to Mother, he thought a thorough-bred horse was the most beautiful thing in this world."[13]

Life changed suddenly for Lewis and his siblings in 1908, when their father died of cancer. Martha reacted with strength and a clear idea of what needed to be done. She let go of the servants, sold off the horses and carriage, and adjusted the family to their new circumstances. The Pullers were never destitute, but young Lewis soon learned the value of work and money. He hawked crabs to tourists visiting the waterfront amusement park in the village, and at the age of sixteen took a summer job as a laborer in a pulp mill. His earnings went to support the family.

The experience of growing up without a father (as his father and grandfather had done before him) undoubtedly had a major impact on Lewis's emerging personality. He thought of his mother as "a strong woman." He emulated her and developed his own deep determination and strength of character. He recalled how she maintained discipline in the family without physical punishment: "She treated me as a man and gave me to know she expected me to act like a man." When one of his sisters married, fourteen-year-old Lewis walked down the aisle to give her away. With the constant reminder that he was the eldest male in the household, he acquired a strong sense of responsibility at a young age. The predominance of females in his life—his grandmother, mother, and two older sisters—probably accounted for his enduring affection for family and close friends, often expressed in an openly tender, warm-hearted manner. Martha also raised her son to respect women and act like a "courtly southern gentleman" befitting his heritage. Another element of his mind-set would surface only many years later, but it was undoubtedly a product of the drastic change in circumstances following his father's death. When Lewis finally had his own family, he wanted very much to provide them with the finer things in life he had lost as a child.[14]

Lewis developed one other trait that would add to his bulldog-like demeanor. In public or in private, he was neither quiet nor verbose—he had a simple, straightforward, "pretty blunt" style in dealing with others. Many of those who knew him well would find that to be his most disarming attribute: "You didn't have to guess what Lewie was thinking—he told you, and he did it so simply you could understand."[15]

Life was not all work and seriousness for the growing boy. West Point sat on the end of a wooded peninsula bounded by two rivers and Lewis fell in love with the outdoors. From an early age his favorite activity was hunting, though he was never noted as a very good shot. He also trapped muskrats and sold the hides and carcasses to pay for his ammunition. Puller often would throw pebbles against a friend's window before dawn to get him up to go hunting prior to the start of class. Lewis fished, swam, and boated, too, and his father had taught him to ride horses at an early age. In his small high school (his class had just fourteen students) he participated in every sport: fullback in football, forward in basketball, and catcher in baseball. In one track meet he competed in the broad and high jumps and ran three races, finally succumbing to exhaustion and cramps in the middle of the 880-yard run. A classmate thought Puller's hallmark was "determination on the fields of play." He enjoyed boxing as well, and arranged bouts between himself and his pals. One friend recalled: "He wasn't a bully and didn't look for a fight, but he never ducked one."[16]

One of the West Point teachers recalled that Lewis was "not what you would call a thoroughly interested student." Academics aside, he was an active participant in school. In his sophomore year he was elected vice president of the small class. As a junior, he was treasurer and secretary of the Social Club. He and one other classmate also created the school's first yearbook. The latter activity indicated that he much preferred romance to academics. In one vignette, he and Miss Mary Hudson were listed as "instructors" for a group with the motto: "If study interferes with loving, give up studying." Other passages in the annual showed that he enjoyed a good joke on himself. "(Mary Hudson out strolling with Lewis Puller): Mary: 'These boys tease us unmercifully.' Lewis: 'Yes, and if they don't stop I'll give them a piece of my mind.' Mary: 'Oh, please don't do that! You need it so badly yourself.'" His pranks were not limited to the pages of the yearbook. Toward the end of his final year at West Point High School, he was "the ringleader" when the senior class skipped out for the rest of the day during a ten-minute recess. Puller's sense of humor may have accounted for another feature of his personality that appeared from time to time. He seemed to relish the role of contrarian, astonishing smug people who thought they knew him by saying and doing the unexpected.

Despite occasional antics and his modest achievements in the classroom, his teachers found him "kind and always considerate." When the principal completed Puller's recommendation for college, the educator gave no praise for scholarship, but rated his student's seriousness of purpose as "exceptionally good" and noted that he was "unusually manly and well raised." Two of Lewis's classmates would recall years later that he exercised informal leadership among his peers (evidenced, no doubt, by the hooky incident): "We always did everything he told us to do." He was the epitome of the class motto: "Climb 'tho the rocks be rugged."[17]

Puller's indifference toward academics did not extend to reading, which he relished from a young age. His first favorites were the historical novels of G. A. Henty, who glamorized heroic figures such as Hannibal of Carthage. One of Lewis's teachers never forgot the time she ordered him to gather his books and leave class for misbehavior. She was astonished to see him pull an armload of his own volumes from his desk to add to his school texts. He studied Caesar's *Gallic Wars* in Latin class, but grew impatient with his slow pace of translation, so he bought his own English language version and devoured it in a night. Throughout his life, his unpretentious attitude and rough manner of speech "gave the impression of being a little bit illiterate," but his intense interest in books more than made up for the deficiencies in his formal education.[18]

His passion for reading was exceeded only by his desire to be a warrior, like the heroes in the stories. Aging Confederate veterans further stoked his interest in martial deeds with accounts of his grandfather's wartime exploits and their own service. Andrew Willis Eastwood, mayor of West Point and a former corporal in the 5th Cavalry, was Lewis's favorite storyteller. The old horseman liked to recount how John Puller had continued his charge even after a cannonball had torn through his stomach. The tales had grown very tall over the years, but Lewis readily absorbed the lessons of fearlessness and fidelity. In the process, he inherited his grandfather's sense of devotion to duty and a devil-may-care attitude toward death. The youth also keenly felt the sting of defeat in what he preferred to call "our second War for Independence." He may even have attributed part of his own tight economic circumstances to the ensuing "poverty from which the South has not yet entirely recovered." When he was too young to know better, he had chided the surviving war veterans with the haunting question: "But how did we lose the war, when there were so many of them left alive? Why didn't we fight until everybody was dead?" Lewis's close connection to the Civil War engendered an aversion to military failure that would never fade.[19]

☆   ☆   ☆

Puller's high school years were punctuated by increasing unrest in the world. American forces landed at Veracruz, Mexico, in 1914, and the European powers embarked on a global war the same year. But he was not old enough to join the military until the Mexican border campaign against Pancho Villa in 1916. That crisis caused President Woodrow Wilson to activate National Guard units in mid-June. Lewis, just a few days shy of eighteen, tried to join the Richmond Blues, a highly regarded Virginia outfit. His mother refused to provide the required permission.

In the spring of 1917, as Puller neared the end of his senior year, the United States finally declared war on Germany and jumped into the cataclysmic struggle in Europe. Strangely enough, Lewis did not join the hundreds of thousands of Americans who rushed to enlist. Instead, he accepted an appointment to the Virginia Military Institute. The motivation might have been his deep desire to follow in the footsteps of his forebears as an officer, since he was not yet old enough for a commission (the minimum ages respectively for the Army and Marine Corps were twenty-one and twenty), nor did he have the requisite education to pass the examinations to become a lieutenant. A year or two at VMI would solve both those problems and provide him with some basic military training as well. Another factor may have been his mother's influence, since she was determined to have her sons earn college diplomas. Whatever the reason for Lewis's decision, it would be the only time in his life that he did not jump immediately at the chance to go where the action was.[20]

☆   ☆   ☆

Lewis took a train to Lexington and enrolled at VMI on September 1, 1917. He was a state cadet, which meant that he received financial assistance from the government in return for two years of post-graduate service as a National Guardsman, teacher, or highway engineer.

The storied military school had a reputation for stern discipline, extremely spartan living conditions, and rough hazing of new students (officially forbidden but still prevalent). The 1918 yearbook gave one small indication of life at VMI when it rhetorically asked: "Have you ever been awakened about two a.m. with a bucket of water, and the sudden contact of your face with the floor, as a gentle reminder that it was time to go on guard?" It was not for nothing that upperclassmen commonly referred to freshmen as "rats."[21]

In addition to stoicism, the school imbued its students with the heritage of their predecessors. Many graduates had fought with distinction in the Civil War and the cadets themselves had participated as a unit in the May 1864 battle of New Market. A former instructor, Thomas J. "Stonewall" Jackson, had been one of the South's leading generals until his death in battle in 1863. Lewis, already enamored with the glory of the Confederacy, adopted the bold general as his idol. Puller especially admired his hero's leadership skills: "Jackson built the esprit shown at Chancellorsville—his men thought they were better than their foes and proved it."[22]

The rats began their ordeal at VMI with a week of instruction in close order drill and sentry duty. Then classes opened, but the regimen of drill, guard, and parades continued. Freshmen could not leave the campus except for two hours on Saturday afternoons; Puller liked to spend his precious free time filling up on waffles at a nearby eatery. The only other relaxing pastime was attending the school's frequent dances. On Christmas Day, the rats received their first and only overnight liberty of the academic year, which ended all too quickly with reveille the next morning and a return to the punishing routine. Occasionally Lewis had lunch on the weekend with a relative, Colonel George A. Derbyshire, the Commandant of Cadets. Other official diversions included sports and the traditional snowball fight between the rats of each company. Puller tried out for football and baseball, but was not good enough for either team.

Lewis's performance in the classroom was mediocre. Overall he stood 177th out of 233 at the end of the year. His worst subject was math (200th) and his best, not surprisingly, were history (102d) and military science (89th). He also studied English (149th) and German (138th). His self-discipline and maturity paid off, as he managed to receive no demerits for misconduct or poor performance of duty. It was a distinction he shared with George S. Patton, Jr. (a very distant cousin), who had completed his rat year in 1904. Other than that, Lewis's freshman days at VMI were unremarkable.[23]

☆   ☆   ☆

When school let out for the summer, Puller went straight to Plattsburgh, New York, without even taking time to visit his family. He and a few VMI classmates spent the next several weeks there attending the Army's Reserve Officer Training Corps camp. Lewis completed the course but was still too young for an Army commission. Officials held out the possibility that a pending change in law might allow him to become a lieutenant and they suggested that he could remain on the camp staff until that time came. He rejected the offer. The Battle of Belleau Wood, which had taken place in France in June, almost certainly intensified his eagerness to join the fray. This was the first serious combat in the war by U.S. ground forces. The conflict had been largely an abstraction in the States till this point; now Americans were fighting and dying overseas. The idea of spending more time in a classroom in Lexington or in Plattsburgh, while others were engaged in a titanic struggle, was probably more than the adventurous young Puller could tolerate. (Many of his fellow rats must have had similar notions, for at least thirty-three of them resigned to join the military that summer.)[24]

The only surprise was how Lewis decided to get involved in the war. Despite weeks of Army training, he selected the Marines. One factor that influenced him was the action of his cadet company commander, Sam B. Witt. He had just graduated from VMI and then enlisted in the Corps in search of a commission. (In the spring of 1917 the Corps had announced its intention to draw all wartime officers entirely from the Naval Academy and its own enlisted ranks, a policy change that prevented students of other colleges from obtaining direct commissions.) Puller had great respect for Witt as one of the three VMI leaders who had "finished making a man and a soldier out of me." Equally important, Lewis was twenty years old now and qualified by age for a Marine commission. He apparently calculated that his chances of being commissioned from the ranks in the Corps were greater than the likelihood of a change in the Army's minimum age.[25]

Another consideration in his choice likely was Belleau Wood. Due to a quirk of fate, the 4th Marine Brigade initially received the lion's share of credit not only for its own valiant actions, but also for the deeds of its parent 2d Division, a mixed Army and Marine Corps organization. The publicity bonanza resulted in record recruiting for the Corps, which took in 8,500 new men during July. Puller may have been swayed by the Marine claim of being "First to Fight."[26]

On July 25, 1918, Lewis went to Richmond and enlisted at the recruiting station. Four days later his mother notified VMI that he would not return. Although Lewis would regret not finishing his civilian education, he always would feel he had made the right decision. Years later he would categorically state that "service in camp and in the field is the best military school."[27]

☆   ☆   ☆

The Marine Corps was not entirely ready for its vast wartime expansion, from barely ten thousand officers and men in August 1916 to nearly seventy-three thousand in November 1918. It had just established its primary recruit depot at Parris Island, South Carolina, in the fall of 1915 and the once minor naval base and prison was ill-prepared for the deluge of enlistees in the spring of 1917. The training program underwent many changes during the course of the conflict, but senior leaders decided from the beginning to maintain high standards and devote a minimum of eight precious weeks to shaping future Marines. They achieved this in part by making some efforts serve two purposes. As an example, recruits spent a lot of their time doing heavy manual labor, which not only helped build the burgeoning base, but also increased their strength and endurance.

By the time Puller arrived at Parris Island in late July 1918, the recruit depot was functioning smoothly. Enlistees reported to the Receiving Barracks, sometimes called the Quarantine Camp. There they had their heads shaved, exchanged their civilian clothes for uniforms, underwent physical examinations, received inoculations, and listened to an inspirational two-hour talk by Edwin Denby (a middle-aged enlistee and future Secretary of the Navy). Marines using megaphones controlled the movement of the large groups of untutored civilians and kept them on their toes when necessary with the command, "Snap out of your dope." One Marine officer likened Receiving Barracks to the precision of a Ford assembly line. During this administrative phase, Lewis established an allotment to send part of his pay home, claimed his mother as a dependent, and applied for a family allowance.[28]

Their in-processing complete, the raw recruits met their drill instructor (DI), the NCO who would guide them and drive them through boot camp. These critical billets normally were filled by veteran sergeants, but those experienced men were being commissioned or transferred to leaven the multiplying field units. As the war progressed, the Corps began to send the cream of each graduating recruit company directly into a special NCO school. Many of these freshly minted corporals returned to the drill field a few weeks later to turn other enlistees into Marines.

Each DI was responsible for overseeing as many as sixty-six recruits, from reveille in the early morning until taps late in the evening. They had to teach each man everything about military life, from personal hygiene to wearing uniforms to marching. Of necessity, the DIs leaned heavily on the assistance of any men in the company who had prior military experience. One of Lewis's fellow recruits later recalled that the former VMI man's "military etiquette, neatness, and snap set him apart" from the rest of the "awkward" company.[29]

The next stop in the recruit cycle was called the Maneuver Grounds. The DIs hiked their companies the six miles to the new tent camp, often with men struggling in the heat under their heavy loads of unfamiliar gear. Each recruit battalion, composed of several companies, stayed here for three weeks while the men learned the basics of close order drill, bayonet fighting, and swimming. Physical training included hiking, scaling walls, climbing ropes, exercising with and without rifles, and laboring to build the base. Recruits hauled buckets of oyster shells from the reefs to pave roads, pushed wheelbarrows of crushed rock, pulled heavy rollers by hand to pack it down, and carried hundred-pound bags of cement. At the end of this period, the recruit battalions marched, often with a band at the head of the column, to the Training Camp. Here they conquered the complexities of advanced close order drill and basic tactical formations, learned the requirements of interior guard duty, and received an introduction to boxing and wrestling.

At the end of the fifth training week, the battalions moved yet again, this time into their first barracks building. They spent the next three weeks on the rifle range; the first one learning the techniques of marksmanship and the last two actually firing their weapons. Specialists handled the initial work, but on the firing line each recruit had his own coach. Those men were themselves recent boot camp graduates who had demonstrated superior skill with the M-1903 Springfield rifle. The Marine Corps took great pride in marksmanship and throughout the war continued to invest this large chunk of training time in shooting practice. As a result, nearly 90 percent of Marine recruits achieved a minimum qualification with their basic weapon. Puller's average boyhood skill with weapons was not improved by three weeks of additional work and he scored only 226 out of a possible 300, which placed him in the marksman category, the lowest of the three levels of qualification.[30]

With the completion of the rifle range on September 20, Puller was just about through with boot camp. The senior recruits polished their drill skills and stood guard duty while the Corps digested their performance. Those who had failed to qualify with the rifle often found themselves assigned to the noncombat specialties, such as cooks and bakers—the least desirable assignments. The top shooters remained at the range as coaches. The best overall graduates usually went to advanced training in the bayonet, physical instructor, or NCO schools. The vast pool of men in the middle shipped off to France as replacements for the Marine Brigade or joined other units in Haiti, the Dominican Republic, or stateside.

Puller's company commander, a lieutenant up from the ranks named Barton I. Jenson, gave Lewis a surprisingly low final mark in military efficiency—just a 3 out of a possible 5. He did give Puller 5s in obedience and sobriety. Despite the low grade, Lewis received orders to NCO school and reported to another part of Parris Island for duty on October 1. His year in college and his VMI training made him an excellent candidate. Most of the other selectees were former college students, athletes, or slightly older men who already had been successful in civilian careers. One of his new classmates was Tom Pullen, a teacher prior to the war, whose family had once lived in West Point. The two soon became fast friends.[31]

Training at the NCO school consisted largely of the same subjects taught in boot camp, except that now the instructors went into greater detail to prepare the students to teach others. The standards also were higher, since long-serving senior enlisted men jealously guarded the entryway to noncommissioned officer status. One former private remembered: "It was an endurance contest as well as hard training." Here Puller began to form his first impressions about Marine officers now that he was in closer contact with them. He noted the important role played by a number of mustangs—officers risen from the enlisted ranks—who seemed to ramrod most activities at Parris Island. In addition to Jenson, there were Bror G. Brodstrom and Leslie G. "Jimmy" Wayt, the captains running the NCO school. Lewis came to believe that the former NCOs made better officers than did graduates of universities or military schools. That was only natural, since the older men had long experience in the service and knew how to work with enlisted men. Junior officers fresh from college were still learning the ropes in the confusing swirl of a rapidly expanding Corps. Puller had little time to observe and compare, however. The course was a month old when Headquarters Marine Corps (HQMC) canceled the class.[32]

In August 1918 the Corps finally had won approval to send a second brigade of Marines to France. (Since the Army's publicity defeat at Belleau Wood, it strenuously had opposed any increase in the size of Marine forces committed in Europe. Only a summer of heavy losses in France and a shortage of trained units had forced the War Department to relent.) The Corps quickly formed the 5th Marine Brigade and shipped it overseas during September. The 4th Brigade meanwhile had fought its way to additional bloody victories at Soissons in July, the St.-Mihiel salient in September, and Blanc Mont Ridge in October. Heavy casualties in the 4th and expected losses in the 5th required the Corps to increase the flow of replacements to France. Moreover, a worldwide epidemic of a virulent strain of influenza was sweeping through military units and further boosting the need for fresh men to replace the dead and sick.[33]

On November 5, Puller and the other members of his NCO school class boarded a train on the mainland. Fresh from months of spartan living on Parris Island, they were startled to find themselves ensconced in luxurious Pullman sleeper cars for an overnight journey. They arrived at Quantico, Virginia, the next morning convinced that only aviators and Marines rated such special treatment. The men, all still privates, joined the 11th Separate Battalion, a replacement unit forming for deployment to France. They drew field equipment and began training, but there was free time in the evenings. It was their first taste of the outside world in three months and they relished the small delights of walking the streets of Quantico and eating out in a restaurant.[34]

The excitement of going to war was short-lived. On November 11, 1918, Germany signed an armistice with the Allies and the fighting came to an end. There is no record of whether Puller was elated or disappointed at this turn of events, but he may have felt the same as one Parris Island sergeant: "As long as I live, I'll never live down the fact that I did not get to go to France. But I'm glad it's over for the boys over there."[35]

There no longer was a need for combat replacements in France. The Corps was heavily committed, though, with two brigades still in Europe, one each in Haiti and Santo Domingo, and, soon after, a small detachment in Vladivostok, Russia. There also was a requirement to provide a readily deployable Advance Base Force for any contingency involving the seizure or defense of overseas naval installations. The United States had stepped forward as a major international power and for the moment would continue in that role. Most of the 5th Brigade had come from the Advance Base Force at Quantico and the Corps now had to reconstitute that capability. To achieve that end, the war-strength 11th Separate Battalion became the core of the new peace-strength 15th Regiment on December 1, 1918.

Given the Corps' continuing operational commitments, the need to replace combat casualties in the officer ranks, and the absence of any decision on future manpower levels, Headquarters decided to proceed with the selection and training of a new group of candidates for commissioning. These men would constitute the third batch to go through Officers' Training Camp, the mechanism the Corps had used during the war to turn college men and enlisted Marines into officers. All Marines had a chance to apply if they met the basic requirements. Puller and

Pullen submitted their applications and then went before a review board. The privates answered questions about their training, experience, and goals, and had to demonstrate the capability to send a message by semaphore signal. Both men received a positive endorsement and their names went forward to Headquarters.

Just after Christmas leave, Lewis received word that he and his friend had orders to OTC. They reported there for duty on January 10. And once again, Puller's desire to become an officer frustrated his hopes to see combat. Not long after his transfer, the rebellion in Santo Domingo heated up and the Corps dispatched the 15th Regiment there. His mother also was disappointed, but for a different reason. She "had hoped he'd go back to VMI" now that the war in Europe was over. Apparently he informed her after his selection to OTC that he would gain his commission without finishing school. She wrote a friend at VMI with the news: "I think Lewis will continue with the Marines."[36]

☆   ☆   ☆

The Quantico base was even more a product of wartime expansion than Parris Island. In 1917 the Corps had acquired the land around the village of Quantico, nestled in wooded, rolling hills along the Potomac River south of Washington. Civilian workers had thrown up over a hundred temporary buildings that looked like overgrown shacks—long, wooden, single-story affairs on low stilts, with tarpaper roofs and small, screened windows. The primary training area was a large complex of European-style trenches and bunkers carved into the hills above the rifle range. Marines preparing for the Western Front had cut down trees for construction materials, cleared brush for fields of fire, strung miles of barbed wire, and dug a warren of fortifications. The denuded, torn-up terrain was an eerie replica of the battlefields of France.

With the cessation of major hostilities, the Corps decided that the 3d OTC would be much more thorough than its wartime predecessors. Whereas the other classes had lasted about ten weeks, Puller and his fellow candidates would undergo five months of training and evaluation. The course was a mix of book learning and hands-on work. Classroom studies covered everything from military law to administration to guard regulations. The tactical exercises emphasized the control and movement of units up through regimental size. And the school devoted considerable time to weapons familiarization, hikes, calisthenics, bayonet practice, and drill, the staples at that time of Marine training at all levels. As with boot camp, many of the instructors were themselves recent graduates of the course. One was Lieutenant Sam Witt, who had won his commission via the 2d OTC.

Puller did not fare especially well in the classroom work, but did not let that bother him. He once remarked to Pullen that he took heart from the belief that in any such group there probably always would be "at least one S.O.B. dumber than I am, so I keep on plugging and have confidence that I will not be at the bottom." Lewis did get the chance to fire the rifle range again and this time improved his score to 256 (3 points more than the minimum needed for an expert badge, the highest marksmanship qualification). His overall performance was average; he finished 128th out of 231.[37]

The students completed all graded portions of the course by June 4 and many went to a short machine gun school while waiting for graduation and commissioning. The class celebrated its success with a grand dance at a Washington hotel on Friday, June 13, 1919. The inauspicious date turned out to be an omen of bad luck. Congress was finalizing its work on the naval appropriations bill and it was now clear to Marine leaders that all the military services would be cut drastically. Under this legislation, the Marine Corps would shrink from its wartime high of 73,000 to about 1,100 officers and 27,400 men, with additional reductions likely in the future. In mid-June, in anticipation of the cut, Headquarters directed the discharge of 1,200 officers.

The size of the cuts came as a shock to most Marines, but the announcement was not necessarily unwelcome to all. A sergeant who finished fourth in the class probably expressed the prevailing view: "I for one wanted out. For me a military career was useful only in war." On June 19, three days after graduation and commissioning, Headquarters issued orders to Puller and his classmates that would transfer them to inactive status on the 25th of the month.[38]

Lewis remained determined to become a military leader. He told classmates: "I know I can lick this game . . . I'm going to stay in." Years later, he recalled that he briefly considered volunteering for service with a group of Americans going to Poland to support that newly independent nation in its struggle against the Communist forces of Russia. That idea evaporated when he and a fellow graduate of OTC, Laurence

R. Muth, talked to Captain William H. Rupertus, one of their instructors. Rupertus suggested they would be better off resigning their reserve commissions, enlisting in the regular Marine Corps, and asking
for duty with the Gendarmerie d'Haiti, which was looking for Marine
NCOs to serve as lieutenants. The choice was undoubtedly an easy
one—they would be on active duty again, serve as officers, and likely
see some action in that Caribbean country.[39]

On June 28, 1919, two days after his twenty-first birthday, Puller
signed a four-year enlistment. He spent two weeks of leave in West
Point, then he and Muth reported to Charleston, South Carolina, for
transportation to Haiti. After three years of false starts, Private Puller
finally was heading off to a war.[40]

2

"The Great Lessons of Warfare"
Haiti
1919–1921

The ship carrying Private Puller and Sergeant Muth approached the coast of Haiti near the capital of Port-au-Prince on July 30, 1919. From a distance, the Caribbean nation had all the earmarks of a tropic paradise. Looking out across the emerald water, they could see the red-tile roofs of the city standing out sharply against the lush green mountains that formed a dramatic backdrop. As they drew closer, that initial pleasant impression melted away. One Marine officer who arrived just a few months later recorded that his nose gave the first hint of misery: "The gentle offshore breeze brought the acrid odor of many charcoal fires tainted at the last by passage over the 'Gut,' a mess of several acres of filthy straw shacks that sprawled at the water's edge." In the first few hours ashore, Puller likely realized that his home for the next few years was about as far from heaven as one could get.[1]

☆   ☆   ☆

The island of Hispaniola had a long, troubled history. Spanish colonizers disposed of the Indians who lived there and imported African slave labor. The French took over the western third of the island in 1697 and christened it Haiti. These eleven thousand square miles—75 percent mountainous interior and 25 percent coastal plain—produced an abundance of coffee, sugar, and other cash crops. By 1791 the rich colony had a population of twenty-five thousand whites, thirty thousand free

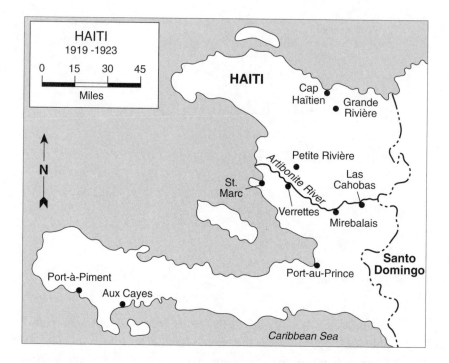

mulattoes, and half a million black slaves. The slaves rebelled that year.
A decade and a half of conflict brought the creation of an independent
state and the death of 70 percent of the inhabitants, including all the
whites. The nation never again achieved prosperity or stability due to an
unending series of revolutions and coups. The mulattoes, advantaged
by their status under colonial rule, maintained French culture and governed the country. The true power brokers, however, were the *cacos,*
lawless rural blacks who formed gangs and provided a violent boost to
any would-be leader willing to pay for their assistance. With their interests ignored by both the mulattoes and the *cacos,* the vast majority of
the population remained illiterate, poor, and sickly.

Between 1908 and 1915, the Haitian presidency changed hands
seven times, with four of the incumbents dying by violent means and
the others fleeing the country. In response to this persistent crisis, President Woodrow Wilson ordered forces to Haiti in 1915 to protect American interests and restore order. A brigade of two thousand Marines
soon combined vigorous offensive action with an offer of a generous
bounty for anyone turning in a weapon. Fighting was limited and casualties low; Marine losses were three dead and eighteen wounded. The

United States also persuaded the Haitian legislature to sign a treaty that essentially made the Caribbean country an American protectorate. Haiti became stable for the moment.

One of the provisions of the U.S.-Haitian agreement created the Gendarmerie, a constabulary force designed to replace the former army and police. Marine officers and NCOs would provide the experience and political neutrality necessary to get this organization off to a good start. The NCOs received commissions as Gendarmerie lieutenants; officers served in billets one or two grades above their American rank. The Marines received a salary from the Haitian government in addition to their regular pay from the United States. For a Marine corporal working as a second lieutenant, the extra $720 per year more than doubled his income.

The Gendarmerie grew to 120 officers and 2,600 enlisted. The force was divided into geographic departments, each commanded by a Gendarmerie colonel. A department consisted of a few districts, each about a company in strength and commanded by a captain. The district consisted of several subdistricts headed by lieutenants, who were responsible for the small garrisons within their zone. It took considerable time to organize and train this force, especially since the native recruits spoke only Creole. To complicate matters, the new soldiers brought with them the illiteracy, illness, and indolence endemic in a chaotic society. Some Marines, in turn, carried the difficult baggage of racial prejudice. The Chief of the Gendarmerie did not certify his force as fully effective until late 1919, after three years of training and the "transfer of several white officers for inaptitude." Nearly one third of the eighty-eight Marine enlisted men in the Gendarmerie were shipped out for unsatisfactory performance during late 1919 and early 1920. The attempt to develop Haitian officers was just beginning.[2]

The high failure rate for Gendarmerie officers was rooted in their duties, which went far beyond those of Marine counterparts. In addition to being a soldier, a constabulary officer had important civil powers. He enforced the laws, ran the jails, prepared criminal cases for the courts, approved all local government financial transactions, and personally paid teachers and other civil functionaries in cash. He kept an eye on education, sanitation, agriculture, and the judicial system and reported problems to higher authorities. Finally, he supervised all military construction and the maintenance of all roads. A semiofficial report on the

Gendarmerie noted that the civil duties required a leader with "exceptional tact, judgment, and patience."[3]

In order to foster economic progress and improve military mobility, the constabulary undertook a vigorous road-building program in 1918. Since the government had little money, the Gendarmerie turned to a forgotten law that required citizens to devote time each year to work on the roads. With characteristic zeal, constabulary officers drafted men into this effort, known as the *corvée*. Those opposed to the American presence equated the *corvée* to the reinstitution of slavery. The dormant *cacos* took advantage of the discontent to resume their bandit activities.

The *cacos* were never a serious military threat, since they were poorly armed and untrained in marksmanship and tactics. Only about one bandit in four carried a rifle and many of these were older, large-caliber weapons; shortages of ammunition often forced the *cacos* to fire rounds wrapped in bull hide or wire to make them fit these unusual bores. Nevertheless, their brigandage, concentrated in central and northern Haiti, threatened the effort to create a stable, prosperous country. The Gendarmerie and the Marine brigade patrolled the countryside, but *caco* sympathizers provided news of government movements and the bandits rarely were surprised. Most contacts occurred when the *cacos* ambushed Marine and Gendarmerie units. The forty small battles during the first half of 1919 resulted in three Marine deaths.[4]

☆   ☆   ☆

Puller recalled later that he received a brusque reception upon his arrival in Haiti. A Gendarmerie captain simply pointed the newcomer toward the hotel and told him to observe drill the next morning. That evening in the bar, a lieutenant gave him his first lesson in Creole and told him to learn a few new words and phrases each day. Puller's lasting impressions of the following day were of *cocomacaques* and camp followers. Haitian NCOs used the former—long, hard walking sticks—to strike the head of any soldier making a mistake during drill. The latter—wives accompanying their men in the constabulary—did all the cooking and laundry for the unit.

Puller soon had more challenging work. The primary means of supplying inland units was by mule train. These missions required an armed escort to ensure their safety against *caco* attacks. They were also a good way to break in new officers unfamiliar with the Gendarmerie or the countryside. Within a week or so of his arrival Puller received orders to take charge of a run to Mirebalais and Las Cahobas. These small towns were located in a region infested with *cacos* under the leadership of Benoit Batraville, one of the foremost bandit commanders.

Puller's force, about twenty-five mounted men plus pack animals, departed early in the morning for Mirebalais. This village of 1,500 souls was located some forty miles up the main road heading northwest from Port-au-Prince. He began this first mission with a number of handicaps. There were no accurate maps of the country; he had only a verbal description of the route to guide him. His troops spoke no English and he as yet knew almost no Creole. He also apparently had little knowledge of how to care for a mule train. His main concern, he decided, was reaching Mirebalais that day to avoid risking a night attack by bandits. The young leader kept his force moving rapidly. At frequent intervals his Haitian sergeant approached and spoke excitedly, obviously complaining about something but unable to make himself understood.

Late in the afternoon the small force ran into an equally surprised column of about one hundred *cacos* coming from the opposite direction around a bend in the road. Puller's innate aggressiveness came to the fore at this critical moment; he instinctively ordered a charge and spurred his horse forward. His soldiers may or may not have comprehended his command, but they loyally followed their leader. *Cacos* seldom stood their ground when attacked and this time was no exception. They loosed just a handful of shots in the direction of the onrushing patrol and then scattered. Since the pack mules made it impossible to pursue, the clash was over in a matter of minutes. Puller found one dead bandit. It was a small encounter, but Confederate Major John W. Puller certainly would have been proud of his descendant's courage and coolness under fire. The skirmish also established a pattern the young Marine would follow for the remainder of his career: aggressive action and leadership from the front.

The supply train finally reached Mirebalais around 2100 and delivered half its load to the unit there. Puller asked a Gendarmerie lieutenant what had made the sergeant so irate. The older officer soon discovered that the NCO thought the pace had been much too fast for the troops and the animals. Unfazed by this knowledge, Puller overrode the continuing protests of his Haitian assistant and ordered him to have

the column ready to move out prior to dawn the next morning. Then the
fledgling officer reported to the commander of the Mirebalais district
and received congratulations on his first victory in battle.[5]

Puller made the thirty-four-mile round-trip to Las Cahobas and back
the next day and then returned to Port-au-Prince the day after that. He
recalled that he "beat at those damn pack mules all the way." The department commander, Colonel Walter N. Hill, saw the outfit coming
into town and was amazed that the young officer had accomplished his
mission so quickly. He promptly assigned his subordinate to permanent
duty with the supply trains. When Hill asked about the state of the animals, Puller responded they were okay. They were in poor condition,
though, and the Haitian sergeant had been right all along. The lieutenant had violated a cardinal rule of operations with beasts of burden:
"Do not attempt to make speed records." Puller knew he was in trouble
after Hill promised to inspect the animals in the morning, but a fellow
lieutenant came to the rescue, offering to "cure" the animals for $10. To
Puller's surprise, he did so by secretly substituting different horses and
mules prior to the colonel's appearance at the stables. On the positive
side, Puller's speed of movement may have brought about his successful
first contact, since he was running ahead of the schedule anticipated by
the bandits. Luckily for the young Gendarmerie leader, his mule team
days would be short-lived.[6]

☆   ☆   ☆

The brigade commander, Brigadier General Albertus W. Catlin, had inspected the Mirebalais district in early June and come to the conclusion
that the Marines and *gendarmes* there were "badly worn out." As overall commander of military forces in Haiti, he shifted additional troops
to this troubled region. These were mainly Marine units, but included
an experimental Gendarmerie force designated Provisional Company A.
Its purpose apparently was to provide a sizeable force dedicated solely
to patrolling. Other Gendarmerie units were dispersed in small packets
guarding towns and villages and thus found it difficult to conduct offensive operations.[7]

The commander of Company A took sick soon after and Colonel
Hill assigned Puller to this new duty. He inherited a force of one hundred men, supported unofficially by about the same number of female
camp followers. His chief assistant was Acting Second Lieutenant Au-

gustin B. Brunot, a fluent English speaker and one of several NCOs recently promoted from the ranks to begin the process of creating a Haitian officer corps. Puller was pleased with his subordinate: "He was very smart, comprehended anything I told him, and got it over to the men." Another standout was Private Cermontout Jean Louis, whom Puller had sought after observing him return from patrol with the heads of two bandits. He was better known throughout the Gendarmerie as one of a small detachment of Haitians who, in the constabulary's dark days of early 1919, had stood by their wounded American lieutenant and fought through a large *caco* force to bring him to safety. Years later Puller also would recall with fondness three other senior leaders in his unit—Lyautey, Clairmont, and Calixte—who proved valuable in molding him and his small command. (Demosthenes P. Calixte's ramrod-straight posture and piercing eyes gave him the look of a leader. He would rise to command of the constabulary in the 1930s.)[8]

Brunot and Lyautey introduced the American lieutenant to the new tactics being used in the district. Typically patrols moved by daylight and camped in the evening, but the Mirebalais command was experimenting with night movements. The Haitians explained the logic. Chance encounters such as Puller's pack train episode were rare because the *cacos* knew the terrain and had good intelligence of constabulary activities. If the bandits thought they held the upper hand, they would set up an ambush; if not, they would scatter to avoid contact and regroup later. However, the *cacos* camped at night, so patrols moving in the dark had a better chance of surprising the enemy. Government forces also were learning that it was best to operate in small groups. That made it easier to move about undetected. It also might tempt the bandits to attack, thus increasing the odds for making contact. Company A's commander eagerly accepted these ideas.[9]

The tactics produced results in short order. As Puller and a detachment of his unit patrolled along a ridge-top trail one night, he observed campfires and heard drums nearby. Closer investigation by the lieutenant and a few NCOs revealed a *caco* force bivouacked in a clearing and apparently engaged in an evening of revelry. He returned to his unit and issued orders for a classic L-shaped ambush. Most of the patrol stealthily formed a line facing the bandit camp, while a smaller group, heavily armed with three Lewis machine guns, placed itself beyond the flank in a position where it covered the rear of the *cacos*. As Puller pre-

dicted, when his main body opened fire at first light the surprised bandits fled away from the source of immediate danger and ran unwittingly
into the fields of fire of the machine guns. The last *caco* was dead or
gone within minutes. The victorious *gendarmes* investigated the battlefield and found seventeen bodies, dozens of machetes, and a large flock
of gamecocks. The patrol launched its own celebration and spent the
day fighting the birds against each other and feasting on the losers.[10]

As the days passed and Puller participated in more patrols, he
learned the peculiarities of small wars. He marveled at the things he
saw—the ability of his men to butcher a steer in the field and store
the unused portions for future use on the trail, a camp follower giving
birth while the patrol halted for a rest, and the iron discipline meted out
by the NCOs. In one case, Lyautey tied a straggler to a mule and had
him dragged along the ground to motivate him to keep up. Puller accepted this "brutal kind of treatment," because the alternatives were
worse—the unit failing to achieve its mission or a *gendarme* falling behind (which inevitably would lead to his capture and death by torture).
Lyautey also explained his views of leadership, which required the
commander to show no fear in battle and the troops to obey every order
without question. The naive American lieutenant soon saw the dark side
of such loyalty. As his patrol stopped one day at a river near the border
with Santo Domingo, he casually remarked how much he would like to
have the beautiful white horse he saw on the other side. Brunot issued
an order and one of the *gendarmes* shot the rider. Puller was startled
and upset, but he did not punish the Haitian lieutenant, who explained
that he had merely assumed it was a command.[11]

Lyautey's notions about leadership conformed with and reinforced
what Puller already had learned in studying Stonewall Jackson and
other heroes of the Civil War. "Every ounce of authority," one officer in
the Confederate army had observed, "had to be purchased by a drop of
my blood." Puller would take to heart and more than live up to the
words and example of his Virginia forebears and the Haitian sergeant
major.[12]

☆   ☆   ☆

The disorders reached a climax in October 1919, when Charlemagne
Peralte, the most charismatic *caco* leader, brought his large band to the
outskirts of Port-au-Prince and demanded that the president surrender.

He marched into the capital that night, but a combined force of *gendarmes* and Marines easily drove him out of town. This impudent attack provoked the brigade commander to step up efforts to destroy the enemy. In particular, he ordered a major increase in operations around Mirebalais and Las Cahobas, a center of unrest.[13]

As part of this aggressive offensive, Puller left Mirebalais on October 28 on patrol with Brunot and a mixed force of fifteen Marines and *gendarmes*. They would stay out ten days, at which time another group would relieve them. The unit, using night movements, made contact on October 31 with a small band, killing two of the enemy and capturing four rifles and several machetes and swords. On November 1 they arrested three suspected bandits. Late in the afternoon of November 4 they entered a small village of grass shacks ten miles west of Mirebalais. A priest told Brunot that Dominique Georges, a bandit chieftain, had a camp about fifteen miles distant.

Despite a heavy rain, Puller ordered the patrol to move out immediately. He, Brunot, and the redoubtable Private Cermontout Jean Louis were scouting out ahead of the small column about 0230 when they came upon the remains of a bonfire drowned out by the rain. This typically indicated a bandit guard post and, sure enough, a man with a rifle challenged the approaching figures. Without the light of his fire the sentry had only his ears to go by and he accepted without question Brunot's Haitian-accented reply, "*Cacos.*" Beyond the outpost, the three men came upon a clearing with many huts and lean-tos. As Puller remembered the encounter years later, he and Jean Louis took firing positions on the ground inside the camp while Brunot went back to bring up the rest of the patrol for an assault. Puller aimed his rifle at a man he later believed was Georges, but waited for the main attack instead of firing, a decision he soon regretted. A *caco* approached the two prone figures and demanded to know who they were, at which point the American shot him and the battle was joined.

The Marines and *gendarmes* rushed forward, but the estimated two hundred *cacos* scattered according to their usual practice. Puller and Jean Louis fired as fast as they could at fleeting figures in the dripping darkness. After the government soldiers had sole possession of the camp, they found one body, twelve rifles, and the typical assortment of swords and machetes. They might have achieved much greater success but for the vigilance of the *caco* inside the bivouac and the poor conditions for marksmanship. They had one consolation—among the booty was Georges's personal rifle, identified by his initials in the stock. The patrol spent the night there, then headed back to its base at Mirebalais the next day. Puller eventually would receive his first combat award, Haiti's Médaille Militaire, for this "dangerous and brilliant attack."[14]

Company A's commander spent the next three days in camp conducting drill and holding school for the men and NCOs. On November 9 Puller and Brunot led out a force of thirty-three *gendarmes* on patrol. Just prior to dawn they located a camp and attacked, this time killing ten *cacos* and capturing two rifles. The patrol then took a circuitous route back to Mirebalais, where they again fell into garrison routine for a few days.

During one of his forays Puller met up with Louis Cukela, a Marine lieutenant who had won the Medal of Honor as a gunnery sergeant during the World War. The Serbian-born officer spoke critically about the conduct of the campaign. He believed that garrisoning the towns was a waste of effort, that all the combat forces should be gathered together and placed in the field to pursue the bandits until they finally were destroyed. Looking back at the end of his career, Puller would say of that conversation: "I learned one of the great lessons of warfare from him—concentration of force. It was familiar to me from having read Caesar and Napoleon, but no one had put it like Cukela, and he was one of the first critics of American warfare I had met." Puller eventually would build his own reputation as a harsh, realistic judge of military policies.[15]

While Puller was in Mirebalais, he also had his first contact with military aviation. A small Marine squadron was working with the ground forces in Haiti and the Gendarmerie lieutenant made several flights in the backseat of a fragile Curtiss JN Jenny. His job was to point out landmarks to the pilots and familiarize them with the region. Although the planes usually attacked the *cacos* with machine guns, the Marine aviators were pioneering techniques such as glide bombing. These personal encounters with early aerial operations gave Puller a rare appreciation for the potential utility of airpower.[16]

☆   ☆   ☆

The brigade commander came to Mirebalais on an inspection tour on November 14. He expressed his displeasure with progress against the bandits and took measures "to greatly increase activities of units stationed in this district." The pressure probably resulted from the much more impressive success recently registered by units in northern Haiti.[17]

Herman H. Hanneken, a Marine sergeant and a Gendarmerie captain, had performed an outstanding feat of personal initiative and daring. He recruited a Haitian agent named Jean Conzé to infiltrate Peralte's force and hopefully lead the *cacos* into an ambush. When the operation did not go according to plan, Conzé alerted Hanneken, who immediately set out with Lieutenant William R. Button (a Marine corporal) and twenty *gendarmes*. Disguised as *cacos* and armed with a password provided by Conzé, they proceeded through several outposts and gained entry to Peralte's camp. In the predawn hours of November 1 Hanneken killed the *caco* leader with a pistol shot while his small force opened fire on several hundred bandits in the immediate vicinity. The *gendarmes* beat back a few halfhearted attacks by Peralte's followers, then brought the body to Grande Rivière. The brigade circulated photos of the dead leader around the country and the number of bandits turning in arms and accepting amnesty increased dramatically.[18]

Now the primary *caco* chieftain was Benoit Batraville. A few days after the brigade commander's visit, Puller and Brunot each took a part of the company out on patrol. The Haitian lieutenant actually saw a force that turned out to be Batraville's, but the enemy broke camp and melted away before Brunot could get his force into position for an attack. Puller's detachment had slightly better luck, making a contact that resulted in two *cacos* killed and sixteen captured.[19]

Puller returned to Mirebalais on November 25 and received a report on the district commander's inspection of the garrison the day prior. A senior lieutenant pronounced the physical condition of the barracks much improved, the troops clean and well drilled, but marksmanship remained "poor." Following a few days of rest and training, Puller took out another patrol. He found nothing and returned to his base at 1700 on December 2 to discover that he had orders transferring him from Company A. The next day he turned over the unit to his replacement and rode to Port-au-Prince. The new commander of the Department of the South, Major Alexander A. Vandegrift, told Puller he was going to become the subdistrict commander at Aux Cayes.[20]

The transfer likely was the result of Gendarmerie policy requiring "frequent changes of officers at isolated posts" to reduce the ill effects, mental and professional, of a Marine NCO or junior officer being left on his own for too long. It also allowed Gendarmerie officers from quiet regions to gain experience in the *caco* campaigns of central and north-ern Haiti. It was now Puller's turn to take a shift in the tranquil hinter-land. Although he had not won any spectacular victories during his four months of active operations, he could take some of the credit for "a marked improvement throughout the entire district." On December 6, the young officer boarded a small sailing vessel and made the three-day coastal voyage to his new assignment.[21]

☆   ☆   ☆

With a population of fifteen thousand, Aux Cayes was the third largest city in Haiti. Its prominence was due in large measure to its being the principal seaport along the country's long, narrow southern peninsula, which had no good overland connections with the rest of the nation. In addition, it was a major center for the hiring and transportation of Hai-tian men who worked for high wages in the Cuban sugar fields. These men and their money generally returned in the off-season and boosted the local economy. Despite its relative prosperity, Aux Cayes was a pesthole built on marshy land in the delta where two rivers met the sea. During the rainy seasons in spring and fall, water and mud covered the streets. Malaria and other tropical fevers were common. A telephone line indirectly connected the town with Port-au-Prince, but messages had to be relayed by a dozen intervening operators and usually took twenty-four hours to cover the 125 miles to the capital.[22]

Puller arrived in Aux Cayes on December 10, 1919, and reported to the district commander, Major Keller E. Rockey. The Gendarmerie lieutenant soon settled into the dull habits of a garrison outpost far from any action. His daily report of events seldom varied from the refrain "drill, inspection, and office routine." The biggest threat to public order was petty thievery on the docks and the main challenge was recruiting new *gendarmes* given the competition from the Cuban cane fields. The district had barely half its authorized strength and many of those re-cruited were substandard. During this brief period, Rockey found his newest lieutenant to be "a very satisfactory officer."

Two days after Christmas, Puller received a present of sorts when the district commander told him to take over the subdistrict of Port-à-Piment. This very small town farther west along the peninsula was even more remote from civilization, but it was an improvement over Aux Cayes. The citizens were of "the better class" and it had a much healthier climate. On the other hand, the subdistrict had gone without an officer for six months and the men and barracks showed it. The young commander spent his first three days inspecting his outposts and paying government workers. Then he found himself back in the same garrison rut, with the added duty of supervising the construction of a new jail. The only highlights were the January 10, 1920, visit of Vandegrift and Major Bill Rupertus and the arrival on January 27 of Puller's commission as a full-fledged Gendarmerie second lieutenant.[23]

At the end of March the stout Marine came down with fever, probably malaria. He first tried quinine pills, then began drinking large quantities of rum. On his fifth day of lying in bed racked by pain, he lost consciousness. When he woke up the next morning, his orderly claimed he had poured a gallon of rum into him and then had the audacity to present him with the bill. Puller finally got better when he received injections of quinine, a common method in Haiti for dealing with severe malaria attacks. Afterward he joked with Tom Pullen that the Caribbean alcohol had provided the real cure.[24]

In testament to the wisdom of the Gendarmerie rotation policy, Puller began to show the effects of illness and isolation. He was just getting back on his feet on April 7, when he rode to Aux Cayes to pick up cash for the monthly salaries of his subdistrict. The major was absent, so Puller, "not wishing to return to the hills too soon," waited there for him for nearly a week instead of going back to his post. It was a rare lapse in diligence for the hardworking lieutenant.

After his lengthy stay in Aux Cayes, the subdistrict commander rode the thirty-nine miles of rocky trail back to Port-à-Piment. He barely had arrived there at 2000 when a *gendarme* caught up with him to tell him to report immediately back to district headquarters. Puller saddled up a fresh mount and headed off into the night. After a few hours' sleep at one of his outposts along the way, he completed the journey to Aux Cayes late the next morning. He soon wrote Pullen about the incident: "You can rest assured that I was relieved when I found I had been ordered in to Port-au-Prince to be decorated for killing . . . and not to be court-martialed for the same." (His words echoed a cynical joke then common among Caribbean Marines. One man stationed in Santo Domingo asks: "Hey, Bill! Wot's a Specification?" Instead of explaining that it is a military term for a criminal charge, his counterpart in Haiti replies: "Oh, nothin'! Just a Citation [for a medal] with the date and place changed.")[25]

After Puller recovered from his long round-trip on horseback, a vehicle took him to the capital the next day. On the 17th, the President of Haiti pinned the nation's Médaille Militaire on the lieutenant's chest. That honor placed Puller in a select group. Only twenty American members of the Gendarmerie received Haiti's sole medal for valor during the 1919–1920 campaign. But the award did little to lift his sagging morale. He counseled Pullen: "You don't want to come down here. . . . It's a dog's life here." He also told his friend about a letter from Headquarters Marine Corps asking 3d OTC graduates if they wished to be considered for an active duty commission. "I replied that I did. Unless I get back into the Corps, I have a pretty rotten looking future ahead of me." Another officer who served in Aux Cayes would come to a similar conclusion about a tour in that remote region, calling it "man-killing work." When Puller answered the query on his Gendarmerie fitness report regarding whether he intended to reenlist, he was less than enthusiastic: "Depends on conditions."[26]

☆   ☆   ☆

Puller's reference to a court-martial was a reaction to a rising concern over the possibility that Marines had committed atrocities during the current rebellion. General Catlin had raised the issue after he took command of the brigade in 1919. He noted that "several rumors have reached these headquarters that prisoners have been shot" and he wrote a letter to all officers promising to prosecute any offenders. Command interest went up a notch when the Commandant of the Marine Corps was alarmed by a statement in a court-martial transcript. A lieutenant, acting as defense counsel for two enlisted Marines accused of killing a captured *caco,* tried to excuse their acts by admitting that he himself had ordered wounded bandits shot, had seen others order executions, and doubted "whether a treacherous guide need expect a trial if made prisoner." The Commandant ordered an investigation of the matter in September 1919 and vowed to bring perpetrators to justice.[27]

These initial attempts to deal with the situation went awry. The brigade did write a report in accordance with the Commandant's order, but it mysteriously disappeared in the mail between Port-au-Prince and Washington in March 1920. When John A. Lejeune, the respected commander of the 2d Division in France during the World War, succeeded to the commandancy at the end of June, he was greeted by a scathing magazine article attacking the Corps for abuses in the Caribbean. The Secretary of the Navy ordered him personally to inspect the forces in Haiti and determine what had happened. During September Lejeune visited many of the posts and interviewed witnesses. He found there was some truth to the allegations; a few Marines and *gendarmes* had committed atrocities. But he believed the vast majority of the men had acquitted themselves honorably. A Senate committee eventually conducted its own investigation in 1921 and substantiated Lejeune's conclusions. It found credible reports of several murders, but insufficient evidence at that late date to take legal action. Cukela was one of those under suspicion and the Corps transferred him to Santo Domingo.[28]

Senior Marine leaders had failed to take stronger corrective action at the first hint of trouble and thus had allowed a handful of offenders to bring discredit upon the Corps. The problem also highlighted the lack of accepted doctrine for small wars. One school of thought popularized at that time by the British strategist C. E. Callwell held that only punitive methods designed to inflict casualties and economic harm could subdue a population. He felt the "lower races" were most effectively impressed by force. To support his theory, he quoted a Russian general named Skobolef: "Do not forget that in Asia he is the master who seizes the people pitilessly by the throat and imposes upon their imagination." The Marine Corps, partly as a result of bad publicity over atrocities in Haiti, eventually would adopt a more benign strategy based on the premise that small wars should be prosecuted "with a minimum loss of life and property and by methods that leave no aftermath of bitterness or render the return to peace unnecessarily difficult." The *caco* rebellion thus contributed to the birth a decade later of the *Small Wars Manual,* the Corps' first doctrinal bible for counterinsurgency campaigns.[29]

The outcry also made senior Marine leaders overly sensitive about how they presented their operations to the public. Lejeune began censoring news bulletins generated by units in the field. One of the first stories to fall victim to this scrutiny was an account of Hanneken's feats. A Headquarters staff officer sent it back with the notation that the Commandant "does not desire any publication which refers to the 'shooting and killing' of bandits to be released."[30]

Puller was never tarred with the atrocity brush, but he felt strongly that he and his fellow Marines were being unjustly second-guessed in carrying out U.S. policy. He wrote Pullen: "It seems funny as hell to

me; every once in a while some fool . . . up in the States sets up a howl
over a few [Haitians] being knocked off. Well, someone has to be the
goat and it is generally a Gendarmerie officer." Those sentiments
notwithstanding, Puller seems to have understood and readily adapted
to his complex role in the strange cultures of Haiti and the Gendarmerie. He denigrated the *cacos* (boasting that he could "lick two
score of the black dogs") and he used then-common racial slurs in private, but he never demonstrated signs of prejudice toward his Haitian
soldiers or the population at large. A Marine lieutenant who served with
him at Mirebalais noted that Puller, "by his tact, common sense, and
dignity of manner, won the confidence and respect of his command of
black troops." One of his commanders in the Aux Cayes district observed that "he made friends of the Haitians of all classes and by so
doing inspired confidence in their minds of our mission in Haiti." A
subsequent commander felt that Puller was "liked by the Haitian officials." Judging by his sentiments expressed decades later, he also developed a genuine regard for the *gendarmes* with whom he served. His
feelings may have been influenced by Vandegrift's tutelage, since the
senior officer frequently "sound[ed] off . . . on the belief that loyalty
down must occur simultaneously with loyalty up."[31]

☆   ☆   ☆

As the months progressed Puller managed to improve his small command. Rockey noted that the subdistrict commander "has worked hard
and has brought his men to a better state of instruction," though still
"handicapped by a lack of knowledge of the language." On fitness reports, he gave Puller marks from very good to excellent and described
him as "calm, forceful, even tempered, energetic." In a reorganization
of the Gendarmerie in spring 1920, Colonel Joseph A. Rossell became
Puller's new reporting senior. He thought his subordinate had "all the
attributes of a splendid young officer." Perhaps aware that Puller was
seeking to regain his commission, Rossell also took the unusual step of
adding lengthy remarks: "My impression of this officer is that he is of
exceptional high moral character; possessed of qualities which are outstanding and that he is deserving of promotion not only to higher grade
in the Gendarmerie, but that he is also qualified for commissioned
grade in the Marine Corps."[32]

   In line with the rotation policy, at the end of June 1920 Puller received orders to a new duty station. The records do not properly ac-

count for his whereabouts during the next ten weeks, but it appears that he became a subdistrict commander at Verrettes, a small town in the Artibonite plain. This valley, described as "the most important" in Haiti, consisted of fertile low ground ten to twenty miles wide, surrounded by mountains, and bisected by the Artibonite River. It extended from the coast all the way to Mirebalais. This placed Puller near the heart of *caco* country, but he had returned to the region too late to see any additional action. The rebellion had weakened considerably in the aftermath of Peralte's death in November 1919 and then collapsed altogether when a Marine patrol killed Batraville on May 19, 1920. A month later, the last significant *caco* leader turned himself in and the brigade commander declared victory: "This practically completes the surrender, capture, or death of all the prominent active bandit chiefs. The pacification of Haiti may therefore be said to be complete."[33]

There remained a few hundred holdouts in the mountains, so government forces in the central and northern regions continued their aggressive operations. They averaged 225 patrols per week, but in the following year they made just thirty-eight contacts and killed only eighty-five bandits. Hanneken achieved another coup in September 1920 by penetrating a *caco* camp in disguise and arresting five chiefs and killing another. By June 1921 the brigade commander could justifiably report that "the country is completely tranquil." Puller likely did his share of patrolling during these final months of the rebellion but made no contacts.[34]

One of the rare friendly casualties in the latter stages of the war was Sergeant Muth, who had come to Haiti with Puller. *Cacos* under Batraville had ambushed Muth's patrol on April 4, 1920, and the lieutenant went down in the first fusillade with several wounds. The remaining three Marines and a handful of *gendarmes* fought their way out of the trap, but left their commander for dead. Patrols converged on the scene the next day and recovered the remains. After hearing what the *gendarmes* had found, Puller hoped that Muth had died before the *cacos* had gotten to him: "There wasn't a piece of flesh or bone as large as my hand. His head is stuck up on the end of a pole somewhere now, out in the hills." Puller already had become hardened toward death in battle and he accepted Muth's demise, but he was bitterly angry with the men who had deserted their leader. He "damned" them for failing to look out for a comrade on the battlefield.[35]

In all, the *caco* rebellion of 1918–1921 had resulted in the death of roughly two thousand bandits. The Marines lost seven killed and perhaps a half dozen wounded. There were less than seventy-five casualties among the Haitian *gendarmes*.[36]

☆   ☆   ☆

With the end of the fighting the Gendarmerie finally could focus on building itself into a professional institution. Up till this point districts had recruited men locally and given them on-the-job training. The constabulary likewise obtained most of its officers by commissioning Marine and Haitian NCOs, who merely changed their rank insignia and kept on working. Now the Gendarmerie created recruit depots and started officer candidate schools, one for Haitians and another for Marine NCOs. In addition, each post held school half of each day to teach the men reading, writing, and arithmetic. The force also built its first real rifle ranges and instituted regular marksmanship training. (At the 1924 Olympic Games, a Haitian team composed entirely of native *gendarmes* would win the silver medal in the rifle team event.)[37]

On September 17, 1920, Puller took over as commander of a sub-district centered on Petite Rivière, a town of five thousand strategically placed in the heart of the Artibonite plain. During this tranquil period he made frequent patrols, but his primary focus was the same as the rest of the Gendarmerie—putting the organization on a permanent footing. He spent much of his time supervising the construction of barracks. Both soldiers and prisoners provided the labor and it was up to commanders to procure materials cheaply, given the Gendarmerie's extremely tight budget. The constabulary cut lumber, quarried stone, made bricks, and hauled sand and coral from the sea. About the only item it purchased was the galvanized iron for the roofs.[38]

Puller seemed to bounce out of the mental slump he had been in during his tour in Port-à-Piment and he took to the task with renewed energy. His district commander gave him special mention in a monthly report for "excellent work." A new commander soon after would second that endorsement with more glowing praise: "Lt. Puller has his command in excellent shape, well disciplined and drilled. This officer has taken great interest in the building of barracks at Verrettes and La Chappelle and deserves the credit for their construction. He speaks Creole very well and is liked by Haitian officials. His Sub-District is the largest one in the District and all reports, correspondence, etc. rendered by him are correct. He is interested in his work and is fully capable of handling a larger command." Later the commander noted that his lieutenant "has repaired and improved the barracks at Petite Rivière beyond what was considered possible with the means at his disposal." On his fitness reports, Puller now expressed an intention to extend his enlistment in the Marine Corps when it expired.[39]

On March 6, 1921, he transferred yet again, this time to be the subdistrict commander at St. Marc, a seaport of thirteen thousand located sixty miles north of Port-au-Prince. This also was the seat of the district headquarters and for his first month he was the acting district commander pending the arrival of Major Rockey. During this brief stint he oversaw a region of hundreds of square miles and more than 100,000 people, though he was familiar with much of it since it included his old posts at Petite Rivière and Verrettes.[40]

In the spring of 1921 Puller received tangible recognition of his superior work. On April 7 the Marine Corps promoted him to corporal and four days later the Chief of the Gendarmerie recommended him for elevation to first lieutenant in that force. Before the month was over he received a long-awaited Good Conduct Medal for his first enlistment during the World War. Most important of all, it appeared that he finally would have the opportunity again to pin on the coveted gold bars of a Marine lieutenant.[41]

3

"I Have Some Perseverance"
A Junior Officer in Peacetime
1921–1928

Almost since his arrival in Haiti, Puller had been striving to regain his commission in the Corps. In December 1919, under the mistaken impression that the Corps would be giving an examination for officer candidates, he made a formal request to participate. A few months later, the Commandant did write to all former wartime officers, telling them they could apply for vacancies if Congress granted a request to expand the Corps. The letter came to Mrs. Puller and she forwarded it to Haiti, but also replied to Washington that her son was interested in being considered. He received the letter at Port-à-Piment and made his official preference known.[1]

The anticipated manpower increase did not materialize, but fate gave Puller an opportunity. In 1919 a board under Colonel John H. Russell had selected those temporary wartime officers the Corps would maintain on active duty. Composed of senior Marines who had not fought in France, it ignored combat records and gave preference to factors such as education. (Russell supposedly told his fellow board members to pick those young men they would be willing to let their daughters marry.) Both the Secretary of the Navy and Congress were upset with the results. In June 1920 the legislators directed the Marine Corps to reevaluate its decision. Upon his assumption of the commandancy at the end of that month, Lejeune appointed a new board under Brigadier General Wendell C. Neville, a veteran of the Western Front.

All of the 1,200 surviving temporary officers of 1917–1919 were eligible for one of the 750 spaces allotted to lieutenants and captains in the postwar Corps. Lejeune regretted that the boards created "much unrest among the officers owing to their uncertain status." The process gave some hope, however, to Puller and others seeking to regain their status.[2]

The Neville Board issued its findings in March 1921. Three Marine NCOs in Haiti made it. Puller did not. As expected, the board had favored combat veterans, not only in selection but also in establishing precedence on the seniority list. Some who had done well in France vaulted from lieutenant to captain while others who had not gotten overseas went in the opposite direction. The changes, made without regard to dates of original commissioning, created some hard feelings and resulted in a few resignations. Puller would harbor his own resentment, as he felt that he should have been selected based on his record in Haiti. He was especially incensed that an NCO in the brigade headquarters in Port-au-Prince made the cut. Puller believed that his rear-echelon competitor was selected solely due to his status as an NCO, while his own service on the front lines with the Gendarmerie had delayed his promotion to corporal in the Corps. In reality, neither enlisted rank nor longevity as an officer had governed the board's decisions.[3]

That was still not the end of the line for Puller. In addition to openings created by angry resignations, some of the Neville Board selectees could not pass the required physicals, others had left the service for civilian opportunities, and a few senior officers had retired or died. In June 1921, the Corps decided to acquire 150 new second lieutenants from the Naval Academy, Army ROTC programs, and its own enlisted ranks. Marines desiring a commission had to be NCOs, undergo both physical and mental screening examinations, receive a recommendation from their commanding officer, and then pass a final battery of academic tests. Puller cleared the initial hurdles and earned a recommendation from the Chief of the Gendarmerie. He received transfer orders within a few days and sailed for the States on June 17. In mid-July he reported for duty at the Marine barracks at the corner of Eighth and I streets in Washington, D.C.[4]

This was the Corps' first attempt to screen officer applicants since the end of the 3d OTC two years before. For the Naval Academy and ROTC graduates, the Corps accepted diplomas as evidence that the candidates possessed the necessary mental qualifications. The NCOs posed a separate problem, since most of them had much less education. To afford these men a reasonable opportunity to meet academic requirements, Headquarters established a Candidates School at the Washington barracks under the command of Major Clayton B. Vogel. It essentially was a cram course for the final examinations, though it also provided a means for senior officers to observe and evaluate the applicants in a number of areas. Sixty-five NCOs took up residence in the post gymnasium and began a demanding program of several months duration.

Their daily schedule called for reveille at 0535 and taps at 2200. In between they had an exercise period before breakfast, an hour of drill, five hours of class, and three hours of supervised study. On Saturdays they took academic tests or received practical instruction in tactics and similar topics. They had liberty each weekday evening and Saturday night through Sunday night. The subjects covered were mathematics, English, history, and geography. In addition to academic grades, the candidates received weekly efficiency reports from all instructors, who were supposed to score each man on a list of twenty qualities desired in future officers.[5]

As the course progressed, the instructors dropped eleven men who were not measuring up. Puller very nearly fell into that category after he returned more than two hours late from liberty. Vogel assigned the corporal to a summary court-martial. Puller pled guilty and received a $45 fine, about a month's worth of pay. The major might have thrown him out of the school, too, but elected not to do so. On the positive side of the ledger, the former Gendarmerie lieutenant had good recommendations from several of the senior officers he had served under. Rockey gave him the strongest praise: "Corporal Puller possesses the instincts and bearing of a gentleman, a fine character, and an unusual sense of responsibility and attention to duty."[6]

Puller did not fare well in the demanding course. His efficiency reports initially placed him in the excellent category with a 3.7 out of a possible 4.0, but those scores dropped each month and ended up at 3.26, which placed him thirty-third in the class in that area. Academically, he flunked five of the eleven subjects and had a failing average overall. That mediocre performance in the preparation program did not prevent him from taking the officer qualifying examinations, however, and he did so beginning on December 19 along with the rest of the class.

The examining board issued the results on February 8, 1922. It recommended nineteen men for commissioning, with the minimum examination score being a 3.19. Puller had a 2.54 average. His failed compatriots included two other Gendarmerie officers and Corporal Ernest E. Linsert (who would earn a commission later and head the development of the amphibious landing craft that helped win World War II). One of the successful candidates was Corporal Vernon E. McGee—he would become a four-star general and a leader in the development of close air support doctrine. The Corps needed many more officers than it finally approved, but Headquarters was determined to keep the standards high. A semiofficial statement on the program noted that the door to a commission was open to any NCO, though "it is not open for the mob to rush in but only to those who by hard work have adequately prepared themselves to 'carry on' successfully." Puller certainly was not one of the "mob," but he had let a splendid chance slip through his grasp.[7]

☆ ☆ ☆

Headquarters transferred Puller to an infantry unit at Quantico. A number of his classmates, including the other former Gendarmerie officers, took yet another examination, this one to qualify them for duty in Haiti. Puller did not take the test, but Major Vogel recommended him for a slot. The Gendarmerie seconded that nomination. The twenty-four-year-old corporal soon was on a transport bound for Port-au-Prince. He arrived on March 29, 1922. Although his commission as a Gendarmerie first lieutenant had come through in June 1921, his transfer that summer had forfeited that rank. Now he had to rejoin the constabulary as a second lieutenant. He did receive one promotion soon thereafter, to sergeant in the Marine Corps on May 11. That $10 increase per month in U.S. pay did not begin to offset the $40 he had lost in his Haitian salary—a bitter postscript to his failed attempt to regain his Marine commission.[8]

Vandegrift, commander of the Department of the South, selected Puller to be his adjutant. It was a headquarters job in Port-au-Prince, but the aggressive young officer was not missing out on any combat operations in the now quiet country. He lived with other American junior officers and led a comparatively easy existence in the capital. The city of 125,000 consisted largely of slums, but it did have amenities rarely available elsewhere in Haiti. One luxury was the American Club, which provided athletic facilities and hosted frequent social activities. There also was a well-stocked post exchange, telephone service, electricity, motion pictures, and the brigade hospital. Puller also found plenty of time to participate in baseball and other sports. It was a far cry from the isolation and hardships he had experienced previously in small Haitian towns.[9]

☆   ☆   ☆

Historically the duties of an adjutant had been wide-ranging. In the days when a general could see the entire battlefield from his horse, his adjutant wrote out the orders and collected information from subordinate commands. The growing complexity of warfare had rendered that method of operational control outmoded. Many professional military forces had adopted a general staff system that divided work among several sections, usually personnel (G-1), intelligence (G-2), operations (G-3), and logistics (G-4). The Corps moved in the same direction during the World War, but some Marine officers viewed that as a mistake and yearned for the old days of a minuscule operational staff.[10]

In 1921 the Chief of the Gendarmerie had tried to adopt the general staff system for his organization but could not obtain the necessary increase in officers to man it. As a consequence, the headquarters of the Department of the South in 1922 consisted of the commander, the adjutant, a medical officer, an NCO, and three privates. This tiny group controlled a force of 750 men and half of Haiti's eleven thousand square miles. That gave Puller much to do, but also allowed him to learn quite a bit about the various tasks involved in running a large outfit.

His primary duty was processing a multitude of reports. Some of these concerned intelligence and operations, though most were related to the constabulary's civil work. He also had to deal with personnel, pay, and quartermaster issues. His department commanders were thoroughly satisfied with his ability to handle these tasks and gave him superior ratings for "administrative and executive duties" in his fitness reports. In fact, on two of his three evaluations it was the only superior ranking he earned among the thirteen performance-related topics. Both Vandegrift and his replacement found their adjutant to be an efficient, reliable hard worker. Perhaps the only shortcoming of Puller's tour as a staff officer was the absence of field duty. He did not experience the planning of tactical operations or the requirements of supplying them and thus missed out on what would have been the most educational aspect of his billet.[11]

☆ ☆ ☆

There was one small irony in Puller's return to Haiti. The issue of the *Gendarmerie News* that carried a notice welcoming him back also featured an article on Marine commissioning programs. It emphasized that a stint as a constabulary officer "opened up an unusual opportunity for promotion from the ranks," because it gave an enlisted man the chance to "bring out his abilities to the front." While that statement might have felt a little bit like salt in the wound for Puller, it did represent the strongly held views of the Chief of the Gendarmerie, Lieutenant Colonel Douglas C. McDougal. The constabulary leader had a long record of trying to obtain Marine commissions for NCOs and that would greatly benefit one certain Marine sergeant.[12]

In the fall of 1922 the Commandant sought comments on a list of Marines nominated for warrant officer. Puller was among those being considered. Vandegrift provided a solid endorsement. He noted that his adjutant was "a man of sterling qualities and conscientious in the performance of his duties." The promotion never materialized, probably because Puller was far short of the ten years of service normally required.[13]

Senior Gendarmerie officers did not give up on Puller's situation. In January 1923 Headquarters solicited nominations for NCOs to take the qualifying exam for that year's officer candidate school. Vandegrift submitted his adjutant's name along with a two-page recommendation. McDougal added the endorsement that Puller had "the ability to make an excellent officer." When the department commander went home on leave soon after, he stopped in at Headquarters to plead Puller's case and ensure he was not prejudiced by his previous failure. The Corps allowed the Gendarmerie adjutant to take the preliminary exam on May 5. He passed. Vandegrift's intervention was undoubtedly crucial in gaining a second chance for Puller. In the 1930s, the senior officer would claim, without exaggeration, that he was "more or less responsible for Puller's receiving a commission."[14]

Puller's four-year enlistment ended on June 30, 1923, as he waited for transportation to the States. With the incentive of yet another shot at a Marine commission, he had no difficulty deciding to sign on for three more years of service. McDougal had a parting gift for him. Technically Puller was not eligible for a second award of the Good Conduct Medal due to his summary court-martial, but the constabulary chief asked for a waiver of the rule given his "exceptionally good" service. Headquarters issued the bar designating a second award. McDougal drew the line, however, at the government bearing the cost of Puller's second transfer home from Haiti before the completion of a full tour—he made the sergeant pay his own way.[15]

Puller had spent the past four years as a Gendarmerie lieutenant or an officer candidate, so he had a wealth of valuable experience. That by itself meant little, as Stonewall Jackson's biographer observed: "Whether a young soldier learns much or little from his first campaign depends on his intellectual powers and his previous training." But the young Marine, like his hero, "was no thoughtless subaltern, but already an earnest soldier." For four months Puller had patrolled Haiti in active combat operations, resulting in several engagements with the enemy. He had been at the heart of the constabulary's flirtation with a mobile striking force, an innovation that would appear again in the Corps' next small war. He participated in some of the early work of aircraft operating in support of troops on the ground. He had gained an appreciation for the abilities of native troops and had an understanding of the civil-military intricacies of small wars. He even had mastered some of the basic skills of a staff officer. He certainly was not "one of the most seasoned combat officers in the Corps," not even among those who had served in Haiti, but he was as well groomed for a commission as any officer candidate could ever hope to be.[16]

☆   ☆   ☆

The Candidates School of 1923 operated in much the same fashion as that of 1921. Puller started off strong again, with a military efficiency grade of 3.6 and no academic score lower than an 81 during the first month. His performance did decline in some areas during the course and he ended up failing three subjects: trigonometry, geometry, and (surprisingly) history. His overall academic average was an anemic but passing 78, while his military efficiency grade actually increased to 3.7, the second highest in the class of seventeen NCOs. In terms of the leadership qualities that the instructors evaluated, they gave him the strongest marks for his bearing and conduct and found him weakest in mental endurance and quickness of perception. Other than a short bout with acute tonsillitis, there was nothing remarkable about this tour at the Washington barracks.[17]

For the 1923 final examinations, Headquarters established slightly different criteria, which decreased the importance of the academic results. The candidates took written tests in ten subjects, but also received a separate score based on their record of service, with the latter constituting a third of the overall grade. The men still had to attain a passing mark in each individual test, however. The former Gendarmerie lieutenant had one additional factor in his favor; the two senior members of the board were Majors Rossell and E. A. Ostermann, both of whom had commanded him in Haiti and previously recommended him for a commission. The examining board began its work on January 14, 1924, and remained in session for a period of two weeks. Puller finished fifth out of the ten men who made the cut.[18]

Puller pinned on his gold bars on March 6, 1924, at the Marine barracks in Washington. He had started the long, hard trail to a commission nearly seven years before at VMI and now, finally and permanently, had achieved his dream. He remarked to a friend: "I may not have much else to go on, but I have some perseverance." He should have added that some of his senior officers had been persistent, too, in their efforts to help him reach his goal. Vandegrift later would cite Puller's second chance at the Candidates School as proof of General Lejeune's philosophy that a young man "should be allowed one mistake without having it held against him."[19]

☆   ☆   ☆

The next stop for the new lieutenants normally would have been the Basic School. This course for fledgling officers had existed in one form or another (to include OTC) since 1891. Its purpose was to teach them how to function effectively as junior leaders. In the spring of 1924 the school moved from Quantico to the Philadelphia Navy Yard. Due to space limitations at the barracks there, Headquarters instituted a schedule of two semiannual classes. So, four of the former NCOs reported directly to Philadelphia, while Puller and the others went to the Marine barracks at the Norfolk Navy Yard pending the start of their course in January 1925.[20]

The six new lieutenants, later reinforced by two graduates each from the Naval Academy and ROTC, were a godsend to the barracks commander, who suddenly had a pool of labor to help out his small command. Puller assisted the adjutant. All of them took turns as the officer of the day, which required them to inspect guard posts and serve as the commander's representative for a twenty-four-hour period. In July a new colonel reported aboard to head the barracks. He added academic study to the practical work experience. There were two hours of class each day, with the curriculum modeled on that used at the Basic School. Puller performed adequately in this informal program and he again finished fifth among his ten compatriots.[21]

On January 2, 1925, Puller and twenty-five other lieutenants began their five-month course in Philadelphia. The Basic School was housed entirely in a two-story brick building with classrooms and offices on the lower level and student living quarters on the second deck. Each bachelor lieutenant had his own room and a servant. Married students were allowed to reside in town.

The routine was not demanding but it was confining. The day started with reveille at 0630, followed by a period of physical exercise and breakfast. The students attended four one-hour classes in the morning, usually devoted to academic studies, and two sixty-minute sessions in the afternoon, generally involving practical application such as close order drill, weapons, sand table exercises, or mock trials. Three afternoons per week they participated in some form of outdoor physical training. They had free time for the brief period from the close of the workday till 1900, then had a study period lasting till 2200 and taps. Instructors used Saturday mornings for examinations and practical exercises. Students who had passed all graded events for the week received liberty from Saturday afternoon through Sunday evening. Approximately once every four weeks a student had to stand watch as the junior officer of the day.

The new lieutenants resented the level of supervision under which they labored. The junior officer of the day, for instance, had to ensure that each man was in his room for the evening study period and that there was no loud talking or socializing. The lieutenants were confined to quarters from taps to reveille. Even during authorized liberty, they could not leave the environs of Philadelphia without permission. Instructors inspected their rooms daily. Russell N. Jordahl, a student in the class after Puller's and a future general, thought he and his class-mates "were subjected to rules and regulations suitable for high school boys."[22]

Academically the course focused on eleven subjects: administration, military law, topography, field engineering, interior guard duty, tactics, musketry (field firing), drill regulations, marksmanship, first aid and military hygiene, and boats. Tactics, which included the study of company-level operations and all infantry weapons, was the largest block of instruction at 176 hours. The subject of boats—how to command the small launches carried on naval vessels—received just three hours. Each of these major headings was further subdivided into specific topics. Some of the most important elements (judging by the time devoted to them) were mapmaking (sixty-nine hours), practical drill (forty-two hours), combat principles (thirty-three hours), and machine gun indirect fire (twenty-nine hours). The only field training consisted of two weeks on the weapons ranges.[23]

Puller may have been bored by much of the package, since he had gone through OTC and spent several years already working as an officer. However, despite having served as a commander in combat, he had little knowledge of the formalized tactics required for large-scale conflicts. He also had little familiarity with crew-served infantry weapons such as Browning machine guns, mortars, and 37mm guns. As it turned out, his lowest score was in weapons and tactics (65 percent). His best subjects were interior guard (94 percent) and marksmanship (91 percent). He qualified as an expert on the rifle range, but could attain only a marksman's badge with the pistol. He finished the course with a 75.7 percent average, which placed him twenty-second out of twenty-six.[24]

Puller was now a full-fledged member of a very small fraternity. In the Corps of the mid-1920s there were barely one thousand officers and it did not take long to get to know most of the others, by reputation if not in person. They had different motivations for choosing to serve, but these did not include money or rank. A second lieutenant earned just $125 per month, less than Puller had made as a corporal and Gendarmerie first lieutenant. Since promotion was solely by seniority and the vast majority of officers had joined during the World War, there was little prospect for advancement. The Basic School graduates of 1925 could look forward after a thirty-year career to retiring as senior captains or perhaps majors if they were lucky. There was some adventure to be had, with Marines serving in exotic locales such as China and aboard Navy vessels all around the world. There was an unusual lull in action, however, as the Corps found itself in a rare period of peace. With no sound of the guns toward which he could march, Puller requested duty at either Quantico or Parris Island. Headquarters granted his first choice.[25]

☆   ☆   ☆

Puller reported on July 1, 1925, for duty with the 6th Battery of the 10th Regiment, the artillery arm of the East Coast Expeditionary Force. This organization—composed of the artillery regiment, two infantry regiments, aviation squadrons, and support units—was designed to seize or defend overseas bases or conduct other operations ashore in support of the Navy. It was the successor to the Advance Base Force, Puller's parent unit for a short period in late 1918. In this era, Marine officers were supposed to be able to handle any field assignment; they received no advanced schooling for specialties such as artillery. When Puller joined the battery, he knew nothing about the unit's 75mm field pieces, French-designed weapons acquired by the Corps during the World War. He was not alone, as there were only three officers left in the entire regiment who had served with it during field maneuvers in the Caribbean the summer before.[26]

The new lieutenant had been with his outfit for just two weeks when the battery commander took leave. One of the other officers was at the rifle range and the third was also on leave, so that left Puller in charge of the ninety-four enlisted men. He later recalled that he was faced with an upcoming live-fire shoot but still lacked the knowledge required to run his four-gun battery. He was especially concerned because several senior officers would observe the exercise. He turned to his NCOs and asked for their advice and assistance. The battery's ordnance man, Gunnery Sergeant Nicklos Mihnowske, taught him about the weapons and their employment.

As Puller remembered it, the gunny explained that the battery fired adjustment rounds from a base gun, with an observer providing input for necessary corrections after he spotted the explosion of each shell. Once the base piece was on target, the gunners applied the same settings for elevation and deflection to the others and the entire battery fired together. The goal was to have the base gun on target by the third shot. The veteran NCO also said that the senior officers scheduled to attend the shoot had notoriously bad eyesight and would not really know where the shells were landing. He suggested that the lieutenant order the entire battery to fire after the third adjustment round, no matter where it fell, and then inform the commanders that he was right on target. Puller probably did not have to follow this advice, since three captains joined the battery in early August prior to the regiment's September live-fire exercise. He drew the conclusion, however, "that the Corps was in fact operated by its senior noncoms and that too few officers knew the basic details of their trade."[27]

The regiment began a two-day motor march to Camp Meade, Maryland, on August 21 and completed the trip after an overnight stop at a park near Washington. The batteries spent the next several days training and practicing with live shells in preparation for the regimental shoot on September 2. The observers for this final exercise included Commandant Lejeune and Brigadier General Dion Williams (former commander of the 10th Marines). A squadron of seven Marine planes supported the event by picking out targets for the artillerymen.

When the excitement of the shoot was over, the regiment resumed the dull routine of peacetime military service. In addition to Puller's daily work with the men and guns, he was the battery mess officer (in charge of the cooks and bakers) and took his turn as the regimental guard officer. It did not take long for him to seek something more adventurous and challenging.

Almost as soon as the 10th Marines returned to Quantico, Puller took the first step to become a pilot by passing a special physical examination. Although he never explained this decision, the flights in Haiti clearly had piqued his interest and the work of the squadron at Camp Meade must have rekindled that attraction. The timing of his request may have been driven by his association at Camp Meade with a lieutenant from the aviation section who was attached to the battery. The debate over the future of warfare may have influenced him, too. Some military leaders, such as Army Brigadier General William "Billy" Mitchell, were advocating airpower as the arbiter of conflict. On a more personal level, flying was fun and aviators received a 50 percent increase in pay. Undoubtedly all these factors were appealing to someone as ambitious, aggressive, and audacious as Puller. Headquarters, always starved for pilots, quickly informed Puller they would grant his wish early in 1926.[28]

Anxious to get a start on his new career, Puller requested that he be transferred to the aviation group at Quantico pending his orders for flight school. He managed to spend two weeks at the Quantico airfield during October. Then Headquarters assigned the base to prepare a platoon of Marines for an annual interservice drill competition sponsored by the governor of Massachusetts. The mission landed in the lap of Captain Jimmy Wayt, the new commander of the 6th Battery. The mustang officer probably received the task because he had helped run the NCO school at Parris Island during the war—he undoubtedly knew a thing or two about drill. He called on Puller, one of his former students, to assist him in training the platoon and to command it during the competition. There was considerable pressure to do well, as the Army had won the trophy the past two years and would get to keep it permanently with a third successive victory.

The two officers and their picked men worked hard for a month, then traveled to Boston for the December 3 event. The senior Marine officer in the region attended the competition and telegraphed the results to the base commander at Quantico: "The drill was splendid, the uniforms and appearance of the men were very fine, Lieutenant Puller was an inspiring drill officer." That assessment was seconded by the judges and the Marines marched away with the trophy. The only blemish of the trip came that night, when the men celebrated their victory in downtown Boston. One Marine, probably with a few drinks under his belt, climbed aboard a camel in a passing circus parade, only to fall off and end up in the hospital. General Lejeune, equally pleased with the triumph, wired congratulations to the unit and formally commended Wayt and Puller.[29]

November had been a busy month for Puller, as he also had taken the professional examinations to complete his period as a probationary lieutenant. That must have set him to thinking about his career, since he took time to pen a lengthy request to Headquarters asking that his Gendarmerie fitness reports and the citation for the Médaille Militaire be made a part of his official officer records. In addition, he repeated an earlier complaint that the 1925 register of Marine officers had omitted mention of his ten days of previous commissioned service.[30]

At the beginning of 1926, Puller finally received the transfer to the 1st Aviation Group that he had requested in September. The Quantico fliers gave him a month of preliminary instruction before sending him on to flight school at the Naval Air Station at Pensacola, Florida. That extra training should have given him an advantage at the upcoming school, but the lieutenant had not been a gifted pupil. The group commander, Major Thomas C. Turner, a mustang who had learned to fly after sixteen years in the service, found Puller "hardworking but slow."[31]

☆　☆　☆

During one of his leave periods in the mid-1920s, Puller went back to West Point, although there was little left to attract him there. His mother had died in April 1923. His sister Pattie now lived in Richmond, while Emily had married and moved to California. Sam had been tossed out of VMI after he accidentally struck an officer with a potato in a mess hall food fight. He was now working on his degree at St. John's College in Maryland. Many of Lewis's friends had moved away or gotten married, and the bachelor Marine felt out of place. He went on to nearby Urbanna to visit with relatives. At a dance there, he encountered Virginia Evans, the daughter of an old friend of the family. He had remembered her as a youngster with freckles. Now she was an attractive brunette and herself visiting home from Saint Mary's College in North Carolina. He fell in love at first sight. He was able to take his turn with other young men and have a few dances with her, but he found that his martial skills did not prepare him for this type of contest. He didn't know how to carry on a conversation with a charming young woman. True to form, he determined to try the one tactic that worked when he was in a tight situation—he charged straight ahead. In the middle of their next number together, he impetuously asked her to marry him. The confident, levelheaded student was not swept off her feet by the dashing lieutenant—she refused. Even so, she was impressed that he ignored the other girls and waited patiently by the sidelines the rest of the evening to get an occasional dance with her. He had not won the engagement, but he also knew that it often took a sustained campaign to wear down a determined challenger. He returned to duty at the end of his leave, resolved to regroup his forces and try again.[32]

☆　☆　☆

At the beginning of 1926 Marine aviation consisted of just fifty-six active pilots even though it had an authorized strength of nearly one hundred. The dearth of fliers was easy to explain. One cause was a policy that required aviators with five years in a flying billet to return to line duty for at least three years. While that rule kept the aviation community closely tied to the rest of the Corps, it created holes that had to be filled. A second factor was the difficult entry-level training program, which resulted in a high failure rate. One Marine who completed the course during this period later noted that "they dared you to get through." The third reason was the most disquieting one—aircraft were still crude machines and the accident rate was high. In 1922, for example, the Corps had trained seventeen new pilots and lost a total of nine in fatal crashes. The year prior to Puller's request for aviation duty, eleven Marines earned their wings and four were killed. In all, forty-one Marines died in flight accidents from 1920 through 1925 (eight of them at Pensacola). Flying promised equal parts danger, excitement, and career opportunity—if one lived long enough.[33]

The Pensacola flight school lasted five months. It began with four weeks of theoretical study, known as ground school. These classes then continued while students underwent a month of flying under instruction, which consisted of several short flights per week with a qualified pilot in the plane. The aircraft used in this stage of the course was the Curtiss N-9 Jenny, a two-seat, biwinged seaplane that could land and take off only on water. The syllabus was designed to teach the student to solo by the tenth hour of instruction in the air, with reevaluations every five hours of flight time thereafter until graduation.[34]

Puller got off to a bad start at Pensacola and never recovered. He performed very poorly in ground school, failing six subjects and standing last in his class of sixty-three. The five- and ten-hour flight reports rated him below average in many skills. His Marine instructor thought he was "slow to learn" and "couldn't fly at all until his tenth hour." The Navy pilot grading Puller's first solo attempt rated it unsatisfactory, but he passed the lieutenant on his second try. Another Marine instructor checked him out after five hours of solo work and noted that his performance was poor in a number of areas. Puller made two check flights at the ten-hour mark and both the Marine and the Navy pilots rated him unsatisfactory.

On May 5 a review board evaluated Puller's case. Three aviators voted to retain him even though they noted his serious deficiencies. Four others, including the chief flight instructor and the squadron commander, thought he should be dropped. Given a chance to make a statement in his behalf, the student pilot acknowledged his difficulties through the first ten hours: "Up to that time I think that all my instruction was wasted, but I believe I can fly all right now. My ground school record I know is low but I can correct that; I can make those examinations up. When most of the other students were going to school, I was in the Marine Corps at that age." (While that was true, it conveniently ignored his two long academic stints in Candidates School.) The officers asked only one question, whether he had received "considerate treatment while under instruction." Puller replied that he had. The board then issued its recommendation that he be dropped from the school rather than be recycled into a subsequent class.[35]

In a specialty with so little margin for error between life and death, it was probably a good thing that the aviators were not as willing as the rest of the Corps to give second chances—Puller would survive to fight another day. Nor would his lack of success as a pilot count against him. It was a distinction he would share with Merritt A. Edson, Evans F. Carlson, and Merrill B. Twining, three other renowned Marine ground officers of World War II.[36]

The day after the board, Puller asked for assignment to the Gendarmerie again. Failing that, he hoped for duty with the 1st Marine Brigade in Haiti. Headquarters issued orders on May 14 for the lieutenant to report for transport to Hawaii, where he would join the Marine barracks at the Pearl Harbor Navy base. In the Corps of the mid-1920s, when money was often more valuable than time, Puller had to wait for space on any government vessel headed for Hawaii. He finally made it to Pearl Harbor on July 17.[37]

One of Puller's last acts before leaving the States was to send three orchids to Virginia Evans. The token of love had cost him $10, but it had the desired effect. She replied with an excited letter. He answered her from his new post in the same direct fashion that had marked his first proposal: "Marry me, and I'll buy you three dozen orchids, every month of your life."[38]

☆ ☆ ☆

The Hawaiian Islands were a comparatively sleepy outpost in the 1920s. Although the United States had been developing plans for years to deal with a war with Japan, everyone assumed that the struggle would take place in the Philippines and at sea in the Western Pacific.

The Navy's presence in Hawaii was small; most of its ships and planes were stationed along the Atlantic and Pacific coasts of the mainland or with the Asiatic Fleet in China. Hawaii had an Army garrison, some old coast defense forts, and a few hundred Marines guarding the naval installations. The Marines were all part of the barracks at Pearl Harbor, though several detachments of this force performed various functions elsewhere on Oahu and on the outlying islands.

Puller joined the 92d Company and received command of one of its two platoons. The other lieutenant in the unit was Merrill Twining. The cash-strapped young officers spent a lot of their free time talking and became "lifelong friends" even though they had different natures. Twining was an extremely intelligent Marine who would fashion an outstanding reputation as a superior staff officer. He found Puller to be a good storyteller but rather set in his opinions.[39]

The daily routine of the barracks in Hawaii was like that of any other similar Marine unit at Navy bases around the world. The men stood guard at the gates and other critical locations, conducted close order drill, participated in occasional training events, and attended to the work of maintaining the spit-and-polish image of Marines. The lieutenants supervised the men and took turns as the officer of the day. The twenty-four-hour-a-day, year-round schedule of guard duty made it easy to forget that the barracks had an additional mission. Since the early days of the Corps, barracks detachments had served as the manpower pool for the creation of provisional field units in a crisis. Lejeune had changed that to a degree by creating a standing expeditionary force on each coast of the mainland, but these were well under war strength and Headquarters still expected the barracks units to fill them out. The barracks at Pearl Harbor also was part of the defense force for the Hawaiian Islands. According to the contingency plans, the 92d Company would serve as a machine gun unit armed with the Browning .30 caliber water-cooled model.

Not long after Puller reported aboard, he learned of his platoon's wartime role and investigated its readiness to execute the mission. He discovered that the company never trained with the guns and that the weapons lacked many of the accessory items such as water cans and hoses required to make them operational. He raised the issue with his company commander and then the barracks commander. Colonel Newt H. Hall was a twenty-nine-year veteran who had served in the Boxer

Rebellion of 1900. He had graduated last in his class from the Naval Academy in 1897 and Twining thought him unaggressive. True to that characterization, Hall expressed surprise when Puller told him about the state of the unit's machine guns. Soon thereafter Puller initiated a training program, the quartermaster requisitioned the parts, and Hall commended his subordinate for being "an officer well above the average second lieutenant."[40]

In January 1927 Hall gave Puller a new assignment as the officer in charge of the rifle range detachment. For the next three months he supervised the permanent range personnel and handled the requalification firing of all Marines and sailors in Hawaii. One of the senior enlisted coaches took Puller under his wing and taught him advanced marksmanship techniques. With that special assistance and plenty of opportunity to practice, he raised his expert rifle score even higher. In April Puller moved yet again, this time to the big island of Hawaii. Here he had what must have been the most relaxing tour of his long career—commander of the guard detachment at the Navy Health and Recreation Center. He remained there till early December and then returned to Oahu to resume his old duties as a platoon commander at the main barracks.[41]

Puller began to consider his next assignment. He submitted a request to take another crack at flight school and Headquarters quickly denied it. Undaunted, Puller tried again, this time with a lengthy argument concerning his lack of flight training prior to Pensacola and the particulars of his failed checks. This request went all the way to the Navy's Bureau of Aeronautics. Captain Ernest J. King, the acting head of the branch, noted that the Marine lieutenant had failed both in ground school and in the air and refused to grant a waiver.[42]

An extremely tight manpower situation and a desire to economize on travel costs ended up dictating Puller's new duty station. Each summer the Corps held a series of regional marksmanship competitions. The Marine barracks in Hawaii had to send its team to the Western Division competition in San Diego, so it nominated Puller and a captain, both due for transfer, to head its team. Headquarters agreed to the choices and announced that the two officers would belong to Marine Corps Base San Diego at the conclusion of the matches.[43]

The Pearl Harbor contingent left Hawaii aboard the SS *City of Los Angeles* on April 7, 1928, and arrived in California a week later. They spent a month practicing at the rifle range before firing in the three-day matches in mid-May. There is no record of Puller's scores, but he did not qualify for the next level of competition. That might have been due to illness, as he entered the hospital a few days later with acute tonsillitis and remained there for a week. For the next few months he drifted through a series of short jobs in the San Diego area. He spent three weeks at the base headquarters, two weeks on leave, five weeks as the assistant rifle range officer, five weeks as a platoon commander at the recruit depot, eight weeks as the guard commander of the naval air station, and then another week back at the recruit depot. All of his seniors were pleased with his performance and the Navy captain commanding the air station noted that Puller had "made marked improvement in efficiency of the Marine Guard of this station."[44]

☆   ☆   ☆

The lieutenant's nomadic existence was due to a severe manpower crunch brought on by a spate of emergency overseas deployments. China exploded into a virulent civil war in early 1927 and the United States dispatched a force to the great port city of Shanghai to protect American lives and property. Almost the entire Marine barracks at Guam went in February, followed by the 4th Regiment from San Diego a few weeks later. In May a brigade headquarters, the 6th Regiment, and supporting units arrived to reinforce them. The 3d Marine Brigade totaled nearly 4,500 officers and men, a quarter of the entire strength of the Corps, and HQMC had been forced to create a third battalion from scratch for each of the two regiments. A civil war in Nicaragua resulted in American intervention there. Marine detachments from Navy ships went ashore in January 1927 and soon were reinforced by the 5th Regiment from Quantico. By May the 11th Regiment and other units joined them to form the 2d Marine Brigade, a force of 3,300 men. On top of these expeditions, the Corps still maintained the legation guard in Peking, the 1st Marine Brigade in Haiti, and its usual scattered detachments on ships and at Navy bases overseas.[45]

The rapid deployment in the space of a few months of more than 40 percent of the Corps had stretched the tiny service to the breaking point. As an example, nearly the entire 10th Regiment was cannibalized to fill out its 1st Battalion at war strength to serve as the artillery component of the 2d Brigade. The vast majority of students and instructors at the Marine Corps Schools in Quantico had shipped out with one or another of the units. Of the 17,861 enlisted men in the Marine Corps in May 1927, fully 64 percent were outside the continental United States. Among lieutenants, 57 percent were overseas.[46]

During the summer of 1927 things seemed to quiet down in both China and Nicaragua and a few of the Marine units headed home. Puller had not volunteered for the deployments; instead he had focused his efforts on getting back to flight school. With that goal squelched in 1928, he finally began to look overseas for an assignment with one of the expeditionary forces. In May he asked for a transfer to the brigade in Nicaragua or its counterpart in China. His seniors, noting his recent return from an overseas billet and "the marked shortage of officers" at San Diego, recommended disapproval. Headquarters agreed and told the lieutenant he would stay put. In October he submitted a similar request, this time asking for the new Guardia Nacional de Nicaragua or the Gendarmerie d'Haiti. With the turmoil of the emergency deployments fading and the situation in Nicaragua heating up, the chain of command was more amenable to the idea. On November 5, 1928, HQMC issued orders for Puller to report to Nicaragua for duty with the Guardia. For the second time in his career he was sailing to the sound of the guns.[47]

4
"Days of Hard Marching"
First Tour in Nicaragua
1928–1930

Puller's time in Haiti had not given him any special reputation as a combat leader or constabulary officer. In December 1927 and again in October 1928 the head of the Nicaraguan Guardia had sent HQMC a list of officers whose services he desired. Neither roster included Puller. Most of the Marines were not available, however, so Headquarters asked the colonel if he would accept Puller, who had a transfer request on file. The reply was in the affirmative. When the aggressive second lieutenant arrived in Nicaragua on December 5, 1928, he was undoubtedly surprised to find that he would be on the Guardia staff as the personnel officer (G-1).[1]

☆   ☆   ☆

The United States had a history of intervention in Nicaragua dating back to 1853. Many of these operations were the result of civil wars between the dominant political movements, known as the Liberals and Conservatives. In 1926 the Liberals revolted. In early 1927 President Calvin Coolidge ordered several ships' detachments and then a Marine brigade into the fray. By May this show of might allowed the United States to broker a peace treaty. The United States promised to supervise honest elections and assist Nicaragua in establishing a nonpartisan constabulary. Most of the revolutionaries agreed to turn in their arms. Some of the American troops headed home.

One minor Liberal leader, Augusto César Sandino, took his small group of armed men into the unmapped, sparsely inhabited north-central highlands. He called for a patriotic war to oust the North Americans from the homeland and sweetened the pot for potential recruits with loot from a pillaged mine and town. Eventually other groups sprang up, some working with Sandino and others merely using his name. Marine leaders universally referred to all these fighters as bandits and in some cases that was an accurate description.[2]

In July 1927 Sandino led a force of several hundred men against an outpost of Marines and Nicaraguan constabulary at Ocotal. Backed by aerial firepower, the defenders inflicted heavy casualties on the attackers and easily drove them out of town. Soon thereafter Marine planes and ground troops chased the rebel leader out of his supposedly inaccessible mountain fortress. At this point in the war the revolutionaries were poorly equipped. Only a third of the men had rifles; the others carried machetes. Sandino thereafter vowed to avoid conventional battles.

He maintained no fixed base and melted into the eastern region or over the border into Honduras whenever government forces made things too hot in the central highlands. He resorted to the classic strategy of the weak—a guerrilla war.

☆   ☆   ☆

The agreement creating the Guardia stipulated that its American leaders would come from the Marine Corps. This was a natural outcome of previous joint efforts in the Caribbean between the State and Navy departments. The Army tried to place some of its officers in the constabulary, but the Corps squelched this initiative. Once again a handful of Marine officers and NCOs would assume responsibility for molding a dependable military force out of raw native clay in the middle of a civil war. The leader of the Guardia (a Marine lieutenant colonel bearing the title *jefe director*) followed most of the precedents established by his predecessors in the Gendarmerie d'Haiti. By late 1928, the constabulary had reached a strength of 173 officers and 1,637 enlisted men, well on its way to its goal of 190 officers and 2,200 enlisted.[3]

The Guardia never became as enmeshed in civil functions as the Gendarmerie, but it experienced the same early problems. In one six-month period the Guardia transferred out thirty-one Marines who were ineffective as constabulary officers. The *jefe director* felt compelled to issue a series of orders regarding the treatment of Nicaraguan soldiers. One directive stated that "an officer of the Guardia Nacional must not hold either consciously or subconsciously contempt for the enlisted men." It further noted that it was "unfortunate" that some leaders cursed their soldiers or used "epithets which are insulting." Another order pointed out that being "manhandled" was a special affront to a Nicaraguan's sense of honor. These leadership problems were reflected in statistics for the Guardia's first year—159 men deserted, three died in mutinies, and only six were killed in action. Conversely, the Nicaraguan soldiers developed great personal loyalty to good commanders and did not understand the system of transferring personnel between units.[4]

☆   ☆   ☆

Puller, the new G-1, had some experience as an adjutant from his tours in Haiti and Norfolk, but this was his first exposure to the general staff system. At times the headquarters in Managua seemed to go overboard in its desire to follow bureaucratic procedures. One order specified that patrol leaders would make a written report in *"quadruplicate"* of all engagements with the enemy. Before long the Guardia staff was producing a weekly newsletter that kept track of the minutest details about the force. This obsession with paperwork may have initiated Puller's lifelong disdain for staff officers and their efforts.[5]

Whatever reservations he may have had about his billet, Puller performed his duties in an exemplary manner. The *jefe director* remarked on the lieutenant's fitness report that he was "an excellent officer, capable and efficient." The head of the Guardia also commended his adjutant for contributing to the "successful organization" of the outfit.[6]

Puller's stint in Managua was short lived. On March 6 he took command of the garrison in Corinto, the major seaport on the west coast. Policing a large town was no simple task, especially when the population was split by civil war. The *jefe director* thought the lieutenant handled the difficult situation with "force, tact, and good judgment." Puller did equally well on the examination for promotion to first lieutenant in the Marine Corps. He earned his silver bars effective May 24, 1929, and advanced to the rank of captain in the Guardia at almost the same time. He had spent five years as a second lieutenant. He was now too senior for the platoon-sized Corinto detachment and returned to Managua late in May to command the guard force of the national penitentiary. That job lasted barely a week—he finally received the assignment to the field forces he had wanted since his arrival in Nicaragua.[7]

☆   ☆   ☆

Puller's new unit, the 1st Battalion, was headquartered in the town of Jinotega and was responsible for the Central Area (the departments of Jinotega and Matagalpa). The small city nestled at the juncture of two rivers in the middle of a valley surrounded by wooded mountains. The Marines had an airstrip four miles to the north. The main economic activities were raising cattle and coffee, mostly on large ranches (known as *fincas*). To the west was the Northern Area (the departments of Nueva Segovia and Estelí). By 1929 Sandino and his *compadres* were operating primarily in these rugged regions in north-central Nicaragua.[8]

The biggest peril in the Jinotega area was Pedro Altamirano, often referred to as simply as Pedrón. He was rumored to be an illiterate former peasant, but he had become one of "the most powerful Sandinista gen-

erals." He also was one of the least politically motivated in the movement. Many of the true believers thought he was "completely independent from Sandino." Even in Nicaragua, where ritual execution of
opponents had a long history, Pedrón was considered particularly brutal
and outrageous. Many of Sandino's followers regarded Altamirano as a
"murderous assassin." Guardia leaders agreed that he was "the most
savage, cruel, and sanguinary" rebel leader. They also believed he was
their most effective opponent—wily enough to avoid battle when he did
not have the upper hand and a master at using his knowledge of the Nicaraguan wilderness to achieve surprise. Those rare occasions when
government forces fought him resulted in "many of the most desperate
encounters of the Guardia." Pedrón would be the prime protagonist in
Puller's Central Area odyssey.[9]

The 1st Battalion came into being in 1929 as part of the Guardia's
developing concept of how to organize itself to fight. In 1921 the
brigade commander in Haiti had lamented the lack of a striking force, a
unit not tied to the defense of towns and therefore able to conduct offensive operations whenever and wherever necessary. The first *jefe* of
the Guardia had wanted to create a "mobile battalion," a mounted unit
that would serve as his striking force. For a short time in the summer of
1928 he did field a small unit known as the Mobile Patrol, but the lack
of manpower (fewer than two thousand men to police fifty-four thousand square miles) brought the experiment to an end. In the fall of that
year the American chairman of the electoral mission directed the *jefe* to
create two similar units—*"free to move at their own discretion"*—for
the purpose of tracking Altamirano. The two patrols totaling forty men
were unsuccessful and short lived.[10]

Colonel Douglas McDougal had been in command of the Guardia
less than a month when he established the 1st Mobile Battalion on
March 25, 1929. He planned to bring this unit to a strength of fourteen
officers and two hundred men by taking slices of manpower from other
outfits around the country. He wanted the battalion's three companies to
operate as "mobile columns" in the Central Area. For the next several
months the battalion was well short of authorized manpower and it fell
into the recurring trap of garrisoning towns and *fincas*. Its patrols were
infrequent and short.

In early August 1929 McDougal finally achieved the elusive goal of
placing a truly offensive force into the field on a permanent basis. He
stripped sixty men from various units and placed them under the com-

mand of Herman Hanneken, now a Guardia captain. The *jefe director* designated it Company M (for mobile) and issued definite instructions on its role. It would be used solely "for active pursuit of bandits," would disregard department boundaries, and would receive "great latitude." Although initially it was supposed to be a national asset, it soon became a part of the 1st Battalion (which had lost its "mobile" designation).[11]

☆ ☆ ☆

Puller reported to Jinotega on June 4, 1929. He was eager for action, but received yet another disappointment. He became the area quartermaster, in charge of all supply matters. He had minimal training in this field and inherited a mess left by his predecessor (the *jefe director* noted with sarcasm that the prior quartermaster had "felt the duty too onerous"). Budgetary shortages also forced McDougal to cut spending on rations and transport. The daily allowance per man for food dropped by a third and Puller had to figure out how to make do.

The brand-new quartermaster expressed his unhappiness to the battalion executive officer, Captain Edward A. Craig, but dug into the task with a will and performed admirably. Another battalion officer, Graves B. Erskine, would recall Puller's response to the situation: "The Marine Corps was his religion and his life. . . . He never tried to bug out on anything. If a job needed doing I could always depend on Lewie to get the job done one way or another." McDougal praised his subordinate in a fitness report: "This officer took over and organized the QM office of the Central Dept. and out of confusion and chaos has a well running and efficient office."[12]

One task epitomized the oddities that sometimes cropped up when staff officers in a tiny headquarters tried to follow rules laid down by faraway bureaucrats. When it appeared that a few dollars might be missing from the small battalion post exchange, the acting area commander, Erskine, wrote a formal letter to himself appointing himself and Puller to a board to investigate the matter. They interviewed the few lieutenants involved, but the board members also had pertinent information. So Erskine stepped out in front of the table to be questioned by Puller. A few minutes later they traded places and the acting commander interrogated his quartermaster. The lengthy transcript of testimony and the final report met the requirements of the regulations, but cost far more in time and effort than the sum in question.[13]

Puller was not content merely to do his assigned duties and soon

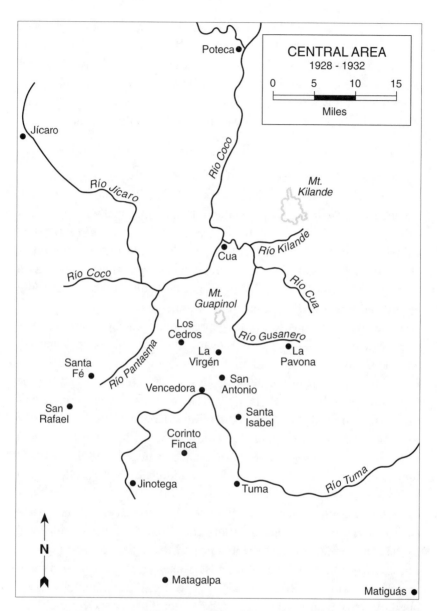

begged his seniors to let him operate in the field when he could spare
some time. The battalion commander and other staff officers went out
on patrol, so the major was willing to oblige his quartermaster on occasion. Puller commanded a sizeable operation during the first half of
July 1929, a force of four patrols totaling five officers and eighty men.
The groups moved northward on parallel courses to sweep an area for
bandits, but saw no significant action in eleven days. Their sole success

was coming across a bandit storehouse with food for thirty men cooking on the fire; they ate the meal and burned the shack. Puller's patrols had flushed Pedrón's force—the first of many encounters between the two leaders. The quartermaster rarely was able to indulge his desire for action, however, and usually left Jinotega only when inspecting outposts or taking supplies to combat patrols.[14]

In January 1930 Puller led three patrols, one of them sent out in response to a report of Altamirano's whereabouts. Those rumors proved false and all he captured was an unattended bull loaded with salt and a Marine poncho. He was not the only one coming up empty-handed. During all of 1929 the Guardia had engaged in just twenty-six battles, most of them minor in nature despite the heated rhetoric of the after-action reports. In August, for example, an estimated sixty bandits attacked the town of Jícaro in the middle of the night. The Guardia captain recounted that "each time a wave of the enemy came over, they were swept with a devastating fire" from his machine guns. The garrison then "dogged the trail of the bandits for hours." Despite this withering fire and hot pursuit, the defenders found no trace of enemy casualties nor did they suffer any themselves. Some of the engagements did spill real blood, but the Guardia still was feeling its way toward effectiveness. It lost just two men killed in action during the period October 1928 through September 1929, while forty-seven died from other causes and 480 deserted. Marine units were turning over most field duties to the Guardia at this time and returning to the States or garrisoning the larger towns. During 1929 they lost four killed and three wounded.[15]

In February 1930 the area commander gave Puller ambitious orders to search a swath of territory north of Jinotega and then check for a bandit camp on top of Mt. Kilande, a remote peak. On the 12th the Guardia captain, a Nicaraguan lieutenant, and twenty men marched out in the middle of the night, probably to reduce the likelihood that bandit sympathizers would observe the move and report it. Surprisingly, Puller seemed slow and unaggressive on this mission. The patrol went only a little way the first night, then departed its rest site at 0800 for a three-hour move to the outpost at Corinto Finca. There it joined up with another unit of one lieutenant and eighteen men. The combined patrol spent just five hours on the trail the next day and went into camp at 1300 in the village of San Antonio. On February 15 it did not move at all because there was no food in the area and Puller sent back to Corinto Finca for rations.

At 0800 on the 16th the patrol got underway again. In accordance with standard procedures in the Central Area, Puller had divided his force into a point, main body, and rear guard and had an officer with each section. He was moving with the eight men at the head of the column. They were just three miles down the trail when an estimated thirty-five bandits sprung an ambush. The enemy position, well concealed in trees and heavy brush, was parallel to and seventy-five yards from the trail. A rebel Lewis gun opened up on the point while rifle fire rained down on the main body. The *guardias* hit the dirt and unleashed a heavy volume of return fire from their Browning automatic rifles (BARs), Thompson submachine guns, Krag rifles, and grenade launchers. The enemy machine gun soon went silent. With rifle bullets still spattering the column, Puller led the point in a charge against the inactive Lewis gun. The handful of *guardias* barely had begun advancing when the remaining bandit fire died out. By the time Puller reached the position the enemy had fled with their weapons. The patrol briefly moved after them in the thick foliage but could not regain contact. The entire action had lasted just twelve minutes.

The patrol marched for several hours after the battle and spent all the next day on the move, too. Puller determined at that point that there was no usable trail to Mt. Kilande and he did not have enough rations to sustain him for the time needed to cut one. After making a brief foray across the Coco River, he headed home because seven of his men had worn out their shoes. On the way in they passed the site of another recent engagement and discovered that someone had disinterred the one *guardia* killed there, mutilated the body, and hung it from a tree.

The results of Puller's first battle in Nicaragua were inconclusive. A search of the site had yielded just a single cartridge for the Lewis gun. There were some spots of blood, but no dead or wounded bandits in sight. There also were no Guardia casualties and the patrol leader was generally pleased with the conduct of his men. He asked the area commander to commend the two lieutenants and the members of the point for their actions, but noted that his troops needed "rifle instruction on the range as soon as possible." Erskine recommended that the *jefe director* also recognize Puller because the staff officer had volunteered for patrol duty and "exercised unusual skill and judgment" in handling the ambush. In all probability, however, the patrol's slow movement and day of delay at San Antonio had created the opportunity for the rebels to ambush the unit. Although Puller never indicated that he learned such a lesson from this operation, his methods would change dramatically in the future.[16]

The quartermaster made no patrols for the next three months. March passed quietly except for the day a private shot and killed his officer; Puller had to escort the body to Jinotega's landing field for transport to Managua. (Several Marine officers and NCOs died in Nicaragua at the hands of mutinous or simply irate *guardias*.) Puller spent much of April and May moving supplies to outposts and accompanying his new area commander, Colonel C. A. Wynn, on inspection tours of the region. During this period Major James W. Webb reported for duty as the battalion executive officer. Finally, in the middle of May 1930, Puller received his long-awaited assignment to a real combat billet. In a reprise of his work with Company A in Haiti, he would take over the Guardia's sole dedicated field force, Company M. Wynn certainly did not realize it at the time, but he had launched the man and the unit toward a rendezvous with destiny.[17]

☆ ☆ ☆

Despite its official title, by the summer of 1930 Company M consisted of just two officers and fewer than three dozen enlisted men. Since Hanneken's departure from Nicaragua earlier in the year, Lieutenant M. K. Chenoweth had led the force. In the middle of March Gunnery Sergeant William A. Lee joined the Guardia and became the second in command of the company as a constabulary second lieutenant. Lee, just shy of thirty years old, had enlisted in the Corps in May 1918 but missed the fighting in France. He was a strapping, athletic Marine who had spent part of his youth learning woodcraft from Cherokee Indians in North Carolina. He could track men and animals and maintain a fast pace with a heavy load on the trail. His energy, endurance, and tenacity soon would establish him as a fearsome opponent of the Sandinistas.[18]

The company had been in operation for eight months when Puller replaced Chenoweth, but it had yet to achieve any significant success in combat. The new commander wasted no time and departed almost immediately on a patrol. He moved eastward for a five-day sweep, but soon received orders from McDougal to head northeast. The patrol moved by day and camped each night in a village. Early in the afternoon of June 4 the company was at San Antonio cooking a steer in preparation for a trek into the uninhabited area around Mt. Kilande. Hearing three shots to the north, Puller sent thirteen men to investigate.

A thousand yards beyond the town, on the same trail where Puller had been ambushed in February, six bandits walked into the *guardias*. In thirty seconds of shooting the soldiers killed one man, but the others escaped. The dead bandit was unusually well armed with a Springfield rifle, Colt revolver, and plenty of ammunition.[19]

Just after noontime on June 6 the patrol was moving toward the village of Los Cedros when it came under fire. The enemy were on top of a brush-covered hill that sloped about 175 yards down to the trail. The company returned fire. With barely a pause, Puller dashed up the rise while yelling to his men to charge. The two officers and thirty-five men of the unit followed, shooting as they went. Thick foliage and heaving lungs made it hard to see or hit anything. The bandits kept up a steady fire at the onrushing *guardias* and began to throw dynamite bombs. (These were crude grenades—a cowhide sack shrunk around jagged stones or scrap metal with a stick of dynamite in the center.) Lee proved his physical prowess and courage; he and a private dodged explosions and were the first to reach the position. While many of the enemy had fled by now, their leader had stayed to the last, heaving bombs until he was cut down at a range of twenty yards.

It turned out that the patrol had not walked into a prepared ambush but merely stumbled upon a bandit camp. The Sandinistas had been equally surprised, but at least had seen the government troops first. A search turned up seven rebel bodies, one of them hit in the head by a rifle grenade. No *guardias* were wounded, though one man was shaken up by a dynamite bomb.

Puller thought the favorable casualty ratio resulted from the relative position of the two forces. He believed that men firing downhill had a tendency to aim high while those shooting up a slope did not do so. Another factor may have been the shortage of bandit arms; the patrol found just two rifles, one pistol, and ten machetes. In addition, the rebels were even more unskilled as marksmen than the *guardias*. Both Puller and Lee later admitted that any professional military force lying in ambush would have slaughtered a unit caught in the open on the trail.

The patrol leader learned another lesson that day about the difficulty of estimating the size of the opposition. He had thought in the midst of the fight that he faced at least thirty enemy, but a roster of the bandit gang found in the camp listed just twenty men. The papers included recent letters from Altamirano and also revealed that two of the dead were the leaders of the group. The company returned to Jinotega the next day with something to show for their hard efforts.[20]

The unit departed on a new patrol on the 12th. They searched fruitlessly and arrived back at their base after midnight on June 20. Major Webb and forty other men were preparing for a mission to check a bandit camp bombed by planes the afternoon before. Company M joined in and headed out with just a few hours to rest and replenish. The large patrol reached the site that day and found one dead rebel. The next day Webb split the force to cover more territory. Puller and his men remained out in the field till late on June 23. Webb's unit returned to Jinotega at the same time with the battalion executive officer reporting his rations exhausted, all three officers of his group sick, and "many men footsore and worn out."[21]

Company M, with much more time already logged on the trail, apparently was in better shape. Puller, Lee, and their men joined Chenoweth and thirty others for a new patrol that left Jinotega at 0730 on the 24th. At Santa Fé he picked up an additional fifteen *guardias*. After five days in the field, Puller went to Yali, where he could check in with the area commander by telegraph. He reported that his outfit had encountered lone bandits on two occasions and killed both of them. Wynn told him that planes had been looking for them for two days to drop orders and that his patrol was now under temporary control of the Northern Area. Puller's large group operated for nearly two more weeks, often split into two patrols with one following the other at a distance. The reinforced unit finally returned to base on July 12. The ten bandits Company M had killed during June were the only ones bagged by the Central Area for the whole month.

In his report of this long patrol Puller stated that he thought Guardia units made few contacts because they moved too slowly, mainly due to pack mules and the mounts of the officers. In addition, the animals confined the patrols to the established trails. In Company M, by contrast, the officers walked and supplies and equipment were kept to the bare minimum. He believed that spare uniforms and even ponchos were excess baggage—"within a week one gets used to being wet and dirty." He cited his own recent experience as the proof of his methods:

> After becoming hardened a foot patrol can average 25 miles per
> day whereas a patrol with animals will only average 18 miles and

> this will be on the main trails. One day since I have been in com-
> mand of Company M, the company marched 36 miles without
> undue hardship to officers or *guardias*. When I say a foot patrol
> can average 25 miles per day, I mean for a period of 30 days with a
> lay over of not more than one day per week. Company M has had
> only one day lay over in the past 31 days, no officer or *guardia*
> mounted, and on the afternoon of the 31st day the company
> marched 21 miles in four hours and thirty minutes.[22]

Puller expressed other strong opinions to his superiors. He preferred
the BAR to the Thompson because of the latter's short effective range.
He thought part of the patrol should wear civilian clothes to allow it to
conduct "reconnaissance work." And he considered the issue binoculars
useless. Those points made no impact, but at least one senior Guardia
commander eventually would agree with Puller's tactics: "The only
successful offensive operations have been by small very mobile patrols
capable of living off the country and of following the bandits wherever
they have been able to go."[23]

One issue Puller did not address was the major difference between
the tactics he and fellow Gendarmerie leaders had used in Haiti and the
ones now prevalent in Nicaragua. In the earlier campaign Marines had
learned to operate largely at night and had won important victories in
the hours of darkness. The brigade commander in Nicaragua initially
directed his subordinates to employ "heavily armed patrols moving secretly at night and resorting to ambushing in order to obtain surprise
against outlaws during the *daytime*." But before long both Marine and
Guardia units worked almost exclusively when the sun was up and
camped each night. Nearly all contacts with the enemy occurred during
the day and the rebels initiated most of the rare night battles. No one ordered this doctrinal about-face, it simply became accepted practice.
And it proved to be a workable solution given the superior firepower
and marksmanship of the government forces—they had a decided advantage in any engagement in which the opposing sides could see each
other. Unlike the Gendarmerie, however, the Guardia would never inflict the type of knockout blows to its enemies that actually pacified the
countryside.[24]

Another important factor in Nicaragua was the problem of communications. A few Marine units had heavy radios that they could carry

into the field on mules, but the most common means of passing information was via aircraft. The planes dropped messages in weighted bags or picked them up from the ground using a system of ropes, poles, and a hook. The infantry also could talk to pilots, after a fashion, by laying out colored panels in specified configurations. The Guardia had no radios, however, and seldom had planes at its disposal. The only means of communication was via runner or stopping in at an outpost and using the telegraph. It was common for a constabulary patrol to remain out of touch with headquarters for days at a time. That placed a special premium on junior leaders who could think for themselves, take initiative, and not worry about being alone in hostile country with no means to call for help.[25]

Puller's commander thought his subordinate was perfectly suited for this independent style of warfare: "He was probably the bravest man I ever knew. His was a cool courage, not one of desperation. About the only way to contact the enemy was to let them ambush him. He would go anywhere without support, knowing if he got in a jam he had to get himself and his men out. He not only never hesitated, he invited that kind of work." The senior officer was mistaken about one thing—Puller would be ambushed in less than half of his twenty-two contacts in Nicaragua.[26]

☆　☆　☆

Puller spent several days of mid-July in the dispensary recovering from conjunctivitis, an infection of the eyes that sealed them with pus. The day after the doctor pronounced him fit for duty, he and Company M embarked on a new operation, this time reinforced by another lieutenant, a medical officer, and fifteen *guardias.* On the 22d, acting on information that a wounded bandit *jefe* and a few men were hiding out on a mountain a few miles north of San Antonio, the patrol climbed toward the summit. In the midst of pushing through heavy vegetation the unit "blundered into the camp." The rebels probably had a few minutes' warning from the noise of men moving in the brush; the *guardias* saw only fleeting targets through the foliage as they rushed forward shooting. The contact lasted five minutes and the patrol fired less than two hundred rounds. There were no casualties on either side. Puller estimated there had been ten men in the camp and his patrol collected six firearms, a horse, a mule, rations, and equipment.[27]

The unit continued north toward Mt. Guapinol. On the afternoon of

July 24 the *guardias* detained a man carrying a pack full of fruit. He admitted that it was destined for a rebel group, which would pick it up the next day. Puller stationed an outpost near the man's cabin and placed his company in a nearby ravine. The next morning the outpost observed a Sandinista a few hundred yards away and alerted the patrol. As Puller led his company in that direction, a concealed sentry fired at him from a range of ten yards, but missed. The *guardias* rushed forward and found a deserted camp; they had slept that close to an enemy bivouac. Most of the bandits had pulled out quietly during the night and scattered in small groups.

The patrol followed several trails but saw nothing and returned to camp in the early afternoon. Soon afterward an outpost sighted a lone bandit and wounded him. Before he died, the man admitted being a rebel captain and claimed that both Sandino and Altamirano had been at the base with two hundred men. There was proof in the form of a paper, signed by Sandino, granting the captain a five-day leave that expired that afternoon. Company M returned to Jinotega on July 28. Although the operation had resulted in only one enemy casualty, the company was keeping the Sandinistas on the run.[28]

On August 8 the area commander sent Puller and Company M to track down a bandit group operating south of Jinotega. The *guardias* kept on the move for five days and slowly circled their way north to Corinto Finca, where they received orders to head west to the Río Tuma. On the evening of the 15th an informant told them that eighty mounted men had crossed the river two days prior and headed north. Although the bandits had a big head start, they went into camp on August 17 to rest their animals. The next day they made a foray on foot and ambushed a Guardia patrol, then ran into another while making good their retreat. That afternoon a plane discovered the enemy corral and bombed it. The unlucky band had stumbled into the middle of a combined offensive launched by the Northern and Central Areas on August 15.[29]

Puller's unit kept up its hard pace along the hot, humid, hilly jungle paths. Rain and mud were more than an irritating nuisance, but did not stop the intrepid company. Late in the afternoon of August 19, the force hounded down its quarry. The rebel camp was located "in an excellent defensive position" on a ridge bisecting the trail. Puller immediately ordered two thirds of the company straight forward in the assault to fix the enemy, while he and a dozen *guardias* moved around the flank. The bandits foiled that tactic by firing a few rounds and then fleeing on their horses. The company pursued and the rebels began abandoning their mounts to make better time over the difficult, soggy ground. Puller called off the chase at nightfall. The *guardias* found two dead in the vicinity of the camp and captured fifty-two animals, two rifles, and a substantial quantity of equipment and food. There were indications that the previous day's aerial action had killed another two bandits and nine horses. The patrol burned what they could not carry and returned to Jinotega on August 21. As usual, Puller's report commended his subordinates: "The conduct of both men and officers was excellent during this engagement and the 14 days of hard marching, especially Lieutenant Lee for his courage, coolness, and indefatigability."[30]

The *jefe director* issued an order praising Puller and his unit for this entire operation:

> The fact that this patrol left Jinotega on 8 August 1930 to gain contact with this group of bandits and continued persistently on their trail until they made contact on 19 August showed a spirit of determination and aggressiveness that is highly commendable. The success attained could only have resulted from the splendid manner in which Captain Puller maneuvered his men and their ready and willing response to orders, setting a fine example of excellent training and discipline. . . . Captain Lewis B. Puller and Second Lieutenant William A. Lee are especially commended for their courage, coolness, and aggressiveness.

McDougal went one step further, recommending Puller and Lee for the Navy Cross.[31]

Company M continued its active existence. Puller took the unit out for a three-day operation on August 28, then hours after their return they departed at midnight for a nine-hour patrol. The captain and Lee each led out small detachments two nights later. (These occasional one-night patrols probably set security ambushes around Jinotega.)[32]

On September 5 Puller departed with Lee and twenty-five men and joined up with another twenty-three *guardias* from Corinto Finca. Their destination was the Mt. Guapinol region. The patrol reached the mountain but found no enemy. Puller sent Lee and part of the men back to Jinotega and continued on with thirty-five *guardias*. They headed southeast to the Río Gusanero and moved along its banks. On the 10th they discovered a well-used trail, which in this sparsely inhabited region usually indicated a bandit path. The patrol followed it and the next morning sighted a camp. The terrain prohibited any movement off the track so Puller launched an immediate attack up the trail. The rebels scattered, but not before the *guardias* downed three of them. One survived long enough to say that Sandino had been there a week before and was probably now in Cua.

A search of the site turned up four firearms and the usual assortment of machetes, dynamite, equipment, and papers. The documents confirmed Sandino had been there. Puller wanted to pursue this lead, but his unit had gone three days without meat and had only a little rice left for the march back to Jinotega. The food situation forced him to head home—his desire to travel light had both benefits and drawbacks. (Earlier in the intervention the brigade had supplied some Marine patrols by air, but the Guardia never had the opportunity to try this.)[33]

Company M spent much of the next thirty days in the field, but had only one contact by a small patrol under Lee. Puller took several days of well-earned leave in Managua in mid-October. Meanwhile the Central Area received a new commander, Colonel Julian C. Smith, with new ideas. In early November he issued an order encouraging his subordinates to think and act quickly: "Action promptly initiated and rapidly carried through will invariably produce better results under present conditions than plans requiring elaborate preparations and considerable time." He placed less emphasis on combat patrols in favor of more frequent police patrols of a few men each designed to safeguard the *fincas* and the rural population from lesser bandit depredations. He also reorganized the command and cut Company M's enlisted complement from thirty-five to twenty-five. The small force now had two BARs, three Thompsons, and six grenade launchers mounted on Springfield rifles; everyone else carried the venerable Krag rifle.[34]

The company's next call to arms came on November 6. The ten-man garrison in Matiguás had come under attack by 150 rebels the previous evening and retreated after running out of ammunition. Puller, Lee, and twenty-one men left Jinotega within a few hours to search for the enemy. They had no luck, but the patrol eventually picked up the trail of about thirty bandits who were pillaging small ranches near Santa Isabel. They caught sight of the enemy about 0900 on November 19, pursued them for three miles, and wounded at least one of them.[35]

One incident during this patrol illustrated the difficulty of trying to move surreptitiously in order to surprise the bandits. Company M was hidden in an ambush site along a trail when a manager of a local *finca* walked up to provide them information on a rebel band—apparently he knew exactly where to find the nearest constabulary outfit. Often the enemy seemed to be equally well informed. During the August general offensive a patrol had captured a letter from Sandino warning his subordinates of the operation; it was dated the day the movement began and just a few hours after orders had been distributed to the field units. One Guardia leader suspected the source of information was the Nicaraguan telegraph operators.[36]

The company reported into Corinto Finca on November 20 for supplies and pack animals, then left the same day to check out a report of a rebel concentration under Altamirano near Mt. Guapinol. Heavy rains, muddy trails, and flooded rivers made the going rough, but Puller was not deterred. On the morning of the 25th the patrol came across a bandit trail. The *guardias* followed this track and at 1030 the point sighted about ten rebels amongst some fallen trees. Puller's men opened fire and the enemy took off running. A thousand yards farther along the trail the pursuers came upon the camp—four buildings with log barricades in front and a hundred-foot cliff in the rear. The forty or so rebels fought only briefly as they threw their belongings and even three wounded men into the ravine and then clambered down on ropes and ladders, which they pulled down after themselves. By the time some of the *guardias* worked their way down into the draw the enemy had disappeared. The patrol found two dead bandits and some supplies. Puller was certain that the three wounded who had gone over the cliff had died. Captured documents also proved that Company M had wounded a minor chief in its August 19 contact. The unit returned to Jinotega on November 27 after three weeks of hard patrolling.[37]

Puller took a rare break from the field and remained in Jinotega for the entire month of December. While in garrison he participated in two conferences with McDougal, Smith, and their respective staffs on the 15th and the 22d. The area commander lauded the mobile unit: "Captain Puller and the members of his patrol displayed the qualities of courage, persistence, physical endurance, and patience to the highest degree. . . . The work of the officers and men of this patrol is worthy of the highest praise." The *jefe director* gave Puller a higher honor and pinned the Navy Cross on his roving patrol commander. The award was for his cumulative efforts in engagements between February 16 and August 19: "By his intelligent and forceful leadership without thought of his own personal safety, by great physical exertion and by suffering many hardships, Lieutenant Puller surmounted all obstacles and dealt five successive blows against organized banditry." This was Puller's first U.S. medal for valor. Lee received his Navy Cross soon after.[38]

☆ ☆ ☆

With Lee temporarily in charge in December, the company went on patrols that resulted in contacts on the 12th, 15th, and 19th. The outfit killed at least four bandits, but lost the first one of its own men, a private killed in the engagement at Vencedora on December 12. This battle was easily the most severe fight up to that point in the unit's history. Lee and twenty men attacked an estimated two hundred bandits. They expected the enemy to scatter, but instead the rebels put up a strong defense backed by the firepower of two Lewis guns and four Thompsons. The fire was so intense that it forced the *guardias* to break off their charge and seek cover. The fight went on for thirty minutes and twice the bandits actually counterattacked. Lee feared his small band would be overwhelmed, but each time the enemy retired. Another group flanked the Guardia line and began firing on the patrol from the rear. In desperation, Lee then led a new charge that finally broke the enemy position to his front. With that, all the rebels fled.[39]

The war did seem to be taking on a new and deadlier character as 1930 came to a close. The Sandinistas were fighting harder and with better arms. On December 31 a patrol of ten Marines checking the telegraph line northeast of Ocotal walked into an ambush set by a hundred rebels. After an hour of fighting the Sandinistas withdrew, leaving eight of the Marines dead and the other two wounded. On New Year's Day a Central Area patrol struck a large force entrenched behind a stone wall and could not dislodge it till another constabulary unit arrived on the scene an hour later. That night the enemy used machine guns to fire on Ocotal from long range. The Guardia also was expanding its role in the war as the Marines withdrew. From twenty-six contacts with the enemy in 1929, the number leapt to 120 in 1930 and would rise to 141 in 1931. Guardia performance remained spotty, although it continued to improve. During fiscal year 1930 it lost twelve men killed in action, while two hundred went to prison and 323 deserted (of a total strength of

2,200). The following year the figures would be eight killed, ninety-two imprisoned, and 270 deserted.

Julian Smith, the proponent of four-man police patrols, seemed depressed by the worsening character of the war. He reported many instances in which his forces had scattered rebel bands without inflicting serious harm and lamented the "comparative futility of small patrols attempting to destroy large bandit groups." He asked for more officers, men, and automatic weapons: "With the present numbers only a futile sort of war of attrition . . . can be carried on."[40]

Puller briefly rejoined Company M's heavy schedule of patrolling at the end of December. He went into the field on the 30th, returned to Jinotega on January 10, and departed again on the 13th for a four-day foray. The roving patrol maintained this intensive effort in the coming months but made no contacts. Part of the reason may have been a shift in rebel activity to the Northern Area, which fought thirteen engagements in January 1931 compared to five in the Central Area. It grew even more quiet in the latter zone in February and March with only one contact each month, neither by Company M. During the same period the Northern Area engaged in seventeen firefights.

In February Puller had to go on a limited-duty status due to a severe bout of skin ulcers on both legs. By the time he reported to the doctor on the 25th he had a dozen dime-sized lesions, with many more small eruptions in earlier stages of development. The medics cleaned and treated them daily, but it took more than a month for them to heal. Many years later Lee recalled that his commander "looked bad" and needed a rest at this time. Puller continued to work, though he had to stay close to Jinotega. He ran escort missions to the aviation field outside of town or led halfway patrols (going half the way to an outpost to meet a detachment coming from the opposite direction for the purpose of transferring people or supplies).[41]

☆ ☆ ☆

On March 31, 1931, an earthquake hit Managua and in the span of two minutes devastated the city. Then fires broke out and raged throughout the urban area for several days. Both the Guardia and the brigade went to work rescuing trapped people, fighting the flames, and succoring the injured and homeless. Of the city's population of thirty-five thousand, 10 percent were injured and nearly 5 percent died. On April 2 the Central Area dispatched Puller to convey relief supplies donated by the residents of Jinotega. The Guardia captain remained in the capital until April 20 leading a group engaged in burying the dead.[42]

Two weeks after his return to Jinotega, Puller made one last patrol with Company M. The captain, Lee, and twenty-two men headed northeast toward Poteca, once the stronghold of Captain Merritt Edson and his Coco River Patrol. The withdrawal of Marine forces had left this remote region unprotected for some time and intelligence indicated Sandino might be there. On the way Company M passed through its old haunt around Mt. Guapinol. In testimony to the reduced bandit presence in this area, the patrol commander noted how vegetation was obliterating many of the trails. On May 9 the unit reached the Río Cua and proceeded southeast along its banks. At mid-morning, four bandits in two canoes appeared around a bend in the river. The two sides saw each other at the same time, but quick shooting downed two of the rebels as they tried to jump overboard. The other two escaped. The patrol recovered the canoes, bodies, and two shotguns. Since there was no food in the boats, Puller surmised there must be a camp nearby.

Company M continued up the river to the mouth of the Río Kilande, where the point discovered a recently abandoned sentry post and a track leading along the Kilande. The patrol followed this trail and discovered a large abandoned bandit camp about a mile away. The guardias destroyed nine buildings and a large quantity of supplies and equipment, including several pole-climbing sets, which Puller suspected had come from the ambush of the Marine patrol on December 31. The company backtracked to the Río Cua and joined up that evening with another patrol along the river. The combined force started to move north along the Río Coco the next day, but high water made it necessary to cut a path through heavy brush the entire way. Puller decided to abandon that slow effort and Company M returned to Jinotega on May 13 having marched an average of sixteen miles a day.[43]

☆   ☆   ☆

The Guardia captain's thirty-month tour in Nicaragua was drawing to a close. In January 1931 he had requested a seat at the Company Officers Course in Quantico, the Army Infantry School, or the Army Motor Transport School. If none of those were available, he wanted to extend with the Guardia for another year. Both Julian Smith and the *jefe direc-*

tor strongly endorsed his application for professional education. On June 1 Headquarters ordered Puller to the Army Infantry School. The next day, Colonel Smith rode out to the Jinotega airfield with his captain and saw him off on a flight to Managua. Puller sailed from Corinto on the 12th. One of his last acts in Nicaragua was to recommend Lee for promotion to first lieutenant in the Guardia and Marine gunner in the Corps.[44]

The commander of Company M did not go unrecognized for his own performance. Nicaragua awarded him the Presidential Medal of Merit (that country's highest decoration) and he received glowing praise on his fitness reports. McDougal called him "the most active patrol leader in the Guardia." Smith remarked: "An excellent officer in every respect. Possesses highest moral and physical courage, persistence, patience, loyalty, endurance, and sound common sense. One of the very best officers I have ever known." Most telling of all, dozens of citizens of Jinotega signed a letter to the Central Area commander and asked that Puller be retained there: "Captain Puller was one of the few officers of the Guardia Nacional that worked brilliantly on the task of pacifying this area where for a long time he revealed himself as the strong and efficient man for this kind of campaign, carried out among all kinds of danger in an untamed and wild tropical wilderness." Smith acclaimed Puller and Company M in an interview with an American reporter: "[They] have never fought a battle in which they were not outnumbered at least five to one. . . . They have never failed me . . . nor come back whipped. Is it any wonder they are called the Terror of the Bandits and that their commanding officer is known as the Tiger of the Mountains?" El Tigre had won more than a nickname in Nicaragua—he now had a well-deserved reputation as one of the best junior combat leaders in the Corps.[45]

"The Toughest Proposition"
Fort Benning and Nicaragua
1931–1932

First Lieutenant Puller reported to Benning on September 11, 1931. The Army welcomed the students with hospitality and bureaucracy. The Marines received complimentary memberships in the officers club as well as volumes of post regulations. Before classes began, the faculty let it be known that they expected "an honest day's work" but would require no onerous after-hours efforts. That did not mean the course would be easy.[1]

The Army had inaugurated its Infantry School at Fort Benning, Georgia, just as the World War drew to a close. Its purpose was to teach lieutenants and captains how to handle units up through the regiment. It focused almost entirely on weapons, tactics, and field skills with little effort devoted to staff work. Benning's 100,000 acres and three regiments (two infantry and one cavalry) served as the laboratory for a program devoted heavily to practical instruction and hands-on training as opposed to theoretical lectures. The school oversaw two programs, the Advanced Course for senior captains and the Company Officers Course for junior captains and lieutenants.

The Army assigned high-caliber instructors and students to Benning. In 1929 Lieutenant Colonel George C. Marshall became the assistant commandant of the school, overseeing the faculty and the curriculum. He was a rising star in the Army and had served with distinction as a staff officer in France. He also was a recent widower and he threw himself into raising the school to an even higher plane of professionalism. His instructor group included several men who would serve as distinguished generals in World War II.

During his tenure Marshall tried to inculcate the idea that war was uncertain and did not lend itself to textbook rigidity. He lessened the importance of the once almighty school solution (the only answer accepted as correct for tactical problems) and forced faculty to look at each student's work on its own merits. He attempted to simulate "how little information you actually have in war" by making students use imperfect maps and by adding surprise events to field exercises. Night maneuvers, previously unheard of, became a staple of the course.

Marshall also led the drive to redesign Army doctrine and organization. He pushed for a triangular structure in which each level of command had three subordinate maneuver units and a fire support unit. He introduced the holding attack as the basic method of operation; while one element of the force fixed the enemy in place, another sought an open flank, and the third remained in reserve. One Marine in the 1931–1932 course summarized Marshall's passion for simplicity and realism: "The next war like the last will be fought by men and officers with three months experience or thereabouts. Nothing complicated is going to get across in the early stages of such a war." Marshall's work came to be known around the Army as the Benning Revolution.[2]

The Infantry School had a superior reputation within the Corps. A seat there was a "coveted assignment" and Marine graduates invariably were posted to instructor duty in Quantico. Puller would not have been a prime candidate if the Benning program had been a theoretical course, but he was a good fit for the practical curriculum of the Army school. He was a hard worker and a proven performer in actual operations. He also carried himself well and was impeccably uniformed in garrison. He would make a fine representative before a sister service.[3]

His Marine compatriots in the class of 1931–1932 were Captains Gilder D. Jackson, Jr., and Oliver P. Smith in the Advanced Course and Captain Dudley S. Brown and First Lieutenant Gerald C. Thomas in the Company Officers Course. Puller would serve with three of the four in future billets. Jackson had received two wounds and six citations for valor in France. Smith was a quiet, intellectual officer, but also a capable commander. At first glance, Puller and Smith seemed to be opposites, but they soon became good friends. The older officer also had lost his father at an early age, been raised by a strong-willed mother, and worked his way through school. Smith developed great respect for the lieutenant's deep interest in reading and self-tutored knowledge of history. Thomas was a top-notch staff officer, but could hold his own as a field leader. He had enlisted in 1917 and earned a battlefield commission while fighting at Belleau Wood, Soissons, Blanc Mont, and the Meuse-Argonne. Brown had seen duty in Santo Domingo and spent a year in Nicaragua with the 2d Brigade. Puller was in excellent company. The Marines in the Company Officers Course were surprised to discover, however, that about half of their class of 134 officers was made up of lieutenants only recently graduated from the Military Academy at West Point.[4]

☆   ☆   ☆

Thomas thought Benning boasted "the greatest school of weapons in the world." More than a third of the schedule was devoted to tearing apart, reassembling, and firing all the infantry arms—pistol, rifle, BAR, machine guns, trench mortars, and 37mm gun. The students also worked with grenades, bayonets, and artillery. There was a course on horsemanship, since students spent much of their time riding over the post to do map reading, terrain analysis, field sketching, and tactical exercises without troops. Part of the curriculum looked back at the tried-and-true role of animals in transportation while a newer portion looked forward to the use of motor transport. The 1931–1932 class spent a considerable amount of time learning the mysteries of radios, too.[5]

In the spring the junior officers received their dose of tactics instruction, which included classes on command posts, combat orders, intelligence, and tactics up through the battalion level. The culmination of this phase of both the Advanced and Company Officers Courses was a series of field exercises with the base's three regiments. The students held command slots from the platoon to brigade. Each day the student officers rotated to a new billet without regard for their rank. Twice a day there was a critique of everyone's performance. In the first exercise the students commanded a simulated force in action against the regiments. The following week the student body divided into halves, took charge of the real units, and conducted a two-sided exercise. Umpires determined the results of each battle between the "blue" and "red" forces.[6]

Puller put his small-wars experience to use in these training operations. One day he commanded a machine gun platoon complete with mule-drawn carts to transport the weapons. His battalion commander happened to be Smith. Although the later memories of participants conflicted a great deal, the Marine lieutenant apparently engineered a successful ambush of an opposing cavalry unit well in the enemy rear. That evening, Puller's machine guns and an infantry platoon served as the covering force while the remainder of the battalion made a withdrawal. Cavalry scouted the lightly held line and demanded the surrender of the tiny force. Puller refused and hustled his men and mule carts to the rear, outrunning the horse soldiers in the thick terrain. The instructors must have been pleased with the Nicaraguan veteran's tactical solutions; he received a grade of excellent in that portion of the course.[7]

Puller had one superior grade, in instructional methods. The faculty had asked the Marine students to make a presentation on Nicaragua. Puller drew the assignment since he had the most extensive experience there. He was supposed to talk about the country itself and not the war, so when he ran out of background information he provided some spicy rumors about the private life of the Nicaraguan President. He then sidestepped into a lecture on the threat from Japan. His extemporaneous performance apparently also was a hit with the student body, which enjoyed his uninhibited style in an otherwise "staid Army school."[8]

For all the seriousness of the subject matter, the students were inventive in creating their own amusement. Smith described some of the antics for a fellow Marine scheduled to attend the 1932–1933 class: "It is worth your life to sit in front when out on terrain exercises. The people in the rear begin to throw pine cones and rocks on the heads of those in front. In the school room it is ash trays and wads of paper; or they may put a bag of water on a man's seat or coal in his desk or set his map afire when he is not looking." The gruff, rumbling voice of Puller sometimes sparked the mischievous side of his fellow students. When the Marine lieutenant answered questions in class they would shout that they could not hear him. He would play along and boom out his words even louder, which invariably dissolved the room into laughter.[9]

In spite of the occasional clowning, Puller "was in the dumps" for much of the year worrying about his grades. He had not performed especially well in previous schools and there was considerable pressure to uphold the honor of the Corps in this Army course. When the final scores came out in May 1932, Thomas thought his compatriot had rea-

son to "go away happy." Puller's marks were about evenly divided between excellents and satisfactories and he joined the "Order of the
Horseshoe" (a U for unsatisfactory) only on the machine gun course.
He did superbly on the range with the rifle and pistol. Nevertheless, his
overall performance was less than HQMC desired and that eventually
would affect his future assignments.[10]

☆   ☆   ☆

Many years later, Puller scorned his year at Benning. While many other
Marine graduates looked back at it as great training, he regarded it in
retrospect as a waste of time: "You just simply cannot learn warfare in a
schoolroom, or anywhere else except in combat. And you'll never know
whether you're a fighting man until you're under fire." It seems unlikely
he actually felt that way at the time. He had asked for the opportunity to
go there and would seek to return to school in the future. Moreover,
under Marshall's direction the school was trying hard to paint a realistic
picture of war. Undoubtedly the Marine lieutenant must have absorbed
many things that he had not yet encountered in his brushes with small,
poorly equipped enemies. In any case, he soon would have the opportunity to put his education and his experience to good use.[11]

Puller had submitted his request for his next assignment in December 1931. His choices were the Guardia Nacional, China, or a ship's detachment. Probably motivated by his initial experience in Nicaragua, he
specifically added that his preference in the constabulary was for field
duty. Headquarters slated him for an instructor position in Quantico,
where he could pass along his fresh knowledge. Barely a week later the
jefe director "urgently requested" the services of Puller. The Guardia
commander noted the lieutenant's previous performance in Nicaragua
and argued his expertise would be invaluable during an approaching
"critical" period. The request had the intended effect. Headquarters issued new orders for Puller to report to Managua.[12]

☆   ☆   ☆

The character of the war against Sandino was changing dramatically.
Since 1928 there had been significant opposition from the U.S. public
and Congress to the intervention in Nicaragua. The onset of the Depression in late 1929 added fiscal considerations to the mix. The death of
eight Marines in the December 31, 1930, ambush near Ocotal was the
final spur. The United States announced its intention to withdraw all

American servicemen, to include those in the Guardia, following the Nicaraguan presidential election in late 1932. The *jefe director* asked for more time to allow an orderly turnover of the Guardia's senior positions to Nicaraguan officers. President Herbert C. Hoover remained firm on the January 1, 1933, deadline for the departure of the last Marine. If the Guardia did not break the back of Sandinista resistance prior to that, it seemed likely that the country would descend into anarchy yet again.[13]

The scale of the rebel threat continued to grow while the Marine withdrawal reduced the strength of government forces. The Sandinistas purchased substantial quantities of arms and ammunition in Honduras, and instigated occasional mutinies in the ranks of the constabulary. In one instance, a Guardia sergeant and fourteen of his men killed their American officer and made off with the detachment's weapons, including a heavy machine gun. In August 1932 a Central Area report noted that everywhere north of Jinotega, "the inhabitants live in perpetual fear of the bandits; they practically all pay tribute, which is the only way they can exist." Sandino was content to bide his time, however, and avoid major operations until all the Marines were gone. That made the task of finding and destroying the rebel forces that much harder.[14]

☆   ☆   ☆

Puller departed Fort Benning on June 1, 1932. A front-page story in bold type greeted his arrival in Managua on July 7. The article announced that "El Tigre" had returned to help with the "worsened" situation. The newspaper predicted he would go to the Caribbean coast, currently suffering through a major Sandinista raid. The reporter's sources proved inaccurate. A week later Puller flew to Jinotega, where the Central Area commander assigned him to lead Company A, a unit of four officers and sixty men garrisoning some small towns.[15]

Puller led several short forays during his first days with the company. On July 26 he departed his base with one officer and twenty men for an extended operation. Just after dawn on the 31st, the patrol came across a freshly cut trail. The Guardia captain put his unit on to the new track and sped up the rate of march. Four hours later they caught up with a small rebel group. The opposing forces saw each other at the same time and the bandits scattered as the constabulary patrol opened fire. In the brief contact the *guardias* killed two men and captured their weapons. The patrol returned to base on August 6.[16]

Several officers transferred out of the Central Area at this time and

Puller again took charge of Company M. The roving patrol of two officers and thirty men still worked out of Jinotega. Lieutenant Lee remained the second in command. Before twenty-four hours had elapsed Puller was in the field with a reinforced unit of Lee and thirty-nine men, part of an offensive of seven patrols. The objective was a reported rebel concentration in the Pantasma valley, though patrol leaders had wide latitude to go where they wished. No Guardia units had been in the area for several months. Puller avoided the known trails and cut across the valley in search of any hidden bandit byway. He found one on the morning of August 12 and headed northwest on the well-worn path.

That afternoon the company came upon a group of ten rebels driving eleven cattle. The *guardias* fired and were certain they wounded one man, but the others escaped, though not with their rations-on-the-hoof. Two hours later the patrol encountered and scattered another ten bandits and captured fifteen head of cattle. The next day the trail appeared to end at a river, just at the point where the waterway entered a rocky gorge. Puller suspected the path followed the bed of the shallow river. He waded into the water and his men followed. They slogged along for five miles between canyon walls as high as eighty feet. They discovered several prepared defensive positions along this "death trap," but none were occupied. As Puller had guessed, a trail appeared at the water's edge on the far end of the gorge.

Not long after the patrol emerged dripping from the river, the point man spotted a sentry and heard many voices. The lead *guardia* silently alerted the others. Puller took fifteen men and quietly moved off through the underbrush in the hope of getting on the flank of his quarry. After a suitable delay, Lee and the others attacked straight ahead. They achieved a rare surprise, but the foliage was thick and neither wing of the Guardia force was able to shoot effectively. They killed just two rebels. The patrol then destroyed eight bunkhouses and a large quantity of stores.

After two hours of work the company got back on the trail. Much to Puller's chagrin, he immediately came upon a much larger camp, apparently abandoned by its 150 or so occupants at the sound of the nearby attack. His force barely had begun exploring the site when rebels started shooting from the hills overlooking the area. The *guardias* took cover and returned fire, but they were pinned down by many rifles and two Thompson submachine guns. Puller decided to try a ruse. He quietly passed the word to cease firing all automatic weapons and then shouted a report that the patrol was running low on ammunition. He hoped the rebels would attack. They did not. He pondered an uphill charge through heavy brush against a superior force, but rejected that option. Instead, he ordered his rifle grenadiers to open a sustained bombardment against the Sandinistas. Under the concentrated rain of explosions, the enemy broke and ran. The *guardias* recovered one bandit body, but the patrol's civilian guide also died in the battle. The Guardia captain felt lucky to escape without more casualties. He believed, as he had in his first tour, that the tendency of untrained marksmen to shoot poorly from high ground had decreased his losses.

Company M continued to scour the Pantasma valley and three days later skirmished with a band of fifteen rebels. All escaped but the *guardias* believed they had wounded at least one man. On the morning of August 19, the patrol encountered eighty Sandinistas in an ambush position near Santa Fé. The enemy had chosen a bad site, however. Their firing line on a ridge paralleled a spot where the sunken road provided a ready-made trench for the *guardias*. In addition, one Sandinista revealed his location moments before the enemy sprung the trap. With that slight warning, Puller's men took cover before the first shots rang out. The rebels had one automatic weapon and made liberal use of dynamite bombs, but the better-trained government troops soon gained fire superiority. When the enemy fire slackened, the *guardias* charged the ridge and the rebels fled, leaving four dead on the field. The company reached Jinotega that day.

In his first patrol following his reunion with Company M, Puller had fought an unprecedented half dozen engagements with the rebels and seriously disrupted their heretofore easy life in the Pantasma valley. Some of the other six patrols had made contact, too, but nothing to compare with Company M's success. The Central Area commander praised his subordinate for "the consummate skill and daring employed in the conduct of this patrol, the difficulties encountered and overcome, the results obtained, and the desired firsthand information obtained." Puller lauded Lee as "probably the best man in the U.S. Marine Corps today for combat patrol duty." But there was little time for backslapping. Puller estimated there were probably five hundred rebels still in the valley. Hoping to take advantage of the temporary disarray of the Sandinistas, Company M and two other patrols went back into the field on August 22. The area commander adopted Puller's tactic and stressed that they should cut across country to uncover new trails.[17]

On the morning of August 25 Company M approached a mountain

pass. The rebels had prepared yet another ambush, but again a careless Sandinista exposed himself and the *guardias* deployed before the bandits could open fire. There was "excellent cover" available for an assault and Puller's men made ready to charge. Instead of ordering them forward, he employed his rifle-grenade launchers to bombard the rebels until they retreated. Inspection of the ambush site turned up one dead Sandinista. In his report of the battle, the Guardia captain explained that he had used the rifle grenades "mainly in order to save the men of the company." This was the second time in as many weeks that he had relied solely on indirect firepower to defeat his opponent.

For the next two weeks Company M marched through the bandit zone with near impunity. The *guardias* uncovered and eliminated six abandoned rebel camps. They surprised two men in another bivouac site and killed both of them. By September 7 the patrol had worked its way to the southeast and reached the Río Tuma, at a point where the river was forty yards wide, very deep, and fast. Puller took the obstacle as a challenge. A volunteer swam a line to the other side and the unit built a raft to ferry itself and its thirteen mules across. In his report the company commander proudly described the feat as proof that any river was fordable. But the presence of the animals also highlighted another subtle change in Puller's tactics. He was now sacrificing some speed to bring along the supplies needed to remain in the field for an extended period. The use of rifle grenades and mules indicated that perhaps the Benning Revolution had influenced him after all.[18]

Puller and Lee led a small patrol south to Matagalpa near the middle of September, then the *guardias* had a welcome two days of relaxation and celebration in honor of the anniversary of Nicaraguan national independence. The festivities included a parade by Company M and the reading of the *jefe director*'s citation for the unit's performance in August.[19]

☆   ☆   ☆

For some time Puller and Lee had heard rumors of a secret road, said to date from the time of the ancient Indian civilizations. It now served as a major rebel supply route. They believed that if they found this highway it would lead them to Sandino's current camp, thought to be somewhere east of the Río Coco. On September 20 Puller, Lee, and forty men left Jinotega with nineteen mules loaded with thirty days of rations. They planned to cut a trail due east from La Pavona until they came to the road. The area commander arranged for the rare support of a plane, scheduled for September 30.

Just three miles beyond the village, the company discovered its immediate objective. The *guardias* headed northeast on the road and came across two major trails intersecting it. Puller marveled at their width, up to fifteen yards, and found it "hard to believe" that such byways existed in the trackless region. They were lined with dozens of temporary camps, all showing recent use.

For a day and a half the company was aware that two rebel scouts were shadowing them. Puller expected an ambush at any moment. He chose not to employ flank security, however, since that would have slowed him down. Instead he remained ready to react if contact came. At mid-morning on September 26, as the spread-out column moved along the road, a single volley of rifle fire rang out from the jungle. The *guardias* charged into the brush, but found nothing. The rebels had fled after taking their one shot. Puller thought this might have been an attempt to take out the officers and deprive the patrol of its leaders. There were no casualties on either side.

An hour later the company came to a river and saw numerous fresh tracks. It was a good spot for an ambush, so Puller had the Lewis gun unlimbered from the pack mule to cover his scouts as they crossed. When they found nothing, the patrol waded through the cool water, packed up the machine gun, and moved uphill into heavily wooded and broken terrain. Puller was walking behind the point man when the lead *guardia* saw something and shattered the silence with a shout. The patrol had just entered the mouth of a V-shaped ambuscade. As the *guardias* dived for cover, a rebel machine gunner opened up on the head of the column. The first burst cut down the man in back of Puller—blood spattered over the company commander. The entire point element was pinned down by the intense fire, which inflicted other casualties. Lee had taken a bullet in the arm and another had grazed his head, knocking him unconscious. A *guardia* yelled that Lee was dead. Puller looked back, saw the limp, bloodied form, and thought it was true.

In the midst of the fighting cheers rang out for Sandino and Altamirano, an indication that the cunning Pedrón probably was leading the ambushers. Puller estimated that he faced 150 rebels armed with dynamite bombs, several rifle grenade launchers, and at least seven automatic weapons. The shock wave of explosions, the whir of flying shrapnel, the staccato bursts of submachine guns, and the crack of rifle rounds whipped around the men of Company M as they hugged whatever small cover they could find and began to respond in kind. With the possible exception of the veterans of Vencedora in December 1930, it was by far the heaviest fire anyone in the patrol had ever experienced. For a time it looked like the Sandinistas would charge the outnumbered government troops. The *guardias* knew they were taking a toll of the enemy, however, since numerous calls rang out above the din for machete men to evacuate casualties.

The fight had been raging for fifteen minutes when Lee regained consciousness. He was still groggy and weak from his wounds, but he struggled to a pack mule and retrieved the unit's Lewis gun. The *guardia* lieutenant then demonstrated equal parts determination and marksmanship as he employed the weapon "with telling effect" against the rebels. His accurate bursts cooled the ardor of the bandits and incoming fire began to die off. Puller seized the advantage Lee had won. The company commander jumped to his feet, called for a charge, and dashed uphill toward the right half of the enemy line. His *guardias* followed. The Sandinistas in front of them fled. Puller circled to take the other side of the ambuscade from the flank, only to discover those positions abandoned. His scouts fanned out to locate the path of retreat, but the enemy had scattered in all directions.[20]

The company consolidated on a ridge just beyond the ambush site. There were ten dead bandits on the field and the *guardias* were certain they had hit at least six more. The patrol had four men wounded and one dead. (In Puller's years in Haiti and Nicaragua, this was the first time he had seen one of his own soldiers killed in battle.) He had his men bury their comrade in a concealed grave and then decided to return to base. He had little choice given the serious condition of his casualties; carrying their improvised stretchers would slow him down and occupy one third of his remaining manpower. The plane due on September 30 would not be able to land and evacuate anyone, so it was of no help. Lee stoically refused to be a burden and walked the entire way back. The *guardias* rotated carrying the three casualties up and down the hills, but the heavy loads were exhausting even so. One of the injured men died. Puller expected the rebels to strike again, so he kept pressing his men onward to reduce that possibility. He firmly believed:

"You can never stop, you've got to keep going when you're carrying wounded on the trail."[21]

Four days after the battle, the Sandinistas sprung the anticipated ambush. One bandit opened fire too soon, though, and gave the experienced unit all the warning it needed. The *guardias* sought cover, Lee unlimbered the Lewis gun, and the estimated eighty rebels were soon put to rout. A few miles farther on, the trail paralleled a stream with a bluff about twenty feet high on the opposite bank. A few dozen rebels lay in wait here, too, but they failed to open fire simultaneously. The patrol brushed aside this feeble ambuscade in short order. In the two brief contacts the unit suffered no casualties, found one enemy body, and believed it had wounded or killed another ten men. Company M reached Jinotega on October 1. A plane took Lee to Managua for treatment.

Puller's report of the action heaped praise on Lee and unwittingly gave him a lifelong nickname when it described his subordinate's tough walk home: "In the days of wooden ships he would have been an iron man." The patrol commander recommended "Iron Man" Lee for the Nicaraguan Cross of Valor and later the Navy Cross. The *jefe director* was equally impressed with Puller's feats and nominated the Guardia captain for the Cross of Valor and the U.S. Distinguished Service Medal. The constabulary chief felt that "this signal victory in jungle country, with no lines of communication and a hundred miles from any supporting force, was largely due to the indomitable courage and persistence of the patrol commander," who had demonstrated "coolness and . . . military judgment."[22]

☆ ☆ ☆

With Nicaraguan elections coming up in early November, the constabulary launched a major offensive. The goal was to keep the rebels on the defensive and away from the population. Puller left Jinotega on October 8 with two officers and thirty men. He was supposed to meet up in the field with fifty-eight officers and men out of Corinto Finca, but heavy rains interfered with the operation from the beginning. The rivers were exceptionally high and fast and the trails were quagmires. It took five days instead of one for the two outfits to rendezvous, then they held up their advance while a detachment escorted a sick *guardia* back to base. Once on the move again, the pack animals made slow progress in mud that sometimes reached to their bellies.

The patrol observed rebel scouts on occasion and discovered recently abandoned defensive positions located where the trail wound through a mountain pass. Puller theorized that the Sandinistas had changed their plans when they saw the size of his ninety-man patrol, one of the largest ever fielded by the Guardia. He was thankful for the respite: "This pass is the toughest proposition that I have seen and against a resolute defense, it would require trench mortars and mountain artillery to force it." After resting his men and animals on October 21, he decided to head back to Jinotega early, since he was running short of rations. The weather affected the bandits, too, and they subsequently did not disrupt the voting. Puller spent election day on November 6 guarding polling booths near Jinotega.[23]

By early November Lee was well enough to return to duty with the company, which sortied from Jinotega on the 11th. Puller kept his outfit in the field almost continuously through December 10, though they stopped a few times at Guardia outposts for supplies. The lengthy patrol had no success, at least in part due to a complete lack of surprise. Another commander operating in the area reported that the inhabitants informed him that the rebels had been aware of the timing and routes of advance of both him and Puller.[24]

This was the last patrol with Company M for Puller and Lee, as the evacuation of the Marines was at hand. The twenty-three officers and NCOs in Jinotega departed for Managua by truck on December 15. The American *guardia* officers and the remnants of the 2d Brigade were scheduled to entrain for Corinto on New Year's Day. In the meantime, they had little to do but enjoy life in the capital and begin reminiscing about the war. Or so they thought.[25]

☆   ☆   ☆

On December 23 the Guardia chief of staff informed Puller that the *jefe director* had one final mission for the intrepid captain. The outgoing Nicaraguan President wanted to personally dedicate the new railroad line between León and El Sauce. Rumors abounded that Sandino intended to disrupt the event or destroy the railroad. Puller was to lead a patrol to El Sauce to keep things quiet until after the celebration. In addition, the unit would escort a shipment of rifles and ammunition. Many Marines volunteered to help and the Guardia captain picked seven constabulary lieutenants to go along. The group included Lee and a Navy

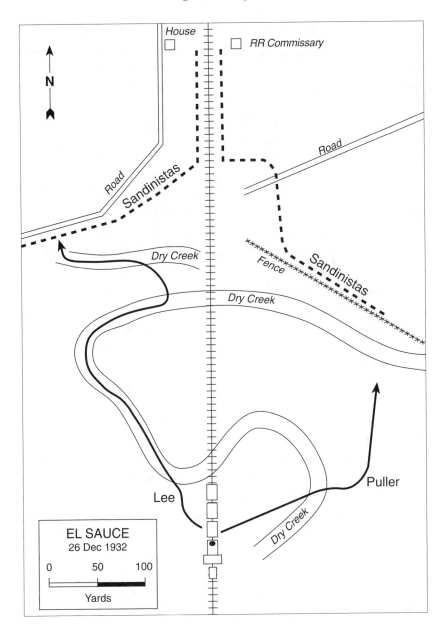

House

RR Commissary

N

Road

Road

Sandinistas

Dry Creek

Fence

Sandinistas

Dry Creek

Puller

Lee

Dry Creek

EL SAUCE
26 Dec 1932

0   50   100

Yards

corpsman who had worked with Company M. They led a force of sixty-four enlisted Nicaraguans.

The outfit boarded a train in Managua on the 26th and set out for El Sauce. Hundreds of workmen were still driving spikes, so progress was slow. Puller, concerned about derailment or mines, had placed the boxcar and his two passenger coaches in front of the engine. Lee and another lieutenant manned a lookout post on top of the lead car. At 1600 the small train was laboring up a low grade a few miles from El Sauce. A bandit force of 250 men was at that moment raiding the railroad company store near the top of the rise. The rebel commander heard the engine and dispatched a hundred men to intercept it. The enemy hastily deployed on both sides of the track. Most of them were behind a fence running off at an angle to the southeast of the northbound line. The rest were along a road and hedge heading southwest. Felled trees and a low stone wall strengthened the position, which formed a natural V-shaped ambuscade.

Lee saw two men on the track and was trying to determine whether they were workmen when the bandits opened fired. The train was still about three hundred yards from the heart of the ambush. That enabled the *guardias* to pour out of their coaches with just one man killed and another wounded. The patrol found shelter in an S-shaped dry creek bed on both sides of the railroad. Puller, with the eastern half of his force, initiated a movement to flank the bandit position but soon discovered that it extended much farther than he thought. Moreover, the remaining 150 rebels now were reinforcing the line. He then dispatched two runners to find out what was happening on the other side of the train. When they did not return he made the trip himself. He discovered that Lee was planning a charge as soon as his *guardias* had fire superiority.

Puller scrambled back to the eastern side through the barrage of rebel fire. He ordered Lieutenant Bennie M. Bunn (a Marine corporal) to make another attempt to flank the enemy. As this group moved out it encountered about sixty bandits attempting to execute the same maneuver against the Guardia position. In a striking display of individual courage, Bunn strode purposefully toward the charging enemy, firing controlled bursts from his BAR. They shot back at first, then fled. Bunn's force struck the end of the bandit line and began to roll it up. At that moment the eastern rebel force dissolved. Their comrades in the west soon followed suit.

The fighting had lasted sixty-five minutes and cost the constabulary unit three killed and three wounded. The rout was so complete that for once the bandits failed to remove most of their dead. The *guardias* counted thirty-one bodies and captured nine weapons and sixty-three horses. It was the biggest confirmed loss inflicted on the Sandinistas since the May 1927 battle at Ocotal. One officer called El Sauce "the most spectacular" engagement of the war, while another found it second only to Ocotal. On the way to El Sauce the Nicaraguan chief of state stopped at the battlefield and received a guided tour from Puller. Ecstatic at the triumph, the President borrowed a rank insignia from one of the majors accompanying him and promoted Puller on the spot. The patrol commander recommended twenty-four of his men for awards. Bunn and Chief Pharmacist's Mate Thomas M. Lynch eventually received the Navy Cross, while others got the Nicaraguan Cross of Valor.[26]

☆ ☆ ☆

The Marines left Managua by train on January 1 and boarded a ship at Corinto the next day. The conflict was far from over—the rebels were stronger than ever, in fact—but henceforth it would be a purely Nicaraguan affair. The small U.S. forces had done all that anyone could expect. They had allowed the country to enjoy a string of relatively clean elections and nonviolent transitions of power and had built the backbone of a competent, nonpartisan constabulary.

Through no fault of the Marines, their rapid withdrawal led to the undoing of much of their hard-won success. It was necessary to appoint dozens of Nicaraguans to fill the senior Guardia billets being vacated. The President opted for political henchmen unfitted to lead a professional military force. Anastasio Somoza, the new *jefe director,* found a reprehensible but effective way to bring the rebellion to a conclusion. Under the guise of a truce in February 1934, he lured Sandino and his main chiefs into Managua for talks and assassinated them. Deprived of leadership, the forces in the field soon broke up and went home. Then Somoza used his control of the Guardia to establish a dictatorship that would remain in power for four decades.[27]

☆ ☆ ☆

Puller's two tours in Nicaragua forever shaped his views of warfare. His long patrols completely cut off from communication with, and support from, higher echelons conditioned him to act on his own with initiative and speed. Many of his battles reconfirmed his Haitian experience regarding the effectiveness of aggressive tactics. These traits would serve him well in most instances in the future. Not every combat situation would be like the small wars of Nicaragua and Haiti, however. Some of Puller's fellow Marines (and later observers) would wonder if he knew the difference or was capable of adapting himself to larger conflicts.

That simplistic view of the man overlooked the subtleties of his performance in Nicaragua. The daring leader who always ordered an immediate charge in the early days developed in time into the wiser commander who employed rifle grenades to break a strong enemy position. The Marine who later would become synonymous with the frontal assault had won several battles by turning the enemy flank. The troop leader noted for his disdain of staff work actually had done quite well as both a personnel officer and a quartermaster. All his seniors and contemporaries in Nicaragua thought he was a highly competent, well-rounded officer with a bright future.

There was no denying that Puller's time with Company M had transformed his career. He had joined the Guardia as a relatively inconspicuous junior officer with some minor skirmishes in Haiti to his credit. Now he was known as one of the Corps' leading fighters. The area commander was not exaggerating when he cited the lieutenant for "exceptional heroism and audacity" and officially concluded that "Puller is probably the outstanding patrol leader of the Marine Corps today." Partisans of Hanneken and Edson might have disputed that claim, but everyone would have agreed that Puller was part of a select group of superb small wars leaders.[28]

On a more visceral level, Puller and Company M fired the imagination of many Marines and a mystique began to develop around the deeds of the unit and its commander. Stories spread around the Corps and grew with each telling. One persistent tale was that Puller's barrel chest came from a steel plate that surgeons had inserted to repair a wound received from the Sandinistas. The less gullible merely viewed his striking posture as a physical manifestation of his innate aggressiveness, courage, and pride. Whatever the opinion held, all came to know Puller by a moniker that connoted far more than his appearance. The crucible of Nicaragua had given birth to the legend of "Chesty" Puller. It would be nurtured by many more battles in wars to come.[29]

6

"An Exceptionally Confident Officer"
On the China Station
1933–1936

Before leaving Nicaragua Puller had submitted his choices for his next duty station. In order of preference he wanted to rejoin the Haitian constabulary (now known as the Garde d'Haiti), go to China to serve with the 4th Regiment in Shanghai or the Legation Guard in Peiping (known till recently as Peking), or do sea duty. The response from Headquarters was confusing, probably because it was in the midst of implementing a 10 percent reduction in the strength of the Corps and finding billets for everyone coming out of Nicaragua. In the space of a few weeks HQMC issued orders for Chesty to report to the Marine barracks in Washington, D.C., then San Diego, then Mare Island, then San Diego again. Shortly after he arrived in southern California, the Corps finally decided to send Puller, Evans Carlson, and several other former Guardia leaders to China. The small group of Marines sailed from San Francisco on February 10, 1933.[1]

In a tribute to Chesty's post-Nicaragua renown, an Oakland newspaper announced his departure for Asia. The reporter may have been the first to inflate the Puller legend beyond the already impressive reality. He referred to the lieutenant as the "most decorated Marine," proclaimed that he had fought twenty battles in his last thirty days in that country, and listed a medal that did not even exist. At that time Puller had just one U.S. award for valor and a second pending, plus three foreign medals (one of them from Haiti). He was definitely not the most

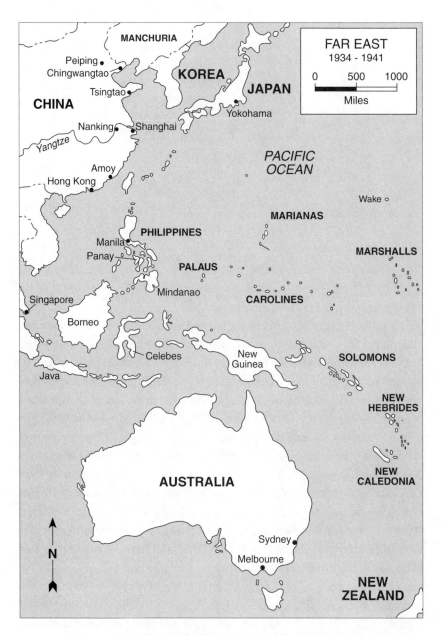

decorated Marine, not even in the campaign against Sandino; Bill Lee
had garnered three Navy Crosses and two Nicaraguan medals in that
small war. Iron Man Lee, in fact, was the first Marine ever to receive that
many awards of the Navy Department's second-highest decoration.[2]

Puller's first journey to the Far East took him to Peiping via Manila and Shanghai. He joined the Legation Guard in the former Chinese capital on March 22, 1933, and received a welcome-aboard present, a star representing his second award of the Navy Cross. The decoration cited his "great courage, coolness and display of military judgment" in the September 1932 patrol in which Lee was wounded. "This signal victory in jungle country, with no lines of communication and a hundred miles from any supporting force, was largely due to the indomitable courage and persistence of the patrol commander."[3]

☆ ☆ ☆

The embassy detachment at Peiping had occupied a place of prominence in the traditions and history of the Corps since 1900, when Captain John T. "Handsome Jack" Myers and fifty Marines participated in the defense of the Legation Quarter during the Boxer Rebellion. The diplomatic missions were located inside the Tartar Wall in an exclusive area adjacent to the Imperial and Forbidden cities. Some of the finest tourist attractions in the world were just a pleasant walk from the Marine barracks. Although the detachment occasionally had to worry about disorder arising out of political turmoil in China, its main preoccupation was maintaining an elite status among the embassy guards. The competition, both official and informal, ran from drill and marksmanship to sports and entertainment. The U.S. force of twenty-six officers and five hundred men was the largest of the international units, but Japan, France, Britain, and Italy also maintained big detachments.[4]

Puller joined Company A, which manned the organization's ten Browning machine guns. Company B was a rifle unit, Company C handled the mortars and 37mm guns, and there was a platoon-sized mounted force. Each unit conducted cross-training with all other detachment weapons, which meant that "junior officers have to be . . . artillerymen, machine gunners and riflemen." The twin requirements for skill and a certain amount of dash meant that officers selected for the embassy guard had to be not only of "good standing and ability," but also able to "fit into the picture of Peiping." Captain John W. Thomason, the acclaimed Marine writer-artist and a member of the detachment, described the citizens of the Legation Quarter as "a slick, highly polished lot—very much on the social side, and they discuss international politics and the menace of the moment and their neighbor's wife with equal freedom and gusto." Chesty's selection for this sort of duty was an indication that he had a solid reputation as a professional. Despite years on the trail in the company of Nicaraguan peasant-soldiers, he also apparently remembered how to display the manners of a Southern gentleman when required.[5]

Despite the high standards, the daily routine of the Legation Guard was not too arduous. The Marines usually conducted garrison training in the morning and spent the afternoon engaged in organized athletics. Periodically the companies practiced tactics on the glacis, an open area just beyond the walls of the Legation Quarter. It was designed to provide clear fields of fire in an emergency but otherwise served as a place to play sports. The units also went on occasional hikes or field exercises in the countryside or fired their weapons at a range outside the city. There was liberty every evening and weekend if one was not on guard duty.[6]

The Marines of the Legation Guard took their marksmanship as seriously as the rest of the Corps. Once a year each company marched out to the International Range, a facility jointly maintained by all the foreign units. The two weeks of duty there was a pleasant interlude, with the troops living in wooden-decked tents along a tree-shaded lane. The Legation Guard also fielded a team for the annual Far East Division Match that qualified Marines for the Corps-wide competition in Quantico. Traditionally there had been a triangular match between the Marines of Peiping and Shanghai and the 15th Infantry in Tientsin, but the Army cut back its marksmanship program during the Depression to save money. The Army regimental commander begged out of the 1934 competition because none of his men had fired their rifles in 1933.[7]

Athletic competition was a way of life in the Peiping military community. The Marines held intramural contests between the companies in just about every team sport and chose their best to represent the Corps in matches with Western civilians and the soldiers of other nations. Boxing was the premier activity for the enlisted men while the officers focused their attention on polo. Each officer was responsible for overseeing a particular sport; a standing order told them to "bear in mind that athletics are a part of military duty and every effort will be made to stimulate interest." The detachment commander also made it clear that the commissioned ranks would either play on the polo team or provide financial assistance to those who did.

Chesty, an accomplished horseman, became one of the starters for a relatively inexperienced Marine polo group. The 1933 Leatherneck team did not fare too well, winning only one tournament, but Puller received the Griffin Cup as the best first-year player in Peiping. According to one officer, it was a good activity for a warrior in peacetime: "The thrill of combat is there. There is a call for courage, horsemanship, a keen eye, and a steady hand. And the Marine Corps can't have too much of that." There also was no small amount of danger. Chesty spilled his horse in the autumn of 1933 and fractured several ribs. He had to wear a tight wrap on his torso for a month and ended up with a permanent deformity of his lower chest.[8]

Puller was intimately involved in the other key Peiping sport as well, since he served as the post boxing officer. His fighters participated in frequent intramural smokers and sometimes traveled to Tientsin for bouts in the Army's large gymnasium. Chesty, always looking out for the welfare of his men, officially complained that the 15th Infantry was not giving Marine boxers a fair share of the proceeds from ticket sales. He soon found a facility in Peiping and began sponsoring fight cards and charging admission. His fighters won more bouts than they lost, no small feat against the Army, which had a much larger force to draw upon for talent.[9]

Marines had long considered China a good duty station, but it was especially so in the early 1930s. As a result of the Depression, Congress had cut officers' pay by 15 percent beginning in 1932, and that of enlisted men by a similar amount in 1933. But the American dollar recently had doubled in value against the Chinese currency and labor there was extremely cheap. One could purchase a tailor-made suit for a fraction of the stateside cost and even Marine privates employed someone to keep their uniforms and equipment burnished for inspections. The Chinese economy largely shielded Puller from the loss of his Guardia pay and the drop in his U.S. income.[10]

☆   ☆   ☆

Periodically the legation Marines had to turn their attention to more serious matters. Recent events in China had placed relations between the United States and Japan on a particularly tense footing. For many years Japanese troops had guarded Manchurian railroad lines owned by their nation. To expand their control of this Chinese province, in September 1931 the Japanese leadership accused China of attempting to blow up a railway bridge at Mukden. With that as a pretext, Japan conquered

Manchuria in a few months and installed a puppet government. China invoked a boycott of Japanese goods. Japan responded by attacking the vital commercial center and port of Shanghai in January 1932. After weeks of fighting, China agreed to keep its troops outside the city and end the boycott while Japan withdrew its forces from all of Shanghai except its portion of the International Settlement.

The United States strongly opposed Japan's actions but was unwilling to go to war on behalf of Chinese territorial integrity. American Marines and Japanese soldiers, side by side in both Shanghai and Peiping, regarded each other with barely concealed hostility. One astute Marine in 1932 noted that "the Japanese have embarked upon a course from which it will be difficult, perhaps impossible, to turn back." John Thomason thought "they have an idea they can lick the world and it doesn't matter where or when they start."[11]

Things grew especially tense in Peiping just as Puller reported there for duty. In early March 1933, Japanese forces had advanced into another northern Chinese province and fighting soon spread to the region around Peiping. Chinese forces prepared sandbag positions all over the city and set up antiaircraft guns, while Japanese planes flew overhead. On one occasion three bold pilots buzzed the Marines during their morning parade. There was no fighting within the city, however, despite the presence of the Japanese embassy guard. The two warring nations agreed to a new truce in May and China again ceded territory.[12]

Under these strained conditions there were bound to be incidents between the legation detachments. In one instance a Japanese soldier standing watch at the gate of his embassy put his bayonet to the stomach of a passing Marine officer and then chambered a round after the lieutenant pushed it aside. On another occasion a platoon of Japanese armed with iron bars surrounded an officer riding on the glacis and one of them struck at him. The American commander formally complained each time there was a provocation and his Japanese counterpart invariably replied with a mixture of apologies and regrets that innocent actions had been misconstrued. As officer of the day in March 1934 Puller had to investigate a late night brawl that had erupted when a group of Marines entered a dance hall frequented by Japanese. The two sides employed broken beer bottles and a number of combatants suffered severe cuts.[13]

☆   ☆   ☆

Just after Thanksgiving Day 1933 Puller transferred to Headquarters Company to become the assistant to the officer responsible for intelligence, operations, and training. One of his last acts with Company A was to lead his platoon to victory in the annual drill competition. In early January he assumed command of the mounted detachment, a billet he had held briefly in the spring of 1933. He also continued to perform his staff job as an additional duty.[14]

The Peiping Horse Marines liked to style themselves as the "first organized cavalry unit in the Corps." The unique group had gotten its start in 1912 and since became part of the mystique of the China station. In an emergency the force of one officer and thirty-some men was supposed to deal with unruly crowds or escort American nationals to the safety of the Legation Quarter. During quieter periods, they made weekly rides to verify the residence of every U.S. citizen.

Duty with the mounted detachment was attractive and the requirement that applicants have clean records served as an incentive to good behavior. According to lore the Horse Marines played the opposing force in field problems and were allowed to ride back at the end of the exercises, thus giving them first crack at the wine and women when liberty sounded. Since field training was exceedingly rare during Puller's time, that was not much of an advantage. Men more likely sought to join purely for vanity. They were the elite of the Legation Guard, "noted for their smart appearance, élan in mounted drill, and arrogance." They vied for silver cups in horse races and had an expatriate European countess as their patroness. Even their training and equipment was unusual. Each man carried a Colt automatic pistol and a cavalry saber in addition to his rifle or automatic weapon. The highlight of their year was the saber qualification course. They had to jump obstacles and pierce ten dummies within a prescribed time limit, with extra points for "spirit and fighting manner." Puller was an excellent rider, a perfectionist at drill and appearance, and the right size for the smallish Mongolian ponies; he was made to order for the job. The Legation Guard commander found the Marine lieutenant "exceptionally well qualified in every way."[15]

Chesty's twin posts as assistant intelligence officer and mounted commander gave him an opportunity to learn about the Japanese and Chinese military forces. Although he never saw any combat operations, he observed their training and discipline and formed opinions about their relative worth. He was impressed by both sides, mainly by their toughness and endurance in the face of adverse conditions of weather and supply. Another Legation Marine developed similar views after attending a Chinese army parade: "The men in the ranks appear well-drilled, fairly well-equipped, and sturdy. (They having stood out on the wind-swept plains of Peiping from daylight until ten o'clock with the thermometer hovering around nine above zero, and in wind whistling down from the Western hills.) I couldn't help but think how very unpleasant this outfit and several more like it could make it for our brown friends across the way [the Japanese] if properly led." Puller's reconnaissance forays gave rise to yet another mythic tale. He was supposed to have ridden into the midst of a battle while the "astounded combatants ceased fire" as Chesty calmly trotted along the trench lines to get a good look at their work.[16]

☆   ☆   ☆

In mid-August 1934, with a year remaining on his thirty-month tour of duty, Puller received unexpected orders. The Commander in Chief of the Asiatic Fleet was unhappy with the Marine detachment aboard his flagship, USS *Augusta* (CA-31). The ship's captain, Chester W. Nimitz, also was "impatient with poor performers." The two senior officers had fired a first lieutenant after nine months on the job and sent a captain packing after four. Since the Leatherneck unit was the ceremonial representative of the admiral, the fleet, and the United States, it was no small concern. The admiral and Nimitz did not have to look hard for a suitable replacement already available on the China station—Puller's time with the mounted detachment had only enhanced his reputation for snap and polish. The Marine lieutenant left Peiping on September 8. The Horse Marines, with their usual bravado reinforced by alcohol, gave him a royal sendoff. Mounted on their ponies, they escorted their commander through the train station and right onto the platform, while stunned Chinese hastened to get out of the way of the skittish animals.[17]

Puller's selection for duty on the flagship was an honor since her guard rated a Marine captain. It also gave him the opportunity to prove his mettle in a higher-ranking billet. That was suddenly more important than usual, as Congress finally had reformed the Marine Corps promotion system in the summer of 1934. Henceforth boards would select officers based on merit. The legislation also gave the Corps more field grade officers. Both actions greatly sped up advancement, if one ended up being among the chosen. Instead of waiting up to a decade more for a guaranteed promotion to captain, Chesty would be in zone for consideration in the next year or two. No doubt with that in mind, he asked for an extension of his tour till fall 1936 and requested that he receive another assignment to school at that time. Both steps would enhance his record. Headquarters granted his first wish but held off on his second.[18]

☆   ☆   ☆

Sea duty had been the backbone of the Marine Corps since Leathernecks had served on board American warships during the Revolutionary War. It was in many respects an anachronism now, since the fleet no longer required riflemen to shoot from the fighting tops or storm the bulwarks of enemy ships. The seagoing Marines could still spearhead landings to deal with minor contingencies ashore, but even that role was disappearing as the United States lost interest in intervention and small wars. Now the detachments mainly manned some of the heavy guns and performed ceremonial functions in their dress blue uniforms. Despite this decrease in utility, in 1934 fully one seventh of the strength of the Corps was afloat on such duty.[19]

The *Augusta* was a rarity in the U.S. fleet of the early 1930s—she was a new ship. Following the Washington Naval Treaty of 1922 the government had drastically curtailed construction of warships, authorizing many fewer than the agreement allowed. The Asiatic Fleet flagship had come off the building ways in 1930 and was lucky to be completed. In response to the Depression, President Hoover had deleted all funds for shipbuilding from subsequent budgets. *Augusta* had benefited in one respect from the naval arms limitations; she was a "treaty cruiser" built to the maximum specifications permitted. At ten thousand tons displacement and armed with a main battery of nine 8-inch guns, she dwarfed the older cruisers in the fleet.[20]

Puller reported on board the *Augusta* on the warm, sunny morning of September 11 as she lay anchored at Chingwangtao. His command consisted of a second lieutenant and forty-two men. He had little time to get acquainted with his new home. One of his additional duties involved marksmanship training for both his detachment and the sailors designated to reinforce any landing party. Four hours after his arrival he took this mixed group ashore for two weeks at the rifle range. His impact was almost immediate. He could do little to change "primitive" conditions in the spartan camp, but after a day of "unappetizing and skimpy" meals, he ordered the Navy cook to pack his personal gear. The two men went out to the ship and Puller returned a few hours later with a replacement and a boatload of provisions. The chow immediately improved. So did morale and scores. Chesty's "excellent results" in qualifying the men earned his first kudos from his Navy seniors. Nimitz was no doubt equally impressed by the Marine lieutenant's decisive response to the food situation. More important, Puller's subordinates soon confirmed he "was always personally concerned with the welfare of the men under his command."[21]

As soon as the shooters returned, the ship set sail for the voyage of a lifetime to Australia. The cruiser put in briefly in Shanghai and again at Guam, then shaped course for Sydney Harbor. As the ship plowed southward, the crew turned its attention from work and the anticipated liberty to an ancient nautical custom, the ceremony marking the crossing of the equator. The shellbacks (those who had gone over the line before) prepared a tough rite of passage for the pollywogs (first-timers). On the evening of October 13 the mythical Davy Jones appeared on board to hand out subpoenas requiring all pollywogs to report the next day for trial. Puller's shipmates had gleefully charged him with "unmilitary bearing" and "gross display of medals." Neptunus Rex and his court arrived the following morning to mete out punishment. The initiates suffered a host of indignities, from having to kiss a sailor's fat belly greased with some vile concoction to crawling through a gauntlet of men armed with paddles fashioned from canvas fire hose.[22]

Once the fun was over for the shellbacks the ship got back to the serious business of daily operations at sea. Under the leadership of Nimitz, the men of *Augusta* went about their duties with a greater sense of purpose than most of their contemporaries in the Navy. The skipper set high standards, demanded hard work, and subjected the crew to an exacting regimen of daily battle drills, but he also motivated them to give their utmost. Many of his junior officers would go on to become admirals and they all recalled this tour with fondness and pride. They thought their cruiser was a "pretty hot outfit . . . in everything from gunnery to athletics." They remembered a taut ship, pervaded by a great sense of camaraderie. Their captain delegated considerable authority to his subordinates and doled out the credit for good results. Puller excelled in this environment and was doing his full share to bring his detachment up to the same level. Nimitz was "most favorably impressed" by the rapid improvement in his Marines and was not surprised when the admiral pronounced them "smart and efficient" during his quarterly inspection. The *Augusta*'s captain thought his senior Leatherneck had a "very high sense of duty" and was "a true leader who demanded—and received—the best from his subordinates." The ship's officers and men respected the lieutenant for his "ramrod posture, leathered countenance, bulldog jaw, and general demeanor of relaxed competence," all of which bespoke an "old salt," someone bearing the imaginary white crust of long service in the briny ocean air.[23]

The ship spent six days in Sydney and then arrived in Melbourne on October 29 for a two-week stay. Invitations flooded the *Augusta* and Nimitz had to establish a special scheduling board to ensure that personnel appeared for every social event. Officers had to attend as many as four per day. Here Puller had his first chance to stand pier-side duty as officer of the deck, but he performed a much more memorable service on the evening of November 10. He and a few other Marines had attended a rifle match. On the return trip they were crossing a river on a ferry and were just about to dock when a car ran off the slip and plunged into the water. As others stood by in horror, Chesty tore off his shoes and shirt and dived in. He pulled two women from the sinking automobile before it went down and drowned the unlucky driver. After his daring feat a bystander gave him a bottle of whiskey and he drank freely. When he finally returned to the ship, his fellow officers saw his bedraggled, boozy condition and kidded him for falling off the pier after too much revelry. They discovered the truth only after reading the newspapers two days later.[24]

The *Augusta* sailed around Australia to Perth, then on to other port calls at Java, Bali, Celebes, and Borneo. She entered Philippine waters in mid-December and stopped at the islands of Mindanao and Panay before coming to anchor in the harbor of Manila on the 22d. Puller got his Marines ashore for target practice and took along one ensign to settle a bet. A Navy officer had argued that marksmanship was a talent rather than a learned skill; Chesty won $10 when the one-striper reported back aboard with an expert medal.[25]

After two months of battle practice and repair work, the cruiser headed north in March 1935. She put in briefly at Hong Kong and

Amoy and spent a month moored in the Whangpoo River off Shanghai. This cosmopolitan roadstead routinely hosted visiting warships from the United States, Britain, France, Italy, Japan, and other nations. A new captain replaced Nimitz and the ship sailed for Japan to participate in funeral ceremonies for Admiral Heihachiro Togo, the great hero of the Imperial Fleet for his victory over Russia in 1905. Puller and the ship's captain specially selected the honor guard from the tallest Marines and sailors, so they would stand out amongst the Japanese. After three weeks in Japan, *Augusta* returned to Shanghai and made a trip up the Yangtze River to the Chinese capital of Nanking. In June Puller was part of the admiral's team conducting the annual inspection of the 4th Marines. In the fall the flagship made its winter pilgrimage to warmer waters, with stops in Thailand, Singapore, and Borneo. By November she was back in the Philippines.[26]

Puller spent most of the next several weeks ashore at the rifle range with the landing party. He continued to perform superbly in that role, achieving a 100 percent qualification rate for his Marines in all small arms and over 90 percent for the sailors. It was one of the best records of any warship in the Navy that year and brought a special commendation from the ship's captain. The *Augusta*'s Marine detachment won the Corps' Haines Bayonet Trophy as well. Chesty also acted as the ship's legal officer, an unwelcome part-time billet commonly assigned to a Marine officer. Eventually he filled the same job on the admiral's staff, too, and did well enough to earn special mention in his fitness report. He even qualified to serve as officer of the deck underway when the ship was not in formation, a feat requiring considerable education in seamanship.[27]

In September Puller had taken his examination for promotion and failed ordnance and gunnery. That was a strange outcome, since he now had a year's experience in charge of the ship's four 5-inch antiaircraft guns. But it was a minor setback. On November 9, 1935, a board of senior Navy officers on the cruiser supervised his automatic reexamination and he passed. In February 1936 he pinned on the twin silver bars of a Marine captain. He had waited more than six years for this promotion, but if the new selection system had not cleaned out the deadwood, it would have been much longer. In terms of seniority, Puller had risen to about six-hundredth place among the slightly more than one thousand Marine officers of all ranks on active duty.[28]

Captain Thomason sent his congratulations: "All that I hear of you confirms the opinion I formed of you in Peiping, and I consider you one of the few officers I know who have a genuine military aptitude." The World War hero noted the number of Marines who had performed superbly as platoon and company commanders in that conflict, only to rest on their laurels thereafter. Then he mentioned that Napoleon's recipe "for proficiency in the military art was to study and reflect upon the campaigns of the great captains." It was perhaps a subtle hint for Puller to keep up his interest in military history and tactics and not fall by the wayside as others had. Thomason closed with an admonition: "Take care of yourself. The world does not promise peace and they will need us combat officers before our time is up."[29]

In February 1936 the *Augusta* participated in joint Army-Navy maneuvers in the Philippines. The exercise included live gunnery practice. The simulated combat proved all too real in some respects. The shock of sustained gunfire inflicted considerable minor damage on the ship and one man died from heat exhaustion. The outside temperature was in the low 80s, but it was hell in the confined turrets. The sailors and Marines toiled over their heavy guns while exploding powder charges steadily drove the thermometer higher. (It also was not uncommon for men to lose fingers and hands as they worked at top speed amidst shell hoists, breech blocks, and many other moving parts.)

The cruiser completed its winter with a trip around the Philippine Islands and headed back to Shanghai via Hong Kong and Amoy. The flagship also made its annual upriver visit to Nanking. Upon its return to the coast, a Marine captain and a lieutenant reported aboard as Puller's prospective replacements. (He had been without an officer assistant since December 1934.) *Augusta* sailed to Japan a few days later and arrived on May 25, 1936. Chesty had reached the end of his extended duty in the Far East and had orders to the States. He transferred his gear to a civilian ship and made his last salute to the officer of the deck and the national ensign as he departed the *Augusta*. It had been an eventful tour and the ship's captain specially noted that his Marine subordinate had taken a "marked" interest in the entire profession of arms. Puller had indeed learned a great deal about the Navy, the Pacific, gunnery, seamanship, and a host of lesser topics. He had every reason to be "an exceptionally confident officer."[30]

7
"So Very Happy and Contented"
Basic School and China Again
1936–1941

I n early 1936 Puller had reiterated his request to return to the classroom, asking for the Marine Field Officers Course, the Army Staff
College, or the Artillery School. He partially got his wish. He had escaped an assignment to instructor duty after Benning and Headquarters
had not forgotten. Now he would join the staff of the Basic School in
Philadelphia. He left Yokohama on the SS *President Jackson* on May
26.[1]

☆　☆　☆

The school had not changed in many respects since Puller's days as a
student in 1925. The length of the course had doubled to ten months,
but the focus on small unit fundamentals remained. The size of the
classes grew dramatically beginning in 1935, mainly due to the advent
of promotion by selection. The 1935–1936 class had doubled the normal intake of about fifty students. The 1936–1937 group (Puller's first)
numbered 141. The class size dipped back to just under a hundred
thereafter. The influx was so great that during Puller's three years at the
school, the lieutenants passing under his tutelage constituted nearly one
third of the Marine officer corps.[2]

The quality of the incoming leaders was outstanding. The Corps
continued to commission its annual quota of twenty-five Naval Academy graduates and a select group of NCOs. But the bulk of the new
men now came from an unusual source. During the lean Depression

years the Army made almost no use of its large crop of ROTC students. The Marine Corps astutely took advantage of the situation and offered commissions to the top one or two graduates of the best ROTC programs. The chance for active service persuaded many to accept. In addition, the six Naval ROTC schools provided a few officers. The Corps' fledgling Platoon Leaders Class program also allowed students from colleges without ROTC to earn reserve commissions. The Corps turned the best of these into regulars. And a handful came in via the Navy's aviation cadet program. These lieutenants spent a year flying before they came to Philadelphia for final polishing.

No matter what the source, the Marines were paying almost nothing to develop this talent and were widening the geographic base of the officer corps (previously drawn disproportionately from the South). The backgrounds of the new officers also proved complementary. Midshipmen contributed their knowledge of the sea, cadets brought their expertise in Army skills, and the NCOs chipped in with an enlisted man's perspective on leadership. But most important, in the 1930s the Corps was skimming the cream off the top of the available officer candidates. Many of these superb young men would rise to command battalions and staff the divisions during World War II.[3]

☆   ☆   ☆

Puller made an immediate splash in Philadelphia in 1936. Congress finally had authorized Marines to wear Nicaraguan decorations, so an admiral pinned awards on a number of men in a summer parade at the Navy Yard. Chesty received his Presidential Medal of Merit and Cross of Valor. Another reporter perpetuated the 1933 mistake of his Oakland colleague and referred to Puller as "the most decorated Marine to serve in Nicaragua."[4]

Irrespective of the number of medals, Puller certainly was one of the most experienced officers to come out of the Corps' recent Caribbean intervention. The director of the Basic School made sure that knowledge was put to good use. His newest instructor took over the small wars package. That course constituted a tiny section of the overall program (just thirty hours of a total of 1,200), but many students later would recall it as one of the best parts of the Basic School. The man who had scored his only superior grade at Benning in instructional methods proved he could perform well in a real classroom. Chesty used the Corps' new *Small Wars Manual* as his basic text, but brought it to life with stories of his own patrols or the deeds of others. (He wrote Hanneken for details of his encounter with Charlemagne in Haiti and developed that into one lecture.) This case method of teaching enthralled the students and made the material stick in their minds. They "looked forward to every session" with him. In their eyes, only Captain Russ Jordahl, another Benning-trained man, rivaled him as an instructor.[5]

Puller also served as one of the drill and command officers. Each of the captains assigned to this duty was responsible for a platoon of lieutenants. The senior leaders supervised drill, taught bayonet fighting and hand-to-hand combat, and ensured that their charges acquired proper-fitting uniforms. Puller was a natural for this work, too. Since the 170 hours of drill and command constituted the largest block of training, he had the greatest opportunity to influence new officers here. He instilled in them the need to maintain high standards in discipline, dress, and bearing and advised them that "women, whiskey, and indebtedness" were the surest ways to get in trouble. One lieutenant recalled Puller's introductory speech to his platoon in 1936: "The motto of the Marine Corps is 'Don't let your buddy down!' In the Marine Corps your buddy is not only your classmate or fellow officer, but he also is the Marine under your command. If you don't prepare yourself to properly train him, lead him, and support him on the battlefield, then you're going to let him down. That is unforgivable in the Marine Corps."[6]

He also taught them the finer points of leadership by example. One future general recalled that Puller handled poor performance with a simple comment, not a tirade. "When he inspected the class, if he found something that really wasn't up to standard, he'd merely say in a low voice, 'Robertson, you know better than to come out that way.' And while you'd start shrinking down to about two-inch height, he was down inspecting the next man." On occasion he could resort to a scornful tone to spark a little collective motivation on the parade deck or in the field: "If you high-paid lieutenants can't do it right, how do you expect a $21-a-month private to do it right?" He frequently reminded them that "second lieutenants have no rights and damn few privileges."[7]

In the fall the students went to the firing range for a month to learn everything from grenades to mortars. In the spring they spent another four weeks in the field focusing on combat firing and small unit tactics. This second phase of instruction took place at the state military reservation at Indiantown Gap, Pennsylvania, in the foothills of the Blue Ridge Mountains. That gave the lieutenants ample opportunity to experience the challenge of maneuvering in tough terrain. Puller accompanied them every step of the way. During rest breaks the students often would gather round to hear more of his stories. He also informally passed along his thoughts on topics ranging from combat leadership to living off the land. One of the young officers who absorbed every word was Lewis W. Walt, who later would become famous in his own right with Edson's Raiders. He gave a large measure of credit for his success to Puller's teachings in Basic School: "You have had a greater influence on my performance as an officer than anyone else, with the possible exception of General Edson. . . . You taught us how to train men and to fight and ignore danger as though it didn't exist."[8]

In the spring of 1937, Major General Thomas Holcomb, the new Commandant, spoke to the Basic School. His themes already were guideposts for Puller. Holcomb noted that promotion by selection made it important for a young officer to keep his record clear of "thoughtless mistakes," but he counseled them to seek to do more than that: "The avoidance of trouble is a purely negative virtue. What should be sought is the positive virtue of achievement." He then summarized his views on leadership:

> There is one characteristic of enlisted men that I especially wish to point out to you, and that is their rapid and accurate appraisal of their officers. You will not for long be able to deceive your men, either with regard to your professional ability or your character. . . . Every military organization, by virtue of the power of example, is like a mirror in which the commander sees himself reflected. Whether consciously or unconsciously, men take their cue from their officers. If the officer is diligent, his men will strive to exceed him in diligence; if he is thorough they will be thorough; if he is thoughtful of them, they will constantly be seeking opportunities to do something for him.[9]

Chesty's legendary status as a Marine would come to rest largely on those two traits—his willingness to do more than his share and his ability to cultivate a strong bond of mutual respect with enlisted men.

☆   ☆   ☆

The thirty-nine-year-old captain was still a bachelor in the fall of 1937, but he had not wanted to remain single that long. He had kept his mind on Virginia Evans for the past dozen years, writing to her from his exotic duty stations, sending her gifts, and always reminding her that he still wanted her to be his bride. She had remained in no hurry to get married, however. Her classmates at Saint Mary's College had long ago recognized her strong-willed independence and predicted that she would "refuse many suitors to pursue [a] career." Puller wasted no time in renewing his campaign at close range after his posting to Philadelphia. He found she was still "the belle of the Peninsula," but by then she was considering an offer of marriage from another man. Nevertheless, the brash Marine captain persuaded her to accompany him to the 1936 Army-Navy football game. After that date she decided to give him a chance.[10]

He approached courtship with the same vigor that he applied to everything he undertook. He spent all his weekends and leaves in the Tidewater, and demonstrated a sweet, gentle side of his personality that would have shocked the Marines who served with him. Virginia told others how amazed and pleased she was by his devotion: "I never had a beau like him. He's always so positive about everything. He never pays the least attention to what I say. If I tell him not to come down for the weekend, there he comes anyway. Yet he's the most attentive thing you ever saw. He writes me every day." Those letters were filled with fervent expressions of his feelings:

> I love you so very much, Virginia, that I will never be happy unless you are. I would not want you to marry me, if I had the least idea that I could not make you completely happy. I would rather that you were married to some other man and for me to know that you were happy. You are so fine and you have had too much sorrow in this life. From now on life must be different. Your happiness is all that matters to me.[11]

Rumors of Chesty's romantic campaign apparently were circulating around the Corps. Hanneken closed a January 1937 letter with the brief postscript: "By the way, are you married now????????" He had jumped the gun only a little. In early spring, Virginia finally agreed to marry Lewis. His letters grew even more demonstrative:

I, too, miss you dreadfully, but as you know, I can stand on my head until *The Day*. Oh! Virginia, I am so very happy and contented and we will always be ever so happy. You have made my life worthwhile, now. Colonel Turnage showed me my fitness report today for the past six months and the report was perfect. . . . You are responsible, darling, and from now on all my reports will be likewise. . . . The weather is quite wet here now. Rain most of yesterday and all of today. The sun is shining for me, though, and always will. . . . I would like to phone you every evening but will continue to confine myself to Sundays in order to save *our* money.

He did make one exception to his promises of future bliss. He explained that if he "heard the beat of the drum," he would have to march off to war.[12]

Virginia would prove to be an excellent match for him. Her family roots were equally illustrious and possibly distantly intertwined with his. Her great-grandfather Colonel Edgar Burwell Montague had attended VMI, commanded a regiment of Virginia infantry during the Civil War, and served as a judge. Her grandfather and father also were prominent in the legal field. She had served as a class or club officer during each of her three years at Saint Mary's. She was voted "most enthusiastic" by her classmates, but they noted her zeal was balanced by a judicious temperament: "Excellent in scholarship, faithful in duty, reserved in disposition, unaffected and kind in manner, this bespeaks Virginia to a 'T'. . . . We maintain she'll always be level-headed in the greatest crisis. From the smallest task to the largest deed Virginia puts her heart and soul in all she undertakes." She also had developed a reputation for ensuring the "healthy condition of the [class] money box." After graduating from Saint Mary's in 1927, she had gone to work as a secretary in her father's law office. During the first few summers she also had taken courses at the University of Virginia. She had the education and character to go far. She now would turn that talent to helping her husband.[13]

The wedding took place on November 13, 1937, in Christ Episcopal Church in Middlesex County, Virginia. Lewis did not make her entirely happy that day, mainly because his own excitement embarrassed her. He marched out of his appointed waiting room too early, then prodded the minister to hurry up and join him. The first time his bass voice echoed around the church, the surprised guests from her side couldn't suppress their laughter. When the ceremony was over and they walked down the aisle, she turned crimson as his attempts at stage-whispered compliments about her loveliness were heard by all.[14]

The couple took a weeklong honeymoon in Atlantic City, then moved into an apartment overlooking the north end of the Basic School parade deck. Virginia brought along a family maid. The marriage came as a surprise to many in the Corps, especially Chesty's students, who remembered his harangues that Marines should remain single. A few of the young officers thought that the presence of Mrs. Puller softened him a bit, but he was far from domesticated at first. Lieutenant Robert D. Heinl found that out when he and a small group appeared for an obligatory call on the new couple. The captain made no small talk and his students were afraid to open the discussion. All sat there wordlessly sipping drinks until the sophisticated Heinl recognized Virginia's antique china on display. He commented on it and he and Mrs. Puller ended up in an "animated dialog" on the subject. Later he felt it took him years to convince Chesty that someone with so much knowledge of fine porcelain actually could be a good Marine officer. Mrs. Puller would recall of these days: "After a certain amount of house-breaking, the field soldier became a genial, hospitable host." As time passed, those who knew Chesty both professionally and socially would be amazed by the chameleon-like switch in his personality whenever he shifted between the two realms. Fellow officers would recall that "he was entirely different [at home] than when he was out standing in front of troops."[15]

Virginia brought much more to the marriage than skills as a hostess and homemaker. She had considerable experience as an office administrator and was adept at managing money. From this point on, Lewis turned the family finances over to her with only one admonition, that they would never go into debt. She eventually assumed responsibility for many other functions normally handled in those days by the husband—in fact, just about everything not directly related to his professional life. Her Southern upbringing showed through in one respect; she took pains to conceal this unladylike expertise from the rest of the world.[16]

☆   ☆   ☆

During his time as an instructor Puller did not give up trying to become a student again. In March 1937 he asked for an early release from his tour in Philadelphia to attend advanced schooling that fall. He was not choosy and listed the Quantico courses for company and field grade officers, as well as the Army's staff, tank, artillery, and cavalry programs. Headquarters turned him down because of his short time on station. He sent a new request in July for the following academic year. In the fall of 1938 he submitted a plea just for the Army's staff college and pointed out that he would be past the age limit after the 1938–1939 class. He also mailed personal letters to Colonel Vandegrift (now the military secretary to the Commandant) and other senior officers asking for their intervention in the assignment process. Vandegrift provided a vaguely encouraging answer to his former Haiti protégé: "I hope that your desire will be realized because I feel that you will make good in that assignment as you have in others." Privately, the colonel thought otherwise: "I understand that his marks and the way he got along at Benning were not too promising. . . . Puller is an excellent field soldier and practical man, but neither of us believe at the present time that he is the type of Marine officer that we should send to Leavenworth." Vandegrift's opinion carried considerable weight with Holcomb. In April 1939, HQMC issued orders to transfer Chesty that summer to the 4th Marines in Shanghai.[17]

Puller's failure to get a school seat, even after he had sought help from friends in high places, was undoubtedly a bitter pill to swallow. The experience may have soured his attitude toward military education, since his opinion changed dramatically after this point. In future years he would express a strong disdain for such academic training and anyone associated with it. His new outlook may have resulted in part from a sense of inferiority in the one area where he had not been able to match or surpass his contemporaries. Whatever the cause, hereafter he would wear his own lack of attendance as a badge of honor and foster the idea that he purposely had avoided being a student because education was meaningless, perhaps even counterproductive. He would argue that "service in the camp and in the field is the best military school."[18]

The three-year tour in Philadelphia had not added much to Puller's education or experience, but it was worthwhile nonetheless since it brought him into contact with a large number of Marine officers. Among others, Chesty would end up working closely in the next war with Major Amor L. Sims, the officer in charge of the curriculum. Puller influenced a great many young lieutenants and in turn got to know several who would serve with him in the future, men such as Russell E. Honsowetz, Lew Walt, James C. Murray, Jr., Stephen V. Sabol, Robert E. Galer, Gregory "Pappy" Boyington, Raymond G. Davis, Jr., and Thomas L. Ridge. Dozens of others would become generals or otherwise have distinguished careers. Nearly all would rise to become lieutenant colonels in barely more time than Puller had spent just as a second lieutenant. The lessons they had picked up at Basic School would have to carry them a long way. Lieutenant Colonel Gilder Jackson, the director since 1937, felt that the students had been privileged to learn from Puller, "one of the best officers of his grade."[19]

☆ ☆ ☆

Lewis and Virginia Puller took some leave in May 1939 and then traveled by train to San Francisco, where they boarded a transport bound for China via Hawaii and the Philippines. They were just a few days into the voyage when a radio message from the commander of the Asiatic Fleet modified Chesty's orders. Instead of joining the 4th Marines, he would resume his old position with the Marine detachment of the *Augusta*. The change likely was a reflection of the sterling reputation Puller had left behind. The couple arrived at Tsingtao on July 9. Virginia took up temporary residence in a hotel while he reported to the cruiser. The Marines quickly noted that their new CO wore more ribbons on his chest than the ship's captain.[20]

Perhaps the most discernible change in the Far East during Puller's three-year absence was a marked increase in the rapacity of the Japanese. In July 1937 they had launched a full-scale war against China. Since then they had seized much of the northeastern part of the country, the lower Yangtze River, Shanghai, and many of the other major ports. The United States again decided not to take military action, but did maintain its small forces in the international sections of Peiping and Shanghai (both now deep behind Japanese lines). For the moment Japan tolerated the extraterritorial rights of the Western powers in those two cities.

☆ ☆ ☆

A few days after Puller reported aboard, the cruiser sailed for Shanghai and Lewis shifted Virginia to the Cathay Mansions in that city. This apartment building was a favorite for married couples in the 4th Marines and it would give her ample companionship during his many absences. With the increase in tensions the flagship was constantly on the move up and down the Chinese coast. She was sitting at anchor in Tsingtao in early September when Germany invaded Poland and Great Britain and France declared war. But the advent of another major conflict in Europe made little impression on the daily life of the cruiser. The deck log contained the usual entries recording the delivery of fresh food and the punishment of minor offenses at captain's mast. Only the frequent notations of the movements of Japanese warships hinted at the ongoing war in Asia. Elsewhere in the U.S. fleet, some seagoing Marines were occupied with such grave concerns as "necktie trouble"—shrinkage in the lining of their uniform ties that left them wrinkled.[21]

Befitting Chesty's own reputation for smartness in appearance, he gave considerable attention to uniform items, too. Every Marine in his detachment was required to take advantage of the low cost of labor in China to acquire specially tailored uniforms that made *Augusta* Leathernecks sharper-looking than their counterparts. A new man on the flagship was limited to duty on working parties or with the brig guard belowdecks until he was outfitted properly. At the same time, Puller maintained his emphasis on marksmanship and other combat skills, and also shielded his men from some of the less desirable duties on a ship, such as chipping paint. One Marine on the cruiser recalled the high level of regard for the detachment commander: "We would do anything he asked—willingly. In fact, we would go overboard to please him."[22]

In November *Augusta* sailed for Philippine waters for the winter, leaving Virginia Puller and the Sino-Japanese War behind. The ship spent more time in gunnery drills these days, but usually put back into Manila or nearby Subic Bay each evening. The regular supply of ice cream coming on board from the San Miguel Brewery, of all places, partially made up for the exhausting combat exercises. The only excitement of the stay in the Philippines came in late March when *Augusta* struck a coral head. The sudden and unexpected jolt threw everyone on board into bulkheads or onto the deck. The damage to the propeller and rudder necessitated an extended visit to the floating dry dock in Subic Bay. Lewis wrote Virginia about the ill-timed accident: "It is tough luck on me, as my happiness in joining you will now be delayed about ten days."[23]

The war in Europe did have one major impact on Puller and his fel-

low Marines. In September 1939, President Franklin Roosevelt authorized the Corps to add seven thousand enlisted men and increase the officer cadre by 50 percent. Promotions, already spurred by selection,
accelerated even faster. Whereas the 1938 board had picked just twelve
new majors, in December 1939 the Corps was able to advance eighty
captains. One of those on the list was the *Augusta*'s Marine detachment
commander. Accelerated promotion had not meant easier selection,
however. Of the fifty-two captains senior to Chesty, only fifteen joined
him in making the grade. The pending promotion brought fresh orders
for Puller, as he would soon have too much rank for his billet. On May
21, 1940, a month after the cruiser returned to Shanghai, he left the
flagship and joined the 4th Marines.[24]

☆   ☆   ☆

Prewar Shanghai had been the commercial heart of China and one of
the most cosmopolitan cities in the world. The British had bargained for
extraterritorial rights in part of the metropolis following their victory in
the 1842 Opium War; other nations later gained similar concessions.
The resulting International Settlement covered 5,500 acres and had a
population of one million, about 10 percent of them foreigners. The
zone had its own municipal council and police force. Military units of
the various powers divided up responsibility for external security, with
each defending a designated sector. Another million and a half Chinese
lived in the rest of the city surrounding the foreign area. Japan occupied
the latter as well as its own portion of the International Settlement.

The 4th Marines had been in Shanghai since 1927, but it now was
only the shell of a regiment. It had just two infantry battalions, each
composed of two rifle companies and a machine gun company. The line
units were severely understrength, as the regimental headquarters alone
monopolized nearly three hundred of the 1,010 enlisted men in the outfit. The commander of the Asiatic Fleet remarked upon this imbalance
between fighters and support troops following his annual inspection in
May of 1940.

The readiness of the regiment was further reduced by the lack of
training opportunities and a garrison mentality. The Japanese conquest
had cut off access to traditional maneuver areas outside the city. Due to
the rising tensions, the admiral also had ordered the Marines to cease
rotating companies to their range complex along the north China coast.

The regiment cleared an area for use as a subcaliber firing range and maneuver area, but Price Field measured just two hundred by four hundred feet. Otherwise the 4th Marines had occasional use of a city park and the racecourse, both nearly as tiny. The only significant training consisted of short hikes in the city and marksmanship practice with .22 caliber weapons on Price Field and at three indoor ranges.

Like their counterparts in Peiping, the Marines in Shanghai spent much of their time focusing on parades and similar noncombat aspects of military life. When they were not marching smartly in their dress blues they stood guard duty at one of the perimeter outposts or at the power plant in the Japanese sector. (In the strange life of the International Settlement, the Japanese also maintained detachments at two of their cotton mills in the American zone. The Italian and British contingents, meanwhile, worked side by side even though their compatriots were on the verge of fighting each other in Europe.) The Marines also conducted roving patrols throughout their own territory. For men not actually on guard duty, afternoons were devoted to sports and evenings to liberty. The regiment boasted ownership of "the finest club for enlisted personnel in any branch of the service." Senior leaders considered that facility one important part of the effort to keep Marines away from the inexpensive vices of the city. The venereal disease rate in the command was 35 percent and the number of disciplinary cases was not much lower.[25]

Life for officers and their families was generally pleasant. Currency exchange rates were now even more favorable than they had been during Chesty's stint in Peiping. Coupled with the low cost of labor, that allowed senior Marines to live like "Shanghai millionaires." All married officers were billeted on the local economy. The Pullers took up residence in an apartment on Avenue Joffre, a broad, tree-lined boulevard. That was in the French Concession, but only two blocks from the U.S. zone of the International Settlement and not far from the racecourse and the French Sports Club, two of the centers of Shanghai social life. Like most other families, the Pullers employed Chinese servants to handle all the domestic chores.[26]

Other than cheap labor, Shanghai had lost much of its prewar luster. It was overcrowded with refugees, most of whom slept on the streets and spent their days begging. Sanitation was consequently much worse than it had been. Poverty and a scarcity of food further fueled the spread of disease. Each morning there was a new host of lifeless, rag-clad forms on the sidewalks of the city. The onetime Pearl of the Orient now was permeated with the "Shanghai stench."[27]

☆   ☆   ☆

Puller served his first month in the regiment as its assistant intelligence officer, then moved over to the 2d Battalion, where he simultaneously held down the billets of executive officer and operations officer. For a month in late summer he fleeted up to command the battalion until a lieutenant colonel reported in to take over. The only professional excitement came during an occasional incident with the Japanese. In July a number of armed policemen entered the American zone and soon after two Japanese light tanks briefly raced down the streets. Similar episodes occurred every few weeks, but none led to violence. In October Puller received his promotion to major with an effective date of August 29, 1940. He had been a captain four years.[28]

The transfer to shore duty had come none too soon for Lewis's personal life, as Virginia gave birth to a baby girl on May 27, 1940. They named her Virginia McCandlish. Chesty was delighted at the addition to his family: "Ordinarily I don't brag but I believe that I have a right to now." Puller's joy was offset by concern for the safety of his wife and daughter. Although he reassured Virginia's mother in letters home, it was "one of the happiest days of his life" when the admiral ordered all military dependents out of the country due to the threat of war. The two Virginias left for the States in November and took up residence in Saluda, Virginia, with Mrs. Evans. They were only gone a day when Lewis wrote them: "I miss you more each moment." He continued to write nearly every day. His letter of January 14, 1941, covered the details of his routine—drill and training in the morning; sports in the afternoon (usually riding for him); reading, writing, and card playing in the evening; followed by a prayer for his family just before taps: "Thus the days go by—they are almost just the same and pass so slowly."[29]

☆   ☆   ☆

The situation around the world was growing ever bleaker for the Western democracies. In May 1940 Germany had conquered France. That left Britain alone against the Nazis and she withdrew her 1,800 men from Shanghai in August. The defeated French were no longer a partner against the Japanese, while the Fascist Italians formally joined Japan and Germany in the Rome-Berlin-Tokyo Axis in September 1940. That same month the United States warned Japan not to move against Indochina, but the Japanese soon began occupying that French colony anyway. In response, President Roosevelt embargoed the shipment of American steel to Japan. The economic war escalated in July 1941 when the United States, Britain, and the Dutch government-in-exile froze all Japanese assets, which effectively cut off their access to oil. Since the island nation imported 90 percent of this vital commodity, war became inevitable unless one side backed down. In the summer of 1941, Germany also launched its invasion of the Soviet Union, while Hitler's Afrika Korps pushed the British back toward the Suez Canal.[30]

In his letters Lewis tried to calm Virginia's fears. He asserted that the Japanese "would back down just as soon as they knew that we would fight for our rights." But he also expressed dismay at his own government's policies: "I do not understand why we have taken all their guff the past few years. . . . Our leaders do not know history or else they are blind to it." He admitted, too, that "sooner or later we will be involved with the Axis powers" and he hoped that once the fighting was over in Europe the United States would "put the Japs back to where Perry found them."[31]

The precarious position of the 4th Marines heightened Puller's keen interest in events. In one January 1941 note he explained: "I read the papers and listen to the radio and try to determine what will happen next." He believed that the Japanese likely would continue their southward expansion toward the resource-rich areas of Malaya and the Dutch East Indies. If they were to do so, he thought "the movement will commence in the early spring" and he hoped "the regiment will be withdrawn before they start."[32]

The United States already had moved the 15th Infantry out of Tientsin. As Marines went home from Peiping at the end of their tour, they were not replaced and attrition cut the Legation Guard in half by summer 1941. The 4th Marines remained at reduced strength while naval leaders were pressing for the withdrawal of all U.S. forces from China. The regimental commander made plans for his unit to make a break for the coast or the Chinese-held interior if war came and Puller himself kept up a cocky front, allegedly boasting: "I don't know what the United States Government will do, I don't know what Marine Headquarters will do, and I don't know what the regiment will do, but—no orders to the contrary—I'll take my battalion and fight my way the hell back to Frisco." But everyone knew they could not hope to escape the encircling Japanese and Puller was much concerned about the possibility of becoming a prisoner of war. He counted down the days till the end of his tour. Meanwhile, he and his compatriots kept up the facade that all was normal. After the 2d Battalion did poorly in a regimental parade, the major decided he would "have to bear down a bit on close order drill." Soon thereafter he spent an entire morning putting the unit through its paces in preparation for the next weekly ceremony.[33]

The Japanese continued their provocative acts and grew bolder as time passed, though Chesty sometimes was inclined to give them the benefit of the doubt. In one instance a Japanese civilian attempted to assassinate a member of the International Settlement's Municipal Council. The man claimed he was irate over a pending increase in taxes while government leaders refused to take a cut in salary. Puller sympathized with the taxpayer: "Perhaps the shooting will result in more good than harm. . . . I absolutely believe in law and order, but the people that make the laws should be held responsible for the laws being good and for the benefit of all and not for the few." Most of the bombings and shootings in the International Settlement, however, were directed at people or institutions allied with the Chinese government.[34]

Puller figured prominently in one of the major incidents between the two armed forces. Around 2100 on March 14 a report came into regimental headquarters that the sentries at one of the Japanese cotton mills in the American sector were arresting dozens of Chinese on the streets. Chesty took the officer of the day (Lieutenant Russ Honsowetz) and a handful of Marines to the scene. They confronted the Japanese commander, who explained that a Chinese gunman had fired several shots and he was collecting suspects. The Marine major made it clear that the Japanese had no police power within the American zone. Chesty threatened force if the Chinese were not freed. Honsowetz recalled that Puller gave a short deadline and then calmly kept an eye on his watch while refusing to listen to the arguments of his opposite number. When the Japanese commander realized that the Marines were not about to back down, he let the prisoners go.[35]

☆   ☆   ☆

While Puller showed a tough face to the Japanese, he continued to demonstrate a gentle, affectionate side to his family. Every letter home was filled with protestations of his love and poignant reminders of how much he missed his wife and daughter. He told Virginia to buy a camera and send him a monthly photo of her and their daughter. He kept close track of the arrival and departures of ships carrying mail and asked his spouse to use air mail more often. He also provided occasional advice on taking care of "Virginia Makkee" but refused to get involved in one aspect of the child's upbringing: "Whenever (if) her behavior is not good, you must punish her. You will have to, Darling, I just could not; it would be like punishing her Mother." It was not an idle statement—his wife served as the disciplinarian throughout their marriage.[36]

The separation of the Puller family was about to come to an end. Lewis had put in his request for his next duty station in January 1941. With war close at hand and the Marine Corps Schools closed down due to a shortage of officers in the burgeoning operating forces, he had quit applying for an academic slot and instead asked for assignment to an infantry regiment. Headquarters complied and issued orders for his transfer to the 1st Marine Division. Feeling "fortunate" that he was getting out while there was still time, Chesty departed Shanghai on August 14 and arrived in San Francisco two weeks later. The Marine major was so anxious to get home that he arranged for an airline flight at his own expense to take him to Washington, D.C.[37]

"The Enemy Are on the Hill"
New River and Samoa
September 1941–August 1942

During Puller's two years on the China station the Marines had quadrupled in size as the United States geared up for the war no one wanted but everyone expected. By the summer of 1941, activated reservists and fresh recruits were bringing the Corps up to its recently authorized ceiling of 75,000 men and 4,200 officers. Without the United States having fired a shot in anger in World War II, the Corps had equaled its peak strength during World War I. For the first time in their history, the Marines also fielded a division. In February 1941, while the 1st Marine Brigade was conducting amphibious exercises in Cuba, Headquarters redesignated it as the 1st Marine Division. The 5th Marines gave up a slice of its personnel to form the 7th Marines. The 1st Marines soon came into being, but only on paper initially. In April the division sailed back to the States, with the 5th Marines returning to Quantico and the 7th going to Parris Island.[1]

While Puller was on leave, he stopped at Quantico to visit Lieutenant Colonel Merritt Edson, the commander of 1st Battalion, 5th Marines (1/5). "Red Mike" was in the early stages of converting his outfit into the 1st Raider Battalion and Chesty believed he would become 1/5's executive officer. That potential pairing of small wars heroes was not to be. By the time Puller reported off leave on September 20, 1941, he had found a plum position for a relatively new major. He would take command of his own rifle battalion just as soon as he and the 7th Marines joined up at the brand-new base at New River, North Carolina.[2]

The commander of the 7th was Colonel Jim Webb. The former executive officer of the Central Area in Nicaragua was a spare, balding man who looked more like an accountant than a warrior. And in a career spanning twenty-four years he had not had the chance to demonstrate that his appearance might have been deceiving. He had joined the Corps in March 1917, but sat out World War I with the Legation Guard in Peiping. Despite two tours of expeditionary duty in China and Nicaragua, he had never been in a battle and had no decorations for valor.

The former commander of 1/7 and new regimental executive officer, Lieutenant Colonel Amor Sims, had a background that was undoubtedly more to Puller's liking. He had quit Ohio State University in April 1917 to enlist in the Corps, and then earned a Silver Star, a Purple Heart, and a battlefield commission in France. While Puller was fighting *cacos* in Haiti, Sims was next door helping to put down a similar rebellion in Santo Domingo. He had gone on to a tour in the Guardia Nacional's tough Northern Area at the same time Chesty was leading Company M. He had a reputation for being "absolutely unflappable" in a tight situation, but was also "cold and distant" toward his subordinates. He had served two tours commanding guard forces at naval prisons, duty that did not improve his irascible nature. He sported jet-black hair and a small matching mustache, carried a swagger stick, smoked cigarettes in a long holder, and was every inch a martinet. His personality and appearance won him the nickname "Black Duke."[3]

The division was populated with other officers who had long associations with Chesty. Jerry Thomas was the operations officer and Vandegrift, now a brigadier general, soon took over as assistant division commander (ADC). Merrill Twining became Thomas's assistant. Hanneken commanded 2/7. And there were a number of Puller-trained Basic School graduates.

☆　☆　☆

The rapid expansion of the Corps was lifting its officers to heights many had never expected to reach. The once small service now had two divisions and was providing the leaders and staffs for a pair of corps headquarters as well. Some Marine officers, such as Major General Holland M. "Howling Mad" Smith, were well prepared for these great responsibilities by schooling or experience. Smith, commander of the two-division Amphibious Force Atlantic Fleet, had served as a brigade adjutant and assistant corps operations officer in France in World War I. After that conflict he graduated from the Naval War College, worked as a war planner in Washington, completed the Field Officers Course at Quantico, and served on several senior staffs. The careers of many other Marine leaders, however, had not groomed them for higher duties.[4]

In many respects, Puller fell into the latter category. He had spent more time in staff billets than he later would care to admit, but he had not gained much useful experience. As the quartermaster in the Central Area he ran mule trains of beans and bullets (and little else) to tiny outfits at fixed posts. His tour as operations officer of 2/4 taught him nothing about controlling a battalion in wartime since it never went to the field. His only significant preparation as a staff officer came when he was the assistant intelligence officer in Peiping; there he had evaluated information on real forces in the midst of a campaign. Attendance at a senior school would have remedied his lack of knowledge of staff procedures, but Headquarters had never granted his many requests for advanced professional education. For all his experience as a combat leader, Puller rarely had commanded a force in the field larger than fifty men. And in every fight his unit had been alone; he had never needed to coordinate his actions with adjacent units or supporting arms.

Chesty was handicapped by these shortcomings in training and experience, but he had offsetting virtues. He was a keen student of military history and readily quoted from works such as Henderson's *Stonewall Jackson*. (Puller told one of his captains it was "the greatest book ever written" and he treated the biography like a "professional Bible.") He was physically and mentally toughened by long, hard periods on the trail. He had an easy way with men and could inspire them to follow him into danger. But most important of all, he had proven in combat that he was an aggressive, fearless fighter. The Corps would need such leaders in the bitter battles to come.[5]

☆   ☆   ☆

Late in September 1941, Chesty and the division (less 1/5) boarded trains for the movement south to New River. At the end of the month Puller formally took over 1/7. From the first moment in the change-of-command parade, when his bellowed words echoed with vibrant authority, he began to make an indelible impression on his men. His renown as a hero of the Nicaraguan campaign rapidly radiated through the ranks. He wasted no time in reinforcing the tough image. Following drill on one of his first days in charge, he called his command together. He explained that he had overheard a Marine from another outfit remark out loud: "There goes the God-damned 7th Regiment." He expressed amazement that no one had broken ranks and punched the man; he enjoined them from this point forward to take pride in their unit. The eager Marines "really enjoyed" this kind of rousing talk from a senior officer. The battalion's Navy surgeon, Lieutenant (jg) Edward L. Smith, as new to the service as many of the young privates, was impressed by Puller's attitude: "We like his fighting spirit. I think we are going places now."[6]

☆　☆　☆

The Marine Corps had purchased the 110,000-acre New River site on the Carolina coast in February 1941 to provide a suitable place for amphibious training. The undeveloped, wooded land lacked all the requirements of a base, but construction crews soon swarmed over the area building roads, rifle ranges, and all the other necessities. Barracks were a low priority, so the units lived under canvas. Sun turned the olive drab tents into ovens. Dust billowed up onto everything, including the food. Rain converted the dust into mud. Mosquitoes attacked in hordes. Winter eventually brought a numbing cold into the poorly heated structures. Kerosene lanterns were the sole source of light. On those infrequent occasions when the men had liberty, usually from 1100 Saturday till Sunday evening, there was nothing to do. The closest town was tiny Jacksonville; transportation was seldom available for more distant forays. Married personnel were separated from their families, since there was no available housing on base or off, so Puller's wife and daughter remained in Saluda with his mother-in-law. Chesty made the most of the situation and went on occasional hunting expeditions with friends.

The daily regimen was almost as spartan. Everyone turned out at 0600 for physical exercise prior to breakfast. Afterward they hiked ten or fifteen miles, then spent the afternoons in classes learning the fundamentals of their trade. Sometimes the training consisted of cutting down trees and brush to clear areas for new firing ranges or other facilities. As the younger officers and men grew harder physically and acquired some basic skills, the units spent more time on field problems. During breaks in training, Puller's officers frequently gathered around while he regaled them with stories of his experiences and instilled lessons he had learned in Haiti, Nicaragua, and China. One of the things he considered most important was the use of camouflage. The Marines were even more impressed by their commander's stamina. He always walked up and down the length of his hiking column, talking to his troops and inspiring them by example. One sergeant recalled that the forty-three-year-old CO "drove us unmercifully."[7]

Given the rudimentary experience of most of the officers and men, tactical exercises necessarily were limited in scope. A tale supposedly went around the battalion at one point that Puller actually berated a lieutenant for making a flank assault with his platoon: "Old man, there's mighty little room for fancy tactics below the division level. The enemy are on the hill. You go get 'em. In the end you'll save men. There are times when you'll have to flank, but don't forget that the shortest distance between two points is a straight line."[8]

But other Marines remembered one field problem in which Puller's unit was to attack 2/7 as it conducted a linear defense of a peninsula formed by two creeks. Hanneken anchored his right flank with a tank positioned near a swamp. While a small part of 1/7 kept its sister battalion occupied with a simulated frontal assault, Chesty sent a team to infiltrate the lines and cut all the field telephone wires to 2/7's command post. Then he led the remainder of his force through the swamp and into the enemy rear, where they captured the tank and Hanneken's headquarters. This second story likely provides a more accurate picture of Puller's views on tactics. He had made use of flanking moves with Company M (a unit rarely bigger than a platoon) and underlined passages in his favorite book about the value of such maneuvers. It thus seems unlikely he would have told his officers to focus on straight-ahead attacks, unless it was a temporary expedient until the small unit leaders and their men learned how to conduct more complex operations. Such a policy would have been in accord with Marshall's prescient teachings at Benning about the need for simplicity with inexperienced troops.[9]

Chesty also tried to pass along his views on leadership. After one four-day exercise in early November, he gave a "roaring pep talk . . . full of piss and vinegar" to his officers and senior NCOs. He challenged them not just to be the first battalion of the 7th Marines, but to be the best outfit in the entire Corps. Then he gave them his secret for reaching that goal: "Gentlemen, if you want to get the most out of your men give them a break! Don't make them work completely in the dark. If you do, they won't do a bit more than they have to. But if they comprehend they'll work like mad." During one maneuver he gave them a subtle lesson in positive motivation. Both the division commander and the Commandant had visited 1/7. As soon as they left the area, Puller penned a message to his company commanders recounting the compliments handed out by the two generals. He told them to read it to their men. The battalion surgeon noted how it "peps up an organization when you pass along the good things as well as the bad."[10]

When it came to maintaining order in the unit, Chesty followed a middle ground. Dr. Smith observed: "He never objected to the men's drinking and raising hell off duty, but if they got into trouble, discipline was quick and just." A Marine recalled that "there was always a kindly approach whenever he was chewing anyone out that displayed a touching empathy with the miscreant." A sergeant remembered "many cases where [Chesty] made a good man out of a bad one, with his strange mixture of understanding, gentleness, and strict discipline." After watching the battalion commander "bawling out" a private for wasting water in the field, Dr. Smith noted that Chesty did not always appear so temperate: "Puller gets so angry sometimes words seem to get stuck in his throat and he has to cool off before the words are intelligible." But the Navy surgeon also observed the final outcome of the incident, with Chesty quietly taking the time to show the Marine how to fill his canteen properly from the water trailer. In most cases, Smith thought miscreants felt their commander's "scorn was more humiliating than punishment."[11]

☆   ☆   ☆

When the Japanese attacked Pearl Harbor on December 7, 1941, Puller was in Saluda on a rare weekend visit to his family. He listened to radio reports for a while, then headed back to base in a bitter mood over the plight of the Peiping Marines (Bill Lee among them). He knew they would have to surrender. (The 4th Marines only recently had won a temporary reprieve with a transfer to the Philippines.) The division immediately stepped up its training tempo. Henceforth the battalions

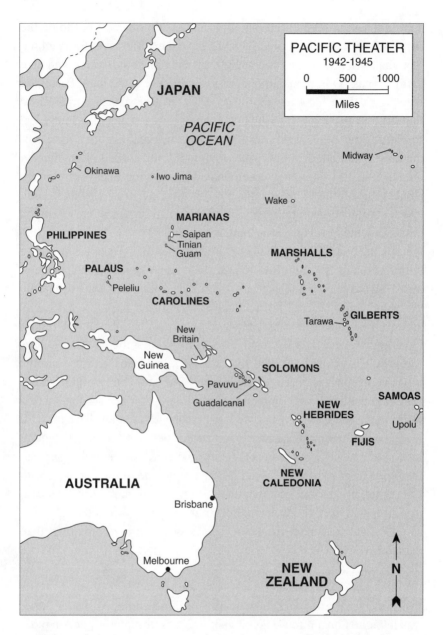

spent most of their time in the field. They returned briefly to the tent camp each week or so to clean up and rest. But even 1/7 could keep only about half its men on maneuvers at any given time. The hospital was overloaded, many of the patients sick with respiratory infections. Other Marines were siphoned off to the ongoing work of building the base.[12]

Despite years of planning for an amphibious campaign against Japan, the Corps had difficulty preparing itself for war. Some of the wounds were self-inflicted, while others were beyond the control of the service. The siren song of the 1940 German success with parachutists and gliders led the Corps to devote precious manpower and money to develop those capabilities. Several factors, including pressure from President Roosevelt, resulted in creation of the raiders. The demands of these new units caused tremendous personnel turbulence in the line organizations. One entire battalion of the 1st Marine Division disappeared when 1/5 became the 1st Raiders. The glamorous appeal of the specialist outfits also caused some of the best men to request transfers just when their capabilities were sorely needed to train the young lieutenants and privates pouring into the divisions. Puller did his best to convince his men to stay in 1/7. He claimed that he had "as good a raider battalion as anybody."[13]

The regular infantry formations were hurt by these crosscurrents in another way. The divisions devoted a lot of time to demolitions, rubber boat operations, and air landing techniques, often to the detriment of the basics of shooting, maneuvering, and communicating. A shortage of ammunition for target practice only compounded the problem. The resulting deterioration in marksmanship skills would adversely affect the Corps through much of the war. Puller was not entirely immune to the fascination with commando tactics—he gave an enthusiastic reception to a British captain who spoke to 1/7 about the elite units. In a letter home, the perceptive Dr. Smith probably spoke for many of his compatriots: "No one understands what we are training for. [We are] experimenting with a vast number of new ideas."[14]

Some leaders found it hard to shift out of their peacetime focus even after Pearl Harbor. Colonel Robert Blake, a World War I hero and the highly regarded commander of the 5th Marines, was one of those who were slow to react. In October 1941, while his unit had been adjusting to the hard life of the New River tent camp, he had devoted much effort to stamping out vulgar language. He issued a written order and threatened offenders with five days on bread and water. That action brought forth an irreverent ditty that closed with the lines: "Oh! Shameful day for the Fifth Marines! For you we've lost all hope! We'll just have to spank you and march you off, And wash out your mouths with soap." There must have been some high-level interest in the perceived problem, for Puller also raised the issue with his command. His solution, however, was more in keeping with the times. He merely told his subordinate leaders: "For Christ's sake, don't swear at your men."[15]

In March 1942 Vandegrift assumed command of the division and began weeding out ineffectual officers. He relieved one colonel for failing to conduct realistic exercises with live ammunition. Twining recalled that Vandegrift referred to the regimental commander as "nothing but a damn old school teacher." Puller, on the other hand, sought out opportunities for his troops to work near artillery fire or experience the deprivations of war. During a bitterly cold January hike, he allowed no overcoats. Dr. Smith recorded how one NCO silenced his griping men during that exercise: "All right you bastards. Compared to what the Russians are facing, this is summer weather." Chesty would have been in perfect agreement with the sergeant.[16]

Colonel Webb came close to losing his job, too. He did not act like a leader in the field or in garrison. Oftentimes he remained in camp during field exercises and merely drove out in a station wagon for a few minutes each day to observe the battalions. He had opposed Puller's practice of camouflaging his men, until the division commander overruled him. On one occasion Webb tried to invigorate his officers with a speech, but read most of it and came across "flat." He ended up admonishing his subordinates to be "bright eyed and bushy tailed." Sims, in turn, upbraided men for petty violations of uniform regulations and haughtily informed a lieutenant that it was "very unmilitary" of him to be washing his own socks. The actions of both leaders caused a "good deal of unfavorable comment" within the division. Chesty would recall that many privately derided Sims as the regimental "police sergeant" (the title of the NCO charged with keeping the area clean and neat). One veteran of the 7th was "reasonably confident that I never heard a kind word said about [the XO—executive officer]." The regimental operations officer, Major William R. Williams, created more friction due to his high-handed treatment of the battalion commanders. Thomas thought he was "a mean devil" who "tried to take a curry comb to Hanneken and Puller." The division operations officer believed that the 7th Marines "wasn't a very happy outfit."[17]

Events intervened to save Webb for the moment. In mid-March 1942, HQMC activated the 3d Marine Brigade and assigned the 7th Marines and the 1st Raider Battalion to it. An order warned the command to prepare to move overseas by the end of the month. Although these steps were tightly controlled secrets, the officers and men of the regiment became aware that something big was about to happen. Their stay in the field ended early, then personnel from the 1st and 5th Marines joined the 7th to bring it to full strength. They also received first priority on equipment and supplies, at the expense of other units. With the prospect of action, morale soared, deserters returned, and the sick recovered sufficiently to get out of the hospital.[18]

Many of the officers and men of the brigade were convinced that they would be the first Marines to strike back at the Japanese. Thomas later recalled that Puller could not resist the temptation to crow over his regiment's good fortune. Just before his departure he made his farewells and told Twining: "You stay here and train the division and when it's ready to fight, bring it out and help us in the Pacific." Chesty did indeed feel confident that he and his outfit could handle the challenge. He had great faith in his own experience from the Banana Wars and in his knowledge of the enemy, gleaned from "close observation of the Japanese Army" in China.[19]

Puller made his personal preparations for war. He visited his family and then sent Virginia a letter detailing financial arrangements in case the worst should happen. There was little to discuss, just two small insurance policies and service-related benefits. He was optimistic about his chances, though, and told her she would not need to deal with his will "for many long years to come." He had not yet left for overseas but already was looking forward to his return: "I am just living for our life together after this war is over. . . . And when that day comes I will provide for you and Virginia McC. much better than I am able to do now." He also sent his brother-in-law money to buy a dozen red roses for Virginia on the 13th of each month. This sentimental side sometimes showed through to others. One young officer approached Chesty for authorization to get married. The CO merely asked his subordinate if he loved his fiancée. Assured that was the case, Puller replied: "Well, never forget to tell her so, every day of your life. Permission granted."[20]

☆ ☆ ☆

In early April 1942 the 3d Brigade headed overseas. Puller's battalion loaded onto the USS *Fuller* (AP-14) and joined a strongly escorted convoy. The ships sailed out of Hampton Roads and into the Atlantic on April 10. Most of the officers and men had no idea where they were

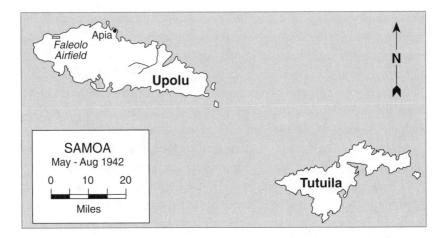

going and many soon lost interest; foul weather and rough seas made them too sick to care about anything. After two days the ocean became calmer and the Marines gained their sea legs. The embarked troops participated in the ship's drills and tried to get comfortable in the hot, crowded berthing compartments. Puller whiled away his free time playing bridge in the wardroom and rereading the copy of *Stonewall Jackson* that Virginia had given him in 1937.

On April 18 the convoy transited the Panama Canal and heard the news that Lieutenant Colonel James H. Doolittle and his squadron of sixteen Army Air Forces B-25 bombers had made an air raid on Japan. Two days later the brigade headquarters passed the word that the command was headed for Samoa. They would defend the island of Upolu, presently garrisoned by a tiny force of New Zealanders. The 2d Marine Brigade had been protecting nearby Tutuila since January. Both of these islands had good harbors and terrain suitable for airfields. That made them likely targets for an enemy attempt to cut the seaborne supply line between the United States and Australia.[21]

Unit briefings on the mission were interrupted on April 23 for the traditional ceremony marking passage of the equator. Shellback Puller had the honor of serving as Davy Jones. He and the rest of Neptune's royal entourage were staged on a platform over the side of the ship, doused with salt water, and then hoisted on board as if they were just coming, dripping, from the sea. Davy was arrayed in a raincoat, a peaked hat decorated with a skull and crossbones, and a life belt sash. He brandished a cutlass as he supervised the day-long rite of passage of the pollywogs. Despite the war, they received the complete treatment, which included "the liberal use of red paint, multitudinous shocking devices, paddling, eating of soap, drinking of kerosene, drinking in the waters of the Pacific, and general bodily punishment."[22]

Just before the convoy reached Samoa, Puller wrote his wife in his usual loving vein:

> One month ago today I left you and you have not been out of my thoughts for a moment. . . . Heretofore I have always been eager to go on an expedition. But that was before we were married. The only thing I want now is happiness with you. . . . Please do not worry. I am coming back, and then we will have the home with two chimneys. . . . Germany and Japan must be stopped, and then perhaps I can retire. . . . I am well but I do miss you dreadfully. . . . I know how hard it is to tell Virginia McC of me, but do not let her forget me. I love you, Virginia, and I always will.[23]

☆   ☆   ☆

Upolu is a long, narrow island (roughly forty-seven miles by thirteen miles). A central spine of high mountains slopes down to plains, though much of the low-lying ground consists of rough volcanic flows. Coral reefs surround the coastline. There were about forty-two thousand residents in 1942, only 1 percent of them Westerners. The convoy hove to off Tutuila on the morning of May 8 and discharged reinforcements for the 2d Brigade. Then the ships sailed on to Upolu's Apia Harbor. From afar it looked like a scene from a travel brochure—mist enshrouding the peaks, lush tropical foliage everywhere, surf breaking on the reefs. A closer inspection did not disappoint the Marines. They debarked and set up a bivouac at the racecourse on the edge of the small, sleepy town. The pleasant sounds of tropical birds and the sweet smells of exotic flowers wafted past on fresh sea breezes while the natives struck up friendly contact. The men traded cigarettes for their first taste of fresh-picked coconuts and bananas. The hard work started the next day when it came time to unload the ships. The holds were filled with the supplies and equipment of the brigade, as well as everything needed to construct an air base and fortifications, and support an aviation unit. The last of the ships did not depart empty until May 27. While some men worked as stevedores, the rest set up two defensive lines around Apia.[24]

The interesting environment and the long hours kept the Marines occupied for their first few days on the island. After a while the realization began to sink in that they were not likely to fight anytime soon. That letdown was deepened by the continuing hard, monotonous work of moving boxes, digging holes, and filling sandbags. A regimental hike on May 30 proved to be a poor diversion and even poorer training. They marched just far enough to be on display along the road for the visiting Governor-General of New Zealand, who put in a late appearance. Private First Class Gerald White confided his disgust to his diary: "I fail to see how American–New Zealand relations were improved by keeping two battalions of men waiting in a blazing sun for over three hours." The short return hike proved too much for men unused to the heat and still recovering from a month at sea; many fell out along the way. An officer observed that "it is beginning to be more than a little difficult to keep the men in high spirits." One event provided some personal motivation to Puller—on May 22 he received a temporary promotion to lieutenant colonel.[25]

☆ ☆ ☆

The plan for the defense of Upolu centered on airpower, which would be based at the airfield and seaplane ramps under construction at Faleolo on the northwest end of the island. The raiders had left the 3d Brigade to become the mobile reserve on Tutuila and 3/7 went to Wallis Island, but the 7th Defense Battalion joined the Upolu garrison and more than made up the difference with its heavy firepower. Most of the brigade moved to Faleolo during the first half of June and set up a defense-in-depth. Puller's battalion had to leave Company C to garrison Apia and send a platoon from Company D to set up an outpost on the south side of Upolu. A company from 2/7 went to the nearby island of Savaii. If the Japanese landed on Upolu, the remainder of the 7th Marines would counterattack. If that failed, the regiment would fall back on the Faleolo bastion. If the position there became untenable, the Marines would destroy the field and disperse into guerrilla bands to disrupt the occupation from the mountains.[26]

The 7th Marines made its move to Faleolo on June 12. Reveille came at 0330 and the units were on the road at 0600. The men carried field packs, weapons, ammunition, and rations—a full combat load. The first few hours of the twenty-five-mile hike went well, but after a break for noon chow the heat began to do its devilish work. "Men were falling out by the dozen" and some made it to the end only because Puller allowed them to place the heavy crew-served weapons on vehicles. Captain Joseph H. Griffith thought it "the toughest ordeal I have undergone so far." Private White's condition after the march was typical: "My shoulders felt as if they'd been thumped all day with a blunt stick, my back ached, and my calves were knotted up with cramps." He noted, however, that Chesty came to the platoon areas and personally thanked those who had done more than their share in carrying the machine guns, mortars, and other weighty items.[27]

The 3d Brigade had established a viable defense of the western Samoan islands, but its employment as a garrison force was a "stop-gap" measure. Admiral Ernest King, the head of the Navy, wanted to use the amphibious capability of the Marines in offensive operations. The brigade knew it was less ready than King thought, since 40 percent of its men were recent recruits in need of "further training in fundamentals such as weapons and marksmanship." On the positive side, the command believed that the work of unloading ships and constructing fortifications had given the troops training in the defense and put them in "first-class physical condition." (The June 13 hike indicated the latter assessment was overly optimistic.) The brigade did realize that it had a long way to go before it was fully ready to go on the offensive.[28]

The Marines of 1/7 initially had little opportunity to train. Once they settled into their ant-ridden bivouac site at Faleolo, they went to work constructing fighting holes and bunkers. They also cut down trees and brush to make fire lanes ten yards wide and eight hundred yards long for every machine gun and 37mm antitank gun. Then they had to build firing ranges. Day after day the skies poured forth rain while the cooks dished out a monotonous ration of corned beef. The men lived in their two-man field tents or whatever other shelter they could rig. They washed when they could with a helmetful of water. It was New River all over again, only worse, and everyone was "wet, smelly, and continually miserable." One report noted that the "rain and heat and bugs" at least served a useful purpose as excellent preparation for future service in any "jungle hell." The men were able to get a few hours of liberty most evenings. But they were limited to watching old movies, attending band concerts, nursing their ration of two beers, or purchasing a rare treat from the post exchange or the Samoans. Puller spent his free time play-

ing bridge, usually with his executive officer and the battalion's two
Navy doctors.[29]

By early July work on the defenses was sufficiently advanced that
the regiment finally started training. The battalions made two or three
hikes each week, beginning with twelve miles and working their way up
to twice that distance. The platoons and companies practiced land navigation, scouting and patrolling, jungle warfare, weapons drill, and
small unit tactics. On a couple of occasions Puller and Hanneken were
able to square off against each other in battalion-versus-battalion exercises. A good portion of the training took place at night. Ammunition
was still scarce; Private White shot five rounds at the rifle range one day
and ten rounds from his machine gun the following week. The late July
arrival of the 22d Marines freed the 7th Marines from some security duties and allowed 1/7 to recover its far-flung detachments. After a month
of effort the improvement in the brigade's readiness was notable.
Puller's battalion hiked for fourteen hours on August 5 and the 7th
Marines conducted its first regimental field problem on the 10th.[30]

The hard training kept Puller busy, but he was not very happy. He
had left New River expecting action and now felt marooned on Samoa.
The closest the brigade had come to combat was a false midnight air
raid alarm. His frustration grew after news reached Upolu of the 1st
Marine Division's August 7 offensive in the Solomon Islands. The 1st
and 5th Marines had met little opposition in seizing an incomplete airfield on Guadalcanal, but the 1st Parachute Battalion and elements of
the 2d Marines had fought hard to take the islets Gavutu and Tanam-
bogo. The 1st Raiders had spearheaded the contested capture of Tulagi.
Perhaps for a moment Chesty regretted the orders that had diverted him
from Edson's unit in the summer of 1941. He expressed his fear to fellow officers that the 7th Marines would "rot on this damned island with
no fighting."[31]

Much of the regiment was feeling equally low, but not necessarily
for the same reason. Webb and Sims continued to irritate their officers
and men. When the 7th Marines procured a bit of cement to make a
deck for the dentist's work area, the CO diverted most of it for use in his
own quarters. The XO devoted the organization's motor transport and
its contingent of hired local labor to fixing up the regimental headquarters area while the battalions were struggling to build the frontline defenses. He also held garrison-type inspections of the bivouac areas that

"took up infinitely more time than [they were] worth." Even Puller felt compelled to watch his step around the XO. One afternoon Chesty was playing bridge in his CP (command post) when Sims unexpectedly drove up. Dr. Smith noted in his diary: "We hid the cards, felt guilty, looked innocent." The order for a regimental hike indicated that Webb would lead the marching column. Junior officers were certain he could not finish and laid bets on when he would drop out. The man who chose the first mile won because the colonel was out front in a vehicle. His constant reliance on a car instead of his feet inspired an irreverent 7th Marines "fight" song with the refrain: "Break out the station wagon, We are off to the wars again." One of the regiment's staff officers thought Webb "simply had no concept of what the conduct of a commanding officer should be in the way of example and guidance and care of his troops."[32]

Many officers in 1/7 were not particularly happy with Puller, either. Some of this may have been unjustified resentment at his inability to shelter his battalion from the more ridiculous actions of the regiment. Another factor was his treatment of commissioned subordinates. Both officers and enlisted men agreed that he was often gruff and unforgiving with the former. Lieutenant James M. Hayes, Jr., an admirer of Chesty, characterized his CO's attitude toward his captains and lieutenants as "peremptory," while a private in the intelligence section described Puller as "occasionally ruthless" toward the junior officers. Dr. Smith felt that the colonel was "tougher on the officers than the men." Although Chesty was in a sour mood as he fretted over his distance from the fighting, the roots of the situation probably went much deeper.[33]

This was Puller's first big command with American troops under field conditions. It was here that he began to earn his Corps-wide reputation as a leader who genuinely identified with, and looked out for the welfare of, enlisted men. He saw to it early in his tour that officers would eat last in the chow line, and he encouraged them to pitch in and work with their men instead of merely supervising them. His methods were not unique, as the Corps was transitioning from an old culture where officers put great store in their privileges to one in which they placed greater emphasis on leading by example even when they were not on the battlefield. Evans Carlson would go even further in trying to democratize the service. A newspaper columnist would argue in early

1942 that the Marine Corps was the most effective of the military services because of its efforts to do away with the traditional "caste system" that separated the ranks.[34]

Puller stood out as a premier proponent of the new style in part because he cultivated the image that his enlisted men were more important to him than his officers. Although he had shown a few indications
of this approach to leadership in prior years, his attitude may have been
shaped or reinforced by his reading of Henderson's biography of
Stonewall Jackson. Chesty had underlined passages in his copy that described a similar philosophy:

> It is manifest that Jackson's methods of discipline were well
> adapted to the peculiar constitution of the army in which he
> served. With the officers he was exceedingly strict. He looked to
> them to set an example of unhesitating obedience and the precise
> performance of duty. He demanded, too—and in this respect his
> own conduct was a model—that the rank and file should be treated
> with tact and consideration. . . . His men loved him . . . because he
> was one of themselves, with no interests apart from their interests;
> because he raised them to his own level, respecting them not
> merely as soldiers, but as comrades. . . . He was among the first to
> recognize the worth of the rank and file.[35]

One story that gained wide circulation in the battalion reflected that attitude. Supposedly Puller came upon a Marine repeatedly saluting a
lieutenant. The young officer explained to Chesty that the private had
failed to salute and was being taught a lesson by having to do so one
hundred times. Puller interjected that it was proper for the senior man
to return each one and then made sure it was done. The butt of the tale,
of course, was the lieutenant, portrayed as being overzealous in enforc-
ing his position of authority. Whether or not the incident actually took
place, the men of the battalion believed it was something their commander would do. Iron Man Lee recounted similar stories of how Puller
had handled new lieutenants operating with Company M. Instead of
simply telling them that they were to eat after the men, Chesty would
send them on repeated errands until everyone else had collected their
rations. Eventually they got the hint.[36]

There were some officers in 1/7 who needed the leadership train-

ing. Captain Griffith recorded in his diary that his men (whom he flip-
pantly referred to as "feathers") did well in an inspection: "However, I
laid them out in fine shape for a lousy [job]." Such misguided notions
of how to motivate men were precisely the type of thing Puller sought
to stamp out. Regrettably, his less-than-direct approach to educating his
subordinates sometimes alienated his officers or failed to get the point
across. Years later, one observer would record that Puller was "the idol
of his enlisted men and the bane of all second lieutenants."[37]

Another source of grumbling was the feeling that Puller was pushing 1/7 too hard. Griffith complained that there was too much work and
too little reward: "This lousy outfit has failed completely in giving the
men anything to look forward to. . . . The men just don't give a particular damn about anything." He "intensely disliked" Puller and considered him a "great lunkhead." Hayes believed such sentiments were
widespread: "The younger officers were critical of Puller behind his
back and low-rated his efficiency; he was thought too rough." While
some junior leaders would continue to chafe at Chesty's treatment of
them, after their first brush with combat none would regret his insistence on tough training. One officer would recall: "No one could
toughen an outfit better than Puller. . . . He was one tough bastard and
the men loved him."[38]

☆   ☆   ☆

Chesty's days of training and waiting were drawing to a close. On August 16 the 7th Marines saddled up and marched back to Apia as the
22d Marines hiked in the opposite direction to take over the Faleolo defenses. To his rare credit, Webb used this administrative shift as a training opportunity and conducted it as a regimental movement to contact.
Puller went one step further and told his officers that it was a test of the
battalion's endurance and combat proficiency. Hayes remembered that
he exclaimed: "I want nobody to fall out unless he falls on his face unconscious." In a repeat of the move out to Faleolo, the sun broiled the
heavily laden troops. Captain Charles W. Kelly, Jr., felt that the heavy
marching order—a full pack with blanket roll—seemed "as big as a
house" on his back. Puller added to the burden when he refused to let
the crew-served weapons go into vehicles this time. He also kept up a
fast pace, but when he saw someone struggling, he put part of their load
on his own shoulders until they were reinvigorated enough to take it

back. He did not hesitate to enlist his staff officers to help out, too. The long column reached Apia blistered and tired, but largely intact. The battalion commander directed a scathing tirade at his communications officer, however, when he discovered that Griffith had trucked out much of the gear his men were supposed to carry.[39]

The next day reveille came at 0500 and the 7th Marines began a forty-eight-hour field problem. The first part of the exercise simulated a counterattack against a Japanese landing to the east of Apia. Puller's unit moved down the coast road to serve as the anvil while Hanneken circled inland through the high ground and then attacked toward the sea to hammer the enemy. On the second day, the Japanese were supposed to be defending Apia. This time 2/7 attacked along the coast while 1/7 used "a treacherous mountain trail" to gain the opponent's flank. When the 7th Marines returned to their bivouac site, there was a swap of personnel with the 22d Marines, as promotions had left the older regiment with too many senior officers and NCOs. Men who had left New River as second lieutenants were now captains.[40]

The first definite word about the regiment's future was not good. An August 20 dispatch earmarked the 7th Marines and the 5th Defense Battalion to land at unoccupied Ndeni Island and protect yet another air base under construction. Many evenings Chesty railed about missing the war and tempers grew short in his command post. One night Puller got into a heated argument with Dr. Smith over a hand of bridge. Smith later recalled that his battalion commander was animated by the news that the 1st Marines had killed nearly everyone in the seven-hundred-man Ichiki Detachment in the August 21 battle known as the Tenaru. "He was as excited as a schoolboy as he repeated the figures again and again. . . . I think that at last he had something tangible for a goal, something that he most certainly resolved to equal or improve. . . . He did not put that into words but you could sense his grim determination to slaughter more Japs than anyone else."[41]

One of Puller's letters home contained a strange mix of optimism and references to death:

> I am just living for our life together when this war is won and I will return to you and Virginia McC. . . . Please do not worry, even a little bit, sweet. . . . Life is so short. And when I was a child, I thought it would last forever and ever. My love for you will, Vir-

ginia, even into the next life, and then on. The hardest thing that I have ever done was to tell you goodbye. That was a black Tuesday and I pray there will never be another separation.[42]

☆   ☆   ☆

The 3d Battalion rejoined the 7th Marines on Upolu in mid-August and for the first time since March the entire regiment was together on dry land. Transports and cargo ships began arriving on August 25 and the units loaded on board. Most of the Marines assumed they were headed for the Solomons and the crucible of war. Among those who were excited at the prospect, some of the adventurous appeal wore off when they came into contact with casualties being brought to the rear on the ships and heard lurid battle stories.

The brigade headquarters pronounced the regiment "well prepared to enter into actual combat." Even a pessimist like Griffith thought that "these men [are] mentally and physically ready to fight." Puller was also confident that his battalion was as ready as it could be. He even had stoked the martial ardor of the unit with a bit of bravado: "I told the officers and men that if they followed me they would get the medals." But his outward optimism was tempered by inner realism: "I was the only member of the battalion that had been under enemy fire previously and had the slightest idea what a bloody mess we would go up against." He had withheld part of the truth about the decorations to be garnered: "I did not tell them what the cost would be."[43]

The inexperience of 1/7 was reflected in its XO, the second-most-senior officer in the outfit. In civilian life Major Otho L. "Buck" Rogers had supervised the issue of new stamps for the U.S. Post Office. He had enlisted in the Marine Corps Reserve at the age of thirty-one in 1932, a time when boot camp was not required of reservists. The following year, after a two-week reserve officer candidate class, he earned his reserve commission. In several years as a part-time company commander he gained a reputation as a "conscientious officer" who always had "well-trained units." He was activated in November 1940 and became a company commander in 1/7, then the XO of the battalion in early 1942. He was promoted to major on Samoa. His experience as a Marine in September 1942 consisted of about two years of actual training time; a steep drop-off from Puller's twenty-four years of service and dozens of battles. What Rogers lacked in seasoning he tried to make up in enthusiasm. He thought of war as "something glorious" and joked in a letter from Samoa: "I am well and happy and about the toughest Marine you ever saw." He was, in fact, "mild-mannered, soft-spoken, sociable, politically-oriented," almost the opposite of Chesty. The XO was "a brave man and a good gent," but ill-prepared for leading nearly a thousand men into battle. He was not alone in that regard as the Corps expanded rapidly.[44]

☆   ☆   ☆

The convoy took its time moving west toward Ndeni. Meanwhile Vandegrift, facing a shortage of infantry to defend the Guadalcanal airfield and several adjacent islands, was pleading for the 7th Marines. On September 12, as the ships laid over in the New Hebrides, senior Navy leaders decided that the regiment would go to Guadalcanal.[45]

9

"You're Not Going to Throw These Men Away"

The First Weeks on Guadalcanal

September–October 1942

The goal of the August 7, 1942, amphibious assault in the
Solomons (the first such U.S. operation in the war) had been to
stop a southward Japanese thrust toward the sea lanes between Australia and the States. Surprised by the counterattack, the enemy wanted
to recapture the vital Guadalcanal airstrip (now christened Henderson
Field). The Marines weakly held a small perimeter around the runway
located near Lunga Point on the north coast of the island. Across
Sealark Channel they were masters of Tulagi and neighboring islets
Gavutu-Tanambogo. There were not enough planes at Henderson to
command the skies overhead, though the mix of Marine, Navy, and
Army fliers made the Japanese pay dearly for each aerial assault. The
Imperial Navy generally avoided the area in daylight in deference to
U.S. airpower, but enemy ships appeared almost every night to land
troops and shell the Marine positions. Allied warships operated at their
peril day or night and a number had been sunk by enemy air, surface,
and submarine action. The overconfident Japanese army committed
troops piecemeal to the island and they attacked recklessly with little
fire support. The Marines thus were able to inflict crushing defeats on
the Ichiki Detachment in August and the Kawaguchi Brigade in mid-
September.

☆ ☆ ☆

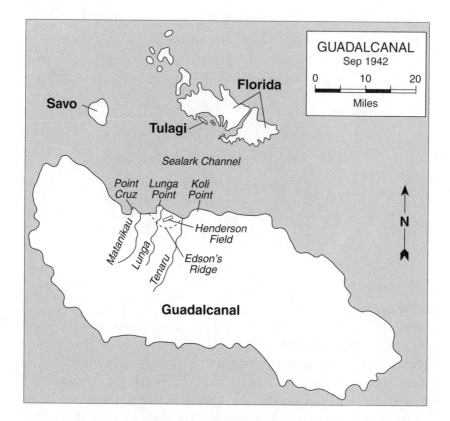

Following spirited debate between Vandegrift and his Navy superior, the admiral finally agreed to place the 7th Marines ashore at Lunga Point. The expected arrival date was delayed two days while the convoy countermarched at sea to avoid a Japanese task force near the Solomons. Word passed among the Marines about the threat of enemy air and the need for rapid unloading to get the vulnerable amphibious shipping away from deadly Sealark Channel (soon to be rechristened Ironbottom Sound). By the time the ships hove to off Lunga Point at dawn on September 18, the Marines and sailors were keyed up to expect the worst. That nervous energy brought forth a barrage of fire from naval crews and embarked troops that downed an American plane flying low over the convoy on an approach to Henderson Field. Luckily the pilot survived.[1]

According to legend, when Puller came ashore he immediately asked where the enemy were located. After perusing one of the poor maps (made from aerial photos and full of blank spots marked "clouds"), he exclaimed: "Hell, I can't make head nor tail of this. . . . Just show me where they are!" Told that the Japanese were in the hills beyond the perimeter, he responded: "All right. Let's go get 'em." Thomas remembered it differently. In his version Twining ribbed his old friend as he stepped off the landing craft: "Well, Puller, you finally found the war. Did you get lost on the way? Where have you been?" One officer who landed that day recalled there were frequent gibes from the veterans of the division: "It's about time that you got here, now that the fighting's over." There was little time for showmanship on this busy day, though; the 7th Marines moved at a feverish pace to unload every-thing it could before the convoy departed. One Marine recalled that Puller patrolled the beach supervising the job and ensuring that every-one got a break for a hot meal. The ships were nearly empty when they sailed away at 1800.[2]

As dusk approached the regiment settled into a temporary bivouac site in a coconut grove just behind the beach. There was no doubt they were now in the war. Many of the trees were shattered from bombard-ments, wrecked planes and vehicles lay scattered among the broken trunks, and hollow-eyed, scraggly men stood watch on guns trained up to the sky or outward over a shoreline sprinkled with the flotsam of sea battles. Puller passed the word for everyone to dig in, but most of the men were too exhausted and many unit leaders failed to supervise, probably due to a combination of fatigue and the onset of darkness.

The Japanese on Guadalcanal had reported the landing to their su-periors at 0630. The area headquarters at Rabaul immediately launched air and surface forces to attack the convoy. Bad weather prevented the pilots from reaching their destination. The swift departure of the am-phibious shipping then foiled the hopes of the cruiser *Sendai* and four destroyers, which arrived off Lunga Point in the middle of the night. The Imperial Navy task force had to content itself with a shore bom-bardment. Just after midnight the men of the 7th Marines were roused by an aircraft dropping flares to illuminate the target area—the airstrip next to their coconut grove. The ships opened fire and those Marines and sailors without fighting holes hugged the ground or frantically scraped at the earth with helmets, bayonets, and bare hands. There was little Puller could do except to shout calmly to those around him to keep their heads down. The shelling lasted for half an hour. In this baptism of fire, 1/7 lost three dead and two wounded. When it was over, the battalion commander walked through the area smoking his pipe and quietly reassuring his men. One Marine recalled that the aroma of the colonel's tobacco and the sound of his favorite expression—"Everything will be all right, old man"—did much to soothe frayed nerves.[3]

☆   ☆   ☆

The ships had deposited 4,262 men, nearly all their equipment, and large quantities of food, ammunition, and aviation gasoline, all critically needed on the island. The only thing the 1st Marine Division had no shortage of in mid-September was colonels, as a recent promotion board had selected six of the command's officers for advancement to that rank. The Commandant already had asked Vandegrift to send some of the excess colonels home. Webb stepped ashore in the midst of this personnel shake-up and did not improve his already weak reputation. Twining felt the colonel's "attitude was such and his reactions [such] that he seemed to be completely demoralized by the situation." Thomas later hinted that the relief of the 7th Marines commander "had all been arranged" before the regiment had arrived. That seems certain, as Vandegrift elevated Sims to command the 7th Marines on the morning of September 19. In the same shuffle, Thomas moved up to be the division chief of staff, Twining replaced him as operations officer, and Edson was slated to take command of the 5th Marines a few days later. Lieutenant Colonel Julian N. Frisbie, who had led 3/7 in 1941, transferred from the 1st Marines to become the new executive officer of the 7th. Like Sims, Frisbie had quit college in 1917 to enlist in the Marines, then earned a commission in 1918 after a year as a drill instructor at Parris Island. His campaign experience included stints in Santo Domingo and Nicaragua.[4]

The change in leadership of the regiment did not necessarily please Puller, who had no great respect or affection for Sims. And it only marginally improved the readiness of the outfit, which was saddled with several problems at the command level. The battalions were individually well led and comparatively well trained, but there had been no opportunities for the entire regiment to work together. One captain in the outfit later reflected that several of the senior leaders were "colorful individualists" and there were definite jealousies between some of them. Webb had not melded his subordinates into a cohesive unit and consequently "there were no team players in the 7th Marines." Sims was a strong enough leader to solve some of these problems, but he did not do so. His approach to leadership has been described by some of his officers as "pompous," "rather cold and distant," and marked by "regal overtones." His haughty attitude did little to foster unity of effort within the regiment. These shortcomings would be magnified in combat, when he was "usually far too remote to influence the action."[5]

☆   ☆   ☆

The arrival of the 7th Marines gave Vandegrift a force of ten infantry, one raider, and four artillery battalions on Guadalcanal, plus assorted supporting units. For the first time the division had sufficient strength to establish an unbroken defensive line around the Lunga Point lodgment. Thomas and Twining assigned the engineer, amphibian tractor, and pioneer battalions to protect the beach and divided the inland perimeter into seven sectors. The 1st, 5th, and 7th Marines each received responsibility for two of them, which allowed them to put two battalions on line and maintain a third in reserve. The 1st Raiders served as the division reserve while 3/2 occupied the remaining defensive sector. The Marines would not simply wait for each Japanese attack, however, but would use the four reserve battalions for offensive thrusts to keep the enemy off balance.[6]

The value of the 7th Marines lay not only in the number of battalions it added to the division, but also in their size. All were close to full strength, while Vandegrift's other units were badly depleted by casualties and sickness. Puller had thirty-four officers and 857 enlisted men out of the thirty-six and 875 that he rated. His three rifle companies each had three rifle platoons (consisting of an eight-man BAR squad and three nine-man rifle squads), plus a weapons platoon of two 60mm mortars and two light machine guns (M1919A4 air-cooled models). The weapons company had twenty-four heavy machine guns (M1917A1 water-cooled versions), four 81mm mortars, and two .50 caliber machine guns. The regimental weapons company possessed additional .30 and .50 caliber machine guns, plus 37mm and 75mm antitank guns. The riflemen still carried the bolt-action Springfield, but it remained a formidable weapon despite its age.

The 7th Marines brought a high level of quality, too. While the regiment lacked the combat experience of those outfits already on Guadalcanal, it was better trained than the 1st and 5th Marines had been on

August 7. More important, Puller and Hanneken provided exactly the type of leadership Vandegrift desired. Fighting on Guadalcanal was less like the large-scale, conventional warfare of Europe and more like the small unit, jungle combat in which the two old banana warriors excelled. They were a welcome addition to the senior stalwarts on hand such as Edson and Colonel William J. Whaling.[7]

Just days later, Vandegrift would tell his superiors: "The coming of the Seventh has made all the difference in the world in our activities and what we have been able to accomplish."[8]

The division wasted no time in putting the 7th Marines to work. On September 19 the 2d and 3d Battalions moved into the two southern sectors. They covered the area from the bank of the Lunga River running east to the flank of the 1st Marines, in position along Alligator Creek. It was flat ground blanketed by jungle, except in the center where there was a low, north–south rise covered with kunai grass. This latter feature bore the name of Edson's Ridge following the desperate battle of September 11–13. In two nights of bitter fighting the raiders and parachutists, supported by artillery, had beaten off the Kawaguchi Brigade and killed more than six hundred of the enemy. The remainder, many of them wounded, retreated into the interior. Vandegrift wanted to ensure that the Japanese were not regrouping for another assault, so he ordered the 1st Raiders and 1/7 to reconnoiter beyond the perimeter and disrupt any enemy concentrations. Edson's men would move down the east side of the Lunga while Puller's battalion operated on the west bank. Division informed Chesty of his role early in the afternoon on the 19th.

After a morning of moving supplies off the beach, the rifle companies of 1/7 formed up and headed south at 1430. The long column crossed the Lunga at Pioneer Bridge, where it encountered scattered rifle fire from a few Kawaguchi Brigade stragglers. One Marine went down. Puller, accustomed to poor enemy marksmanship and much tougher numerical odds, strode along the narrow trail and told his troops not to worry about this "small stuff." His cavalier attitude in the face of enemy fire impressed his officers and men and increased their confidence. Most Marines were not about to take chances. In the middle of the firefight three Japanese looked as if they might be surrendering, but men in Company A shot them.[9]

The battalion stopped for the night on a low ridge, but the Marines got little rest. Like the men of other untested units before them, they saw the enemy in every shadow and shot at these ghosts or fired simply because someone in the next foxhole did so. Puller tried to put a stop to it, without much success. (That same evening the rest of the regiment opened up on the raiders as they tried to reenter the perimeter.) When the sun came up 1/7 resumed its patrol. The battalion commander had warned his troops about the scarcity of water, but they drank as freely as they shot. The concept of water discipline then espoused by military leaders simply did not work in the face of oppressive heat and steep hills. Soon every man had emptied his single canteen and all struggled forward with parched throats. A number fell by the wayside with heat prostration. The Lunga appeared like an oasis in the desert in mid-morning. Many Marines raced for it and drank deeply without taking time to purify the water with iodine.

After fording the river, 1/7 neared the site of a suspected enemy bivouac. Chesty called in an artillery barrage before advancing into the area, which proved to be unoccupied. The battalion did come under fire several times during the day from small bands or individual Japanese. In one of these micro engagements, Major John P. Stafford, the commander of Company B, was wounded by a rifle grenade that exploded prematurely. The pace of the battalion slowed to a crawl thereafter as men bore his stretcher up and down the rough terrain. The force finally reached friendly lines late in the evening and went into reserve between the airfield and Edson's Ridge. At a cost of three casualties, 1/7 had killed twenty-four Japanese and confirmed there were no organized enemy near the southern perimeter. They also had weathered their first ground action and made strides along the road to becoming a veteran outfit.[10]

That night there was considerable firing in the front lines of 3/7 and 2/7. The regimental command post thought it was under attack. Sims called out Puller's battalion to reinforce the area, but the weary troops found no enemy. The "trigger happy" 7th was "the subject of much scorn and merriment" among the rest of the division, though most of those who were laughing had acted the same way just a few short weeks before. Thomas arranged for Martin Clemens, a coast watcher and head of the native scouts, to give the officers and senior NCOs of the regiment a class on nighttime jungle noises. Word went around that Vandegrift also forbid them to fire at night anymore without orders from division; they were otherwise to rely solely on their bayonets. (One nervous but obedient sentry promptly stabbed a fellow Marine the very next evening.) Puller lost patience with the uncontrolled shooting and his angry reprimands helped instill calm. Dr. Smith observed that the problem gradually disappeared as the green troops of the regiment had the "chance to taste actual combat, to get the feel of their weapon, to kill, to be fired at, to hear the noise of battle, and to get over their first fright." Before long they would be amused by newer arrivals going through the same process of adjusting to war.[11]

☆   ☆   ☆

The 1st Marine Division was aware that Japanese ships were making nightly runs to Guadalcanal and dropping off supplies or troops at the western end of the island. The staff was concerned that these reinforcements might include artillery. Although the Japanese so far had made sparing and incompetent use of that combat arm in the campaign, the shallowness of the Marine perimeter made it theoretically possible for the enemy to place the airfield under constant bombardment and thereby deprive the division of its aerial firepower. There were not enough Marines to expand the lodgment, but Twining came up with an idea that would allow them to dominate the area reaching to the Matanikau River and thus keep enemy artillery out of range.

The plan called for 1/7 to find and reconnoiter a trail that led from south of Edson's Ridge to the headwaters of the Matanikau. Along the way, Chesty's force would search for a suspected enemy observation post on the slopes of Mt. Austen, the high hill to the southwest that overlooked the entire perimeter. The battalion then would cross the river and move down the far bank to clear it of Japanese. After that the raider battalion would establish a patrol base farther to the west and be in position to give advance warning of any Japanese activity in the region. Thomas later recalled why they selected 1/7 for the mission: "We thought if any person could get a battalion up the river and get it across and get above the Japanese, it would be Lewie Puller."[12]

Unbeknownst to the division, the Japanese had gathered about four thousand men in the vicinity of the Matanikau. Most were west of the river, but one company was in the foothills of Mt. Austen to collect stragglers from the battle on Edson's Ridge.[13]

☆   ☆   ☆

Chesty decided to take only his three rifle companies on the operation. The force of just under six hundred men departed the perimeter on the morning of September 24, with A Company in the lead, followed by the command group and B and C Companies. They had a native scout and Marine Gunner Edward S. Rust from the 5th Marines to guide them, plus a liaison team from the 11th Marines to direct artillery fire. The lieutenant acting as forward observer stayed close to Puller and found that meant he was "always right up in front." It was not the way most senior commanders operated, but the artillery officer thought it "was good for the men's morale."[14]

Under a cloudless sky the Marines made their way through thick jungle lowlands and over precipitous grass-topped ridges. The terrain played havoc with the formation; the column slowed while the lead unit went uphill, then suddenly the tail found itself scrambling to catch up as the head went downslope at a rapid clip. After their earlier experience on patrol, many men were carrying field-expedient canteens fashioned from sections of bamboo. Even with this extra supply they were fast running out of water, until a cloudburst in mid-afternoon brought welcome relief. But the rain also made the slopes treacherously slick and further slowed the advance.

Late in the afternoon the point squad under Corporal Harold L. Turner started looking for a suitable bivouac site. He investigated a grassy rise. His platoon commander, Captain Regan Fuller, followed close behind and stumbled upon two Japanese squatting beneath a tree over a pair of cooking pots full of rice. He shot one and Turner's squad got the other. Puller, in his habitual position near the head of the column, quickly came up to the scene. The battalion commander was reaching down to sample the captured chow when Japanese machine guns began to rake the area. The Marines had surprised an outpost of the enemy company, which used the brief warning to occupy defensive positions. Chesty escaped the initial burst of fire and managed to work his way back to cover. His runner and several other men were not so lucky.

Company A was pinned down by "withering" fire, so Puller called for B Company to come up and deploy. First Lieutenant Alvin C. Cockrell, Jr., of Baker Company led the 1st Platoon up the right-hand side of the trail, while First Lieutenant Walter B. Olliff took the 2d Platoon toward the left. Olliff thought the enemy fire was so heavy "the bushes and leaves waved and bent over as if there were a gale." His men tried to move up by rushes whenever the shooting seemed to slacken, but progress was halting and they sustained a number of casualties. Olliff

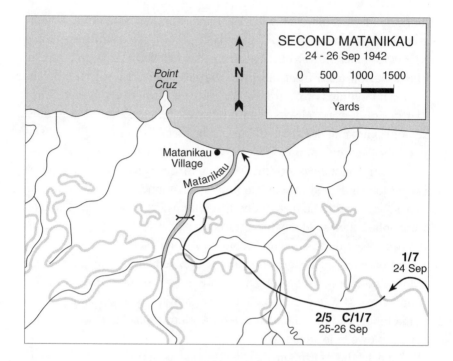

was hit in the hip after he rose to his knees and threw a grenade. Cockrell died charging forward and yelling for his men to follow. This loss of
leaders further slowed the maneuver. Puller shouted curses at Cockrell
when he failed to respond to repeated calls; it would be some time before Chesty realized that the young officer would never answer.[15]

The 1st Battalion could not gain the upper hand. The enemy were
dug in on ground they knew and they maintained fire superiority with
their heavy weapons (a capability 1/7 could not match). The forward
observer called in an artillery mission, but the first adjusting round
landed on his own lines and he gave up trying to establish his location
on the poor map. An A Company NCO recalled: "This was our first real
fire and we were having a little trouble putting into practice our tactics
which we had so thoroughly been drilled in." Puller responded aggressively to the situation. He was "on his feet throughout, organizing, moving, exhorting," and trying to rally his unit. One officer called it "the
greatest exhibition of utter disregard for personal safety I ever saw." But
the problem of deploying an inexperienced battalion from a column on
a trail into a line against an unseen enemy as darkness fell was simply

too much. He concluded it would be wise to break off the action and re-group. He ensured that the wounded were gathered up and then ordered a withdrawal of three hundred yards to another ridge, where 1/7 set up a perimeter for the night.[16]

At 2030 Puller made his first report to division. The terse message gave a rough location of the battle and listed friendly casualties of seven killed and twenty-five wounded. (There actually were twenty-eight wounded. Most of them were in poor shape and unable to move under their own power; three would die during the night.) He also requested air support the next day to bomb the enemy position and drop stretchers and water. Chesty made no estimate of Japanese losses, but there was a feeling among some in the battalion that the Marines had gotten the "worst" of the fight. Private White, wounded slightly that day, thought "they could have slain us all that night; I'm sure of that." Puller made the rounds of his "weary and dejected band" to reassure them that all would be well. A squad leader who had experienced the "terrible feel-ing being under enemy fire the first time" thought that the colonel's dis-play of courage and calm during the fight "really raised our morale." Even those who had not seen their commander firsthand benefited from the tales that circulated around the perimeter. In one story, he had lit his pipe in the dark, then quickly hit the ground and rolled away in an effort to draw fire from a Japanese machine gun and locate its position.[17]

Vandegrift realized that it would take a large number of men to es-cort the wounded and carry their stretchers over the rough terrain, so he ordered 2/5 (temporarily commanded by a captain) to depart prior to dawn and join up with 1/7. The general informed Puller that the addi-tional battalion would come under his command and left the next step up to him: "Continue attack or return as you decide [in] accordance [with] your situation in morning. Well done and good luck." Vandegrift gave the acting CO of 2/5 verbal instructions that differed slightly by emphasizing his desire that the combined units "push a little bit if ter-rain suitable."[18]

The 2d Battalion covered the five miles to 1/7 in less than four hours, arriving at 0845. Puller already had discovered that the Japanese had withdrawn from their "well-prepared positions" during the night. He called off the requested air strike. Chesty gave his A and B Compa-nies the mission of taking the wounded back to the perimeter. He then buried his dead and prepared to continue the operation with his C Company and 2/5. This was a strange decision since it placed him in charge of a force he did not know. Possibly he thought this veteran but depleted unit was in better shape for action than his recently bloodied companies. He also might have considered it important that his own men take care of their wounded comrades. In any case, this odd concoction would characterize the remainder of the operation.[19]

On September 25 the combined unit advanced along the trail but encountered no enemy soldiers. That evening, Puller informed division that he would return to the perimeter the next day along the coast road. The Marines moved out early in the morning of the 26th and finally reached the Matanikau. Chesty did not cross as originally planned, though he did send one platoon of 2/5 to make a brief reconnaissance of the opposite bank. Twining later would call this an "unfortunate decision."[20]

Puller's force moved down the east bank of the river through the narrow, steep valley and received some desultory fire from the far side. At 1400, Company E, the lead unit, attempted to cross the river at its mouth. The men were barely in the water when Japanese on the far bank opened up with mortars and machine guns. The Marines withdrew with six wounded. Chesty immediately got on the radio to report this opposition to his crossing. The division operations section thought he already was on the other side and asked for clarification. Twining also offered supporting arms and advised that the raiders were moving up the coast road in accordance with the original plan. In the meantime, E Company provided a base of fire for two assaults by platoons from G Company, both repulsed. The first difficulty with the mixed battalion arose at this point, since Chesty seemed reluctant to listen to officers from 2/5. When a lieutenant who had commanded one of the failed attacks insisted that the enemy defenses were too strong, Puller ignored him. Then Chesty refused the request of 2d Battalion's doctor to ask division for ambulances and a resupply of battle dressings. Approached moments later by his own surgeon, Chesty acquiesced and wrote out the message himself.[21]

Puller did react to the failure of his initial tactics; he called off the infantry assaults and resorted to firepower. He requested support from artillery and air, while Private First Class Johnny Smolka (a signalman from 2/5) went out to the beach under fire and used semaphore flags to contact the *Monssen* (DD-436). The destroyer's boat picked up Rust, who pointed out targets for shore bombardment. While high explosives softened the position, Chesty pondered what to do next. He already had twenty-five casualties requiring evacuation. At 1630 Lieutenant Colonel Samuel B. Griffith's 1st Raiders arrived on the scene, accompanied by high winds and rain. Just minutes later, Twining radioed Puller that division had dispatched Edson to "command combined forces in continuation [of the] attack." Although the original plan had not contemplated much enemy opposition, Vandegrift and his staff were resolved to achieving their objective despite the changed circumstances. They still believed there were no more than four hundred enemy in the area.[22]

Edson and Puller conferred and the commander of the 5th Marines issued orders for the next day. In an effort to envelop the enemy, the raiders and 1/7's C Company would move two thousand yards south along the Matanikau, cross over, and then attack back toward the coast. To keep the enemy fixed in place during this flanking maneuver, 2/5 would conduct a frontal assault across the river mouth. The third element of the plan called for the remainder of 1/7, now back in the perimeter under Major Rogers, to make an amphibious landing near Point Cruz to seal off the enemy's avenue of retreat.[23]

After a night of continuing rain, the raiders and Company C began their movement. At 1050 they ran into a Japanese company that had crossed the river the previous afternoon to secure a lodgment for a future attack. Mortars on the far bank peppered the Marines in their confined space between the river and a ridge. Major Kenneth D. Bailey, the executive officer and a hero of Edson's Ridge, went up to the front to help break the impasse. He died in a burst of machine gun fire. Griffith then took both Charlie Companies up onto the high ground in an effort to flank the stubborn resistance. The enemy had this approach covered, too, and Griffith was hit in the shoulder. There were thirteen other casualties. With the two senior raiders down, there must have been some confusion in the battalion command group and that translated into an ambiguous report of progress. Both division and Edson interpreted the message to mean that the raiders were fighting on the western side of the Matanikau. At 1030, 2/5 had launched Company G in an attack across the river mouth, but the Marines were turned back yet again.[24]

Major Rogers had not received word of his part in the battle till 1000 that morning, when he was called away from Sunday religious services. Captain Charles W. Kelly got A and B Companies and a few

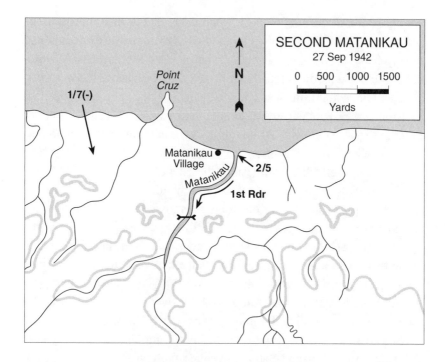

crew-served weapons moving toward the beach, while Rogers reported
to division headquarters for instructions. The 398 Marines embarked in
landing craft and Rogers joined them, still wearing the shiny, starched
khaki uniform he had dug out of a footlocker for church. He made a
quick speech about 1/7 being the "finest body of fighting men in the
world" and exclaimed: "I hope every man gets the Navy Cross." The
only plan he passed to his force was that they would land in two waves at
1300. Division had arranged for the seaplane tender *Ballard* (AVD-10)
to provide fire support, but a Japanese air raid came in and the ship sped
away to take evasive action. The small boats bored ahead and deposited
1/7 ashore just beyond Point Cruz. Rogers led his force toward a grassy
ridge about five hundred yards in from the coast road.[25]

The Japanese had been anticipating a landing for three days and reacted quickly. Mortar shells began to fall as the lead elements of the Marine battalion reached the high ground. One of the first bursts killed
Rogers and wounded Captain Zach D. Cox (only recently elevated to
command of Baker Company). Kelly succeeded to command of the force.
Meanwhile a Japanese battalion came up the coast road from the west
and a company counterattacked from Matanikau village in the east. The

tail of 1/7 was clearing the beach when it saw the enemy approaching. Lieutenant Richard P. Richards and Platoon Sergeant Rufus A. Stowers set up a machine gun and inflicted numerous casualties until the onrushing Japanese overwhelmed the position. At that point the Marines were effectively cut off from the sea. They formed a perimeter on the ridge.

Due to 1/7's hasty departure from Lunga Point, it was not well prepared. The rump battalion had brought only one 81mm mortar and just forty rounds. Kelly also discovered that his outfit had no radio; he had no means to request supporting arms or even inform division of his plight. An attack across the Matanikau mouth at 1310 by 2/5's F Company failed to reach the far bank, while the raiders remained bottled up on the east side of the river. Kelly's unit, surrounded and under attack by superior forces, was on the verge of reenacting Custer's Last Stand.

Marine pilot Lieutenant Dale M. Leslie came to the rescue. As his dive-bomber circled overhead, Kelly's men used their white undershirts to spell out "HELP" on the ground. Leslie radioed the news to division, which relayed it to Edson's command post. Puller argued for a renewed attack by the units on the east side of the river in an attempt to break through to his own outfit. Edson refused to order yet another hopeless charge across the open water into a strong enemy defensive position. He also authorized the raiders to withdraw. Chesty was livid: "You're not going to stop them when they've had only two casualties? Most of my battalion will be out there alone, cut off without support. You're not going to throw these men away."[26]

The angry battalion commander took matters into his own hands. He walked out to the beach and had a signalman contact the *Monssen,* which was steaming by. At Chesty's request, a launch picked him up just after 1600. Once on board, he explained the situation to the ship's commander, who readily agreed to assist. Puller, familiar with the mechanics of naval firepower after his two tours on *Augusta,* huddled with the gunnery officer, while the destroyer's captain radioed Lunga Point for landing craft. When *Monssen* reached the scene, Chesty sent messages by blinker and semaphore flags to his troops ashore. Looking through his field glasses, he saw a Marine (Sergeant Robert D. Raysbrook) standing on the fire-swept ridge wigwagging a reply. Puller directed the destroyer to lay down a barrage between the coast and the ridge and then shift it to the flanks as the Marines withdrew. After he passed that plan to the men ashore, *Monssen* fired thirty-eight 5-inch rounds.

Kelly got his outfit underway, but artillery fire (apparently from Marine howitzers) came crashing down and the column split up. Japanese infantry rushed forward to cut off most of A Company. Platoon Sergeant Anthony P. Malanowski, Jr., picked up a BAR from a casualty and covered the withdrawal until he was killed. The rest of the battalion made its way to the beach about two hundred yards to the east of Able. The first boats to approach shore came under heavy fire and three coxswains were hit. The others backed off. Lieutenant Leslie then strafed the Japanese and circled low over the landing craft to shepherd them to the coast. Captain Thomas J. Cross also swam out to the boats to bring them in. Chesty already had boarded one of the small craft. He ordered it into shore and shouted at others to follow him. The battalion laid down additional covering fire and the landing boats finally came in at both locations. The Marines carried their wounded out into the surf, but had to leave the dead behind. As Puller's force pounded over the waves toward Lunga Point, division directed the withdrawal of the troops along the Matanikau.[27]

The fighting on September 27 had cost the raiders two killed and eleven wounded, while 2/5 suffered sixteen killed and sixty-eight wounded over two days. Puller's unit had lost twenty-four dead and thirty-two wounded (three casualties from Company C during its operations with the raiders, and all the rest from the amphibious landing). There was no way to determine total Japanese casualties, though Chesty believed 1/7 had killed about eighty enemy near Point Cruz. The engagement was a clear defeat for the Marines, however, since they had failed to achieve their objective and been forced to retire from the field. All concerned felt lucky to have escaped without greater bloodshed.[28]

☆   ☆   ☆

The official division report cited the "good judgment of senior commanders" in preventing a debacle, but off the record there was considerable finger-pointing. Puller thought Vandegrift and Thomas had erred by mixing three unrelated battalions. This was a reasonable critique, but he was guilty of the same behavior when he sent most of his own unit to the rear instead of giving 2/5 the mission of evacuating his casualties. Chesty also scorned "the much-vaunted Raiders." This was their only defeat of the campaign, but they were fighting at less than half strength due to previous losses and all present were physically debilitated. Many of their leaders were gone, too. Vandegrift already had decided to send the unit off the island for "rebuilding." In addition, the lightly armed raiders had never been designed to break through strong defensive positions. On the 27th they were hemmed in by a river and a ridge and had none of the support from air, artillery, or naval guns that had made it possible for 1/7 to fight its way clear of encirclement.[29]

Twining placed some of the blame on Puller "for disobeying orders in going down the right bank of the river instead of the left." That was not a completely accurate assessment, as Vandegrift's September 24 radio message had given Chesty freedom to do as he saw fit. However, things might have worked out differently if Puller had crossed the upper Matanikau on the 26th when it would have been easy to do so. Edson had made mistakes, too. He had created a risky plan that divided his force and left him no reserve. Twining also accepted a share of responsibility for the outcome. Division had vastly underestimated enemy strength, pushed ahead anyway when the original plan fell apart, cobbled together a bastard command for the job, and provided too little supporting firepower. Twining admitted that it was "a good example of how not to run a battle." There was plenty of blame to share among the leaders of this engagement, generally known as Second Matanikau.[30]

The men involved rated some glory, though. One participant accurately observed that "individual heroism" had saved the day. Puller nominated a number of his Marines for medals and officially praised the work of Rust, the boat crews, and the *Monssen*. Leslie, Raysbrook, Malanowski, and two Navy coxswains would receive Navy Crosses and Coast Guardsman Douglas A. Munro would be awarded a posthumous Medal of Honor. Captain Kelly thought his entire force had displayed "fine fighting spirit." Thomas believed that Chesty also merited commendation, since his "force of will" had played a decisive role in rescuing 1/7 from the trap.[31]

Coupled with the fight on the 24th, 1/7's casualties for the operation totaled ninety-one, more than 10 percent of the battalion. The losses included not only the battalion XO, but all three rifle company commanders, too. As the officers and men returned to the perimeter on the night of the 27th, the extent of their losses set in and morale plummeted. Puller called his officers together the next day and tried to buck them up. He told them that everyone had to die sometime and doing it for one's country was a fine way to go. Then he stressed what they should learn from their hard-won experience. Above all, he enjoined them to be more than just commanders—he wanted them to lead their men from the front, not simply issue orders to attack. He reminded them what he had been taught since his earliest years: "That in the Confederate Army, an officer was judged by stark courage alone and this made it possible for the Confederacy to live four years. There are other qualities in the make-up of a man, but stark courage is absolutely necessary in the make-up of an infantry leader." (He reinforced his point when it came to his attention that one of his four shell shock cases was a lieutenant who had collapsed in terror just as the landing boats deposited Rogers and most of 1/7 near Point Cruz. Chesty asked Vandegrift to give the young officer a general court-martial.) Puller would admit years later: "I have as much fear in me as the average man. . . . For the sake of your men you had to appear fearless." He believed that he personally had demonstrated his own fearlessness as "the battalion leader" in the first nine days on the island. His men certainly would have endorsed that opinion.[32]

☆   ☆   ☆

Division gave Puller's battalion no time to contemplate the results of the battle. On September 28, Vandegrift issued orders for 1/7 to move up and replace 2/7 on the perimeter. The assigned zone was south of Henderson Field in jungled flatlands. On the right flank was 3/7, occupying Edson's Ridge. On the left was the 1st Marines' sector, which looked out over a field of kunai grass and then curved north till it reached the coast. The new home of 1/7 had been largely unoccupied until the arrival of the 7th Marines; Hanneken's men had been building defensive works there for the past week. Chesty immediately set his outfit to the task of improving what it found.

The battalion set about replicating the fortified line it had built on Samoa to defend another airfield. The troops carved out the undergrowth to create wide, interlocking fire lanes for their machine guns and antitank guns, which they placed in bunkers covered by logs and sandbags. They strung double-apron barbed wire fences and attached ration cans containing pebbles to prevent intruders from silently cutting through the barriers. The deep fighting holes of the riflemen stretched along the entire sector; many of these sported overhead cover as work progressed. Roughly a hundred yards to the rear, the men hacked out a path paralleling the front line, so they could move from flank to flank without being observed by the enemy. In the west this narrow lane tied in with the dirt road snaking down from Edson's Ridge and leading back to the airstrip. In the opposite direction it connected with a similar communications trail in the 1st Marines' zone. About fifty yards farther back from the trail, near the left end of the line, was a log- and sandbag-covered bunker housing Puller's command post. Each day, while two thirds of the battalion dug and cut and built, a company-sized patrol penetrated the jungle in search of signs of the Japanese. They found none, but did uncover a "well-beaten" east–west trail about three thousand yards from Marine lines. Everyone assumed this had been made by the Kawaguchi Brigade during its advance on Edson's Ridge.[33]

Not long after 1/7 moved into the perimeter, Nimitz flew into Guadalcanal to assess the situation for himself. Vandegrift took the theater commander on a quick tour of the small American bastion. The next morning, the admiral decorated about two dozen Marines with the Navy Cross. Puller was one of the few present to observe the quiet ceremony and Nimitz took the opportunity to chat for a few minutes. The two *Augusta* shipmates traded pleasantries about the old days until it was time for the admiral to depart.[34]

With the passage of time and the establishment of some semblance of routine, the officers and men of the 7th Marines began to adjust to the situation. They found Guadalcanal "hotter, more mountainous, more rugged, wilder" than Samoa, but they were growing used to the "strange jungle noises" that permeated the night. Mosquitoes and midnight nuisance raids by enemy aircraft, however, continued to rob everyone of precious sleep. Food remained in short supply despite the stores brought in by the regiment. Even with the supplement of captured Japanese rations, there were just two meals per day. One officer noted in his diary: "Everybody more than hungry. The men can't seem to get enough to eat." Water also was hard to obtain, since it had to be lugged in five-gallon cans hundreds of yards from the nearest river. The Marines of the 7th began to look like the other veterans of the campaign, gradually acquiring the rail-thin appearance of the undernourished and the hollow-eyed visage of the exhausted.[35]

During this lull, Puller tried to maintain the mental and physical well-being of his force. He had the companies dig wells and then ordered the men to start shaving, in part to make them feel sharp again. He was particularly worried about Regan Fuller. The hard-charging young captain was letting the drama of the campaign go to his head; he was growing a beard and taking a swashbuckling attitude toward his duties. Chesty offered him a drink of bourbon and some sage advice: "Old man, you're getting carried away with this war business. You're feeling too self-important. Clean yourself up." Dr. Smith, 1/7's surgeon, also noted his commander's emphasis on the spiritual: "Not an outwardly religious man himself, he encouraged divine services to be held frequently up on the front lines for the men who wanted them. Puller would much sooner have given services himself than not to have any. On several occasions he was dissatisfied with a chaplain's talk, and he grumbled to me that maybe it was time he tried his hand." Smith noticed, as well, that "it was the colonel's wish always to keep the men well informed with whatever news there was." Every day Puller moved among the growing defensive works and stopped to chat with the troops. One afternoon he gave them some uplifting news. He told them the remainder of the 2d Marine Division would soon be arriving from New Zealand, while the Corps was readying a third division in the States. He also described his recent meeting with Nimitz and passed along the admiral's solemn promise that he eventually would lead them on to Tokyo. Chesty elaborated that the Marines would have the chance to "kill hundreds of thousands of the sons of bitches" along the way. One man thought the colonel was "much too bloodthirsty a gent for my tastes," but an officer noticed that "the boys are beginning to feel better."[36]

Puller also radiated confidence in his letters home. On October 4 he wrote Virginia: "I will return to you safe and well; never doubt it, not even for a moment. . . . My command is one to be proud of. It has proven itself to be such." He already was looking forward to the holidays and enclosed a $500 check as a down payment on a diamond pin for his wife. "Merry Christmas (make it a merry one for our precious daughter's sake). I will be merry because you two are safe and well. I love you with all my being."[37]

☆   ☆   ☆

While the division strengthened its defenses in early October, patrols from the 5th Marines revealed a continuing buildup of Japanese forces west of the Matanikau. Other intelligence indicated that the enemy was planning to launch a large offensive in the near future. Vandegrift, Thomas, and Twining decided to strike first, secure the river crossings, and keep the foe out of artillery range of the airfield. Their plan looked very much like the one that had failed at Second Matanikau, but this time the forces involved would be much larger and better supported. Two battalions of the 5th Marines would seize the near bank of the river and serve as the anvil. A composite force of division scouts and 3/2 under the command of Whaling would cross over south of the Matanikau forks, with two battalions of the 7th Marines close behind. The Whaling group would attack north along the river, while Sims's outfit followed suit in echelon to the west. The result was supposed to be a three-battalion hammer that would smash the Japanese against the sea and the 5th Marines. A battalion of the 1st Marines would remain in readiness to execute an amphibious envelopment if needed. Aviation and three battalions of artillery would bombard the area the day prior to the attack and support operations thereafter as required.[38]

Command arrangements were as haphazard as those of the previous battle. Some participants thought Edson was in overall command, while others believed that division retained control. There also seemed to be no clear demarcation of responsibility between Whaling and Sims. Communications difficulties further complicated matters. The lightweight TBY radio did not have enough power to carry over the jungle-covered hills. The larger, more reliable TBX sets were a bulky three-man load, which meant that they could not be employed while on the move. Field telephones were also unwieldy due to the reels of wire, but Sims preferred them to radios. However, it would be difficult to lay and maintain the lines along heavily traveled, narrow trails. These shortcomings in command and communications inevitably would result in confusion.[39]

Puller and a few of his staff officers spent most of October 6 at the regimental CP receiving the operations order. Sims picked Hanneken's battalion to follow in trace of 3/2 as it crossed the Matanikau; 1/7 would bring up the rear and eventually hold down the left flank of the sweep to the north. Frisbie told John Hersey, a civilian reporter, that the tactics were "very much like a plan [General Robert E.] Lee used at the Chickahominy." The XO of the 7th Marines was confident "it'll work," but they were prepared if it did not: "The advantage of our scheme is that Whaling goes in, and if he finds the going impossible, we haven't yet committed Hanneken and Puller, and we can revise our tactics." Chesty would have heartily seconded Sims's final instructions, issued to his

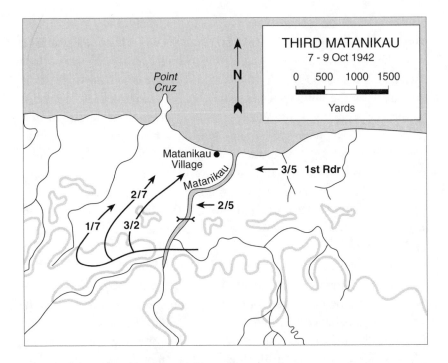

mess officer: "Breakfast in the morning must be a good, solid, hot meal. And if we get back from starving ourselves for two or three days out there and find that you fellows who stay behind have been gourmandizing, someone'll be shot at dawn."[40]

After what passed on Guadalcanal for a veritable feast—sliced pineapple, beans, creamed chipped beef, rice-and-raisin stew, and hot coffee—the 7th Marines moved out at 0830 on October 7. The force crossed the Lunga and followed the coast road before turning southwest. It was a blistering hot day and the Marines soon drained the single quart of water in their canteens. During a break in a palm grove near the coast, some men got temporary relief by drinking milk from coconuts. A water trailer also was available, but it proved painfully slow filling hundreds of canteens from the single spigot. When the long column snaked into the high ground in the early afternoon, heat prostration became a real threat as troops staggered uphill under heavy loads. The Japanese provided a respite to the 7th Marines around 1400 when they hit 3/2 with mortars and machine guns after it crossed the east fork of the upper Matanikau. Everyone stopped while Whaling's force cleared the area of opposition.

The delays for watering and fighting had thrown the Marines behind schedule. Sims told Puller to press on in spite of the approaching darkness. Chesty asserted: "That's fine. Couldn't be better. My men are prepared to spend the night right on the trail. And that's the best place to be if you want to move anywhere." Frisbie kidded his fellow lieutenant colonel: "We know your men are tough. The trouble with the trails along these ridges is that there's not enough horse dung for your men to use as pillows." (The two officers often traded good-natured barbs. The XO insisted that "little guys like Chesty made up what they lacked in size with a lot of noise." Puller retorted that "big guys like Frisbie had all their energy used up growing bones and meat so there was not enough left for brains.") The banter died out long before Whaling drove off the Japanese, so the battalions settled in for the night well short of their intended attack positions.[41]

As it turned out, the enemy was in the midst of securing crossing sites for his own upcoming offensive. A company was dug in just to the east of the Matanikau mouth and 3/5 had its hands full after sunset as small groups of Japanese probed its lines. The men of 1/7 could hear the sounds of battle all night long from their position atop a ridge barely a mile to the south. A heavy rain and the sight of casualties from 3/2 passing back along the trail contributed to a sleepless evening. At least Chesty's Marines were able to catch water in their helmets and ponchos to slake their thirst and fill canteens for the next day.

The downpour continued throughout the morning of October 8, disrupting air support and turning the trail into a quagmire. Fresh intelligence also came to the division that strong air, sea, and land forces were preparing to depart the Japanese bastion at Rabaul. It was apparent they soon would make a determined effort to retake Henderson Field, possibly with a direct amphibious assault on Lunga Point. Vandegrift decided to scale back his objective to a quick envelopment of the west bank of the Matanikau followed by a complete withdrawal back into the original perimeter in preparation for the enemy attack.

The rain let up enough at midday to allow a resumption of flight operations by the Cactus Air Force—Vandegrift's aviation arm. The enveloping force had been on the march since 0600 despite the weather. Heat and water were no longer a problem, but mud and slick grass presented their own challenge. Puller's force had the worst of it as it tried to negotiate a trail churned into a morass by Whaling's and Hanneken's outfits. The Marines of 1/7 worked their way slowly down one ridge, up another one, and down into the valley of the Matanikau. Puller made it over both forks of the river with Company C in the early evening, but he knew the rest of the battalion would have a tough time negotiating the passage in darkness. At 1815, he telephoned Twining with a less-than-confident update: "Only one company across river. Remainder will cross if possible." There were two problems. One was the single log that served as a bridge over the western fork. The other was the river's far bank, which was "an exceptionally steep and muddy cliff." Hanneken had found it "extremely difficult" during daylight. That night, one of Chesty's machine gunners thought it "the toughest thing I've ever encountered." It was barely a couple hundred yards from the waterline to the top, but it took more than an hour for each Marine to climb and crawl up that short vertical distance.[42]

Hanneken's battalion had set up for the night along a wide, grassy ridgeline. Puller and Charlie Company joined 2/7 at 1930 and went into position on the left flank, facing to the west. The remainder of 1/7 stumbled in as the night progressed and all were in place by 2300. The men spooned some cold rations out of cans and drifted off to sleep. Meanwhile, Sims had established his command post on the eastern side of the river, not far from the previous night's bivouac site. That was three kilometers from the front lines. By contrast, Edson's regimental CP was less than four hundred yards back from his lead units. Chesty, like his hero Stonewall Jackson, thought a commander should always be up front where he could observe and make informed decisions.[43]

Puller's Marines were awakened by heavy fire at 0500. Hanneken's right-flank company had spotted a small group of Japanese moving into position farther along the ridge. Fox Company wiped them out. An hour later, Hanneken passed word to Chesty that Whaling had set 0645 as the time for the assault to the north. The attack would kick off on the heels of a fifteen-minute artillery barrage. Whaling also wanted 1/7 to follow just to the left rear of 2/7. The lead elements of 3/2 and 2/7 moved out as the sun rose into a cloudless sky, but Hanneken's Easy Company (on the left flank) ran into heavy machine gun fire about 0800. More than two hours later that unit was still stalled, so Hanneken directed Chesty to send one company to the northwest to get behind the Japanese position and secure the next ridgeline to the west. Puller dispatched Charlie Company on this mission.

Captain Marshall Moore moved his unit down into a jungled ravine and then up onto his objective. His Marines immediately began exchanging fire with the same strongpoint that was holding up 2/7. This action had barely gotten underway when Hanneken received a message from division via airdrop: "The Commanding General directs that you occupy the west side of the sand spit at the Matanikau River at once. Start moving north." Hanneken informed Puller that he was breaking off the action and heading for the river mouth as ordered. As Chesty digested this news, a signalman telephoned from the regimental CP with a message from the colonel: "Execute reconnaissance with your battalion along the coast road toward Kokumbona. Do not become involved in large action. Be prepared to withdraw on order. Maintain communication. Sims."[44]

Puller had been receiving his marching orders for the past twenty-four hours from Whaling or Hanneken; Sims had remained at his command post east of the river. Chesty was already upset at Hanneken's action, since 2/7's hasty move to the northeast was leaving 1/7 on its own in the midst of a battle with a potentially strong enemy force. Sims's message then asked 1/7 to move farther west, without support, and told the battalion commander to stay out of a large fight, when he already was embroiled in one. The uninformed directive drove Puller over the edge into a rage. He bellowed into the field phone that he was fully engaged, that regiment didn't understand what was happening and was in no position to issue orders. At least a few officers and men at the scene thought he was talking directly to the colonel. Captain Fuller recalled much later that Chesty boomed: "If you'd get off your ass and come up here where the fighting is, you could see the situation." It seems very likely that Puller was not talking to Sims at that point, but merely was directing his justified anger at the collective "you" at the regimental CP.[45]

As Hanneken's men broke contact and headed northeast, Puller fed Able Company in to take their place. Soon Baker and Headquarters Companies further extended his right flank. He contacted the regimental commander on the phone, explained the circumstances, and asked that the order to move toward Kokumbona be revoked. Sims told Chesty to join 2/7 at the mouth of the Matanikau, then follow that unit across. That was easier said than done. His battalion was now heavily engaged with a Japanese force holding the crest to the northwest and the ravine in between. Puller called for artillery fire to his right front and brought his

81mm mortars to bear to the left front, but he thought that the light mortars and the rifle grenades of the line companies "were most effective." That was due to the intrepidity of young Marine lieutenants and sergeants, who stood exposed on the barren ridge to direct the fire of their units. The rain of high explosives soon flushed the enemy from the jungled low ground, some of them charging at the Marine positions, but most trying to escape in the opposite direction. The next day, Chesty would laconically note: "Our machine guns then took a heavy toll as they attempted to gain the next ridge to their rear, the slope of which was bare." The devastating show of American firepower slackened only when 1/7 ran low on ammunition. By that time, Japanese resistance was broken and Puller ordered his battalion to head for the river mouth. Some of the Marines, elated at their first unblemished victory, took a few minutes to scrounge for souvenirs among the enemy dead.[46]

Chesty estimated he had routed a force of three hundred Japanese and killed at least 130. This was no motley group of survivors from earlier battles, either. One Marine officer observed that the enemy were "well equipped and in seemingly fine physical condition." Subsequent intelligence would reveal that Hanneken and Puller had faced a battalion of the recently arrived 4th Infantry Regiment, which lost 690 men in that action. Although 2/7 was responsible for some of the casualties, 1/7 undoubtedly had accounted for the major share. The cost had not been cheap—Puller's battalion had suffered six killed and twenty wounded, while 2/7's losses were seventeen killed and twenty-six wounded—but the casualty ratio greatly favored the Marines. More important, the offensive had spoiled a Japanese attack scheduled for the same day and captured important papers. The documents detailed the enemy's seaborne reinforcement, dubbed the Tokyo Express, and plans to establish artillery east of the Matanikau to interdict the airfield. That information would have a major impact on future operations. Puller thought the battle had left the Japanese "seriously depleted and disorganized." Vandegrift agreed: "We did a pretty good job, and it was well worthwhile."[47]

Chesty's battalion reached the mouth of the Matanikau at 1600. A Higgins boat took off the worst casualties and 1/7 crossed to the friendly bank. A few trucks transported the weary Marines, one group at a time, back to the airfield. From there they hiked back to the lines, where the cooks provided coffee and a hot meal that "tasted sublime." Puller ended up having to walk all the way back with the last twenty men when their truck broke down. They finally reached the battalion CP at midnight. Kelly recalled that Chesty cranked up the telephone and loudly reported his outfit's return, then slammed down the handset. Moore, already back at his company area, claimed he could hear the colonel's voice carrying through more than a hundred yards of jungle. After three days of fighting and marching, Puller had some reason to be angry with higher headquarters, but he also had every right to be proud of the fine performance of his own outfit.[48]

A few senior Marines at division were equally displeased with one aspect of Puller's actions and thought he had mainly himself to blame for the conflicting orders of October 9. Twining agreed with Chesty that Sims should have been west of the river with his units during the battle. But the division operations officer also felt that the root of the problem was the failure of the battalions to keep higher headquarters informed. He later would say that division would never have issued the orders it did to Hanneken if it had known 2/7 and 1/7 were in the midst of a fight. Twining ascribed the problem to "a habit common to all old Coconut Warriors, whose credo was 'once you clear the camp, tell 'em nothing.'" The staff officer lumped Whaling and Hanneken into the same group, though he allowed that Edson and Carlson (also experienced Nicaragua hands) "never engaged in this dubious tactic." Thomas concurred that Puller and Hanneken "were inordinately bad in the matter of communications." Vandegrift thought both battalion commanders "were terrible" in that respect. One of Chesty's staff officers would later admit that "communications within and beyond the battalion did not break down unless it was intentional, as was the case when [Puller] would rather not discuss a situation with the higher echelon."

On the positive side of the ledger, Vandegrift and Thomas valued the fact that Puller and Hanneken "were tremendously quick in the matter of striking at any objective that presented itself." Such aggressiveness was not necessarily a common commodity among battalion commanders early in the war. Vandegrift already had relieved several senior Marines for timidity in battle, but he knew he could depend upon Puller's combativeness. Chesty would have more opportunities to demonstrate that quality in the near future.[49]

"You've Got Bayonets, Haven't You?"
The Battle for Henderson Field
October 1942

The Third Battle of the Matanikau was only the prelude to a rapid-fire series of major actions in the seesaw campaign for Guadalcanal. On the night of October 11–12, 1942, an American fleet under Rear Admiral Norman Scott defeated an enemy force escorting a reinforcement convoy to the island. The victory was not complete, however; the Japanese landed four large-caliber artillery pieces destined to shell Henderson Field. Vandegrift already was taking steps to prevent any such bombardment. In addition to manning the main defensive lines, the division now would occupy a position astride the Matanikau to keep Japanese guns out of range. The key to this scheme was the arrival of a U.S. convoy on the morning of October 13. It disgorged the Army's 164th Infantry Regiment, a North Dakota National Guard outfit with a proud heritage from previous wars. With this added manpower, Vandegrift could afford to establish a two-battalion, horseshoe-shaped outpost along the Matanikau.[1]

As part of the reshuffling of forces, 3/7 would go out to the new position in the west, 1/7 would go into reserve near the main airstrip, and 2/7 would take over responsibility for the entire 7th Marines sector. Chesty's Marines knew their new location would put them into the Henderson "V ring"—the center of the bull's-eye for Japanese air and naval bombardments. What no one foresaw was the vast increase in the scale of enemy attacks. Puller's battalion luckily avoided the worst of it. During their last night in the front lines on October 13–14, two Imperial Navy battleships pounded the main field and the recently opened auxiliary fighter strip with nearly a thousand 14-inch shells. For the balance of the night, Japanese planes harassed the perimeter. The deluge of steel put much of the Cactus Air Force out of commission, destroyed nearly the entire stockpile of aviation gas, and killed forty-one men. The dead included two lieutenants in 1/7, lost when their small shelter suffered a direct hit from a bomb.

Large-scale air raids and the first shells from the enemy 150mm guns added to the devastation the next day. Puller's outfit threaded its way down to the airfield between attacks and went into reserve. That night two cruisers fired more than 750 8-inch shells into the perimeter, one of them killing a 1/7 Marine. The following evening another task force hit American positions with nearly 1,300 8-inch and 5-inch rounds. Thomas found the onslaught "worse than anything he had experienced in World War I." An intelligence man in Chesty's CP recalled the battleship bombardment as "the most terrifying night of my life." Captain Kelly, the battalion XO, spent the night in the dugout with Puller and afterward felt "there is nothing more demoralizing than naval gunfire—you can hear each round leave the ship and come in like a freight train." A sergeant in 1/7 recorded in his diary: "I shook and trembled all through the first night, more afraid of my life than I've ever been before." The continuous blitz caused more than physical wounds— the number of shell shock cases rose significantly.[2]

Through herculean effort, the Cactus Air Force managed to get some planes aloft to attack a six-ship convoy unloading troops and supplies on October 15. American fliers eventually managed to destroy three of the transports, but not until most of their contents were deposited onto the beaches west of the perimeter. The reinforcements included about 4,500 men and more 150mm howitzers. The routine runs of the nightly Tokyo Express during October added another nine thousand troops and additional supplies to those totals. With this fresh strength, Japanese leaders planned a new offensive that would dwarf their previous efforts to retake the airfield. Their scheme called for a two-pronged diversionary attack along the Matanikau. A tank company and two infantry battalions would strike across the river mouth, while three infantry battalions moved to turn the inland flank of 3/7. These twin assaults would be coordinated with the main thrust by Lieutenant

General Masao Maruyama's Sendai Division, which would hit the southern side of the Marine perimeter. Despite the experience of the Kawaguchi Brigade at Edson's Ridge, the enemy was certain that the southern sector was undefended. They conducted no reconnaissance to verify that assumption. The scheduled date for the three attacks was October 22.[3]

Before the Sendai set out toward Edson's Ridge, Maruyama apprised his officers and men of the stakes: "This is the decisive battle between Japan and the United States in which the rise or fall of the Japanese Empire will be decided. If we do not succeed in the occupation of these islands, no one should expect to return alive to Japan. [We] must overcome the hardship caused by the lack of material and push on unendingly by displaying invincible teamwork. Hit the proud enemy with an iron fist so he will not be able to rise again." The lead elements of the division began their approach march over a hilly, narrow jungle trail on the 16th. In addition to normal loads, each soldier carried extra food, plus an artillery shell for the mountain guns being manhandled in pieces over the rough terrain. Despite their general's exhortation, the mood of the Sendai was downcast. The troops were limited to a half ration or less per day; often they could not even cook their rice. The hungry men only grew weaker as they fought up and down steep ravines and endured sleepless nights under the chill tropic rains. One lieutenant recorded in his diary: "Many soldiers fear the enemy gunfire and the morale of the soldiers is very poor."[4]

☆   ☆   ☆

The officers and men of 1/7 had very little knowledge of what was happening in the larger campaign. The battalion communications officer, for instance, saw the flashes of nightly naval battles and heard that Japanese transports had made landfall, but he received "little dope" about the results of these events. Vandegrift and his senior staff were only slightly better informed. They expected a renewed effort by the Japanese, but hard evidence consisted only of a captured map that indicated the enemy would strike with a division each from the east, west, and south. Marine planners discounted that document since they were reasonably sure from reports by Martin Clemens's native scouts that there were no Japanese to the east. Frequent patrols to the south also found no enemy there, so division headquarters focused on the Matanikau River.[5]

American forces faced an increasingly bleak picture in mid-

October. Back in the States, the government began providing the press with gloomy assessments that seemed designed to prepare the public for possible defeat. Some Marines and sailors on Guadalcanal were in a "pretty dejected mood." They were worn down from fatigue, hunger, and unrelenting combat. There also was a sense they were not being fully supported, given the enemy's ability to bomb, shell, and land reinforcements almost at will. A lieutenant in 1/7 thought he now "knew to a certain extent how the boys on Wake and Bataan must have felt." The usually ebullient Dr. Smith "for the first time had serious doubts about our plight." Even Thomas was letting occasional "notes of doubt creep into his letters home." Chesty was not pessimistic, but he admitted in a letter to a VMI friend that the constant pounding was having an effect: "I am O.K. but a bit banged up."[6]

While 1/7 remained in reserve waiting for something to happen, Puller drafted a recommendation that one lieutenant and four enlisted men receive the Silver Star for their part in the Third Matanikau. He closed out that document with an unusual statement not directly pertinent to the awards process: "This battalion has suffered thirteen percent casualties of its total strength in action against the enemy to date. Officer casualties total thirty-seven percent." The declaration foreshadowed opinions that he subsequently would express more directly. In later campaigns he would use casualty levels as a means to judge how aggressively a unit was fighting. He also would point with pride to officer-enlisted loss ratios in his own outfits as proof that his senior subordinates were leading from the front.[7]

Chesty was equally prepared to take stern action with anyone he thought was failing to do his duty. While he had waited near the mouth of the Matanikau on October 9, he had noticed that the men of a mortar platoon seemed agitated. He asked them what the problem was. They said they thought one of their fellows had secretly discarded his shells rather than carry them over the rough terrain. Puller already knew the man was a disciplinary problem after reducing him to the rank of private on Samoa for unauthorized absence. The battalion commander was so incensed that upon his return to the perimeter he wanted to initiate a court-martial. Jimmy Hayes, a former 1/7 platoon commander now serving as the division legal officer, recalled that Chesty's anger was driven by the belief that good Marines had died as a result of the private's dereliction.[8]

☆   ☆   ☆

On October 20, 1/7 moved back into the lines, reassuming responsibility for the left half of the 7th Marines sector, while 2/7 contracted into the right half. The men went to work again improving their defenses, which Puller considered only 30 percent complete. Despite his low estimate, it was a formidable position. In addition to the fire lanes, barbed wire, bunkers, and fighting holes, both battalions were generously equipped with heavy weapons. Each had its normal complement of mortars (six 60mm and four 81mm) and .30 caliber machine guns (twenty-four heavy and six light). Infantry battalions also rated a pair of .50 caliber machine guns. The regiment had three antiair/antitank platoons, each with five .30 caliber and two .50 caliber machine guns and four 37mm antitank guns. The 7th Marines had emplaced all these platoons in the front lines of its sector in September and kept them there throughout the movements of the battalions. Enterprising members of the regiment also may have scrounged some extra machine guns from wrecked aircraft or other sources. As a result, the defenses bristled with automatic weapons and direct-fire cannon. In terms of manpower, 1/7 was in good shape by Guadalcanal standards, with 80 percent of its authorized strength on hand and reasonably fit for duty. (Malaria, the worst threat to health on the island, had a relatively slow gestation period, so few men in the 7th were affected at this time.) One officer in the battalion believed that "not since WW I had there been such a picture perfect example of a fixed military defensive position." Vandegrift took a visiting General Holcomb to the sector on October 22 and described it as "a machine gunner's paradise." The division commander asserted: "I feel confident that if we can have fifty to one hundred yards of cleared space in front of us, well wired, mined, and booby-trapped, that our fire and grenades will stop any assault they can make."[9]

On the 21st, Sims told Puller to place a platoon-sized outpost on a knoll 1,500 yards south of the left flank of his lines. Chesty and his operations officer, Captain Charles J. Beasley, were not very happy. In the event of a major attack, they assumed the small OP would be overwhelmed. Nevertheless, Puller sent a platoon to the site and thereafter replaced it with a fresh group each day. Unbeknownst to anyone in the 7th Marines, the mission of the outpost was to hold on to the one piece of terrain that dominated a large, flat grassy area. The Cactus Air Force commander intended to use this ground as a dispersal strip in the event of another emergency at Henderson Field. The open field was a few hundred yards wide and stretched south for about two thousand yards from the very left front of 1/7's position. The 164th Infantry, which now held the sector to Chesty's left, aptly nicknamed this narrow plain "the Bowling Alley."

Regiment continued to run daily patrols, but now it was using several squad-sized elements rather than a single company. On the 22d, a 2/7 unit saw one Japanese with binoculars about three thousand yards south of the American lines. The Marines tried to capture him, but he escaped. Four of five patrols the next day reported some sign of the enemy. A squad from Company A found a soldier's equipment on a ridge eight hundred yards west of the OP.[10]

These bits of information notwithstanding, Vandegrift and his staff were convinced even on October 23 that "all signs point to a strong and concerted attack from the west." Division decided to reorganize its forces and place troops from a single regiment in the Matanikau outpost. Marine leaders finally were learning from earlier difficulties along

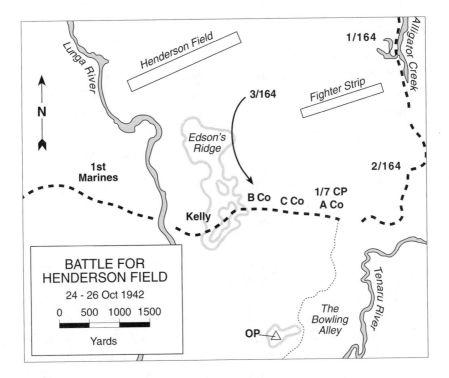

that river—they wanted to fight the next battle with a cohesive unit operating under its normal commander. The 7th Marines drew the assignment, but the reshuffling of forces required a juggling act to keep every mission covered. The 164th Infantry would continue to hold the eastern flank of the perimeter, with its right tying in to the old 7th Marines sector in the south. The 1st and 5th Marines remained responsible for the areas southwest and west of the Lunga. Both the 164th and the 5th had a battalion in regimental reserve, while 3/2 served as the division reserve. Vandegrift elected to send Sims and 2/7 west on October 24, where they would join 3/7 in the Matanikau outpost and relieve 3/1 for reassignment to Hanneken's former position. While that swap was underway, 1/7 would defend the entire southern sector by itself, supported only by a rump regimental CP under Frisbie. It was a calculated risk, but division was confident there was no immediate threat to that zone. Thomas, for one, actually thought it would be an opportunity for Chesty's battalion to avoid another battle and rest up after "two pretty rough shows."[11]

At the urging of Holcomb, the division commander then flew to Noumea for a meeting to try to limit Navy interference in land operations. Brigadier General Rupertus came over from Tulagi in Vandegrift's absence, but immediately was bedridden with dengue fever. For the next few days, daily direction of the division devolved on Jerry Thomas.

Upon receipt of the change in plans, Puller and his XO conferred and decided it would be too complicated to shift the entire battalion to spread it over the 2,500 yards of frontage. They also figured that the high ground of Edson's Ridge presented a more defensible position. So, Kelly would take one platoon from each rifle company, plus a slice of the weapons company and the battalion CP, and occupy 2/7's old position (where half of the regiment's heavy weapons remained in place). Puller also sent the majority of his headquarters personnel up to bolster the line. The battalion settled into the new arrangement on the afternoon of the 24th. From left to right, it was Able, Charlie, Baker, and Kelly's provisional outfit. This tactical layout had one grave weakness—there was no reserve. Puller could do nothing else, however, given the small number of troops at his disposal. Captain Fuller was especially uneasy about his part in the setup. His A Company had only one rifle platoon in its "sadly undermanned" zone, since one was with the battalion XO and the other was at the OP for the night. To add to the captain's concern, a jeep trail led out from his position to the grassy field. But battalion had this likely avenue of approach into Marine lines covered with at least four heavy machine guns, two 37mm cannon, and preregistered mortar targets—"an awesome concentration of coordinated fire."[12]

☆ ☆ ☆

The Japanese also were making their final deployments. The diversionary force continued its successful efforts to deceive the Americans, with artillery fire on October 18 and a probe by tanks on the 20th. The main force, however, was falling behind schedule as it struggled over the forbidding terrain south of Henderson Field. One soldier noted in his diary that he was "very exhausted." On the 21st, Maruyama received permission to delay the attack of his Sendai Division till the night of the 23d. But things only grew worse as time passed. The plan called for an assault by two regiments, with the 29th Infantry striking at Edson's Ridge and the 230th Infantry punching through just to the east. The 16th Infantry would follow up in reserve. During the day on October 23, the commander of the right wing argued for a shift farther to the east and he moved his force in that direction. Maruyama promptly relieved his unruly subordinate. The general also discovered he was not as close to Marine lines as he had thought. And his units were becoming disorganized as they spread out into attack formation and pushed through the dense vegetation. Again, he sought and was granted a one-day delay. That word did not reach the diversionary force, which launched a tank assault across the mouth of the Matanikau on the evening of the 23d. Marine antitank guns destroyed the armor; artillery killed hundreds of infantrymen in assembly areas on the west bank. The cost to the Americans was thirteen dead and wounded. Only one thing went right for the Japanese, but for the wrong reason. The other wing of the diversionary force did not attack—it also had failed to reach its jump-off point on time.[13]

The next day, the Sendai Division prepared for its assault, now scheduled for 1900. Late that afternoon, as the two lead regiments moved toward Marine lines, "torrential rain" began to fall. A Japanese admiral out at sea considered it "a heaven-sent phenomenon" that would mask the final approach of his army colleagues. Maruyama and his men were not so ecstatic. The combination of slippery footing and thick foliage, plus the onset of absolute darkness, slowed and confused the deployment of forces. In a repeat of earlier mistakes by the Kawaguchi Brigade, the Sendai also had failed to reconnoiter and mark approach lanes leading to the American perimeter. As a result, the right wing veered off to the northeast over the course of the evening. It largely would end up missing the Marine defenses. The left wing drifted eastward as well. Instead of making contact at Edson's Ridge, it headed toward the center and left of 1/7's position.[14]

As the Japanese floundered forward, their presence finally came to the full attention of the defenders. Around 1600, native scouts entered the right flank of the 164th Infantry sector and reported they had observed about two thousand enemy soldiers not far from the lines. One of Whaling's scout-snipers also arrived at division with news that he had earlier observed what appeared to be "the smoke of many rice fires" to the south. The final confirmation came around 2100, when Platoon Sergeant Ralph M. Briggs, commander of the 1/7 OP, telephoned the CP that he could hear large numbers of enemy soldiers moving past the knoll. Battalion ordered the platoon to stay put until the Japanese were clear of the area; after that, Briggs could attempt to move his men across the Bowling Alley and out of the line of fire. Puller passed the word to hold fire until the last possible moment. That would give the OP time to escape and would maximize the effect of Marine heavy weapons. Chesty also directed units to man their phones continuously.[15]

This was not the only threat that evening. During the morning, Marines in 3/7 briefly had observed the second wing of the diversionary force moving toward the left or southern flank of their position along the Matanikau. The battalion immediately began working over the likely routes of approach with air and artillery. Division also changed the mission of 2/7. Instead of replacing 3/1 on the seaward side of the Matanikau outpost, Thomas directed Hanneken to form a south-facing line to cover the left flank of 3/7. The battalion was in position by dusk.

Around 2130, Briggs and his OP unit reached the jeep road bordering the Bowling Alley. There they observed a battalion of the enemy silently moving down the track toward 1/7. Briggs ordered the platoon to break into smaller groups and make their own way back to friendly lines. By this time, the rainstorm had passed and bright moonlight filtered down through openings in the jungle canopy. Occasional cloudbursts returned, however, over the course of the night.[16]

The first of the Japanese units reached the American perimeter around 2200. This outfit (probably the one that had passed Briggs) attacked from the vicinity of the jeep road toward the junction of the 7th Marines and 164th Infantry sectors. The enemy poured forth from the shadows at the edge of the jungle, running headlong toward the double-apron barbed wire and the muzzles of American guns. The defenders opened up with everything they had and called down mortar and artillery barrages. Division devoted two battalions of howitzers (a normal supporting complement for two infantry regiments) to answer the repeated calls from forward observers working with 1/7. The adjoining units of the 164th added the weight of their mortars and machine guns against the flank of the enemy. The bullets and shells did their usual deadly work, but the 37mm guns added an extra dimension. Their crews employed canister rounds—essentially huge shotgun shells spraying small steel balls, designed specifically to deal with massed infantry in the open. More than one Marine was awed by the devastation wrought by these cannon: "It really blows the living hell out of everything around." The courageous but foolhardy Japanese charge simply dissolved in the face of this overwhelming firepower.[17]

The sudden, unanticipated threat to the southern perimeter worried Marine leaders. Puller's men had fended off one thrust, but there were almost certain to be more before the night was over. The lines of 1/7 were very thin and the battalion had no reserve, so there was a real chance the Japanese might punch a hole in the defenses. Any sizeable enemy force breaking into the rear areas could quickly shut down the artillery and the aviation that were the linchpins of American strength. The division CP was still distracted by the ongoing battle at the Matanikau, but it took immediate action to deal with the situation. As a first step, Thomas ordered the 164th's 2d Battalion to provide its local reserves to 1/7. Soon after, three platoons of E and G Company were moving along the communication trail that led to Puller's zone. When the Army units reached Captain Fuller's rear area, he promptly brought them into his lines, where they occupied empty fighting positions or replaced casualties in Marine-manned bunkers.[18]

Puller was glad to have these soldiers and the extra firepower of their semiautomatic M-1 Garand rifles, but he knew he needed many more men to hold the battalion's long line. Around 2300, Chesty got on the phone to Frisbie and requested additional reinforcements. A little before midnight, Thomas agreed to up the ante and Twining directed the 164th to dispatch its reserve battalion to reinforce 1/7. Lieutenant Colonel Robert K. Hall left for the front immediately; his 3d Battalion formed up in its bivouac site near Henderson Field and was headed south by 0200. The recent arrivals on the island did not know exactly where to go, but Frisbie, Puller, and their staffs already had worked out that problem. The regiment's Catholic chaplain, Father Matthew F. Keough, had been to the perimeter on numerous occasions. He guided the soldiers up to Edson's Ridge and then onto the communications trail. As the long column moved along that path, Marines came back from the front lines and each led an Army platoon through the last hundred yards of jungle. In the same fashion as the first wave of reinforcements from 2/164, the men of the 3d Battalion filled the empty bunkers and fighting holes. The process was largely complete by 0330. The additional men and the higher rate of fire of their M-1 rifles made an audible difference; all along the line "the sound and tempo of firing picked up tremendously."[19]

The Japanese had been busy with their own maneuvering. The second significant assault of the night came about a half hour after midnight, when the lead elements of a battalion of the 29th Infantry reached the edge of the cleared zone directly in front of Able Company. The first company crawled across the open space and began to cut through the barbed wire. This stealthy attempt failed when a few soldiers recklessly revealed themselves before the breach was complete. The combined Marine-Army force blazed away again with all available weapons and slaughtered the exposed unit in less than half an hour. Subsequent assaults were made with equal bravery, but much less skill or tactical thought. There was little or no attempt by Japanese commanders to coordinate efforts; most units attacked as soon as they came to the cleared zone that marked the Marine lines. The enemy also failed to bring much supporting firepower to bear. Very few rounds were fired from Sendai mountain guns and mortars, and machine guns were seldom employed to duel with their American counterparts. One 29th Infantry company launched a typical charge against 1/7's Charlie Company at 0115. The Japanese infantrymen rushed forward aided only by the sound of their own shouts of "Banzai" and "Blood for the Emperor." Within the space of a few minutes, all were dead or dying in front of the double-apron fence. Kelly later remarked: "It could not have been a more ideal situation from the defense standpoint."[20]

Puller and his staff counted six major assaults on their lines by 0330. So far the Marines and soldiers had held, but the continuous attacks were taking their toll. Ammunition was running short and weapons were wearing out. Sergeant John Basilone, leader of two sections of heavy machine guns in the Charlie Company zone, performed magnificently in keeping his weapons operating. When a pair of guns were knocked out of action, he brought up a replacement for the surviving crew members, repaired the other one, and then operated it himself until additional men arrived on the scene. In the midst of enemy attacks, he moved along the line doling out fresh belts of ammunition. The high rates of fire boiled away the water in the cooling jackets of the guns; Basilone told his men to urinate in them to keep them going. Not far to the rear, mortarmen were using brief lulls in the action to dig out and resite tubes pounded down into the rain-soaked soil by the recoil of near continuous firing.[21]

Through it all, Puller remained calm. For most of the night, he and a very small group of staff officers and enlisted men worked by flashlight in the command bunker, while Japanese rounds pierced the jungle above. They supervised the flow of reinforcements and ammunition up to the front, and kept Frisbie and division abreast of the action. When the 3d Battalion arrived on the scene, Chesty went out to the communications trail to greet Hall and bring him into the CP. The two lieutenant colonels conferred briefly and agreed that Puller should continue running the show, since he already had a handle on the situation. More than once, the Marine commander's bulldog attitude steadied his hard-pressed men. At one point Regan Fuller called back to the CP with the news that he was running low on ammunition. Chesty replied in his typically brusque, devil-may-care manner: "You've got bayonets, haven't you?" Puller knew "there was no such thing as falling back." His troops were in the best possible defensive positions and there was not much ground to give in any case before one reached the vital airfield. A Marine on Frisbie's staff voiced the opinion of many in the perimeter that night: "Christ, I'm glad Colonel Puller is there!" Twining later would say: "Puller's presence alone represented the equivalent of two battalions."[22]

The final Japanese assaults of the night came just around dawn. Colonel Masajiro Furimiya, commander of the 29th Infantry, led one attack, accompanied by the regimental colors and the company charged with guarding them. In the last minutes of darkness, he led his small force across the open ground and through the battered wire. The defenders were tired, short of ammunition, and distracted by a large, simultaneous thrust just to the west. Casualties also had thinned the line. The Americans exacted a toll, but Furimiya and about sixty of his men made it past the bunkers and into the jungle behind the line. It was the only significant penetration of the night. It also proved futile, since the Japanese had not stopped to destroy the Marines and soldiers in the fighting positions and create a hole for follow-on forces to exploit. Instead, the colonel's force constituted a small pocket in the American rear. Another attack just after sunrise failed miserably. In addition to Furimiya's enclave, a few dozen other Japanese soldiers had infiltrated in ones and twos. Maruyama wisely called off further attempts and pulled back his forces. The Sendai would try again that night.[23]

☆   ☆   ☆

Daylight on October 25 brought clear skies above and a scene of utter carnage on the ground. Hundreds of bodies carpeted sections of the narrow cleared strip fronting the eastern half of Puller's sector. In a few spots, the corpses were stacked two and three deep. Near Company A's left flank, the dead lay in windrows, scythed down by 37mm canister rounds as their formations had moved along the jeep road and emerged from the Bowling Alley. The debris of war was everywhere: broken weapons, ripped-open ammunition containers, lost equipment, dirty bandages, bits of uniforms, lengths of broken barbed wire. In the midst of this charnel house, American officers and NCOs automatically began the process of reorganizing their men, resupplying ammunition, and responding to occasional small arms fire from Japanese stragglers in front of and behind the lines. Marines and soldiers moved in on Furimiya's small force and squeezed it out of existence, killing fifty-two enemy in the process. American infantrymen accounted for an additional forty-three enemy scattered about the perimeter.

Chesty walked his lines and conservatively estimated there were more than three hundred dead in the fire lanes, plus hundreds more inside the jungle beyond the cleared ground. He saw more than two dozen officers among the corpses, including a lieutenant colonel. Furimiya was not one of them. For the moment, he and ten of his men had escaped detection, with the colonel secreting "the honoured regimental flag" inside his uniform. It was a spirit-crushing situation for a commander who had rashly vowed to "bravely rush to the enemy and anni-hilate them."[24]

The Americans had decisively won the first round, but Puller dis-patched a hastily scrawled report that gave no cause for immediate cele-bration. He was certain the enemy had a strong reserve and was ready to use it: "Believe Japanese will assault with large forces tonight." Chesty was still trying to determine the extent of his losses, but knew he had more than the one dead and twelve wounded already counted. There was a bit of positive news. Early in the afternoon, men in Company A's zone observed the Japanese shooting at someone in the kunai grass of the Bowling Alley. Seeing that the targets were survivors of the OP, Regan Fuller ordered his men to provide covering fire while he drove a jeep out to get them. A mad dash left the vehicle riddled with bullet holes, but he brought in a few of the Marines. Soldiers from the 164th duplicated the feat with a weapons carrier and rescued the remainder of the group. Much of the platoon was still missing, but it seemed a miracle that any-one had made it through the Japanese encirclement.[25]

Briggs was one of those who had run the gauntlet. Chesty called for him and asked for details about the enemy. The platoon sergeant re-counted as much as he could and noted that the battalion commander "digested [it] calmly, as though he was sitting in his tent in New River, instead of in the mud and blood." Puller already was focused on prepa-rations for the coming night. With most of the Japanese infiltrators liq-uidated, he and Hall were beginning to sort out their forces. They decided that the Army battalion would take over the left half of the sec-tor, while 1/7 consolidated astride Edson's Ridge.[26]

☆   ☆   ☆

It was a trying time for everyone on Guadalcanal. The Cactus Air Force struggled all day to get planes off the ground from shell-pocked Hen-derson and the muddy fighter strip. Enemy air attacks were heavier and more frequent than usual, and Imperial Navy destroyers put in a rare daylight appearance off Lunga Point. American and Japanese artillery also traded fire. Both sides drew blood in the air, at sea, and on land during the course of what would come to be called "Dugout Sunday." The enemy directed most of his effort against the airfields, but a few planes bombed and strafed the perimeter defenses and the 150mm guns lobbed shells in that direction.

While the fighting raged elsewhere, the Sendai Division regrouped in the jungle and prepared for its second attempt. The much depleted 29th Infantry again would serve as the spearhead, despite having its 3d Battalion "practically annihilated" the previous night. In recognition of that regiment's losses, the 16th Infantry would abandon its reserve role and reinforce the effort. The 230th was destined to miss the fight a second night in a row. The regimental commander feared a flanking counterattack by the Americans, so he deployed his force in a defensive posture facing toward the east. The Japanese were attempting to rectify some of their errors. This time Lieutenant Colonel Kusuhichi Watanabe, commander of Furimiya's 2d Battalion, reconnoitered the front himself prior to leading the renewed assault. And the Sendai mustered their few mountain guns and mortars for a preparatory bombardment of the American lines. Some leaders were deluding themselves about the situation, however. The orders of the 16th Infantry for October 25 were based on the supposition that Furimiya and the "main strength of the left flank unit broke through a part of the enemy line last night."[27]

The American reorganization of the southern sector was complete by evening and the defenders girded themselves for another rough night. They did not have long to wait. The Sendai Division fired its limited supply of shells in a weak barrage beginning at 2000. Then Japanese infantrymen surged out of the jungle in an attempt to cross the few dozen yards of deadly open ground in front of the American lines. Their focus seemed to be the point where the jeep road from the Bowling Alley entered the perimeter. The assaults lasted all night long, but none came against 1/7's positions. Puller's battalion was on the receiving end of only a handful of shells and some "minor sniper activity." The 164th Infantry, with the assistance of elements of the 7th Marines Weapons Company, repulsed every effort and inflicted hundreds of fresh casualties on the Japanese. The inland wing of the diversionary force finally launched its attack against the line occupied by Hanneken's outfit. This enemy effort fared no better than the others.[28]

Maruyama admitted defeat the next day, October 26, but some survivors of the Sendai continued the action that night. The Army's 164th Infantry repulsed what it described as several "massed" assaults during the hours of darkness, and a brief evening mortar barrage hit the left flank of 1/7, killing five men. A few of these probes were attempts to reclaim the colors of the 29th Infantry, though given the state of Japanese communications, several units may not have received the order to withdraw. It would take some time for the exhausted Japanese to disengage fully and begin the arduous return march to the sea, but the battle was over.

The losses of the Sendai were heavy. On October 27, the 164th began the gruesome job of supervising the burial of enemy corpses, many of them already decomposing after two days of tropical heat. The task was so large that bulldozers and dynamite were employed to assist the Japanese prisoners assigned to the job. Among the dead was Colonel Furimiya, who had burned his colors and committed suicide. A general and another regimental commander also had died. By the time the burials were finished, the 164th counted more than 1,075 bodies in and around the lines, and estimated there were another 1,500 scattered through the jungle beyond. The Japanese 29th and 16th Infantry regiments were no longer effective fighting organizations. Casualties for the second diversionary force likely exceeded a thousand.[29]

The three-day struggle along the southern perimeter and the Matanikau came to be known as the Battle for Henderson Field. American losses were significant, but they paled when compared to those of the enemy. The 164th Infantry counted twenty-nine dead and seventy wounded. The units on the Matanikau had suffered sixteen killed and forty-three wounded, most of them in 2/7. Puller initially informed division that his battalion lost nineteen dead, thirty wounded, and twelve missing. Deaths from injuries and the eventual return of others from the platoon outpost brought the final totals to twenty-four dead, twenty-eight wounded, and two missing. Chesty closed his official report on the battle with the observation that his outfit's casualties on Guadalcanal now totaled 24 percent.[30]

Several factors accounted for the lopsided victory. The strong perimeter fortifications proved critical, since they significantly reduced friendly losses and helped 1/7's thin lines hold on during the night of October 24. A sergeant in the 164th felt that the barbed wire "must be given a great deal of credit for slowing and confusing the Japanese." The nature of casualties in 1/7 also attested to the abundance of overhead cover in the American fighting positions (and the paucity of Japanese indirect fire). In a remarkable deviation from the norm, shrapnel accounted for only two of the twenty-eight wounded; the rest were all gunshots. A Japanese company commander in the 29th Infantry credited the "intense machine gun and mortar fire" and noted that the Marines "had excellent detectors set up which discovered our movements." Another captured enemy document stressed the "cooperative firing" of the Americans, who "never fight without artillery." Puller himself implied in an October 28 note to division that mortars and howitzers had inflicted most of the casualties. Years later, he would state: "We held them because we were well dug in, a whole regiment of artillery was backing us up, and there was plenty of barbed wire." A staff officer from the Japanese theater headquarters laid the greatest blame on "poor command and leadership," which included such failures as "insufficient reconnaissance," weak staff work, quarrels between senior officers, and incompetence. He also emphasized the middling quality of his own forces: "The [Sendai] Division had little hard combat experience, as it had engaged only in the easy Java campaign. Though high-spirited, they were not expert fighters. The [29th Infantry] knew nothing but bayonet charges." Surprisingly, one Japanese officer thought the Americans "lack initiative," but admitted "they do more duty than they are told." Advantages in firepower and field fortifications notwithstanding, Marines and soldiers had done much more than their duty. And they had been well trained and well led by men like Puller, Basilone, and Hall.[31]

☆   ☆   ☆

Although the 164th had borne the brunt of the fighting during the last two days of the battle, 1/7 had stood alone during much of the crucial first night and barred the way when American defenses were thinnest. Puller was proud of his battalion's performance, but he gladly credited the Army's assistance. Considering that the inexperienced reinforcements had been thrown into a confused situation in the middle of the night, he thought the conduct of the soldiers had been "exemplary." He also believed they had "arrived just in time" and he told reporters a few days later: "I was damned glad to see them." Vandegrift, upon his return to the island, issued division commendations to both 1/7 and 3/164. Chesty nominated a number of his officers and men for personal awards, to include a Medal of Honor for John Basilone. The machine gun section leader would become one of the first enlisted Marines to receive that high honor in World War II. (Another was Sergeant Mitchell Paige, also a machine gunner, who had made a critical stand in 2/7's battle at the Matanikau outpost.) Chesty's Company D soon would claim the title of being the "most decorated" outfit in the Corps.[32]

As always, there was considerable discussion after the battle about recommendations for awards. Puller nominated Father Keough for a medal and later was upset when it was not approved. Regan Fuller and his fellow company commanders all received the Silver Star, but the young captain thought several enlisted men had done more to merit that recognition. The greatest debate, however, centered around Chesty himself. Vandegrift already had established a routine on Guadalcanal of ensuring that commanders of successful actions received a significant award, usually a Navy Cross. After the 1st Raider and 1st Parachute Battalions defeated the Kawaguchi Brigade in mid-September, the division commander had recommended Edson for the Medal of Honor. There were some parallels between Red Mike's dramatic stand on the ridge that came to bear his name and 1/7's successful defense against heavy odds on October 24–25. Naturally, then, some thought that Puller should receive a similar accolade. Frisbie, based on his position as Chesty's immediate superior during the battle, directed the adjutant to draft a recommendation for the nation's highest award for valor. Sims approved of the effort when he learned about it. Unbeknownst to the leaders of the 7th Marines, Twining already had broached the idea to Vandegrift and Thomas. He later recalled that their reaction was emphatically negative, though he was not certain why. The division commander never formally acted on the recommendation for a Medal of Honor and ultimately Sims submitted paperwork simply requesting a "suitable award." The eventual result would be Puller's third Navy Cross.[33]

Everyone agreed that Chesty fully merited the praise contained in the medal citation:

> Courageously withstanding the enemy's desperate and determined attacks, Lieutenant Colonel Puller not only held his battalion to its position until reinforcements arrived three hours later, but also effectively commanded the augmented force until late in the afternoon of the next day. By his tireless devotion to duty and cool judgment under fire, he prevented a hostile penetration of our lines and was largely responsible for the successful defense of the sector assigned to his troops.[34]

11

"Evacuate Me, Hell!"
Final Days on Guadalcanal
October–December 1942

O n October 27, with a few Japanese stragglers still taking pot shots, Chesty walked down the lines to examine the results of the Battle for Henderson Field. After looking over the piles of yet unburied corpses, he felt his initial report of enemy losses had erred. The next day, he penned a note to Twining: "I find that my estimate of the Japanese casualties [inflicted] by our mortar and artillery [fire] to have been smaller than it actually was." (In reality, his first educated guess may have been more accurate, since enemy losses had grown considerably during the subsequent nights of fighting by the 164th.) Dr. Smith noted that Chesty's eyes had a "sparkle" when he recounted the number of Japanese dead. The incident reminded the surgeon of the day back on Samoa when news of the slaughter of the Ichiki Detachment had piqued Puller's interest.[1]

Daily small contacts continued as patrols scouted to the south and squads mopped up in the rear. One officer noted in his diary that "everyone [is] exhausted but still working hard to complete new positions." On the evening of the 27th, a Japanese force of unknown size probed the lines of 1/7 near the Lunga River. The next day, the Marines captured two survivors, one of them a badly wounded warrant officer, the other a private. Puller thought the enemy "may still be in the area south of our lines," but would not attack again "without extensive reconnaissance." Since he believed the previous night's activity had been just such an intelligence-gathering operation, he took a personal interest in the prisoners. The junior man responded to Chesty's interrogation like most Japanese, who talked freely because they had never been told how to act after surrendering. The officer, however, refused to answer questions. In frustration, Puller picked up an entrenching tool and used the flat of the blade to slap the man. Chesty was surprised when the force of the impact knocked teeth out on the ground. They turned out to be a set of dentures, but the unexpected result of the blow brought the proceedings to a halt. He gave up the effort at interrogation and the prisoner died soon after from his original wounds.

Lack of sleep over several days and Puller's concern over a possible subsequent attack by the Sendai Division undoubtedly spurred his actions. He had a certain admiration for the Japanese because of their willingness to die for their country, but he would go to great lengths to prevent the needless deaths of his own men. The incident also was a reflection of the no-quarter approach to warfare being waged by both sides. In response to Japanese treachery on past occasions, Marines had become very reluctant to risk their lives in taking prisoners. Some junior officers and men in Hanneken's battalion openly asserted this view: "Be mean and kill 'em. Kill 'em dead. Our motto in this platoon is 'No prisoners.' "[2]

☆　☆　☆

While the last embers of the Battle for Henderson Field slowly cooled in late October, both sides planned to light fresh fires on the island. The Japanese launched a major new reinforcement effort in preparation for another offensive. Vandegrift wanted to take another crack at the Matanikau and finally attain his objective of keeping enemy artillery out of range of his airfields. The latter operation began on November 1. Two regiments of infantry, powerfully supported by air and artillery, bulled their way across the river and trapped an enemy force at Point Cruz. Meanwhile, on November 2 the Japanese sent three cruisers and eighteen destroyers down the Slot, the channel separating the twin strings of islands forming the Solomons chain. These ships were carrying the first wave of supplies and men for their upcoming push. A reinforced company of this echelon would land to the east of the Marine perimeter near Koli Point. It was supposed to marry up with the remainder of the 230th Infantry (the former right wing of the Sendai

Division), which was retreating in that direction. Intelligence gave Vandegrift warning of the seaborne operation on the 1st. With much of his force committed to the Point Cruz attack and the rest holding the perimeter, he had little to draw upon. He decided to commit his only reserve, 2/7, to the mission of frustrating the Koli Point landing.

Hanneken's force, still recovering from its part in the Battle for Henderson Field, hastily saddled up and moved out at 1430 on November 1. The Marines completed their tough trek the next day, reaching the Metapona River at dusk. It had been hard marching, especially when many of the men's socks had long since rotted away. With blistered and bloodied feet, the Marines passed over the sandbar at the mouth of the estuary and took up positions along the beach. At 2230, the right flank unit reported that it could see ships arriving and offloading a thousand yards to the east. Judging from the number of ships, Hanneken believed that a substantial force had come ashore. He tried to contact division, but his radios were wet and inoperable. The two forces came to blows the next morning when the Japanese stumbled into Marine lines. Rapidly running out of mortar ammunition and unable to reach division for support, Hanneken conducted a fighting withdrawal to the Nalimbiu River. He took up positions on the west bank and finally made contact with higher headquarters at mid-afternoon on November 3.[3]

Division decided to commit more forces to the battle on the east flank. The 7th Marines headquarters and 1/7 were to move by landing craft to reinforce 2/7. Later in the day, Vandegrift also added the 164th Infantry command element and its 2d and 3d Battalions. The Army outfit's mission would be to head overland and come in on the south flank of the enemy. This decision to vastly expand the operation was another calculated risk, since it would leave the entire southern sector of the perimeter temporarily uncovered. (The 164th's 1st Battalion already had moved out to the west to aid in the battle near Point Cruz.) For additional support, division sent a battalion of 75mm pack howitzers across the Ilu River and launched strike aircraft. Vandegrift also implemented a new command setup to control his far-flung operations. He gave Army Brigadier General Edmund B. Sebree control of everything west of the Lunga River and Rupertus, the ADC (assistant division commander), all forces to the east. Vandegrift maintained overall direction of the campaign.[4]

The marshaling of strong U.S. forces in the east was based on faulty information, since Hanneken had vastly overestimated the numbers that had landed. However, the enemy's 230th Infantry began to arrive east of the Nalimbiu that same evening. These men were nearly exhausted after their difficult circumnavigation of the Marine perimeter, but their losses in the Battle for Henderson Field had been light. Revived by the rations delivered the previous night, they would be a formidable foe. In this case, when it came to evaluating the enemy's dispositions, luck proved to be a more important factor than good intelligence for the Americans.

As soon as Puller received the order on November 3, he directed a hasty issue of field rations and extra ammunition and put 1/7 on the trail at a fast pace. He and his men reached Lunga Point by 1800. An hour later the battalion and Sims's command post were aboard landing craft and plowing east into the approaching twilight. The reinforcements knew roughly where Hanneken was supposed to be, but as darkness fell, it became difficult to pick out landmarks on the coast. There was considerable confusion and gaggles of Higgins boats straggled in small groups to the right location. By the time the last of 1/7 made it to Koli Point, it was 0100. Sims let the battalion sleep on the beach, then ordered Puller to deploy at first light into a defensive line on the west

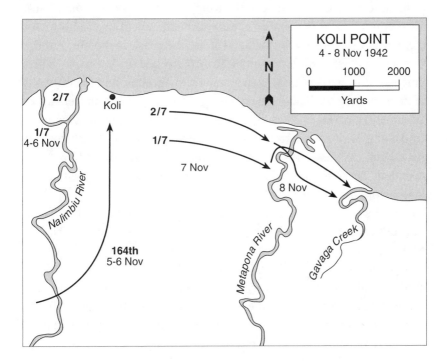

bank of the Nalimbiu, stretching inland from the right flank of 2/7's position.[5]

Believing (correctly now) that there were strong enemy forces to the east, Rupertus was reluctant to make any offensive move until all his forces were ready. The 164th had only left the perimeter that morning. Sims passed on the general's "explicit orders . . . that *under no circumstances*" would the battalions "bring on an action." As Puller's outfit was moving into its assigned position, a patrol reconnoitering his open southern flank observed Japanese activity. Company A headed south to investigate further. The Marines soon tangled with an enemy company with heavy machine guns. The Americans called in mortar fire, then launched a fresh assault, which also failed to crack the position. Chesty realized he was crossing the line into a real battle and Able Company disengaged early in the afternoon. When stretcher bearers brought six wounded and ten dead to his CP, he was momentarily taken aback by the losses in the small action and let out an exclamation of dismay. That evening, Colonel Bryant Moore's 164th Infantry moved into position about a kilometer to the southwest of 1/7.[6]

Rupertus, anticipating that the Japanese were dug in on the far side of the river, decided to launch an enveloping attack against their flank. On the morning of November 5, the two battalions of the 164th waded the upper Nalimbiu and turned left toward the coast. In the midst of this river-crossing operation, mountain storms swelled the waterway. Thick jungle, occasional contacts with small enemy groups, and the difficulty of maneuvering the battalions through a 90 degree wheel further slowed the drive. Two American cruisers and a destroyer shelled the vicinity of Koli Point while the Army units thrashed northward. After stopping for the night, the 164th resumed its advance, with the 3d Battalion reaching the coast that evening. The Japanese easily had withdrawn long before the trap was sprung.

At first light on November 7, landing craft ferried 2/7 to a beach near the village of Koli. The boats returned and picked up 1/7. The 7th Marines passed through the Army lines, with Hanneken along the coast and Puller on his inland flank. For once Puller was frustrated by his inability to communicate. Chesty wanted to coordinate the advance with Hanneken, but grew increasingly exasperated when he could not make solid voice contact. Finally, the lieutenant colonel "muttered a stream of unintelligible profanity and threw the field telephone in the mud."

Those difficulties notwithstanding, the Marines reached the west bank of the Metapona at 1600, having made no contact with the Japanese. Landing craft brought up 2/164 to join the 7th Marines, but division recalled Moore and 3/164 to the main perimeter in preparation for renewed offensive action west of the Matanikau.[7]

The Navy had delivered the fresh 8th Marines to Lunga Point on November 4 and 5. At the same time, an Army regiment and part of the 2d Marine Raider Battalion went ashore at Aola Bay, about twenty-five miles to the east of Koli Point. Vandegrift had opposed this diversion of assets from the start, and now saw a way to pry away some of that force. He received permission to order Lieutenant Colonel Evans F. Carlson's raiders to move eastward and threaten the rear of the enemy at the Metapona. The two companies of Marines were on the march toward the river on November 6. Meanwhile, the Japanese 230th Infantry already had received orders to retrace its steps and take up new positions far to the south. The commander left about five hundred men as a rear guard near Gavaga Creek, east of the Metapona. He began moving the remainder of his force away from the coast at roughly the same time the American pincers operation was taking shape.[8]

Rupertus's staff renewed the attack on November 8 even as the general fell increasingly ill. Before the day was over, he would be evacuated to the rear with dengue fever, and General Sebree would take command of the eastern sector. The morning opened with both battalions of the 7th crossing the sandbar at the mouth of the Metapona. Once on the far side, Sims's outfit formed a semblance of a line and advanced to the east, with 1/7 along the coast and 2/7 taking the interior route. Hanneken's force generally had it easier, since there were large grassy areas in his zone. The coastal flat was heavily jungled and swampy, so Puller's force fell into two loose columns. One rifle company and the command post moved just inside the tree line from the beach, while the other two companies cut their way forward on the southern flank. At this point, the Americans were marching right off their maps, which ended just beyond the Metapona. The next distinct terrain feature they could see along the coast was another waterway spilling into the sea. They would come to find out later that the natives called this Gavaga Creek.

The Marines had only minor contacts during the morning. The thick vegetation slowed 1/7, and 2/7 gradually pulled out in front of its sister battalion. Eventually Puller's command group migrated onto the beach where the going was easier for men carrying heavy radios and large reels of telephone wire. Around noon, the Japanese opened up on this lucrative target with a field gun and machine guns located east of the Gavaga. The initial fusillade savaged 1/7's CP, which was just behind the lead infantry elements and only a few hundred yards from the creek. Before the clerks, communicators, and corpsmen could scramble to safety, nearly twenty men were down. One of them was Puller, hit once in the arm and several times in his left leg and foot. His long run of good fortune in the face of enemy fire finally had come to an end.[9]

Chesty's wounds were significant, but not immediately life-threatening. As his battalion reacted to the fire and attacked, he remained firmly in command. Another of the casualties in the CP was the artillery observer, so Puller got on the field telephone to request fire support. To his dismay, the line had been cut by the Japanese barrage. With much of his communications section knocked out, he crawled out onto the beach and repaired the break. Still in the open to obtain a field of view, he rang up the 10th Marines and called in a mission. The pack howitzers were not in range. Puller moved back into the tree line and tried to arrange air support, but none was available. Meanwhile, his men moved forward under increasing fire until they gained the near bank of Gavaga Creek, where they dug in for the evening. Kelly, the XO, was with the rifle companies. When he learned that Chesty was a casualty, he called the CP and asked if he should move back there to assist in running the battalion. Puller told him to "stay up forward where [he] was most needed." The artillery finally was ready to fire late in the afternoon and Chesty moved onto the beach to spot the fall of the shells and call in corrections.[10]

Hanneken's force had made no contact and had kept moving forward. Early in the afternoon, Sims ordered the 2d Battalion to turn north and hit the enemy in the flank. The right wing of the regiment crossed Gavaga Creek upstream and headed for the coast. The Japanese position proved to be rather shallow, however, and Hanneken missed it. He reached the coast late in the afternoon without opposition. He dug in on a north–south line, facing to the west, back toward the lines of 1/7 just several hundred yards away. The enemy was now cut off on three sides, by 1/7, the sea, and 2/7. Sebree and Sims decided that night to seal the box by ordering 2/164 to fill the gap the next day between the southern flanks of the two Marine battalions.

Landing craft came up the coast that evening to remove 1/7's five dead and twenty-six wounded. A doctor inspected Puller, filled out a casualty tag, and told him he would be sent to the rear. Bloody bandages on his arm and leg notwithstanding, Chesty rose up and shouted: "Evacuate me, hell! Take that tag and label a bottle with it. I will remain in command." His reaction came not from mere bravado, but from a genuine concern about the fate of his outfit. Casualties and disease had greatly reduced his officer complement and the next senior leader in the battalion was Kelly, a junior captain. The strength and capability of the Japanese were unknown, but they had artillery (which Chesty had come to respect the hard way). He expected they would launch a night counterattack. In his opinion, "the situation was far from good . . . [and] I had no officer of sufficient experience to take over the command." As the night wore on, however, Puller's leg stiffened and he realized that his ability to run things was severely handicapped. When Sims called after midnight to say that Major John E. Weber (a company commander in 3/7) would report to assume command of 1/7, Chesty accepted the news without complaint.[11]

Weber arrived at the command post around 0700 and took over the battalion. Puller's troops placed him on a landing craft for the short voyage back to Lunga Point. From there he was taken to the division field hospital. There were several holes, possibly as many as seven, but the doctors were able to remove all of the metal except one piece, which was embedded deep in his thigh next to the bone. The surgeons indicated he would have to be evacuated from the island to have that extracted. Chesty opted to stay near the sound of the guns. Having been raised on stories of Confederate veterans "walking around with enough iron in them to start a junk yard," he actually may have been pleased at the prospect of having his own permanent souvenir of war.[12]

While Puller lay in the division hospital, 1/7 remained dug in along Gavaga Creek. The 2d Battalion, 164th Infantry had difficulty closing the encirclement on November 9, 10, and 11, leading to the relief of the battalion commander by Sebree. The Army outfit finally sealed the gap, however, and Hanneken's force fought back to the west through the pocket. The soldiers and Marines snuffed out the last resistance on November 12. There were roughly 450 enemy bodies in the vicinity, but most of the Japanese 230th Infantry had escaped to the south. The Americans had lost about 160 dead and wounded since the initial deployment of 2/7 on November 2. The Battle of Koli Point was not a stunning success for the United States, but it did clear the eastern flank of the perimeter, which would never again be threatened by the enemy. It also contributed to the slow campaign of attrition that was sapping Japanese strength and will.[13]

Puller was barely out of surgery and apparently not yet entirely lucid when he drafted his report on the battle. His description of the action was generally accurate, but he confused east and west several times. He closed the account with his now standard recapitulation of 1/7's casualty rates. His officer losses for the campaign had risen to 50 percent, while the figure for enlisted men was 23.5 percent (another mistake, actually it was 29 percent). He believed that "casualties inflicted on the enemy during this period are known to be more than twice our own."[14]

A different opponent was imposing even greater losses on American forces in this phase of the campaign. In October, malaria had begun to take a dreadful toll among those who had made the initial landing. Since the 7th Marines had arrived later, the debilitating disease only started to make its full presence felt in that regiment's ranks during the stint around Koli Point. Several officers and men were evacuated with high fevers and severe chills while the fighting was going on. Many more followed once Sims withdrew to the Metapona on November 12 and set up a defensive line. Although Atabrine pills were available to suppress the symptoms of the illness, many men did not take the required dose on a regular basis. It did not help that this swampy jungle area constituted the "worst living conditions" that most of the men would encounter during the Pacific war. The oppressive equatorial heat was broken only by frequent downpours that added to the misery. The poor quality and quantity of food compounded the problem. Dr. Smith estimated that the average man in 1/7 already had lost about twenty-five pounds. Weakened bodies could not withstand the ravages of illness. Once sick, a man was able to eat little, thus creating a vicious downward spiral.

The division registered more than five thousand cases of malaria during October and November. Only those with very severe symptoms were hospitalized, and they were allowed to stay only a few days till the fever dropped. Even so the spartan medical facilities were overflowing. Deaths were rare, but the sick were unfit for duty for extended periods and a large number had to be evacuated off the island. Regan Fuller was airlifted from Henderson Field in mid-November when his 104-degree temperature nearly exceeded his withered weight of 107. Marshall Moore, another of Puller's stalwart captains, would follow soon after, diagnosed with malaria, jaundice, and amoebic dysentery. The men of the 7th Marines also began to encounter a disease all their own—filariasis, picked up during their stay on Samoa. As the days dragged on along the Metapona, the situation grew worse. On November 18, 1/7's staff noted in the daily journal: "Health of command poor and on decline—malaria & skin disease."[15]

With some chance to rest, better food, and slightly easier conditions in the hospital, Puller recovered rapidly from his wounds and regained strength. He also dutifully took his Atabrine and avoided malaria. The medical facilities were hardly a safe haven, however, as they were subject to bombardment from artillery, aircraft, and ships. Heavy air raids took place on November 11 and 12. During the night of November 13–14, Japanese float planes dropped flares that lit up the sky bright enough "that you could read a newspaper." Under this glow, cruisers shelled Henderson Field. Whenever the alarm sounded for these threats, doctors, corpsmen, and the ambulatory patients had to move the bedridden wounded and sick to shelters.[16]

Beginning on the afternoon of the 14th, Chesty had the pleasure of listening in on the radio chatter of American pilots as they exacted a terrible revenge on the enemy. The Imperial Navy was attempting to send an infantry division to Guadalcanal in a large convoy under strong surface escort. The Cactus Air Force caught eleven of the transports in the open a hundred miles north of the island. Unrelenting attacks destroyed seven of the ships by nightfall. The remaining four fell victim to American planes and coast artillery as they tried to unload the next morning. This success was coupled with two night battles between U.S. and Japanese warships on November 12–13 and 14–15. In both cases the American Navy took major losses, but the enemy flotillas suffered even more and were turned away before they could bombard Henderson Field. The Japanese no longer owned the night and they were running out of resources to throw into the meat grinder of Guadalcanal. As Chesty absorbed the fragmentary reports of these air and sea battles, he realized that the tide of the campaign definitely had turned in favor of the Allies.[17]

There were other signs that the worst was over. After a hiatus of several weeks, mail arrived on November 19. Food shipments were improving, too, and soon there was finally enough to meet normal daily requirements. Puller was especially ebullient when he received long-overdue letters from home. He took great delight in showing off new photographs of his daughter and recounting cute stories passed along by his wife. In one tale, little Virginia interrupted her evening prayers to ask her mother what God's last name and rank were. Mrs. Puller cleverly replied that his surname was "Almighty" and he was a general. Thereafter, the girl addressed him each night as General God Almighty.[18]

As Dr. Smith passed the hospital wards one day, he was pleasantly surprised to hear Puller call out: "Hey Smitty, let's get together for a bridge game." Then the surgeon poignantly recalled that two of their Samoa foursome were gone—Rogers dead and 1/7's other doctor evacuated with wounds. Although Chesty often appeared indifferent in the face of casualties, Smith was certain that was a facade. The Navy officer wrote his wife: "We all noticed as time went on how deeply [Puller] felt the loss of his men, and became more and more thoughtful of them and became almost fanatical in his desire to see that they were properly cared for. If a man's body were lost [the colonel] was greatly disturbed." Others remembered that their commander's eyes sometimes misted over when he saw his Marines carried in. Chesty's concern was tangibly expressed in the form of letters signed personally by him. One went to each of his wounded that had been evacuated. It conveyed appreciation for their efforts, wished them a "speedy recovery," and hoped they would return to action with 1/7. It closed with Puller's solemn promise on behalf of the outfit: "They further assure you that until you return and thereafter until the enemy is destroyed, they will continue the fight with ever increasing vigor and determination."[19]

☆ ☆ ☆

On November 21, Sims and the 1st Battalion pulled out of the Metapona position and took landing craft back to Lunga Point. By 1800 that evening, the men of 1/7 were again manning the Edson's Ridge sector they had vacated seventeen days before. The 3d Battalion, 7th Marines was on the left flank. A few days later, 2/7 came back into the perimeter and moved into position to the left of 3/7 (filling in the area that 2/164 had defended during the Battle for Henderson Field). For the first time since mid-October, the entire 7th Marine Regiment was together and under the control of Sims. The first individual replacements of the campaign arrived on the island during this period and just over two hundred joined 1/7, nearly bringing the battalion to full enlisted strength. Puller, released from the hospital on the 18th, resumed command.[20]

Although division issued no formal declaration, officers in 1/7 believed there was a "promise that we had done our work and unless absolutely necessary would not be called upon for more offensive action." Captain Robert H. Haggerty probably spoke for many when he expressed the belief that the outfit was in no shape to fight: "The spirit was sore distressed. . . . Seasoning in battle is invaluable in making soldiers but the point can be reached where a prolonged strain negates the value of what is learned under fire and reduces men to worse than the greenest greenhorn because nerves are strung so tightly." Despite the arrival of adequate food supplies, to include everything required for a traditional Thanksgiving Day dinner, the physical condition of the veterans continued to deteriorate. The holiday meal was an unforgettable feast, but some could not hold it down. Atabrine pills were now plentiful, too, but enforced doses came too late to stem the tide of malaria. Many men continued to lose weight and significant numbers were evacuated by air in late November and December.[21]

It was a tough situation for a leader—the men knew the campaign was largely won and they were not likely to fight again, but there was no end in sight for their ordeal on the island. Many were also "pessimistic about the public at home." The news from the States, sometimes available by radio, spoke of labor strikes and demands for higher pay in the same breath as the sacrifices of fighting men on the front lines. Puller did his best to keep up morale, often in subtle little ways. He washed his clothes and swam in the river with everyone else, in the process revealing his scars and his tattoo (a Marine Corps emblem emblazoned in blue on his upper right arm). He had no use for a separate officers mess, and fell in line for chow like any private. Many senior officers on Guadalcanal, Chesty included, received a steady stream of gifts of whiskey from friends in the rear. He gave many of his bottles to the troops, often with the simple admonishment: "Pass it around, just leave a sip for me." During every encounter with his Marines, he had words of encouragement or merely chatted idly about chow and other mundane topics. He displayed a common touch that his troops loved, because they knew it was no act on his part. Dr. Smith realized that Puller walked a fine line—developing strong ties with his men, but still maintaining his mantle of authority: "He was always approachable. No one feared him, but no one was a close intimate. He never played favorites. He kept himself somewhat aloof, [but] not because he was proud or stern. Everyone had sense enough not to encroach on his privacy or authority. How he did this and still won the admiration of everyone was due to his genius for leadership." Chesty's fatherly approach in the difficult closing days of 1942 solidified the place he had won in the hearts of nearly all his subordinates.[22]

The officers and men of 1/7 were almost universal in their praise of his courage and leadership. Captain Charles J. Beasley described him as "probably the bravest man I'll ever meet." Private Ralph Tulloch thought Puller was "a relentless leader in combat" who was "revered by those who knew him." Lieutenant Frank Sheppard (recently field promoted from sergeant major) considered the colonel "the most fearless man I ever knew and the most aggressive." Platoon Sergeant Briggs recalled that Chesty "was in the middle of everything . . . at all times an inspiration, and a man whom any guy in the battalion would have unquestionably followed anywhere." He was one of that rare breed "who got things done when the going was tough." Corporal Frank Cameron admired Puller for his "bravery at the front" and his "leadership qualities," because "it means so much to us to have a leader who enters into the thick of battle with his men, regardless of the danger to himself." Dr. Smith wrote home: "[The colonel] is a man of enormous drive, indomitable will, more fearless than anyone I've ever known. I am proud to have him for my commander." Marshall Moore believed 1/7 was "very fortunate to have Chesty Puller as our battalion commander. He was a tough commander but was always very fair. . . . He instilled confidence in all of us" because "he was so full of confidence himself." The young captain thought he knew why "the boys are sure crazy over old Louie"—"He was an outstanding leader and had that rare gift which few people have of having an outfit which would follow him to hell and back and enjoy every moment of it." Private First Class Gerald White agreed: "No commander on Guadalcanal was so well endowed with men who fairly worshiped him." Months later Chesty would say that "the respect of the Marines and Corpsmen serving under me is all the honor that I desire." In that regard, he would come away from Guadalcanal with something much more precious than a Medal of Honor.[23]

Even those who were not completely won over by the Puller mystique had to concede that he had many positive virtues. The regimental communications officer's assessment was typical of this group: "I think Lewie was a fearless man. I don't think he had the slightest concept of what it was to be afraid of anything. I don't think he ever did anything he wouldn't have wanted his men to do, or expected them to do anything that he was not also willing to do; but he did a lot of damn fool things that shouldn't have been done. . . . There are a lot of things you had to like about the man. He was certainly a leader." Captain Kelly appraised his CO as "a gutsy little guy with a big heart." Although the acting battalion XO did not agree with all of Puller's field decisions, he readily admitted: "I learned a great deal from him about handling men and inspiring their loyalty." Vandegrift did not think much of Puller's academic skills or his attitude toward communications, but he readily granted that Chesty was "one of the best combat patrol officers I know."[24]

☆　☆　☆

The 7th Marines remained on the southern perimeter for more than a month. On Christmas Eve, the regiment was relieved by the Army's 35th Infantry. The Marines went into bivouac near Lunga Lagoon, their days on the island nearly over. The 1st and 5th Marines and division headquarters already had departed. On January 5, 1943, the 7th boarded the old president liners—*Hayes, Adams,* and *Jackson*—the same ships that had brought them to Guadalcanal. Getting aboard was no easy task, since everyone had to scale the tall sides of the ships via cargo nets. Many Marines and corpsmen were "just completely washed out" and needed help to complete the last steps of the journey. Although life on crowded transports was almost always uncomfortable or worse, this time was an exception. By comparison to their hellish lot of combat and deprivation on the island, it "was like going to heaven." When they arrived in Australia a few days later, Twining met them at the dock and "was shocked at their condition," until he remembered that he and the rest of the division had looked the same a month earlier.[25]

The 1st Battalion, 7th Marines had lost eighty-nine dead, 156 wounded, and three missing in action on Guadalcanal. Those figures would pale in the face of much higher casualty rates in shorter time spans in later campaigns in the Pacific, but they were severe nonetheless. The roll call of battles the battalion had fought was as long as that of any other unit in the division, and much longer than most. Puller was completely proud of what his outfit had accomplished. In later days, he would inscribe information about the campaign into the blank pages at the end of his favorite book. Among the entries was a listing of his casualties, as well as a comparison of awards received. He recorded that the entire regiment had earned a total of fifty-six medals and commendations, forty-five of which had gone to officers and men of 1/7. In writing to a friend, he expressed special pleasure in the Battle for Henderson Field, where his outfit "stopped and virtually destroyed one enemy regiment." (He also claimed, with less justification, that this was "more than any other Marine battalion has ever done in this or any other war." In a first sign of an emerging feeling that his accomplishments were not fully appreciated, he further noted: "No other battalion had an equal record although the two other battalions [of the 7th Marines] received far more publicity.")[26]

Puller's respect for the Japanese as a tough opponent remained intact: "They could live on nothing and they didn't mind dying. It was an honor to die for their country." But he knew that the Marines had proved themselves superior in a drawn-out campaign of attrition: "It was a wonderful victory. We just bled the Japanese Empire white." Vandegrift had an equally simple assessment of the struggle: "We needed combat to tell us how effective our training, our doctrine, and our weapons had been. We tested them against the enemy, and we found that they worked. From that moment in 1942, the tide turned, and the Japanese never again advanced."[27]

Platoon Sergeant Briggs did a much better job of capturing the essence of Guadalcanal in a diary entry written shortly after his arrival in Australia:

> The horror of Guadalcanal is over and done. Of course I can never forget it or describe it—blood, sudden death, drudgery, disease, insanity, heroism, toil, acute pain, hopelessness, a boy covered in blood and crying in great sobs, mounds of stinking dead humans, blankets of flies, fear, and lack of it, bad food, thirst, mud to sleep in, the whirring sound of a bomb coming down and its terrible

whumph, the peculiar ripping sound of naval artillery striking, a bayonet through a man's chest, a hand grenade blowing a man over backwards, a Jap Zero and two Grummans putting on a beautiful aesthetic show in the sky, so hard to realize they really mean it, naval gunfire at night, fox holes, mosquitoes, malaria, guts, beaten men, rows of crosses, a skeleton in the jungle, two-toed tracks, skulking gibbering yellow bastards, monkeys, smells, bamboo, barbed wire, tin cans, dirty clothes, machine gun fire like hail thudding the ground sideways, mangled trees, Jap writing, Jap bivouac areas, fresh stinking equipment. It would take days and millions of words, and then, what would you have. No man can tell another.[28]

12
"A Great Deal of Hard Work Ahead"
Interlude in the Rear
January–December 1943

Puller did not make the voyage to Australia with his battalion. On December 31, 1942, he received a radio dispatch ordering him to "proceed first available air transportation to Washington DC [and] report [to] MARCORPS [for] temporary duty period [of] two to three months." Chesty flew out the very next morning from Henderson Field. He kept his eyes fixed on Guadalcanal till it disappeared from view. It would not be his last glimpse of the fateful island.[1]

He arrived in Washington on Saturday, January 9, 1943. Virginia was on hand to greet him at the airport. He still bore the physical marks of the long campaign, but she found great "relief and satisfaction to see him whole and unbroken by the terrific strain." After a brief check-in at HQMC, they drove home to Saluda and Virginia McC. On Monday, Chesty phoned in a request for a week's leave. He passed the time relaxing and getting reacquainted with his wife and nearly three-year-old daughter. During one walk through the village, Lewis and Virginia stopped at the offices of the local newspaper and chatted with the editor. Puller was tight-lipped about where he had been and what he had done. His only reference to the conflict was that he intended to reside in Saluda once "the war was over and things were normal again." (After the Marine Corps ensured that he made the national news a few days later, Virginia remarked: "He is *so* retiring and a man of action, not words, that I was surprised at the acclaim he got.")[2]

Puller returned to headquarters on January 18. The Commandant's staff was now located in the pale-brick, four-story Navy Annex, one of several warehouse-like office buildings thrown up around the capital as the government expanded after the outbreak of the war. This one sat on high ground immediately adjacent to the south side of Arlington National Cemetery and overlooking the just completed Pentagon to the east. If General Holcomb and his assistants needed any reminder of the human cost of war, they merely had to look out their windows at the rows of headstones marching up the gentle slopes of the parklike burial ground.

There had been no hint in the original message regarding the reason for the trip, but it was tied all the way back to Puller's stint at Fort Benning. George Marshall, former assistant commandant of the Infantry School, was now a four-star general and chief of staff of the Army. In an effort to "secure the point of view of the fighting men in the Solomon Islands," he had sent Lieutenant Colonel Russell P. Reeder, Jr., from the War Department to glean what he could from Guadalcanal veterans. Reeder interviewed dozens of officers and men, including Chesty shortly after his release from the division hospital. The Army officer subsequently published their oftentimes conflicting opinions in a classified pamphlet titled *Fighting on Guadalcanal.*

Colonel Sims and Puller agreed on several points. The regimental commander advocated the value of big guns: "Don't spare your artillery. . . . Even if the target is not profitable, get artillery fire on it. They hate it." Chesty certainly would have seconded Sims's idea that "field manual knowledge is fine, but it is useless without common sense [which] is of greater value than all the words in the book." And Puller also was an adherent of Sims's emphasis on aggressiveness: "Try to get the Japs on the move. . . . When you let them get set, they are hard to get out. . . . If you make the mistake of 'milling around,' you will expend men's lives." Hanneken voiced a similar notion after noting that units sometimes failed to move forward in the face of fire. "We have got to get to the point where the men go ahead when ordered, and damn the hindmost. Corporals must be indoctrinated to overcome this, and all ranks have got to have the 'hate.' "

Puller did not hesitate to disagree with his commander, however, in a few fundamental areas. Sims emphasized the importance of communications, especially by wire, and the necessity for his subordinates to report information "at once." Chesty vigorously dissented: "To HELL with the telephone wire with advancing troops. We can't carry enough wire. We received an order: 'The advance will stop until the wire gets in.' THIS IS BACKWARDS! . . . The 'walky-talky' the Japs have operates. Why can't we have a similar one?" Puller also vented his displeasure with the employment and size of headquarters elements: "The staffs are twice as large as they should be. The regimental staff is too large. I have five staff officers in the battalion and I could get along with less. . . . In order to get a true picture of what is going on in this heavy country, I make my staff get up where the fighting is. This command post business will ruin the American Army and Marines if it isn't watched. . . . As soon as you set up a command post, all forward movement stops. . . . Your leaders have to be up front. . . . Calling back commanding officers to battalion and regimental CPs to say, 'How are things going?' is *awful*."

Chesty had little to say about equipment, except to argue briefly that the troops needed more shovels, a better grenade launcher, and the M-1 rifle. His sole comment on tactics involved battalion patrolling. In a clear reference to 1/7's first contact near the headwaters of the Matanikau (and perhaps to his Nicaraguan experience), he stated: "It is okay to say that an outfit cannot be surprised, but it is bound to happen in this type of warfare; so therefore, your outfits must know what to do when ambushed." His solution was simple. Move in column, with a machine gun platoon attached to each of the rifle companies, and the command element and 81mm mortars near the center. (He had not taken the heavy tubes on the Second Matanikau operation, so his interview with Reeder indicated he now realized their value even on patrol.) Each company would watch out for its own flanks. If contact occurred to the front, the lead company automatically deployed to the right of the trail, the middle company came up on its left, and the last company moved up into a reserve position while securing the rear of the battalion. "This is a time-tested and proven formation which works. If attacked from a flank, face and adjust."[3]

Marshall had been greatly pleased by Reeder's draft report and had ordered a million copies printed. The four-star general at least partially shared Chesty's distaste for "the staff type" and believed that the Army needed more "officers who know how to get soldiers out of the rain." He also apparently liked Puller's bold, aggressive, confident assertions. Marshall reputedly kept a black book throughout his career, in which he noted the qualities of all the officers with whom he came in contact. Those who had favorably impressed him had assumed important positions after he became the chief of staff in September 1939. If he did indeed check his rumored black book after poring over Reeder's pamphlet, he might have noted Chesty was a Benning graduate with a superior grade in instructional methods. In any case, just before Christmas, Marshall singled out Puller for an important mission. The chief of staff wanted the Marine lieutenant colonel and several other successful combat leaders to tour major Army training facilities in the States and tell the soldiers about Guadalcanal. Marshall's goal was to dispel the myth that the Japanese were invincible supermen who possessed some special ability to fight in the jungle. The request for Chesty's services went to HQMC, which promptly arranged his trip to the States.[4]

Marshall wanted to provide some guidance to the group before the tour began, but he was in Morocco at an Anglo-American summit. In the meantime, HQMC put Puller to work. The staff could make good use of a veteran of Guadalcanal, drawing on his experience to help formulate policy and trading on his increasing fame to garner favorable publicity. Chesty started with a day at the Army's Aberdeen Proving Ground in Maryland to evaluate the new weapons being tested. One was the carbine, which favorably impressed him.[5]

The director of public relations was equally quick to take advantage of Puller's reputation. He picked out a Marine combat correspondent's file story and issued it as a press release. The piece was short on facts about battles, but the author heaped praise on Puller from the opening words: "On Guadalcanal, where heroes are made, I have found a man whom many call 'the perfect soldier.' I picture my perfect soldier to be an inspiring leader of men, a 'fighting fool,' a kind and tolerant officer, and above all a fearless warrior. Fitting this picture to perfection is Lieutenant Colonel Lewis B. Puller." The story recounted highlights of his career and quoted those who served under him. Focusing on his habit of living simply, like his men, it cited him as "one of the most highly admired officers in the Marines."[6]

Newspapers made little use of the release, but it did attract reporters to a January 22 press conference. After two weeks of stateside food, Puller was rapidly filling out, and at least one correspondent thought he looked "tanned and rugged." But Chesty was still subdued in the spotlight; he spoke so quietly that *Newsweek* magazine later described him as "mild-mannered." In his unique Tidewater drawl, Puller provided the hard news reporters really wanted—a quick summary of the campaign and a snapshot of the current situation. In an unusual display of service unity, his account praised the quality of the Army's 164th Infantry, talked about the expansion of aviation forces on the island, and cited the naval battles of mid-November as the turning point. He also confidently asserted that the Japanese there "are through so far as a real fighting force is concerned." While events would soon prove him correct in that respect, he seriously underrated the enemy's determination to go down fighting: "As far as I can see, we will have no trouble in cleaning up the rest of them. It is possible that if we pocket them, they might even surrender." His remarks made headlines the next day, because they were "the most optimistic to come out of Guadalcanal" up to that point.[7]

A few days later, HQMC staff officers sat down individually with Vandegrift, Colonel Clifton B. Cates (former CO of the 1st Marines), and Puller to pick their brains for lessons about infantry organization and equipment. Chesty provided the most extensive comments of the three. Armaments were his prime focus. He favored reducing the weight of crew-served weapons and suggested means to do so. For individual arms, he preferred the BAR to the rifle and the carbine to the pistol, but considered the Reising submachine gun a piece of junk. When it came to ammunition, he observed that "it was remarkable how little was used" by the riflemen, though machine gunners often ran short. He had high praise for mortars, artillery, and the 37mm canister rounds, all of which had played such an important part in the Battle for Henderson Field. He acknowledged that friendly supporting arms occasionally had fallen on his own position, but "it is better to have a few shorts and some casualties rather than no artillery or mortars close enough to be of use." He recommended an increase in 105mm howitzers over 75mm pieces, as he "would rather have more heavy shells than a lot of light ones." He was enthusiastic about tanks, believing they had not been used "as much as the situation justifies" and "should be in the first wave" of the amphibious assault. Although some viewed jungle terrain as unsuitable for larger medium tanks, he felt they would work there. "I believe if tanks were used more, casualties would be less."

He had strong opinions about organization, too, although he believed the present battalion setup was generally good. He was in favor of the move already underway to expand the rifle squad from nine men to twelve. The battalion staff was "larger than needed, but should be retained to take care of casualties." He was much less charitable to the regiment and division: "Higher staffs are usually taking officers from companies who are urgently needed, for filling staffs to overstrength." Prodded about a move to adopt distinctive shoulder patches for the divisions and aircraft wings, he was emphatic: "No unit insignia is required. Marine is enough." Asked if he had any final comments, Chesty suggested that old China hands should be sprinkled through every unit going overseas: "Such men know how to handle the Japs."[8]

There was no way to gauge whether Puller's input into *Fighting on Guadalcanal* had any effect on subsequent combat performance, but he eventually would see with his own eyes that much of the Army disagreed on the subject of headquarters staffs and their employment. Chesty probably felt some satisfaction, though, when it came to his discussion of lessons learned at the Navy Annex. The director of Plans and Policies took them seriously and closely tracked them as they threaded their way through bureaucratic channels. Many would come into reality, because they represented the combat experience of Puller and many other leaders on Guadalcanal.[9]

☆　☆　☆

Marshall returned to the Pentagon in late January and his confidence-boosting road show got underway soon after with a series of presentations in the Washington area. Puller and the other officers in the group spent nearly ten days with the highest echelons of the Army. From there, he went on the road, following a schedule that dedicated about five days each to various schools and units. Chesty gave a typically blunt talk about Guadalcanal to large groups of officers and men. His favorite story was the fight in mid-October, when 1/7 and the 164th Infantry had turned much of an enemy division into piles of bodies. He described the opponent's strengths and weaknesses, but emphasized that the Japanese were no match for well-prepared Marines and soldiers: "Any American can lick three of them if you give them half a chance."[10]

At Leavenworth he caused a stir among the faculty when he reiterated his opinions that staffs were too large and stymied offensive spirit. In a talk to new second lieutenants in Quantico, he declared: "A good battalion commander didn't need a staff, he got out in front of his battalion and led it." He had expressed similar feelings on Guadalcanal. Twining, the consummate planner, recalled that he was often the butt of Chesty's disparaging comments about "paper shufflers" or "potted palms." Puller was not the only one concerned about the sometimes misplaced priorities of staff officers. Vandegrift had reacted to one edict issued from higher headquarters with the observation: "It shows a total lack of knowledge on personnel, and I think is a result of too much staff and not enough command duties in the past." Just a few years prior, Chesty had tried very hard to get to Leavenworth, the Army's citadel of staff education. His attitude had begun to change after his failure to receive one of the coveted school seats. His experience on Guadalcanal accelerated the transformation. It was the first time he had operated in combat under the close supervision of a higher-level staff and he had not liked the results.[11]

Chesty's straightforward narratives and his colorful manner of speaking connected with his audiences. A staffer on the War Production Board enthused over Puller's presentation there: "I have never seen such a stirring demonstration as the one the members of the Board's Operations Training Course recently tendered you. . . . If I were asked to tell which event of the week was the outstanding one, I would say Colonel Puller's talk about Guadalcanal." At the end of Chesty's whirlwind six-week tour of the country, Marshall sent him a note of thanks: "You were given a very heavy and tiring schedule but reports from every organization you visited indicate that your inspirational talks and first-hand information which you brought from actual combat with the Japanese has been of tremendous value in preparing our soldiers for the type of enemy they will soon face. Undoubtedly you have saved the lives of a good many soldiers and have given the veteran's touch to some of our training." The chief of staff sent a short letter to General Holcomb, too: "I wanted you to know of the very excellent impression that [Puller] has made on all of the officers with whom he has come in contact."[12]

☆   ☆   ☆

Puller returned to Saluda on March 16 for another week of leave. He was thoroughly enjoying the time with his family, and had even brought his wife and daughter up to Washington during his two weeks of duty there. They had to stay in a crowded hotel at his own expense, but he considered the cost and inconvenience unimportant. Although he was "most fortunate and thankful" for the opportunity to get to the States at all, the trip had its difficult moments. While in Washington, he and Virginia made a call of condolence on the widow of Major Rogers. She produced a box of cigars and explained that her husband had asked her to purchase them as a gift for the colonel, but Otho had died before she could send them. Now she insisted that Chesty take them. As he uncomfortably smoked one, Virginia was overcome by tears. She undoubtedly wept not only in shared grief with a fellow Marine wife, but also because it brought home that the same fate might yet befall her own husband. Puller had great sympathy for the families of the dead, though he realized there was little he could do to console them. At a minimum, he wrote a friend, he had made it his objective to ensure that the deeds of those who were lost were made known: "I would like for their families to have the glory (perhaps it would help)."[13]

Chesty's view of life in the States left him troubled. He wrote Dr. Smith: "My impression of the home front was about the same as yours. . . . I am unable to understand the necessity of playing the political game at this time; I suppose it is necessary in a democracy. Oh well, we will bungle through and win, with the help of Almighty God. . . . I trust that our leaders will be able to arrange a lasting peace." Virginia took on the same attitude and was reduced to wishing that stories of heroism and hardship overseas would soon "arouse a greater interest for the war effort on our home front." Puller also was beginning to feel out of place in his own country. He explained to an old friend that he had spent so much of his life overseas, the trip to the United States left him with the sense that he was "near to being a foreigner." On January 23, he boarded a plane and started the long trek back to the Pacific and the 7th Marines.[14]

☆　☆　☆

The suffering of the 1st Marine Division had not ended entirely upon its withdrawal from Guadalcanal. The first stop for the exhausted officers and men was Camp Cable, about twenty-five miles south of Brisbane, a city roughly in the center of Australia's east coast. The marshy terrain, hot, rainy weather, and lack of transportation to town for liberty conspired to keep everyone miserable. Malaria also continued to stalk the ranks, with more than a hundred cases reporting to the hospital each day. Vandegrift pleaded with General Douglas MacArthur's Southwest Pacific Area for a shift to a better clime and place, but the theater headquarters initially turned a deaf ear. The local civilian authorities finally weighed in with their worry that mosquitoes feeding on the heroes of Guadalcanal soon would infect the population. In Vandegrift's words, that "really put the fear of God into this General Staff crowd." By mid-January 1943, the 1st Marine Division was ensconced around Melbourne in the cooler latitudes of southeast Australia.[15]

The only drawback to the new location was the wide dispersion of the command. The division headquarters and the 1st Marines were billeted in Melbourne proper, the 11th Marines were thirty miles to the west at Ballarat, and the 5th Marines were thirty miles to the south at Balcombe, with the 7th Marines nearby at Mt. Martha. The 5th and 7th at least bordered Port Phillip Bay, which gave them ready access to sites for amphibious training. They also were in the midst of a prewar seaside resort area, which meant transportation links to all the diversions that a metropolis of a million people had to offer. Although Australia had been at war for more than three years and rationing of just about everything was strict, the population went all out to welcome the troops that had helped turn back the threat of a Japanese invasion. For the first two months there was ample time to enjoy life in a rear area, since the division's emphasis was on rest and recovery. As the weeks passed, men slowly recuperated from the ravages of malaria and regained weight. If Guadalcanal had been hell, Melbourne now seemed almost like heaven.[16]

Puller was not quite so happy when he arrived in Australia on April 5. Not only was home far away again, he also discovered that he had lost command of his battalion several weeks before. Worse still, he had become the regimental operations officer. Given his recent strong expressions about staff duty, the change in billets must have come as quite a blow. He had little time to feel sorry for himself, though, as training was back in full swing throughout the division and it was his job to coordinate all that went on in his regiment.[17]

Chesty had barely begun to tackle his new assignment when the telltale chills and fever of malaria laid him low. The symptoms had appeared as he was flying to Australia. They came on strong on April 11 and he was forced to turn himself in sick. He explained to the doctor that he had fallen out of the habit of taking his regular dose of Atabrine back in the States. It was a foolish thing to do, since a mid-February test at Fort Benning had confirmed the presence of the parasites in his blood. Now he paid the price with a three-week stay in the hospital. Puller, alone among his compatriots in the officers ward, liked the food there, but he was still anxious to leave. At Chesty's insistence, the doctors released him to duty on May 1.[18]

Just a few days later, Puller found himself elevated to be executive officer of the 7th Marines, a billet much more to his liking. Although his primary duty was supervising the regimental staff, he also was the second-in-command and could spend time out in the field observing the battalions in action. Puller naturally gravitated to the latter activity, which intensified as replacements and the recovered sick and wounded fleshed out the ranks. With the bloody experience of combat behind them, the leaders of the division fashioned a training regimen that dwarfed anything they had attempted prior to Guadalcanal. There were frequent battalion and regimental field exercises, often involving live ammunition for every weapon in the unit. As the Southern Hemisphere fall turned to winter, overhead artillery fire was added to the mix, along with night problems. Chesty could not completely sever his understandable sentimental attachment to 1/7 and freely admitted: "I spend all of my spare time with the old battalion." In his mind, it was still "not only the first of the regiment, but also the first of the division."[19]

Puller's new responsibility for staff work did not alter his conviction that its importance was overrated. He rarely visited the tin shack that served as the regimental headquarters. Staff officers soon learned to take their concerns straight to Sims, and the commanding officer seemed to tolerate Chesty's narrow view of the duties of an XO. (Sims was less forbearing when it came time to write Puller's fitness report. He gave the lieutenant colonel all "outstanding" and "excellent" marks, save for administrative duties, where he rated his subordinate "very good," a mediocre grade in the hierarchy of the time.)[20]

☆ ☆ ☆

During June and July 1943, the leadership of the division underwent a significant change. General Vandegrift, slated to replace Holcomb as the Commandant later in the year, transferred to New Caledonia to take temporary command of a corps. He took with him most of his senior staff officers, to include Thomas and Twining. Newly promoted Major

General Rupertus fleeted up from ADC to command the 1st Marine Division. Sims moved up to become his chief of staff, and Frisbie returned to 7th Marines as its new commander. Hanneken, now a colonel, already had left the 7th to become the CO of division special troops. Lieutenant Colonel Odell M. Conoley, Hanneken's old XO, had taken over 2/7. John Weber (Puller's temporary replacement after Koli Point) now had 1/7. The only billet holdover was Lieutenant Colonel William Williams, the former regimental operations officer, who had received command of 3/7 on Guadalcanal. Merritt Edson departed to become the chief of staff of the 2d Marine Division; he was replaced as CO of the 5th Marines by Colonel John T. Selden. Bill Whaling had taken command of the 1st Marines.

It was a rather thorough change of places, if not faces. Certainly the most important shift came at the very top, since Rupertus bore little resemblance to his predecessor. Vandegrift was the archetypical Southern gentleman, gracious and reserved at all times. The new division commander was emotional, snobbish, and vain. Vandegrift first experienced combat as a lieutenant. Rupertus had never been in a battle until this war and had not distinguished himself during the recent long campaign. He had commanded the forces responsible for seizing Tulagi and Gavutu-Tanambogo on August 7–8, 1942, but throughout the bitter fighting on those islands, he had remained afloat. During Vandegrift's absence from Guadalcanal at the time of the Battle for Henderson Field, and again in early November when Rupertus was commander of the forces around Koli Point, the brigadier had been forced to retire to the hospital with dengue fever.

Most important, Vandegrift had a reputation for looking out for the welfare of his men and for believing in "loyalty down [the chain of command]." Bob Heinl (Puller-trained at the Basic School) had served under Rupertus just prior to the war and discovered: "[He] was certainly not a hero to his own valet or to his own officers. He was an officer of little—if any—loyalty downward and intense loyalty upward." Heinl thought Rupertus combined "limitless ambition" with "the most limited professional attainments." He had thrived in the Corps because he "carried off the externals of soldiering very creditably and looked like a great professional soldier," and also was "one of the master politicians in the Marine Corps and in his dealings with the Navy." Rupertus benefited as well from Vandegrift's uneven ability to judge character and competence. The two had served together several times and Vande-grift mistakenly considered his protégé and close friend one of the "finest officers" in the Corps.[21]

Many veterans in the 7th Marines were glad to see Sims move up to Rupertus's staff. An officer in 2/7 thought: "Our colonel was bucking for brigadier general, so we suffered. Our outfit did more training, more boondocking [slang for field work], more parading, and had less liberty than any other outfit in the division." A story had made the rounds that Sims had rejected his staff's request for athletic equipment with the contemptuous remark: "My boys will get their recreation crawling on their bellies." (Sims may not have been the source of all the hardships. Puller later would take responsibility for having the troops sleep out-doors at the rifle range, since he believed it would keep them toughened up.) Not everyone considered Frisbie an improvement, though. One of-ficer found him "profane, arrogant, obtuse, obnoxious, a screamer, hollerer, shouter, just a terrible leader of men." A division staff officer concurred that the new commander of the 7th Marines was a "brutish and bullying CO." Puller acknowledged his superior's ill temper, but downplayed it: "His bark's worse than his bite." Personality aside, no one questioned Frisbie's tactical proficiency, and he was "single-minded" in his pursuit of an objective. His nickname—"Bull"—perfectly fit him.[22]

Everyone welcomed one fresh addition to the division. Brigadier General Lemuel C. Shepherd, the new ADC, was another courtly Virgin-ian, like Vandegrift. He hailed from the Tidewater city of Norfolk and had graduated from VMI in 1917. As a young officer in World War I, he had fought with the 4th Marine Brigade, suffered three wounds (two of them serious), and received a Navy Cross, a Distinguished Service Cross, a Silver Star, and the French Croix de Guerre. He had spent much of the interwar period on sea and foreign duty. Following a stint forming the 9th Marines at Camp Pendleton, he earned his first star and orders to Australia. He had a well-deserved reputation as an outstanding field commander who understood tactics and combat leadership. Like Puller, he was noted for spending time in the front lines with his troops and for-going the perquisites of high rank in the field.[23]

Nothing occurred in Australia to alter the reputation Chesty had built up. The troops still revered him and junior officers still trod care-fully in his presence. One sergeant recalled being summoned to Puller's office late in the evening. The NCO was new to the regiment and as-

sumed a visit to the executive officer could bode only ill. Much to the
Marine's surprise, Puller said: "You have a phone call from a lady, old
man. I'll just step outside and smoke my pipe while you talk." The sergeant was even more relieved when the unexpected conversation with
his Australian girlfriend was complete and Chesty merely inquired if all
was well, instead of chiding him for the disturbance.

It was widely known, however, that the colonel "had no use for second lieutenants" and he occasionally still treated novice officers in a
peremptory manner. One lieutenant had fallen in at the end of the line at
the post exchange and just finally worked his way to the front when
Chesty appeared on the scene. In the mistaken belief that the young officer had walked up to the head of the line, the colonel loudly ordered
him to the rear. Another lieutenant suffered through a public scolding
when he called his resting troops to attention as Puller approached. At
other times, Chesty's attitude was more like that of a father amused at
the clumsiness of an ungainly child. A platoon commander in 2/7 remembered his first inspection, where he nervously tried to present his
carbine to the regimental XO for examination instead of rendering the
required salute and report. Puller merely smiled and said, "Having trouble, Lieutenant?" Captain Joseph Sasser, a veteran of Guadalcanal,
thought Chesty had "mellowed a little" in Australia, though that simply
may have been a sign of the XO's respect for those who had gone
through the crucible with him.[24]

Puller had no need for additional awards to confirm his bravery, but
one came in the middle of 1943—a star in lieu of his third Navy Cross,
for his actions during the Battle for Henderson Field. Many years later
he would argue that medals were given out too easily, but at the time he
was justifiably proud of the accolades. He also wanted the record to fully
reflect what he and his outfit had accomplished. After reading the 7th
Marines Guadalcanal after-action report, he drafted a long letter to correct errors that did not do "justice to the 1st Battalion, 7th Marines,
A Company thereof, and myself." In a similar vein, he had been quick to
ensure that the division commendation for that battle was made a part of
his personnel record. He was equally ready to look out for the interests
of courageous junior Marines. When he discovered in July 1943 that
Corporal Smolka (the signalman who had helped him at Second
Matanikau) had received no recognition, he submitted a recommendation for a Navy Cross. One officer remarked in a letter: "They are passing out the decorations and citations again as only Louie can do it."[25]

The third Navy Cross again placed Puller's name in the newspapers at home. He received additional publicity when 1/7's former surgeon, Dr. Smith, published an article on Guadalcanal in *Harper's,* a leading national magazine. The battalion commander was not the focus of the piece, but it quietly lauded his courage. The decorations and the renown were well deserved. Colonel Sims did not like Chesty's staff work, but his departing fitness report had captured his subordinate's true value: "One of the best combat officers in the service."[26]

The increasing acclaim did not appear to affect Puller in any significant way. While some of the major heroes of Guadalcanal succumbed to the flattery of Melbourne society, Chesty seemed to keep his feet firmly planted on the ground. When officers were given permission to censor their own outgoing mail for the first time, he insisted that the regimental intelligence section continue to review his. The captain who glanced through Puller's correspondence noted that nearly all of it went to his wife and they "were the most sensitive loving letters that one could imagine." Chesty's occasional brief notes to other family members or friends were always thoughtful, sincere, and empty of conceit or boasting. In one letter, he apologized for not being able to say goodbye before heading back to the Pacific: "Of my aunts, you were always more like my Mother and I regret that during the years since her death, I have been unable to see more of you." Tom Pullen, the old friend from 3d OTC, wrote when he saw Puller's name in the papers. Chesty's reply never mentioned his own achievements, but applauded Pullen's career as an educator: "I was delighted to hear from you and to learn that you have made a success of life; to my way of thinking the future of our country depends largely on our public schools. As for me, I have been a Marine all these years and have a lovely wife and daughter."[27]

☆ ☆ ☆

The quiet interlude in Australia was rapidly coming to an end. Throughout 1943, Allied forces were steadily pushing back the Japanese in the Solomons and New Guinea. Now it was time to pull the noose tight and finally strangle the enemy sea and air bastion at Rabaul, at the eastern end of the large island of New Britain. Since June, the 1st Marine Division staff had been planning the next operation, scheduled to commence in late December 1943 against the western end of New Britain. To acclimatize the assault troops and move them closer to the objective, MacArthur's headquarters decided in August to shift Rupertus's command to New Guinea. Since the theater command envisioned employing the Marines in three discrete groups, the division would be parceled out to three widely separated staging bases. The 1st Marine Division created three independent combat teams, each one composed of an infantry regiment and a slice of all supporting units. Division headquarters and Combat Team B (built around the 1st Marines) were destined for Goodenough Island. Combat Team A (the 5th Marines and attachments) were headed for Milne Bay. The 7th Marines were joined by two battalions of artillery, a battalion of engineers, more than a company of tanks, and other elements to form Combat Team C, which would end up at Oro Bay. Frisbie and Puller now were in charge of nearly six thousand men.

The first echelon of Frisbie's force departed Australia on September 19 and arrived in Oro Bay on October 2. Puller and the remainder of the combat team, as well as much of the rest of the division, sailed on September 27. For most of the men, it would be their last look at Melbourne, which the division had appropriately code-named "Hospitable." The staff historian in the 1st Marines waxed eloquent at the parting: "Our regiment's leaving Melbourne could be compared to a bridegroom's leaving his newly acquired wife after a pleasant honeymoon—full of memories of a new grasp on life and of a determination to perform the task facing him better than ever before." An officer in the 7th Marines laconically noted in his account: "The holiday was over." Apparently one member of the 1st Marines (or perhaps an Australian friend) was not quite ready for it to end; an anonymous telephone call reporting that two ships were going to blow up had brought a temporary halt to loading operations the day before.[28]

Puller was aboard the USAT *Both,* which sailed north with eight other Liberty ships. The convoy put in to the northern Australian city of Townsville for a day on October 4, before passing through the Great Barrier Reef and crossing the Coral Sea. Six vessels broke off for Goodenough Island and Milne Bay. The *Both* and two companions arrived at Oro Bay on the 9th. They were greeted by a Japanese air raid. The combat team sustained no losses, but an Army engineer unit already in the area suffered casualties of seven dead and six wounded. The period of rest and recuperation definitely was over and they were back in the war zone.

The troops spent their first several days in New Guinea unloading

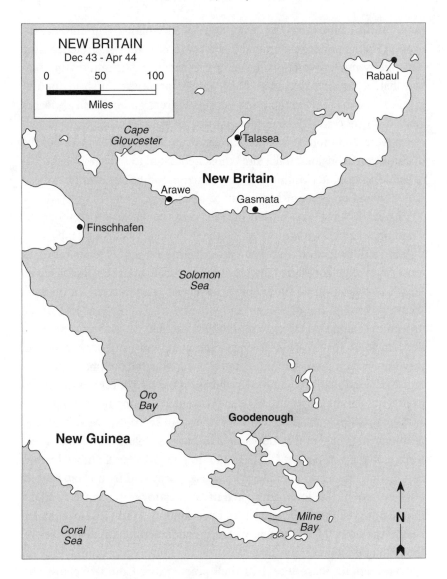

the ships and moving their gear to the Samboga Staging Area. There, at a dogleg in the coast called Cape Sudest, the Samboga River spilled into the Solomon Sea. Just a few miles to the northeast were the villages of Buna and Gona, the scene of a three-month siege lasting from November 1942 till January 1943. Two divisions of Allied troops had starved and blasted the enemy out of existence, suffering greater casualties than the Japanese in the process. Nightmare terrain had complicated that campaign. A coastal plain roughly ten miles wide separated

the foothills of the towering Owen Stanley Mountains from the sea. Elevation in this flat area averaged just a few feet, and vast stretches were
covered by mangrove-choked swamps, especially during the rainy season that began in November. Thick jungle occupied much of the dry
ground. The average temperature was 96 degrees and humidity hovered
around 85 percent. Malaria, dengue, and a host of other tropical diseases were common. It was an altogether unwholesome place, but the
division staff considered the site "most beneficial to the troops as it was
possible to conduct training under climatic conditions similar to that
which would be encountered in future operations."[29]

Frisbie's force was settled into its new tent camp on October 17.
Training resumed with a five-mile hike, followed by classes on bayonet
fighting and tropical living. Thereafter the program grew even more intense than that conducted in Australia. Forced marches increased in
length to twenty-three miles. Field problems ranged from the platoon
level up through the regiment, and stressed every likely aspect of the
upcoming campaign, from tank/infantry tactics, to river crossings, to
the attack of fortifications. When companies and platoons were out
training on their own, senior headquarters conducted command post exercises. Division placed heavy emphasis on the rare opportunities it had
to practice landing operations, since it would be using new equipment.
American shipyards were just beginning to turn out a wealth of amphibious shipping in a wide variety of classes, many of them entirely
foreign to the veterans of Guadalcanal. In late October, Combat Team C
had its one chance to exercise with vessels provided by a Navy mobile
training group. The force embarked in fast destroyer transports (APDs),
tank landing ships (LSTs), and infantry landing craft (LCIs). It sailed
east to the tip of New Guinea, where it conducted landing exercises on
the 28th and again on the 31st.

Throughout these weeks of final preparation, Combat Team C focused on rapid exploitation following the initial landing. Unit training
emphasized "speed of movement in offensive action, the coordinated
employment of supporting weapons in the attack, and assault techniques against well dug-in enemy positions." The regimental command
post exercises concentrated on "offensive tactics following landing on a
hostile shore." The operation order for the final training exercise downplayed a traditional control measure: "Phase lines will be used merely
to indicate relative positions of unit concerned. Units will not halt and

reorganize on them." This stress on swift offensive action may have given rise to the code name for Frisbie's outfit, the Greyhound Group. Chesty was pleased by the emphasis on aggressiveness; he was only too happy to go immediately for the enemy's jugular. He also still had a distinct distaste for staff work. When the regimental operations officer brought the final draft of the order for the actual assault, Chesty declined to read it over before it went in for the colonel's approval.[30]

On December 9, 1943, senior leaders briefed the units on the forthcoming invasion of New Britain. A few days later, Frisbie's force conducted its culminating training event. The entire combat team staged on a beach in groups, each equivalent to the load for one ship involved in the assault. At the appropriate times after H-Hour, the units "landed" and executed their assigned missions for D-Day. Combat Team C was primed for action. The Japanese even had obliged with small air raids every few days throughout October and November to add to the realism of the outfit's preparations. The other combat teams were equally ready. There was only one shortcoming—the 1st Marine Division had not operated in the field as a unit either in Australia or in New Guinea. It would come together, for the first time in nearly a year, on the field of battle.[31]

Combat Team C received one last-minute addition to its numbers. Major Ray Davis, a Puller trainee from the Basic School in the 1930s, was now commander of the 1st Special Weapons Battalion. Since his batteries were parceled out to the regiments, he was slated to remain behind with the rear echelon. Davis approached Chesty and explained that the weapons battalion would need its commander in combat, that he could do a great deal to support his troops even if he no longer was formally responsible for the detached batteries. The major was not disappointed by Puller's reply: "I'll tell you, old man, anybody who wants to go to war, they can go as far as I'm concerned." A few minutes later Davis was on the roster and on his way.[32]

☆   ☆   ☆

D-Day for the pending operation was December 26, 1943. Early in the month, Puller wrote two holiday letters to his wife. One contained a check, with the firm command that it was for her to buy a gift for herself "and NOTHING ELSE." He also noted with relief that she had finally acceded to his wishes and hired a servant to relieve her and her mother of some household chores. He never mentioned his own situation, instead presenting his usual sentimental side: "Merry Christmas! Do not be sad; just think of those to come when we will be together and completely happy. I can picture you all at Evanslea [Virginia's family home] and I am with you in spirit. Kiss Virginia McC for me. I love you, Virginia, and I always have and I always will. . . . If I could only be with you all at Evanslea that day! Having you with me is all the happiness that I will ever desire." He expressed a similar objective, but with somewhat less confidence, to an old friend: "When this war is finally won, if I am alive, I will be more than satisfied to retire and sit on the front porch of our home in Middlesex County." But he knew that goal was a long way off: "There is a great deal of hard work ahead of us here." For Chesty and the rest of the 1st Marine Division, the holiday season would bring precious little peace as they toiled in the very front lines of the war effort.[33]

13

"Directing the Attack from Forward"
Cape Gloucester
December 1943–February 1944

The 7th Marines and the remainder of Combat Team C finished loading aboard amphibious shipping at Cape Sudest on the afternoon of December 24, 1943, and sailed before dawn the next morning. Puller and part of the regimental command group were aboard LST 67. The tropic heat hardly made it seem like Christmas and the discomfort of the troops was increased by the conscious choice of planners to fill the ships beyond their designed capacity. The convoy of small vessels, escorted by six destroyers, did not look like a major invasion fleet. The covering and bombardment force of eleven cruisers moved toward New Britain by its own route; there were no battleships or carriers.

☆ ☆ ☆

The 1st Marine Division's assault on New Britain had its genesis in Cartwheel, the plan to isolate and bypass the Japanese bastion at Rabaul, at the eastern tip of the island. A key part of the final version of Cartwheel was the capture of two airfields located 350 miles to the west on the opposite end of New Britain, at a place called Cape Gloucester. A less important piece of the operation involved the seizure of the small peninsula of Arawe, on the south-central coast of the island. General MacArthur selected Lieutenant General Walter Krueger's Alamo Force to command ground operations. The Arawe mission, scheduled for December 15, eventually went to an Army regiment. That last-minute de-

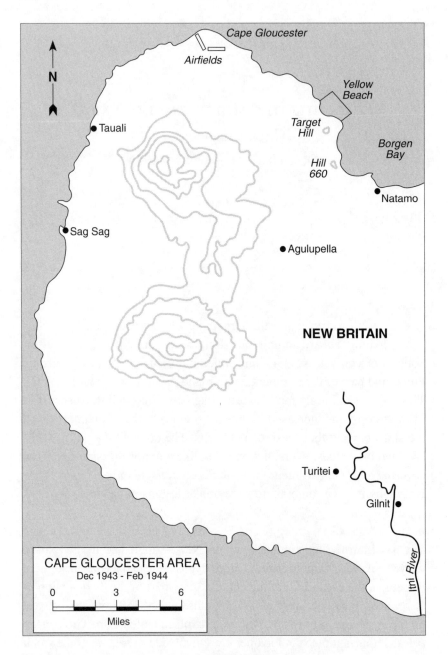

cision allowed the 1st Marine Division to concentrate on the cape.
Combat Team C would seize the beachhead. Two thirds of Combat
Team B (1st Marines) would follow Frisbie's force ashore and spear-
head the assault against the airdrome. The remaining battalion of the 1st

Marines would land to the southwest of the cape and block any counterattack from that direction. Combat Team A (5th Marines) served as the division reserve.

The landing force depended heavily on Army land-based aviation for fire support. Pre–D-Day preparation fires consisted entirely of almost daily aerial attacks during November and December. Although these constituted the heaviest bombing raids up to that point in the Pacific war, the Marines were not about to rely solely on airpower. Just prior to the landing, cruisers and destroyers would bombard the objective for ninety minutes, while Army bombers and fighters made their final attacks. Given the bloody lesson of Tarawa just the prior month, that was shockingly little, but the division planners were placing much of their faith in their selection of a landing site. They had bypassed suitable beaches nearer the airfields in favor of a stretch of sand seven miles to the southeast at Silimati Point, now dubbed Yellow Beach. They expected very few defenders at that out-of-the-way location.[1]

☆   ☆   ☆

Shortly after 0745 on December 26, with bright, clear skies marred only by the drifting smoke of bombs and shells, the 1st and 3d Battalions of the 7th Marines stormed ashore. They met no resistance and soon learned why. The narrow beach was backed by a thin strip of dense jungle. Beyond that was a wide area marked "damp flats" on the maps. The intelligence experts had realized this was the monsoon season, but they also expected the terrain would "absorb this excess rainfall rather well." The surprised infantrymen encountered a swamp that was neck deep in many places. To make matters worse, the pre-landing bombardment had created numerous underwater holes, felled many trees, and left others tottering precariously. The Japanese, well aware of the morass, were astonished that the Americans would choose to land there.[2]

The Marines slowly worked their way through the obstacles created by nature and friendly fire. They encountered their first Japanese on the flanks. As Puller's old battalion advanced to the east, it destroyed a small force and two field guns. Before noon, 1/7 had seized Target Hill, the dominating feature in the area. To the west, elements of 3/7 received only some long-range machine gun fire. By 0845 the 2d Battalion was ashore and moving forward to take the center of the regimental zone.

Frisbie, Puller, and the command group landed at that time and took charge of a situation that was already well in hand.[3]

Rupertus, one of the few senior officers in the division to miss the most intense fighting on Guadalcanal, misread the lack of opposition. He believed that the short bombardment had forced a regiment of Japanese to retreat. Despite the absence of bodies, he felt that "they undoubtedly lost a lot of their men due to this heavy fire." His misplaced faith in the efficacy of preparatory fire would come back to haunt the division nine months later at a place called Peleliu. Puller and others, somewhat wiser for their sufferings at the hands of Japanese air and naval forces, realized that the most they could count on was forcing the enemy to keep their heads down.[4]

A large Japanese air attack sank one ship and damaged three others, but did not prevent the fleet from placing eleven thousand men ashore on D-Day. The division's tracked landing vehicles proved invaluable in moving supplies and artillery across the swamp to relatively dry terrain. By dusk the 7th Marines had secured a perimeter nine hundred yards deep and more than a mile wide, with the front lines mostly resting on solid ground. Two battalions of the 1st Marines had landed behind the 7th and made good progress in their attack to the west to seize the airfields. Many of the division's casualties—twenty-one killed and twenty-three wounded—came as Whaling's regiment fought through a small bunker complex astride the coastal track. That night, a Japanese battalion launched a counterattack, concentrating on 2/7 in the center. In the midst of a "terrific" rainstorm and "pitch blackness," Puller organized headquarters personnel and men from an attached antitank battery to carry ammunition across the swamp and reinforce the front lines as riflemen. Not long after dawn the enemy withdrew, leaving roughly two hundred dead on the field.[5]

The 7th Marines slightly expanded and strengthened the perimeter over the next two days, while the 2d Battalion fought off additional probes by the same Japanese unit. With all three battalions and the regimental weapons company in the lines, Frisbie's entire reserve consisted of about three dozen men from the replacement pool. The colonel seemed to give an unusually large role to his executive officer. Puller was frequently at the front, directing the shifting of the reserve platoon and other units to meet each enemy attack. On the morning of December 30, Army aircraft bombed and strafed beyond the perimeter. Since the Japanese attacks did not recur after Puller's first brush with friendly close air support, he felt it was "very good." Frisbie's regiment lost eighteen killed, fifty-eight wounded, and three missing during this first seventy-two hours of the campaign.[6]

Two battalions of the 5th Marines came ashore on December 29 and reinforced 1/1 and 3/1 in the drive toward the airfields. Using excellent tank-infantry tactics, they systematically cleared a reinforced battalion of Japanese from successive lines of bunkers blocking the coastal road. By the morning of December 30 the Marines had complete possession of both landing strips and the low ridges around them. Rupertus sent a boasting situation report to his commander: "First Marine Division presents to you as an early New Year gift the complete airdrome of Cape Gloucester. . . . Rupertus grinning to Krueger." Informed of the successful seizure of the objective, MacArthur forwarded congratulations to his field force in his typically grandiose manner: "Your gallant division has maintained the immortal record of the Marine Corps and covered itself with glory."[7]

The 1st Marine Division was now divided between two widely separated perimeters along the coast of Cape Gloucester. In recognition of this situation, Rupertus gave his ADC command over forces at the original landing site. Shepherd received reinforcements before the last day of the year when Lieutenant Colonel David S. McDougal's 3/5 joined the enclave and became his reserve. Major General Iwao Matsuda, the Japanese commander in western New Britain, was making his own dispositions for the next phase. He ordered one of his two remaining infantry battalions to march overland from the Gilnit area and deal with the Marines at Silimati Point. Beginning on December 28, patrols from the 7th Marines observed the enemy digging in opposite the 2d Battalion. Five Marines saw a wounded Japanese soldier and tried to capture him, but walked into an ambush. The one man who escaped the trap reported that the others were clubbed and bayoneted to death. Although intelligence personnel continued to emphasize the need to take prisoners to gain information, this incident reinforced the average infantryman's reluctance to take risks with an opponent reputed to be treacherous. Puller had his own close call on the night of December 30 when a Japanese air raid scored a lucky hit on the 7th Marines CP, killing four and wounding seven.

Rupertus directed his ADC to expand the Yellow Beach perimeter

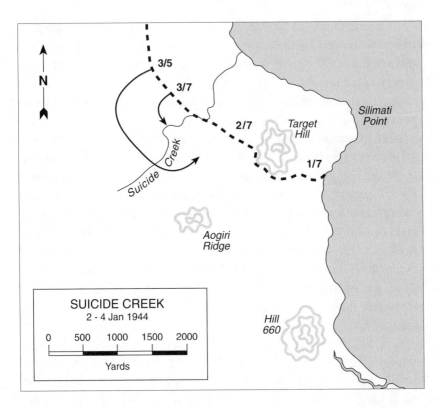

and Shepherd issued orders for an attack to commence on January 2. His scheme of maneuver was highly unusual but promised to be equally effective. Instead of launching 2/7 in a frontal attack against the identified Japanese position, he planned to have 3/7 and 3/5 swing like a gate, with the right end of 2/7's line as the hinge. When the two 3d Battalions were perpendicular to 2/7's south-facing line, they would advance abreast to the east with the men of 2/7 supporting the attack by fire. In theory this roundhouse punch would strike the Japanese in the flank and rear. Luckily for the Marines, they would have the benefit of three straight days of remarkably dry weather to conduct this offensive.

As always happens in war, even the best-laid plans do not survive the opening shots. During the morning of January 2, 3/7 successfully made the sweeping turn, but instead of a dangling enemy flank the Marines ran into a steeply banked stream parallel to their front. As the leading squads began to ford it, the thick jungle erupted with fire from rifles, machine guns, and mortars. The Japanese, seemingly prepared for the Marine maneuver, were deeply burrowed behind the natural moat in well-camouflaged bunkers hid among the extensive root systems of large trees. In the midst of the dense, dark foliage the attacking riflemen could not even find targets to return fire. While 3/7 tried to inch forward, 3/5 was encountering its own difficulties. From the outset of the advance, it had struggled to keep pace on the outer edge of the swinging gate and a gap had developed between the two battalions. McDougal's outfit finally gained the stream after 1500, crossed it, and soon made contact with the enemy, but not with 3/7.

Puller spent the early afternoon arranging for half-tracks to support 3/7 and joining King Company on the battalion's right flank to spur them on. He returned to the regimental CP at 1330. The vehicles arrived, but could not cross the ravine. Their 75mm guns, firing as blindly as the infantry, also seemed to make no impression on the Japanese. The commander of King reported he had tied in with 3/5, but McDougal insisted his left still hung in the air. Late in the afternoon Shepherd visited the 7th Marines command post. Perhaps feeling a bit of pressure with the general looking over his shoulder, within ten minutes Frisbie dispatched Puller to 3/7 "with orders to continue the attack immediately." Barely an hour later the executive officer relieved the King commander, probably as much for his inaccurate reporting as for his failure to advance. Since Puller took that drastic action without seeking input from the colonel, it revealed a lot about Chesty's wide authority in the regiment. While the XO was dealing with the right flank, Frisbie was trying to remedy another gap that had opened between his 2d and 3d Battalions at the hinge. He ended up covering the hole with fire from the regimental weapons company. Before darkness fell, part of King had reached the far bank, but most of 3/7 dug in on the west edge of the stream. McDougal's battalion, still without physical contact, established a perimeter defense on the eastern side. Lieutenant Colonel William Williams, the CO of 3/7, reported that he had lost eighty-eight men. His Marines quickly dubbed the vexing obstacle "Suicide Creek."[8]

For January 3, Shepherd's plan was a miniature version of the previous day's effort. McDougal's battalion would pivot on its left and attack to the northeast in an attempt to get behind the flank of this new Japanese position. The enemy had prepared hasty positions during the night, however, and resistance increased with each yard. Williams's battalion made some slow progress, with the rest of King and the right flank of Love reaching the far bank. Now that 3/7 was firmly established there, Frisbie ordered 3/5 to bear left to establish contact. He was still not satisfied with the rate of advance and at mid-morning again sent Puller to King Company "to get them moving forward." Problems also were arising as a result of the converging attack—McDougal's battalion was now pushing directly toward the front lines of 2/7 barely a thousand yards away. Mortar rounds from 3/5 began to strike in the 2d Battalion's front lines and artillery observers were reluctant to fire into the constricted battlefield.[9]

Williams had been asking for tank support since noon on January 2 and the engineers were rapidly building a corduroy road through the swamp to get them there. Puller thought the armor could get across the creek near the right flank of 3/7. Frisbie directed the Shermans to go there. The banks were too steep, though, and Puller called for engineers to make a crossing. The first two bulldozer operators to attempt it were shot, but the third finally completed the task. By then darkness had arrived and the Marines went into the defense. The remainder of 3/7 had fought its way to the east side during the afternoon and King Company was now in sight of 3/5's left flank. The 7th Marines had lost eighty-seven men that day (most of them in 3/7), while 3/5 had suffered fifty-eight casualties. Puller now was remaining continuously with Williams's battalion. The regimental journal clerk noted around noon that the XO was "directing the attack from forward."[10]

That evening Frisbie telephoned orders for the next day to his subordinate commanders. He also dispatched a senior staff officer to each battalion to "coordinate" the execution of the plan. Puller filled that task for 3/7. The scheme called for Williams to hold King Company's portion of the front with machine guns and mass that unit behind the armored thrust going in between 3/7 and 3/5. The attack kicked off at 0800 on January 4 after a fifteen-minute artillery barrage into the pocket confined by the U-shaped Marine lines. Not long after, the Shermans reached the front lines and quickly disposed of three bunkers with point-blank cannon fire. With that, resistance crumbled and the Marines gained ground rapidly. (A U.S. Army colonel observing the Marines would note the enemy's fear of American armor: "I am convinced that the medium tank is not only usable in jungle warfare, but one of the most effective offensive weapons obtainable." That confirmed Puller's faith in armor, expressed at HQMC a few months earlier.) By 1330 3/7 had come abreast of 1/7's lines, reaching the original objective set for the operation.[11]

As Williams waited for 3/5 to catch up for a coordinated continuation of the offensive, Frisbie told him that he was relieved of command and that Puller would temporarily replace him. The regimental commander cited "lack of aggressiveness in the previous attack" for his action. Shortly afterward he informed Shepherd and Rupertus of the change. In the course of the evening the battalion advanced against little opposition until it was just forward of Target Hill, where it dug in. As the company commanders huddled in a meeting with Puller, a resupply amtrac appeared. One of the crewmen presented a container of hot coffee to the new battalion CO, with the compliments of the mess officer. Puller flew into a rage: "If that S.O.B. can get that up here to me, he can get a hot meal up to these troops!" He passed the can to a nearby group of enlisted men and backed up his tirade with a message to 3/7's rear echelon, ordering them to have "plenty of hot coffee and chow" for the men in the morning.[12]

Although Shepherd and Rupertus accepted Frisbie's decision to relieve Williams, it was controversial with some Marines. The ADC's intelligence officer, Major Frederic Peachy, thought the regimental commander had acted unreasonably given "the bitter fighting and impossible terrain" faced by 3/7. He believed that the real motivation was "personal animus of long standing," a view seconded by others. One officer writing about the relief to a friend who had served in 1/7 prompted the recipient to "recall the feud between" Frisbie and Williams. Shepherd's operations officer, Major John S. Day, was certain the mutual ill will had started during the division's stint in Cuba in 1941. Frisbie had commanded a battalion in the 7th Marines and gotten into an angry dispute with Williams, then the regimental operations officer. Jerry Thomas thought the bright but often caustic Williams later had created considerable resentment in Puller and Hanneken, and they in turn "really worked him over" when they moved to more senior billets. Thomas had no sympathy for Williams: "He earned everything that happened to him."[13]

Puller's part in the affair does not appear to have been significant. There is no indication that the regimental XO tried to influence Frisbie's debatable decision. The charge of insufficient aggressiveness rang hollow given the casualties sustained by 3/7. In addition, the attack ultimately got moving largely as a result of the arrival of tanks, a factor entirely beyond Williams's control. Finally, it was strange that the regimental commander did not place the same emphasis on jump-starting

3/5 when it was equally stalled, nor did he seek a replacement for McDougal, who had been attached to him. There was evidence, however, that Williams was not as effective as he might have been. Two days after the change in commanders, a platoon leader in King Company noted in his diary: "Puller is really snapping battalion headquarters out of it. Just what they need." The same lieutenant remembered that Puller made a definite impression on the men because he was always in the front lines and seemed to understand what was going on there.[14]

After a night of heavy rain, the Marines spent January 5 reorganizing and preparing for a resumption of the advance. The lines now faced south, with 1/7 occupying a narrow front on the coast and 3/7, 3/5, and 2/7 located progressively farther inland. Puller sent out patrols but they found no enemy, only more rough, jungled terrain. The regimental intelligence staff pored over a captured Japanese order that said Aogiri Ridge must be held at all costs. Regrettably, it was impossible to determine from the accompanying hand-drawn map where this feature was located.

Shepherd's plan called for a fresh attack on January 6, with all the battalions jumping off except Puller's, which would remain in place and become the reserve. More torrential rain delayed the start of the operation that morning. As the Marines waited for the weather to improve, three Japanese mortar shells landed on the adjacent CPs of 3/7 and the regiment, wounding one man in Puller's command group. The attack finally kicked off at 1100. The left flank made good progress with the aid of tanks, but in the center 3/5 met strong, seemingly invisible resistance reminiscent of that along Suicide Creek. The failure to make much headway there created a large gap between 3/5 and 1/7. Frisbie had Puller deploy a company behind the hole.

The next day was basically a repeat, except that the predawn thunderstorm was heavier, causing flash floods that washed out several units. When the attack resumed, the flanks again moved forward, while the center (the right of 1/7 and most of 3/5) gained little ground. Casualties in 3/5 were light—about a dozen—but half were officers, including McDougal, his executive officer, and five others. At 1745, Frisbie gave Puller command of 3/5 pending the arrival of a replacement. The colonel ordered his triple-hatted XO to place two companies of 3/7 in a supporting position to cover the void between 3/5 and 1/7. The busy regimental executive officer soon reached the battalion, but found that all its phone lines were out of order. He sent a runner back to report that he "could do nothing tonight but hold what 3/5 has." He believed there were "not many of the enemy but they have a mortar." The 5th Marines wasted no time in dispatching Lieutenant Colonel Lew Walt to take over 3/5, but he arrived at the 7th Marines CP after dark and Frisbie told him to wait there until daylight.[15]

Walt assumed command of 3/5 on the morning of January 8 after conferring with Puller as the two crouched among the roots of a huge banyan tree. The young lieutenant colonel later recalled that his former Basic School instructor told him: "I have never been faced with a tougher situation. We've got machine guns ahead of us and snipers over our heads." Walt received a quick introduction to the situation when a burst of fire cut through their covering roots and interrupted their hurried conference. The predicament they faced mirrored that at Suicide Creek—without the support of armor the Marines were making no progress against the well-hidden defenses. The engineers were trying to build yet another corduroy road forward from the beach, but having little success due to the deep mud. The only result of the day's effort was that the men of 3/5 realized the ground was beginning to slope upward as they fought slowly forward through dense growth. It was becoming obvious that this was the base of Aogiri Ridge. The role of 3/7 was limited to patrolling around the left flank of the enemy position to see if there was an opportunity to envelop it. Puller accompanied one of the probes, which established that there were no Japanese between the main center of resistance and the sea. Late in the afternoon, due to cumulative losses in 3/5, Frisbie attached two of 3/7's companies to Walt, leaving Puller in command of only Company L.[16]

On the 9th, Shepherd ordered a double envelopment of Aogiri Ridge. On the left, 1/7 attacked to the southwest and soon ran into bunkers guarding that approach. On the right, Walt sent King Company of 3/7 to the southeast and up that end of the ridge. That prong of the attack encountered equally tough positions. The men of King had two advantages, however. One was a 37mm antitank gun that 3/5 had manhandled to the front lines. The other was the courageously aggressive Walt. The crew of the cannon got off only a few shots before small arms fire cut them down. When Walt called for volunteers to keep the gun in operation, no one came forward. He and his runner then helped the remaining gunners alternately shoot and push the piece forward a few paces. Within minutes others rushed to assist. There were fresh casualties around the gun, but now there was no shortage of men willing to replace them. The increase in firepower and the huge leap in morale soon carried the gun and the battalion to the top of Aogiri Ridge.

By the time the sun set, the Marines had a foothold in the midst of the enemy line along the crest. The Japanese still held much of their original defensive system, to include positions on the reverse slope. After midnight the increasing level of noise rising from below forewarned the Americans that the enemy was preparing a counterattack. At 0435 on January 10, they came surging upward in a classic banzai assault. Marine artillery and infantry weapons decimated them, with canister rounds from the 37mm gun doing particularly deadly work. The attack finally petered out near daylight, with more than two hundred enemy bodies covering the slope. In deference to the courage of 3/5's new CO, Shepherd renamed the objective "Walt's Ridge."

At noon on January 9 Lieutenant Colonel Henry W. Buse, Jr., had reported to the 3/7 CP to assume command from Puller. That allowed Chesty to focus on his normal duties as the regimental XO, which meant frequent morale-boosting visits to the front. One officer recalled that Puller walked along the lines, stopping at each fighting hole and greeting the troops: "How's things going, old man?" One time a young, frazzled Marine replied, "We ought to get the hell out of here, Colonel!" Puller took him aside for a fatherly pep talk and promised that he would get more hot chow for the men. The colonel's jeep driver noted: "He always wanted to be on the go. He could not stand it when Colonel Frisbie would make him stay in the CP."[17]

By the afternoon of January 11, the 7th Marines secured all of Walt's Ridge and discovered why the enemy had fought so stubbornly for it. Just beyond was a rough, narrow road that ran from Borgen Bay to the south, apparently all the way to the other coast of New Britain. This was the only significant avenue available for Japanese reinforcement or withdrawal. Barely two hours after the first squad reached it, Puller was there to see for himself. He noted that 3/5 now occupied "an excellent defensive position on the military crest of a steep ravine," thus freeing 3/7's companies to return at last to their parent unit. After resting on January 12, the regiment resumed its attack to the south and seized Hill 660. This was the last terrain feature needed to complete the Marine perimeter.[18]

☆ ☆ ☆

Rupertus was pleased with the outcome in the southeast and division headquarters later labeled this phase "one of the outstanding achievements" of the campaign. The 7th Marines and 3/5 had together accounted for two thirds of all casualties inflicted on the Japanese. The commanding general recognized the hard efforts of the 7th Marines with a tangible reward, replacing it in the line with the 5th Marines and shifting Frisbie's regiment to the quieter perimeter around the airdrome. The movement was complete by January 18. The change in scenery also got the Marines away from the mosquito-laden swamps and the smell of enemy bodies rotting in the jungle. The troops now could swim at the beach and wash their ragged uniforms in a stream. The Navy also delivered the first shipments of frozen meat, while Puller pressed the quartermaster to get more fruit and juices for the men. The weather even cleared on January 21 and the Marines enjoyed an unprecedented dry spell for the next ten days. The only downside to the move was the nightly Japanese bombing raid against the airfield, never very serious but sufficient to disrupt sleep. Other than that, the men of the 7th found their new home "quite good."[19]

In a letter to his wife, Lewis echoed the sentiment that life on Cape Gloucester was "very good and steadily improving." His only regret was that the heavy rains had ruined the photos of Virginia and his daughter that he had been carrying in his pocket since D-Day. He took a bow for himself, noting that "I have been personally thanked by [Rupertus] for my efforts," but he also complimented those who had made it possible: "The men and junior officers have been splendid." Virginia confided to a family friend at this same time: "The papers tell me my husband is now in the thick of the Cape Gloucester fight, so of course, I am very jittery. My great anxiety is not to be compared with his hardships, of which I am yet to hear one complaint. . . . Truly he has an inner stamina and more control than any person I ever knew. I cling to my belief that God will help to bring him through." She also recognized his special bond with his troops: "He is a wonderful judge of human nature, and will *never* let them down."[20]

Frisbie was inclined to agree with the positive assessments by Rupertus and Virginia Puller. During this lull in the action he recommended his XO for a Distinguished Service Cross (the Army's equivalent of the Navy Cross). He cited Chesty not only for his effectiveness in temporary command of the two battalions, but for the way he did it: "Without regard for his own personal safety, while under the fire of riflemen, machine guns, and mortars of the determined enemy in well-entrenched positions, he moved from company to company along his front lines."[21]

Some officers thought that Puller was developing an equal indifference to the lives of Marines. Lieutenant Colonel James M. Masters, Jr., recalled years later how the 7th Marines executive officer received him when he reinforced the perimeter with his 2d Battalion, 1st Marines. Puller inquired about a battle 2/1 had fought earlier in the campaign. He asked how many Japanese died and gave his approval when Masters reported 256 bodies recovered and buried. Then Chesty wondered about friendly losses. When the battalion commander replied that he had fewer than twenty killed and wounded, Puller exclaimed: "Hell, Masters, you didn't have no fight!" The younger lieutenant colonel was "shocked" and "never could understand" that reaction. The executive officer of 1/7 remembered a similar incident while his unit was driving toward Walt's Ridge. Puller asked for the number of friendly casualties and consulted a small notebook. He remarked that 1/7's losses were higher than those of the other battalions, then concluded: "Good work, old man. Keep up the good work." The major came away with the impression that "Puller's assessment of your combat effectiveness was directly related to the number of casualties sustained. . . . The more casualties you had, the better job you had done."[22]

Based on these brief encounters, there was justification for both officers to believe that Puller had a cold-blooded attitude toward his Marines. It was more complicated than that. Some who served closer to Chesty thought that he "agonized over every wounded and killed member of his command." His well-demonstrated interest in the welfare of his troops would seem to support that more benevolent assessment. In all likelihood this aspect of his battlefield philosophy was close to that held by another Marine hero. During the fighting on Guadalcanal, Edson had complained about commanders so concerned with possible losses that they were stymied by light resistance. The raider commander believed that a bolder leader pushing ahead would achieve the objective sooner and often at lower cost. In one case he admonished a subordinate reluctant to press the attack: "You've got to take a chance on getting hurt. Somebody has to get hurt in these things. I want it done!" In Puller's own less-than-subtle way, his use of friendly casualty figures as a yardstick of offensive spirit was a means of instilling that sort of aggressiveness in subordinates. Future operations would put that notion to a severe test.[23]

☆ ☆ ☆

By January 20, the Japanese commander on New Britain realized that he had no more hope of retaking the airfields and he ordered the shattered remnants of his forces near Cape Gloucester to withdraw to Rabaul. Five days later, Alamo Force informed Rupertus that "special intelligence deserving of high credence" (undoubtedly super-secret ULTRA code breaking) indicated the enemy had given up the fight. In contravention of wise strategy and MacArthur's original goal of a limited campaign, both Krueger and Rupertus decided to pursue the retreating Japanese, even though the cost would far outweigh any possible gain in security for the airdrome. The division commander's actions were particularly odd given his expressed hope that his outfit would be relieved soon and made ready for a new assault. Keeping it engaged in offensive operations over a wide swath of territory only made that possibility less likely.[24]

The operation built up slowly in a piecemeal fashion. On January 22 a composite company from 1/1 under Captain Nikolai S. Stevenson departed the airfield perimeter heading south, while another composite company from 1/7 and 2/7 under Captain Preston S. Parish (1/7's operations officer) took landing craft to Sag Sag and then struck out to the east. The two patrols were to scout the trails, join up near Agulupella, and "clear the area of Jap remnants." Over the next few days, Stevenson's outfit had several contacts with the enemy rear guard. Each time the Japanese withdrew before they became decisively engaged, skillfully gaining time for every bit of terrain surrendered. They were assisted by the jungle, which was denser than anything the Marines had seen before, making it nearly impossible to circle around the trail blocks and trap the defenders. Since the 1/1 force was running out of ammunition and food, the 1st Marines dispatched Captain George P. Hunt's Company K (less its weapons platoon, to speed movement). Following a rapid advance down the trail, he relieved Stevenson on January 26. Parish had only minor contacts and linked up with Hunt on the

27th. The next day Hunt attacked a company-sized enemy position and was repulsed. The Japanese advantage in firepower outweighed the superior mobility of the lightly armed Marines (a lesson Puller had learned in his first days on Guadalcanal). Division then dispatched heavy weapons and a company of 2/5 as reinforcements, along with Major William J. Piper, Jr. (the XO of 3/7), to command this rump battalion composed from all three regiments in the division. Shepherd also ordered Major William H. Barba's 1/5 to conduct a reconnaissance in force along the trail leading south from Natamo.[25]

Division headquarters realized that it was building up a sizeable force in the interior under divided command—the Piper patrol reporting to division and 1/5 working for the ADC group. To remedy that problem, Rupertus called in Puller during the afternoon of January 29 and told him to take charge of both outfits. One Marine general later pointed this out as "a good example of how not to assemble a task force." Chesty might have been reminded of the genesis of Second Matanikau, but he took on the mission to join the two forces at Agulupella, move south to Gilnit, and clear all enemy west of the Itni River. He put together a small command group with personnel from his own regiment and the division, plus a few officers from the Australian–New Guinea Administrative Unit (an outfit composed of Australians with experience in the region).[26]

Puller departed the perimeter at 0700 on January 30 by jeep, caught up with 1/5 at Agulupella at 1045, and took command of the newly designated Gilnit Group. He set up his command post in a native hut in the village and went to work while the occasional rat scurried to and fro. He found Barba's battalion arrayed in a perimeter defense, but down to its last meal and short of socks, shoes, and other critical items. The trucks dispatched by the ADC Group could not negotiate the poor trail winding over washboard terrain, so Chesty immediately recommended that future resupply runs come by jeep. In a sign that he was becoming more attuned to the value of communications, he also asked 5th Marines to lay a phone line all the way to Agulupella, since radios were behaving temperamentally in the hilly, humid jungle. Most of the elements of Piper's outfit arrived over the course of the afternoon. He was in only slightly better shape in terms of supplies. Native carriers had been shuttling back and forth from Sag Sag to the patrol, but the bearers carried only about thirty pounds apiece and had to eat part of that themselves. Problems with logistics and communications would dog the Gilnit Group for the duration of its short life.

Puller's first order of business was launching patrols to gather information and guard his main force. Overnight he took stock of his situation and discovered that his outfit had fifty-nine officers, 1,339 enlisted men, three Australians, and 150 natives (who served as guides and bearers). The locals informed him that hundreds of Japanese had departed the area several days before, marching east. Many were sick and all were hungry, stealing everything they could from the villages, to include the dogs. Results of the recent actions confirmed those reports, as the primary food found in enemy packs was coconuts. The only thing the retreating Japanese had in plenty was ammunition. Chesty correctly surmised that the resistance encountered by Stevenson and Hunt had been delaying actions and there was little prospect of him engaging any large force. The natives also informed him that Gilnit was four and a half days away on foot. Adding in forty-eight hours to scour the region around the objective, the group commander estimated it would take eleven days to accomplish his mission. In addition to supplying his own large force, he also was faced with the prospect of caring for hundreds of villagers left destitute after the passage of the ravaging Japanese. Agulupella and points south were so far from Sag Sag that it was no longer practical to bring supplies by bearer, so the jeep trail from Walt's Ridge was the only overland option. Puller passed all this along to division and placed his men on two-thirds rations to stretch out his meager stocks. Higher headquarters was doing its own analysis. At noon on January 31, Rupertus issued orders for the Gilnit Group to send 1/5 and another 5th Marines company back to the ADC in order to reduce supply requirements. Division also added a mission; Alamo Force now wanted the Marines to link up near Gilnit with an Army patrol from Arawe.

That same day, one of Puller's patrols discovered a large building in the jungle conveniently posted with a sign designating it as Matsuda's headquarters. It was an unusually "elaborate" structure, three stories high, with designs inlaid in the hardwood floors. The general's personal quarters were complete with a four-poster bed and other fine furniture. Intelligence personnel scoured the area and dug up large chests filled with official papers. Puller immediately sent the potentially valuable documents to division. In a gesture he obviously knew would please

Rupertus's vanity, he added Matsuda's wicker easy chair to the shipment.[27]

Getting anything back and forth between Cape Gloucester and the
interior was growing increasingly difficult. The daily rains had returned
and the dirt trail was becoming impassable to any type of wheeled vehicle. Small tractors, normally used to tow artillery, were employed to
move some food forward, but even this expedient fell by the wayside
when the rivers began to rise. On the morning of February 1, headquarters queried Puller about the feasibility of supplying his force by airdrops. The engineers had repaired enough of one strip to allow the
division to operate its nine Piper Cubs. These light planes, designed for
artillery spotting, could carry only two cases of rations per flight. The
first drops, made without parachutes, took place that afternoon, just in
time to provide enough to eat for the evening meal. With the food situation so precarious, the Gilnit Group remained in place and continued
patrolling the area. To add to the woes, malaria and dysentery began to
appear.

Puller ensured that his troops did not sit idle and contemplate their
troubles. He assigned each unit a sector in the perimeter and put them to
work digging strong defenses. One officer recalled the instructions
Chesty passed to the company-level leaders: "Their place was with their
men and he didn't want them coming around the command post. . . .
[He] let everyone know just what he wanted and just where each one
stood in relation to the operation so that there would be no question of
authority or misunderstanding." Given the confusing composition of the
force, that was no small matter. Puller also circulated around the
perimeter, eating with the troops and regaling them with stories from his
days in China, Haiti, and Nicaragua.[28]

That night a fierce storm savaged the western end of the island. Inside the Marine perimeters lightning killed three men; another two died
from falling trees. Swollen streams and toppled trunks blocked the trail
to Agulupella. Continued poor weather prevented aerial resupply on
February 2 and division began to look at the possibility of requesting
runs by heavy cargo planes based in New Guinea. The Cubs resumed
their work on the 3d and made forty drops.

Puller's patrols kept busy. One discovered it would be necessary to
bridge a river on the way to Gilnit, so the group commander requested
engineering supplies to accomplish that. Another patrol found nineteen

dying Japanese soldiers on a trail. Since they were in very bad shape and there was no way to carry them back to Agulupella, the patrol leader put them out of their misery. Chesty seconded this decision in reporting it to division. Rupertus did not question the action, but division headquarters was "uneasy" about the incident. A subsequent message directed the Gilnit Group to "capture prisoner if possible."[29]

Army Air Forces B-17s made their first supply run on February 4 and delivered more than 1,700 rations in a single drop. Division also ordered the Gilnit Group to send back more men, to include its platoon of pioneers. Puller reminded headquarters he needed help to build a bridge and the staff relented on the latter unit. Those reductions left him with a little less than five hundred Marines, plus his native support force. Rupertus offered to send fresh troops to replace those who had been in the field for two weeks, but Puller demurred since he found "conditions very good." With a small reserve of food on hand, the group commander finally felt able to embark on his main mission. He headed south with two companies and reached the proposed bridge site before noon on the 5th. That afternoon B-17s dropped most of the engineer supplies and enough rations to sustain the patrol for several days. The profusion of items falling from the sky also injured three men. Puller complained to headquarters that the aircraft were not hitting their designated target. Since he now had plenty of food, he recommended that only the Cubs be used in the future.[30]

Communications continued to be a major headache. The group was rarely able to directly raise division on the radio. Messages were relayed through other units, sent over land lines when they were operating, carried by messenger, or dropped from planes. There were problems even when the radios worked. Division had sent out a coding device, but then demanded it back because regulations prohibited its use outside the main perimeter. The daily changes to the replacement code seldom made it to the patrol in time. After Puller departed Agulupella and lost his telephone connection, he wanted to employ a panel code like that used in Nicaragua to communicate with aircraft. Division was slow to provide such a system. Even when the words arrived at their destination, there was difficulty. The use of village names to identify a location on the ground proved confusing, since their map coordinates were often wrong. Division staffers also were surprised at a request for seven hundred bottles of mosquito repellent, given Puller's

often-expressed contempt for creature comforts in the field. One man
on the patrol later explained the need: "The colonel knew what he was
about. We were always soaked and everything we owned was likewise.
That lotion made the best damn stuff to start a fire with that you ever
saw."[31]

While the main body of the group waited for completion of the
bridge, Captain Hunt requested permission to take a small patrol and
reconnoiter a short distance beyond the river. He crossed over on the
5th with eleven men. A newspaperman in civilian life, Hunt's curiosity
got the best of him and he proceeded nearly all the way to Gilnit by
nightfall. The next morning the small patrol crossed the Itni River and
captured a single sick Japanese. Hunt got word back to Puller, who dispatched an interpreter and natives to bring in the prisoner. The soldier
had no worthwhile information, but Chesty was happy to fulfill Rupertus's directive to return a prisoner. He assigned an intelligence officer to
get the man safely back to division and made it clear that he would accept no excuse for failure. Despite Hunt's coup, Puller was angry with
the rambunctious captain because he had exceeded his orders in going
all the way to Gilnit. When he caught up with the young officer, he relieved him of his command and threatened a court-martial. (Chesty
never followed through, probably because he secretly admired his subordinate's aggressiveness. In the next campaign Hunt would more than
justify the reprieve.)[32]

Puller's force completed a bridge of tree trunks and saplings on the
evening of February 6. He took one company across immediately. Piper
followed with the other company the next day while Chesty pushed
ahead toward Gilnit. Hunt already had confirmed native reports that
there were no enemy units in the region. The main body reached Turitei
on February 8 and established a new base there. Patrols reconnoitering
the west bank of the river found only some matériel abandoned by the
Japanese a month earlier.

At this point, communications snafus turned the operation into a
comedy of errors. The bridge had not been able to accommodate the
radio jeep, so Puller had sent the vehicle back to Agulupella, along with
his only copy of the code. His sole source of contact with division was
now via runner or with portable radios relaying through Agulupella or
the Cubs. The unreliability of the smaller sets made the latter methods
hit-or-miss. The greatest source of confusion, however, came from the

rear echelon in Agulupella using the Gilnit Group call sign. The staff at Gloucester did not realize for quite some time that it was talking to two separate entities and was surprised when the patrol sometimes could not read coded messages. Likewise Puller was often puzzled by division queries regarding signals he had neither received nor sent. Chesty's exasperation showed through when he closed one report: "Request more competent radio operators at relay station." The division staff was equally frustrated and insisted that the Gilnit Group send back a receipt for every message.[33]

Puller took his main body over the river by boat and occupied Gilnit early in the morning on February 10. He reported this by native runner and told division he would remain there for forty-eight hours in the absence of other orders. Headquarters received the message that afternoon. It immediately replied that he should stay put until further notice, but that word did not get to Chesty. Division apparently wanted him to loiter there until he fulfilled the Alamo Force directive to link up with the Army patrol from Arawe. From February 6 on, that unit had reported that it was held up by enemy opposition just east of Gilnit. Puller's force busied itself on February 11 with destruction of equipment and supplies in the area and then recrossed the river on the morning of the 12th. He rejoined the remainder of his force at Turitei, where he finally received the message telling him to stay in Gilnit. His response, again sent by native runner, reported that he was sending half his men back over the Itni. He also ruefully noted that he already had destroyed all boats along the river and could not cross it without them.

The next morning Puller and one company of Marines sat on the west bank of the Itni. The evening before six native scouts had gone up-river to cross there. Now eight Marines were going over in one of the "destroyed" boats, which they had repaired overnight. (The official historian of the campaign would later wonder in print about the quality of destruction wrought by Chesty's band.) The destination of both patrols was Attulu Hill, the site east of Gilnit where hundreds of Japanese supposedly were holding up the Arawe patrol. While Puller waited, he drafted a long message to division containing thinly veiled complaints against the Army and his own higher headquarters. He repeated reports from the local population that there had been no enemy in the vicinity for a month and listed evidence supporting it. He insinuated that information from Arawe was too old to be accurate, requested delivery of radios capable of contacting the Cubs, and blasted back at division about communication procedures: "When my messages to you are received it is requested that I be notified by plane drop."[34]

Division, probably concerned with its inability to direct events, had dispatched a platoon aboard two landing craft on the morning of February 12. They were to sail around western New Britain and then up the Itni River to Gilnit. As the seaborne patrol approached its objective, the division staff issued a frenetic stream of orders and counterorders to Puller and the platoon. At noon on the 14th, the Gloucester headquarters directed the Gilnit Group to return "immediately" to Agulupella. Less than an hour later that was slightly amended; the ground force was to leave someone at Gilnit to contact the seaborne element and tell them that they were to return right away, too. That evening, division changed its mind; the Gilnit Group now was supposed to pull back only as far as the bridge site, where it would remain until a reinforced company arrived to garrison the area. Chesty first heard about the immediate withdrawal to Agulupella late in the afternoon, when a Cub pilot asked by radio when he was departing for the village. The aviator explained the reason for his question after the group commander wondered why he would ask such a thing. It was only that evening, however, that Puller drafted a message seeking clarification, which he again dispatched by native runner. The next morning Chesty asked headquarters for an extra twenty-four hours near Gilnit, so he could destroy enemy equipment and installations discovered at Attulu Hill. This communication got to division almost immediately, via radio to a Cub. Division granted Puller's request for an extra day and told him to leave a small detachment behind after that to make contact with the Army.[35]

The series of frustrated messages from Chesty—wrapped in waterproof paper salvaged from K rations and delivered by breathless native runners—apparently created a stir at headquarters. On the evening of February 15, Rupertus personally drafted a lengthy reply that opened with the salutation: "My dear Puller." He blamed the "confusion" arising from the "seeming discrepancy in the orders" on his operations section for "not writing exactly the orders that I desired issued to you." The general proceeded to give Puller "the complete picture" in great detail. He also twice commended Puller and his men "for the excellent job you have done."[36]

Rupertus's intervention finally cleared up the miscommunications.

Puller received the message on the morning of February 16 and promptly got the major part of his force on the trail for Agulupella, with one platoon remaining behind to make the linkup with the Army. The patrol from Arawe showed up on landing craft just a few hours later and the last mission of the Gilnit Group was finally complete. Puller's outfit made it to Agulupella on the 17th and reached the perimeter at Borgen Bay the next day, where trucks picked them up for the last leg back to the airfield. Chesty celebrated the event with a swig of scotch offered by his Australian adviser.[37]

Puller drafted a report of the patrol on the 20th, but proved very sparing with his words. Over half of the relatively brief document was taken up by a detailed listing of all enemy matériel destroyed (to include such mundane items as "2—Cases, Nuts and Bolts"). He did make some pithy observations about future operations. He thought that the Marine Corps should adopt both a panel code and the Army's portable SCR 610 radio for air-to-ground communications. The troops needed better training in maintaining silence, as well as hobnailed shoes to improve footing. Patrols had to bring along 60mm mortars and machine guns to deal with enemy firepower. And he sensed that the Japanese war machine was running out of steam: "Equipment is now not of as good quality as that seen by the undersigned in Japan and China and Guadalcanal; web equipment is of inferior quality and a linoleum is being substituted for leather. Until now the undersigned has never seen rice in only one layer of sacking." Although it did not appear in his report, he had observed that the enemy possessed a high percentage of sniper rifles, with scopes better than those available to American infantry. That may have accounted for the judgment in the division after-action report that "these troops were individually far better shots than any Japanese our men had previously encountered." Japanese industry and logistics were faltering in some areas, but Puller undoubtedly knew that the Imperial Army's warrior spirit remained unbroken.[38]

14

"Until the Downfall of the Japanese Empire"
Cape Gloucester and Pavuvu
February–August 1944

Puller received a very pleasant surprise upon his return to the Cape Gloucester airfield perimeter on February 17, 1944. The 1st Marine Division had received a message promoting him to temporary colonel effective February 1. He pinned on his silver eagles on the 21st. Other promotions and the new rotation system brought changes in leadership throughout the division. Colonel O. P. Smith, a companion from Fort Benning, reported in to take over the 5th Marines. Those heading back to the States included Sims, Frisbie, and Whaling. Puller may have hoped he would get command of the 7th Marines, but Hanneken was senior and apparently laid first claim. At the end of the month, though, Chesty took charge of the 1st Marines. His long partnership with this old regiment would become as storied as his association with Company M.

Like his hero Stonewall Jackson, Chesty was revered by his men for his courage and his devotion to them. He quickly demonstrated to the 1st Marines that the reputation was for real. As the colonel pinned a medal on an awardee, he noticed the photographer was focusing on him, not the recipient. Puller quietly admonished: "If you don't mind, old man, this is the man being decorated." Captain Nikolai Stevenson believed that Chesty also had developed a "chemistry" with the enlisted men because he was one of the few senior officers who was up front alongside them when the going got tough. The new regimental commander trumpeted that attitude in his first talk to his officers. Chesty already had submitted a typically terse message to Headquarters Marine Corps requesting that his "present assignment to a combat unit be extended until the downfall of the Japanese Empire." The substance of his equally short speech was that every one of them should stay with him, even though the Corps was beginning to offer transfers to the States to those with two campaigns under their belt. Although most of the officers were taken aback by the exhortation, only a handful were surprised. Even fewer were willing to take up his challenge, but no one could deny that he was leading from the front yet again.[1]

It remained to be seen whether Puller was equally well prepared for other aspects of command at this level, such as the requirement to coordinate supporting arms and several large maneuver elements. He had not been to a formal school in many years and had no experience in combat as a senior staff officer. O. P. Smith believed that the task of fashioning the disparate units of the Gilnit patrol into an effective organization had given Chesty some appreciation of the importance of a good staff. But Puller gave no outward indication that was true. He certainly showed no respect for the war-shortened staff course in Quantico. Major Bernard T. Kelly, a graduate who joined the regiment at Gloucester, first met his new commander as Chesty sat on a ration box in his tent playing solitaire. Apprised of Kelly's professional education, Puller grunted "School . . . Huh!" and then asked "What can you do?" He ended up making the major his operations officer, a possible grudging admission that the staff course was not a complete waste.[2]

Notwithstanding Smith's opinion, Puller definitely was frustrated during the Gilnit operation by poor logistical support, miscommunication, and changing orders. The experience undoubtedly had fueled his disgust with staff officers (he referred to them disparagingly as "those division hotsie-totsies") who tried to micromanage distant events. Chesty probably preferred his Nicaraguan days, where he was free of interference from higher up once his feet hit the muddy trail. Now he was a senior commander and he would have to reconcile the similar feelings of his subordinate leaders with his own desire to run the battle. He would solve that problem, in part, by continuing his practice of staying up in the front lines, where he could see the situation for himself and directly pass on his orders.[3]

☆   ☆   ☆

While the Gilnit patrol had been scouring the interior of western New Britain, Rupertus had been advancing other elements of his division along the northern coast. As Puller took over the 1st Marines, his 2d and 3d Battalions were just completing a move to the Borgen Bay perimeter to relieve Smith's regiment for an amphibious assault on the Willaumez Peninsula. On March 4, 1/1 took landing craft eastward to the Iboki Plantation, where they would serve as the reserve for the upcoming landing. Division also placed the 1st Marines on alert for an amphibious seizure of Garove Island to the north. The Japanese soon evacuated that garrison, however, and Rupertus canceled the operation. On March 11, most of 1/1 jumped ahead on the coast to the Linga Linga Plantation. The 2d Battalion replaced them later in the month and remained there till April 9, when the 3d Battalion came forward to take its turn.

Throughout these operations, the major focus of the unengaged units was training. By division order, companies spent at least thirty-six hours each week working at marksmanship, hiking, small unit combat problems, and patrolling. Puller ensured that even the combat patrols at Linga Linga served as a form of training. Since many of the retreating Japanese were too weak from starvation and illness to pose a strong challenge, he saw that "all personnel, including cooks," joined the units in the field. He believed that "the experience gained from operating with the natives and from patrolling under the direction of seasoned jungle scouts proved of incalculable value." These efforts also aided the division in assimilating the replacements coming out from the States. The only shortcoming in the program was its emphasis on jungle operations, as the 1st Marine Division's next campaign would be in a decidedly different environment.[4]

During the course of the Linga Linga patrols, Marines sometimes came across enemy stragglers who had been left behind when they were no longer capable of keeping up. At least one captain followed the example set by another patrol leader during the Gilnit operation; he ordered the mercy killing of those he could not help. While it is impossible to say whether that officer was influenced by the earlier incident near Agulupella, some junior leaders in the 1st Marines had gained the mistaken impression that Chesty encouraged the killing of prisoners. When Captain Everett P. Pope captured an enemy officer, he did not turn him into regimental headquarters for that very reason. The Puller legend was still growing, sometimes for the worse.[5]

When the units were not in the field fighting or training, life on New Britain was not always bad. The Gloucester perimeter now boasted good roads, orderly rows of hard-back tents, a PX, and a laundry service. The food was sometimes decent, the division band gave occasional concerts, and there were outdoor movies three times a week. Other than continuing problems with tropic illnesses, one Marine thought the only thing wrong with the Borgen Bay camp was the roar of the nearby surf, which was "very noisy for sleeping." Puller had his own reasons to be happy. At a division parade on April 12, he received a gold star in lieu of his fourth Navy Cross, for his actions in temporary command of 3/7 and 3/5.[6]

The award put Puller in a class by himself, as no other Marine had ever been decorated as many times with that medal. He was not entirely satisfied, though, and was taking steps to ensure he received everything that he believed he was due. Just prior to Sims's departure for the States, Chesty reminded his old commander that no action had been taken on a recommendation for a medal for the Koli Point action. Sims promptly resubmitted the paperwork. Then Puller wrote HQMC to ask for a change in the wording of the citation for his third Navy Cross, to reflect that he and his men had been responsible for "the virtual annihilation of an enemy regiment." Chesty's reputation was becoming mixed when it came to looking out for his subordinates in this regard. Those who had served under him in the 7th Marines thought that he had been generous in making recommendations. But after he became a regimental commander and member of the division awards board, a perception arose that he was tightfisted when it came to approving commendations. The apparent change may have been due to his attitude toward awards that did not involve direct combat. A member of the board recalled that "both Lewie and Hanneken would insist on 'real' evidence that the Marine had a bayonet between his teeth." Puller also might have acted out of deference to Rupertus, who was notoriously stingy with medals.[7]

☆ ☆ ☆

Unbeknownst to most everyone in the 1st Marine Division, their fate had been the subject of heated debate all the way up to the Joint Chiefs of Staff. MacArthur wanted to hold on to them as long as possible, while Nimitz insisted that the organization should return to his control for the next campaign. The Navy ultimately won out. The division found out about the pending transfer on April 9. On the 23d, three trans-

ports brought in the initial Army relief regiment and the next day the 1st
Marines loaded on board in their place. On April 27 they hove to off
Pavuvu, a low-lying, palm-covered isle that looked as if it came right
off a South Seas travel poster.[8]

The New Britain campaign was over and it had been a thorough
success for the 1st Marine Division. They had wrested a good portion
of the island away from the Japanese and inflicted significant casualties
at comparatively low cost (438 dead and 815 wounded). It was Rupertus's first operation as a commander, however, and he did not come off
looking as good as his organization, at least not in the eyes of those subordinates who served close to him. Colonel Smith observed many of
the general's worst traits as the 5th Marines prepared for the Willaumez
Peninsula landing. At the initial planning conference, Rupertus "did
most of the talking" and laid out the main features of the scheme, which
he had developed prior to any consultation with his staff. Despite "an
absolute dearth of information" and a wealth of native rumors about
strong enemy forces, "the general did not believe there were any [de-
fenders], that we would walk ashore." Smith also was concerned about
the selection of a beach without any reconnaissance. He quickly
learned, however, that "it was not politic to show other than enthusiasm
for the operation." In short, Rupertus loved his own ideas, evinced a
strong optimism that was often not grounded in reality, and did not
want to hear opinions that disagreed with his own.[9]

Rupertus also was the opposite of Puller when it came to privileges
in the field for officers. Matsuda's chair, which had graced a comparatively ostentatious residence for the enemy commander, came to sym-
bolize for some the same sort of excess on the American side. At great
effort, Puller's men had brought it out of the jungle so that Rupertus
could rest upon it and brag about its capture to the press. Major Henry
J. "Hank" Adams, Jr., once one of Edson's raiders, recalled that the
piece of furniture caused hard feelings among some in the division. A
bold Marine in the division intelligence section described another such
sore point in the official journal, noting that Rupertus had led a patrol to
"loot village so that CG 1stMarDiv might have native totem pole for his
collection." One officer would refer back to the general's patrician attitude as one of the "real bad cases of that [in the Corps] in World
War II." Another believed that Rupertus "didn't give a damn about the
people under his command," just as long as he kept "on the good side"

of his superiors. A division staff officer recalled that the CG (commanding general) "was not all that considerate of his troops." Even a fellow general felt that he was primarily "interested in making a reputation for himself." Several thought he did not want anyone in the division to "receive a higher award than he himself had." Yet another officer cited Rupertus's bombastic "gift" of the airfield to Krueger as symbolic of "a man whose desire for personal safety and comfort was exceeded only by his vanity for military glory, which he did little to earn." The relative weakness of the Japanese at Cape Gloucester had masked Rupertus's own deficiencies, but there was no guarantee the enemy would always be so obliging.[10]

☆   ☆   ☆

Pavuvu, the largest of the Russell Islands, lay thirty-five miles northwest of Guadalcanal. From the air, it took the form of a hand. The southern, palm-shaped area consisted of low, rugged mountains covered with rain forest. Five broad, flat, sandy peninsulas, largely taken up by coconut plantations, pushed out to the north like the splayed fingers and thumb. Adjacent Banika was home to airfields and supply depots. By contrast, the only inhabitants of Pavuvu were islanders and a construction battalion. Although it looked beautiful from afar, it was no tropic paradise.

When the 1st Marines came ashore on April 29, 1944, they found themselves in a "virgin" area with "absolutely no facilities." Since no one had worked the plantations for three years, the ground was carpeted with rotting coconuts. For the next month, Marines were kept busy hauling them off to dumps for burning. It took two weeks to clear enough land to get all the tents up. A combination of frequent rain and poor drainage turned the bivouac areas into a sea of mud that never seemed to dry up. Drinking water, on the other hand, was in short supply and fresh food was a rarity. There were no showers, mess halls, or any of the other basic amenities at what was supposed to be a rehabilitation area. At night, hordes of rats provided "a constant source of annoyance." The arrival of the remainder of the division in early May only increased the misery.[11]

Rupertus almost immediately flew to Washington for six weeks of leave and conferences at HQMC. He left behind orders for the construction of a CP on a hill overlooking the base. This was no small challenge. Building materials were in very short supply and most of the division's engineering equipment was useless after months of wear in the field. The situation would not improve soon, as the warehouses on Banika had been emptied by outfits departing from Guadalcanal for the Marianas campaign. Work forged ahead with what was available and by mid-June there were Quonset huts for work spaces, as well as a small wooden-frame house for the general. While "not pretentious," the quarters had built-in drawers, venetian blinds, two iceboxes, and ample screening. At a time when the men were bathing in their helmets and eating out in the rain, this use of scarce resources caused resentment. Rupertus seemed not to notice upon his return to Pavuvu. He knew there were shortages, "but these are being taken care of and I am not worrying. . . . Our camp is more bedded down every day, my CP area is excellent." His letters to Vandegrift focused as much on his concern that the Commandant arrange for Mrs. Rupertus to christen the new aircraft carrier *Cape Gloucester.*[12]

The wretchedness of life on Pavuvu spurred some enterprising Marines to write a letter to Vandegrift in early June. Since they realized it "would not get very far through channels," they sent it directly to him. It referenced "The Commandant's parting words, 'I will not forget you men.'" Their chief complaints were delays in applying the rotation policy; poor food; severe shortages of clothing items, water, and beer; the lack of mess halls and recreation facilities. They reminded him that their performance on "the 'Island' . . . undoubtedly got you in the drivers seat" and asked him "to do something to relieve this condition." Vandegrift sent it back to Rupertus, who was not about to "allow any anonymous letters to annoy me." He did acknowledge that the problems made it "a very inconvenient period to the command." Selden, the chief of staff, reported in mid-July that the complaints had been justified, but most were now remedied or currently being fixed. Conditions did improve, but Pavuvu remained a primitive rehabilitation area with bad water, a "marked deficiency" of fresh food, and no decks for the tents.[13]

In the squalor of Pavuvu, Puller's stock among the men soared. As always, he waited like the lowest private in the endless lines for chow or the PX and was the first to berate any newly joined officer who thought rank gave him the privilege to go to the front. In contrast to Rupertus, he lived in an "austerely furnished" tent. When a few NCOs jury-rigged a shower for him by placing a 55-gallon drum on top of a small shed, he made it available to everyone and personally hauled a 5-gallon can to replace the water he used. At the same time, he did not take it easy on his Marines. On the morning of departure for the first wave of men heading home on rotation, he scrutinized them to ensure their appearance met standards. The next day, he welcomed the replacements, then inspected the entire regiment and its camp, thus "setting a precedent" to the newcomers regarding his high expectations. He was out with his regiment early every morning doing calisthenics and did not issue the regulation thin mattresses for the cots, because he wanted to keep the men toughened up. His operations officer believed Puller was a successful commander because "he personally followed those precepts of leadership which many preached but not everyone followed; the troops came first."[14]

Some junior officers still felt that Puller unduly singled them out for censure. Captain James M. Rogers recalled the day he formed his headquarters unit for the colonel's inspection. The troops occupied a relatively dry portion of the company street, but the spot where he should have been positioned was a deep mudhole, so he stood to the right of it. When Chesty arrived, he corrected his subordinate, then started checking the troops as the captain marched into the morass. Although some officers took offense at what they perceived to be Puller's attempts to gain the affection of the men at their expense, Rogers accepted the colonel's emphasis on reducing privileges for leaders. "He set the example and it was a good one. I think it did bring us closer to the men we led, and their respect. It did contribute to what we call esprit de corps."[15]

By nature, Chesty seemed to be gruff with any officer he did not know well. One of the enlisted men in the regimental headquarters observed that Puller seemed to have few close friends among the officers. He spent much of his free time with Hanneken and Captain Joseph W. Buckley, another old mustang who commanded the regimental weapons company in the 7th Marines. But Major Victor H. Streit of the 7th Marines felt that once Puller got to know and respect the abilities of an officer, he was much friendlier and would stand behind their decisions. Captain John Todd, CO of the 1st Marines Headquarters Company, found Puller tough but fair and "admired him greatly." Lieutenant John J. Aubuchon, who had served on the 7th Marines staff, "thought the world" of Chesty. Major Jonas M. Platt of 3/1 agreed that Puller was "widely respected in that regiment." Puller could be harsh with junior officers, but most of those who served under him came away with a positive recollection of that time.[16]

If Puller sometimes seemed to be hard to get along with during this period, it may be that even he was tiring of the war. His affectionate letters home grew more sentimental than usual. "You are the only thing that matters in my life . . . there is not sufficient room for other things. I love you, Virginia, completely and am living for our reunion." "I love you, Dear, completely and your welfare and happiness is all that matters. I realize how you long for me as I am in the same 'boat,' Sweet." He began to talk of going back to the States, and not just for another visit: "I may get home for the Thanksgiving turkey, but if not, I will be with you for Christmas; you can count and plan on this date. . . . We will have a lovely home wherever I am stationed. . . . I am hoping for New River but any place with you will be perfect. I will check the remaining days of our separation off." "We will have a house before long now and when I retire we will have the two chimneys." The change in heart over remaining in the Pacific may have been fueled in part by his wife's well-being, since she underwent a major operation during this time. At one point he was concerned that "you never mention your health anymore." He voiced worries over "what the past four years have done. . . . I deeply regret our separation and the anxiety and other things that have resulted from it." Another factor may have been a visit with his brother, Sam, XO of the 4th Marines, who was on Guadalcanal in June preparing for the invasion of Guam. Puller flew over to the big island and the two spent three days "discussing everything from rabbit traps to tactics" and walking over Lewis's old battlefields. When Chesty headed back to Pavuvu, his last thought was that both of them were "getting old."[17]

Puller spent much of his limited free time alone. When the division received a half day off for a performance by Bob Hope's troupe, he passed it up, although he used it as a foil in his daily letter home. He wrote Virginia that he overheard one Marine regretting his attendance because it reminded him that there were women. "If I had seen the performance, I would not have been so effected as I have not forgotten that you are waiting for me and I have never been contented since leaving you, Sweet, and I never will be until we are reunited." The colonel went to the movies on occasion, though he did not find the diet of westerns and gangster pictures very satisfying: "A lot of shooting but no one hurt; I wonder how the movie companies can sell such films."

He whiled away many of his leisure hours reading and went through Douglas Southall Freeman's *Lee's Lieutenants* more than once. (On those occasions when someone complained in his presence about conditions on Pavuvu, he usually pointed out that the Confederate soldiers in the Army of Northern Virginia had undergone "much worse.") O. P. Smith, one of the Corps' most intellectual officers, later recalled Puller's love for books: "He gave the impression of being a little bit illiterate, but he wasn't. . . . He [was] more scholarly than you think . . . and he read a great many military books." Lieutenant Colonel Russell Honsowetz, one of Puller's former students at the Basic School and now commander of 2/1, reached a similar assessment: "He was a great student of history. He read every history book he could lay his hands on. Although he talked in a manner which gave you the idea that he was not highly educated . . . he actually was." Chesty even gave a critical eye to his readings: "I do not think that Freeman's second volume is as good as the first or at least it does not seem to be as well written; I suppose his works on the Confederate Army are closer to the truth than any books written previously."[18]

On July 27, Sam Puller died from a gunshot wound in the chest as he stood in the 4th Marines CP, located near the front lines in the battle to retake Guam. Honsowetz "could tell it really hurt" Puller, but Chesty said little other than remarking that he would make the Japanese pay. He replied enigmatically to offers of condolence: "Those who live by the sword must die by the sword." The news did prompt Lewis to write a rare long letter to his mother-in-law, though he did not dwell on the unhappy event. He recalled briefly that his younger brother had gone off to the battle determined to "do his duty" and took heart from that: "He did and I am proud of the performance of his passing; others have been inspired by the manner of his death." He reiterated his plans to be home for Christmas: "I too realize that I have been away too long. . . . The time of my homecoming is drawing near." He included a check for Mrs. Evans to purchase red roses for his wife on their anniversary— "my greatest day, seven years of happiness with only one regret . . . the separation that this war has caused." In another letter to a Saluda friend, he was equally reticent about his loss: "My brother's death was a blow but a man has to die and he went out in a good manner and I am proud of his performance of duty." Puller's reluctance to make more than a short reference to his brother's passing reflected his unwillingness to talk about the subject with anyone. That may have contributed to his aloofness on Pavuvu.[19]

☆   ☆   ☆

The 1st Marine Division had known since April that its next target was in the Palau Islands, at the far western end of the Caroline chain. The Japanese had seized the Palaus from Germany during World War I and maintained a secretive hold on them since then. MacArthur was approaching the end of his campaign in New Guinea and looking toward his imminent return to the Philippines. The location of the Palaus roughly 430 miles east of Mindanao theoretically placed Japanese airpower in position to threaten an American force invading the Philippines. Conversely, in friendly hands, those same airfields could support MacArthur's amphibious assault. The Joint Chiefs of Staff directed Nimitz to seize the Palaus beginning on September 15, 1944. The landing force would be Major General Roy S. Geiger's III Amphibious Corps, composed of the 1st Marine Division and the Army's 81st Infantry Division. (Rupertus was not happy about the Army's participation and had lobbied Vandegrift to get the 5th Marine Division to fill that role.) The code name, STALEMATE II, would prove to be a nightmarishly apt title.[20]

The final plan called for the Marines to land on the west coast of Peleliu, the second-largest island in the chain, and seize the airstrip located there, as well as the one on tiny Ngesebus, just off the northern end of Peleliu. Planes flying from these captured fields then would support an assault by two regiments of the 81st Division on Angaur, a relatively flat island seven miles to the south that was suitable for the construction of additional air bases. The remaining Army regiment would serve as a floating reserve. Lobster-shaped Peleliu was six miles long from its tail to the tip of its larger western claw and two miles in girth at its widest point. The airfield was located on the southern flatlands. Steep coral ridges, known collectively as Umurbrogol Mountain, covered much of the northern half, but thick vegetation concealed just how rough this terrain was.

Preparations for the operation benefited from the work of other Marine outfits in the Central Pacific campaign. Documents captured at Saipan in June caused intelligence analysts to revise the number of defenders of Peleliu and Ngesebus upward to ten thousand men—five reinforced infantry battalions and supporting units. The 1st Marine Division also would follow the lead of the 2d at Tarawa and use amphibian tractors as troop carriers to cross Peleliu's fringing coral reef. Some of the wounded from Saipan, Tinian, and Guam returned to Guadalcanal; Rupertus believed that his staff had "picked up some interesting and valuable points" from them.[21]

Strangely, the senior leadership at division and above seemed to miss the real lesson of the Marianas, the change in Japanese tactics toward a more deliberate defense-in-depth based on strong fortifications backed by heavier indirect firepower. The June 15 invasion of Saipan had been preceded by three days of bombardment and the invaders still suffered heavy casualties against a barely impaired Japanese force of thirty thousand men. Twenty-five days later the island was finally secure at a cost of sixteen thousand Americans killed and wounded. By contrast, American planes, ships, and artillery tubes blasted the nine thousand defenders of nearby Tinian for forty-four days. After a daring assault over constricted beaches, the 2d and 4th Marine Divisions captured the island in eight days at the comparatively low cost of less than 1,900 casualties.

The Japanese were learning from each new American landing and now understood the scale of American firepower. On Peleliu, mining experts constructed underground warrens designed to withstand the fury of U.S. shells and bombs. While the thick jungle covering Peleliu's ridges concealed the extent of these stronger fortifications, the experience in the Marianas should have indicated that a short bombardment was wholly inadequate against any island where the Japanese had time to perfect their defenses. Amazingly, U.S. Navy leaders ignored those lessons and scheduled just two days of naval gunfire preparation for Peleliu, basing their decision in part on a shortage of ammunition after the exhaustive bombardments of Tinian and Guam. More astonishingly, senior Marine leaders did not dispute that judgment in any serious fashion. When Geiger finally joined the planning in mid-August (after overseeing the seizure of Guam), he argued for and received an increase to three days, but with no additional ammunition. Rupertus never expressed any concern. In June, he told Vandegrift that he had "great hopes for a quick and successful job." In mid-July, after hearing the experiences of Saipan survivors, he was still flush with optimism: "I feel sure of success, and a rapid one at that." His opinion remained unchanged in early September: "There is no doubt in my mind as to the outcome—short and swift, without too many casualties." The man who had been amazed at the results of less than two hours of naval gunfire at Cape Gloucester was in all probability counting heavily, and mistakenly, on a major payoff from three days of preparatory fire for the upcoming fight.[22]

☆   ☆   ☆

Building its own base had eaten away a fair portion of the time the division should have devoted to rest and training. When the housekeeping chores finally were completed, the Marines faced continuing shortages in equipment, including such key items as individual weapons, landing craft, and tracked landing vehicles (LVTs, also known as amphibian tractors). The shift to a squad organization of three fire teams, for instance, meant a deficiency of one BAR in every squad—as well as an additional requirement to learn new small unit tactics. The Marines also had to master unfamiliar weapons that arrived late, such as the armored amphibian tractors mounting 37mm or 75mm guns [LTV(A)s], backpack flamethrowers, and their larger LVT-mounted cousins (which could shoot a jet of burning napalm 150 yards). But one of the most significant handicaps the division faced was simply a lack of training space. The coconut plantations provided the only open terrain on Pavuvu and the division's base took up a good portion of that limited area. Units conducted amphibious landings by sailing across from one finger to the next and Marines frequently found themselves maneuvering through their own tent camp as twenty thousand men sought a place to practice their skills. Leaders did emphasize coordinated tank-infantry tactics and assaults on fortifications, which would prove valuable, but no one made use of the rough terrain on the south side of the island. Unbeknownst to the Marines, that would have been excellent preparation for what they would face. In spite of these handicaps, the division managed to reach a high state of readiness.

Rupertus played an extremely limited role in overseeing the rejuvenation of the division. Not long after his return from the States in June, he had fallen from an amtrac and broken his ankle. He told Vandegrift about the accident, but reassured him that he was "carefully scrutinizing all the plans and details from my chair on the porch of my house." The CG's convalescence placed even greater importance on the role of O. P.

Smith, now a brigadier general and the ADC. Although Rupertus expressed "utmost confidence" in his regimental commanders, Smith had some slight reservations about the "limitations" of Chesty. The ADC knew that "it had taken a long time to convince [Puller] that in a unit the size of a regiment a staff was essential and should be used." To compensate for that attitude and weakness in experience, Smith saw to the assignment of Lieutenant Colonel Richard P. "Buddy" Ross, Jr., as the XO of the 1st Marines. Ross had been an "exceptional" battalion executive officer for Smith years before and "was exactly what Puller needed." Chesty was leery of his XO's lack of combat experience, but eventually rated him as "very good." The ADC had no qualms about Puller's performance in combat: "His strong point was fighting." Smith was amused by one of the ways in which the CO of the 1st Marines demonstrated that trait. During a practice landing, Smith looked for Chesty:

> Starting from the beach, I found the command posts of the two assault battalions, but found no trace of Colonel Puller. I asked one of the battalion commanders where I could locate the regimental commander. The battalion commander replied: "Oh, he's up ahead." After a search, sure enough Lewie's command post was located in advance of his battalion commanders. I jokingly observed to Colonel Puller: "Lewie, you know that according to the book, the regimental command post should be located in the rear of the battalion command posts." Lewie's rejoinder was: "That's the way I operate. If I'm not up here, they will say, 'Where the hell's Puller.'"[23]

Chesty's interest in the output of his staff officers remained limited. When Major Kelly brought the 1st Marines operations order for Peleliu to his CO, he expected him to "go over it word for word before signing it." To the surprise of the regimental operation officer, Puller glanced at it for only a moment, then affixed his signature. Concerned that he might let his commander down, Kelly went back to the rest of the staff and they spent hours reviewing every line before finally releasing it.[24]

Puller was much more attentive to the performance of his subordinate commanders. During the summer he received three lieutenant colonels from the States and gave them command of the battalions, although he was reluctant to do so given their lack of prior service on a battlefield. Major Ray Davis, executive officer of 1/1, noted that the new CO of his outfit, used to the strict safety practices at home, was "pretty horrified" to see squads making "no-holds-barred" live-fire assaults on bunkers. Shortly before the regiment was to mount out for Peleliu, the battalion commander received permission to visit Banika, but stayed there well beyond the authorized time. When the officer finally returned to the camp, Puller relieved him in a brief but vocal outburst heard all over the area: "I don't give a damn where you go, get out of my regiment!" Davis took over the battalion. Puller also held occasional evening sessions with his senior officers in his darkened tent. He posed tactical situations and puffed on his ever present pipe while he waited for a response. He invariably belittled "school book" solutions and emphasized that the place of Marine leaders was up front with the riflemen.[25]

The division staff briefed regimental and battalion commanders on the scheme of maneuver for Peleliu on August 11. The senior planners had concluded that the best course of action was to attack the west coast with all three regiments abreast. The 1st Marines would land a battalion each over White Beaches 1 and 2 on the left, the 5th Marines would do the same over Orange 1 and 2 in the center, and the 7th Marines would put ashore two battalions in column across Orange 3 on the right. The 1st and 5th would each have a battalion in regimental reserve; 2/7 would act as the division reserve. While Hanneken's regiment drove south to clear out that end of the island, Colonel Harold D. "Bucky" Harris's 5th Marines would push straight ahead to seize the airfield and the east coast. Puller had by far "the most difficult" assignment. Like the 7th Marines, the 1st would have to pivot 90 degrees after landing, but instead of heading into a flat, narrowing promontory, it would go north into a widening zone of action. To cover the longer front, Chesty would have to place his third battalion in the line, leaving no reserve. He would have to conduct this difficult maneuver in open terrain under the guns of Japanese defenders in the spiny central ridge. Then he would have to attack that high ground. The division headquarters expected the 5th and 7th Marines to accomplish their missions rapidly, after which they would relieve the 1st Marines. In the meantime, Puller's regiment would bear an unequal burden. Rupertus selected him for this critical mission in part because "I can depend upon him to push the attack." The division operations officer thought the colonel was perfect for the job because he "was a fearless fighter, was tenacious and

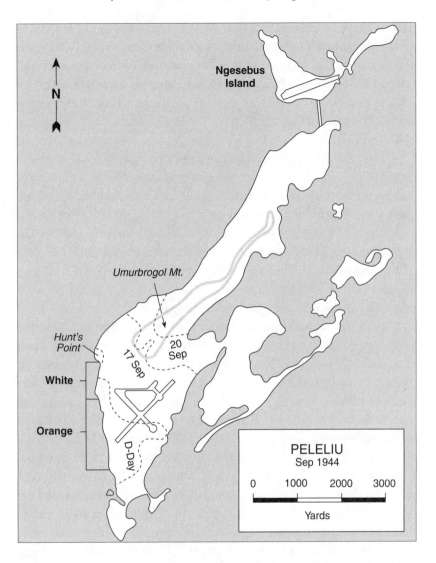

stubborn, would never admit defeat, and above all hated the Japanese."[26]

There was one additional feature that made the job of the 1st Marines potentially even more difficult. The White Beaches were flanked by a low coral bluff on the left and a tiny peninsula on the right; both offered the enemy positions from which to direct deadly enfilade fire down the length of the regiment as it splashed ashore. Aerial photos had not revealed any defensive works at either place, but the Japanese were noted for their skill at camouflage. Senior officers in the 1st

Marines were concerned about the danger and asked that these sites receive strong attention during the pre-landing bombardment. Puller himself repeated the request at a final planning conference after the rehearsals. In addition, he assigned King Company the mission of seizing the point on the left flank as soon as Captain Hunt and his men landed. (Lieutenant Colonel Stephen Sabol's 3/1 would land on White 1 and Honsowetz's 2/1 on White 2.)[27]

The division began loading aboard ships on August 16. During this time, Puller gathered his regiment together at the outdoor movie theater and gave a short, rousing speech to steel them for the coming operation. Kelly remembered him bellowing out exhortations, such as "Remember Pearl Harbor," and getting an enthusiastic response to each one. Nikolai Stevenson, the XO of 1/1, recalled that the colonel described the scale of the pre-landing bombardment and the men cheered. Then Chesty added: "Still, I wouldn't mind having insurance policies on some of you." The Marines roared at that black humor, too.[28]

There were rehearsals on Guadalcanal on the 27th and 29th, the second including naval gunfire and air strikes. On the 30th there was a critique for Marine and Navy officers. Smith found that the open-air meeting produced "nothing particularly constructive. . . . Everyone was pleased with everyone else." Rupertus voiced his optimistic assessment that the battle would be tough but brief, an opinion he later circulated to all his Marines via a letter published to them the day before the landing. At the end of his speech, perhaps with Matsuda's chair in mind, he looked down at Puller and said that he wanted the 1st Marines to capture the sword of the Japanese commander when they swept through the enemy's barracks area on the first day. His "pep talk" received a less-than-enthusiastic response. One captain recalled: "I don't believe I knew a single officer or man who had the slightest confidence in General Rupertus." The Army's official observer noted, however, that the general's blind faith in the effectiveness of the preparatory fire had a definite effect: "This expectation was widely circulated among the troops with the resultant belief of all concerned that the landing would be made with practically no opposition." Rupertus also used the layover at Guadalcanal to lobby for the job he wanted after Peleliu—command of the Marine Corps Schools. Upon hearing that Smith was being considered for that billet, Rupertus told his ADC to write to the Commandant and turn it down.[29]

15

"If There Is Such a Thing as Glory in War"

Peleliu

September 1944

As the men of the 1st Marine Division sailed toward Peleliu in mid-September 1944, they kept busy with the usual last-minute preparation of gear and detailed briefings on the plan. They also endured typically hot, cramped, miserable conditions. Puller suffered added discomfort, as the leg bearing the Japanese shrapnel began to swell and hurt. Unbeknownst to everyone as they sailed west toward the objective, the division almost received a reprieve. Navy carriers conducting strikes on the Philippines reported surprisingly weak Japanese air and ground defenses. Their commander, Admiral William F. "Bull" Halsey, fired off a message on September 13 recommending that MacArthur skip his November 15 invasion of Mindanao and go directly to his eventual objective of Leyte as early as October 15. Nimitz, MacArthur, and the Joint Chiefs all approved it in short order. Suddenly, the original rationale for the Palaus operation no longer made much sense, but Nimitz was unwilling to cancel the Peleliu assault just hours before its scheduled execution.

Beginning on September 6, three fast carrier groups struck at the Palaus for three days. To maintain tactical surprise, their efforts were spread throughout the island chain. On September 10 a single carrier group replaced them and kept up the pressure. Two days later, surface ships and escort carriers of the fire support group arrived to initiate full-scale bombardment of Peleliu and Angaur. Five battleships, eight cruisers, and fourteen destroyers alternately shelled the objectives and then stood off while planes roared in to bomb and strafe. The Japanese were so well dug in and concealed, however, that the Navy soon ran out of obvious targets. The admiral in charge did not want to waste ammunition, so he ceased fire and reported that fact to the amphibious task force. The news filtered down to the troops and "cheered all hands immensely." It seemed to be further proof that Rupertus's optimistic prediction was coming true. The Japanese used the respite to shift units from other beaches to the western coast, where the work of underwater demolition teams tipped off the location of the imminent landing.[1]

At 0530 on September 15, the fleet unleashed final neutralization fires. The cumulative effects of days of bombardments had denuded Peleliu of much of its vegetation and the terrain looked much different, and much more rugged, than it had in aerial photos. But for now, the island was wreathed in smoke and barely visible. Many of those watching from the sea thought it impossible that anyone could survive this impressive display of firepower. As Puller prepared to shove off from his ship, the Navy captain nonchalantly asked if he would be coming back for dinner: "Everything's done over there. You'll walk in." The colonel was much less confident: "If you think it's that easy why don't you come on the beach at five o'clock, have supper with me, and pick up a few souvenirs?"[2]

At 0832, a line of twenty-six LVT(A)s touched the sand and began firing their 75mm guns. At five-minute intervals thereafter, six waves of troop-carrying tractors splashed ashore to deliver the assault battalions of the 1st Marines. A group of DUKWs (amphibious trucks) carrying radio jeeps and 37mm guns followed them. The reserve battalion lay beyond the reef in landing craft, waiting to board returning LVTs. True to his motto of keeping up front, Puller and a small staff were in the third wave, while Ross and the remainder of the headquarters would come in with 1/1.[3]

Contrary to the hopes of the invasion force, the hurricane of high explosives from the sea and air was answered by a storm of steel from ashore. Japanese mortars and artillery pieces hidden in the Umurbrogol fired preregistered barrages onto the shallows and beaches. Once Marine tractors touched shore, a 47mm antitank gun opened up from a casemate built into the low coral bluff on the left flank. Machine gunners located nearby also raked the men and vehicles spread out in a line before them. Automatic weapons in fortifications on the point on the right flank wreaked similar havoc from the opposite end. The combination of indirect and direct fire knocked out about twenty tractors and DUKWs in the initial waves in the 1st Marines' zone. Puller heard the ping of shrapnel and small arms fire splattering off his tractor in the final minutes of the ride. As it crunched onto the rocky sand, he jumped off and sprinted forward. He set up his CP at the center of the White Beaches, a few dozen yards from the water, in what remained of a coconut grove. Moments later he radioed division aboard ship to confirm that he was ashore.

As the infantry leapt from the landing vehicles and advanced, most of 3/1 ran into a coral ridge about thirty feet high and roughly parallel to and about one hundred yards inland from the beach. It had not appeared on the map. The ridge was honeycombed with defensive works. Fronting the seaward side of the rise was an antitank ditch guarded by another 47mm gun firing in enfilade from a bunker on the north end. This combination of obstacles stopped the attack of Item Company short of its initial objective. It also pinned down the 2d Platoon of Hunt's King Company. The men of his 3d Platoon avoided it as they charged north along the beach, straight into the fire pouring from the left-flank point. Within minutes they were reduced to a squad in strength and Hunt committed his reserve platoon. The Marines fought forward and slowly killed or drove off the riflemen in open foxholes. The attackers then worked their way into position to hurl grenades into the apertures of the main fortifications. At 1015, Hunt announced the point was secure. His men had destroyed five pillboxes constructed of reinforced concrete blanketed by five feet of coral. The positions had housed four 25mm machine cannons and the 47mm antitank gun. In and around the fortifications were 110 Japanese dead. Of the hundred men Hunt had led in the attack, only thirty-three had reached the objective unscathed. The company commander noted ruefully that "the entire point and its defenses were untouched by naval gunfire."[4]

The landing area was still under fire from the Umurbrogol, the low coral ridge, and the right-flank point. Honsowetz's battalion nevertheless reached its initial objective, the edge of the airfield and a road, by 0930. It could not advance beyond there, however, due to the heavy fire sweeping the exposed airstrip. As the morning wore on, those LVTs still operating brought in 1/1. Davis's lead company destroyed the defenses in the right-flank point after landing, then established a reserve line near Puller's CP. The tractors carrying the regimental command echelon took several hits; many of the communicators became casualties and much of their equipment was lost. This complicated Chesty's attempts to stay in touch with subordinates and division, though he sent a steady stream of radio messages, many of them over the naval gunfire net. A 0940 dispatch to Honsowetz captured the communication difficulties in the 1st Marines: "We have no contact with third battalion. Can you send a runner to determine their position?"[5]

At mid-morning Puller moved down the beach to check on 3/1. He found that Sabol had committed his reserve company in an effort to close the gap between Hunt's Point and the rest of the battalion pinned down before the coral ridge. Love Company was soon caught in the same web of fire as Item and the 2d Platoon of King (the latter already reduced to squad size). Then the Japanese began launching small counterattacks to regain the critical point. Puller reported to division that King Company was "broken through by enemy" (probably a reference to the gap between Hunt's force on the point and his 2d Platoon at the ridge). Chesty promptly ordered a company of 1/1 to fill the breach. Regrettably, Company A used the antitank ditch as its covered approach and came under withering fire. In trying to extricate themselves from the trap, the Able Marines did storm and seize the southern end of the ridge, the first toehold on that key feature. Chesty started his tanks toward the threatened zone, while Sabol brought in mortars and naval gunfire to help drive off the enemy attacks. Meanwhile, Hunt remained cut off, with about two hundred fire-swept, enemy-filled yards separating him from the rest of the regiment.

Following the failure of Able Company's attack, Sabol again sought Puller's help. Regiment dispatched Baker Company, which soon found itself also bogged down in the killing ground before the low ridge. The tanks might have carried the day, but they could not get forward due to enemy obstacles, mines, and the jumble of trees felled by the prelanding bombardment. Nine of the original eighteen already were out of action. Indirect fire continued to strike throughout the shallow beachhead. One shell scored a direct hit on the regimental CP early in the afternoon, killing three men and wounding several others. Chesty shifted his command group to the lee of the Marine-controlled end of the ridge, which placed him closer to the threatening gap and gave him some shelter from mortar and artillery fire. It was so near the front lines that 3/1 had to send runners forward to get information to the regiment.[6]

Things were going only somewhat better for the rest of the division. The 5th Marines had gotten ashore with much lighter losses since they were not subject to enfilading fire. While Harris's left battalion was held up near the airfield along with 2/1, the right flank of his regiment had found concealment in vegetation south of the strip and nearly reached the eastern shore. The 7th Marines had bogged down in front of fortifications south of Orange 3. The large number of burning amtracs and DUKWs and the lack of progress on the flanks surprised Rupertus. In the middle of the day he had sent the division reconnaissance company in to reinforce the 7th Marines. Late in the afternoon he tried to commit his last reserve, 2/7, to bolster Hanneken's drive. He hoped these forces would "save the day," as the outlook appeared "pretty grim" aboard the command ship. (The lack of LVTs prevented 2/7 from actually going ashore that evening.)[7]

Smith had set up an advance division CP on Orange 2 prior to noon. When the ADC finally was able to talk to the 1st Marines late in the afternoon, Puller gave him a reassuring report that he occupied most of the desired beachhead and would hold. A radio message dispatched from Chesty's CP at 1808 sounded a similar note: "Repulsed enemy counterattack on our left front. Several enemy tanks knocked out. Receiving small arms, mortar, and arty fire. Recommend that we stay on O-1 tonight." Strangely, neither Smith nor Rupertus had reacted to Puller's early afternoon report of a break in King Company's lines. The command post ashore may never have received the message, but division headquarters afloat certainly did. Rupertus's attention nevertheless remained riveted on the 7th Marines in the south.[8]

The Japanese counterattack in Puller's message had occurred around 1700. Fifteen light tanks and infantry had come boiling out of the eastern lee of the Umurbrogol. They rushed across the airfield toward the juncture of the 1st and 5th Marines (placing them on Chesty's right, not his left). Shermans, 37mm guns, and bazookas easily dispatched the thin-skinned enemy tanks and the action was over in minutes. With sunset only an hour away, Smith ordered the regiments to dig in. The ADC was confident about the situation, but unaware there was trouble with the division's left flank. If the Japanese exploited the

gap there, they would have an unfettered path to the supplies and support units on the beach and could roll up the entire Marine line.

Puller was working hard to handle the problem. Behind the intermingled remains of Able, Baker, and Love Companies, he established a
secondary position manned by Company C, his last reserve. He bolstered that unit with headquarters personnel and a hundred Marines of
the 1st Engineer Battalion, borrowed from duty on the beach. He asked
the ships to maintain a continuous barrage of star shells over the front
lines and queried division: "Request approximate time when arty will
be available." The 11th Marines had several batteries of howitzers in
place, so Chesty's battalions arranged for harassing fires. The firepower
provided some measure of security to the infantrymen, whose losses
had been heavy; 250 men in 3/1, 85 in 1/1, at least several dozen in 2/1.
Hunt's beleaguered group also was a little better off once an LVT swam
to the point with machine guns, ammunition, and supplies. Platt
thought regiment "had as good a handle on it as anybody could have
under the circumstances." In all likelihood Puller had not expressed
concern to Smith because he really was not worried about the outcome.
He had beaten equally tough odds in the Battle for Henderson Field.
Even if the ADC had been aware of the problem, there was little he
could have done about it. He had no reserve ashore.[9]

Despite Puller's optimism, the severity of enemy firepower and the
number of casualties had jolted many of his Marines. They also were
surprised by the quality of Peleliu's defenders in comparison to those
encountered on New Britain. The few dead they came across were "well
fed and equipped and rather large in stature." These Japanese constituted a "ferocious and wily foe." As the day wore on, some Marines
found that "the cry, 'Corpsman!' and 'Stretcher bearers!' became more
nerve-wracking than the crump of mortar shells or the whine of bullets." And it was even more "disheartening" when those pleas were followed by "Never mind the corpsman."[10]

The Japanese commander had believed "that if we repay the Americans (who rely solely on material power) with material power it will
shock them beyond imagination." He was only partly right—the men of
the 1st Marine Division had been staggered by an unexpected blow, but
they had reservoirs of moral power more than equal to that of the
enemy.[11]

The evening was relatively quiet until midnight, when a mortar barrage paved the way for an attack on Hunt's Point by a hundred Japanese. Marine grenades and machine guns took a deadly toll of the enemy, who were backlit by illumination rounds as they charged toward the tiny bastion. Just before dawn the Japanese tried a stealthy approach; Hunt's alert force stopped them again. The rest of the perimeter was subjected only to harassment from infiltrators. As the sun came up, Puller could tell division: "Dispositions and situation same as last night."[12]

Early in the morning on September 16 tractors delivered more supplies to Hunt, along with badly needed reinforcements. He had been down to just eighteen effectives. Puller arranged for thirty minutes of preparation fire from air, artillery, and naval guns, then launched his regiment in the attack at 0800. Honsowetz's battalion initially made good progress on the right, sweeping over the airfield in conjunction with 1/5. As 2/1 executed its turn to the north, however, it met strong resistance in the complex of shattered buildings between the strip and the Umurbrogol. Casualties soared. Depleted companies also struggled to maintain contact on their flanks as the battalion's line stretched between the 5th Marines moving west and 3/1 on the left, still stuck at the low ridge. Despite the heavy fire support, 3/1 and the attached companies of 1/1 could make no headway against determined Japanese in the low ridge and in the gap reaching toward the point. Chesty gave Sabol the last reserve, C Company, which attacked north along the ridge. In the afternoon tanks reached the area. With this assistance, the infantry began to destroy caves and pillboxes one by one in a steady move up the length of the coral ridge. As enemy fire from the flank diminished, A and B Companies linked up with Hunt's outpost at 1530. The gap was now closed and with it the last remote chance of Japanese success.

During the morning, division finally began to focus on its left flank, as all units except 3/1 were making steady progress. Puller also was asking for reinforcements to reconstitute a reserve. Since his regiment was facing the bulk of the remaining enemy, Rupertus decided to have 2/7 back him up. Lieutenant Colonel Spencer S. Berger's battalion arrived on White Beach 2 in the afternoon and came under Puller's control, though Chesty was not allowed to commit them without division's consent. Rupertus was confident about the outcome again and now hoped to keep 2/7 intact to seize Ngesebus. At the close of the second day, the situation of the 1st Marines was much better, but hardly bright.

The companies on the left had reassembled themselves into coherent units, though 3/1 remained split, with King on the coast, Item and Love on the right, and the units of 1/1 in between. Chesty told division that he was "very much pleased with naval gunfire this morning." He estimated enemy losses at eight hundred dead and at least that many wounded, but also had to report: "Our own casualties nine hundred plus."[13]

That night the Japanese concentrated mortar fire on King and Baker, then several hundred soldiers charged recklessly over open ground into the teeth of automatic weapons fire and artillery and mortar barrages. Others waded along the coast to outflank the front lines. Hunt's men discovered the latter ploy and stopped it cold as well. The action finally subsided about 0200. An effort of that scale on the previous night might have made a difference, but at the end of D+1 it merely led to slaughter. Sabol estimated that his outfit inflicted about 70 percent casualties on the attackers. A smaller thrust against 2/1 just before dawn also failed. After the sun came up on September 17, the 1st Marines began a planned reorganization of the lines. Major Davis took control of his companies in the center for the first time. Later in the day, Love and Item Companies would pull out of the line and shift left to rejoin King. The goal was to consolidate the battalions, with 3/1 and 2/1 flanking 1/1 in the middle of the regimental front.

After another preparation by artillery and naval gunfire, the 1st Marines jumped off at 0800 on September 17. Davis's battalion soon ran into a major obstacle, a huge blockhouse sixty feet square and twenty feet high, untouched by supporting arms. He requested naval gunfire and two 14-inch rounds from a battleship tore through the four feet of reinforced concrete. The 1st Battalion resumed its advance. By mid-morning it had reached the base of the Umurbrogol, which stared down ominously on the open flats. Shortly after, Japanese guns in caves on the steep slopes began to fire. At point-blank range they could not miss and 1/1 took heavy casualties. The Japanese also brought down indirect fire from mortars and artillery pieces. The 1st Marines called in fire missions on suspected locations for the defiladed weapons, and Puller twice reported the problem to division, but the rain of fire continued. Tanks and bazooka teams eventually knocked out the direct-fire weapons and 1/1 seized the forward slope before sunset.

On the right, 2/1 also made good initial progress. But as Honsowetz's men moved into the plain east of the Umurbrogol, they walked into the same situation as 1/1, with heavy fire raining down from the heights on their left. Honsowetz faced most of his force to the west and the Marines began to fight their way up the sharp slope. The withering fire inflicted heavy casualties on the infantry and knocked out a number of tanks and armored tractors, but by the end of the afternoon, 2/1 was in possession of the long ridge. The Marines now looked west across a steep-sided valley at a slightly higher, enemy-held ridge known as Hill 210. Farther to the west was 1/1, partially facing back to the east. Hill 210 thus constituted a deep salient in Marine lines.

Only 3/1 on the left had it comparatively easy. Sabol's men met light resistance as they advanced seven hundred yards along the coastal flats. At the end of the day, the 1st Marines controlled most of the nose of the Umurbrogol. That greatly reduced the threat of direct fire and observed indirect fire against the beaches and airfields. Puller's men also had driven so close to the Japanese commander's bunker that he was forced to fall back to a new location.[14]

The cost had been high. In the first reasonably accurate count of casualties, Chesty's staff reported that the regiment had suffered over 1,200 killed and wounded since the operation began. The rifle companies had borne the brunt of the sacrifice. Of the 473 effectives remaining in 3/1, almost half were headquarters and heavy weapons personnel. Officer and NCO casualties were particularly high; PFCs were now leading some platoons. Three days of heavy fighting and temperatures in excess of 100 degrees also had inflicted a toll on those still standing. Potable water was in short supply and men were falling victim to heat prostration. Cases of combat fatigue were beginning to appear as well. An officer in Davis's battalion described the cause: "Those who have experienced the constriction of the blood vessels in the stomach and the sudden whirling of the brain that occurs when a large shell burst near by or a friend has his eyes or entrails torn out by shrapnel can easily understand the man who cannot control his muscles and who stares wildly. It isn't fear alone that causes the shock to the system. Often it is the knowledge of his impotence—his inability to help his shipmate who is whistling through a hole in his chest—that momentarily snaps a man's brain." The "sickening stench of decaying bodies" contributed; it was impossible to bury the dead before the "intense heat" went to work on the corpses.[15]

The first seventy-two hours on Peleliu had been bad, but they were merely purgatory. In the next few days, the 1st Marines learned the true meaning of hell. The terrain in the Umurbrogol was worse than anything the division had encountered in the war:

> The rocky spine was heaved up in a contorted mass of decayed coral, strewn with rubble; crags, ridges, and gulches were thrown together in a confusing mass. There were no roads, scarcely any trails. The pock marked surface offered no secure footing even in the few level places. It was impossible to dig in; the best the men could do was pile a little coral or wood debris around their positions. The jagged rock slashed their shoes and clothes, and tore their bodies every time they hit the deck for safety. Casualties were higher for the simple reason it was impossible to get under the ground away from the Japanese mortar barrages. Each blast hurled chunks of coral in all directions, multiplying many times the fragmentation effect of every shell. Into all this the enemy dug and tunneled like moles; and there they stayed to fight to the death.[16]

As the Marines advanced deeper into the central spine, they became enmeshed in this unbelievable tangle of ridges, cliffs, and gullies and found themselves assailed from every side. Each cave, bunker, and crevice held a howitzer, machine gun, or rifleman. The more elaborate ones had multiple levels, with firing ports covered by camouflaged sliding steel doors. Sheer cliffs or drops channelized movement into Japanese kill zones and provided natural protection to defensive works. At night it was impossible to establish continuous lines with clear fields of fire. The enemy made use of every tiny gap to infiltrate to the rear and create havoc. Rupertus's "short and swift" operation had turned into a nightmare.

☆   ☆   ☆

In the struggle to take the high ground on September 17, both 1/1 and 2/1 had kept going until dusk. They consolidated their lines in the dark, leaving a gap between the two battalions near the tip of the enemy salient. The Japanese tried to exploit it with a counterattack at 2000. Regiment, already aware of the situation via reports from 1/1 and 2/1, received permission to use 2/7's Fox Company, which plugged the hole just in time. Davis also arranged for repeated salvos from the USS *Mis-*

sissippi (BB-41). The enemy scaled back the infantry assault after an hour, but kept up a steady shower of mortar and artillery rounds all night long. A little before dawn, Puller reported: "Our casualties fairly heavy. We will attack on time."[17]

Chesty had spent the night mustering forces for a 0700 jump-off on September 18. The 1st Pioneer Battalion provided 115 replacements. He also sent every man to the front lines who was not absolutely essential to support operations. Rupertus gave him authority to utilize all of 2/7; just after dawn it moved forward and relieved 1/1. Davis's weary men fell back several hundred yards to reorganize. At the same time, Puller moved his CP forward to a small quarry, within easy rifle shot of Hill 210. Even prior to that shift, 2/7's Berger had been amazed when he first reported to Chesty: "I was embarrassed to find him operating behind some outcropping of coral, closer to the enemy than [my] command post was. In fact, it was difficult to get out an operations map and read it without exposing ourselves."[18]

After thirty minutes of preparation fire by planes and artillery, the regiment attacked. Or at least it tried to advance. Both 2/7 and 2/1 launched assaults to pinch off the Hill 210 salient at its base. They gained some ground, but the enemy retaliated with extremely heavy mortar and artillery bombardments and repeated infantry counterattacks. Casualties were so heavy on 2/1's barren ridge that Honsowetz called for immediate reinforcements and a smoke barrage to screen his men. Under this concealment, he withdrew his battalion halfway back along the ridge it had fought so hard to gain the day before. Later, when the lieutenant colonel ordered elements of Company E to retake some of the ground, a lieutenant refused to send his depleted outfit into the cauldron again, but offered to go by himself. Junior leaders were beginning to realize that even Marine spirit could only do so much in the face of heavy fire. Honsowetz got on the phone to regiment to emphasize his need for more troops to continue the attack. Chesty had little to offer except determination: "Well, you're there, ain't you, Honsowetz? You get all those [remaining] men together and take that hill." Taken aback by these rebuffs from higher and lower echelons, the battalion commander looked for another way to crack the enemy position.[19]

In the middle of the afternoon Puller gave Company B to 2/1 and Honsowetz ordered it to take Hill 205. The senior officers hoped this knoll northeast of 2/1's ridge would command the Japanese approach

route and stem the enemy attacks. The Marines from 1/1 found the going surprisingly easy and seized the crest by 1630. Honsowetz decided
to push on against this apparently weak opposition and Company B
moved off at 1730 toward a steep coral ridge. The Japanese responded
with intense machine gun fire from the front and flanks and heavy barrages. This feature, soon christened "Bloody Nose Ridge" and subsequently renamed the "Five Sisters," was the southern rampart of the
main enemy redoubt. Here, in a series of ravines surrounded by high,
sheer terrain, the Japanese had most of their mortars and artillery. They
wheeled the pieces out of caves to fire, then pulled them back in when
return barrages threatened. This would be the center of enemy resistance on Peleliu until the bitter end. The Company B Marines were
pinned down in front of Bloody Nose until darkness allowed them to
pull back to friendly lines behind Hill 205.

The 2d Battalion, 7th Marines fared little better than 2/1. After a
morning of heavy fighting and no gains, Berger arranged for an air
strike followed by a 2,500-round artillery barrage. The rough terrain
made it impossible to get tanks into position. He brought up a flame-
thrower LVT, but Japanese small arms fire drove off the unarmored vehicle. The deadly work of knocking out enemy fortifications fell almost
entirely to backpack flamethrowers and bazookas and casualties soared
among these crews. The fresh battalion lost 124 Marines and "suffered
a number of heat prostration cases which were complicated by the fact
that many men upon becoming physically exhausted also snapped mentally." At the end of the day, 2/7 had gained about two hundred yards on
the left and assisted 2/1 in taking Hill 210. Coupled with the partial
withdrawal of Honsowetz's outfit, the line was now straight. On the left,
3/1 had again met little opposition, but Puller limited Sabol's advance
to avoid opening a gap at the juncture with 2/7.[20]

While the 1st Marines struggled in the Umurbrogol on September
18, Hanneken's regiment extinguished Japanese resistance in the south.
The 5th Marines also began a rapid advance through the flat, lightly defended eastern peninsula. Although occasional artillery rounds still
landed on the airfield, engineers and Seabees already were repairing it.
Marine spotter planes began operating from the field on the 18th. Two
regiments of the 81st Division had landed on Angaur on September 17.
The Japanese battalion defending that island had withdrawn to rough,
cave-pocked terrain and the Army was soon fighting a miniature version of the Umurbrogol.

September 19 began like previous days, with a heavy bombardment by mortars, artillery, and naval guns—"all support fire that could be mustered." In the center, 2/7 advanced slowly in the difficult terrain. Berger again tried to use tanks and an LVT flamethrower, but without much success due to the terrain. Liberal use of air strikes and naval gunfire brought only temporary relief from enemy mortars and artillery. He broached the idea of having 3/1 plow ahead along the coastal plain, without worrying about contact with his own battalion, in hopes that might redirect some of the attention of the Japanese. Puller was not in a position to risk that option, since he was responsible for defending the left flank of the beachhead. By the end of the day, 2/7 had gained perhaps two hundred yards along its portion of the front.[21]

Honsowetz's battalion sidestepped Bloody Nose Ridge early in the morning and gained more than five hundred yards on the right flank. To keep up the momentum, Puller fed A and C Companies of 1/1 back into the fight. Regiment also arranged for heavy artillery and naval gunfire support. Around noon, Able prepared for a flank assault along a coral hogback pointing from the west toward Bloody Nose. But the company soon reported: "We cannot move out. There is heavy machine-gun fire raking the entire ridge." Honsowetz was unrelenting: "It is necessary that you move out at all costs. I am giving you a direct order. You will move out at once. If you move in small rushes your casualties will not be great." Fifty-six men of Able's rifle platoons started out along the fire-swept high ground and reached the far end, only to find their way barred by a vertical drop. The heat rising from the sun-baked crest caused more men to fall from heat exhaustion than enemy action. When the survivors returned to friendly lines, there were only six men still able to fight. Able Company as a whole was down to sixty-seven effectives. Baker Company, in a reserve position on the right flank, came under direct fire from a large-caliber gun. "The shells whistled in with the sound of ripping silk and exploded with a blast that could be felt for 100 yards." The Marines eventually were able to withdraw to a safer area, but not until their strength was whittled to two officers and thirty-five men.[22]

Baker Company's frontal attack of the previous day against Bloody Nose had failed, as had Able Company's recent attempt from the left flank. Now it was Charlie Company's turn to take a shot from the right side. Around midday the outfit moved forward to seize Hill 100 to the northeast of Bloody Nose. Captain Everett Pope's three officers and

ninety men reached the base of the knoll but were turned back by raking machine gun fire. Two Shermans led the second attack late in the afternoon, but both slipped off a narrow causeway and into a lagoon. The
infantrymen sprinted forward in squad rushes and then attacked up the
hill in unison, capturing the summit despite fire coming in from all directions. To the dismay of Pope and his men, this was merely the end of
a ridge and the next, slightly higher nob dominated their position.

Pope asked for reinforcements and received the reply from 2/1 that
there were none available. He thought his line was "flimsy as hell," but
he decided to hold on to his isolated outpost won at such great cost.
That night the Japanese counterattacked repeatedly. In the last hours before dawn, with their ammunition exhausted, the Marines were involved
in "the most desperate hand-to-hand conflict of the campaign." When
the sun came up on September 20, they still owned the crest of Pope's
Hill, but the Japanese moved machine guns onto the higher elevation
and opened a withering fire at point-blank range. Pope ordered a withdrawal. Of the ninety-four who had started the attack the day before,
only nine returned to friendly lines without serious wounds. Along with
the survivors of his mortar platoon, he now had just fifteen men left in
his company.[23]

The combat power available to the 1st Marines was dwindling rapidly. The regiment was down to seven Sherman tanks. Heat prostration
temporarily had whittled Company E of 2/1 down to one effective
squad. The loss of officers forced Honsowetz to combine F and G Companies. For replacements the evening of the 19th, 2/1 had received a
squad from the 4th War Dog Platoon. Honsowetz already had committed most of his headquarters personnel; his CP now consisted of his
XO, three communicators, and a journal clerk. In 1/1, Davis scraped together his intelligence men, cooks, and jeep drivers to form a machine
gun platoon under his adjutant. His Able Company was down to just
twenty-six riflemen. Berger had combined his E and G Companies, too.
Puller reduced his staff even more to add a few officers and men to the
line outfits.[24]

Chesty was now practically in the front lines himself. That morning
he had moved his CP into the Umurbrogol and so close to the action
that when Berger had gone forward to visit his men, he had stopped in
to see the regimental commander, too. A correspondent found Puller
under a poncho and a piece of tin to ward off the sun. The colonel was

"weary and unkempt," his eyes bloodshot, a broken cigarette temporarily replacing the customary pipe. A mortar round landed nearby, causing everyone to hit the deck, except Chesty, who merely growled: "The bastards." Asked how his men were digging the Japanese out of their defenses, he replied: "By blood, sweat, and hand grenades." He thought "this is the roughest ground you could ever find to fight over" and described the debilitating effect of the heat on his men. Another reporter overheard Puller's response to a battalion commander's query whether the attack should continue: "Yes. Go ahead and smash them." Chesty then turned to a staff officer and ordered up additional stretcher bearers "because we are going to need them."[25]

Smith also visited him around this time. Puller was stripped to the waist and spitting orders out the side of his mouth while he clenched a pipe between his teeth. A sniper interrupted the visit, so the regimental commander organized a patrol from his CP to take care of the problem. Given the ADC's experience on Pavuvu, he was not surprised that Chesty was set up forward of his battalion command posts: "The location . . . reflected his desire to be where he could make his presence felt." There was a potential price to pay for this proximity, given the danger from infiltrators, snipers, and shells. The operations officer recalled that "small arms fire was not unusual in the CP." But the payoff could be substantial, as one reporter observed after talking to the colonel's men: "They will follow him to hell." Honsowetz agreed: "His men loved him, they'd do anything for him, and they'd see him up there poking around where he shouldn't have been. 'Hell, Goddamn, the old man's up here. Let's go.' So it was his way of leadership."[26]

Puller maintained that personal presence was the key to successful command: "I've always believed no officer's life, regardless of rank, is of such great value to his country that he should seek safety in the rear. . . . Officers should be forward with their men at the point of impact. That is where their character stands out and they can do the most good. I've noticed that our greatest commanders never hesitated to expose themselves. Things work better that way. Men expect you to, and men look to officers and NCOs for example."[27]

☆   ☆   ☆

Puller placed everything he had into the attack on the morning of September 20. In addition to the standard bombardment, he organized crews to man every working machine gun, mortar, and 37mm antitank gun and got them into firing positions. All of the division's flame-thrower LVTs came up to support the regiment. Japanese mortars and artillery pieces remained largely secure in their defiladed positions, though, and they opened a counterbombardment that savaged the front lines of the 1st Marines and destroyed one of the flame amphibians. At mid-morning Chesty arranged for the 11th Marines to fire every five minutes on selected targets. The observer group with 1/1 directed twenty-seven naval gunfire missions, eighteen air strikes, and numerous artillery barrages. Honsowetz's 2/1 also frequently called in supporting arms.

Even with this assistance, the skeletal rifle companies could not make headway. The pitifully small knots of men, physically exhausted and emotionally drained, had depleted their reservoirs of strength and will. They were simply no longer an effective fighting force. They moved forward for a few minutes in the face of heavy fire that inflicted more casualties, until survivors gradually melted into the folds of coral that provided a bit of shelter from the storm. One young officer likened it to "a wave that expends its force on a rocky shore." Gradually, like tiny rivulets finding their way back to the sea, the remnants of the regiment crawled and staggered back down the slope to their starting point.[28]

Able Company lost over half the men in its rifle platoons in an unsuccessful attempt on one hill, then tried again and failed again with what it had left—a second lieutenant and eleven Marines. Fox Company was down to ten men in the front lines; Charlie Company had nine. Honsowetz reported to Puller at 0820 that the 1st and 2d Battalions had about 150 effectives and insisted that "we must have reinforcements in order to hold our positions." At the same time, 2/1's CO was insisting that his companies "hold at all costs as we are preparing to advance." Late in the afternoon, Honsowetz directed Pope to retake Hill 100 via the draw to the west. The captain looked around at his handful of spent men and called on Davis to intervene. As Pope issued orders for the assault, his last lieutenant fell mortally wounded. Minutes later, a messenger arrived with word that the attack was canceled. Berger's battalion made small gains, but only 3/1 changed its position appreciably, moving ahead several hundred yards against slight opposition. As the day wore on, Sabol's lines slipped steadily right, up into the high ground to maintain contact with 2/7, which contracted its own frontage as losses mounted.[29]

That afternoon, Puller reported that his casualties now exceeded 1,800. The number of Marines available for duty in the line companies of the 1st Battalion was representative of the regiment as a whole: Able—thirty-seven, Baker—twenty-two, Charlie—sixty. With the 81mm mortar platoon, headquarters personnel, and attachments such as forward observers and pioneers, Davis's entire outfit totaled 350 personnel. He had come ashore with 1,147 officers and men on September 15, just five days earlier. Honsowetz reported that he was down to sixty riflemen in his three line companies. For the past two days, the 1st Marines (reinforced by 2/7) had borne almost the entire brunt of the fighting on the island. Now division took steps to spread the load. Rupertus ordered the 7th Marines to take over the zone occupied by 2/7, 1/1, and 2/1. Puller's regiment would maintain responsibility for the coastal plain and the west face of the Umurbrogol. As the remnants of his 2d and 3d Battalions filed down out of the ridges, the enormity of their losses came into stark relief. Chesty asked one small group of men which platoon they were and received the reply: "Platoon, Hell, Colonel, this is Charlie Company."[30]

The division resumed offensive operations the next morning (September 21), but for the first time since the landing, the 1st Marines did little fighting. Sabol's battalion repeated its recent experience and advanced a few hundred yards, mainly on the left, since it kept its right tied in with the 7th Marines, which made very little progress. Puller gave 1/1 and 2/1 a badly needed rest back near White Beach 1. Davis reorganized his outfit into two rifle companies and fleshed them out with "clerks, cooks, mess sergeants, intelligence section, jeep drivers, mail orderlies, and communicators." Infiltrators inflicted casualties even as the units tried to regroup.[31]

On September 22, 3/1 got more heavily involved in the fighting on the western slope of the Umurbrogol. Item Company, anchoring the right of the line, fought off a strong enemy counterattack at mid-morning. While these Marines held the pivot, King Company attacked to the east and finally seized a section of the crest late in the afternoon after bitter close-quarters fighting. Puller committed Charlie Company to fill the gap in the line between Love and King. Able moved along the face of the ridge in the rear of Love, cleaning out bypassed caves. That night the first significant rainstorm occurred, bringing a welcome relief from the heat. The Japanese also used its cover to send reinforcements to Peleliu by barges, which landed on the north coast. During these two days of fighting, the 7th Marines had been unable to make any appreciable advance against the same Japanese bastion that had stymied the 1st Marines.

The soaring casualties and lack of progress were making an impact at higher echelons. Lieutenant Colonel Harold O. Deakin, the division plans officer, recalled Rupertus sitting on his cot, head in his hands, muttering in despair: "This thing has just about got me beat." That attitude was apparent in the general's decisions. Despite the obvious failure of current tactics, his only contemplated change consisted of a plan to bring the 1st Marines out of the line for a rest, replace them with the fresher 5th, and "continue the attack in zone." Geiger was more in tune with the situation than Rupertus, who seemed rooted to his CP near the airfield (in part due to his bad ankle). The corps commander had made almost daily visits to the front lines since D-Day, including one to the 1st Marines on September 21. On that occasion, the corps intelligence officer thought Puller was "very tired" and seemed "unable to give a very clear picture of his situation." When Geiger asked Chesty what corps could do to help, he responded that he was doing okay with what he had. Photographer Joe S. Rosenthal stopped by and noticed that Chesty responded slowly to questions, seemed downcast at the size of his losses, and "was a tired guy."[32]

Puller was not in good physical condition by this point in the campaign, and perhaps had not been from the very start. His leg had been bothering him since the rehearsals at Guadalcanal. In the heat and stress of Peleliu the thigh swelled dramatically and caused considerable pain, to the point where he could hardly walk. Although he kept his command post well forward throughout the battle, he had to abandon his customary practice of prowling the front lines. One platoon commander later recalled that "gradually it dawned on us that we hadn't seen him since the landing." Ray Davis was convinced that the inflamed old wound saved the colonel's life: "If he had been able to walk around the way he was prone to do, he was going to be killed."[33]

Geiger had left the front lines on the 21st full of concern, which was reinforced when he read casualty reports at the division CP. He was further dissatisfied with Rupertus's insistence that he could secure the island in just a couple of more days. The corps commander already had been contemplating reinforcing the division with one of the Army regiments. Against Rupertus's wishes, Geiger now ordered the 321st Infantry from Angaur to Peleliu to relieve the 1st Marines. He also directed the division to adopt a new approach; the fresh Army outfit would become the "main effort" and move forward as rapidly as possible along the west coast. The hope was that exploitation of light resistance there would lead to an early seizure of northern Peleliu and Ngesebus and perhaps open up an easier avenue of approach in the rear of Japanese defenses in the Umurbrogol. The discovery of empty barges on the morning of September 23 made the plan more urgent, since it also would cut off the possibility of future enemy reinforcement efforts.[34]

The 321st Infantry began moving up into the line on the 23d, but the Marine regiment was not quietly waiting to be relieved. A King Company patrol moved a thousand yards up the coast, destroying several abandoned heavy weapons and demonstrating that the plain was nearly devoid of the enemy. From its positions on the western crest, Love Company observed a column of Japanese moving along a defile toward the 7th Marines. It was a rare sighting of a large body of enemy in the open and Sabol's men wiped out the exposed unit with artillery, mortars, and hand grenades. Davis's battalion continued its work of blasting bypassed caves in the face of the ridge. The 321st was in place by mid-afternoon, but the regimental commander was surprised when he met up with Puller in close proximity to the front lines. Believing he must be in the 1st Marines forward observation post, he asked for the location of the CP. Chesty replied in his usual gravelly voice: "Right here." Thinking he had been misunderstood, the Army colonel asked again with more emphasis: "I mean your *command post.*" Puller spat and repeated with similar stress: *"Right here!"* The story circulated soon after that the Army commander promptly set up his own headquarters a thousand yards to the rear. The legend, for once, was not very exaggerated.[35]

After the exhausted Marines came off the lines, a lucky few boarded waiting trucks, but most of them had to march the several miles to new positions on the east coast. The regiment took over defense of the sectors seized by the 5th Marines, which now became the division reserve. There were daily patrols and a few minor engagements with Japanese stragglers, but mostly the men rested. They received their bedding rolls and knapsacks from the transports, bathed, swam, ate hot food, put on clean uniforms, slept in hammocks, and read their mail. Smith visited the 1st Marines on September 24 and noted the CO's badly swollen thigh. The old wound notwithstanding, Puller insisted he could have his outfit ready to go into the lines again with three days of recuperation. The ADC told him Rupertus already had decided to return the regiment to Pavuvu. The colonel was unhappy, but his arguments did not change the orders.[36]

Puller received nine letters from his wife and scribbled off a hurried reply on the 24th that indicated he knew his part in the operation was over: "I am well and safe and there is nothing further for you to worry about. . . . God willing I will be with you around the first of December. . . . God is good to us." A few days later he was looking beyond Peleliu to the States: "After reorganizing the 1st [Marines] and getting it back into shape, I will only have to await the arrival of my relief. . . . Now that I know I am returning, I am so very impatient to have you with me." He reiterated his old promise that "some day we will have the home with the two chimneys."[37]

During a visit to the regimental CP, Major Day was surprised at Puller's condition; the colonel "looked like hell" and was limping badly. Chesty confirmed the seriousness of his physical state when he made a rare mention to his wife of something that was not upbeat. He told her that he "could hardly walk," but "could not quit before . . . my regiment was relieved." At a memorial service to dedicate the division cemetery, Puller was the only senior officer to show up in combat gear, but even without that equipment, the marks of his old wound and the recent battle were evident. He appeared thinner than usual, his face craggier, his eyes sunken and dark, his demeanor sullen. Years later, he would call Peleliu his "toughest operation" of the war.[38]

Major Day had been struck during his visit by "how depressed [Puller] seemed at the casualties the 1st Marines had taken." It was not what the major had expected from a man with a gung ho reputation. In letters to friends and family, Chesty admitted "the fight was costly" and sympathized with those who had paid the high price: "May God rest the souls of our dead and make life less bitter for our maimed and crippled." But he said no more, giving his feelings for these men no greater space than he had accorded the loss of his own brother. He preferred instead to dwell with pride on what his outfit had done: "The performance of my officers and men was grand. They never failed to move forward when ordered to, and gained ground continually regardless of the enemy. If there is such a thing as glory in war, they have won it."[39]

By the end of September, the plan to bypass Bloody Nose Ridge partially had worked and all of the island was in friendly hands except for a pocket approximately a half-mile long by a quarter-mile wide. This was the zone the 1st Marines had struggled to reduce during its final days in the line. The last square yard of it would not fall until November 27, but Rupertus decided there was no further need for Puller's "badly mauled" regiment. On September 29, the remaining ninety-two officers and 1,612 men of the 1st Marines began loading aboard transports. Rain, strong winds, and heavy seas complicated what should have been a simple administrative movement from shore to ship. A few landing craft were swamped. No men were lost, though, and the regiment sailed for Pavuvu on October 2. Their time in hell was over.[40]

☆ ☆ ☆

The 1st Marine Division and its attached units had paid a high price for Peleliu: 1,397 Marines and sailors dead or missing and 5,699 wounded. The 1st Marines (not including temporary attachments) had suffered the worst: 311 killed and missing and 1,438 wounded out of the 3,251 who had made the landing. That casualty rate of 54 percent exceeded losses in the 5th Marines (43 percent) and the 7th Marines (46 percent). It routinely (and mistakenly) has been cited ever since as the highest figure for any Marine regiment in any battle of the war. In the eyes of some, Peleliu became a black mark against Puller, an indication of his lack of fitness to command at that level. Some angry survivors of the battle later would call Chesty a "butcher." The bare statistics give some veneer of credence to these condemnations, but they do not tell the whole story.[41]

One of the most serious criticisms leveled against Puller concerned his use of firepower. Deakin believed he was "charitable" in saying that the 1st Marines CO "didn't have a total grasp of the use of naval gunfire, artillery, and supporting arms in general." Lieutenant Colonel F. P. Henderson, a member of the corps operations staff, agreed: "Puller refused to let you help him with fire support. He insisted that he was going to do it with Marine infantry, ram it in there." Major Gordon

Gayle, a battalion commander in the 5th Marines, while not criticizing Puller, felt that Harris's regiment performed better and suffered lower casualties because it employed the lion's share of all the supporting fires requested during the campaign.[42]

Later attacks against the Umurbrogol did benefit from much greater firepower, but the 1st Marines made as much use of supporting arms as the situation allowed. On D-Day, the Navy tallied twenty-six calls for naval gunfire. Fifteen were initiated by observers in the 1st Marines, with one third of those coming from the regimental headquarters. On D+1, it was thirteen of twenty-four, with seven coming from Puller's CP. The 1st Marines' share of recorded missions did not change appreciably till the end of its stay in the lines, when only one battalion was engaged. The war diaries and staff journals also show frequent use of air and artillery by the regiment. This activity may have been driven by the battalions and the regimental staff rather than Puller himself, but one item proves he was thinking about supporting arms. On D+1, the division received a message commending the ships for the naval gunfire provided that day. It began: "CO, 1st Marines very much pleased . . ." An aversion to using firepower was not consistent with his prior record either. Back in Nicaragua he had employed rifle grenades rather than an infantry assault "to save the men." On Guadalcanal he had repeatedly called in fire to support his infantrymen. In describing enemy casualties inflicted by 1/7, he had observed: "In the operations where supporting artillery, planes, and destroyer fire was furnished . . . the figures are much higher." During the struggle at Suicide Creek on New Britain he had led the effort to get half-tracks and tanks into the battle. Possibly Puller was not the most skilled employer of supporting arms, but he was certainly aware of their value and used them when they were available.[43]

The 1st Marines were less creative in utilizing firepower in this difficult situation. Later in the battle, other units would come up with some unique ways to attack the Japanese defensive system. They used 155mm guns for direct fire against caves in the face of ridges, hauled 75mm pack howitzers onto the heights to hit more inaccessible targets, and rigged long hoses to spray fuel where LVT flamethrowers could not reach. While Puller and his subordinates were not as innovative as others, they also had little time to react. They first encountered the unexpectedly tough terrain and defenses of the ridge on D+2 and were relieved from the Umurbrogol barely seventy-two hours later. The ability of others to develop better ideas likely stemmed from their opportunity to understand the enemy's defenses before they confronted them.[44]

The perception that Puller did not make full use of supporting arms also may have resulted from the fact that he had much less available than other regiments had when they fought in the ridges. At the start of the battle, the 1st and 5th Marines each had only a 75mm howitzer battalion in direct support, whereas the 7th Marines had a 105mm howitzer unit. The division had three battalions in general support, one each of 105mm and 155mm howitzers and 155mm guns. The 155mm howitzers were not in place until D+2, however, and then directed half their attention to the south in support of the 7th Marines until D+4. The 155mm guns did not go into action for the division until D+4. Thus the 1st Marines did not have a full complement of artillery available until September 19, at which point the regiment was on the verge of being combat ineffective due to casualties. An Army observer thought the division's slow deployment of the heavy guns was inexcusable, since "their fire was badly needed on the ridge." In the meantime, Puller's regiment had tried to obtain additional artillery support whenever it could. On D+1, for instance, the 1st Marines had called in fire missions from the 5th Marines' direct-support artillery battalion.[45]

By the same token, the regiment conducted its entire fight with only Navy air support, whereas other units in the later stages of the battle would benefit from the presence of Marine aviators more skilled in attacking ground targets. The Marine fliers also made much greater use of napalm and 1,000-pound bombs, which had more effect than the ordnance generally used by the Navy. In addition, during the landing the 1st Marines' air liaison parties lost their jeep-mounted radios. These were not replaced till D+3 or later, which hampered the control of close air support. The regiment also suffered from the limited availability of other assets, such as tanks and flamethrower LVTs, which were not concentrated against the ridges early in the battle. Moreover, other outfits would benefit from the efforts of engineers to build roads into the Umurbrogol to give these weapons better access. Major General Julian Smith, the overall Marine commander for the operation, recognized that Puller's men "had a terrifically hard job because the infantry had to fight its way forward without customary air and artillery support."[46]

Before the battle was even joined, the 1st Marines had been victim-ized by the poor preparatory fire. The enfilading bunkers on the White Beaches could have been knocked out if they had received attention. The 1st Marine Division had asked for fire "against areas which a study of the terrain and a knowledge of Japanese tactics would indicate were fortified" and Puller had identified the points as a major concern. But Sabol's after-action report ruefully noted: "More NGF [naval gunfire] and some napom [napalm] on the point just north of White One would have been a big help. This point was undamaged by preparatory fires." As a direct result, the 1st Marines suffered large losses that hampered the outfit throughout the rest of the battle.[47]

Puller has been condemned more frequently for the tactics he employed. George McMillan, a Marine correspondent on Peleliu, summarized the "stereotype" that has come to haunt Chesty's reputation: "He . . . was a tragic caricature of Marine aggressiveness. Puller overdid it. In the minds of many Marine officers—I think the impression was widespread throughout the Corps—Puller crossed the line that separates courage and wasteful expenditure of lives." Captain Pope knew Chesty was personally brave, but also thought that his CO understood only one method of attack—"straight ahead." The company commander could never understand the orders from above to make repeated assaults against Bloody Nose Ridge: "Why he wanted me and my men dead on top of that hill, I don't know. Don't know what purpose it would have served." Nikolai Stevenson agreed that there was no question of Puller's "bravery," but he "never cared about flanks, just straight ahead." He recalled that the regimental commander often answered the battalions' requests for assistance with the unhelpful response: "Just keep pushing."[48]

There is no doubt that Chesty ordered repeated assaults into the teeth of the Japanese defenses and the results were heavy casualties and minimal gains. It is less clear how much responsibility he bears for that. On one level, the operation required a speedy conquest of Peleliu, not only to provide support for the upcoming Philippines campaign, but also to allow the fleet to withdraw to safer waters. The former reason had evaporated by D-Day, but there is no indication that Geiger or Rupertus was aware that was true until it was too late. The latter requirement had been driven home in the late 1943 Gilberts campaign, where the Navy had lost a carrier while Army units dawdled in seizing Makin. In planning the Tarawa phase of that operation, senior admirals had forced the 2d Marine Division to make a direct assault on Betio Island in order to complete the conquest in a shorter time. On Saipan in the summer of 1944, Lieutenant General Howling Mad Smith had relieved an Army division commander for his failure to maintain rapid progress in frontal attacks. One senior Marine defended Smith's action by arguing that the very nature of amphibious operations required "bold, hard-hitting, relentless assaults."[49]

While it might have been in Puller's nature to drive straight ahead in all situations (and that is open to debate), Marine Corps doctrine and Navy command decisions would have pushed him to that style of warfare at Peleliu in any case. O. P. Smith later would give an estimation of Chesty's tactical views that would have described most of the senior Marine commanders in World War II: "He believed in momentum; he believed in coming ashore and hitting and just keep on hitting and trying to keep up the momentum until he'd overrun the whole thing." General Lem Shepherd, one of the most respected Marine division commanders of the war, would press the offensive on Okinawa with a similar outlook: "We will attack and attack vigorously, and we will continue to attack until the enemy is annihilated." General George Patton, a premier practitioner of the amphibious art in the European theater, expressed the same philosophy: "We must attack . . . a commander, once ashore, must conquer or die." One need only look at Buna-Gona, Tarawa, Biak, Saipan, Guam, Iwo Jima, and Okinawa to realize that both the Marine Corps and the Army often employed straight-ahead, attrition-style tactics against strong Japanese bastions.[50]

On Peleliu, Puller faced a situation that gave him no opportunity to adopt elaborate schemes of maneuver. Within the Umurbrogol, the nature of the interlocking defenses meant that any assault quickly deteriorated into a frontal attack. There were attempts to get at Bloody Nose Ridge from the flanks, but in each case the Marines ran into supporting Japanese positions. There simply were no weak areas to exploit. As the CO of 1/1 would put it years later: "We did not discover the defenses until we were in the middle of them being fired at from three sides." The only real option for maneuver was that employed after the 1st Marines was relieved, the move along the lightly defended west coast. There is no indication that Chesty seriously considered that idea even after Sabol had broached it, but it was beyond his capability to execute it in any case. The vital beaches and rear areas had to be protected and that required the 1st Marines to maintain an unbroken line throughout its zone. By the time the nature of the Umurbrogol defenses became apparent, the regiment already had exhausted its own reserve and that of the division, as well as a good portion of its frontline combat power. The forces available to Puller were too weak to exploit the coastal flank and guard all of the uncovered portion of the ridges. It only became possible once the 5th and 7th Marines had completed their missions and the 321st Infantry had reinforced the division. Thus it was a decision for Rupertus, not Chesty, to make.[51]

The only practical alternative Puller had was one advanced by Julian Smith, who felt that the division should have cleaned up the rest of the island and then attacked the Umurbrogol with all its resources, instead of letting a weakened regiment go it alone. Of course, that choice also was not Puller's to make, as Smith pointed out: "I wouldn't have assaulted as soon as the 1st Division did with Puller's regiment. . . . I would have put him on the defensive, and he would have been in fine shape." That undoubtedly was the best solution, but Rupertus was in a hurry to take Peleliu and all his subordinates knew it. Years later Puller would complain privately that the general gave him no options: "Orders were to attack dead ahead, and that was the only thing we could do, to take ground regardless of losses. . . . It was more or less of a massacre. There was no way to cut down losses and follow orders."[52]

Other senior officers at Peleliu felt the same way. Colonel Harris later reported that there was "plenty [of] pressure from above to speed up the attack." He felt "roughly used" when Rupertus pushed him too hard and believed that only Geiger's intervention had prevented his relief by the division commander. The operations officer of the 5th Marines agreed that his outfit was "under the greatest of pressure from headquarters" and that Harris launched some attacks with "great reluctance." He remarked sarcastically: "You can imagine the fine impression we had at that time of division." The Army's senior observer was equally astonished by Rupertus's orchestration of the operation: "There was not much effort on the part of the Division Commander to coordinate the action of the regiments or assist them by means at his disposal. . . . There were instances when it is believed that coordinated artillery fire and assistance from the 5th Marines would have aided the 1st Marines. . . . It was not until D+4 that the Division Commander visited any of the regimental command posts." That same officer found no problems with subordinate echelons: "The regimental commanders appeared to know their jobs and had superior records as leaders in previous combat." Lieutenant Colonel Arthur M. Parker, Jr., the XO of the 3d Armored Amphibian Battalion, placed the blame entirely on the general: "The cold fact is that Rupertus ordered Puller to assault impossible enemy positions at 0800 daily till the 1st [Marines] was decimated." Major Day agreed: "To blame Puller for the day-to-day attacks on the ridge line is really unfair. He was carrying out Rupertus' orders."[53]

If Puller is to be faulted for heavy casualties in his regiment, it can only be in two areas. One was his failure to raise whatever concerns he might have had with his commander. By his own admission, he never made a serious attempt to challenge orders that he later said he found tactically unsound, but instead merely asked for more replacements. Had he lodged a protest with Rupertus, there was a possibility he would have been relieved of command, which was not just theoretical in view of Harris's concern. In addition, he may have faced an internal conflict given his own past emphasis on pushing ahead regardless of losses. Perhaps most important, Chesty undoubtedly would have been extremely reluctant to do anything that might call into question his own aggressiveness and courage—during a lifetime in the Corps, he had never turned down any mission, no matter how difficult. In all likelihood, his bulldog character never allowed the thought of protesting orders to rise very close to the surface. As O. P. Smith later observed: "As long as there was fighting going on, he wanted to be in it." In the end, none of Puller's fellow regimental commanders bucked Rupertus, either.[54]

One might also question the zeal with which Puller executed his orders after D+3, though there is mixed evidence regarding how much pressure he did apply to his subordinates. Davis did not think there was any: "I never felt driven or forced, I felt supported." Davis's response to Pope's plea to cancel the attack on the afternoon of September 20 backs up that claim. But some others believed they were compelled by Puller to go beyond the call of duty. One snippet of conversation overheard by a reporter on September 19 lends support to that view; Chesty's "Go ahead and smash them" sounds like a call for an all-out assault, not a slow, probing attack. That, of course, may have been pure media hype, but the regiment did send companies into the attack again and again, long after they had lost their effectiveness. If Puller did not create or pass along the pressure, neither did he take action to damp it down.

Like Jackson at Chancellorsville, Chesty was a leader "whose resolution was invincible," who would push forward until the mission was accomplished or he and his men "had been annihilated." The 1st Marines had the reputation of being "the most aggressive of the regiments" and it lived up to that billing for the entire nine days it spent in the thick of the battle. While that aggressiveness might have increased casualties in the latter part of that period, it was crucial to securing the vulnerable left flank of the division during the first two days of the operation, when a lack of determination in the face of enemy fire might have resulted in defeat.[55]

The unknown factor in any evaluation of Puller on Peleliu is just how much his inflamed leg affected his ability to command. It is conceivable that pain and fever may have had a significant impact on his judgment, while his lack of mobility prevented him from developing a true picture of what was happening to his regiment. He certainly was aware of his high losses, but he may not have realized just how little he was achieving in return for those lives. It is significant that Geiger's action to relieve the 1st Marines appeared to be motivated as much by his assessment of Chesty's condition as it was by casualty figures.

If there were some Marines who came away from Peleliu feeling that Puller was a butcher, there were many others whose respect and admiration was undiminished. A rifleman in 2/1 revered Chesty for his leadership from the front: "He was one of you. He would go to hell and back with you. He wouldn't ask you to do anything that he wasn't doing with you." Another Marine, wounded on D+1 at Peleliu, voiced almost exactly the same sentiment: "He was one of us! He led by example— not by sitting 500 yards behind the lines, issuing orders. . . . He *earned* all his honors and accolades and perhaps some he never received." General O. P. Smith also had praise for the colonel's leadership: "I went over the ground he captured and I don't see how a human being had captured it, but he did. . . . There was no finesse about it, but there was gallantry and there was determination."[56]

16

"Nobody's Got Use for a Combat Man"
A Hero Without a War
October 1944–June 1950

The physical state of the 1st Marines was such that a good portion of them sailed for Pavuvu aboard a hospital ship, the USS *Pinkney* (PH-2). Puller was among this group. The convoy was barely underway on October 2, 1944, when he went into surgery. A doctor put him under local anesthesia and began probing his swollen thigh for the offending Japanese shrapnel. After more than an hour of exploration, the surgeon finally located the inch-long fragment close to the bone and got it out. He left the wound open for a few days to drain, and the infection and swelling subsided. By the time the ships arrived off Pavuvu on October 10, Puller's leg was "almost healed" and he felt he would be "in fit shape to play baseball within the month." The doctors did indeed restore him to full duty, but another colonel joining the 1st Marine Division from stateside thought Chesty still looked "pretty exhausted."[1]

In spite of Lewis's "cheerful reassurance" in letters home, Virginia was very concerned about him. She also was distressed over the "coarse" portrayal of her husband published in *Time* magazine in early October. Correspondent Robert Sherrod had painted a picture of a tough, hard-bitten combat leader, revered by his men for his courage and his devotion to their welfare. Virginia recognized it was meant as a tribute, but she hated the description of his appearance and demeanor. She wrote Admiral Thomas Hart, a friend from China days, and lamented that the public did not read about her husband's "fine gentle side." Hart replied immediately:

The article . . . makes me particularly proud. . . . Proud when I can point it out and say "That is one of my old gang." I'll go further and tell you that in my estimation you *must* have a feeling of entire pride that your husband should be so written up in a publication of such wide circulation. . . . Now your husband is one of those few who have stood out as superlative in that war in the Pacific. We must thank the Lord that we have a few like him. . . . What he has had to do, of course, is horrible but the point is that he had to do it. He has been doing it better than almost anyone else and your feeling must be absolutely confined to that of pride—pride that such a man is your own. . . . I can imagine nothing worse for him, when he returns, than a realization that you look upon his past accomplishments with anything other than pride. Despite what he has been through you will not find him changed insofar as you are concerned. This other side of him is what he carries to the office, so to speak, and has no part in your daily lives together. Please do your best, Virginia, to effect such mental readjustment as is needed.[2]

Puller and his regiment found Pavuvu bustling upon their return. More than 4,500 replacements had poured onto the island in the previous few days. While Chesty waited for his transfer orders, division decreed a well-deserved period of rest for the veterans. By the end of the month the 7th Marines were also on Pavuvu and the 5th Marines were just departing Peleliu. Rupertus flew back to his "beautiful base camp" on October 21 and likened it to "the Garden of Paradise." It was a more agreeable place than it had been and it was better by far than the bloody cauldron the Marines had just left behind, but it was still a long way from the States. The general, himself awaiting orders to command the Marine Corps Schools, offered to let his senior subordinates depart prior to the arrival of their replacements. On November 4, Puller, Hanneken, and several other officers started the long journey home.[3]

At the time Puller seemed unconcerned that he was leaving the combat zone. While he did prompt division to fire off a request about the status of a recommendation for an award for his part in the Battle of Koli Point, he made no effort to have his orders canceled. There was no hint of regret at not fulfilling his desire to remain in the Pacific "until the downfall of the Japanese Empire." He was worn down by two years of hard fighting and tough living conditions and he may have recognized just how badly he needed a period of recuperation in a healthy environment. He also thought—along with many others—that the war would go on for a very long time to come. His letters to friends in October 1944 contained his analysis of the conflict:

> I hope our people realize the magnitude of the Pacific War; we not only have to destroy the Japanese on the islands but we must fight them on the continent of Asia as well. Russia is an unknown quantity out here and from the Quebec Conference [of Allied leaders] I believe that we can expect little or no help from the British when the war in Europe is finally won. We will win but we will have to pay for a victory with tens of thousands of lives. Several years ago our government was told by the Japanese that in the event of war, they were prepared to lose ten million men. Perhaps after the election next month, our people will be told the truth. I am thankful that the Peleliu operation is over; our losses were great but we are now one step nearer Tokyo.

As he flew across the Pacific in November 1944, he undoubtedly assumed he would be back again in a year or so to participate in the final campaigns leading to the Japanese home islands.[4]

Rupertus had sent Puller off with only muted praise for his performance. The general's sole comment on Puller's fitness report was very positive—"an outstanding officer, aggressive and a leader"—but he gave the colonel mostly second-tier marks. The only outstanding grades came in regular duties and loyalty. He did recommend Puller for a medal, but it was the Legion of Merit, an award ranking below the Silver Star. The citation credited Chesty with successfully establishing a D-Day lodgment at Peleliu and "masterfully maneuver[ing] his assault elements" against the Umurbrogol. "The combat efficiency and bold tenacity displayed by his regiment was the culmination of Colonel Puller's leadership in attaining its high state of combat efficiency."[5]

Puller arrived in San Francisco on November 6. There he found orders to report to New River, now renamed Camp Lejeune, with a delay of thirty days for leave. He traveled east by train and finally reached Saluda in the middle of the month. Both Virginias had been anticipating the "glorious reunion" and they were not disappointed. Chesty enjoyed the opportunity to get reacquainted with his daughter, now a four-year-old capped by bobbing brown curls. After a few days of ease at the Evans home, he was ready for some time alone with his wife and they went to New York City. With his heroic reputation, the Pullers had no trouble finding a good hotel room and getting tickets to Broadway shows. Virginia thought of the brief "fling" as a "second honeymoon," but she was overjoyed simply to have him home again. Chesty was equally glad to relish the respite and called HQMC to ask for a twelve-day extension of his leave.[6]

On December 27, 1944, Puller reported to Camp Lejeune. Quarters were just as scarce as they had been in 1941, but this time the family took up temporary residence in a fishing lodge forty miles away. After a two-week stint as the executive officer of the Infantry Training Regiment (ITR), Chesty took command of the outfit. It was an important billet. The Training Center at Camp Lejeune and its twin at Camp Elliott in California had been in operation since 1942, with the mission of teaching advanced skills to freshly minted boot camp graduates. One arm of the Lejeune center, the Specialist Training Regiment, produced communicators, engineers, cooks, bakers, and so forth. Puller's command was responsible for turning out riflemen and crewmen for machine guns, mortars, antitank guns, and bazookas. There had been frequent complaints from the Pacific about the shortcomings of personnel in the replacement drafts. In January 1944, Red Mike Edson, now a brigadier general with the 2d Marine Division, had protested to Jerry Thomas that few ITR graduates had ever dug a fighting hole and some had spent much of their time serving as messmen or barbers. Vandegrift and Thomas took action. In the summer of 1944, the Commandant decreed an expansion in the ITR training syllabus from eight to twelve weeks and ordered more combat veterans to instructor duty. It may have been pure chance that Puller took command of ITR a few months later, but in all likelihood Vandegrift chose him for his demonstrated interest in tough training. It was probably no coincidence that Hanneken took charge of the West Coast ITR at the same time.[7]

Ironically, the early withdrawal of the 1st Marines from Peleliu contributed to the undoing of these reforms. Commanders were pushing HQMC to provide excess replacements to each division just before their next campaign. During the initial days of the landing these men would unload supplies at the beach. As units suffered casualties, this manpower pool would keep them up to fighting strength. The goal was to prevent regiments from having to leave a battle due to losses. To prepare for the February 1945 assault on Iwo Jima, thousands of men were pulled out of ITR after a few weeks. Okinawa in April repeated the cycle. The enormous human cost of storming Japanese bastions in the last two years of the war was outstripping the ability of the Marine manpower system to produce high-quality replacements. And the surrender of Germany in May 1945 had no effect on the Corps, which was focused almost entirely on the Pacific war.[8]

Puller had his hands full running the large outfit, which far exceeded the strength of an infantry regiment. The Marines were formed in units designated either as rifle or weapons battalions. All went through the same initial four weeks of training as basic infantrymen at the Tent Camp. They specialized in a particular advanced skill thereafter. A typical week consisted of sixty hours of classroom instruction and field work, with emphasis on team and squad tactics and live-fire exercises. Based on the experience of the Marianas and Peleliu, jungle warfare classes disappeared and the focus turned to assaulting fortified positions. At times, ITR had as many as fifteen battalions—roughly twelve thousand men—somewhere in the pipeline. Puller had over one hundred officers and a large number of NCOs to teach and supervise, but theirs was an uphill battle. It was difficult to build any organizational esprit since the men knew they soon would be farmed out to real units in the Fleet Marine Force (FMF). An awards parade every Saturday morning may have been designed as much to motivate the young Marines as it was to honor Pacific veterans on the staff. The "colorful" Puller, with his chestful of ribbons topped by an unprecedented four Navy Crosses, was also a source of inspiration.[9]

The demanding schedule wore down Chesty and he succumbed to a high fever in July 1945. It was a recurrence of malaria and he ended up spending a week in the infirmary. In mid-August news of the atomic bombing of Hiroshima became public. A week later, while most of the men were enjoying the evening movies, radio stations broadcast the Japanese acceptance of surrender terms. In one theater at Tent Camp, the operator turned off the projector in mid-reel and announced the news. The audience erupted in wild cheers. They eventually resumed watching the show, only to dissolve in laughter when an actor portraying Admiral Yamamoto boasted that he would dictate peace terms in

Washington. For young men who no longer had to worry whether they might survive the next amphibious assault, it was a cathartic release.[10]

The atomic bomb brought about an almost equally rapid termination of Puller's command. On August 17 Vandegrift ended advanced infantry schooling and scaled back all training to peacetime levels. Veteran instructors flowed out to discharge centers and the trainees shipped directly overseas. On September 14, at a final Saturday parade, ITR folded its colors and passed into history. Although Chesty had never been given the time to completely turn "awkward gawky youngsters into smoothly efficient fighting men," he and his instructors had made a difference. Major General John Marston, the commander of Camp Lejeune, lauded Puller for "his unusual qualities of leadership" and "his success in developing men to be excellent combat Marines with high morale." Brigadier General Alfred H. Noble, head of the Training Center, praised the ITR commander, remarking that Chesty had brought the school "to maximum efficiency" and was "highly regarded as a troop leader." The two officers must not have gotten along well, though, as Noble gave his subordinate an unusually low mark in cooperation.[11]

The end of the war did not leave Puller completely happy. According to legend, he told the officer who broke the surrender news: "Now there's nobody left to fight. And I want to fight so bad you better get out of here before I go after you." Chesty wrote O. P. Smith in a sullen mood on September 12: "I regret that Marine Corps Headquarters saw fit to order me back to the States before the Japanese were finally defeated." He had not complained when he left the Pacific, but the surprising onset of peace now made the transfer look like a mistake. Worse still, Puller became the commander of the cooks, bakers, and communicators of Specialist Training Regiment. He was "thankful to be with it" only because "it is at least a regiment in name." But it was a far cry from any hopes he might have had about leading a division in battle against the Japanese. At least a few Marines thought that he should have reached that level. A warrant officer who had served with Chesty in Shanghai and then spent the war as a Japanese captive wrote: "I have heard of your distinguished war record with great pleasure. When we were prisoners in those dark and dreary days we used to speculate: 'If Chesty Puller doesn't get killed, he will surely make Major General.' To the sorrow of your old men of Shanghai the prediction did not come true, and we are all terribly disappointed that you are only a colonel. I can truthfully speak for all of your old men—that we never, never forgot the best Marine officer we ever had the privilege of serving under. . . . Your well-nigh incredible career is the admiration of us all."[12]

Some Puller partisans later would assert that he had advanced in rank more slowly than his performance warranted and was a "colonel longer than anyone in Marine Corps history." They believed this occurred because "he had enemies around Headquarters" or had "none of the guile that slips up the ladder of promotion." In reality, he had moved ahead as fast as anyone in his situation could expect. The thing that had worked most against him was the time he had spent as an enlisted Marine during his years in Haiti. By way of comparison, his commissioning date of March 1924 placed him six and a half years behind Merritt Edson, who had earned his gold bars in October 1917, and five and a half years behind Jerry Thomas, who had gained a battlefield commission in September 1918. Red Mike made the jump to colonel after sixteen months wearing silver oak leaves. Thomas took only fourteen, but he benefited from an early spot promotion for assuming the division chief of staff slot (a colonel's job) on Guadalcanal. Puller spent twenty-one months as a lieutenant colonel. His somewhat slower advancement was due to his position on the seniority list behind the World War I hump and the leveling off of Marine strength in 1944. He did not fall behind any contemporaries, and in fact jumped ahead of several.[13]

Promotion to brigadier general was a much tougher hurdle. Edson attained that rank in December 1943, primarily as a result of his rare combination of bravery in combat and exceptionally strong skills as a staff officer, both demonstrated anew at Tarawa that November. Although Thomas had not commanded units in battle during this war, he picked up his star in January 1944 because Vandegrift relied so heavily on his extraordinary talents as a planner and wanted him to play a key role at HQMC. Edson and Thomas had spent about sixteen months as colonels and had vaulted over the heads of more than one hundred other officers, an unprecedented feat at that rank during World War II. Puller did not have that much time as a colonel until the war was over. There also was very little room for any colonel to advance in the latter part of the war. Although twenty-four men had made brigadier in 1942, Edson had been only the fourth man to achieve that rank in 1943. The stagnating strength of the Corps in 1944 imposed a similar constraint on the number of generals. Even if there had been more opportunity, Chesty still would have had to jump over more than two hundred senior officers to make the grade. Among that group were other successful regimental commanders such as Edward Craig, Herman Hanneken, Harry Liversedge, and Bill Whaling, plus a number of superb staff officers such as Merrill Twining and John Selden. There had been no secret cabal holding back Puller.[14]

Chesty and every other Marine officer soon had a much more immediate career concern than promotion. Vandegrift was determined not to repeat the failed personnel policies of the post–World War I era, when the Corps had held on to all its senior leaders. As a result, junior officers had been separated from the service or reverted to lower rank in order to meet reduced manpower levels. The Commandant pressed for and got a law in early 1946 that created a twenty-year retirement, reduced the maximum age to sixty-two, and authorized the establishment of boards to select officers for involuntary separation. Vandegrift was especially pleased that the last provision would allow the Corps to get rid of "a good many regular officers—especially in the colonels grade —who failed miserably when put to the test [of war]." The chopping block started near the very top, with Lieutenant Generals Holland Smith and Roy Geiger and a three-star admiral serving as a panel to evaluate major generals for retention. Other boards reviewed officers in each rank. With this pruning at all levels, men who had proven their worth in combat would be able to hold on to their hard-earned promotions. Headquarters announced the provisions of the law on March 7, 1946, and offered all officers the chance to send letters to their board "inviting attention to any matter of record in the Navy Department, or to any other official matter concerning yourself which you deem to be important in the consideration of your case."[15]

Puller evidently had been following the progress of the legislation and preparing to bolster his position. He fired off a five-page, single-spaced, typed letter to the board the very next day. He opened with a straightforward statement of his intent (copied in part from a description of Stonewall Jackson in Chesty's favorite book): "I do not wish to be placed on the retired list as I am physically fit for field duty, am in the prime of life, and believe that I am fitted by natural instincts, by education and study, and by self-discipline, for command. From the year 1917, when I was a cadet at the Virginia Military Institute, to the present time, I have been trained mentally, morally, and physically for the position to which I aspire." He noted that he had "recently" examined his personnel file at HQMC and was surprised to find that promotion boards looked at only that material gathered on an officer since his previous selection. He indignantly commented on this practice: "This has resulted in my record containing practically nothing more than that of any reserve colonel with only World War II service." He had little to worry about in that regard, however, since few colonels, regular or reserve, had compiled a résumé consisting entirely of successful regimental command, both in battle and with a major training program.[16]

The main thrust of Puller's letter, however, was that he had received a raw deal when the post–World War I retention panel had not reinstated his commission. Given his service with the Haitian Gendarmerie, he expressed wonderment that the Neville Board had overlooked him, "notwithstanding my position of responsibility at that time and the fact that I had proved my fitness to command troops in battle." He was certain he had been rejected because he was a private in the Corps, rather than an NCO: "If I had been serving in the Marine Corps at that time as a junior non-commissioned officer instead of in the *Gendarmerie d'Haiti* as a company commander, I would have been selected for a commission by the Neville Board, and would now be senior to a number of officers now in the Marine Corps who are about my age, but did not enter the service and remained in school during World War I."[17]

Puller went on to note he also had been rebuffed in his attempt to get his Gendarmerie fitness reports made a part of his officer personnel records, while the policy of reviewing only recent material had subsequently removed from consideration his years of service in Nicaragua and China. "Believing that foreign station and sea duty are the primary assignments for which a Marine officer should prepare and qualify himself in order to develop his capacity for command, I have bent every effort to serve beyond the continental limits of the United States as often and as long as I have been permitted to." In his opinion, he had been hurt by all those circumstances: "I believe that if my military record at Marine Corps Headquarters had presented a truer and more comprehensive picture of my experience and qualifications, my services might have been employed to a greater extent during World War II." He obviously meant to imply that he would have served at a higher rank and thus would have held weightier responsibilities.

The long letter revealed a great deal about Chesty. It was clear that he had built up a deep-seated resentment over his loss of seniority in the early 1920s. He also was concerned that another postwar board again might adversely affect his career, this time bringing it to an end. True to his character, he was not about to let that happen without a fight and he had pulled no punches in making his case. But the speed and strength of his response indicated that he had been brooding on the subject for some time and felt that his chances were not good. He apparently believed that an undue emphasis on education or staff experience might work against him.

His bias against school and staff duty came through strongly in his letter to the board. He denigrated those who had stayed in college during 1917–1918, conveniently ignoring the fact that part of his seniority problem stemmed from his own decision to attend VMI during the first year of the war, while men such as Jerry Thomas and Amor Sims had enlisted immediately and won their commissions under the guns of the enemy or as meritorious NCOs. Throughout the interwar period, Puller had sought repeatedly to attend military schools, but had been denied that opportunity except for the single stint at Benning. Now he chose to emphasize that all he had ever wanted was overseas duty and that he always had believed that "service in the camp and in the field is the best military school."

In a similar fashion, he chose to believe that the thing he had excelled in during his time in the Corps—command—was by far the most important aspect of being a Marine officer. In describing his time in Haiti and Nicaragua in the letter, he mentioned only his leadership billets, leading the unwary reader to assume that he had never served on a staff in those campaigns. In that same vein, he thought himself "fitted . . . for command" and believed that the only concern of a Marine officer should be "to develop his capacity for command." He later would admit that "there must always be staff people, of course, or we'd never get anything done," but he did not see any value in such experience as an element of preparation for greater responsibility as a commander. Increasingly, he viewed staff officers as a breed apart from true leaders. In his mind, those who served on a staff were, by definition, "a bunch of bastards that have never been under fire, have never commanded troops, except at [school]." He would lament: "The combat people run things when the chips are down and the country's life is at stake—but when the guns stop, nobody's got use for a combat man. The staff officers are like rats: they stream out of hiding and take over." Where he once merely sought to keep himself out of staff duty, now he avowed an open dislike for those who occupied the billets. Strangely, he never seemed to realize that his own attempts to avoid such duty helped create the very dichotomy between staff and command he so despised—any staff he served on would have been responsive to the needs of the men in the front lines.[18]

As it turned out, the combat-proven Puller had nothing to worry about and he was not among those plucked for early retirement. The closing lines of his appeal to the board (borrowed in part from John W. Thomason's 1936 letter to Chesty) were prescient, however: "In my opinion, the world does not promise peace, not even the United States internally, and our government will need experienced command officers before I shall have outlived my usefulness as a Marine." A semiofficial Marine publication seconded that sentiment not long afterward: "He has good years ahead, if someone starts another shooting war."[19]

☆ ☆ ☆

Part of Chesty's increasingly hostile attitude toward staff officers may have resulted from his frustration with the awards system. Sims had recommended him in February 1944 for the Silver Star for Koli Point. Ultimately, the awards board at FMFPac (the senior Marine headquarters in the Pacific) had disapproved it. In April 1945, Puller, guessing that "some staff officer acted upon it himself without reference to higher authority," asked Sims to resubmit the request with additional details. Chesty was at least partly right. The colonel in charge of the board, who had spent the war in rear echelon billets, tried to dash cold water on the renewed recommendation, saying that Puller already had received enough medals for Guadalcanal. Chesty persisted and ultimately the review board at HQMC authorized a Bronze Star in the spring of 1946. But the recipient was upset that "some jerk" had reduced the original recommendation: "What right have those people back there got to put their damned cotton-picking hands into a thing like that? They didn't see the action. How in the hell can they have the gall to reduce the award?" His disgust with the process of recognizing him for Koli Point must have deepened when HQMC simultaneously disapproved a recommendation that he be awarded a letter of commendation for his leadership of the Infantry Training Regiment. Puller was not concerned just about himself. When he found out that his attempt to get a Navy Cross for Honsowetz for Peleliu had resulted in a Legion of Merit, he intervened and got it upgraded.[20]

Toward the end of the war it was tougher to get unit decorations, too. Julian Smith had nominated the 1st Marine Division for a Presidential Unit Citation for Peleliu, but Holland Smith, the commanding general of FMFPac, had rejected it. He was willing to consider subordinate units on a case-by-case basis. Buddy Ross, former XO of the 1st Marines, suggested that Puller instigate a move to get the award for their old regiment. Chesty felt he was "not much good at hinting," so he simply forwarded Ross's letter to O. P. Smith: "I owe the officers and men of the 1st Regiment much and would like to feel that I have done as much as I could for their splendid work." Smith was only too willing to comply, since he believed that Puller's outfit was more entitled than any other group. (Eventually Smith's efforts would result in the award of the Presidential Unit Citation to the entire division.)[21]

Chesty may have been concerned about his career and awards, but this was otherwise a happy period for him. For the first time in years he was in a peacetime billet that allowed him to come home every evening to his family. His household also had grown with the arrival of twins in August 1945—Lewis Burwell, Jr., and Martha Leigh. Virginia was pleased to have another "cozy little girl," while her husband was ecstatic to have a "boy from stem to stern" to carry on the Puller name. For Christmas that year, Lewis bought his son a platoon of tin soldiers, but Mrs. Puller was "hoping he will be a Bishop!" Major Victor Streit, the former operations officer of the 7th Marines, lived next door and recalled that the colonel was a congenial social host, surprisingly "gracious and genteel" in contrast to his on-the-job reputation for gruffness. In all things concerning his family, Chesty remained tenderhearted to a fault.[22]

His tour with the Specialist Training Regiment was uneventful. The officers and NCOs, "accustomed to the peaceful serenity of the former organization," were jolted out of their complacency by his arrival, but there was little opportunity for Puller to make a major impact. The main business at hand was folding up organizations and discharging Marines, tasks that included returning war dogs to their owners. He would recall later that one of the most contentious issues he faced involved a canine owners' association that disagreed with his report on the unsuitability of Dobermans for combat missions. Many Marines of the two-legged variety were anxious to get home and the base newspaper headlined each reduction in the number of points needed to qualify for release from active duty. Some Army soldiers held public demonstrations to press for a speedier return to civilian life. There was only one such incident in the Corps, a small protest in Hawaii that was promptly squelched by General Geiger. A cartoonist for the Lejeune newspaper highlighted the difference with a drawing of a grizzled Marine on a Pacific isle looking disdainfully at a crying toddler wearing diapers marked "U.S. Army." By the middle of 1946 the Marine Corps had shrunk to 155,000 troops, well on the way to its authorized peacetime strength of seven thousand officers and 100,000 men. The biggest landmark of the drawdown at Camp Lejeune came in December 1945, when bulldozers pushed the last wooden frames and decks of Tent City into a pile and engineers turned the remains of the once bustling complex into a massive bonfire.[23]

With the onset of peace, the Corps itself was in some danger of ending up on the trash heap of history. The Army had proposed a merger of the War and Navy Departments and a reorganization of the operating forces into land, sea, and air components. Notably absent was any provision for a dedicated, combined-arms, amphibious component. With the guns silent, the Army's idea attracted strong support. The elevation of Harry Truman to the presidency also had placed a World War I National Guard veteran with an anti-Marine bias in a key position. The plainspoken Missourian saw unification as a means to save money and balance the government's budget; in his eyes, the Corps was merely an expensive anachronism in the atomic era. Due in large measure to Vandegrift's distaste for political battles, the fight to save the Corps fell heavily on Thomas, Edson, Twining, and a handful of assistants. Most of the other leaders in the Corps sat on the sidelines in the absence of guidance from the Commandant.

Puller played a part in a rare supporting counteroffensive, launched by Marston in late 1945. The general tried to stem the tide of the Army's "far-reaching and rather well-planned campaign to put their ideas over." He dispatched his senior officers to North Carolina cities to make influential citizens aware of the Navy Department's position. Chesty drew the state capital, Raleigh, and met with the only major rejection in the otherwise pro-Navy state. Surprisingly it came at the hands of Josephus Daniels, a newspaper publisher and former Secretary of the Navy, who refused the colonel's request for support. In all likelihood, the result had nothing to do with Puller's persuasive skills, since Daniels was a staunch Democrat and undoubtedly motivated by party loyalty to Truman. The fight would drag on in the media and the halls of Congress until the contending parties achieved a compromise in the National Security Act of 1947. That far-reaching legislation placed the Navy and War Departments under what would become the Defense Department. But it also solidified the existence of the Corps as an independent service.[24]

☆   ☆   ☆

The ongoing demobilization struck the Specialist Training Regiment in 1946, so Puller was due to have a second command disappear from under him in July. He received temporary duty orders to HQMC in late June and was ushered in to see the Commandant. Vandegrift informed Chesty that he would take over the Eighth Marine Corps Reserve District, headquartered in New Orleans. The unexpected news came as a blow. The reserve component had been a backwater of the Corps prior to the war and he perceived this new assignment as a sort of exile.[25]

While it was not the assignment Puller desired, neither was it the career-ending billet he feared. The Marine Corps Reserve had disappeared when it mobilized for World War II and Vandegrift had been trying in the postwar period to reestablish it as a large, vibrant adjunct to the active-duty force. To achieve that goal, he was placing regular officers whom he trusted in key positions. The Director of the Marine Corps Reserve, for instance, was Colonel Randolph McC. Pate, who had served as G-4 of the 1st Marine Division during the early days of Guadalcanal. He would go on to become the Commandant in 1956. Another district director was Colonel John C. McQueen, the chief of staff of the 6th Marine Division during the battle for Okinawa. He would become a general, too. His former division commander was Major General Lemuel C. Shepherd, now the assistant commandant, who also happened to be the godfather of Lewis Puller, Jr., and a cousin of Pate. Clearly, Vandegrift and Shepherd were not sending Pate, Puller, McQueen, and other close associates into dead-end jobs. Both generals believed that men and women who volunteered to sacrifice time away from their civilian careers and families to maintain a connection to the Corps had "every right to expect a return in well-planned and efficiently executed instruction programs," something that had been lacking in the prewar system. For the second time in as many years, it appears that the Commandant selected Puller in order to bring his reputation as a superior trainer to bear in a critical area.[26]

The Specialist Training Regiment ceased to exist in early July. A week later, the base commanding general pinned the Bronze Star on Puller for the Battle of Koli Point. This time the newspapers correctly cited the colonel in their headlines as "One of Marine Corps' Most Decorated Officers." After the ceremony, the Pullers packed up their household and went to Saluda for a month of leave before heading south to New Orleans.[27]

☆ ☆ ☆

Puller arrived in Louisiana with only a wish from the Director of Reserve for "good luck in your search for living quarters and office space." Chesty soon arranged with the Navy to occupy a few of their unused rooms in the New Orleans Customshouse Building. Although he commanded all reservists in a region comprising the tier of Southern states from Florida to Texas and up to Tennessee, his immediate staff consisted of two active-duty officers and four NCOs, a far cry from the large units he had grown accustomed to in the Pacific and at Camp Lejeune.[28]

The change in circumstances did not alter Puller's informal approach to leading Marines. He no longer had front lines to walk and he had little interest in the administrative details that dominated the work of his staff, but he always was wandering through the work spaces and offering encouragement and praise to the men. He also enjoyed shutting down the office from time to time and taking his small band down to the coffee shop, where he regaled them with tales from the Banana Wars. Occasionally he spent weekends hunting with one of his sergeants, whose family owned property out in the countryside. When it was necessary, the colonel was a stern disciplinarian. He tore up the promotion warrant of one young NCO who was getting into trouble in the notorious French Quarter, but also arranged a transfer to a place with fewer temptations. When the orders came through for the corporal, Chesty reinstated the promotion and told the young Marine to "keep your nose clean." The legendary colonel managed to retain the awe and respect of his staff and still create a relaxed working environment.[29]

With the Marine Corps Reserve just coming back into being in 1946, there was much to do. The Commandant hoped to build the strength of the part-time force to 128,000 officers and men, with a quarter of this manpower in the Organized Reserve (units), a small fraction in the Women's Reserve, and the remainder in the Volunteer Reserve (individuals not affiliated with a unit). The Marines in the Organized Reserve participated in a two-hour session of instruction each week, known as a drill, for which they received a day of pay. They also performed a two-week period of active duty once each year. Members of the Volunteer Reserve had no training requirements, but could participate in the annual exercises. New reserve recruits did not go to boot camp or specialist training—their sole education as Marines came through drills and summer camp. A small group of active-duty Marines, known as inspector-instructors, served with each unit to provide the necessary training and administration. Puller's marching orders called for him to gather 4,400 officers and men into Organized Reserve units. He had to supervise the recruiting of manpower, find homes for the organizations, and see to their training and supply. He also had to enlist and then manage an even larger number of Volunteer Reservists.[30]

The task of generating interest in the Reserve was not simple. There was no reserve recruiting service and no budget for advertising to reach the large number of recently discharged Marines or young civilians considering a future in the military. Initially the manpower acquisition process relied on word of mouth and unpaid volunteers. Puller's fame and "picturesque" character provided a boost to enlistments in his region, however, since he made "good copy" for the local media. One New Orleans paper announced his arrival with the headline "Great Marine Corps Hero to Lead District Reserves." The article recounted the highlights of his career and Marine plans for reserve forces in the area. Trips around his domain to speak at various functions, such as the annual Navy Day observance, helped spread the news.[31]

Chesty made his biggest splash in the press on November 10, 1946. The *Times-Picayune* built the cover of its Sunday magazine around a colorful photograph of Puller in dress blues, with his sword and five rows of ribbons. The feature article opened with his sobering assessment of the postwar world and the role of the Corps in national defense:

> You've got to have a good cop on the beat if you want to have a peaceful neighborhood. What goes for a neighborhood goes for the world. The United States Marines have been patrolling the world's tough neighborhoods, protecting American lives and property, ever since there was a United States of America. We're the cops on the beat. We've learned, like good cops, that when the tough boys get lawless, there's more law in the business end of a riot-stick than in a Supreme Court decision. These days of 1946, it looks like time for America to get realistic instead of starry-eyed.

He also argued that technology had little impact on the nature of war: "Whether they've got atomic bombs and rockets or not, we can lick 'em if America gets hard and American fighting men are trained to march 30 miles a day with a pack, and hit whatever they shoot at with any weapon they're trained to use. Just as long as Americans have the will to fight." Although he had "tremendous respect" for nuclear weapons, "we'll need the Marines to get the enemy launching bases and to make the landings. . . . The foot soldiers and the Marines will play a big part."[32]

The article was significant because it marked the first time that Puller spoke out publicly about issues beyond his own billet. Even during his tour of the country in 1943, he had confined his comments to the fighting on Guadalcanal. His personal letters had long expressed strong views about larger themes involving national defense; from this point on he would be increasingly willing to share those thoughts with the media.

The *Times-Picayune* piece heralded another change in Puller's public persona. Reporters were always hungry for gripping tales that snared public interest and the colonel's prodigious legend provided no shortage of such material. But the writer in this case spun the facts of Chesty's career into pure myth. The penetration of Dominique Georges's camp in Haiti became an attack by Puller and Brunot, working entirely alone, that boldly routed seventy-five *cacos*. The ambush at El Sauce was "the last old-time Indian battle in the Western Hemisphere." According to the author: "250 Indians rode in a whooping, shooting circle around the stalled train. Colonel Puller calmly detrained his 100 men and they shot the circling Indians off their horses like shooting gallery targets." Other battles were only slightly more recognizable. The overactive imagination of the reporter undoubtedly was the main culprit, but Chesty may have egged him on. Puller had been raised on the romanticized recollections of Confederate veterans and apparently enjoyed embroidering his own experiences to make them more engaging. As time passed, his penchant for weaving enthralling yarns and tossing off amusing anecdotes increasingly would obscure the real story of his amazing career. Nor was he the only source of such material. A reporter for *Leatherneck* magazine observed in 1948 that any account of Chesty's career "will require much sorting of facts from the scores of fanciful tales concocted by the men of Puller's command."[33]

☆   ☆   ☆

The first of Chesty's reserve organizations to stand up was the 10th Infantry Battalion, also headquartered in New Orleans. Lieutenant Colonel Robert C. McDonough, a paratrooper who had fought at Bougainville, arrived in September to serve as the inspector-instructor for that command. The challenges he faced in building the unit from scratch were indicative of the program nationwide. Recruiting relied heavily on press releases timed to coincide with newsworthy events such as the Marine Corps birthday. His armory consisted of a wooden barracks at the local naval air station—one of thousands of similar temporary buildings thrown up for the war. It was not designed for classrooms or the storage of weapons and equipment. The Navy owned the facility, but was taking no action to alter it for its new use. The Director of Reserve soon acknowledged that the acquisition of suitable drill sites for his units was the "most serious problem" facing the entire program. That did not slow down the creation of new organizations. In Puller's first year on the job, he also oversaw the formation of two other battalions and two independent companies. In 1947, the Eighth District garnered valuable publicity and local goodwill when Chesty arranged for his units in New Orleans to help repair breaks in the levee following a hurricane.[34]

In its campaign to reestablish a more robust Reserve, Headquarters focused on the quality of the annual training sessions. Vandegrift acknowledged that prior to World War II there had been "too many examples of reservists spending two weeks of active duty as forgotten observers of the daily routine of a post or station." To prevent that from recurring, he directed active-duty commands to develop and supervise meaningful training. He established the goal that reservists should seek to "attain individual and unit proficiency based insofar as practical, on the standards applicable to the regular Marine Corps." Subsequently, Headquarters decided to extend the requirement for annual visits by the inspector general to include reserve units, despite opposition from the IG's office, which dreaded the extra time on the road. Puller strongly agreed with the latter initiative. When he noted that the inspection schedule for 1948 failed to include one of his newest outfits, he "respectfully recommended" that the IG modify his itinerary. The general relented, probably to the chagrin of the inspector-instructors and reservists in Chattanooga, Tennessee, who now had something else to worry about.[35]

By 1948 the reserve program was in full swing all across the country. Headquarters expected twenty-four thousand members of the Organized Reserve to report to Camp Lejeune and Camp Pendleton for "the largest training schedule for Reserves the Marine Corps has ever held." Puller and the Eighth District had done more than their share. He now had sixteen units with 7,560 officers and men, roughly one quarter of the total strength of the Organized Reserve. Another eight thousand men had enrolled in his Volunteer Reserve program.[36]

With the end of his two-year tour approaching, the colonel submitted his preference for a follow-on assignment, seeking duty with the 2d Marine Division at Lejeune. He hoped to participate in operations in the Mediterranean region, where a Communist-inspired insurrection was underway in Greece and war was brewing in the British mandate of Palestine. Relations between the Soviet Union and the Western allies also were deteriorating rapidly in the aftermath of coups that installed Communist regimes in Hungary and Czechoslovakia, to join those already established by Russian occupation forces in Poland and East Germany. The "Iron Curtain" had fallen into place and the Soviets were seeking to expand their influence throughout Europe. Puller reminded Headquarters that he had service in Haiti and Nicaragua and was "well qualified for GUERRILLA warfare or any other type of warfare that might develop." The bold capital letters indicated that he thought Communist insurgencies were more likely than World War III.[37]

The manpower people at HQMC had their own ideas. In March 1948 they informed Chesty that he would transfer in the summer and take command of the Marine Barracks at Pearl Harbor, where he had served as a young lieutenant nearly a quarter-century earlier. He considered this yet another form of exile from the operating forces. The unwanted assignment undoubtedly further soured his attitude toward staff officers at Headquarters. His public disdain for higher learning remained equally strong. While answering a routine request from Washington for personal information in the spring of 1947, he had restated his position that education had no bearing on proficiency. Noting that he still believed that "service in camp and in the field is the best military school," he felt that his time in Haiti had "fitted me for a career in the Marine Corps far better than a degree from any university or military school."[38]

Puller may not have been happy with his new assignment, but he was proud of the job he had done with the Eighth District. He was certain his region had outperformed all others and he told a reporter: "I hate to leave New Orleans just when we're getting things going." The Director of Reserve agreed that he had done "a fine job." Little did Chesty know that he would see the results of his handiwork in action in the not-too-distant future.[39]

☆ ☆ ☆

Despite the intervening years, the nature of the Marine Barracks at Pearl Harbor had not changed very much. Marines still performed the same missions they had in the mid-1920s—providing routine security for the installation and serving as a defense force in case of attack. For the latter mission, Puller's new command possessed nearly all the weapons of a normal infantry battalion, including heavy water-cooled machine guns exactly like those that had occupied his attention twenty-three years earlier. It also was one of the largest barracks in the Corps, with eighteen officers and nearly seven hundred men. If it was not the infantry regiment that he wanted, it at least bore some similarities. And though he felt that it was yet another backwater billet, many senior officers considered it "one of the juicy jobs in the Marine Corps." The climate was pleasant, the duties not too onerous, the social life convivial, and the company of other senior Marines plentiful.[40]

In the letdown after the war, the previous commanding officer had not maintained the normal high standards expected of a Marine barracks. The inspector general's visits in 1947 had uncovered a slide into sloppiness. The inspectors noted that "most of the men needed haircuts," some wore nonregulation uniform articles, and there was a general "lack of smartness." The supply section also had accumulated large quantities of surplus items. A housecleaning brought forth 120 truckloads of excess material, a good portion of it hauled directly to the dump, and a team of outside specialists needed six months to properly inventory and warehouse that which the command retained. The training program was wholly inadequate and the troops had rehearsed the emergency defense plan only once in the past six months. Most damning of all: "The companies are not organized according to military principles, with NCOs responsible for squads or sections or platoons. There appeared to be no line of responsibility or chain of command."[41]

The inspection system itself was running into its own problems as peacetime doldrums settled onto the Corps and some senior leaders succumbed to the siren song of mindless bureaucratic activity that Puller loathed. The director of personnel at Headquarters was a case in point. Concerned that "interest in hobbycraft is lacking at many posts," he asked the IG to "pay particular attention" to this program and gather data "in order that the emphasis which should be placed on hobbycraft in the Marine Corps may be properly evaluated." At least a few staff officers at HQMC tried to maintain the proper perspective. A colonel in Plans and Policies ignited a heated debate when he recommended the consolidation of major inspections to reduce their frequency and the resulting disruption: "Even though prior announcement is made that normal routine will be carried out during an inspection it is common knowledge that once notice of a forthcoming inspection is received every one gets in a 'tizzy' and 'spit and polish' is inaugurated to the detriment of everything else." The inspector general was not pleased by that characterization, though he conceded it might be worthwhile to have "one great inspection festival" to save effort. The assistant commandant, O. P. Smith, finally ordered a reduction in the number of inspections to decrease "interference with training."[42]

Puller went right to work and corrected many of the glaring deficiencies in his outfit. Each Monday he prominently posted the schedule for the following Saturday's inspection, which he frequently conducted himself. "Monotony" did not figure into the plan—one week it was a thorough look at every man's rifle; the next, an inventory of the contents of field marching packs. "Neatly pressed and heavily starched khakis, with spit-shined shoes" quickly became the uniform of the day for sentries. The effort devoted to combat training increased markedly, with an emphasis on weapons firing. Chesty's demands for higher standards were tempered by greater concern for the well-being of his men. His reaction to absenteeism and petty police problems in Honolulu was not an imposition of draconian punishments, but instead the opening of an on-base club for the junior enlisted personnel. He boosted off-duty sports by building a baseball diamond and attending boxing matches. Young privates soon noted that Puller lived up to his "reputation as a man who held his enlisted Marines in high regard and treated them with respect." One man recalled the colonel's speech to a group of newly promoted corporals. True to his interest in military history, he began with a reference to Leathernecks in the Mexican War. He then told them they could not go wrong if they focused on three principles of leadership: "First, be technically and tactically proficient. . . . Secondly, know your Marines and look out for their welfare. . . . Thirdly, and most importantly, as a Marine NCO, you must set the example."[43]

While a subsequent inspection revealed some continuing shortfalls in training, the IG felt that the overall results were "excellent" and "showed marked improvements over last year." In testimony to the reestablishment of a solid chain of command and good discipline, the report noted "percentage needing haircuts—none." The general was particularly impressed that the barracks put on a parade for the inspection party that featured a drum and bugle corps, an indication that the commander knew how to soften up his guests with a little martial entertainment. But Chesty also found that bureaucratic creep was no easy monster to tame. His predecessor had been criticized for devoting too much manpower to administrative tasks; the numbers actually worsened under the new regime. Nevertheless, the base commander was pleased by the positive changes and he praised Puller as "an outstanding, capable Marine officer." The admiral apparently also was impressed by Chesty's self-education, since the Navy officer noted that his subordinate was "well informed."[44]

Puller's stress on combat skills came through loud and clear when a board of senior Navy officers came to Pearl Harbor. They were looking for sites that could be shut down to save money in the cash-strapped post–World War II era. One of the installations in their sights was the rifle range at Puuloa Point (which Chesty had operated in the 1920s). The CO of the Marine barracks proved to be a convincing advocate for keeping the marksmanship complex in operation. A Navy captain re-called the Marine colonel's appearance as a witness: "We found Puller to have a marvelous command of profane English and the ability to ex-press himself in graphic terms, and he quickly persuaded us to let the Marines keep their rifle range. He said that the Marines without a rifle range were no better than the damned soldiers. And that was one of his milder statements."[45]

Hawaii was an idyllic tour for the Pullers. The barracks comman-der's house was large, with well-maintained grounds and a hibiscus hedge fencing it off from the street. Chesty was very pleased that he finally was "able to provide, if only for two years, a home that is the proper setting for my family." It lacked the two chimneys, but he thought it was "great" anyway: "I wish that we could transplant the whole setting back to the States when we finally retire and have it for a residence for the rest of our lives." The children spent much of their free time at the pool and were "brown as natives" from the sun. Lewis Jr. did not care for the water at first, and would not swim despite his father's cajoling. Chesty finally solved the problem by taking his son to the brig. With the admonition that "Marines do not disobey orders," the colonel told Lewis he would stay "locked up" until he changed his mind, which the young boy quickly did. Little Virginia took dancing lessons every week to com-plement her swimming and diving. Their father was proud that they were "developing rapidly and nicely," which he ascribed to "the constant care of their mother, who I think some what overdoes the job." The fam-ily joined in the active social life of the base and Puller came home every day at noon for lunch and a game of canasta with his wife. Vir-ginia's only complaint was her graying hair, which kept Lewis busy try-ing to convince her that it was nothing to worry about. Chesty was absolutely content and wished the same bliss for his brother-in-law, Bob Evans, after his upcoming wedding. "I have been married eleven years now, I like the life very much, and I hope that in your wife you will be as fortunate as I am in mine." He had not lost his tender side, either. He sent money and told Evans: "One evening during your honeymoon when you and Betty are having dinner alone, I want you to buy a bottle of good wine and make believe that the Pullers are present and drinking to your good health, long life, and happiness."[46]

Chesty's own health seemed to be good. Since his last attack of malaria in 1945, his only complaint had been recurring ear infections in early 1949. A week of hospitalization in the spring and heavy doses of penicillin finally cleared up the problem. He was showing some of the normal effects of middle age and the lack of physical training, with his weight slowly rising from his pre–World War II level of 150 to the high 160s. But otherwise he passed his annual physicals with nothing more noteworthy than a catalogue of scars from old wounds, injuries, and illnesses.[47]

As 1950 rolled around, Puller submitted his request for his next assignment. His first choice was the same as 1948—the 2d Marine Division—but this time he added two other options that were surprising, the Marine Corps Schools at Quantico and the Recruit Depot at Parris Island. Although he noted, as usual, that most of his experience was in "field training and command," he uncharacteristically highlighted his time as an instructor at the Basic School. He must have done so to boost his chances for his second and third selections. Chesty obviously was looking at this next assignment as his twilight tour in the Corps. The only common denominator of the three duty preferences was their location on the East Coast. If his primary desire had been another chance at an infantry command, he would have made the 1st Marine Division in Camp Pendleton a choice. His ironic request to join the schools he so disdained could only have been motivated by proximity to Saluda, where he planned to spend his remaining years.[48]

Puller felt he had not advanced as far as he should have in the Corps and he believed that his last two billets were a sign that senior Marines did not hold him in high favor. He would later say of early 1950: "I knew I was through." Although the maximum age limit was sixty-two, he could reach that only if he received future promotions, which were few and far between in the shrunken Corps of the late 1940s. Only a tiny handful of officers were making it to general and he apparently did not rate his own odds too highly. He must have reasoned that a tour near his ancestral home would give him a chance to find the house with the two chimneys and settle down after thirty-some years in the service of his country. The only question then would be how he would spend his leisure time. He recently had listed "military service" as his only hobby.[49]

Headquarters, as usual, would not cooperate. The personnel division issued orders for Puller to report to the 1st Marine Division in mid-July 1950 after the arrival of his replacement in Hawaii. While the thought of rejoining his old outfit may have had some appeal, the current version was a far cry from the powerful organization that had stormed its way across the Pacific just a few short years before. Under peacetime tables of organization, the 1st and 7th Marines did not exist and the three battalions of the 5th Marines each had only two rifle companies with just two rifle platoons apiece. With 1,900 officers and men, the regiment had barely half its designated wartime strength. Things were even worse from Chesty's personal perspective. Lieutenant Colonel Raymond L. Murray was slated to take command of the 5th in June, which would leave only staff billets for the infantry colonels in the division. Puller could not complain too loudly about the selection, as Murray had commanded 2/6 through Guadalcanal, Tarawa, and Saipan and garnered a Navy Cross, two Silver Stars, and a Purple Heart in the process.[50]

The situation might have been even more unfortunate for Chesty, except that O. P. Smith, now a major general, was shifting from his billet as assistant commandant to take charge of the division in August. Headquarters was sending Colonel Edward W. Snedeker to be the division chief of staff and Smith was concerned that Snedeker was junior to three other officers who would join at the same time, one of them Puller. By tradition and necessity, the chief of staff was the senior billet after the commanding general and assistant division commander. Smith was not about to give up Snedeker, who "was the only one with suitable qualifications that could be made available," so he arranged for two of the colonels to go to the barracks at Pendleton instead. He opted to keep Puller despite the seniority problem (probably because Smith knew Chesty would not use that as a lever to demand the billet responsible for all staff work). Smith's decision saved Puller from being shunted into a garrison staff job. If this were to be his final tour, it would at least be in some capacity with a field organization.[51]

"A Chance to Excel"
The Inchon Landing
June–September 1950

On June 23, 1950, Puller performed one of his last duties at Pearl Harbor when he shipped a company of Reserve infantrymen to California via flying boat for two weeks of duty. The Hawaii Marines were joining thousands of other reservists converging on Pendleton for their yearly maneuvers. Although the Marine Corps Reserve still had shortcomings, one of its strengths was the presence of many World War II veterans. As an example, Major Edgar J. Crane, a battalion XO, had received a Navy Cross as a company commander during the Guadalcanal campaign. The readiness of these citizen-warriors would be of major importance in the weeks to come.[1]

Halfway around the globe, another force leavened by combat veterans was also on the move. On June 25, the North Korean People's Army (NKPA) stormed across the border into South Korea with nine infantry divisions supported by three tank regiments. Many of the 100,000 invaders had fought with the Soviet army against Hitler or with Mao Tsetung in the Chinese Civil War. They were well armed and well trained. Their opponent, the Republic of Korea (ROK) Army, was much less ready for battle. The United States had equipped the sixty-five thousand ROK troops with lighter weapons, in part, to prevent the southern President, Syngman Rhee, from carrying out his desire to unify the peninsula by force. They had 105mm howitzers, 81mm and 60mm mortars, bazookas, light antitank guns, scout cars, and machine guns, but no

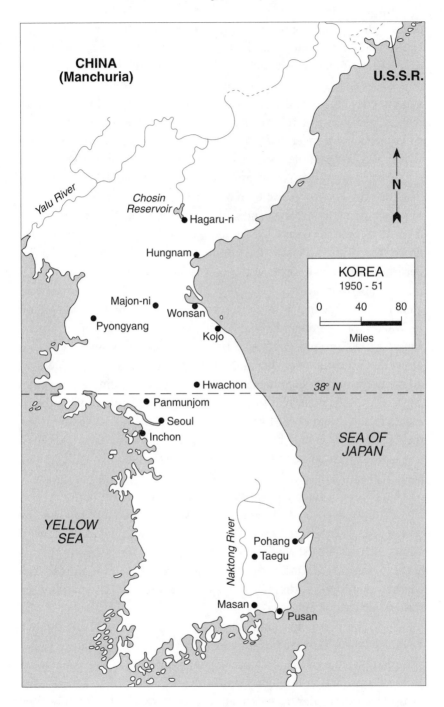

tanks, fighter planes, or heavy artillery pieces. The greater weight of the NKPA told immediately. The capital city of Seoul fell June 28 and some of the ROK forces reeled back in defeat. The South's only hope lay in outside assistance. On June 27 the United Nations Security Council authorized member nations to help repel the invasion; President Truman immediately ordered American forces under the command of General MacArthur to intervene. Less than five years after the end of World War II, the United States was involved in another major conflict.[2]

The arrival of U.S. Army units in Korea beginning on July 1 did not turn the tide. The troops were unprepared for combat after the easy life of occupation duty in Japan and they were initially no better armed than their ROK counterparts. The desperate nature of the situation also drove American leaders to feed outfits piecemeal into the battle. The best these small task forces could do was delay the enemy for a bit before being overwhelmed. By July 26, however, the reinforcements amounted to three divisions and a regiment. Lieutenant General Walton H. Walker took command of the Eighth Army (composed of all American and ROK ground forces in Korea) and issued a dramatic edict: "I direct that all commanders take immediate steps to forcibly impress on all members of their commands the importance of fighting to the death. . . . There will be no retreat from Korea." Supported by heavy bombardments from air and naval forces against NKPA units and supply lines, the Eighth Army slowly began to stabilize the situation. The toehold in the southeastern corner of the Korean peninsula soon became known as the "Pusan Perimeter."[3]

On the same date that the first U.S. ground forces set foot in Korea, MacArthur made a formal request for a Marine regiment supported by an air group. The Corps quickly assigned Brigadier General Edward Craig, ADC of the 1st Marine Division, to command the newly created 1st Provisional Marine Brigade, composed of the reinforced 5th Marines and Marine Aircraft Group 33. The force would depart by sea for the Far East on July 14.

Suddenly, orders to Camp Pendleton looked extremely good to one colonel in Hawaii. Instead of contemplating the end of his career, Puller was reanimated by a desire to participate in the war: "I knew if I got to Korea I wouldn't be through." He firmly believed that "war was what prosperity was to the businessman, a chance to excel." On July 5 he fired off telegrams to the Commandant (now General Cates) and O. P.

Smith, asking for permission to report immediately to Pendleton instead of waiting for the arrival of a relief. Chesty argued that his service in Haiti, Nicaragua, and the Far East would "prove of value in assignment to combat duty in Korea" and he expressed his "earnest desire to carry out my orders as soon as possible." Smith was sympathetic since he was trying to speed up his own transfer to the division, but Cates was unwilling to act on Puller's request. The assistant commandant told his old friend to work on getting Shepherd, now head of FMFPac, to release him from the barracks without a replacement.[4]

MacArthur soon expressed his desire for the services of an entire Marine division. But Camp Pendleton had been wiped clean of combat forces by the departure of the brigade, while the 2d Marine Division in Lejeune had only four battalions of infantry. Smith now had just the job for Chesty: "It appears that we may have to activate another regiment at Camp Pendleton when we get the personnel. . . . I believe Puller would be an excellent man to whip this new regiment into shape and I am going to recommend to the Commandant that Puller now be detached in advance of the arrival of his relief." In the end, Cates authorized FMFPac to immediately release Chesty "in event services [of] Col Puller can be spared." The message departed HQMC on July 14. That same day Shepherd directed the colonel to head for California. The Puller family packed furiously, then he and Virginia attended a long-scheduled bash. Chesty wanted to enjoy one last night out before another protracted separation. She recalled: "Lewis was the life of the party. Did the hula, even, and brought down the house." He had reason to celebrate. At the cost of a few telegrams and with the help of two friends, he was on his way to war again.[5]

☆ ☆ ☆

On July 25, the Joint Chiefs of Staff bowed to MacArthur and authorized release of a division, although it would include the ground elements of the Marine brigade already headed for the Pusan Perimeter. That same day, the Commandant told the 1st Marine Division that it would expand to full strength and must be ready to mount out for the Far East as early as August 10, barely two weeks hence. The G-3, Colonel Alpha L. Bowser, was flabbergasted. His organization had 3,386 officers and men, nearly all of them assigned to headquarters and support elements. There was not a single combat unit in Camp Pendleton. A reinforced Marine division, less one regiment and its attachments, totaled almost twenty thousand Marines and sailors. Bowser thought the idea of sailing off to war that soon was "just impossible." He was probably right, but in the days to come the entire Marine Corps would work with a will to make it happen.[6]

Smith arrived in Pendleton on July 25 after a cross-country drive and was as dismayed as his G-3 at the rapid turn of events. Headquarters already had turned on the manpower spigot. At the Commandant's request, President Truman had authorized activation of the Marine Corps Reserve on the 19th. Cates also decreed that nearly all subordinate units of the 2d Marine Division in Camp Lejeune would pack up and go to the West Coast. The CNO chipped in his share, directing a 50 percent reduction in the strength of Marine forces guarding Navy bases. That freed up 3,630 officers and men. Congress then extended all enlistments for a year, thus freezing the departure of those nearing the end of their contracts. The troops began to pour into Camp Pendleton by the end of the month.[7]

The Puller family flew out of Hawaii on July 20 and parted ways in San Francisco, with Virginia and the children heading home to Saluda for the duration. A few days later, Smith announced Chesty's new billet—he would have the daunting task of re-creating his old 1st Marines in short order out of a wide array of materials. The situation called for a leader who would drive forward through all obstacles to meet the objective. Smith knew he had picked the right man in Puller and "was glad to have him."[8]

Chesty pitched in to prepare for the arrival of his troops. The outfit would come to life at Tent Camp 2, nestled in a small valley bordered by low, brown hills. It was fifteen miles of poor road away from the main part of the base and had not been used since World War II, but it had one advantage—firing ranges for all infantry weapons radiated outward from the site, placing training venues within easy hiking distance. Puller started the work of reopening long abandoned mess halls and erecting tents.[9]

Chesty quickly found out that he would be able to build his regiment on a solid base. The 1st Marines and the division headquarters would depart as directed in mid-August; the 7th Marines would come into being and follow them overseas by the end of the month. Smith thus gave Puller priority, which meant that he would receive the bulk of the units from Camp Lejeune. The first troop train reached California on August 3. The next day Puller took command of the 1st Marines, consisting of the redesignated 2d Marines (headquarters company, 1/2, and 2/2) and 1/6. These outfits were based on peacetime tables of organization; each battalion had just two rifle companies of two platoons each and there was a proportional shortage in heavy weapons and support units. As a consequence, three rifle companies, six additional rifle platoons, and a number of other elements had to be built from scratch. In all, Puller needed about 1,200 men to reach his full authorization of just over 3,900 Marines and sailors. He also had to take under his wing the newly created third rifle companies for each battalion of the 5th Marines. A good portion of these men came from the regulars released from Navy stations. The rest were members of the Organized Reserve who had combat experience or a relatively high level of training.[10]

The 1st Marines did not reach full strength until August 10, the date that the division began loading cargo onto ships in San Diego. Two days later personnel were still reporting to and detaching from the regiment in an effort to get specialists into correct billets. On August 13, Smith told Puller to identify fifty volunteers for a commando outfit desired by MacArthur's chief of staff, Major General Edward M. Almond. Although the division eventually would avoid that levy, it was emblematic of the unnecessary turmoil assailing the Marines from all sides.

One of the biggest problems began to appear on August 7, when units started test-firing their weapons. Many of the ordnance items brought from Camp Lejeune were badly worn, since peacetime budgets had provided little money for maintenance. The newer elements of the 1st Marines had received their arms from the Marine logistics depot at Barstow, California, where the Corps had stored huge quantities of equipment left over from World War II. But much of that matériel had been hastily put into preservation without regard for serviceability. Puller was amazed by the high rate of problems with weapons. Armorers worked around the clock. When the last shot went downrange on August 12, the regiment finally was fully equipped with functioning arms. Other major items, such as vehicles, proved equally unreliable and hundreds of civilians worked overtime at Barstow to recondition this equipment.[11]

Other than the test-firing of weapons, the regiment had almost no time to train. One of the battalions managed to conduct a command post exercise. Some units squeezed in a conditioning hike. Whenever there were a few minutes to spare, platoon and squad leaders sat down with their men to review basic subjects. But the vast majority of each day was eaten up by the administrative demands of assigning, equipping, feeding, and housing personnel. Barely four months later, a company commander would remark: "All that I can remember of Pendleton is a hazing blur of reports, insurance and allotment forms, new men coming in, clothing issues, drawing weapons, and bringing our supplies up to wartime [requirements]." Even the familiarization fire was constrained by the lack of ammunition and time. The units from Camp Lejeune were well trained, but there was no opportunity for new squads to work together, for companies to operate with their third platoons, or battalions with their third companies. Puller did not know his executive officer or most of his staff and had no chance to see them or his battalions in action in a field environment. He never even realized that nearly a fifth of his men were reservists, assuming instead that his ranks had been filled out by regulars from the Navy stations.[12]

While the division sorted itself out at Pendleton, loading proceeded apace at San Diego. The mount-out of the division and all its gear was hectic and sometimes disorganized, but completed on time. Puller's troops clambered aboard their ships beginning on August 13. Chesty and his headquarters were the last to embark on the 16th. Ships sailed as they were loaded and all were at sea by the 22d. Smith flew to Japan with his senior staff as the last of the vessels departed. Only then did he discover that MacArthur planned to launch an amphibious assault against the port of Inchon, with the 1st Marine Division in the lead, on September 15. Almond, now the head of X Corps, would command the operation.[13]

Determination and improvisation had carried the day in getting the division organized and out to sea. It remained to be seen how the outfit would meet the test of battle. Puller, for one, exuded confidence. He was not personally acquainted with his officers and NCOs, but he knew that among them were a high proportion who had performed well against the Japanese just a few years before. He would later boast that "there never was a time in the history of the Marine Corps that a regiment was so well prepared by experience." While that was an overstatement, it was not too far off the mark. He would have been even more optimistic had he realized that a startling percentage of his junior officers had previous service as enlisted men, many of them in combat in World War II. Captain Robert H. Barrow's Able Company was unusually blessed. Five of his six lieutenants had been on active duty during that conflict, three as sergeants and one, surprisingly, as a Navy officer. Barrow's own background—as an adviser with Chinese Nationalist guerrillas in the war against Japan—would prove to be especially valuable.[14]

Puller's senior subordinates brought solid experience to the regiment. Lieutenant Colonel Robert W. Rickert had served as a company commander on Guadalcanal and a regimental operations officer on Okinawa. He had been the XO of the 2d Marines when it transferred to the West Coast and maintained that billet when the outfit was redesignated. Lieutenant Colonel Jack Hawkins had commanded the 1st Battalion, 2d Marines (now 1/1) for two years. He had been a platoon leader in the 4th Marines with Puller in 1940 and was captured with the rest of his regiment when Corregidor fell in 1942. He later escaped from the Japanese and fought alongside Filipino guerrillas. He went on to serve in the operations section of the 1st Marine Division during the Okinawa campaign. Lieutenant Colonel Thomas Ridge had been a student of Puller's at the Basic School in 1938 and must have picked up his aggressive attitude. During World War II he worked in high-level intelligence billets, but, as an observer on Okinawa, he spent enough time near the action to receive two wounds. He had just taken command of 1/6 (now 3/1) in June 1950. Lieutenant Colonel Allan Sutter, in charge of 2/1, had served as a communications officer on Guadalcanal and most recently in the operations section of an aircraft wing.[15]

Puller did not know the members of his command, but most of them were familiar with his reputation. A few viewed their new commander with some trepidation, since they had heard that their predecessors at Peleliu had suffered one of the highest casualty rates of the war. They knew only the numbers, not the details behind them, and came away with the idea that "he was reckless [with] the life of the Marines under him." That impression was reinforced when word went around that Chesty had ordered everyone to sign up for life insurance because he didn't want complaints from "widows or sorrowing mothers." The colonel even arranged for civilian insurance agents to come to the tent camp, as long as they sold policies without an exemption from payment in the case of a war death. The regimental chaplain noted that the CO "was very pleased" with himself: "Not least because he felt the insurance companies were getting taken!" There was just enough fact behind the idle scuttlebutt to create "a chill of apprehension" among a few of Puller's subordinates.[16]

For many young Marines, their commander was simply a legend, one of the most decorated Leathernecks ever and the only one with four Navy Crosses. They had heard the stories, both of his bravery in battle and of his devotion to his troops. That aura served an important purpose in the resurrected 1st Marines. Outfits from Camp Lejeune with their own proud lineage had been redesignated and hordes of newcomers had fleshed out their ranks. There was no time to train together or go through all the other experiences that meld individuals into a unit. But Chesty provided a glue that quickly coalesced the 1st Marines into a tight-knit fraternity. Sergeant Harvey Owens believed that "the regiment came alive" at Pendleton when everyone realized Puller was in command. Lieutenant Charles R. Stiles, a staff officer in 3/1, thought the colonel "gave us pride in some way I can't describe." In no time at all, there was a common response to questions about unit affiliation: "I'm in Chesty's outfit." The officers and men of the 1st Marines would have no shortage of esprit de corps when they went into battle less than six weeks after unfurling their colors.[17]

Puller's reputation was larger than life, but he cut a surprisingly low profile in person at Camp Pendleton. He made no speeches and held no inspections. He simply wandered around the ranges and the company streets quietly observing the purposeful preparations for war. His grizzled visage, rumpled utility cap, and sun-bleached field uniform caused many to take him at first glance for an Old Corps gunnery sergeant. Lieutenant Lew Devine, a recent Naval Academy graduate with World War II enlisted service, grew irritated when a scruffy character sitting on the deck of a Quonset hut interrupted while Devine was reporting in to the duty officer. Much to the lieutenant's chagrin, it was only after he made an annoyed reply that he noticed the silver eagles on the collars of the old fatigues. Chesty took no offense. In fact, he seemed to have mellowed in one respect in these later years. Some lieutenants and captains "dreaded the prospect" of working for a commander with a reputation for his gruffness toward junior officers. Most were pleasantly surprised to find Puller "a grand guy" or "a decent guy and easy to get along with." Chesty still took up for his men when the jury-rigged enlisted club ran out of beer or they had to wait in long lines at the post exchange, but, in contrast to World War II, this era would generate no widely circulated tales of lieutenants and captains running afoul of his wrath. Instead, he seemed to enjoy regaling his subordinates with stories during bull sessions on the ship or in lulls in the action in the field.[18]

Puller still appreciated anyone who was equally as eager as he was to do battle. Due to an excess of officers, Captain Carl L. Sitter faced the prospect of being left behind when his battalion sailed off to war. He asked to see the regimental commander and told Chesty that he wanted "to go fight." He discovered that "those seemed to be the magic words" and he soon had a billet as the regiment's athletics officer. The senior chaplain also received orders transferring him out of the regiment. The Reverend Glyn Jones was a veteran of the Pacific campaign and voiced his desire to stay on. When Chesty's positive endorsement of the request was rejected by Navy headquarters, the colonel pocketed the Baptist minister's paperwork and told him to get on board the ship as fast as he could.[19]

Puller was still capable of delivering a fire-and-brimstone pep talk when he deemed it appropriate. Several officers recalled that he gathered them together one evening to welcome them to the regiment. The gist of his brief lecture was that they had enjoyed five years of peace and lived well off the largesse of the taxpayers; now it was time to earn their keep. He peppered his oration with more than a few profane words and the senior chaplain voiced his objection. Chesty sincerely apologized, but subordinates found it humorous that the colonel and the Navy officer seemed to have the same discussion after every subsequent speech. The Reverend Jones would remember his CO as "a good Christian man" whose "personal life could stand muster with anybody's," but "he had a little trouble with language."[20]

☆　☆　☆

The voyage to Japan took almost two weeks and the regiment made as much use of this time as the cramped ships allowed. Puller's headquarters and 1/1 sailed aboard the attack transport USS *Noble* (APA-218). There was sufficient space topside for one platoon at a time to do calisthenics. Small units gathered in other nooks and crannies for lectures on first aid, squad tactics, and similar subjects. Individuals and teams spent hours reviewing the operation of their weapons and cleaning them. Chesty spent much of the transit reading; by the time he got to the Far East, he had devoured nine books on Korea and Manchuria.[21]

The first echelons of the regiment arrived in Kobe, Japan, on August 29 and moved ashore to Camp Otsu. There they commenced an intensive program of physical conditioning, small unit tactical exercises, and night operations. The *Noble* pulled into Kobe on September 2. Since the Inchon plan called for the regimental headquarters and 1/1 to use this same ship, these troops remained aboard and served as a labor pool. They spent the next several days combat-loading the *Noble* and the dozen LSTs that would carry the rest of the regiment. A typhoon on September 3 interrupted the work and soaked all the supplies on the docks. It was an eerie repeat of the division's troubles in New Zealand when it had mounted out on similar short notice for Guadalcanal. Captain Sitter informed Chesty that the losses included all the regiment's recreation equipment. The colonel merely growled: "We came here to fight, not to play."[22]

Information on the Inchon operation remained scarce until Puller flew up to Tokyo for a briefing from the division staff aboard the command ship, USS *Mount McKinley* (AGC-7). Due to the incredibly short time frame—the division had to be loaded by September 9—Bowser and his assistants already had developed detailed plans for the landing and employment of the subordinate units of the 1st and 5th Marines. Such decisions normally were made by the regimental commanders, based on their analysis of how best to achieve the broad mission assigned by higher headquarters. Chesty registered a vigorous protest over this loss of prerogative, but it was impossible to change things at this late date. In any case, the regimental and battalion staffs were more than busy the next few days supervising the reloading and trying to develop an adequate picture of the situation they would face. The 1st Marines received only one set of aerial photos (which did not fully cover the objective) and each battalion was given only a few hours in which to use them. Good information on the beaches did not make it into the hands of the assault battalions until a few hours before they sailed. The handful of days available to prepare for the operation— "probably the shortest period ever allotted to a major amphibious assault"—made such problems inevitable. Matters were complicated further by physical separation. Half of Puller's regiment was fifty miles away at Otsu. He was nearly three hundred miles from the division headquarters in Tokyo, while the 5th was still entangled in fighting in the Pusan Perimeter, and the 7th was at sea. To add to the last-minute turmoil, the Secretary of the Navy decreed that no seventeen-year-olds could go into combat, so the division had to leave five hundred men in Japan.[23]

Puller spent one day visiting his troops at Camp Otsu. It was his first opportunity to ride with Sergeant Orville W. Jones, the driver he had picked out at Pendleton. The strapping veteran of Okinawa maneuvered along the crowded road with speed and aggressiveness, attributes that immediately endeared him to his new boss. The other Marine that soon became a fixture on Chesty's personal staff was Sergeant Jan Bodey, a recently mobilized reservist who also had fought in World War II. He was an expert with small arms and had a reputation for toughness that made him an ideal bodyguard. Puller had precious little time in Japan to get to know the rest of his regiment. He was so busy that for once he could not find a spare moment to write his wife. He started a letter to Virginia on the 9th, but did not get beyond the salutation until after the fleet departed on September 10. Operation CHROMITE, MacArthur's bold gamble to win the Korean War in one blow, was underway.[24]

☆　☆　☆

While X Corps prepared for the Inchon landing, the Eighth Army fought for its life in the Pusan Perimeter. American forces held most of the ninety-mile western front along the Naktong River. South Korean units primarily defended the sixty-mile northern front. There were not enough troops to fully man the long line and there had been too little time to prepare strong defenses. The growing U.N. command now had superior numbers, however. The North Koreans also had outrun their supply lines, which were suffering in any case from unceasing air and sea attacks. The NKPA breached the U.N. line several times in August and early September, but each time counterattacks drove them back. Craig's outfit, soon dubbed the Fire Brigade, played a key role in re-pulsing many of these determined North Korean thrusts. The possibility of a Communist victory was diminishing with each passing day, but the outcome was still far from certain.

The Inchon operation presented both great opportunity and great danger. The seaport was located less than twenty miles from Seoul and the major airfield at Kimpo. Since most transportation routes in Korea passed through the southern capital city, a landing at Inchon would place U.N. forces in position to sever the primary logistics lines of the NKPA forces fighting far to the south around Pusan. At the same stroke, a successful operation would bring Allied ground-based airpower to the doorstep of the North and regain the psychological edge by recapturing the South Korean seat of government. Rapid exploitation of this thrust deep in the enemy's rear also might allow the United Nations to cut off the retreat of the Communist army and totally destroy it.

The potential pitfalls began with hydrography and geography. To reach the port, a task force would have to navigate thirty miles of narrow channel threading between islands and shoals. Mines or shore batteries could easily block these confined waters. The tidal range in the area was thirty-two feet, among the highest in the world. The resulting strong current could play havoc with landing craft and amphibian tractors. At low tide, huge mudflats covered much of the harbor. There were no beaches, only rocky shoreline and concrete seawalls. The Marines would have to use scaling ladders to get over the latter. The island of Wolmi-do lay directly west of Inchon, connected to it by a half-mile causeway. Since defensive positions there could enfilade any landing against the city, this mile-square landmass became the key to the plan.

Operation CHROMITE would begin early on September 15 with

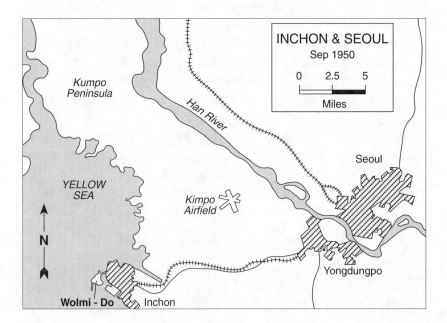

destroyer transports and a dock landing ship negotiating the channel in darkness and disgorging 3/5 to seize Wolmi-do on the crest of the morning tide. That battalion would provide additional covering fire to the main attack occurring during the evening high tide. The remainder of the 5th Marines would come ashore on Red Beach at 1730, just north of the causeway, and seize the waterfront industrial zone and two major hills. The 1st Marines simultaneously would land two battalions over Blue Beach 1 and 2 roughly three miles to the southeast and seize the high ground beyond the urban area. Puller's mission was critical to the operation—to offer a threat to the rear of the enemy in the city and block any reinforcements from coming to their aid. The possibility of NKPA reaction from that direction "seriously concerned" the division staff. If all went well, the next morning the two regiments would complete the conquest of the city, home to a quarter million people.[25]

Intelligence indicated that the Communist forces had not done much to prepare for an invasion—yet. There were just two battalions of recent recruits and eight 76mm coastal guns in the city, though fifteen thousand more capable troops were located nearby in the Seoul-Kimpo area. Intercepts of enemy radio traffic on September 14, however, revealed that the North Koreans now expected a landing at Inchon and were ordering all available units to the scene.[26]

Even without heavy opposition, this was one of the most complex and challenging amphibious assaults ever attempted. But there had been no chance to rehearse it and there was no alternate plan. Some senior officers in the 1st Marines would look back on the lack of a practice landing as a "grievous sin of omission." MacArthur knew the undertaking was a gamble, but he was willing to accept that in pursuit of a high payoff: "For a five-dollar ante, I have an opportunity to win $50,000." The officers and men of the 1st Marine Division had plenty to worry about as they approached Inchon; it was just as well they did not know that the theater commander spoke of them as an expendable opening wager in a high-stakes poker game.[27]

☆　☆　☆

Despite the potential problems, Puller kept up a positive pose throughout the buildup to D-Day. During a briefing session on the *Noble* at Kobe, he interrupted his intelligence officer's detailed report on the difficulties: "We'll find out what's on the beach when we get there. There's

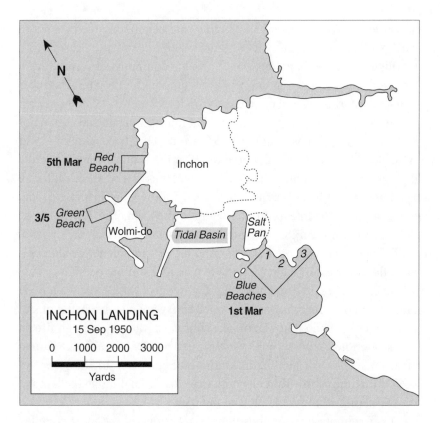

INCHON LANDING
15 Sep 1950

0   1000 2000 3000

Yards

not necessarily a gun in every hole. There's too much goddamned pessimism in this regiment. Most times, professional soldiers have to wait twenty-five years or more for a war, but here we are, with only five years' wait for this one. . . . We're going to work at our trade for a little while. We live by the sword and if necessary we'll be ready to die by the sword. Good luck. I'll see you ashore." (His oft-repeated aphorism about the sword may have been responsible for his CHROMITE call sign—"Blade.") He tried to put on the same game face for Virginia in his last letter before the landing: "The higher echelons appear to be optimistic, so please do not worry or at least worry as little as possible. As I have so often written you, worry does not help—just trust the good Lord to bring me safely back to you—I am confident that he will."[28]

But Chesty's unusually long note to his wife did bear a unique hint of foreboding, something that had never appeared when he wrote from other tough battlefields. He regretted that the landing would not take place on the 13th—their monthly anniversary—"because I know and will always believe it is my luckiest day." He made an effort to clear the slate of any past transgressions, however mild: "Please forgive me and forget the times that I was impatient and not as considerate as I should have been to you. I did not mean to be, Dear, I swear it. I am sorry and I promise to mend my ways and be better when I return to you after this war." He listed his four insurance policies and reminded her: "There is a pension for both you and our precious children. I am sorry that I have not provided better for you." The last paragraph was penciled in on the day of the landing: "I will be unable to write to you again for a few days, but you, Virginia, Virginia McC., Martha Leigh, and Lewis will be continually in my thoughts. May God bless you always and provide for you; giving you much happiness and long useful lives. You, my children, must take advantage of all opportunities and develop into good Christians. Much love to all of you. I love you, Virginia, I always have and I always will." It was not an expression of the fatalism that sometimes grips men going into combat, but he certainly seemed to be arranging his affairs just in case. Ten-year-old Virginia informed her father that she was not the least bit worried: "As our prayers brought you safely home from the last war, surely now with those of the twins added you will be permitted to return from this war."[29]

☆   ☆   ☆

Since Puller typically planned to go ashore with one of the assault waves, he sailed aboard an LST. Rough seas from another typhoon made the shallow-draft landing ships exceedingly unpleasant for two days. While the transports plowed through mountainous waves, planes and warships softened up the defenses at Inchon.

Dawn on September 15 brought final preparation fires. At 0630, 3/5 stormed ashore on Wolmi-do. After five days of sometimes heavy bombardment, many of the Koreans surrendered and there was only sporadic resistance. MacArthur soon radioed one of his usual grandiose proclamations from nearby *Mount McKinley:* "The Navy and Marines have never shone more brightly than this morning." The island was in friendly hands by noon at a cost of seventeen wounded. Enemy losses were estimated to be almost four hundred. A few warships remained behind to provide fire support, but 3/5 passed an otherwise lonely afternoon waiting for the evening tide.[30]

The 1st Marines spent the long day making final preparations. Sutter's 2d Battalion would assault Blue 1 on the left of the regimental zone, Ridge's 3d Battalion would take Blue 2 on the right, and Hawkins's 1st Battalion would land in reserve. Blue 1 was one of the few landing sites without a seawall, but a steep hill just inland limited egress to a road leading through a narrow defile on the left. Jutting into the water on that flank was a salt evaporator surrounded by a rock retaining wall. In the hands of a determined enemy, it had the potential to be like Hunt's Point on Peleliu. The mouth of a creek marked the boundary between Blue 1 and 2. A seawall fronted the entire width of the latter beach and extended a finger into the harbor on the right flank. Behind that projection was a small bay, dubbed Blue 3. Although 3/1 had ladders to scale the wall on Blue 2, the plan called for the tractors to file through the mouth of the creek. Ridge also decided that he would take his amphibian tractor to Blue 3 and investigate it as an alternative if the entryway on the left became a bottleneck.

The weather turned sour as the day progressed, with low clouds and light rain bringing an early gloom to the battlefield. Renewed preparation fires for the evening assault added smoke, soot, and dust to the leaden skies. By the time H-Hour rolled around, the entire Blue Beach area was obscured. The LVTs had no means of navigation, so Navy boats with the proper equipment guided the first line (composed of armored amphibians). Subsequent echelons were left to their own devices. By following the lead vehicles into the smoke, the first two waves of both assault battalions made it ashore in reasonable order. Thereafter confusion reigned.

As Ridge approached shore with the third wave, he saw a tractor bogged down in the creek, blocking that exit. Other landing vehicles were crowded against the seawall as Marines in the bobbing platforms struggled to mount their scaling ladders and clamber over the obstacle. The battalion commander and his XO pointed their LVTs toward Blue 3. Although other tractors were supposed to wait for a signal that the alternate beach was usable, subsequent waves promptly waddled after their leaders like so many baby ducklings. Blue 3 was clear and all the assault troops made it to shore, but 3/1 had lost the unit integrity normally provided by neat landing waves. Disorder reigned for a time until officers and NCOs sorted out the mess and got their outfits moving toward their objectives.

Sutter's battalion fared no better on the left flank. The exit road at Blue 1 was blocked by a landslide caused by naval gunfire, so the small area quickly became congested with LVTs. A Navy control boat, perhaps observing the problem and the mass exodus of 3/1's tractors for Blue 3, directed the third and subsequent waves of 2/1 toward the alternate beach. Sutter suddenly found his battalion split, with himself and his two assault companies on Blue 1 and the remainder of his force mixed up in the temporary jumble on the opposite flank of the regimental zone. The reserve battalion had its own problems. Shortly after H-Hour, Puller radioed Hawkins to land. The Navy control boat attempted to help the LCVPs by shining a searchlight toward their intended goal, Blue 2, but the beam somehow ended up pointed at a seawall well to the northwest. By the time Hawkins detected the error and 1/1 hit the correct beach, it was dark.

Puller had come in with the third wave and was the first from his LVT to climb over the seawall at Blue 2. When he jumped down on the far side, a North Korean machine gun was clattering from a tower five hundred yards distant. Occasional mortar rounds peppered the open ground, though poor visibility prevented the NKPA from fixing on real targets. He called for those members of his command group still in the landing vehicle to debark: "Come on you men, get out of that tractor, they won't hurt you." After a while, he moved inland and set up his CP under a poncho in the small ravine separating Blue 1 and 2. Reports from the battalions began to come in. Despite the confused landing, the assault companies had seized most of the initial objectives. The line was thinly held, and disorganized units would straggle through the rain most of the night trying to link up with their parent outfits. Nevertheless, the 1st Marines were ashore to stay. Casualties in 2/1 and 3/1 totaled five killed and thirty-four wounded. Puller classified the landing as "practically unopposed" and soon expressed disdain for his new adversary: "Compared with the Japanese, these Reds have been very inferior. When I came over the seawall I saw only one dead Communist. If the Japs had been on that side of the wall, there would have been Japs piled up one side and Marines piled up the other." He told a reporter: "These fellows don't amount to much." But he was pleased with his outfit's performance. He realized that "confusion and disorganization" had been inevitable given "the unavoidable circumstance of landing the regiment without a rehearsal, without even a CPX [command post exercise]." In his eyes, the officers and men had rebounded from those initial troubles "with remarkable speed and effectiveness."[31]

Murray had met stronger resistance. His regiment reached its objectives, however, with losses about three times those of the 1st Marines. The night passed quietly, as the mostly inexperienced NKPA defenders had neither the strength, stomach, nor skill to counterattack. The only supporting arms used by the 1st Marines were a few star shells. MacArthur's initial gamble had succeeded, but Inchon was only the prelude to the real payoff—Seoul.

☆   ☆   ☆

In the middle of the night Smith issued an order for the attack to resume the next morning. The 5th Marines were to pass through the urban zone as quickly as possible, leaving the attached Korean Marine Corps (KMC) regiment to ferret the remaining enemy from the midst of the population. The 1st Marines would move due east as well, with the Inchon–Seoul highway as the dividing line between the two regiments. Puller's headquarters performed well its first time out, receiving the division directive just before midnight and issuing orders to the battalions by 0115, which gave subordinate units time to do their own planning. As it turned out, most of the North Koreans had fled and the division made rapid progress over increasingly hilly terrain. Total casualties for the division during the day were four killed and twenty-one wounded, nearly all in the 1st Marines. Because Puller's regiment had a much larger zone of action, it had faced most of the few pockets of North Koreans. The width of the front also caused the colonel to place all three of his battalions in the front lines, leaving him no reserve. On the positive side, the absence of heavy combat was a boon to the outfit. Captain Barrow thought of it as "almost like a training exercise—we had the opportunity to shake down and get set for bigger things."[32]

General Craig had come ashore with the 5th Marines and reverted to his former role as the ADC of the division. At mid-morning on D+1 he was moving forward with Murray's regiment and looking to link up with the 1st Marines. He made contact with the lead elements of 2/1 and asked the infantrymen for directions to the regimental command post. Not surprisingly, it was not very far away. Craig found Chesty, an old acquaintance from Nicaragua, relaxing over a canteen cup of coffee: "Things at his CP looked very calm and collected for the first morning after a landing." The brigadier general would soon learn that "this was the usual way . . . in [Puller's] regiment and reflected his attitude of calmness under trying conditions."[33]

The plan for September 17 was to further expand the beachhead. In a scenario that would become increasingly familiar in the days to come, the 1st Marines did not receive the division order till 0620 (although Smith had approved it the evening before). The contents came as no surprise, however, and most of the regiment stepped off on schedule at 0700. Movement of the 2d Battalion on the left flank was delayed by the first substantial NKPA counterattack. Just after dawn a column of five T-34 tanks and some two hundred infantrymen came down the Inchon–Seoul highway. The North Koreans apparently assumed they were still a long way from the front lines, as they barreled, completely unprepared, into the night roadblock of the 5th Marines. Pershing tanks, recoilless rifles, and rocket launchers quickly destroyed the enemy armor, while machine guns and rifles dealt with the foot soldiers. Sutter's flank company joined in, with Private First Class Walter C. Monegan, Jr., of Fox Company maneuvering to fire his bazooka at point-blank range.

From this point forward the fighting grew more intense, as the Marines began to meet the more capable 18th Division, the defenders of Seoul. The tactical situation also changed as the offensive moved out of the confines of Inchon's peninsula and into the main Korean landmass. Here the 5th Marines diverged to the northeast, moving through Ascom City and up the route to Kimpo Airfield, while the 1st Marines continued due east toward the capital. A KMC battalion guarded the open left flank of Murray's regiment and the division reconnaissance company moved southeast to perform the same mission on Puller's right. During the course of the day, 2/1 shifted to the north side on the Seoul highway and 3/1 attacked directly down the road. Hawkins's battalion advanced cross-country through the hills on the right. Ridge's thrust came to a standstill in a heavily defended defile and it took an afternoon of stiff fighting to clear the surrounding high ground. At the end of the day, the 1st Marines had gained nearly three miles and accounted for 320 enemy killed, wounded, or captured at a cost of one dead and thirty-four wounded.

That morning MacArthur had come ashore with a large entourage of reporters and senior officers. The theater commander went forward to visit the regiments and found Chesty on a hill watching his battalions attack to the east. MacArthur hiked up the rise and greeted the colonel. The five-star general praised the performance of the 1st Marines and explained that he wanted to give Puller a Silver Star as "a symbol of respect" for the efforts of the troops. He found he had no more medals on hand and told his aide: "Make a note of that." The two commanders chatted for a while. Based on prisoner debriefs, Puller estimated there were only two NKPA regiments in Seoul, one of them composed of cadets. MacArthur expressed his hope the Communists would fight outside the city: "It would make it easier for you." Chesty, still influenced by his early estimation of the enemy, was unconcerned: "If they're dug in, we'll hit them with napalm and there won't be any trouble going through them." He compared this war to the last one: "This wasn't the reception we got at Peleliu [where] I lost 62 percent of my men and 74 percent of my officers." MacArthur then reminisced about one of his own amphibious assaults and praised the sea services: "I picked the Morotai date for that reason. I thought I would sneak in under the wing of the Peleliu action." Someone expressed surprise that the 1st Marines commander was forward instead of with his main command post (which they assumed must be well to the rear). Chesty patted a map in his pocket: "This is my CP." That same day the party caught up with Murray, who drew exclamations of glee from MacArthur by showing off the tanks killed that morning. The 5th Marines bagged a much bigger prize that evening, seizing Kimpo Airfield.[34]

After a predawn artillery bombardment, the 1st Marines jumped off at 0645 on September 18. Ridge's battalion again made a mechanized/motorized thrust down the road to Seoul, 2/1 attacked on foot adjacent to the highway, and 1/1 moved across a broad front farther south. The Marines engaged a few pockets of North Korean infantry and gained another two miles, but came under periodically heavy mortar fire. Casualties were the heaviest yet, six killed and more than eighty wounded. The men of the 1st Marines had now advanced halfway to the capital from Inchon. They slowly were growing accustomed to the energy-sapping steepness of the frequent ridges and the sucking, smelly muck of the rice paddies that filled every valley in between.

The enemy and the terrain were not the only problems Puller faced. A Marine jeep driver had started out from the front lines with a load of North Korean prisoners, but none of the NKPA soldiers arrived alive at the 1st Marines CP. The man's CO and the regimental staff were not sure what to do, since there were no witnesses to what had transpired on the way. The colonel took care of the situation with an edict—"There'll be no court martial in this regiment"—and a Solomonic decision— "Give that boy an M-1 rifle and send him up to the front." Chesty applied the same approach to shell shock that he did to wartime legal matters. He informed his officers "there were to be no cases of combat fatigue in the 1st Marines."[35]

Smith visited Puller, noting wryly that "as usual, he had his CP on the top of a hill." The general was not in a particularly humorous mood, however. The corps commander was pushing him to cross the Han as soon as possible. General Shepherd (present as an observer) added to the pressure by "urging speed and boldness." Smith was inclined to be more cautious and was growing concerned over the expanding gap between Chesty's right flank and the coast. The division recon company was keeping an eye on it, but the Army's 7th Division, which was supposed to fill it, had not yet arrived. The CG may have passed on his misgivings about "the tendency to ignore the enemy," though Puller still was not according the foe any great weight.[36]

At 1000 on September 19, 2/1 attacked down the road with 3/1 moving forward in the high ground on the left. Fifteen minutes later, Sutter's force encountered a minefield. While engineers worked to clear the highway, the infantry advanced against NKPA units covering the obstacle with fire. The 2d Battalion used artillery and air to beat down resistance, only to run into another minefield and defensive position. Ridge's outfit met equally tough going in the adjacent hills. The 32d Infantry Regiment of the 7th Division came up late in the morning and relieved 1/1, which boarded trucks for a circuitous eleven-mile trip north to take position on the left of the 1st Marines. The arrival of the Army troops relieved Puller of concern for X Corps' flank, but created another problem. The right boundary of the 1st Marines was now the Inchon–Seoul highway. Instead of continuing the attack, the 32d Infantry spent the afternoon consolidating the line formerly held by 1/1. As 2/1 fought down the road, a gap opened on its right flank. By day's end it was nearly three miles wide and the Marines were taking flanking fire from NKPA positions in the 7th Division's zone. Puller's opinion of the Army had sunk during the debacles that marked the opening days of the war. Now it was personal—the lackluster performance of the 7th Division was adversely affecting his own regiment. He fired off two messages that day informing division of the Army's lack of progress. In private discussions with Smith, Chesty was "caustic."[37]

Puller soon had more reason to be upset. By division order, 1/1 was to relieve 1/5 from Hills 118, 85, and 80, which overlooked the confluence of the Han River and Kalchon Creek and the north end of Yongdungpo. Murray was gathering his regiment to the northwest for an assault crossing of the Han. Due to traffic clogging the poor roads, Hawkins's battalion had gotten off trucks late in the evening about three miles from its destination. Barrow's Able Company reached 118, the nearest hill, after a rapid and exhausting march. The rest of 1/1 could not make it to the more distant knolls in time, and 1/5 vacated them in order to meet its schedule. Hawkins decided to emplace his battalion around 118 rather than move forward in darkness into unknown territory. It was not an improper choice, since doctrine normally called for a thorough reconnaissance before night operations, but it was a conservative decision. Before dawn, the North Koreans reoccupied the two hillocks. The 1st Marines now would have to pay in blood to get them back.[38]

It had not been a good day for Puller. He had an open right flank and no confidence in the adjacent unit. One of his battalions had not fully accomplished its mission and had demonstrated something less than the feisty aggressiveness he prized. The enemy also was becoming "more determined and better organized." The North Koreans were fighting harder and smarter and their mines were reducing the effectiveness of his armor. As he sat that evening in his CP in the middle of a graveyard on the crest of a hill, he could see Kalchon Creek, the large industrial center of Yongdungpo, the wide Han, and then the dense sprawl of Seoul. In its entire history, the Corps could count the number of its urban battles on one hand. The looming fight would dwarf all such previous engagements in scale and intensity. As Puller undoubtedly knew, combat in cities tended to be bloody and drawn out—in its own way, it could be every bit as nightmarish as that which the 1st Marines had experienced in the twisted coral ridges of the Umurbrogol. The colonel and his men were about to find out if Yongdungpo-Seoul would be as tough as Peleliu.[39]

"You'll Take a Lot Fewer Casualties"

The Seizure of Seoul

September 1950

The Marine attack on Yongdungpo and Seoul opened spectacularly and unexpectedly with a North Korean predawn counterattack on September 20. A battalion of infantry led by five T-34s came down the highway toward Inchon. The long column rolled blindly into 2/1's position, a perfect L-shaped ambush with one company blocking the road and the other two dug in along high ground parallel to it. Every weapon in the Marine battalion's arsenal rained fire on the North Koreans, while artillery barrages covered the line of retreat. Private First Class Monegan, the Fox Company bazooka man, repeated his brave act of the 17th and closed in again for point-blank shots. He killed two T-34s with his first two rounds. He was sighting in on a third when machine gun fire cut him down. While the battle raged, Puller listened to radio reports and watched tracers and the flash of explosions light up the horizon. As he puffed on a pipe, he remarked to a reporter, "Cedarbird [2/1] is catching hell." He added: "They've received more casualties to date than any battalion in the 1st Marine Division." The fighting petered out by daylight, with results much better than Chesty expected. Sutter's force had suffered light losses and destroyed two tanks, captured fifty soldiers and a T-34, and killed roughly three hundred Communists.[1]

Half an hour later, the 1st Marines launched its riposte. The 2d Battalion met only "scattered resistance" from the NKPA forces in its area.

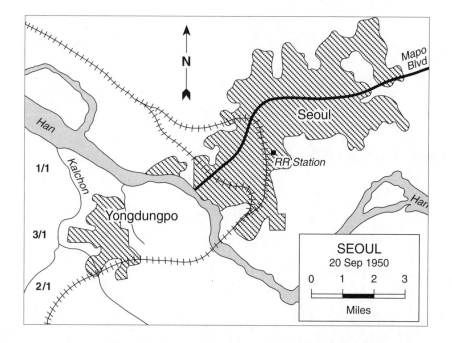

By 1230 it had reached the western fork of the Kalchon and secured a
concrete bridge. Hawkins sent Charlie Company forth to regain Hills
85 and 80, after he softened up the objectives with artillery and air
strikes. Captain Robert P. Wray attacked from the right flank, while the
rest of the battalion supported his movement by fire. He executed three
successive double envelopments, seizing a village, Hill 80, and finally
Hill 85. The last proved the toughest, since the North Koreans were prepared for the maneuver. Lieutenant Henry A. Commiskey (who had
fought as an enlisted man on Iwo Jima) charged ahead of his men,
jumped into a machine gun pit, and killed the crew. Within minutes he
repeated the feat against another emplacement. His determined attacks
caused the remaining enemy to flee. It had taken all day, but the
Marines owned the high ground on the left flank again.[2]

In the center, 3/1 was already well positioned along a ridge overlooking its portion of the Kalchon, so Ridge's outfit remained station-
ary. Puller's center and right might have taken additional ground during
the day, but the regiment was waiting for the Army outfit on its right
flank to catch up. In the afternoon, Sutter tried to call artillery fire on a
strong NKPA outpost in the Army's area that overlooked his line of approach to Yongdungpo. But the challenge of coordinating fires across

the boundary proved insurmountable. Later in the day the 32d Infantry successfully seized high ground that brought it on line with the Marines. The zones of action of all units now were so "greatly extended," however, that there was nothing resembling a continuous front, just a trace of strongpoints on key terrain.[3]

The 5th Marines had crossed the Han River that morning and was now to the northwest of the city, poised to attack down the east bank of the river. The plan called for the 1st Marines to seize Yongdungpo, while Murray uncovered a site nearby for Chesty to get over the Han. The 7th Marines, scheduled to come ashore the next day, would drive north of the capital and block the movement of NKPA forces into or out of the city. The hope was that the KMC regiment would do much of the clearing of Seoul, with some support from the 1st and 5th Marines.

Puller was fully aware of the difficulty of seizing a large, well-defended city and he believed that Yongdungpo was "heavily occupied by enemy troops." In this case, the NKPA had an added advantage, since the low-lying town was surrounded by a thick, high earthen dike. The North Koreans had dug into this man-made feature, which was fronted by the east branch of the Kalchon and the Han. In effect, the industrial suburb was surrounded by an old-fashioned castle wall and moat. Puller took a first step in cracking this hard nut when General Almond, the corps commander, visited the regimental CP. Higher headquarters had restricted the use of firepower to "military targets," but Chesty asked for unlimited authorization to employ supporting arms in the city. Around noon on the 20th, the division operations section recorded that "X Corps has granted permission to 1st Marines to burn Yongdungpo." Puller took prompt advantage of the decision. Throughout that afternoon and evening Marine aircraft struck at targets and two battalions of artillery fired nearly fifty missions, totaling several thousand rounds. The regiment reported that it was "leveling southern part of Yongdungpo which is infested with enemy troops." Chesty also requested extra tanks and engineers, important assets for urban fighting. Division approved the extra armor, but told the 1st Marines that there were no more engineers available.[4]

Almond had come to the 1st Marines in the company of MacArthur, Smith, and the usual bevy of reporters. The generals were so used to looking for Puller near the front lines that they accidentally ended up in the midst of a company flushing snipers out of a rice paddy.

They backtracked a little ways and found the colonel. Chesty enthusias-
tically described 2/1's predawn encounter and proudly emphasized
Monegan's feat. He voiced regret at the loss of a good man and told
MacArthur he intended to recommend the PFC for a posthumous
Medal of Honor.[5]

It was probably during this meeting that Smith made an unusual
arrangement for the next day's attack. He told Puller that 3/1 must remain uncommitted. The general was becoming increasingly uneasy
about Puller's "tendency to get all his battalions in the fight." Captain
Barrow, at the opposite end of the command spectrum, also noticed that
Chesty "was not the kind of person who would like to see an unem-
ployed unit." That practice had been acceptable early in the campaign
when resistance was relatively light, but in the tough fighting ahead the
lack of a reserve force could result in trouble. The CG decided to "dis-
courage this tendency by putting strings on one of [Puller's] battalions."
Smith retained full confidence in Chesty's ability as a commander; he
simply was imposing on his subordinate a certain degree of his own
careful approach to tactics.[6]

Puller, as usual, took no particular care for his personal safety.
Early that evening he, Rickert, and the tank company commander were
on the forward crest of a ridge looking toward Yongdungpo and making
plans for the next morning's attack. A North Korean gun crew in the
distance spotted the small cluster and must have guessed its importance. Without warning, a flat trajectory shell whistled by the small
group. Rickert and the captain dropped to the ground and remained
there as a few more rounds came their way over the next several minutes. Chesty remained standing, carried on the conversation till they
were done, then never mentioned the incident as they went back to the
CP on the rear slope. A correspondent visiting the regiment noted that
Puller was the only one who moved about the battlefield "as if he were
killing time on a hunting trip . . . as if he had contempt for the marksmanship of the enemy."[7]

☆   ☆   ☆

The assault on Yongdungpo began in earnest at 0630 on September 21.
With 3/1 unavailable in the center, the fight devolved into a double en-
velopment. Sutter attacked astride the main road on the right, while
Hawkins advanced on a wider front on the opposite flank. Smith visited

with Puller in the morning and the two watched the operation develop from the 1st Marines' hilltop CP. The general noted that it looked like the whole town "was in flames."[8]

The 2d Battalion had no difficulty getting across the first Kalchon bridge, but it immediately came under heavy fire from the enemy-held hill in the 7th Division's zone south of the highway. Sutter again was frustrated in his attempt to arrange artillery support across the boundary. Most likely with Puller's blessing, the regimental mortars soon fired a bombardment. Sutter then diverted two of his rifle companies to seize the troublesome high ground, while the third continued toward the second branch of the Kalchon. Both of his thrusts fell short of their goal. Fox and Easy were stuck halfway up the ridge and Dog was held up one hundred yards from the river by NKPA units on the dike on the far bank. Casualties mounted at both places.

Reinforcements were needed to break the impasse and Puller got division to release 3/1 to his control. At 1530 Ridge's force crossed the Kalchon in the center of the regimental zone. The lead company encountered the first enemy where the creek split into two branches. When Company G cleared that out, Company I crossed to the west bank and the battalion advanced along both sides of the east fork of the Kalchon, rolling up the NKPA positions from the flank. Just before dusk, the 3d Battalion destroyed the last of the enemy opposing Dog Company. Sutter broke off his attack on the hill and brought his battalion together where Company D had been fighting. At significant cost, Chesty now owned the bridge carrying the Inchon–Seoul highway over the east branch of the Kalchon.[9]

While two thirds of the regiment battered open the southern approach to Yongdungpo, Hawkins's battalion was attempting to take the northern half of the suburb. Captain Richard F. Bland's Company B had led off the drive, using the Kimpo–Seoul highway bridge to cross the Kalchon. On the other side, Baker Company ran into two companies of North Koreans holding the apex of the dike, where the Han and the Kalchon came together. With the assistance of air strikes, Bland made steady progress at heavy cost. He moved about two thousand yards along the northern dike, but finally ran out of steam in the afternoon. He got no help from the artillery battalion, which would not fire to the south of Company B, assuming that to be friendly territory since it was between the positions of the guns and the infantrymen calling for support. As dusk approached, Hawkins sent his reserve company and heavy weapons over the bridge to join up with Bland in a half-moon perimeter backed against the Han.

Able Company, tasked with crossing the Kalchon a few hundred yards to the south, got off to a later start. Barrow and his men cautiously moved up onto the dike, waiting for the expected eruption of enemy fire. None came and they proceeded slowly into the nearly deserted town. The North Koreans had been there, but had withdrawn earlier in the morning. It seems probable that the NKPA commander dispatched his forces from the center to reinforce the wings when the attacks of 2/1 and Baker Company appeared to reveal the U.S. plan of action. By arriving late, Company A walked into a vacuum. What followed would become one of the great small unit epics in the history of the Corps, to rank with Hunt's Point and Pope's Hill.[10]

As Company A advanced deeper into the town, Barrow radioed Hawkins for guidance. The battalion commander did not react cautiously in this instance; he told his subordinate to keep moving forward. Early in the afternoon, as the company neared the Inchon–Seoul highway, it spied a column of North Korean infantrymen on their way to reinforce their comrades trying to stave off 2/1's assault. The Marines opened up and scattered the enemy formation. The company engaged other small groups as it kept moving ahead, until it reached the far side of the town. Here the Kimpo–Seoul road ran atop the dike. On the eastern side was a floodplain; beyond lay the Han River and Seoul. The Marines crested the mound, saw a large body of troops moving across the low ground, and quickly inflicted heavy casualties with machine gun fire. Barrow then had his men dig in along the dike just short of where it intersected the Inchon–Seoul road.

Through luck and daring, Able Company now had its hands around the throat of the enemy defensive system for Yongdungpo. The Marines sat astride the main routes of reinforcement or retreat and could cover secondary approaches by fire. As they searched the immediate environs, they discovered a building filled with weapons and supplies and also accidentally fired into a camouflaged ammunition dump. The ensuing explosion shook the town and sent a cloud of dust boiling into the sky. Barrow's outfit had deprived the NKPA of all the resources it needed to keep up the fight for an extended period.

Now Company A had to maintain the choke hold. It would not be easy. Barrow's mortarmen had exhausted their limited supply of rounds, his radio batteries were drained, and the battalion knew only roughly where Able was located. Worse still, with the rest of the regiment now in defensive positions for the night, the enemy was free to focus its efforts on the isolated unit that most immediately threatened his possession of the town. Later, the regimental headquarters would record that "considerable alarm was felt by all hands of the 1st Marine Regiment for the safety of Able Company." However, Puller and his staff evidently were not aware of Barrow's situation until it was too late to do much about it, since reports made to division through the early evening did not mention the subject. The regimental command post was focused throughout the day on the progress of the attacks on the wings. The failure of Barrow's radios made it impossible for him to keep his superiors informed and thus a golden opportunity had been lost. If Chesty had been able to direct the 3d Battalion to follow Able, he could have used his reserve to exploit success instead of feeding it into the teeth of the enemy's defenses to salvage the 2d Battalion's stalled attack. As darkness fell, he now had to contemplate the fate of nearly two hundred Marines and corpsmen cut off behind enemy lines. Puller decided to wait until morning to send a force to effect a linkup, thereby avoiding a potentially costly night attack in an unfamiliar city. For the time being, Company A was entirely on its own.[11]

Barrow's position at least had some natural strength. It was easy to dig deep fighting holes in the dike and there were good fields of fire. The North Koreans did not wait long to test the small fortress. Just after dusk, the rumble of tanks came out of the blackness from the Inchon–Seoul road. Soon five T-34s turned onto a lane that paralleled the Kimpo–Seoul highway. As they rolled along, they fired at the dike from a range of about thirty yards. Shells and machine gun bullets whipped the western side of Able's position, while Marine bazooka men shot back. The tanks turned and came back down the street, eventually making a total of five passes. In the course of this drive-by counterattack, 3.5-inch rockets destroyed one T-34 and damaged two others. The enemy had gotten the worst of the thirty-minute firefight, since their armor-piercing shells had buried deep in the dirt before exploding. Only one Marine was wounded.

Between 2100 and midnight, Able endured four company-sized infantry attacks. Barrow was growing concerned about his supply of ammunition when two events cooled the ardor of the enemy. One of Company A's prisoners, an NKPA lieutenant, escaped and ran shouting into the town. A South Korean interpreted his words: "Don't attack any more! They're too strong for you." Then Corporal Billy D. Webb moved stealthily off into the darkness and shot the North Korean commander who could be heard a few blocks away exhorting his troops before each onslaught. There were no more harangues that night. One more half-hearted attack took place, but after that Able Company endured only scattered small arms fire.[12]

At first light, the 1st and 3d Battalions attacked with the mission of relieving Company A. To their surprise, the determined enemy resistance of the day before had melted away. Meanwhile, Barrow's men counted 275 dead around their perimeter and found four abandoned T-34s nearby. Able Company's audacious advance and stubborn night defense had broken the NKPA hold on Yongdungpo. The North Koreans had withdrawn over the Han while there was still time to escape in the dark. After losing thirty-four killed and 137 wounded on September 21, on this day the regiment could count its losses on one hand. The city, however, "lay in smoking ruins."[13]

☆   ☆   ☆

The 1st Marines had cleared a fairly large urban area in two days, but X Corps was not happy with the pace of the offensive. On September 23, the men of the 5th Marines were still fighting to break through strong positions in the hills northwest of Seoul. At MacArthur's urging, Almond was determined to retake the capital by September 25, the three-month anniversary of the North Korean invasion. The 1st Marine Division was eager to press the offensive, too. Craig felt that "the eyes of the world are upon us"; he and Smith did not want Eighth Army, now driving from the south, "to get to Seoul before the Marines." To further aid the drive on the northeast side of the Han, Smith wanted the 1st Marines to join up with the 5th Marines on September 24. Rickert received the plan at division headquarters around midnight. The last details of the regimental order were ironed out at 0430 in a conference between Chesty and two of his battalion commanders. (The 3d Battalion would remain near the Han bridges for the time being.) The pressure to move faster filtered down along with the division order. As Puller's force reconnoitered the Han crossing site on the evening of the

23d, it found a large number of mines, but "plans proceeded in view of urgent requirements for speed."[14]

The 2d Battalion went over first the next morning. The maneuver was uneventful, save for some ineffective NKPA mortar fire. Once 2/1 was on the opposite side, it came up on the right flank of the 5th Marines, with a railroad serving as the boundary. Sutter advanced toward Hill 79, the day's objective, with his right sweeping along the banks of the Han. The 1st Battalion did not reach the far side until noon. Hawkins and his company commanders then reported to the regimental CP for orders. Much to their surprise, Puller told them to move up between the railroad and the river and seize Hill 79. The 1st Battalion commander pointed out the obvious: "Colonel, the 2d Battalion is already attacking in that zone." Chesty was not fazed: "Well, you'll just have to move a little faster than they do." He then turned to his driver, Orville Jones, and asked him to hand over a folded flag. He gave it to Hawkins with orders to raise it at the top of the hill.[15]

Word of the change in plans had not even filtered down to Sutter's subordinates when Hawkins's men came trotting up to the rear of the 2d Battalion. A 2/1 company commander demanded: "What in hell's going on here?" Barrow merely replied: "Don't worry, we're conducting a passage of lines on the move." Sutter finally got his outfit stopped and it went into regimental reserve. While the 5th Marines continued slugging it out in the ridges just to the north, the 1st Marines met only scattered small arms fire in their zone. The only serious trouble came when the 1st Battalion encountered antivehicle mines on the outskirts of the city. The infantry pushed on and entered western Seoul, a zone of squatter shacks crammed along narrow alleys. Luckily the enemy was not prepared to fight in this dense maze.

The Marines threaded their way to the summit of Hill 79 and immediately raised the national ensign on a bamboo pole over a ramshackle schoolhouse. At 1707, radios crackled at the division CP: "CO 1st Marines reports American flag now flying on Hill 79, city of Seoul." Murray's regiment was still mopping up in the ridgelines outside of town. Smith thought Puller's coup in entering the city first had "annoyed" the 5th Marines, since that outfit had been fighting for several days to get there. Both regiments would hoist more flags before the battle was over. A story circulated later that a X Corps staff officer was irritated at the Marine penchant for flying the national colors over every

captured site, in obvious imitation of the heroically inspiring flag raising on Iwo Jima. Chesty reputedly growled in reply that the best fighter
was "a man with a flag in his pack and the desire to put it on an enemy
strong point." There was no shortage of such men in the 1st Marine Division in September 1950.[16]

☆   ☆   ☆

Puller's odd order to Hawkins had not created any problems, but it
seemed mystifying to those involved. Years later Chesty would explain
that "the lead battalion showed signs of tiring." He could have relieved
2/1 by halting it to conduct an orthodox passage of lines, but there was
the emphasis on speed coming down from higher headquarters. His
seat-of-the-pants solution also likely reduced the resistance his troops
faced, since it gave the enemy little time to react to this new thrust past
the flank of the NKPA's main defenses on the northwest ridges. In that
respect he followed the doctrine taught in the schools to even the
youngest lieutenants, "that almost any decision they make will be right
if they pursue it aggressively." His action also echoed words he had underlined in his favorite book: "Napoleon never waited for his adversary
to become fully prepared, but struck him the first blow." Although
Puller's risky and awkward tactic worked, it demonstrated his often
breezy attitude toward the finer points of coordinating the activities of
his subordinate units.[17]

In these early days of the Inchon-Seoul campaign, there was no
shortage of senior officers looking over Puller's shoulder. On September 22, an Army major general had appeared at the 1st Marines CP. He
introduced himself as Frank E. Lowe, a reservist acting as Truman's
personal observer in Korea. Since the President was no friend of the
Corps and Chesty disliked most things connected with the Army, this
was not much of a recommendation. The Marine colonel granted his
visitor full access to everything, but quietly passed the word that the officers and men should be wary of "adverse comments regarding political personalities and U.S. Army activities."[18]

Despite Puller's initial misgivings, he quickly developed a "warm
friendship" with Lowe. The general was sixty-five years old, but still
played the part of the aggressive commander who had served in World
War I. During the Second World War he had been a military assistant to
Truman's Senate committee overseeing the administration of the war
effort, but Lowe disdained the comforts of higher headquarters. He re-

ferred to the Inchon flagship, *Mount McKinley,* as "an overcrowded VIP tourist ship" and preferred to get up to the front lines. Most important, Lowe was building up an abiding respect for the Marine Corps based on its performance in the Korean War. After watching the 1st Marine Brigade in action in the Pusan Perimeter, he had become convinced that it was the only reason that "U.N. forces were not defeated, routed, and possibly annihilated." He was more impressed when interrogations of captured NKPA officers revealed that the North Koreans feared fighting the Marines more than any other force.[19]

Lowe quickly came to admire the commander of the 1st Marines. He appreciated Puller's unflappable nature in the midst of battle and shared many of the same opinions. The observer thought "the staff must be the servant of command and not the master" and that Army headquarters required "entirely too many detailed reports." He firmly believed both services started with "the same cross section of the United States," but "the difference is in Marine training and the fact that the Leathernecks disdain a lot of Army frills and non-essentials." His only criticism of the Corps was that "officers and men alike were so courageous and determined that they failed to take cover when they could, resulting in an unnecessarily high casualty list." Of course, he was not averse to getting close to the action himself. After one foray to the front he returned to the CP with sixteen bullet holes in his jeep.[20]

☆　☆　☆

The increasing strength of enemy resistance dictated that experienced American units would have to take the lead in seizing the main part of Seoul. The 1st Marines had moved into the capital in a southeasterly direction on September 24. Now Smith ordered the regiment to make a 90-degree pivot and push northeast through the heart of the city on a front about one and a half miles wide. The 5th Marines would make a "coordinated attack" to the left or north of the 1st, while the 7th Marines guarded the northern approaches to the capital. A battalion of Korean Marines would follow each of the assault regiments and mop up Communist elements trying to hide among the population. Division also sent 3/1 back to the regiment that night.

Murray wondered how the "coordinated attack" was supposed to work in practice, since he had a zone of action about as wide as Puller's. On the afternoon of the 24th, he helicoptered over to the 1st Marines CP, set in the middle of a turnip and onion patch on top of a hill outside of town. It was the first time the younger regimental commander had ever met his counterpart. Murray quickly discovered Puller's favorite method of appraising someone's effectiveness in combat: "The first question he asked me was how many casualties did we have . . . and as soon as I convinced him that I had quite a few, why he figured, okay, you can join the group then. He determined how good a fighter you were by how many casualties you had."[21]

Puller was thinking of an additional category of human loss that afternoon. As a correspondent interviewed him in his CP, Chesty absently tore apart blades of grass and watched children playing nearby while the shells and bombs thundered. The youngsters reminded him of his own family. He remarked with a twinge of sadness: "The North Koreans are defending the city in such a way as to force us to destroy it. There's a billion dollars worth of publicity in it for them." Nodding toward an adjacent hut, he added: "I hate to see people in a shack like that get hurt. Probably the same family has been living for generations in that same dump." The man who had flattened Yongdungpo was not about to quit using firepower, but he realized the unavoidable consequences of employing it in populated areas.[22]

Chesty also had reason to be annoyed with division's tactical scheme for a change. His wide frontage would have been too much territory to cover in open terrain; it was impossible in an urban area, especially when he planned to keep the 2d Battalion in reserve. The late arrival of 3/1 gave him little time to get that battalion forward to operate in the left of his zone prior to the scheduled 0700 attack. There also was some confusion as Ridge tried to identify the line of departure in the unfamiliar city. The 1st Battalion, which was fighting off small counterattacks during the night, had to reorient its lines to assume responsibility for the right half. Puller told division headquarters how difficult it was to get ready for the assault "inasmuch as a simultaneous passage of lines, a change in regimental direction of attack, and coordination of supporting artillery fires from unfavorable positions on the other side of the Han River were involved." To make matters worse, the tanks that were supposed to support his operation did not show up in time.[23]

☆   ☆   ☆

Both the North Koreans and the Marines adopted unusual tactics for this urban battle. Historically defenders worked primarily from buildings, using them as ready-made strongpoints and forcing the attackers to clear each and every one, a costly and time-consuming process. In Seoul, the NKPA chose to fight in the streets. At intersections they built small forts out of dirt-filled rice bags, with walls facing in all four directions. Given the North's limited manpower and time to prepare, these defensive works were concentrated on the main thoroughfares. Puller, with a wide front and far too few troops, would also have to focus on a few narrow avenues of approach. He could have sought out routes that bypassed the Korean rice bag roadblocks, but he elected instead to push up the major byways and meet the NKPA forces on their chosen ground.

Chesty's actions would add to the legend that he based his plans entirely on the precept that the shortest distance between two points was a straight line. An observer of the fighting noted that the colonel's "battle tactics have the subtlety of a sledgehammer." Captain Wesley B. Noren of 1/1 joked that the 1st Marines operations officer had the "easiest job" in Korea, since all he needed was a ruler to draw a path from friendly to enemy positions. Even Smith thought that his subordinate "believes in direct action" and "would have no truck with clever maneuvers." The straight-ahead approach may or may not have suited Chesty, but the situation left him no choice. From MacArthur on down, pressure was building to seize the city quickly. Murray knew that Almond "was raising hell" over the pace of the operation. The Americans could race to the far side of the city by avoiding the enemy's defenses, but that would not have achieved the 1st Marine Division's mission "to destroy the enemy in its zone." Moreover, if the single regiment of barely trained Korean Marines was to have any hope of handling the Communists, the NKPA main units first had to be beaten down to a manageable level by the 1st and 5th Marines. Captain James F. McInteer, a company commander in 1/1, realized that the plan was to "break the backbone of the enemy defense" and leave the survivors "disorganized and [able] to fight only as individuals or small bands." The ROK Marines would then "clean up the enemy left in the city." There was no point in making flanking attacks on individual roadblocks, either, as they were organized for all-around defense. Puller's tactics were exactly what Smith wanted: "When confronting the enemy in practically a face-to-face situation, it is better to punch him on the nose than it is to maneuver around." In the commanding general's view, Chesty "did not sacrifice men uselessly."[24]

The 1st Marines jumped off in the attack shortly after 0700 on September 25. The 3d Battalion moved up Mapo Boulevard, a broad avenue with streetcar tracks running down the middle. The tanks finally arrived around noon, with 131 POWs in tow, the result of a firefight outside Seoul that had delayed their appearance. Puller was not impressed and gave the company commander "a heated tongue lashing" for being late. To complicate matters, there was some confusion about command relationships. The tankers insisted they were not attached to the 1st Marines and would take orders only from their own battalion commander. It was an all-around bad day for the M-26s, as mines disabled two Pershings and heavy fire chewed up radio antennas and periscopes. Despite these setbacks, the armor did assist in clearing the first two roadblocks. A third fortification was so strongly defended by antitank guns and mines that Ridge finally gave up trying to reduce it after repeated requests for indirect fire support generated no assistance.[25]

There were no heavy weapons available because 1/1 already was monopolizing them. After advancing against light resistance early in the day, Able Company reached high ground that overlooked much of the city. From this vantage point, Barrow saw enemy activity around the main railroad station. His observers called in mortars and artillery and the first shells kicked over a beehive—troops seemed to rush from everywhere scrambling for better cover. He decided to keep bringing firepower to bear until he ran out of targets. As the evening approached, the two assault battalions assumed defensive positions for the night. They had gained about two thousand yards.[26]

Puller had been up front most of the day, pressing his men to keep up the advance. He appeared frequently just behind the lead platoons, Jones and the jeep close by, a battered soft cap in place of a helmet, and a cigar or a pipe thrusting from his clenched jaws. Since the Marines were bashing their way down the main streets and ignoring most everything else, there was scattered small arms fire throughout the area. Several men were wounded near Chesty and more than one round spattered against a nearby wall or off the pavement at his feet. The small pockets of bypassed enemy presented a real danger to the unlucky, but that did not change his plan. He remarked to a correspondent: "They're a nuisance, that's all. We can't waste time sending patrols after them or we never would get this war over." The colonel was sufficiently nonchalant that he took time out for a little souvenir hunting and plucked a sword off a dead North Korean officer. Lieutenant Joseph R. Fisher, a company commander in 3/1, thought Puller's calm demeanor in the midst of the action provided a reassuring influence to officers and men who were still new to the business of urban warfare. One of Fisher's platoon commanders, fresh from the Basic School just three months earlier, noted how Chesty's fearlessness emboldened his troops.[27]

Captain Wray found out secondhand how Puller evaluated the strength of the resistance. He was involved in tough fighting on the approaches to the railroad station when Hawkins came up and told him the regimental commander had said "we weren't having enough casualties." Wray registered his shock and expressed his belief that he was accomplishing the mission at the lowest possible cost. His battalion commander agreed: "That's exactly the way I feel, but don't worry about it. About the time he made that statement, you called down an artillery concentration almost on your own position and it sounded to us as if all hell was breaking loose. Colonel Puller just smiled his little, rare smile and drove away." As usual, it was aggressiveness, not losses, that the CO of the 1st Marines truly prized.[28]

Even Chesty's well-known pugnacity was soon challenged, however, by Almond's desire to bring the battle to a quick and symbolic end on the three-month anniversary. Shortly after 2000, the 1st Marine Division CP received an urgent message from X Corps. Aerial spotters had reported the enemy "fleeing" from Seoul and Almond ordered: "You will push attack now to the limit of your objectives in order to insure maximum destruction of enemy forces." Bowser called the corps headquarters to find out what "now" meant. The answer was "at once." Division passed the word to the regiments at 2200. In an effort to let his colonels make the best of a bad situation, Smith told them to "carefully" coordinate the attack and take it slow. After consultation, the 1st and 5th Marines agreed to establish contact with each other by patrols and launch the assault at 0130. Puller also decided he would employ a fifteen-minute artillery preparation, another prudent measure. Everyone except corps headquarters remained opposed, however, to the idea of launching a night attack into unreconnoitered urban terrain. Lieutenant Fisher believed: "Whoever thought it up must have had a brain you could put in a thimble."[29]

The unexpected and hurried change in plans apparently caused some confusion in the 1st Marines CP. Before midnight, someone directed 3/1 to send a patrol three hundred yards to its front down Mapo Boulevard to meet up with the 5th Marines. There was no mention of plans for a heavy bombardment in the area. Eight Marines and three Korean interpreters departed the lines shortly thereafter, with no clue that they were the leading wave of a division night attack. It was not until 0030 that the 1st Marines staff told the battalions about the preparation fire scheduled for 0115 and the assault at 0130. Ridge protested, since that gave him too little time to prepare. Regiment relented and switched the time of the assault to 0200. There was considerable concern about the fate of the patrol, which had no radio.

A little before 0130 the sounds of small arms fire indicated the patrol had stumbled into something. Minutes later, Marines near the front lines heard the ominous rumble of many armored vehicles approaching. The North Korean tanks got in the first shots, but the scheduled preparation fire almost immediately came crashing down around them. Other U.S. supporting arms and direct-fire weapons quickly joined the fray. The firing remained heavy on both sides for the rest of the night, but the North Korean infantry never launched a direct assault through the curtain of American steel. At one point, five battalions of artillery, including an Army 155mm howitzer outfit, were providing "the greatest concentration of firepower in the entire operation." The fighting died out just before dawn. First light revealed a street littered with about five hundred enemy dead and the hulks of seven tanks and two self-propelled guns. The Marines rounded up nearly a hundred prisoners. Ridge had lost two killed and forty wounded. Amazingly, the members of the patrol filtered into friendly lines after hiding out during the height of the battle.[30]

☆   ☆   ☆

The events of the night generated mixed emotions in Puller. He was extremely proud of his outfit's performance. He "firmly believed that no military unit in the history of modern warfare was ever more prepared to meet an attack than the 1st Regiment at this particular time," though he modestly did not ascribe it to his own tactical skill: "Talk about the help of God, we certainly had it on that one." He was much less happy with the high command. When correspondents asked him in the morning about the reports of a North Korean withdrawal, he could barely contain his disgust for Almond's headquarters: "All I know about a flee-

Young enlisted Marines take a break from the rigors of the third Officers' Training Camp in 1919. Puller (second from left) was on his way to his first commission, but he had missed out on the "war to end all wars."

Second Lieutenant Puller cut a dashing figure in 1926, even without the gold wings of a naval aviator, which had eluded him at Pensacola that year.

Puller focuses on the sights of his revolver during target practice.

Following a successful patrol in September 1930, Puller (far left) stands with (left to right) Guardia lieutenants Avery Graves, Bill Lee, and Tom Lynch. Two years later, Puller, Lee, and Lynch would participate in one of the most spectacular victories of the Nicaraguan campaign, at El Sauce.

"El Tigre" poses in 1931 with First Sergeant Carlos Gutierrez (left) and Sergeant Carmen Torrez, two of the steadfast *guardias* who helped him chase Sandino throughout the rugged jungles of central Nicaragua.

Company M marches on parade in September 1932. Puller and the small group of Nicaraguan soldiers had earned an unsurpassed reputation for courage and aggressiveness.

The Pullers on their wedding day, November 13, 1937. It had taken nearly a dozen years, but Lewis had finally convinced Virginia Evans to marry him.

The pronounced barrel chest, a gruff booming voice, and a reputation for fearlessness in battle were all part of the growing legend of "Chesty," pictured here as a captain in Shanghai.

The Marine detachment turns out on the deck of the USS *Augusta* in 1940 with its commanding officer (sixth from the left in the rear rank). It was Puller's second tour on the flagship of the Asiatic Fleet.

During a brief visit to the States in early 1943, Lieutenant Colonel Puller speaks intently about the Guadalcanal campaign. His opinions on tactics, equipment, and the enemy caught the attention of the public and military leaders at home.

The senior staff officers of the 7th Marines on Cape Gloucester on January 10, 1944 (left to right): Major Victor H. Streit (operations officer), Lieutenant Colonel Puller (executive officer), First Lieutenant Frank T. Farrell (intelligence officer), Major Claude B. Cross (quartermaster), Captain R. T. Musselwhite, Jr. (communications officer), and First Lieutenant John J. Aubuchon (assistant operations officer).

During a lull in the Gilnit Patrol on New Britain in February 1944, Chesty rests on an ammunition cart and catches up on mail from home. The frequent heavy rains created many operational problems, and also ruined the family photos that Puller always carried in his pocket.

Amid the coconut groves of Pavuvu in May 1944, Colonel Puller pins a medal on one of his Marines. Chesty enjoyed giving out awards and felt great pride when his men earned more decorations than their contemporaries in other units.

In the field, Puller boasted that the map in his pocket was "my CP." In the rear, he lived as austerely as his men, in a modestly furnished tent. His Marines revered him for his simplicity and lack of pretense.

An admiral visits the frontline command post of the 1st Marines on Peleliu on September 18, 1944. The hellish heat aggravated Puller's Guadalcanal wound and left him hobbled during much of the battle.

Major General Pedro del Valle, the incoming commanding general of the 1st Marine Division, is greeted by Colonel Puller on Pavuvu in late October 1944, while Major General William Rupertus (far left), the outgoing commanding general, looks on. Chesty was still recovering from Peleliu and would soon be on his way home.

The commander of the Infantry Training Regiment at Camp Lejeune in July 1945. Puller's combat reputation and his chest full of medals were an inspiration to the men he prepared for battle.

Colonel and Mrs. Puller chat with Lieutenant General Lem Shepherd during a Fourth of July barbecue at the Marine Barracks at Pearl Harbor in 1950. The next day, Chesty sent the first of his telegrams in an effort to "march to the sound of the drums" in war-torn Korea.

During the Inchon invasion of September 1950, the commanding officer of the 1st Marines stands ready to disembark from his amphibian tractor. Chesty thought he and the officers of his regiment were lucky to have another "chance to excel" at their trade so soon after World War II.

A jeepload of stars—General Douglas MacArthur, Major General Ned Almond (driving), Major General O. P. Smith (left rear), and Lieutenant General Lem Shepherd (right rear)—stop to visit with Puller as the 1st Marines drive on Seoul on September 20, 1950.

Brigadier General Edward Craig, the assistant division commander, confers with Chesty on a hilltop overlooking Seoul as the 1st Marines battle their way into the city.

During the Commandant's visit to the 1st Marines on October 3, 1950, Puller presents the first American flag flown over recaptured Seoul to General Clifton Cates. Chesty believed that the best fighter was "a man with a flag in his pack and the desire to put it on an enemy strong point."

In celebration of the 175th birthday of the Marine Corps on November 10, 1950, Puller cuts the traditional cake with a captured North Korean sword and serves it up to his men. In a short, fiery speech he had declared: "We can knock the hell out of anything that comes before us—that's why we are the best fighting unit in the world."

Brigadier General Bill Whaling (left), Major General Jerry Thomas, and Brigadier General Puller chat for a moment on the day of Chesty's departure from the 1st Marine Division and Korea in May 1951. Puller firmly believed that there had "never been a better division in the history of the world."

Following a chant of "We want Puller," Chesty spoke briefly at the 1st Marine Division Association banquet in August 1951 and received an enthusiastic response from fellow veterans.

The 2d Battalion, 3d Marines of the 3d Marine Brigade undergoes a typical Puller inspection in September 1951. Among other things, he wanted to instill in his junior leaders the importance of looking out for the feet of their men.

Chesty chats with
Colonel Lew Walt, one of
his former Basic School
students, during a land-
ing exercise at Camp
Pendleton in 1952. The
two legendary Marines
had fought shoulder-to-
shoulder on Guadalcanal
and New Britain.

Major General
O. P. Smith presents
Puller with his fifth
Navy Cross at Camp
Pendleton in February
1952. Many of Chesty's
admirers thought he
should have received
a Medal of Honor for
at least one of his
countless feats of
heroic leadership.

Lewis and Virginia with retired General Holland M. "Howlin' Mad" Smith and his wife at the November 1953 Marine Corps birthday ball. Even though both men had well-deserved reputations for speaking their minds, they had risen to high rank in the Corps.

Sergeant Major Robert L. Norrish pins the third star of a lieutenant general on Puller at Chesty's retirement ceremony on October 30, 1955. There was no joy in the promotion for Puller, who had fought with every means at his disposal to remain on active duty.

WITNESSES

The appearance of Puller as a witness for the defense in the McKeon trial at Parris Island in 1956 electrified the courtroom. Chesty was more than happy to have yet another opportunity to champion the emphasis on tough training that had guided his entire career.

Chesty enjoys a quiet moment at his home in Saluda, Virginia. He kept to his retirement promise to his wife: "I will live only for you and our precious children and my requirements will be your great love, a little food, and a daily can of tobacco."

ing enemy is there's over two hundred of them out there that won't be fleeing anywhere—they're dead." He was pleased with the assistance rendered by the Army 155mm howitzers, though, and sent a message of appreciation to the battalion. But Chesty continued to regret the destruction he was wreaking on the population: "I am sorry I had to use that [heavy] stuff last night. The Koreans won't forget this in 500 years. I'm convinced the Reds are holing-up deliberately to force us to use artillery and flame throwers. I hate to see people in houses like these burned out."[31]

Puller obviously was concerned some people might think he was employing firepower indiscriminately. Murray would draw a comparison between the two regiments in that respect: "Chesty used a lot of artillery and you could almost see a boundary line between the two of [us], the smoke coming up from his sector and very little smoke coming up from mine. I'm not saying that I was right and he was wrong by any manner of means. I'm just saying that this was two different philosophies." The pendulum had swung from the opposite extreme at Peleliu; now Chesty was being singled out for using too much firepower. But the opinion of those who counted was in Puller's favor. Craig already had registered his belief that the division was not using all its available supporting arms and that any resulting destruction inside the city "was necessary." Throughout the day South Korean civilians were posting hand-lettered signs of thanks for their freedom, despite the high cost. One read: "Welcome U.S. Marines, Angel of U.N. Army." Chesty's own troops were grateful, too, since the firepower increased their odds of survival. One enlisted man would later tell him: "I realize how you saved so many lives."[32]

Puller had good reason to consider how people viewed his actions. Since the battle to reclaim Seoul was dominating the headlines back home, he was fast becoming a fixture in the news. As usual, the reporters were not too careful about the facts of his career, as long as the tales added color to their articles. One piece claimed he had earned a battlefield commission in World War I. Supposedly he also had been charged with but not convicted of murder in Nicaragua for shooting four suspected Sandinistas in the street in Bluefields (a town in which he had never set foot). One man wrote: "There is no more fabulous character [in the Corps]. . . . Colonel Puller is a Marine's Marine, an uncouth, profane, tough fighting man." The same reporter also astutely observed there was a lot more to Chesty than that simple image: "Although in reality a well-educated man, Puller delights in tormenting his visitors by posing as a rustic."

The correspondents also enjoyed mining new myths from the ranks of the 1st Marines. One story illustrated Puller's penchant for keeping the headquarters close to the action. Supposedly the colonel had radioed back to his staff to move up to the front lines. The XO received the message, stood up, and shouted: "CP attention! Two paces forward." All reporters quickly uncovered one truth, that Puller was held in high esteem by his subordinates. One officer observed that "all the men are crazy about him" and vowed he would "follow him to hell." Another Marine leader called the colonel "the fightingest man we have [in the Corps] and that makes 'Chesty' quite a fighter." A reporter noted the apparent contradiction in Chesty's status: "Known as a 'mankiller' because— fighting the toughest battles—he always loses a high proportion of men, and yet beloved, if not worshiped, by those who serve under him." A stateside columnist summed up the laudatory reports with prescience: "If frontline dispatches from Seoul mean anything, there may soon be even more Navy Crosses on this most outstanding chest."[33]

☆   ☆   ☆

On the morning of September 26 Puller moved 2/1 forward to resume the attack in place of a very tired 3/1. His orders were simple: "Keep your troops moving. . . . If you keep moving you'll bypass most of the snipers . . . and you'll take a lot fewer casualties. Let the Korean Marines coming in behind you do the mopping up." Sutter's battalion passed through the previous night's carnage by 0900, rounded a bend in the road, and discovered it was not going anywhere fast. From that point on, Mapo Boulevard was studded every few hundred yards with a rice bag fort, each one boasting antitank guns, automatic weapons, and an occasional T-34 or artillery piece. Minefields covered the approaches. Chesty encouraged his troops to use heavy weapons "to maximum extent." The tankers, engineers, and infantrymen soon developed a methodical system for coordinating their assaults. The Pershings shot up their ammunition too quickly, however, and each time they withdrew to the rear for replenishment, the attack stalled. Puller found the process "agonizingly slow" and pestered division for more tanks. After his early requests went unanswered, he grew more insistent: "Imperative additional company of Tank Battalion [be] placed in support this organization." Hawkins's men advanced at a similar crawl as they cleared pockets of resistance from the wreckage of the train station and rail yards. At dusk the regiment settled into defensive positions after gaining less than a mile.[34]

The next day 2/1 continued its step-by-step advance through the barricades, but it moved faster as the day wore on. Sutter's companies began to bring air strikes on each redoubt, while the tankers mastered the process of rotating vehicles to the rear for resupply so that a few were at the front at all times. The 1st Battalion cleared the troublesome rail yards and then made steady progress through a similar series of NKPA strongpoints in the streets. During the course of the day, the 1st Marines raised the American flag over the U.S. embassy and the French and Soviet consulates. By late afternoon, enemy resistance crumbled and there was little hard fighting at the roadblocks. The regiment gained five thousand yards and reached the eastern outskirts of the city. Except for mopping-up operations by the Korean Marines, the battle for Seoul was over.

Throughout the day, Puller was in his customary position up front. He saw Lieutenant Lew Devine's unit make short work of a barricade. The colonel put his arm around the platoon leader (who was wearing an NCO's jacket) and congratulated him: "Great work, Sergeant." Rickert recognized Devine and pointed out the mistake. Chesty was chagrined; he spat, said only "Lieutenant?" and walked off. Devine, a mustang, was not upset: "I knew, as most junior officers around me did, that he preferred sergeants to second lieutenants, but all the same, the junior officers were strong for him, too." A similar story circulated later about a captain who wanted to obtain a battlefield commission for one of his men because the NCO was "better than a sergeant." Chesty supposedly replied: "Captain, there's *nothing* better than a sergeant."[35]

The regiment faced almost no opposition when it resumed the attack on September 28. The 2d Battalion occupied its final objective, high ground east of the city, by 0740. The 1st Battalion linked up at 1040. The Eighth Army, which had been fighting its way north from the Pusan Perimeter, finally reached the southern flank of X Corps. The NKPA was in full retreat.

Smith came forward to visit Puller at the 1st Marines CP on the grounds of Duksoo Palace. The CG found Chesty looking over a North

Korean bugle he had picked up as a souvenir for Lewis Jr. Both men were surprised to see a column of Korean civilians armed with brooms, apparently a crew of volunteers beginning to restore their city. Puller was ready for a cleanup himself. He dispatched Jones to find a bathhouse and the colonel was soon luxuriating in hot water. When it came time to pay, he had no small American bills, but his driver came to the rescue with a large-denomination Korean banknote salvaged from a destroyed building. The two Marines enjoyed the look of glee on the face of the attendant when they paid him a fortune.[36]

The war seemed almost over, but that night the NKPA launched a counterattack against Sutter's lines. For the first time the enemy relied on stealth and infiltration rather than an all-out charge. Achieving some surprise and using a lot of hand grenades at close range, the North Koreans killed four Marines and wounded twenty-eight more. The companies had failed to put out any trip flares or concertina wire, and the artillery responded slowly to calls for illumination. Puller knew this was an expensive "lesson" for his troops—there still was fighting left to do.[37]

MacArthur and President Rhee entered the city on September 29 for ceremonies restoring the South Korean government to its proper seat of power. Ridge's outfit drew the primary responsibility for security, with orders to remain out of sight of the dignitaries. The 1st Marine Division was allowed a total of six attendees at the event, which took place in the damaged Government Palace. Smith, Craig, Puller, Murray, and two aides were thus the only Marines in view. There were some hard feelings that the conquerors of Seoul largely were shunted aside when it came time to celebrate the outcome. Chesty resented it even more when he saw the spit-shined Army military policemen flown in from Tokyo to line the hall where MacArthur and Rhee spoke to a crowd of well-groomed officers who obviously had not participated in the fighting. Craig agreed with him that "the men who captured Seoul should have had that place of honor." Puller told a correspondent: "I wanted to bring some of my men and officers with me, but they tell me they don't have enough room. . . . You know, I lost 25 men—four of them killed—while these cookies were coming in for the ceremony."[38]

Puller highlighted his regiment's work in his initial report on the campaign: "It is particularly desired to point out here that at no time during the advance through the heart of Seoul were any other American or friendly Korean units ahead of this regiment's assault battalions. Throughout the entire advance friendly adjacent units on both flanks were generally to our rear. . . . All missions assigned were accomplished." That was no small feat for an outfit that had come into being on August 4 and "less than a month and a half later had landed at dusk on an enemy-held shore." Chesty was equally proud of the manner in which it was done: "Missions were accomplished with spirit and drive characterized by superior leadership and individual initiative inherent in the Marine Corps. The regiment at all times advanced so aggressively that the enemy was demoralized, routed, and/or destroyed wherever he was encountered." General Smith's aide echoed that assessment: "A fiery drive under inspirational leadership that was in a sense unique . . . it was a sort of inspirational drive, a pride instilled in them, a leadership that made this unit what it was." Smith agreed that the effectiveness of the 1st Marines "was a tribute to the leadership of Colonel Puller."[39]

"Not My Way of Fighting a Battle"
On to North Korea
October–November 1950

The 1st Marine Division moved to new positions farther outside Seoul on September 30. While elements of Eighth Army passed through and kept up the pressure on the retreating enemy, MacArthur held X Corps out of the fight in contemplation of another amphibious hook. In the meantime, the Marines launched patrols to search for remnants of the NKPA. They also recuperated a bit from two weeks of combat.

Puller set up his CP in a pleasant pine grove on a hillside and soon found he had "little to do except get my reports prepared." His experience as a reader told him the facts would not necessarily speak for themselves: "I wish I had a flair for writing, as then I am certain this regiment would get the credit due them when the history of this operation is finally written. Now every one knows, but in a few years what is written will govern. I will do a better job of getting the facts in my reports than I did in the past war. I will also claim everything due the regiment." He also was not averse to a little back-scratching to advance the interests of the Corps. He suggested that General Smith nominate Truman's observer for a Distinguished Service Medal. "Major General Lowe stated on more than one occasion that he was advising the President that a ready force of four war-strength Marine Divisions, with corresponding Marine aviation units and adequate amphibious shipping readily available, was a minimum requirement for the nation's defense.

. . . It is my conviction that General Lowe can help the Marine Corps immeasurably and will willingly do so. . . . I believe that such recommendation, coming from the Division Commander, would cement an already friendly feeling and ultimately benefit the Marine Corps greatly."[1]

Puller had gathered quite a collection of souvenirs and began distributing them. The Commandant visited the 1st Marines and received the first flag flown over Seoul. For Smith, the regimental CO had a North Korean sword. He passed his captured bugle to Honsowetz, now one of Cates's assistants, and asked his former battalion commander to take it back to the States for Lewis Jr. Befitting his protective fatherly attitude, Chesty sent along instructions that Virginia should not let their son play with it till she had boiled it in soap and water "for at least an hour."[2]

Puller felt the war was winding down. He wrote his wife that he thought the division "may not be further employed" and he expected to be back home "before too long . . . perhaps in another month." He was more than happy to see the end of this campaign: "I am getting more homesick now for you and our children and pray that we will soon be reunited. I will not be content or happy till then. . . . I just want to go home to you and our children and get sufficient pay for you to be comfortable and to educate them." Virginia certainly was tiring of the separations and the worry. News accounts had indicated that the "battle for Seoul was a grim one" and it had caused her several "most anxious days." She was looking forward to the time when Lewis would "retire to a quiet life." Little Martha wanted him back so she could receive her father's habitual evening greeting—"Hug me tight and give me a little kiss." Although Chesty had once promised his wife he always would march toward "the beat of the drums" when war came, the pull of family life was beginning to wear down his ardor for the fray. He promised Virginia: "Rest assured that I am never volunteering for duty that will take me away from you again."[3]

As Puller's thoughts turned to his place in history and the future of his family, he made a rare admission to Virginia that he envied those who had better schooling and a way with words. "Many times I have regretted that my English education was cut short during the first war. Please do your best to impress on our children the necessity of taking advantage of every opportunity that presents itself to improve themselves in all ways. Later in life I have found out, it will pay off many times over and if they don't, they will certainly lose out in this hard old world of ours."[4]

☆   ☆   ☆

The war entered a new phase when Truman authorized MacArthur to launch operations north of the 38th parallel with the goal of reuniting the Korean peninsula. There was some small concern about intervention by the Soviet Union or Communist China. The Chinese foreign minister made a specific threat to do so on October 2, though he vowed that his country would remain neutral if only ROK forces crossed into North Korea. Given that China had just finished a long, destructive civil war the year before, few U.S. leaders took the warning seriously.

On October 6, the 1st Marines trucked back to Inchon and went into bivouac in an industrial complex. For the first time since he had come ashore, Puller slept in a cot that night. Although the division staff was busy planning an amphibious assault against the east coast port city of Wonsan, the rapid progress of Eighth Army was making it increasingly likely that area would be under friendly control before X Corps could arrive by sea. Chesty was still hopeful the Marines would "not be employed further," though he had little confidence in the rest of the U.N. force. He assumed "we will be shoved into it in a hurry . . . [if] the other crowd (ours) again bogs down," but "Red China and Russia appear to be keeping out of Korea and if this continues, our Army should not have much trouble in winding up the Korean War." He found it "funny how so many persons have regained their courage since the 15th of September."[5]

His opinion of the U.S. Army was not enhanced when Almond invited Smith and his three regimental commanders to dinner on October 9. Puller was amazed that "the Army staffs even live better than our staffs." The food was flown in fresh from Japan and served by white-uniformed enlisted men on linen-covered tables complete with fine china and silver place settings. In contrast, the CO of the 1st Marines had eaten only canned field rations since the Inchon landing and his men were sleeping in a bombed-out foundry covered with coal dust. Chesty did not envy the rear-echelon luxury; instead, he thought it was an unconscionable waste in a war zone. He told a reporter inquiring about Marine chow: "Hell, no, we like that canned stuff cold. Besides, we need the trucks to haul ammo."[6]

During the dinner, Puller inquired about the size of the corps command element: "The answer of over three thousand left me dumb with astonishment and rage; enough to form an additional infantry regiment." Two days later the incident still rankled him. He thought of his unit's "dead and cripples" and the misused manpower that might have made the fight easier: "If we become involved with Russia, our Army must change its ways and in a hurry, or else we will go down in defeat. This is not my way of fighting a battle and if I had the authority, I would change such things in less than twenty-four hours. Our country and leaders had better wake up and that in a hurry. May God protect us if we do not!"[7]

The 1st Marine Division began loading aboard ships on October 8 and set sail on the 15th. The official objective was still Wonsan, though ROK forces already had taken the town on the 10th. The Navy also was having difficulty clearing the heavily mined approaches. Puller concluded the operation would be canceled: "I suppose we will be a floating reserve and I do not believe we will again land unless the Army again bogs down. . . . I trust we Marines will shortly return to Kobe, pick up our seabags and trunks, which were stored there, and then return home." General Craig, the ADC, also wondered in his diary: "Will our landing be necessary?" Chesty was enjoying the interlude with the Navy, though: "This ship is very nice after being ashore. The country here is just like China with all the dirt and poverty and disease. . . . The rest, good food, and a clean-up will do us all a great deal of good." His biggest concern was his wife's complaint concerning a quote attributed to him in a newspaper: "I assure you, Virginia, that I, never in my life, have ever made a statement that 'I like to fight.' "[8]

From MacArthur on down, everyone was hopeful the war would be over soon and they would be home by Christmas. But that holiday was a long way off yet. The 1st Marine Division staff already was arranging for the issue of mountain sleeping bags and winter underwear. There might not be much fighting ahead, but it could get uncomfortably cold in the high terrain of North Korea. And, contrary to Puller's hopes, MacArthur needed every man he could lay his hands on to speed the process of securing the Communist half of the peninsula. The landing at Wonsan would take place just as soon as the Navy cleared the last of the mines blocking the coast.[9]

Continuing problems with the minesweeping effort resulted in a postponement of the amphibious operation. On October 19, the transports turned about and headed south. A rumor swept the ranks that the war was over for the 1st Marine Division. The scuttlebutt was wrong. The ships spent the next five days sailing up and down the Korean coast, shifting direction each morning and evening. The troops soon dubbed it "Operation Yo-Yo." There was every expectation at higher echelons, however, that the conflict was rapidly winding down. On the 21st, MacArthur publicly announced the end was near and Smith received word that the Navy wanted to keep one Marine regiment in Japan following "the conclusion of hostilities."[10]

To the embarrassment of all those responsible for getting the 1st Marine Division ashore, Bob Hope and a troupe of entertainers flew into Wonsan on October 24 and gave a show to elements of the 1st Marine Aircraft Wing operating there. The men at sea had long since ceased enjoying the relative comfort of a ship; fresh food was running low and dysentery had broken out. But the wait was almost over. On October 25, Smith finalized the orders for the administrative landing and subsequent operations. The 5th Marines would move north and occupy the vicinity of Hungnam, the 7th Marines would strike out from there to relieve ROK units pushing toward the Chosin Reservoir, and the 1st Marines would control a wide swath of territory around Wonsan. The next morning, the main elements of the division finally hit the beaches.[11]

Puller came ashore early in the day. Craig immediately gave Chesty the news that he had been selected for promotion to brigadier general. The general-to-be felt that his performance in the Korean War had been the key. It certainly had not hurt his cause. But Honsowetz, from his position as the Commandant's aide, thought there had been little doubt: "With the record he had, he had to be selected." Smith had agreed in his most recent fitness report on his subordinate: "This officer has proven himself to be a highly competent regimental commander in the field in World War II and Korea." The division commander's opinion had played a critical role. The selection board knew Puller was "an excellent field soldier, but one [who] had had little or no staff work." Smith's glowing input sealed their decision. Back home, Virginia received the news in a phone call from HQMC and was so excited she drove to Virginia McC's school and pulled her out of class to tell her. One newspaper reporting the selection stated that Puller had "emerged as one of the most aggressive and colorful leaders in the Korean War."[12]

There was no time to celebrate or rest on laurels. The 1st Marines were under orders to get a battalion to Kojo as soon as possible to relieve a ROK unit guarding a supply dump. Lieutenant Colonel Hawkins drew the mission. The only intelligence he received was that North Korean guerrilla bands were active around the small port, located nearly forty miles to the south. A "rickety" train, consisting of a "wheezy old engine" and fourteen coal cars, carried the troops in two trips. As it turned out, most of the supplies in Kojo had been used up by the ROKs. With his vague mission now irrelevant, Hawkins deployed the bulk of his battalion on high ground northwest of the town, while the platoons of Company B (now commanded by Captain Noren) outposted three hills to the south.[13]

That night the North Koreans infiltrated close to the Marine lines and launched surprise attacks with grenades and small arms. They struck mainly against Company B's isolated positions. One of Noren's platoons was overrun, with several Marines killed in their sleeping bags, and the other elements of the company soon withdrew to link up for mutual support. Fighting continued sporadically throughout the night and into the morning. With daylight on October 28, Hawkins assessed his situation. He had lost nine killed, thirty-nine wounded, and thirty-four missing. Interrogation of prisoners revealed they belonged to the 5th Division, and it seemed probable there were several thousand Communist soldiers in the vicinity. The battalion commander decided to form a tight perimeter along the coast north of the town to better withstand any large-scale assault. As his units established the new line, he made heavy use of aviation and his one artillery battery against suspected NKPA positions and several large groups of troops spotted in the open.

Hawkins felt his position was "serious" after his significant losses in the night battle; his reports to the regiment during the day reflected that concern. The first called for immediate support from helicopters and an LST to remove casualties. At 1000, he asked for clarification of his mission: "If this position [is] to be held, a regiment is required. . . . Shall we hold here or withdraw to North? ROK supply dump . . . removed. Request immediate instructions." At 1840 he added fresh information and reiterated his appeal for guidance: "NK prisoners revealed large enemy force plans attack over position tonight. Recommend LVTs with LSTs stand by at daylight in case emergency evacuation necessary. In view of large numbers of troops facing us as previously reported and fact enemy on all sides except seaward, consider situation critical. Request higher authority visit."[14]

Hawkins had meant to convey a sense of urgency to division, but fatigue, preoccupation with establishing the new perimeter, and a garbled transmission that omitted the word "casualty" from the evacuation message left his superiors with a different impression. Smith found the series of communications "disturbing." He concluded that "the battalion commander was in a funk and it would be wise for Puller to go to Kojo and take charge." The CO of the 1st Marines agreed that he needed to go "down there to straighten things out." Even so, division was taking no chances in case a big fight might indeed be brewing. The colonel would take 2/1 with him, while an LST would deliver a company of tanks and a destroyer would come along to provide fire support. Chesty and the first trainload of reinforcements arrived in Kojo at 2230 to the sound of Marine mortars, artillery, and night fighters conducting harassing missions. As the 2d Battalion went into position next to 1/1, Puller inspected Hawkins's dispositions. The colonel was satisfied with the 1st Battalion's preparations and canceled the movement of tanks and additional artillery to Kojo. He then moved among the troops and radiated optimism: "Well, by God, we're going to see some Communist asses roll tonight. . . . We'll get our share if the Reds come back."[15]

Over succeeding days the two battalions scoured the vicinity. They recovered a few Marine bodies, brought in several survivors, captured eighty-three men, and counted 165 dead North Koreans at the October 27 battle sites. Final Marine losses turned out to be twenty-three killed, four missing, and forty-seven wounded. A Korean Marine Corps battalion arrived in Kojo by LST on November 1; Puller and 1/1 went back to Wonsan on the landing ship the next day.

The lack of opposition after the initial fighting gave rise to considerable discussion about the strength of the enemy. Hawkins was certain the NKPA force had vastly outnumbered his and only the extensive use of firepower had prevented a major attack the night of October 28. Puller suspected the enemy had merely struck a glancing blow while foraging for food on their way north. The important thing, however, was the perception of Hawkins's superiors. Smith now had some doubts about the lieutenant colonel's steadiness, while the matter heightened Chesty's secret misgivings about Hawkins's experience in World War II. The colonel had a bias against those who had surrendered and believed "no prisoner of war should be permitted to remain in our forces upon his release to us unless he escaped from the enemy." Puller also felt that his subordinate's time in captivity had deprived him of the experience he should have had as a captain and major. Moreover, the regimental commander was certain that a POW "lost something while in the hands of the enemy and was never the same man again." In his mind, the messages of October 28 corroborated that view.[16]

Hawkins certainly did not fit Chesty's stereotype. His capture by the enemy had come as a result of a decision by higher authority. He had escaped and fought behind Japanese lines, then served with distinction on Okinawa. He and his battalion had done well at Inchon and Seoul, and Puller had recommended him for a Silver Star. Nevertheless, the incident at Kojo, rightly or wrongly, had undermined the confidence of his superiors. The uncomfortable situation was solved just a few days later when Hawkins and several others received orders to instructor billets at the Marine Corps Schools, which were looking for personnel with Korean combat experience. Hawkins also had been in command of the 1st Battalion for nearly two years. Lieutenant Colonel Donald M. "Buck" Schmuck replaced him. The small, muscular officer had fought on Bougainville, Peleliu, and Okinawa, but he faced a tough challenge taking over a unit that had been together in combat for several weeks. His intelligence and energy, however, quickly won him the respect of the officers and men.[17]

☆ ☆ ☆

General Shepherd came to Korea on November 1 and visited Puller in Kojo the same day. The two spent part of their meeting catching up on news about each other's family. Chesty seemed to have some doubt about the strength of their friendship, since he wrote Virginia that Shepherd "appeared glad to see me." The colonel was pleased, however, that his son's godfather "stated he knew I would make a good general." Chesty also tried to reassure his wife when she reacted with concern to his letter about his dinner with Almond: "I am sorry you seemed to have gotten the idea that things were not going to my liking. I will be more careful how I write you. I know that higher echelon decisions are none of my business and I only mention them to you."[18]

Puller was looking forward to his promotion in part due to the raise in pay. The $158 per month was a large boost to his current $550 of base pay. He already had ideas how to use it. He told Virginia: "Do not save so much money." Instead, he wanted her to hire a household helper and improve their diet: "I wish you would make sure that the entire family eats fresh beef daily. We can afford it now, Virginia, and beef builds bone and muscle. I want Lewis to be fairly large and now is the time to build his frame. . . . He has to make the football team, you know." He sent Virginia McC a $5 reward for her good grades, along with a fatherly admonition: "I expect you to do well, plus, in everything you undertake. The difference between success and failure in this life of ours is mostly hard work, I believe, so you must constantly try to improve yourself." He was "delighted" to hear that she now owned a cocker spaniel, "but remember you promised to take care of him and you must live up to your promise and never let him be a bother to the grown-ups."[19]

When it came to his troops, the CO of the 1st Marines sometimes felt like a parent torn between imposing stern discipline or laughing at the antics of his youngsters. On Halloween night at Kojo, a "company clown" had fashioned a jack-o'-lantern from a candle and a cardboard box. Puller overheard a typically gruff NCO tell the man to put it out or "he would break his fool skull." "I could not do or say anything, as of course the light was dangerous as it probably would have drawn enemy fire. I felt like telling the sergeant to lay off and the man to go on with his 'trick or treat business.' Later on I gave the fellow a good big drink of whiskey so he at least got one *treat*. Perhaps I am getting soft in my old age?" Puller had his own mischievous streak. In a letter home, he instructed Lewis Jr. how to play a practical joke on the neighbors.[20]

The level of combat had moderated considerably since Seoul, but Virginia's letters were full of concern for his safety. He in turn fretted over her anxiety: "I am distressed to know that you are worrying again. Damn this and all wars. Just keep on praying and I am sure that I will be blessed and permitted to return safely to you and my family, by the grace of God." He tried to free her from the torment of each new report of battle: "If anything should happen to me, and *I am sure it will not*, you will be informed in a matter of hours. So when you read the newspaper or listen to the radio regardless of what is written or stated you can rest assured that I am safe."[21]

☆   ☆   ☆

While Puller had been off in Kojo, the mission of the 1st Marine Division had expanded. MacArthur, still hoping to end the war by Christmas, had decided that U.S. troops should provide greater help to the ROKs in cleaning up the NKPA forces gathering in the far north near China and the Soviet Union. Eighth Army would secure the western half of the country and X Corps drew responsibility for rugged northeastern Korea. The new corps area of operations was shaped like an inverted triangle, with the tip resting in the south at the port of Hungnam and the base running along the border with the two Communist giants. The few roads through the narrow valleys and mountain passes diverged widely as one moved northward into the expanding zone. Yawning gaps thus were bound to open between units as the offensive progressed. Almond, ever impatient, was willing to accept that risk. His plan called for the ROK Capital Division to move along the coast, the 3d ROK Division and most of the U.S. 7th Division to head due north, and the 1st Marine Division to advance northwest to an eventual linkup with Eighth Army. One X Corps officer thought the force was better deployed for "a quail hunt than a military campaign."[22]

For the time being, the 1st Marines would remain responsible for the greater Wonsan area, until the U.S. 3d Infantry Division took over security for the corps rear. As part of that mission, on October 28 3/1 had moved thirty miles west to occupy Majon-ni, a village sitting astride a key road junction. The objective was nestled in a valley between high mountains, and the route from Wonsan "corkscrewed" through a steep-sided pass, a potential "nightmare alley." In a situation that would become all too familiar to the Marines, Ridge set up a perimeter defense, but the amount of ground to be covered necessitated the use of provisional rifle platoons from his attached artillery battery and other supporting units.[23]

Since Puller "believed in concentration," he was not very happy that his regiment was widely split—2/1 at Kojo, 3/1 at Majon-ni, and 1/1 with him at Wonsan. Communication with the outlying battalions frequently depended on written messages delivered by helicopter. The intervening ground was rife with North Korean guerrillas, who could mass against any one of the American positions or interrupt movement between them. Adding to Chesty's headaches, X Corps directed him to hold 1/1 in readiness to conduct an amphibious landing 220 miles to the northeast. To cover all his assigned territory, Puller sent men from the regimental headquarters company on combat patrols. The rest of the division faced the same situation. The 5th Marines were spread over more than fifty miles of ground between Wonsan and Hungnam, while the 7th Marines were moving to relieve a ROK regiment at Sudong, thirty miles northwest of Hungnam.[24]

Smith's unease at having his force dispersed across more than a thousand square miles was greatly heightened when the South Koreans encountered Chinese near Sudong on October 28. In brief but bloody fighting, the ROKs captured sixteen soldiers of the People's Liberation Army (PLA). (In U.N. parlance of the time, the enemy were the Chinese Communist forces or CCF. For propaganda purposes, the PLA styled their expeditionary force as the Chinese People's Volunteers or CPV.) Almond interrogated the ragged-looking prisoners on the 30th and determined that they were indeed Chinese regulars. However, after he tried to put them through some close order drill, he derided them as a bunch of "Chinese laundrymen." Marine leaders—many with experience in China—were not so sanguine. Smith ordered his subordinates to establish all-around perimeters in the defense and he thereafter continually pressed the corps commander to consolidate the 1st Marine Division. While Almond passed along and even amplified MacArthur's emphasis on speed, Smith remained determined to act with prudence and deliberation.[25]

The potential difficulties became reality on November 2, when the NKPA ambushed one of 3/1's patrols and a convoy bringing supplies to Majon-ni, while the 7th Marines ran into strong Chinese opposition. Friendly casualties in the encounter near Majon-ni totaled twenty-five killed and forty-one wounded. For the moment Ridge's battalion was isolated and forced to rely on airdrops. Division directed Puller to reopen the overland route and he dispatched Company A on November 4 to shepherd the trucks. By the time Captain Barrow received his orders and organized his force, it was mid-afternoon. Just prior to nightfall and halfway to the objective, a North Korean roadblock covered by heavy fire stopped him cold. The terrain favored the enemy and there were too many vehicles for Barrow's outfit to guard, so he decided to return to Wonsan.

The Able Company commander, troubled by his failure, reported to Puller in his CP, which was located in a schoolhouse. He found the colonel in a classroom sitting behind the teacher's desk. Barrow did not know what to expect from "the greatest of hard-chargers," but he was relieved when the regimental CO proffered a friendly drink of bourbon. Chesty got right to the point: "What do you need to get this convoy through tomorrow?" The captain wanted only a team to control close air support and an early start to maximize daylight. His simple requirements granted, Barrow set off on the morning of November 5. Halfway up the mountain road a lead element on foot surprised the ambushers as they ate chow and waited for the sound of trucks. The Marines killed fifty-one, captured three, and got the convoy into Majon-ni unharmed.[26]

The next day, Puller ordered 2/1, recently returned from Kojo, to send a company to occupy positions along the road to Majon-ni. Since another of Sutter's companies already was on detached duty, the battalion CO protested this would split his outfit over twenty-five miles. Chesty was sympathetic given his own unhappiness with similar orders from above. He told Sutter to take his entire battalion less the preoccupied unit and, for good measure, threw in a platoon of the regiment's 4.2-inch mortars. The move into the pass precipitated another battle. In a fight that lasted all afternoon, Easy Company lost eight killed and thirty-eight wounded and counted sixty-one enemy bodies. Puller's emphasis on leadership from the front was apparent in the casualty figures; of the seven officers engaged, five were hit. Following several more small engagements over the next few days, units from the U.S. Army and Korean Marine Corps relieved 2/1 and 3/1 on November 14 and 15. The 1st Marines did not realize it then, but the all-hands defense of Majon-ni and the breaking of mountain roadblocks had been an excellent dress rehearsal for what was to come.[27]

☆   ☆   ☆

While Puller's regiment dealt with the NKPA, a hundred miles to the north Colonel Homer L. Litzenberg's 7th Marines was fighting a different enemy. On the night of November 2, the PLA 124th Division had attacked the 7th near Sudong. The Leathernecks held and they soon resumed the advance toward the Chosin Reservoir. The regiment encountered the same Chinese outfit again on November 4. Litzenberg's force made little headway in three days of hard fighting, but on the morning of November 7, the Chinese were gone. The 7th Marines had lost 250 men killed and wounded and inflicted more than two thousand casualties on the enemy. During this same period, the PLA had been equally busy in the west, handing a bloody nose to the Eighth Army and then disappearing. General Lowe told Smith that the situation with Walker's forces was "not good."[28]

These first clashes with the Chinese heralded the tactics each side would employ throughout the campaign. In the offense, the PLA relied on night infiltration attacks. Enemy squads or platoons stealthily approached the front lines and then charged from close range. Sometimes the infantrymen were supported by mortars, but mainly they covered their forward rush with their own automatic weapons or grenades. The initial units merely probed to determine the layout of Marine defenses; following echelons attempted to penetrate weak points or flow around open flanks. In the defense, the Chinese established roadblocks covered by the fire of units on adjacent high ground. In contrast, the Marines made liberal use of supporting arms during daylight attacks to seize overwatching terrain as they moved along the roads, then they settled into perimeter defenses to ride out the night, when air support was rarely available and the only observed targets for artillery were at very close range. The 1st Marine Division had one large advantage in this contest. The Chinese had considerable experience, but mostly in guerrilla campaigns against the Nationalists and Japanese. After this first battle, Smith realized they were wholly unprepared for the hail of firepower unleashed by the Marine air-ground team.[29]

☆   ☆   ☆

Puller celebrated the 175th birthday of the Marine Corps on November 10 at his CP with a large cake that "was among the most ornate in Korea." He read the traditional message from General Lejeune, then launched into a short, rousing speech designed to fire up his troops to "get down and fight." He closed with the confident assertion: "We can knock the hell out of anything that comes before us—that's why we are the best fighting unit in the world." The colonel cut the cake with a captured North Korean sword and personally served the regiment's mess sergeant and the first fifty men in the chow line. Afterward, he was certain his oratory had hit the mark and "the enemy will feel the effect of it, if we are employed against him again." Chesty's pugnacious leadership impressed one Army division commander, who sent a dozen of his officers to the 1st Marines CP with the request that the aggressive colonel "conduct an evening of school for them."[30]

During this period, Puller held award ceremonies for Inchon and Seoul. Among the recipients was Captain Barrow, who received a Silver Star for his defensive stand in Yongdungpo. The colonel enthusiastically congratulated the company commander for an excellent job, but also registered his unhappiness with the final award. Chesty told Barrow's battalion commander to resubmit the original recommendation for a Navy Cross. Sergeant Harvey Owens, another awardee, recalled that the colonel told his group: "This is a thing I like to do, to decorate people. Go out and get some more." As usual, the commander of the 1st Marines was looking out for his officers and men when it came to awards for valor. Five of the first eight members of the 1st Marine Division to receive the Medal of Honor would be from Chesty's regiment.[31]

Despite Puller's promise not to upset Virginia with his unhappiness over high-level policy, he could not keep his disgust out of his letters. On November 8 he wrote: "I hope and pray that now as the elections are over, that President Truman will call out the National Guard. The first Roosevelt stated that it was a good policy to talk softly and carry a big stick. Since the last war we have only had a big mouth and no stick." Two days later he elaborated:

> I pray that our government, by now, realizes what a poor war machine we have and will conduct themselves accordingly. Some of the statements made by our Army and Air generals back in the United States are either false or the makers are ignorant and should be separated from the service. As I have often stated to you, it is my belief that only a terrible defeat will change our present system which is leading us to disaster.

On the 18th he described the visit of a U.S. senator to Korea:

> I did not see him. He made a speech in Seoul several days ago and I have just read it with unbelief. . . . You can bet that he saw nothing and went nowhere, except by plane. Just another case of the waste of taxpayers money. . . . If Knowland came here to find out how the war was going, why didn't he have sense to go forward and see for himself and talk with the officers and men who have done the fighting or lack of fighting. I can assure you that he would have found thousands of both officers and men who would have told him the truth and nothing but the truth, regardless of the consequences . . . [which] would be minor to what might have happened due to mismanagement or what may still happen.

He reassured her that his predicted disaster would not happen while he was in Korea: "There is not much of a war going on in this locality. . . .

The situation shows improvement during the last several days and perhaps the Chinese Government won't send in their troops in great numbers." Events soon would prove, however, that his fears, not his hopes, were grounded in hard reality.[32]

☆ ☆ ☆

With the arrival of the 3d Infantry Division in mid-November, Almond permitted the 1st Marine Division to concentrate somewhat. On the 14th, the 1st Marines began moving to Chigyong, a town about eight miles west of Hungnam. By the 19th, Chesty had his entire force in one place for the first time since sailing from Inchon. Smith then fended off a directive from X Corps to move battalions of the 1st Marines to outlying areas: "I do not intend to put Puller out on a limb where he cannot be supplied." When issuing orders to the regiment, the CG also kept in mind Chesty's tactical propensities: "Maintain minimum one battalion, less one company, in reserve . . . to be committed only on division order." Puller, meanwhile, was upset with division headquarters regarding mail service, since he had expected it would arrive faster the nearer he got to the general's CP. But he went a few days without letters from his wife because "some of the smart staff people sent it south—on the same day that we came north. Can you beat it?"[33]

The rest of Smith's division was heading up the single, narrow road (grandly titled the Main Supply Route or MSR) leading north from Hungnam to the Chosin Reservoir. Beyond Sudong, the route climbed 2,500 feet over eight miles through Funchilin Pass. Here there was just a single lane filling a narrow shelf, with steep terrain rising on one side and a cliff falling away on the other. At the top of the ascent, the road entered a rugged plateau and followed the Changjin River to the reservoir. Major villages along the way were Chinhung-ni near the foot of the pass and Koto-ri two miles beyond the top of the rise. The town of Hagaru-ri was just below the reservoir. The MSR took a twisting path west of the man-made lake through Toktong Pass to Yudam-ni, which was seventy-eight road miles from the port of Hungnam.

The 7th Marines had reached Koto-ri on November 10, Hagaru-ri on the 15th, and Yudam-ni on the 25th. The 5th Marines initially had diverged up the eastern bank of the reservoir, but at Smith's urging Almond assented to having Murray's regiment support Litzenberg in the west. Elements of the 7th Division (two infantry battalions and most of

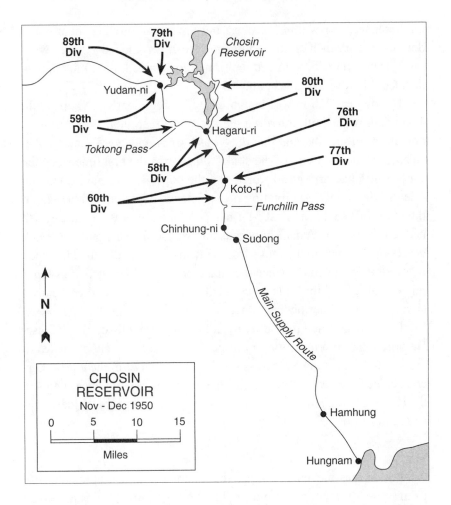

an artillery battalion) replaced the 5th Marines in the east. The 1st Marines finally got on the MSR on November 23, with 1/1 taking over the job of garrisoning Chinhung-ni. The 2d Battalion and regimental headquarters moved to Koto-ri on the 24th and 25th. The next day, 3/1 took over Hagaru-ri, though it temporarily had to leave G Company at Chigyong to guard the X Corps CP.

Puller was pleased to be closer, finally, to the rest of the division, but otherwise was not very happy with the situation. His troops, pierced by an icy wind, surveyed the abandoned village of Koto-ri and proclaimed: "What a hole." Their regimental commander felt the same, but for a different reason. He was in a valley, with steep hills crowding in on every side. The crests were spread out just far enough that he could not enclose them within his lines, but an enemy holding them could dominate every inch of his perimeter. Koto-ri was indeed a "hole," with the Marines in the bottom and the rim up for grabs. Puller immediately decided: "I don't like this at all."[34]

His dissatisfaction was increased by his regiment's mission—split again and, worse still, guarding the division's rear area. While Smith's operations officer thought that duty was *very important,* Chesty considered it "the dirty end of the stick." It also was the first time since the 1st Marines had arrived in Korea that the outfit did not have a leading role. Smith merely was rotating his regiments, however, and he had no intention of keeping the 1st Marines permanently in the rear. The 7th had led the way to Yudam-ni because it was the freshest outfit. The 5th was going to head up the move from Yudam-ni because it "had not been in a serious engagement since the attack on Seoul." The general's long-range plans called for Puller's regiment to lead the assault after the division reached its intermediate objective—if it got that far.[35]

In the meantime Puller did not let his force rest idly on the defense. He ordered a vigorous program of patrols and told his subordinates to prepare to assume the 5th's mission if it should falter in the attack. Circumstances, however, would limit Chesty's ability to influence events in the coming battle since his regiment was spread over three widely separated locations.

☆   ☆   ☆

As the Marines moved north into the mountains, a new opponent rose to the fore—the bone-numbing cold of a high-altitude North Korean winter. Although snowfall was seldom heavy in the region, the prevailing air currents out of Siberia brought subzero temperatures worsened by windchill. The division already had received its cold weather gear, which consisted of pile-lined parkas and shell outer trousers, flannel underwear, leather and canvas mittens or gloves with wool inserts, and soon-to-be-infamous boots called shoepacs. The special footwear made a man's feet hot enough to sweat during exertion, but allowed that moisture to freeze once he stopped, thus creating a severe threat of frostbite. Troops had to change socks frequently and place the used pairs inside their shirts close to their bodies to dry them out for the next switch. The other clothing items were reasonably good, except that all were designed to be effective only down to zero degrees. The services as yet had no "arctic" items for subzero temperatures.[36]

The bitter cold had a tremendous effect on combat capability. It injured exposed skin, sapped mental and physical energy, and made it difficult to eat or drink. Those who wolfed down chunks of frozen rations often succumbed to intestinal disorders. The gloves were too bulky for tasks, such as reloading rifles, that required manual dexterity. As a result, the men frequently had to bare their hands and risk the consequences. The wounded suffered most of all, as the loss of blood increased vulnerability to the cold, while plasma and morphine usually were frozen and thus not readily available. Small arms fired sluggishly or not at all, fuel lines froze up, batteries had a much shorter life, and mortar and artillery rounds became erratic. The Marines found it impossible to dig fighting holes in the rock-hard soil. Dealing with the cold also increased the burden on logistics. During the move to the MSR there had not been enough trucks and the 1st Marines supply officer had left much of the regiment's ammunition behind to make room for tents and stoves. Puller agreed with that priority: "I'll take care of my men first. Frozen troops can't fight. If we run out of ammunition we'll go to the bayonet." The winter conditions in North Korea in November and December 1950 exceeded anything U.S. forces had ever faced in wartime. A Marine who had been a soldier in the 82d Airborne in World War II felt: "The [Chosin] Reservoir was much colder . . . and much worse than my experience in the [Battle of the] Bulge." Puller would say years later: "The Continental Army never went through anything like those boys in Korea. The weather at the Chosin Reservoir averaged 25 degrees below zero, and it doesn't get that cold at Valley Forge." The only positive note was that this was the dry season for the region, which meant "the best sky conditions for aerial operations prevail."[37]

☆ ☆ ☆

The weather turned a bit warmer on November 23, but it rained. Puller spent a good part of the day driving to and from the X Corps CP for another of Almond's feasts. At least this time the colonel's troops also were able to eat well, since the division managed to provide an "excellent and plentiful Thanksgiving Day dinner." Although Chesty was "discontented" at being separated from his family, he believed there was "much to be thankful for." His wife and "precious children" had given him "more happiness and satisfaction than I thought possible." But he felt he had not provided well for them: "You did not make a brilliant marriage, Sweetheart, but I do love you a bit more for saying so. You could have done much better, I am sure. There are so many things that I thought I could give you, when you married me. . . . Maybe some day, I can."[38]

Puller's only other holiday regret was a shortage of cigars. "As long as the newspaper men were around they kept me supplied (more than I could smoke) but they have long since departed, probably had sense enough to get out before the cold weather set in." The correspondents and senior visitors also brought whiskey, which Chesty in turn doled out to his men whenever he felt they needed a lift. He was proud one reporter had said publicly that "whenever he or any other newsman went up to Puller's troops, both Puller and his outfit would be gaining ground and naturally there would be a story."[39]

The colonel's exasperation with the course of the conflict was growing. He was beginning to think that "the Red Chinese will only send in enough troops to prolong this war and keep the United States occupied and Russia will eventually bankrupt us without even having to fight us—maybe." He was even more discouraged by the lack of historical knowledge on the part of fellow military leaders: "I have yet to encounter any officer here who has read an account of the Russo-Japanese War. The Japanese armies went up through Korea, crossed the Yalu River and turned westward to capture Port Arthur. The Japs found out what cold weather would do to the troops under field conditions." He also remained unimpressed by American generalship: "Our Eighth Army headquarters is still in Seoul. I don't understand how they expect the troops to reach the Yalu River without their leaders." The time was not far off when his disgust with the war effort and his reputation for making good copy for reporters would turn into an explosive mix.[40]

☆   ☆   ☆

While the 1st Marine Division was pushing carefully into the Korean highlands, the Chinese were mustering their forces for a decisive blow. The Chinese had moved by night and hid in villages, forests, and railroad tunnels by day, so American forces were uncertain about the size and disposition of the enemy. MacArthur and Almond steadfastly believed that there was no significant Chinese presence in North Korea. In reality, a half million enemy already had crossed the border. The majority were focused on Eighth Army. Twelve divisions had filtered toward the Chosin Reservoir with the primary mission of destroying the 1st Marine Division. (Mao Tse-tung, the head of Communist China, personally had directed more forces against the Marines because they "had the highest combat effectiveness in the American armed forces.") Eight divisions would conduct the initial attack in the X Corps zone and four would remain in reserve. On paper each outfit numbered ten thousand men divided among three infantry regiments and an artillery unit. But wariness of U.S. airpower and limited time and transportation had prevented most of the artillery from crossing the Yalu River. The infantry components were generally understrength as well. That left the average Chinese division in northeastern Korea with about 7,500 men. The Communist troops were poorly equipped for a winter campaign. Their cold weather gear consisted of lined hats and quilted-cotton jackets and trousers. Few soldiers had gloves and most wore rubber-soled canvas shoes. Many of these troops also hailed from Shantung, a coastal region with milder winters than those of North Korea. Nevertheless, roughly a hundred thousand hardy peasant soldiers were poised to strike at the fifteen thousand Marines deployed between Chinhung-ni and Yudam-ni.[41]

"Not All the Chinese in Hell"
The Chosin Reservoir
November–December 1950

eneral Almond's orders called for the 1st Marine Division to attack northwest from Yudam-ni on November 27 and push rapidly toward the distant Chinese border. By this point, General Smith had "little confidence in the tactical judgment of the [X] Corps or in the realism of their planning." While Army staff officers were drawing arrows on a map, the Marines were maneuvering over steep ridges in abominable weather. Although there had been no contact with the PLA since November 6, Smith was very concerned about the prospect of a winter battle at the end of a supply route threading along a narrow mountain road. Hagaru-ri loomed large in his scheme to prepare for the worst. His engineers were constructing an airstrip to handle C-47 cargo planes and he was building up supply dumps. The division CP also was moving there.[1]

Smith kicked off the offensive with 2/5 in the lead. It had not gone far when it bumped into Chinese forces in the hills just west of Yudam-ni. Heavy use of supporting arms enabled the Marines to push forward a little, but gains for the day did not exceed two thousand yards. In retrospect the stiff PLA resistance was a blessing, since the advance merely constituted a bulge in the American lines. The 7th Marines still occupied the high ground around Yudam-ni, while the other battalions of the 5th remained in assembly areas to support 2/5's attack the next day.

That night the temperatures dropped to a harrowing 20 degrees below zero. Beginning at 2100, two Chinese divisions attacked the Yudam-ni perimeter. Another PLA division cut the Main Supply Route just to the south and struck at the two company-sized outposts in Toktong Pass. In every instance the Marines were able to hold or withdraw in good order, but casualties were heavy. On the opposite shore of the reservoir, a fourth Communist division hit the elements of the 7th Infantry Division. The Army force had not been as cautious and was caught in seven small clusters spread out over ten miles. The Chinese overran most of an infantry battalion and an artillery battery and left the survivors badly shaken. The attacks petered out with daylight.

Litzenberg and Murray took stock of their situation on the morning of November 28. The CO of the 5th Marines was "shocked" by the sudden turn in fortunes. He later admitted: "My first fight was within myself. I had to rebuild that emptiness of spirit." In view of the news that Eighth Army's front was collapsing in the face of the PLA offensive, Smith considered it "rash" to push westward. He confirmed the decision of his regimental commanders to stand fast. During the course of the day, the Marines improved their positions around Yudam-ni and managed to bring in one of Litzenberg's companies from the MSR. Fox Company remained isolated at the top of Toktong Pass. It had lost twenty-three dead or missing and fifty-four wounded, but had killed at least 450 of the enemy and still held the vital outpost. Total division casualties in the night and day of fighting were nearly seven hundred, with an additional 259 men lost to nonbattle causes, mostly frostbite.[2]

On the 28th Almond helicoptered from Hungnam to visit the units around the reservoir. That evening he flew to Tokyo for a meeting with MacArthur. In confirmation of Smith's doubts about the grasp of tactical reality at higher echelons, Almond told MacArthur that X Corps could continue the offensive and relieve pressure on Eighth Army, which was reeling in retreat. The theater commander wisely rejected the offer. He ordered Almond to concentrate his entire corps along the coast in the vicinity of Hungnam.

☆   ☆   ☆

The 1st Marines had been spared in the initial Chinese onslaught. Some enemy soldiers had appeared in the hills above Koto-ri on November 26, but Chesty gave orders to conserve ammunition for more lucrative targets. Elements of 1/1 and 2/1 fought small unit actions on November

27. The next day a pilot reported that the Chinese had blown two bridges and built eight roadblocks between Koto-ri and Hagaru-ri. At mid-morning on November 28, Smith ordered Puller to open up that section of the road. Chesty dispatched one of Sutter's rifle companies, but dug-in Communists stopped it cold. Puller could not commit more troops to the task or Koto-ri would be at risk. Throughout the day his men called in air and artillery on PLA units moving about the hills. The heavy firepower appeared to take "a tremendous toll." After a few Chinese tried to slip in among refugees entering the perimeter, the Marines kept all civilians at bay for the remainder of the battle. The cutting of the MSR actually benefited 2/1 that evening. Convoys moving up the line had to remain in Koto-ri, so Puller added the units to his defenses. They included Company B of the Army's 31st Infantry Regiment, 3/1's George Company, the division recon company, and 41 Commando (a 235-man force of British Royal Marines).[3]

Puller's inability to break through caused Smith grave concern at Hagaru-ri. The division commander had two rifle companies to protect a four-mile perimeter enclosing the town, supply dumps, his CP, and the airfield. If the Chinese had attacked on the night of November 27 in conjunction with their assault on Yudam-ni, the division's vital heart probably would have been ripped out. As it was, patrols on the 28th indicated that the PLA planned a major operation against Hagaru-ri that night. Ridge, the commander of the Hagaru-ri defenses, set about strengthening the fragile perimeter. He had his two rifle companies on the likeliest avenue of approach and filled in the remainder of the long line with noninfantry elements. How and Item Companies had been hard at work since the 26th; they had good positions covered by mines and concertina wire. Many of the other units were still getting organized when darkness came.

The Chinese began their assault on Hagaru-ri at 2230 on November 28. They supported their customary probing attacks with an unusually heavy mortar barrage. The main effort, focused where Ridge had expected it, commenced barely thirty minutes later and continued for hours. Not long after midnight, the sheer weight of numbers allowed some PLA soldiers to overrun a platoon of How Company. A reserve of service troops and engineers formed a second line behind the infantrymen. Luckily, many of the enemy who made it inside the perimeter turned to looting food supplies or stripping American casualties of warm clothing, instead of expanding the penetration. The Chinese also attacked East Hill and quickly drove the Army defenders off that commanding terrain. The PLA soldiers never exploited this advantage either, perhaps in part due to How Battery, which concentrated its fire on the gap for the remainder of the night.

In the morning, Marine Corsairs pummeled the Chinese on East Hill. A scratch force of Army and Marine service troops counterattacked up the steep slope, but could not reach the top. In testimony to the dire shortage of manpower, a second effort to regain the summit was made by two squads of Marine engineers. It also came up short. Ridge then formed a new line on the lower slopes and prepared for a resumption of the PLA offensive that night. Smith knew he had to marshal reinforcements as soon as possible. He had lost five hundred men at Hagaru-ri in the past twenty-four hours. Another day like that and the perimeter would collapse. Help appeared to be on the way, however, from Koto-ri. Puller told division headquarters that he was forming the British outfit, George Company, and the Army company into a task force under Lieutenant Colonel Douglas B. Drysdale, the Royal Marine commander. Chesty would launch them up the road the next morning. Smith approved the move.

The lead elements of Task Force Drysdale—the British and American Marines—departed Koto-ri at 0930 on November 29. A long vehicle convoy would follow, with the soldiers of Baker Company providing the rear guard. Puller watched from the outskirts of town that morning as his supporting arms pounded the ridgeline positions that had held up the previous day's attack. Then he saw the two companies of Marines storm up the slope and drive out the Chinese. Chesty radioed Drysdale that four platoons of tanks had arrived in the town and would come forward to join the task force. The British colonel resumed the advance at 1330 with half of the armor in front and the remaining Pershings at the tail of the long column. By late afternoon the task force was still well short of Hagaru-ri. Drysdale radioed division for instructions. Smith was desperate and he ordered the Royal Marine to "push on through if at all possible." Drysdale in turn told Captain Carl Sitter of George Company that the outfit was to "get through at all cost." The long column pressed on. Chinese fire soon destroyed several trucks near the head of the vehicle train. George Company, the lead tanks, and most of 41 Commando were in front of this block and continued to fight their way north. This group reached Hagaru-ri that evening.[4]

Stripped of much of its protection, the convoy was in a bad way.

The senior officer present ordered the column to head back to Koto-ri. The tanks at the rear, barely a mile from the town, managed to fight their way to friendly lines, but the Chinese launched several aggressive attacks that damaged more vehicles and prevented further movement. The American troops abandoned their trucks and coalesced into four groups. Marine staff officers took charge, formed perimeters, and kept the PLA at bay. With the arrival of darkness, the survivors of the convoy lost their air support. They had no way to call in artillery and had few heavy weapons of their own. The Chinese kept up a steady fire on the Americans, who began to run low on ammunition. Well before dawn, the PLA demanded surrender. With no means to keep up the fight and the wounded outnumbering the able-bodied, Marine leaders decided to give up. While a major purposely dragged out the negotiations, some men slipped away toward Koto-ri. When it was over, more than three hundred Americans, Brits, and South Koreans had died or gone into captivity.[5]

The 1st Marines CP initially became aware of the problem late in the afternoon, when an Army officer returned to the perimeter to report that his unit had lost contact with 41 Commando. The regiment also had no communications with the task force. The news grew worse around 2030 when four tanks showed up at the outskirts of town. The armor platoon leader reported that the rest of his unit and everyone else was blocked by stalled vehicles. Around 2200 the tank company commander relayed a request for infantry support via the lieutenant's radio. Koto-ri had none to offer since the defenders had repulsed a battalion-sized attack between 1745 and 1900 and expected a repeat at any time. The 1st Marines CP explained that "every available man was being utilized in the perimeter including cooks, truck drivers, clerks." Puller did offer artillery. The tank captain controlled it by relay through his platoon commander's Pershing and that firepower was enough to drive off the Chinese. The M-26s and a few trucks then worked their way around the blockages in the road and made it into Koto-ri just before dawn.[6]

The Chinese attack on Koto-ri on the evening of November 29 had been a near-run thing. Puller had pulled one rifle platoon out of the line to accompany Drysdale part of the way. That mission accomplished, the unit had resumed its position barely an hour before the enemy struck. The entire focus of the PLA assault came against that small stretch of the perimeter. At a cost of four killed and eight wounded, 2/1 stacked up

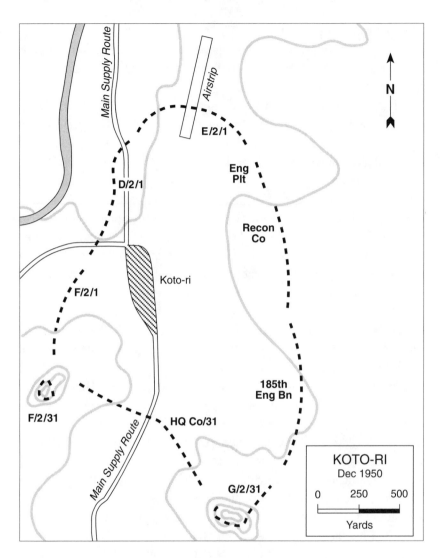

nearly two hundred Chinese in the narrow corridor. Koto-ri received only mortar fire the rest of the night.[7]

The two companies of infantry and two platoons of tanks that pulled into Hagaru-ri during the evening of November 29 were welcome indeed, despite having lost 119 men along the way. Ridge placed them in reserve. Throughout the night 3/1's supporting arms coordinator, Major Edwin H. Simmons, brought heavy barrages down on suspected assembly areas. He even managed to get aircraft into the action after dark by marking targets with the converging streams of tracer rounds from two machine guns. The firepower so disrupted the enemy that no assault took place. The division nerve center had survived for another day and would continue to do so now that it had sufficient combat power on hand.[8]

The Chinese made their last major attacks on the 1st Marine Regiment on November 30. Throughout that day, 2/1 observed "heavy enemy troop movements" in the hills at all points of the compass. Puller and Sutter pounded each group with air, artillery, and mortars. The PLA responded with an occasional shell into Koto-ri, but the heavy American fire again staved off a ground attack. That evening the Chinese struck hard at Hagaru-ri. The first attempt hit square against Item Company again. Bolstered by the support of tanks, artillery, and mortars, the Marine infantry prevented any penetration. At a cost of two killed and ten wounded, Lieutenant Fisher's outfit eliminated more than five hundred of the enemy. A second PLA force drove down the face of East Hill. This time the line was manned by George Company and three platoons of Marine engineers, backed by men of the 1st Service Battalion. The fierce Chinese assault bashed a hole in the perimeter, but the point-blank fire of tanks and artillery onto the slope prevented the enemy from sending many reinforcements into the gap. Before dawn, Ridge fed in 41 Commando and a reserve force of Marine and Army headquarters and service personnel to restore the line.

The PLA did not get a chance to attack the southernmost Marine bastion at Chinhung-ni. Patrols from 1/1 had made contacts with Chinese units outside the village during the first two days of the enemy offensive. Based on that information, Schmuck identified a probable Communist assembly area in a nearby valley. On November 30 he launched his battalion in a spoiling attack that drove the enemy force into the hills, while waiting Corsairs pounced on the fleeing soldiers.[9]

The Marines were holding their own, but they were developing a healthy respect for their new opponent. Chesty already knew that the Chinese were industrious, intelligent, and resolute, but these encounters increased his regard. He decided they were "far superior to the North Koreans," "excellent fighters," and masters of camouflage. He was particularly impressed by their use of a straw mat and a white cloth to cover themselves on open or snow-covered ground so as to avoid detection from the air. Captain Barrow, who had served with Chinese guerrillas in World War II, had a similar appreciation: "Unlike the Japanese, these soldiers are not fanatics [but] they will go about their business with resigned determination. . . . These peasant soldiers are accustomed to unusual hardships, both before and during service. . . . The Chinese is a highly adaptable type and rather quick to learn. . . . They will become a dangerous enemy."[10]

☆　☆　☆

Smith had not been aware at first of the cost of the Task Force Drysdale reinforcing effort. The Royal Marine commander himself had not known what had happened in the center of his column, since he never had radio communications with the vehicle train, the Army company, or the tanks in the rear. The full story only came to light when the men who had avoided capture made it back into friendly lines the next day. Although there was much hard fighting ahead, this was the only engagement where the Chinese destroyed an element of the division. Smith regretted the losses, but accepted them as a bearable price to pay to hold on to Hagaru-ri. Certainly no one could have expected more from the units involved. With the exception of the Army company, which had been fatally handicapped by the assignment of untrained Koreans to its ranks, everyone had fought well.[11]

In retrospect, Task Force Drysdale need not have come to that fate. Its name alone revealed its weakness, for Puller had sent a scratch organization to perform a very difficult mission. Drysdale did not possess the wherewithal to command what was, in essence, a reinforced battalion. The problem was greater than just lack of a staff and communications equipment. The "British didn't exactly understand Marine Corps radio procedure" and the Marines "couldn't understand the British." One officer later cited poor internal communications as a tremendous handicap. While the Army had shot itself in the foot by employing Korean augmentees, Chesty had compounded the cohesion issue by lumping together three companies from different services and even different countries. Many participants felt that they were part of "a jumble of troops" and "rather confused." The difficulty of getting such a disparate force ready for an attack had contributed to the task force's late start. The addition of the large, unwieldy truck convoy made things worse. The last of the vehicles had not cleared Koto-ri until mid-afternoon, which assured that they would be on the road late into the night.[12]

Puller could have done two things that likely would have altered the outcome. He had in hand a cohesive, battle-tested Marine battalion that would have been able to launch the attack shortly after first light and effectively coordinate subsequent action. While that would have left a less capable Task Force Drysdale responsible for Koto-ri, a static defensive mission would have been less of a challenge for the hodgepodge outfit. And the 1st Marines CP would have been able to provide the necessary command echelon that the collection of disparate companies lacked. Sending 2/1 to Hagaru-ri would have increased the risk to Koto-ri, but the division nerve center was far more important. Deciding to pin the convoy onto the tail of Task Force Drysdale drastically complicated the situation and gave the British commander two distinctly different missions that pulled him in opposite directions. Reinforcing Hagaru-ri meant getting there as fast as possible with a maximum of combat power. Safeguarding the vehicle train required the expenditure of time and troops to keep the Chinese away from a vulnerable target.[13]

Although Puller could have made a different choice, he did not bear primary responsibility for the outcome. He had informed Smith beforehand of his plans for the task force and his intention of "pushing supply convoys through under armed guard" in compliance with division's orders to "open up the road." The commanding general had raised no concerns. Division also had assigned 2/1 the mission of defending Koto-ri and would have had to approve any change. In all likelihood, the two officers and their staffs were so busy trying to salvage success from a desperate situation that they did not have the time to consider all the ramifications of their plan. Task Force Drysdale did make one thing obvious to Smith: "The conclusion was inescapable that a considerable force would be required to open up the MSR between Hagaru-ri and Koto-ri. We would not have any such force until the 5th and 7th Marines joined us at Hagaru-ri."[14]

☆ ☆ ☆

On the afternoon of November 30 Almond flew into Hagaru-ri and finally informed the 1st Marine Division that the entire corps was to fall back on Hungnam. He stressed his desire to complete the move rapidly and authorized the destruction of all equipment and supplies. Smith replied that he would need everything to fight his way to the sea. When the division commander described the situation soon after to correspondents, one of them scribbled down a "quote" that captured the attitude of the general and all his Marines: "Retreat, hell! We're just advancing in a different direction." The 1st Marine Division was not about to run to the rear in a rout or be driven backward by force of arms—instead, it would battle its way through strong enemy opposition that threatened every step of the way to prevent it from reaching Hungnam.[15]

Before anyone could think about heading south, they needed to survive long enough to start the trip. Fox Company of the 7th Marines had been fending off nightly assaults at Toktong Pass since the onset of the Chinese offensive. Attempts by the remainder of the regiment to reach them from Yudam-ni had all failed. The only assistance outside echelons could provide was fire support and the delivery of supplies by airdrop and helicopter. Captain William Barber's men held on, despite suffering 50 percent casualties through December 1.

The 7th Division's much larger force on the opposite side of the Chosin Reservoir did not fare so well. On December 1 Task Force Faith loaded its five hundred wounded on vehicles and tried to fight its way south to Hagaru-ri. Even with close air support from Navy and Marine fliers, the Army units could not break through PLA roadblocks. Then control disintegrated as the Chinese launched attacks along the length of the stalled convoy. Many of the able-bodied soldiers and walking wounded escaped across the frozen reservoir. Others surrendered. Most of the stretcher cases died as they lay in the trucks—from enemy fire, the cold, or lack of medical care. The next morning, Lieutenant Colonel Olin L. Beall, commander of the 1st Marine Division's motor transport battalion, organized a rescue effort. He and many others scoured the ice and the banks of the Chosin under fire to bring in hundreds of soldiers, many of them wounded or frostbitten. Of the original 2,500 men in Task Force Faith, barely a thousand reached Marine lines and less than four hundred proved capable of joining the provisional Army battalion formed at Hagaru-ri. A noted Army historian would call this "one of the worst disasters for American soldiers in the Korean War."[16]

The 5th and 7th Marines at Yudam-ni had been spared any major attacks since the opening Chinese assaults on November 27. They were still in a bad position, as they had hundreds of nonambulatory casualties and were cut off from any means of resupply save airdrop. Given that the entire resources of the Air Force in the theater could at best deliver a hundred tons per day and two reinforced regiments consumed more than twice that much, they needed to reach Hagaru-ri soon. The odds were better now that Murray and Litzenberg could attack south with all their combat power. It would not be easy, however, as they also would have to protect the same type of large vehicle train that had helped bring Task Force Drysdale and Task Force Faith to grief. The plan called for the 7th Marines to lead off and seize high ground dominating the road. The 5th Marines would guard the convoys and provide rear security.

In an effort to relieve some of the Chinese pressure on the MSR, Litzenberg decided that 1/7 would make a cross-country advance at night to link up with Fox Company in Toktong Pass. The 1st Battalion's commander was Lieutenant Colonel Ray Davis, who had led 1/1 at Peleliu. The move to Hagaru-ri began on December 1. Davis's outfit started a superhuman trek through the mountains as the sun set and temperatures dropped to 16 below zero. The 1st Battalion neared Fox Company's position just before noon on December 2 and swept the Chinese off the final ridge between the two units. Lieutenant Joseph Owen recalled the moment when they reached the top: "We were astonished by our first view of Fox Hill. The snowfield that led up to the embattled company's position was covered with hundreds of dead Chinese soldiers. . . . We stood in wonder. Men bowed their heads in prayer. . . . Tears came to the eyes of raggedy Marines who had endured bitter cold and savage battle to reach this place of suffering and courage." At least one of the Fox Company Marines was equally overwhelmed by the physical appearance of the relieving force: "Good God! These guys have been through more than we have."[17]

The PLA was determined not to let the Marines escape from the trap at Yudam-ni. In the hours before dawn on December 2, Chinese units launched strong assaults on the rear-guard positions of the 5th Marines. There also were numerous battles along the MSR as Marines broke through roadblocks and the Communists tried to destroy the vehicle train. After much fighting, the column linked up with 1/7 and Fox Company on the afternoon of December 2. On the evening of the 3d, the first elements reached Hagaru-ri. The tail end of the large force did not enter the perimeter until mid-afternoon the next day.

The strain of continuous combat, extreme cold, and poor food began to tell on many. When Ridge had made a report to Smith on the morning of December 1, the commanding general was surprised that his perimeter commander "was pretty low and almost incoherent." But the CG knew "the main trouble was loss of sleep," an increasing problem as the campaign dragged along. Koto-ri had never been in quite as dire straits as Hagaru-ri, but the situation was still grim. Through it all Puller was his usual calm self. He operated in the same fashion he always did, roaming the perimeter, chatting with the troops, occasionally providing them with a swig from a whiskey bottle, bucking up morale. A lieutenant thought the colonel was a very "human sort of guy" who put the men at ease. Smith knew that Chesty played an extremely valuable role at Koto-ri even though he only could influence one of his battalions: "He was a tower of strength. Men felt confident with him in command. . . . His very presence reassured men, and he circulated constantly." One machine gunner recalled: "That man made us all feel invincible." A new Puller legend soon passed among the troops. Supposedly their colonel had nonchalantly told reporters: "We've been looking for the enemy for several days now. We've finally found them. We're surrounded. That simplifies our problem of finding these people and killing them."[18]

He presented the same serene front to his family. In a November 30 letter to Virginia, he explained that he had not written on the 29th (the night of the major Chinese attack on Koto-ri) because his gas lantern had quit working. He filled his note with idle chitchat and a drawing of the size of pipe she should send him for Christmas. He apparently thought that word of the disaster in Korea was being withheld by censorship. On the 1st of December he found out that was not true: "I understand that the news back home is to the effect that the 1st Marine Division is cut off, surrounded by the Chinese, etc. This is not ____ so, although the situation, anywhere in Korea, has been far from good ever since the Chinese crossed the border and moved south. I am terribly sorry that this news has been published on account of the additional worry it has caused you and the families of other Marines here." (Chesty had added his own blank to represent the expletive he badly wanted to use.)[19]

As usual, Puller made light of the situation: "Remember to believe only half of what you read and hear of the news." He also continued to focus on events at home, inquiring for the umpteenth time whether Virginia finally had hired a cook and insisting that she use a forthcoming check to "buy a present for your dear self and not put it in the bank." The only inkling he gave that he might be in danger came in his increasingly fervent expressions of affection for his family: "I miss *you* and our precious children terribly, far more than I can express myself in writing, Virginia, and about my greatest wish is to return home to you and them and then never to leave you again. I love you so very much, completely and with all my being." He also repeated his pre-Inchon regrets for "the worry that I have caused you in the past, and also the many times that I haven't been as nice to you as I should have been." And he emphasized his contentment with her as a wife and mother: "One of the many reasons why I wanted you to marry me, for so many years, was that I knew that I would always be proud of you and I am, Dear, and always will be."[20]

He justifiably wrote her on December 2 that "the situation shows a marked improvement today." Reinforcements had come in the form of the 2d Battalion, 31st Infantry, which had been moving up the MSR to join the 7th Division elements east of the Chosin Reservoir when the Chinese offensive struck. In a replay of Task Force Drysdale, 2/31's rifle companies had fought their way through to Koto-ri prior to dawn on December 1, but they had left much of their vehicle train behind on the road. The enemy overran those elements. When wounded and frostbitten survivors began to appear at the perimeter that morning, Chesty ordered Army infantrymen, reinforced by Marine tanks, to go out and find others who might still be alive. In an amazing turn of events, one of the armor NCOs came upon mail that had been scattered across the ground. He found a letter from Virginia for Puller and delivered it that evening to the colonel.[21]

The Army rifle companies augmented Puller's thin lines, but he had no faith in their leadership. Chesty reacted dramatically that evening when the commander of 2/31 asked about his line of retreat. Puller called up his artillery officer and told him to fire on the soldiers if they abandoned their position, then turned to the lieutenant colonel: "That answer your question? There will be no withdrawal."[22]

Supply had been a major problem, but cargo planes began to deliver ammunition and other critical items to the beleaguered town on December 1. The first flight came in too high and the parachutes drifted in the wind, leading Sutter to record that "a friendly air drop of supplies was made on enemy positions to the west." The next missions came in too low and the parachutes did not open. Heavy pallets hurtled into the crowded perimeter, killing and injuring several Marines. Puller lodged "strong protests" with X Corps. Eventually the "technique of C-119 pilots improved." Chesty also had directed the construction of a new airstrip within the perimeter because the old one was under constant enemy fire from the hills. Initially both fields could handle only spotter planes, but work proceeded on the new one to make it suitable for cargo aircraft, a task completed on December 8. With additional troops and an improving supply situation, the picture was indeed getting brighter at Koto-ri.[23]

The only thing that did not change was the cold. Puller wrote Virginia that he had "good warm clothing," but in reality he was not doing well in the subzero temperatures. Jones, his driver, recalled that the colonel began to show signs of "suffering from the cold" as soon as they moved to Koto-ri and "he seemed to take it harder than most." That was no surprise, since he had served most of his career in warm climates. In addition, he was one of the oldest men in the division and he admitted that he "had not been taking much physical exercise during the past four years." What he did not know was that he also was suffering from arteriosclerosis (hardening of the arteries), which significantly reduced the flow of blood throughout his body. Puller confided to his adjutant: "I can fight in the tropics, but this weather kills me." Chesty thought the weather was so "severe" that "none of us will ever forget it entirely." Throughout the stay in Koto-ri, the colonel shared a heated tent with his executive officer, but still spent much of his time out with his men in spite of his aversion to the icy wind. His only concession was to wear every item of clothing he had, which left him feeling "like a mummy."[24]

☆   ☆   ☆

Engineers operating around the clock had completed enough of the runway at Hagaru-ri to allow flight operations to begin there on December 1. The air bridge operated continuously thereafter during daylight. The planes brought in critical supplies and 537 replacements. More than 4,200 casualties flew out. With the bulk of its combat power now concentrated and more than two hundred Marine, Navy, and Air Force sorties per day dedicated to its support, the 1st Marine Division was a formidable foe. It launched south in the attack on the morning of December 6. The column had a thousand vehicles, each loaded down with equipment and supplies. No one rode except drivers and fresh casualties. Much of the force was still in the Hagaru-ri perimeter that night when the Chinese made a last attempt to break through at East Hill. In one of "the most fiercely contested" engagements of the campaign, 2/5 and reinforcing units killed more than a thousand of the enemy and took two hundred cold and hungry prisoners.[25]

As the last Marine units were battling their way out of Hagaru-ri on the morning of December 7, the head of the column was entering Koto-ri. The fighting along the way was intense at times. Infantrymen fought their way up snowy slopes, artillery batteries fired point-blank over open sights at charging Communists, and support troops defended their vehicles. The rear guard finally reached Koto-ri at midnight on the 7th. Puller and Sutter did as much as they could to welcome the weary newcomers. The galleys worked full-time to provide hot meals. All but a handful of buildings and tents were turned into warming areas, to be used in rotation. For many of the men coming in, it was their first opportunity in many days to enjoy the simple luxury of sleeping while someone else worried about perimeter security.

☆   ☆   ☆

On December 4 Almond had flown into Hagaru-ri to decorate Smith, Litzenberg, Murray, and Beall with the Distinguished Service Cross, then down to Koto-ri to pass out more awards. In a faithful imitation of MacArthur, the corps commander ran out of medals. After pinning a DSC on Puller, the general took it off, placed it on an Army officer, then returned it to the Marine colonel. Strangely, the citations for all officers read exactly the same: "Distinguished himself by extraordinary heroism in connection with military operations against an armed enemy during the period 29 November to 4 December 1950. His actions contributed materially to the successful breakthrough of United Nations Forces in the Chosin area." The fight to the sea, of course, was still a long way from finished and the medals smacked of a theatrical effort to encourage the recipients to live up to the words. The Marines needed no such false motivation. Puller put his award in the mail for Lewis: "It is about the least thing that I care for now and I hope he will get some pleasure out of it." Chesty was much happier at having another battalion back under his control and even more pleased that 3/1 had come down from Hagaru-ri with all its own gear, plus "equipment abandoned by Army units."[26]

Revelation at home of the Chinese offensive allowed Puller to vent his feelings again to Virginia:

Perhaps in the long run it may accomplish the awakening of our people as to the state of affairs and our lack of a military machine. . . . I just hate our leaders who got us into this mess and the far worse mess that may be the consequence of the first decision. The whole affair seems to have developed due to gross ignorance. . . . The leadership, especially that of the higher command, during this operation, has not been of top grade, especially in determining an estimate of the situation and the capabilities of the enemy. . . . On the 24th of last month, General MacArthur announced that the Korean war would be over and our troops withdrawn by Christmas. A few days later he announced that there were six hundred and fifty thousand Chinese soldiers in this country. . . . What do our people think? What are they doing? Do they realize what they have been led into?[27]

With the arrival of the 5th and 7th Marines on December 7, Puller was more confident about the outcome of the campaign, but his misgivings about the war remained:

This concentration means that we are now in better shape than we have been since landing on the east coast of this peninsula. Our losses from battle and from frozen hands, feet, and parts of faces have been heavy but with the help and blessing of the Almighty, the entire Division will be down on the coast within another two or three days and under the protection of our naval gun fire and carrier planes. I hear that the great commander (ours) has recommended to Mr. Truman that all the U.N. Forces be withdrawn from the country immediately. I pray that the recommendation will be approved. No thought should be given to face saving as our country has already lost its entire head and as a consequence has no face left to save.

He felt his opinions were widely shared: "All of our troops will have a lot to say when they get back home."[28]

Puller confined his criticism of seniors to his letters home, but he expressed bleak assessments of the tactical situation to others. Captain Michael J. Capraro recalled that Chesty "was not in the least cocky, but somber." When the young officer asked the colonel about the prospects of the division, there was a long pause, followed by a thoughtful, almost weary response about the importance of concentration and close air support. Puller had faith in his Marines, though: "Old man, it looks black now but after the darkness comes the light and tomorrow we are going to bust out of here with our gear, our wounded, and our dead . . . God willing." In talking to reporters, the colonel was confident about the outcome, but not the cost: "We'll suffer heavy losses. The enemy greatly outnumbers us. They've blown the bridges and blocked the roads . . . but we'll make it somehow." Chesty provided his most optimistic assessment to the regiment's senior officers after the staff outlined their rearguard mission. In one expletive-laden sentence he asserted that no number of Chinese could stop the Marines, then concluded: "And Christ in His infinite mercy will see you safely through."[29]

☆   ☆   ☆

Aerial spotters were observing large PLA units moving cross-country along the flanks of the MSR in an effort to mass ahead of the division. To minimize this threat, Smith decided to continue the offensive to the south immediately. His plan called for an Army battalion to relieve 1/1 at Chinhung-ni, so Schmuck's outfit could attack to the north to seize key terrain in Funchilin Pass. The 5th and 7th Marines would lead off out of Koto-ri and take control of high ground along the road to protect the convoy, now swelled to 1,400 vehicles. Puller's force—2/1, 3/1, and 2/31—would be the rear guard. The 1st Marines would relieve Murray's and Litzenberg's troops on the hills as the column went down the mountains. The last vehicles out would be the tanks, as a precaution against a breakdown that might block the one-lane road through the pass.

All day on December 7, small planes landed and took out casualties. The next day the bold pilot of an Air Force C-47 made it in on the lengthening strip, but the weather was so poor that no others could follow. Enough cargo planes were able to use the field on the 9th to clear out all remaining wounded. Two reporters showed up by air on the 7th, one of them Marguerite Higgins, a well-known New York writer. Puller was not about to assume responsibility for a woman in his perimeter and he sent her back out that day. She came in again two days later.

Chesty did not soften, despite her heated arguments that she should be treated "the same as a man." She was in good company. Shepherd had flown in, too, with the intention of walking down the mountain with the division, but Smith convinced his superior that a three-star general would be a worrisome burden for the division.[30]

There was one last task to accomplish before the division departed Koto-ri. There had not been enough space on the planes to send out 117 bodies. Burying them seemed an impossibility in the frozen ground till someone decided to use the large trench that had been blasted out for use as the artillery command post. The living moved out and the dead took over. The division bid them farewell with a short religious service and a rifle volley. When it was over, Puller mingled with the members of the firing squad and thanked them, as engineers bulldozed chunks of rock-hard dirt over the mass grave. All the bodies were frozen, many of them in the positions in which they had fallen in battle. From the line of corpses, the upraised arm of one slain man seemed to bid a poignant farewell to his comrades.[31]

The division set off on the morning of December 8 in the midst of "a blinding snowstorm" that reduced visibility to a few feet and grounded air support. The 7th and 5th Marines, reinforced by survivors of Task Force Faith, artillerymen, and other support troops, took most of the objectives slated for the first day's advance. Enemy opposition was not particularly strong in most instances, but each battle was an ordeal. The ranks of the infantry units were too thin and the men too worn. One of Litzenberg's battalions, for example, mustered barely 130 effectives in its three rifle companies, less than a quarter of their normal strength.[32]

Schmuck's 1/1, meanwhile, had made a night march into the southern end of Funchilin Pass. During the morning, under the heavy snowfall, the Marines made an agonizing climb from the road up the face of a steep, thousand-foot ridge. That afternoon, they cleaned out several bunker complexes, often surprising occupants focused on the approach from the opposite direction. After surviving a night of 25 below zero temperatures on the windswept heights, 1/1 resumed the attack on December 9. In the midst of the battle, a Marine saw the division column far below, moving into Funchilin Pass. He shouted and everyone paused a moment to see for themselves. The "dramatic sight" sent a jolt of adrenaline through the bone-weary officers and men and they surged forward "in a final burst of energy and guts" to seize the crest of Hill 1081, which dominated the critical choke point in the pass.[33]

In addition to the weather and the Chinese, the division faced one other major hurdle. Just above the hairpin turn, the single-lane road temporarily ended where the enemy had blown up a bridge. On one side of the missing span there was a concrete building backed by a steep slope; on the other, a sheer drop to the valley floor. On December 7, the Air Force had dropped eight large bridging sections by parachute, the first time this had ever been done. Two days later, after Marines had gained control of the site, engineers installed the bridge. Its two narrow steel treadways became the path to freedom for thousands of men.

With 1/1 and the 5th and 7th Marines on the high ground dominating the MSR, most of the long column made the passage to Chinhung-ni with little or no interference from the PLA. The lead element of the division, 1/7, reached the town before dawn on December 10 and the tail end of the vehicle trains arrived there that evening. There was trouble brewing in the rear, however, as thousands of Korean refugees gathered on the road entering Koto-ri from the north. They were no threat, but experience already had shown that the Communists would not hesitate to use the civilians to gain a tactical advantage. The Marines were torn between compassion and their own survival instincts. At times they had to fire above the crowd to keep it away from the perimeter. The hungry, cold Koreans hovered nearby as the division slowly filed out of town.[34]

With everyone else gone, Puller's men began to peel off from their positions and join the procession. The 3d Battalion exited first and relieved units of the 5th Marines on high ground along the highway late in the afternoon of December 9. Ridge's men fought off one serious Chinese attack that night. The regimental headquarters departed around 1500 on the 10th, followed by an artillery battery, 2/1, 2/31, the tanks, and the division recon company. The last man cleared Koto-ri at 1640. Puller's plan called for 2/1 to relieve a unit of the 5th Marines on Hill 1457, the last outpost before the bridge, with 2/31 then taking 2/1's place. After 3/1 pulled off its high ground, it would go down the road, followed by the tanks and recon. The Army battalion would pull in at the tail and cross the bridge last. These arrangements fulfilled Smith's order that the 1st Marines place infantry at the rear to protect the forty Pershings.

The column made slow progress as the vehicles of the 1st Marines inched across the narrow treadways in the inky blackness, guided only by flashlights. The horde of refugees followed down the road. Puller moved through the long snaking trail of men and vehicles, sometimes walking and occasionally taking a break in his jeep. While investigating one of the many incidents holding up the convoy, he found a sergeant from 3/1 stopping each vehicle to see if it was carrying 81mm mortar rounds, which his platoon badly needed. The colonel pitched in and helped obtain a supply from the passing trucks. There was no way for Chesty to be everywhere that night, though he chose not to place himself near the rear, generally the point of gravest danger in a withdrawal under pressure. In this instance, however, the requirement to deal with PLA threats to the flanks and front negated that conventional wisdom.[35]

Shortly after darkness fell on the 10th, Chesty modified the plan, although his reason for doing so and the exact details of what happened remain unclear. The end result was that he authorized 2/1 to return to the road earlier than it would have, while 2/31 did not get off the MSR and onto the high ground at all. He contacted the recon company commander and informed him that he now would be the rear guard and was solely responsible for the tanks. Puller also held a "hasty 30-second conference" with Schmuck as the colonel came through 1/1's position. Chesty told Schmuck that his battalion would assume the rear-guard mission after 2/31 had passed through his lines below the bridge. The lieutenant colonel was soon surprised to find elements of the Army battalion intermingled throughout the regimental column. The recon company commander thought the soldiers simply kept moving forward during the halts of the vehicle train instead of remaining in their assigned position.[36]

The armor was still two thousand yards from the bridge at 0100 on December 11 when the ninth Pershing from the tail end suffered brake lock. The M-26s in the front continued moving, escorted by two of the recon platoons. Thoroughly exhausted and likely absorbed in navigating the narrow mountain road, they were unaware of the break in the column. The stranded crews worked on the stalled tank for forty-five minutes without success. During the delay, dozens of Chinese soldiers filtered through the refugees. The Marines of the remaining recon platoon were soon engaged in a slow fighting withdrawal. Most of the tankers abandoned their vehicles, but the crew managed to fix the brakes of the stalled Pershing. Two tanks finally made good their escape, along with the infantrymen. Seven tanks had fallen into the hands of the enemy, four crewmen were missing, and the recon platoon had lost two killed and twelve wounded. When the survivors crossed the bridge, engineers blew it up.[37]

While this battle went on at the rear of the regiment, the lead elements of the 1st Marines were in trouble, too. Chinese had infiltrated into the village of Sudong. Just after midnight they rushed out of houses to attack Puller's vehicle train. In a matter of minutes they destroyed several trucks and blocked the highway. Chesty had not yet reached Sudong when the fighting broke out, but he went to work arranging fire support in case it was needed. It was not. The drivers drove off the attack. Casualties in this engagement were eight killed and twenty-one wounded.

Trucks were supposed to pick up the Marines at Chinhung-ni, but X Corps had not provided enough. None were available by the time Puller's regiment showed up, so the infantrymen kept walking. They reached Majon-Dong, about ten miles farther down the MSR, around noon, where vehicles finally appeared and carried the exhausted men the rest of the way to the sea. Sutter's 2d Battalion had been marching with little pause since the previous afternoon and had covered twenty-two miles. The last unit of the division to reach Hungnam was the tank column, which finally pulled into the port at midnight. That night, the men of the 1st Marines slept in heated tents and the next day, December 12, "enjoyed a well earned rest."[38]

☆   ☆   ☆

In the regiment's after-action report, Puller expressed the feeling that the Sudong ambush was a "particularly bitter loss" because the Army was supposed to have secured that portion of the MSR. He also briefly described the recon platoon's rear-guard action, but made no comment upon it. Privately, he was at least as upset with the latter event and would later conduct his own quiet inquiry into the matter. The number of casualties had not been high and the loss of the tanks was not critical at that point in the campaign, but it was an unnecessary "tragedy" and a black eye for the 1st Marines, which otherwise had performed superbly during the campaign. Puller blamed the recon Marines for failing to keep the refugees at bay and the tankers for not supporting the infantrymen once the engagement got underway. Smith, for the only time in his life, thought his old friend was at fault: "This is where Lewie Puller slipped up. . . . [His] infantry should have been the last out." The division commander specifically had ordered the 1st Marines to provide a strong escort for the armor; the small recon company did not meet that requirement. The general had reemphasized his interest in the matter by radioing the 1st Marines late in the afternoon to obtain the identification of the "last unit." Chesty's reply should have set off alarm bells at division headquarters: "Last element to leave top of pass will be Recon Co." Apparently neither Smith nor his staff understood that the tanks were the second-to-last unit or that the regimental commander had diverged from his instructions.[39]

Puller had made a strange choice in the first place when he assigned 2/31 to bring up the rear. Up to that point, the battalion's performance had been mixed, but its big failure involved the loss of its own vehicle train in a night movement along the MSR. That record could hardly have inspired confidence on the part of the CO of the 1st Marines. It almost seemed as if Chesty was looking out for his own troops first in assigning 2/31 and then division recon to cover the tanks. That notion is bolstered by the self-reliant tone of his brief note to his wife after reaching Hungnam: "With the help of the Almighty and no other unit or person, my regiment is on the beach." Given his disgust with the high command and his own loss of faith in the war effort, it is possible that he succumbed for a time to the simple desire to take care of his own men first. Captain Barrow had experienced a similar feeling at one difficult point in the campaign: "I was secretly glad that we were to be in reserve and I distinctly remember that I questioned my usefulness— perhaps these men had come to mean too much to me!"[40]

The most likely explanation was the cumulative effect of fatigue and cold on Chesty. The walk down the mountain was no easy task for a man of his age and physical condition. Even many of the youngest men on the road that night had fallen into a zombie-like state induced by exhaustion and hypothermia. In these extreme conditions, no one could make clearheaded decisions, but Puller faced the challenging situation with the added handicap of arteriosclerosis. Under the circumstances, it is not surprising that he might have made errors of judgment.[41]

Whatever the reason, Smith was justified in his belief that Puller fumbled the mission of protecting the tanks. Chesty picked his least reliable outfit to fill the role, then either failed to ensure that it carried out the order or reassigned the duty at the last moment to another unit that was much too small. A stronger rear guard would have kept the Chinese at bay until the Pershings made good their escape or the crews had the chance to render them useless. As it was, air strikes had to destroy the abandoned armor on December 12.

☆　☆　☆

On December 9, when the 1st Marine Division was leaving Koto-ri, it had learned that MacArthur had decided to withdraw all forces from Hungnam. The news was not well received by everyone. There was a belief among the Marine leadership that the division, its supporting arms, the weather, and the PLA's own poor logistics system had thoroughly destroyed the eight Chinese divisions thrown against the Marines. By conservative estimate, Smith's outfit and supporting air forces had inflicted tens of thousands of casualties on the enemy. Captured PLA documents revealed that it had lost equally large numbers from starvation and cold weather. Puller had observed that "the majority of POWs taken were in pitiful condition being severely frostbitten and usually extremely hungry." The 1st Marine Division's casualties from November 27 to December 11 were heavy—561 killed, 2,894 wounded, 182 missing, and 3,657 injured or sick out of roughly fifteen thousand engaged—but it remained an effective organization that could absorb replacements and return immediately to combat if need be.[42]

Shepherd was certain the decision to evacuate Hungnam was wrong. After a conference with MacArthur on December 7, he believed the theater commander and his staff "were licked" and that Walker also "had little fight left in him." In his opinion, the 1st Marine Division and the rest of X Corps could hold on to the port and airfield indefinitely. Murray also thought "we should have stayed there." Craig was confident the division could defeat the PLA. Puller later would express a similar view: "Why the hell they [withdrew] I'll never know, gave up all that ground we paid so much for. Not all the Chinese in hell could have run over us." However, at the time he departed Hungnam, he saw no point in maintaining an enclave there, or anywhere else, for that matter. On December 14 he wrote Virginia: "My prayer now is that our leaders, knowing that we have no war machine, will evacuate Korea completely, have a thorough house cleaning, and then build a real war machine before again becoming involved in another war. May God give us wisdom and common sense!" The highest American leaders had different ideas from both Chesty and Shepherd. They would consolidate U.N. forces in South Korea, hold that territory, and seek a negotiated peace that would reestablish the prewar status quo.[43]

Puller was unhappy with national policy, but he was extremely pleased with the performance of his own outfit. He had brought out most of his dead, all of his wounded, and the vast majority of his own equipment, plus some vehicles that other units had abandoned: "I left nothing for the enemy except planted land-mines." Beyond that, he was perhaps a little too quick to boast when he wrote Virginia that he had made it to the sea with the help of "no other unit or person." The 5th and 7th Marines had seized dominant terrain along the route of march, while aviation had provided critical supplies and fire support. Although he believed his regiment had "covered the withdrawal . . . with utmost success," the loss of the tanks had marred that final chapter of the battle. He and his men had fought as well as anyone else, though, and everyone in the 1st Marine Division had a right to be extremely proud of their accomplishment.[44]

Time magazine recognized the legendary nature of the Chosin Reservoir campaign a week after it was over: "The running fight of the Marines . . . from Hagaru to Hamhung . . . was a battle unparalleled in U.S. military history. It had some aspects of Bataan, some of Anzio, some of Dunkirk, some of Valley Forge, some of the 'Retreat of the 10,000' (401–400 B.C.) as described in Xenophon's Anabasis. . . . It was an epic of great suffering and great valor." Puller would have taken exception to the last historical comparison solely due to its title. He had told reporters as he waited to board ship: "Remember, whatever you write, this was no retreat. All that happened was we found more Chinese behind us than in front of us. So we about-faced and attacked." No matter what one labeled it, the two-week struggle had an impact far beyond the saving of one American division. In the short run, the Marines provided a bright spot for the United States in an otherwise bleak period. That did much to keep the United States in the war, an outcome Chesty loathed, but one that eventually guaranteed the survival of an independent, non-Communist South Korea. Coupled with earlier successes at the Pusan Perimeter, Inchon, and Seoul, it also would ensure the viability of the Marine Corps as an institution in bureaucratic bat-

tles to come. But Marines will remember it forever for the courage, re-
sourcefulness, and fortitude demonstrated by those who overcame one
of the toughest challenges ever faced by the Corps. General Lowe
thought Winston Churchill's quote about the RAF in 1940 was appropriate: "Never have so many owed so much to so few." General Smith
did not wax as eloquent in a memorandum to those he had led through
the trial, but he paid his own heartfelt tribute: "No division commander
has ever been privileged to command a finer body of men."[45]

21

"Befuddled and Disgusted"
Central Korea
December 1950–May 1951

The 1st Marine Division began loading on board ships at Hung-nam on December 11, 1950. When Puller's regiment sailed on the 14th, there were five thousand Marines crowded aboard a vessel designed to hold a third of that number. The conditions were far from ideal, but the chance to eat hot food and sack out in a warm environment, even if only on a steel deck, seemed like paradise to men who had suffered through so much. By the next day Puller was refreshed by ten hours of sleep, two showers, a shave, a haircut, and plentiful helpings of beef, eggs, and milk. He now felt "normal again," but the change did not alter his feelings about the war: "I don't know yet what the high command intends to do but I know what they should do and that is to get out [of the war] immediately and form a new army before getting further involved uselessly and for no purpose except that of face saving. . . . We can do no further good here at this time." He shared that view only with Virginia, though he held forth in the wardroom on a wide range of subjects for a large audience of junior officers. He gave them a history lesson on the Russo-Japanese War, told them all Americans should be "ashamed" of the U.S. Army's failure in the current conflict, and expressed disdain for the Air Force. "Our aviation is practically useless. Before Congress votes to increase the Air Force, they should certainly find out just what they accomplished in Korea and then decide whether the expense involved paid off."[1]

The transport docked at Pusan on December 15. The division moved to Masan, twenty miles to the west, where the brigade had stayed briefly during the late summer campaign. A tent city mushroomed in the "Bean Patch," a cultivated area north of town. Smith emphasized to his subordinates that their mission consisted of the four Rs; reequip, resupply, repair, and rehabilitate. Medical personnel screened everyone for frostbite and treated an epidemic of respiratory ailments. New men began to arrive and the Army opened up its warehouses to replace equipment. Training focused on weapons firing, small unit tactics, and conditioning hikes.

Smith passed the word that it was time for everyone to spruce up their appearance after the slovenly days of the Reservoir campaign. Marine commanders made sure there would be no time for the men "to begin to feel sorry for themselves," but the process of reinvigorating spirit had to begin right near the top. Colonel Murray, for one, experienced "a rather crushing feeling" when he returned to Masan: "Here we'd fought all this hard fight all the way into Inchon and Seoul, and had gone all the way up to the reservoir, only to find ourselves back in the same spot where we'd been at the very beginning." Craig had a similar reaction: "I had the feeling that we had been let down by those in Washington, and in turn that we had let down the Koreans."[2]

Rehabilitating the division involved more than just hard work. Smith wanted improved chow, since the Marines had only had fresh food three times since arriving in Korea. Ultimately the Navy dispatched a shipload of refrigerated rations that arrived just in time to provide a Christmas feast and then some. Smith recalled: "For a while we had turkey coming out of our ears." The PX system soon made beer available, there was occasional access to hot showers, and the division granted brief periods of liberty in town. One Marine noted in his diary that, all things considered, life in the Bean Patch was "pretty comfy."[3]

Puller enjoyed the respite and spent more time thinking about his family. He filled each daily letter with little domestic concerns, inquiring about Virginia McC's progress in school, telling Lewis how to run a rabbit trap, and worrying about their health. In a tender note to his oldest child, he repeatedly told her how "very proud" he was of her achievements. He wrote his wife that his goals were simple now: "To return to you and our precious children in order that I may help to provide for, care for, and protect my family. Furthermore I would like to be given an opportunity to do some little good in this world." He itched to teach his son "how to shoot and many other things that boys and men must know," and wanted all of his children "to look back on a happy childhood." He teased Virginia, telling her that when he returned home he would watch the children so she could make a trip to Richmond, then quickly adding: "Do not believe this, Sweetheart, as I will not let you out of my sight when we are reunited!" He plaintively regretted that he had been the cause of much anxiety and frequent, long separations: "Maybe I would not have permitted you to have married me, if I had known all this was coming on!"[4]

At Christmas, he had to be contented with celebrating the holiday with his other family—the Marine Corps. On Christmas Eve he visited all his units, each of which produced a group singing carols. Afterward he invited his senior officers to his tent and shared a ham and a bottle of whiskey, which he had received from friends in Japan. The next morning, he attended church services and had eggnog at General Smith's quarters. The celebration had all the trappings of home, but without his wife and children he thought "the whole procedure is flat."[5]

☆   ☆   ☆

While the 1st Marine Division recuperated, the situation continued to deteriorate for the allies. The U.N. coalition had ceded all of North Korea by the end of December and had yet to establish a defensive line it could hold. *Time* magazine summed it up for the public at home: "The best to be said of Korea was that the worst had not happened. The U.S. forces threatened with annihilation a fortnight ago had not been destroyed." The magazine subtly noted that X Corps (mainly the 1st Marine Division) had conducted a "fighting retreat," whereas the Eighth Army had merely "outdistanced the pursuing foe" in a "rapid withdrawal." A subsequent issue of the magazine drew an even sharper comparison between the two services. It observed that barely one half of 1 percent of Marine casualties were missing in action, whereas that category accounted for fully one sixth of the Army's losses: "New evidence to support the military axiom that carefully cultivated discipline and *esprit de corps* pay off in combat effectiveness." Hanson W. Baldwin, the highly respected military affairs analyst for *The New York Times,* bluntly stated in print that the United States had "a creampuff army." He felt that "tougher, harder, stronger and far more disciplined, better trained, better led soldiers are essential." Puller privately expressed his own scathing assessment: "I will never be able to understand the great difference between our enlisted men and young officers and those of the Army. There appears to be no example of leadership in the latter organization. No pride and nothing to look up to."[6]

That sad state of affairs began to change on December 23, when General Walker died in a highway accident. The Army dispatched Lieutenant General Matthew B. Ridgway to take command of Eighth Army. The hard-nosed paratrooper had won a well-deserved reputation for combat leadership during World War II. He wasted no time in breathing life into the fighting forces in Korea. One of his first acts was to tour the front lines and instill a new philosophy in his senior subordinates: "The job of a commander was to be up where the crisis of action was taking place. In time of battle, I wanted division commanders to be up with their forward battalions. . . . Their place was up there where the shooting was going on." He also was a strong proponent of the study of military history. It was a mind-set that should have warmed Puller's heart. The three-star general visited the 1st Marine Division for a little over an hour on January 9. Smith thought it was "excellent" that Ridgway exuded confidence in a talk to the senior officers. In turn, the Army commander was pleased with the caliber of the division and its leaders. He later recalled that one look in Chesty's eyes revealed this was someone upon whom he "could utterly depend." The feeling was not yet mutual. Ridgway had not given his command-from-the-front pitch, and Puller left the briefing "not too favorably impressed with the new commander." Murray thought the "firebrand speech" was reminiscent of Almond's overexuberance and he felt "pretty cynical about the whole thing."[7]

Puller privately continued to express his growing bitterness at the direction of events. He felt that the war was now being waged to "save the political life of one man [Truman] and the so-called military reputation of another [MacArthur]." He ridiculed the theater commander's official statement that "the fall of Seoul was a planned operation, executed as planned in an orderly manner." When news accounts described the evacuation of the city as "a disorderly rout," Chesty surmised "the censorship will go on tight now." He remained convinced that "an immediate evacuation is required and should have been ordered weeks ago," because he could "see no chance for victory here as we are vastly outnumbered." Over and over again he referred in dire terms to the crisis facing the nation. "I pray that there is yet time enough for us to take the necessary steps to preserve our freedom. This is how serious I believe the situation is." "It is either that or defeat and slavery." "I can only pray and trust that God will give us leaders who are wise and qualified." He was utterly convinced that "I am right in my estimation of the situation, *beyond a shadow of a doubt.*" On occasion, some of his strong sentiments nearly boiled over in public view. One *Time* reporter asked Chesty: "What is the most important lesson that the Marines have learned in Korea, so far?" An Army officer watching the interview recorded Puller's response: "Without batting an eye, [he] said, 'Never serve under X Corps.' "[8]

His feelings on the subject ran so deep that he had no real desire to see Lewis follow in his footsteps: "I will not influence my son as to choosing a profession. . . . I will not even recommend the service. I have had to stand with my mouth closed on too many occasions and then carry out orders from too many half-wits. If I had a private income, enough to support and educate my family, I would have resigned a month or two ago." Chesty especially regretted the waste of Marines for what he deemed to be a lost cause: "I haven't minded the hardships here but the killings and cripplings of the young men is awful."[9]

On occasion Puller regretted his outbursts because he knew they troubled Virginia. After one explosion, he wrote her: "Please do not worry about my yesterday's letter." And he always sought to put a positive face on his own future: "Remember the situation will never be quite as black as it may seem and that there will always be some way out, God willing. You may rest assured that I will do everything in my power to survive and return home for you and our grand children. I will never quit, believe me. I have much to live for. You! You! You! You! You!" He also held out hope, bolstered by rumors, that his promotion would come soon and result in his transfer home: "I trust that the friend is right and I am ordered back to the East Coast." He was disturbed that another acquaintance was giving the opposite picture to Virginia: "I did not like him telling you that he was willing to bet, and give odds, that I would want to remain out here."[10]

☆　☆　☆

A Chinese–North Korean offensive on New Year's Eve had routed the ROK 1st Division and forced the Eighth Army to fall back rapidly below Seoul. A subsequent attack against the ill-fated American 2d Infantry Division created a large bulge pointing southward in the eastern half of the country. Only poor PLA logistics prevented the enemy from gaining even more ground. Meanwhile, large numbers of NKPA soldiers were operating as guerrillas in the U.N. rear areas. On January 8, 1951, Ridgway decided to get the regenerated 1st Marine Division back in the fight, although only in a limited fashion at first. He ordered Smith to shift his outfit to eastern Korea, where the Marines would scour a large region for NKPA bands and serve as a backstop in the event of a fresh Chinese penetration toward the vital ports of Pohang and Pusan.

Word of the new mission passed down the chain of command. That evening, as Puller and Colonel S.L.A. Marshall (an Army historian) sat in Chesty's tent sharing a drink of whiskey, a captain came in. He reported that a sergeant had spoken up at formation, complaining about the apparent lack of national interest in winning the war. The NCO concluded: "Sir, we'll go because we're Marines. But that's the only reason." The company commander asked Puller how he should respond to the sergeant. Chesty looked at Marshall, who said nothing, then turned to the captain: "He's right. There isn't anything to tell him. But let me say something to you. Until we're backed, don't volunteer for one _____ thing. And don't let your men do so." Perhaps a little taken aback by his own discouragement, he added: "I've never said that before in my life."[11]

After reflection that night, Puller knew he needed to boost the spirits of his command. The next day he spoke to each of the battalions, giving them a pep talk in his booming voice. Once they headed north, he told them, they would have the opportunity to avenge their fallen comrades. He also said they had to be prepared to dig down deeper and possibly do even more than they had at the Reservoir. To emphasize his point, he described his experience at Peleliu and the regiment's much heavier losses there: "And if we could do it then, we can do it again." The reference to high casualties created a stir in the ranks. Barrow recalled: "A few of us looked at one another like, 'My God, what does he mean by that?'" In another move that caught subordinate commanders by surprise, Puller reversed his old approval of the carbine and told the men to throw away the unreliable weapons and replace them with M-1s or BARs. The junior officers were equally unhappy with the lightweight firearms, which did not work well in freezing weather, but a few were now concerned they would be responsible for a host of "lost" carbines.[12]

Most of the Marines did not take Puller's speech literally—there was no rash of missing weapons. But his words provided fodder for gallows humor for weeks to come. Like Chesty, many of those who had served since the beginning of the war were wondering when they would get home. The Marine Corps initially was having difficulty just replacing the division's casualties. It was not until February that some of the veterans got back to the States, although the first rotation draft largely was limited to those who had suffered a wound and returned to duty. Speculation was commonplace about the timing and composition of future drafts. As the 1st Marine Regiment moved up for an operation late that winter, one man yelled out to a friend in a passing platoon: "Hey, Sam, when are the Inchon men going home?" The other old-timer yelled back: "Don't worry about it, Chesty says all Inchon men will be dead by June 1st."[13]

☆   ☆   ☆

The 1st Marines led off the move by truck on January 10 and the entire regiment was in the vicinity of Pohang the next day. Smith assigned each of his regiments a zone of action to patrol. Puller drew the most "critical" one, a twenty-by-twenty-five-mile rectangle along the main road running through Andong. Those five hundred square miles encompassed three airfields and the most likely avenue of approach in the event of a Communist breakthrough. The 1st Marines had few contacts in the hilly terrain, but it was excellent training that helped meld replacements into their units.[14]

The division commander visited the 1st Marines on January 18 and came away a little concerned, because Puller's pessimism about the war was beginning to show through. Chesty had argued that the division should be concentrated around Andong to defend against a breakthrough from the north, rather than spread out over thousands of square miles hunting guerrillas. That night Smith confided his assessment to his diary: "The trouble with the 1st Marines is lack of confidence in the Army. Puller feels that they will take off to the south and leave him holding the bag. On this basis he requested enough trucks to get his whole outfit out, if necessary. This is Army-type thinking." The last comment would have stung the feisty colonel, but it was partly true. Chesty had given up hope the war would be won and was thinking too much about how to save his men if the worst came to pass. Like the Army battalion commander at Koto-ri, he had one eye focused on his

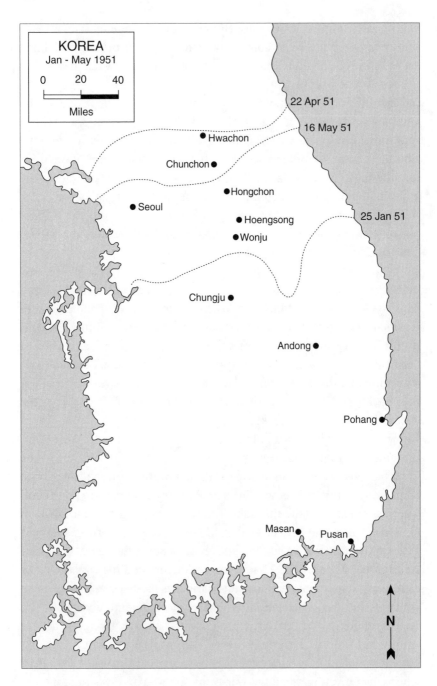

line of withdrawal. That concern notwithstanding, Puller and his Marines could still be counted on to give a good account of themselves in any battle.[15]

Smith also had grown wary about how he issued orders to his subordinate, probably as a result of the incident with the tanks in the Reservoir rear guard. There were four thousand Army and ROK troops in the vicinity of Andong and Puller had asked for power to coordinate their actions for defense of the area. Ridgway granted it on January 19, but the division CG sent Craig to visit the 1st Marines the next day "in order that there might be no misunderstanding regarding the scope of his authority." Smith saw both a weakness and a strength in his regimental commander: "With Puller it is necessary that he thoroughly understand instructions. Once he understands them they will be carried out explicitly." On a subsequent inspection of Andong, the general was not surprised to see Chesty "was making his presence felt" and had the situation well in hand.[16]

Puller demonstrated his thoughtful, noble side when a message arrived informing Captain Barrow that his father was dying. The company commander received emergency leave, but arrived at the regimental headquarters too late to get transportation to Pohang that day. Chesty told the captain to spend the night with him and Rickert. Barrow later recalled: "I think he sensed my deep concern and worry about my father and felt, somehow, that he could maybe take my mind off that by having me there in his tent and having conversation. So we spent a very long time talking, just the two of us. Not so much about Korea but about the Marine Corps and some of his past experiences." The next morning, Puller gave his subordinate a "warm farewell."[17]

On January 24, HQMC authorized the promotion of a number of senior officers in the 1st Marine Division. Smith pinned on Craig's second star that day, as well as Murray's eagle. Gregon Williams, the chief of staff, became a brigadier the next day. Puller flew into Pohang on the 26th and the division commander held a small ceremony in his quarters. The newest general in the Corps headed back to Andong on the afternoon of the 27th. He almost became the shortest-lived brigadier in the history of the Marines. As the helicopter attempted to land near the regimental CP, the pilot caught one of its skids on a telephone cable and the craft jerked down and forward, slamming into the ground. The helo was a complete wreck, but the pilot and his passenger miraculously walked away with nothing more than scratches and bruises.[18]

The promotions left the division overstaffed with senior officers. In deference to Puller's new rank, Smith sent his G-4, Colonel Francis M. McAlister, to take over the 1st Marines. Chesty fleeted up to head of Task Force Puller, a temporary outfit composed solely of his old regimental combat team. It was a stopgap until HQMC determined where to put the new generals. Craig definitely was going home, so one of the brigadiers would become the new ADC. Smith wired the Commandant that he preferred Williams. The CG thought Chesty was "getting tired," and also valued the chief of staff's greater experience around the division headquarters. (In a recent fitness report, Smith had rated Puller as a "highly competent" commander, but argued that Chesty "should be given a different type of duty in the Fleet Marine Force"—i.e., work on a staff—an indication that Smith felt his subordinate lacked enough experience in that area.)[19]

Puller would have been happy had he known that Smith wanted Williams. On the 25th he wrote Virginia: "I am now a general to date from the first [of January] and hope to be detached immediately. The radio announcing my promotion stated the commission would be delivered upon my arrival in the United States; so surely that means I am just about on my way to you, our children, and complete happiness. I am so very thankful." His expectations went up even more when Williams told him that he anticipated remaining with the division (probably the chief of staff knew of Smith's recommendation). The Commandant had his own ideas. Orders arrived just a few days later for Craig and Williams to return home.[20]

The news surprised and saddened Puller. He announced it in somber tones to Virginia: "My orders came in today, not back home to my precious wife and children, but to the division as assistant division commander. A few years ago I would have considered this an honor and thought myself fortunate, but not now. I too, like you write me, 'love you too much.' Even last evening or the day before, I thought and wrote you that God willing I might be reunited with you in less than ten days. This is going to be hard to bear on both of us." He cautioned her to "say nothing and write nothing to any one about my being retained here, or at least expressing our feelings on the subject." He also remained pessimistic about the U.N. coalition's chances against the Communists: "I may get out in the near future anyway. I honestly feel that I will (the whole outfit with me), not only the Marines but the Army as well." Chesty was not alone in his sentiments. At that point MacArthur was telling Washington that if he did not receive an additional 200,000 men, "the U.N. command would be annihilated or it would have to be evacuated." Puller was not as "tired and depressed" as the five-star general then appeared to be, but the brand-new Marine brigadier certainly was not his usual confident self.[21]

Puller's long association with the 1st Marines came to an end on February 1. McAlister provided a platoon honor guard and artillery fired an eleven-gun salute, but Chesty preferred the small ceremony put together by a handful of senior NCOs. They had manufactured a jumbo star and found the smallest man in the regiment to pin it on the general's shoulder while Puller stood on a rock, "so it would look like he was a giant." The sentiment of the sergeants was genuine, but Chesty needed no tricks to create an illusion of stature—he stood across the history of the 1st Marines like a colossus. He had led the regiment from the jungles of New Britain to the searing coral ridges of Peleliu, from the concrete seawalls of Inchon to the rubble-choked streets of Seoul, from the frozen wasteland of the Chosin to the hill country of southeastern Korea; against Japanese, North Koreans, and Chinese. Every time, Puller and his 1st Marines had prevailed. An NCO provided reporters with a simple but fervent tribute: "Puller is one of the roughest Marines I have ever seen. He is more the typical Marine than any Marine I have ever known. His men will do anything for him. . . . They love him and they have complete faith in him." A gunnery sergeant added: "I swear by him. Anything he says or does, I think is right. Anything." One newspaper referred to Chesty, this time with rare understatement, as an "almost legendary Marine."[22]

Before he flew off in a torpedo bomber, Puller thanked the men in the ranks and credited them with his success. Then he published his official farewell statement:

> It is not without some misgivings and a certain reluctance that I carry out these orders. All of you, officers and men alike, realize, I am sure, what the 1st Marine Regiment has meant to me. You may be equally sure that the faith and confidence you have placed in me will continue to receive my attention. . . . Good luck, God speed, and thank you.[23]

☆　☆　☆

In some respects Puller was an excellent fit for the ADC slot. The division was the lowest level in the chain of command where there was a chief of staff to oversee the flow of planning and paperwork in the outfit, thus relieving Chesty of any concern in that realm. In fact, the second senior officer in a division had no inherent responsibilities, other than being available in the event his boss was incapacitated or absent. (Puller explained that element of his new position to Virginia, adding: "Not that I want to get a division in that manner.") Red Mike Edson, who had filled the number two role in the 2d Marine Division during World War II, readily acknowledged that reality: "In most places the ADC is an absolutely negligible personage as far as command and active direction of the Division and its policies are concerned." By tradition (which was only a decade old in the Corps when it came to divisions), the ADC served as a second set of eyes for the commanding general, who was invariably busy pondering weighty decisions back at the CP. Smith agreed that the ADC was "a contact man whose job is to visit the combat units." A good brigadier, then, spent time with the troops, gave them the benefit of his experience, and inspired them by personal example. Puller was eminently suited for that role.[24]

The main drawback was Chesty's disdain for higher echelon staffs, a fact Smith recognized: "Lewie Puller was the fellow who was always saying the Goddamned division headquarters didn't know what it was talking about. . . . Then he came to division headquarters and the shoe was on the other foot. He belonged to this dumb headquarters outfit. . . . His attitude changed a little bit. Not an awful lot." (Colonel Bowser, the G-3, did notice that his relations with Chesty improved considerably once the two began working together.) But it did not help that the new brigadier was not in a position to change any of the things he did not like—for the first time in many years he was not in charge. Despite Puller's well-known feelings, Smith believed that his old friend would be "a very effective Assistant Division Commander" and "a delightful person to have around the command post." Chesty was content to work under Smith, whom he considered "shy, detached, quiet." He thought the CG was "a good planner," but "didn't inspire men," so they would be a "good team."[25]

During his first days on the job, Puller kept busy making the rounds of the regiments. His heart definitely remained with the 1st Marines, since visits there lasted all day; he made much shorter stops at other units. The routine did not take his mind off his perceived misfortune at having to remain in Korea. In one poignant letter to Virginia he lamented: "I can hardly bear to think of it, as the day after tomorrow I would have been with my precious wife and children had I been detached from the division." Forty-eight hours later he was still feeling the same way: "I would have arrived in the United States today and tomorrow I would be reunited with you, My Precious." He managed to take the delay philosophically: "I can wait, though, knowing that you love me and are waiting for me." "I could not love you more than I do, Darling, and the most wonderful part of it is that you love me, too. I often wonder why. Why do you?"[26]

Puller saw some positive aspects in his elevation to division: "I now have very good quarters with a stove. . . . A good mess with plenty of beef and biscuits. Quite a change from the regiment. Also good shower and hot water." He even had time to go hunting on occasion for geese and pheasant. More important, it said something about his stature in the Corps: "Actually my present assignment is an honor . . . and the Commandant thought that I could handle it. . . . General Cates probably thinks that I am competent and also that he is giving me a break."[27]

☆   ☆   ☆

The U.N. coalition had established a stable front by mid-January and even launched a counterattack on the 24th on the left flank of the peninsula that moved the U.N. line steadily back toward Seoul. On February 10 the U.S. 24th Infantry Division recaptured Inchon and Kimpo airfield. The successful offensive seemed to restore some of Puller's faith in the Korean mission, though conflicting reports left him far from confident: "It all leaves me befuddled and disgusted. I do not know where it will lead to, but I pray that it will all lead to victory and an enduring peace." None of the fighting men realized it yet, but the leadership back home was reaching the conclusion that a complete triumph on the battlefield was not worth the cost. That possibility was only slowly beginning to trickle down to the upper echelons of the combat forces. In a February 1 meeting, Ridgway informed Smith that Eighth Army had no present plans to move past the South Korean capital, as "an advance beyond the Han River involved political considerations."[28]

The 1st Marine Division was one of the most "powerful" organizations in Korea and Ridgway was not about to keep it chasing after elusive and largely ineffective guerrillas. The need for dependable units came to the fore on the night of February 11, when a Communist counteroffensive in the center of the country threw back two ROK divisions and forced the retreat of the U.N. IX Corps. The next morning, the Marines received orders to move to Chungju and prepare to counterattack the enemy penetration. Puller flew to the central Korean town on the 13th and conducted a helicopter reconnaissance to select assembly areas. The ADC met with Ridgway, who envisioned dispersing the Marine regiments over a wide front. Chesty, always an advocate of concentration, argued for placing the entire division at Chungju. The Eighth Army commander finally agreed. With the exception of that small victory, Puller returned to Pohang on the evening of February 14 with bad news. The Army's 23d Infantry Regiment was surrounded, an entire battalion of artillery had been overrun and lost, and the 8th ROK Division had disintegrated. The Communist forces proved unable or unwilling to exploit this success, however, and their attack soon halted. On February 18, intelligence indicated the enemy were beginning to withdraw.[29]

Puller returned to Chungju on February 15 and set up the division's advance CP. On the 19th he attended a conference, with Ridgway and the staffs of the IX and X Corps, that laid out the plans for the allied riposte in central Korea. The 1st Marine Division would occupy the right flank of the IX Corps zone and jump off from Wonju on the 21st, heading northeast to seize dominating terrain near Hoengsong. The 6th ROK Division would be on the left of the Marines, and X Corps' 7th Division would be on their right. Ridgway ordered his subordinates to preserve a solid front and not bypass any Communist forces: "Maintenance of lateral contact between all units is of prime importance." Under this directive "even lack of opposition would not justify a unit in advancing ahead of schedule." Operation KILLER, as it was dubbed, would not be a campaign of maneuver—its goal was solely to inflict attrition on the enemy.[30]

The Eighth Army timetable was overly ambitious. Even with Army support, Smith had only enough trucks to move one regiment at a time, not including its required supplies. He partly solved that problem by airdropping rations in the forward area, along with the fuel needed so the trucks could make the return trip. With the exception of the 7th Marines, the division was mostly assembled at Chungju by the 19th, but it still had to get forward to Wonju. To complicate matters, there were only narrow dirt roads in the area and rain was turning them to mud. Smith was convinced from the beginning that he had been given twenty-four hours too little to make the move. MacArthur intervened to make life even more difficult. On February 20 he went to Wonju to visit an Army airborne regiment and a French infantry battalion. All other traffic was stopped to clear the road for his movement, thus snarling the convoys carrying the 1st Marines and Puller's ADC group to the front. The vehicles, in turn, were delayed in getting back to Chungju to pick up the 5th Marines, the other assault regiment. It was obvious to Chesty that Murray's outfit would never make it to Wonju in time and he called the division CP in Chungju for instructions. Smith told him to go ahead with the attack as long as at least one battalion of the 5th Marines was available. He thought the "calculated risk" was "justified by the improbability of serious enemy resistance." Trucks dropped 1/5 off in its assembly area at 0745 on February 21 and the troops dogtrotted forward to the line of departure, arriving just in time for the scheduled 1000 jump-off. Smith was right and the opposition was light on this first day of the offensive.[31]

Chinese forces did not materialize in any appreciable strength until February 23, though rain, melting snow, and mud combined to slow the forward movement of the Marines and make conditions miserable for infantrymen on both sides. On the 24th the division seized its final objective for KILLER, the high ground just south of Hoengsong. That same morning, Smith received an urgent message from corps headquarters. Major General Bryant E. Moore, the commanding general, had died as a result of a helicopter accident. Ridgway ordered Smith to take over IX Corps, leaving Chesty in charge of the 1st Marine Division. The sudden change in status gave even Puller a moment's pause: "Last month I was a regimental commander and today I am a division commander." But his excitement over the elevation was dulled by the reason for it. Chesty had known Moore since Guadalcanal, where the Army officer had commanded the 164th Infantry that fought with 1/7 at the Battle for Henderson Field and Koli Point. Moore had left a positive impression on Puller: "He seemed to be a good soldier and gentleman, and I regret his death."[32]

Puller initially wondered "how long this assignment will last," but was not surprised when he discovered it would be only a matter of days.

Although Ridgway had full confidence in Smith, the Army high command was not about to let a Marine remain in that plum position. Within ninety-six hours, Washington had ordered Major General William H. Hoge to leave Europe for Korea, where he would take over IX Corps. The hasty transfer rankled Chesty: "Unification only works one way and that is that the General Staff Corps of the Army runs (all) the services as they see fit and that only they are fit for the higher commands. What fitness depends on, I haven't been able to find out. You at least have to be an Army General Staff Corps officer. Combat experience doesn't matter. . . . I knew that the Army would never consent for Smith to have the IX Corps." Puller also realized the Army's decision had personal consequences for him: "The tables of organization for a division call for a major general to command it. Ordinarily when a brigadier is given command of a division he is temporarily promoted to that rank." No second star was in the offing for Chesty, but he nevertheless felt it was "a great honor to command a great division." Newspapers back home highlighted his new role and described him as "flint tough," "a fabulous fighting Marine," and "tremendously popular with the enlisted men."[33]

The last days of February were quiet as the U.N. forces consolidated their gains and pushed enough supplies forward through the mud to support fresh offensive action on March 1. Puller issued his first division operations order on the 27th. It called for his two lead regiments to conduct a simultaneous assault across the valley on March 1 to seize their objectives, high ground on the far side of the town. While that simple plan seemed to confirm his preference for straight-ahead tactics, it also was in consonance with Eighth Army's insistence on a linear advance. Late on the afternoon of the 28th, Puller modified his orders in a two-sentence message. The 7th Marines would still attack on the left as planned the next morning, but the 1st Marines would remain at the line of departure and support the movement of Litzenberg's outfit by fire. McAlister's regiment would move forward "at [a] time to be designated by CO 1st Marines and coordinated with CO 7th Marines." The commanders of the two assault regiments went one step further and agreed among themselves to shift the boundary between their zones and have one battalion of the 1st advance alongside the 7th. That maneuver would outflank the town of Hoengsong and Hill 208, the major terrain features in the zone of the 1st Marines. These last-minute changes indicated that Puller was willing to seek an alternative to the lockstep type of attack desired by Eighth Army and to give his subordinates wide latitude in executing their mission. Smith, however, had not overlooked Chesty's eagerness to throw in his reserve. On the afternoon of the 28th, a division staff officer recorded the substance of a telephone call from higher headquarters: "Corps wants string on one [regimental] combat team. Don't care which one but one regiment cannot be employed without approval of CG, IX Corps."[34]

Shepherd flew in on the morning of March 1 and helicoptered forward with Puller to watch the 7th Marines jump off after heavy preparation fires. Litzenberg's regiment made good progress initially, but encountered increasingly stiff opposition. The Chinese were learning how to deal with American firepower—during bombardments they vacated their defenses on the military crest and took shelter on the reverse slopes, then quickly resumed their positions when the fire slackened. With air and artillery support and some hand-to-hand fighting, the 7th Marines finally gained the face of their intermediate objectives in the afternoon. The enemy still held the tops of the hills. The 1st Marine Regiment had to wait for the next day to launch its attack. The division had not achieved its goal, but Shepherd was nevertheless impressed after visiting all the regiments with Puller during the afternoon. In spite of tough challenges from rugged terrain and poor logistics, the senior general found "all hands in high spirits" and he thought the "performance of [the] division under these difficult conditions is most creditable."[35]

There was one other glaring handicap facing the division, the lack of assistance from the 1st Marine Aircraft Wing (MAW). Chesty was mightily displeased and had his air officer provide a detailed brief to Shepherd. MacArthur had allowed his subordinate Air Force commander to establish a Joint Operations Center (JOC) that controlled the employment of all aircraft, including those of 1st MAW. A request for an air strike now went all the way to Eighth Army headquarters, where the JOC responded as it saw fit. Since the Air Force believed that deep interdiction missions were "the most profitable," close air support requests received a low priority. As an example, the division had asked for twelve planes to conduct a strike before H-Hour that morning. It received the assistance of just two photo reconnaissance jets armed solely with .50 caliber machine guns, and that only because the pilots were in the area and volunteered to help. The JOC provided some planes later in the morning, but they were jets with little time on station and less ordnance than that carried by Marine aircraft. Shepherd agreed with Puller's complaints and promised to raise the issue with the Air Force. Two days later, Chesty fired off a message to Smith castigating the JOC's failure to meet his request for night heckler aircraft, since enemy artillery invariably remained silent when they were aloft. Puller was opposed to the idea of an independent air force, but he remained firmly convinced of the value of close air support. His protests did some good—under pressure from Shepherd, the Air Force soon allowed Marine planes on armed reconnaissance missions to divert to support the division if it needed them.[36]

The Marines managed to bring more firepower to bear on March 2. The Chinese put up stubborn resistance in some pockets, but there were signs they were beginning to withdraw. Falling temperatures, gusting winds, and snow brought a brief reminder of the Chosin Reservoir to both sides. McAlister's regiment seized its portion of the division final objectives the next day and Litzenberg's outfit occupied the remainder on the 4th. They uncovered "Massacre Valley," where a 2d Infantry Division task force had been ambushed by Chinese forces. The enemy had destroyed the entire vehicle train and killed nearly three hundred American and Korean soldiers. One Marine NCO called it a "ghastly scene," with frozen bodies, stripped of clothing and footwear, strewn along a dirt road. To Chesty, it was a "disgrace to American arms" and one more piece of evidence that most of the nation's armed forces were sadly unprepared: "The Pentagon is largely to blame for this mess— they were given the money to provide and train an army. When I entered the service, the regulations stated that 'the object of all military training is success in battle.' Since the last war this short sentence has been rewritten on three pages and I defy anyone to read it over three or more times and then explain what the object of military training now is."[37]

During this phase of KILLER, Puller went forward from his CP only once, when he and Shepherd watched the 7th Marines on March 1. The two generals had spent the next day at the division command post following the action over the radio. During the morning of the 3d, a visit from Smith tied the brigadier general to his CP. That afternoon Puller had to fly to IX Corps headquarters for a briefing. He was unaccustomed to remaining so far from the front lines, but he could honestly report to Virginia: "I am taking care of myself and taking no unnecessary risks."[38]

On March 5 General Hoge arrived at IX Corps and Smith returned to Wonju to resume his normal billet. The Marine general was happy to get away from the "defeatist attitude" of Army staff officers and their shameless talk about the times they had "bugged out" (slang for a hasty retreat). Puller was still angry about the Army's haste in replacing a Marine, but pleased that he "at least had the division for ten days." He firmly believed: "There has never been a better division in the history of the world." March 5 also brought several letters from his wife and his Marines suffered "no casualties, so it was a grand day."[39]

There was another reason for Puller's improving outlook. Shepherd had informed Smith and his ADC that the Commandant intended to send out replacements for them by early summer. Chesty now had a fairly definite date to look forward to for his reunion with his family: "I pray that it may be so and even better that I may be detached before June, the sooner the better." Cates announced a few days later that Bill Whaling would become the new ADC on May 20.[40]

The good tidings did not stop there. Smith decided to recommend all three regimental commanders during the Chosin Reservoir campaign for the Navy Cross. Some of the awards board members thought that Puller did not rate it as much as Murray and Litzenberg, since those two had faced more dire circumstances at Yudam-ni. But the division commander believed the defense of Koto-ri and supervision of the rear guard had "called for a high degree of professional competence, for determination, and for a display of heroic leadership" that "fully merits the award." If Secretary of the Navy approved it, Puller would become the first Marine ever to receive a fifth Navy Cross.[41]

☆　☆　☆

Ridgway launched a new offensive on March 7 dubbed Operation RIPPER. His goals were threefold: to inflict more casualties on the Communists, to disrupt preparations for their rumored spring offensive, and to drive a deep salient into central Korea that hopefully would force the Chinese to withdraw from Seoul without a fight. The 1st Marine Division was again in the middle of the fight. Smith's organization attacked due north to seize the town of Hongchon, an important communications hub. The roadless region was characterized by steep hills and extremely narrow draws. The Marines gained ground steadily, however, as the Chinese chose to withdraw their main forces while small elements fought a delaying action.

The 1st Marine Division CP had displaced forward to a site near Hoengsong just prior to the offensive. Smith was mightily glad to be out of the "terrible mudhole" at Wonju. Puller apparently came out of the cold, wet conditions of the old location with a severe illness bordering on pneumonia. Although he was the ADC again and the division was in the attack, he did not venture away from Hoengsong for the next five days. After that unusual hiatus, he resumed his daily trips to the front to visit with commanders and their troops. As always, he showed a marked and understandable predilection to spend time with his old outfit. Tours of the front also gave him the opportunity to mix with the men, something he missed now that he had risen to the solitary loftiness of the general officer ranks. His aide noticed that Puller was discomfited by the isolation. The lieutenant told more than one old hand: "The Old Man is lonesome in that van of his. He likes to talk to his World War II men. Go on over and visit him."[42]

RIPPER took back territory but did not achieve its first two objectives. The willingness of the Chinese to retreat both cut their losses and shortened their supply lines. The United Nations did accomplish one major goal. On March 14 ROK patrols discovered the enemy had abandoned Seoul. Once and for all the capital returned to South Korean control. The inability of Eighth Army to inflict significant casualties on the Communists caused Ridgway to rethink his previous emphasis on linear tactics. In mid-March he directed a change: "It is desired that more use be made of maneuver within and between division zones with a view toward trapping and annihilating the enemy. . . . It is not desirable that units always advance toward the enemy abreast." The Chinese frustrated even this plan by retreating faster. Logistics, rather than enemy opposition, continued to be the main limitation in the rate of advance. In the absence of decent roads, supply devolved upon the backs of Korean laborers who carried heavy loads lashed to simple wooden A-frames. With such expedients, Hongchon fell on March 14.[43]

For Virginia's benefit, Puller was beginning to count down his remaining days in Korea. He now was guardedly optimistic about the war. "Unless higher authority gets too ambitious and again goes to extremes, I do not expect too much trouble during the next two months. I pray that the Russians will keep out of this mess." Ridgway was even more confident about the future and "would only consider withdrawal if the Soviets intervene." No one seemed too worried about the Chinese, even though intelligence indicated they were preparing for a major spring offensive.[44]

For a brief period Eighth Army's greatest source of concern was a Navy chaplain. Lieutenant Commander Otto E. Sporrer had served with the Marines at the Chosin Reservoir and been decorated with the Silver and Bronze Stars for his actions. The courageous Catholic priest had been mortified by the behavior of some soldiers in the aftermath of the Task Force Faith debacle; a significant number had feigned wounds to escape Hagaru-ri by airlift. In an echo of Puller, the chaplain was even more incensed by the use of censorship to cover up Allied failings and by the luxury in which senior Army staffs lived in Korea. In mid-March he published his accusations in an unsigned article in a California magazine. At the end of the month he went public on television and radio, creating a national stir. The Army tried to get the Commandant of the Marine Corps to disavow Sporrer's statements. Cates replied that he would make no comment to the press, but would provide any facts solicited by government officials.

The Army turned to the 1st Marine Division for help: "It is imperative that General Smith . . . make a public statement as to the truth in the matter and clear the good name of the Army personnel involved." Smith thought Sporrer had been wrong to raise the issues in the media, but agreed with much of what the chaplain had said. He refused to issue a press release contradicting the priest. MacArthur's representative then approached Chesty, but received no sympathy. The best the Army could get out of the Marines was permission to photograph the 1st Marine Division general's mess. In contrast to Almond's palatial setup, it was a pyramidal tent with a partition down the middle, the cooks on one side and a simple wooden table for Smith, Puller, and their guests on the other. On occasion the senior Marines did dine on fresh food flown in from Japan—whenever General Lowe visited and brought along a supply of good rations. The Sporrer incident blew over only when other, more serious news wiped it off the front pages.[45]

MacArthur provided the story. The theater commander had emerged from his funk and was now calling for increased military action to achieve a complete victory in Korea. The five-star general was well aware that President Truman already had decided to negotiate a settlement, but MacArthur unilaterally tried to change American policy. He issued a public statement calling on the Chinese to get out of Korea or risk air attacks on their homeland. Soon after, he granted interviews to newspapers and wrote a letter to a Republican congressman ridiculing U.S. strategy and complaining about restrictions on the employment of force against China. Truman rightly considered this "rank insubordination" and announced on April 11 that MacArthur was relieved of command. Ridgway replaced him. MacArthur returned home to a hero's welcome, but his advocacy of a wider war with China soon dulled public enthusiasm. Puller did not like the idea of a stalemate, but he also strongly opposed any increase in American commitment in order to win. Unlike MacArthur, he was certain that air strikes in China would not effect the desired outcome. He believed that similar aerial campaigns behind the lines in Korea had done little to stop the PLA.[46]

The strain of the seesaw Korean War was beginning to tell on some senior officers. Shortly after MacArthur's relief for cause, Litzenberg asked when he was going to get orders home. The 7th Marines CO said he was worn out and feared he might have a heart attack. Puller, impatiently waiting for his own transfer without complaint, wanted to "read him off." The division CG thought Litzenberg had been spending too much time in his tent dwelling on troubles, but Smith also did not want to keep someone in command who no longer wanted it. He borrowed a colonel from Shepherd's staff and sent Litzenberg home in mid-April.[47]

☆   ☆   ☆

With occasional halts to close up gaps in the line or to allow supplies to catch up with the assault elements, the Eighth Army attack ground forward through April 22. The 1st Marine Division, with the 1st KMC Regiment attached for much of this period, had moved up to the Hwachon Reservoir, a gain of forty-five miles since the inception of Operation KILLER in late February. There had been occasional bitter battles with pockets of Chinese, but generally resistance was light and friendly casualties low.

On the night of April 22, the PLA launched its long-awaited spring offensive. Attacks came all along the U.N. line, but the major blow fell upon the 6th ROK Division on the immediate left of the 1st Marine Division. Before midnight the Koreans were shattered and streaming toward the rear. Smith promptly got the 1st Marines, his reserve, into position to cover his flank, while the 7th Marines and the KMC Regiment fought off large-scale assaults to the front. The next morning he received the first in a series of orders to withdraw to a new position. Although the enemy employed a considerable amount of artillery for the first time in the war, they also took a severe beating at the hands of American supporting arms. By the 26th, attacks against the Marine line had dwindled to insignificance, though some sections of the Eighth Army front continued to receive heavy pressure. The U.N. retrograde did not stop until the last day of April. The 1st Marine Division was now near Hongchon, half of the way back to Wonju.

Puller, as usual, was disgusted with the performance of the American and Korean armies. He was especially aghast that one U.S. Army artillery battalion had abandoned twelve self-propelled 105mm howitzers after receiving small arms fire from Chinese infantry. Not all soldiers fought so poorly. The U.S. 92d Field Artillery Battalion had come into Marine lines following the 6th ROK debacle. On the 24th, a large number of PLA soldiers attacked the artillery outfit, but the Army gunners held firm and mowed them down with direct fire at ranges under a thousand yards. (This same unit had supported 1/1 during the breakout from the Chosin Reservoir.)[48]

The Chinese offensive gave rise to one new tale about Puller. As the debacle unfolded on the left flank of the division, Chesty supposedly contacted the headquarters of the disintegrating ROK outfit to determine the strength of the attacking enemy. A Korean answered: "Oh, many, many, many!" The ADC spoke to another ROK officer and received a similar reply. Finally he got through to the young Marine officer acting as liaison with the allied division. The lieutenant, equally excited in the midst of the confusion, blurted out: "A whole damn pot full, sir." Puller finally was satisfied: "Well, I'm glad someone up there can count!"[49]

In the midst of this fresh setback to allied arms, the division received a new leader. Jerry Thomas, promoted to major general in the fall of 1950, had arrived in theater to replace Smith. Puller met him at the airfield on the afternoon of April 25 and escorted him to the CP, providing an update on the situation as they drove. It was the first time that Smith, Thomas, and Puller had been together since their school days at Benning, but it was not a pleasant reunion. At the urging of the new Eighth Army commander, Thomas actually was arriving a few days ahead of schedule. Smith rightly protested that the middle of a fighting withdrawal was no time to change horses, but ultimately he realized the decision was out of his hands. The next morning he turned over the outfit and Chesty accompanied him to the landing strip. Puller already knew that he and Smith would be working closely together again in the States in just a few short weeks.[50]

Puller's time under Thomas was brief and relatively uneventful. During the last few days of April and the first half of May, the ADC made the rounds of the regiments as they sat in defensive positions along the oddly titled No Name Line. Intelligence indicated that the enemy was preparing to launch a second round of their offensive. The blow fell on May 16, this time directed at two ROK divisions to the east of the 2d Infantry Division, which sat on the right flank of the 1st Marine Division. The Chinese swept the Koreans aside and opened a hole twenty miles wide and thirty miles deep in the U.N. front. The unlucky American soldiers of the 2d fared better this time than they had in the past—they were able to reorient their lines to face to the east and hold that shoulder of the penetration. The Marines fended off two regimental-sized probes in their sector and then sideslipped to take over some of the frontage of the 2d Division. The PLA, as usual, ran out of steam in a short time and U.N. reserves prevented the Chinese from exploiting their initial success. By the 20th of May the situation was stabilized. The offensive had failed to achieve anything of substance. In fact, the enemy's action finally was allowing Ridgway to achieve his goal of inflicting severe casualties on his opponent. The PLA was so decimated by its twin thrusts that Eighth Army was able to launch its own counterstroke on May 23 that swept forward to recover all the ground lost since April, and more.

Puller was not around to see this latest swing of the pendulum. His replacement had arrived and Chesty had boarded a plane for the States on May 20. He had been in Korea for just over eight months and the war had given him the "chance to excel" that he had wanted. He and his Marines had played a vital part in the brilliant end run at Inchon, the slugfest through Seoul, the epic fighting withdrawal at the Chosin, and the bitter back-and-forth of the stalemate in central Korea. His performance had not been flawless. Smith felt that Murray had done better as a regimental commander, but the major general also praised Chesty for getting the job done when the chips were down and the division needed leaders who could carry out a mission "with determination and singleness of purpose." Smith's final fitness report accurately captured Puller's valuable contribution to the fight: "An outstanding troop leader. His background, his devotion to duty, and his steadiness in critical situations all inspire a high degree of confidence on the part of both officers and men."[51]

Puller had hoped the war would revive his career. His future in the Marines had never been in jeopardy in the first place, but the mushrooming size of the defense establishment had expanded his opportunities. He now had the coveted star of a general and even had achieved his goal, if only for ten days, of commanding a division in battle. That success, however, did little to soothe the bitter taste of a conflict he had grown to despise. He was more than happy to be leaving Korea, but before he could rejoin his family, he had a long flight home and a lot of time to brood about the past and the future.

"I Hope I Don't Get Hung"
Training and Experimenting
May 1951–June 1952

Brigadier General Puller was coming home to an important, just created job in May 1951. As a result of the sterling performance of Marines in Korea, there was growing sentiment in Congress to double the size of the Corps to four divisions and four air wings. President Truman had a long history of opposition to Leatherneck interests, most recently expressed in an August 1950 letter to a Republican representative. The note had derided the Corps as "the Navy's police force," with "a propaganda machine that is almost equal to Stalin's." It had appeared in the press soon after, embarrassing the President and strengthening the hand of Marine supporters. Under pressure from politicians at the far end of Pennsylvania Avenue, in the spring of 1951 Truman reluctantly granted General Cates authority to add a brigade. At the same time, the Commandant was placing Korean veterans where they could "bring their combat knowledge back to the Marine Corps training centers and planning councils." Cates gave Puller a strong vote of confidence by selecting the junior one-star general to command the new brigade—the third largest combat outfit in the Corps and the only field command for a brigadier.[1]

The assignment heightened media interest in Puller, already known among combat correspondents as a source of "good copy." One article heralding his transfer called him "one of the most colorful figures in Marine Corps history." Stateside reporters also were eager for new angles on the controversial war. Chesty undoubtedly looked like an ideal source to them.[2]

Puller stopped in Hawaii for two days before heading on to San Francisco. As he was departing Honolulu on May 23, he gave a United Press correspondent a brief but perceptive analysis of Chinese capabilities. He pointed out that the Communists "can knock holes [in U.N. lines] big enough to drive Barnum and Bailey's Circus through—but they cannot exploit them." He explained that their poor logistics system could not resupply their forces in combat: "All you have to do is to stand and fight and they run out of ammunition." (Although the interviewer failed to catch the implication of that statement, it was a veiled criticism of the U.S. Army, which frequently had failed to hold its positions.)[3]

When Chesty arrived in California that evening, reporters were waiting for him, so he held a press conference. Their questions focused on the lessons of the war, his thoughts on the Chinese, and his plans for training the 3d Marine Brigade. He probably was tired from the long flight. He also may have believed that he was among the same type of correspondents he had befriended on the battlefield—writers who filed positive stories on leaders who fought well. And he probably had spent much of the long trip brooding over the things that had raised his hackles for the past several months. Whatever the reason, he let his guard down in front of the reporters and poured out many of the frustrations he previously had vented only in private. When the session was over, the representative from the *San Francisco Examiner* accurately captured Puller's attitude toward the war: "It was a savagely realistic message, full of bitterness for what has already happened in Korea and full of grave apprehension for the future." The reporter also had astutely observed Chesty's discomfort in this unfamiliar arena: "[Puller] struggled constantly to express his views in polite language. And he struggled even harder to stay within the rules governing public statements by military commanders. He emphasized repeatedly that he was not criticizing anyone and that his observations should not be interpreted as criticism."

Most of Chesty's statements encapsulated convictions that had developed or deepened over the past few years. Officers "have had far too much schooling and far too little service on the field of battle." "Infantry troops with rifles and bayonets" remained the force of decision—the world was no closer to "pushbutton war" than it had been in the days of Julius Caesar. "The bulldozer was the secret weapon of World War II, but the tent stove has been the secret weapon of the Korean War, and it wasn't developed by a scientist, but by a blacksmith." Too many American infantrymen were armed with carbines, while the enemy preferred "good Russian rifles." Aviation was failing in its self-imposed mission of interdicting Communist supply lines. Bombs blew up railroad tracks, but peasants with hand tools could repair the damage in hours. "Somebody—not so much the aviators as the aircraft manufacturers—sold the American people a bill of goods as to what aviation can do." (Moments later he appeared to contradict that judgment when he repeated his Honolulu assessment that poor logistics imposed severe limitations on the PLA. Both statements were right—airpower had not strangled the Chinese and North Koreans, but it had made it impossible for them to build up stocks of food and ammunition sufficient to support sustained offensive operations.)

Puller provided a candid appraisal of both sides in the conflict. He cautioned against either overestimating the enemy or taking them lightly. Drawing on his knowledge of history, he pointed out the tenacity of the Chinese Communists evident in Mao Tse-tung's Long March in the 1930s. In his mind, it was a feat seldom "equaled in the annals of warfare." However, "they freeze just as solid as we do when things get down to a certain temperature." He then "proudly noted" that the 1st Marine Division had never fallen back except when ordered to do so by higher headquarters. He commended the British, French, and Turks as the best of the allies, giving particular praise to the latter, who were "just as good as the Marines." His pointed reference to Marines standing fast in combat was another clear, though unstated, jab at the U.S. Army.

Up to that point in the press conference, Chesty had carefully skirted the edge of the minefield, but he walked right into it when he explained how to produce first-class fighters. He intended to train his new brigade "as Marines have always been trained." That standard was simple: "My troops are going to get plenty of physical training and training in marksmanship. I want them to be able to march twenty miles, the last five at double time, and then be ready to fight." But he believed men also needed to learn how to endure the hardships of war. Reporters scribbling furiously in notebooks each recorded this last strong statement in a different way. The United Press correspondent quoted the brigadier: "I think a man can be trained so he is proud to be a rough, tough soldier without the conveniences of life. I tell my troops, 'You're men. You don't need ice cream cones to fight.'" Puller supposedly added that American bases featured "too many canteens and ice cream cones . . . we have to get down to fighting and throw out the women and the YMCA." In another version, Chesty allegedly asserted: "Throw all these girls out of the camps. Get rid of the ice cream and candy. Give 'em beer and whiskey—that'll help some. Get some pride in them. Tell them they're men—they don't need ice cream and candy."

Puller went one step further and compared the fighting spirit of the populations of the main antagonists. He ascribed part of the opponent's resolve to Marxist political success: "All [the peasants] want is a piece of land that they can call their own. . . . The Communists all over Asia are giving them just that. Did South Korea ever give anyone any land? Hell no!" He reserved harsh words for his own countrymen. "What the American people want to do is fight a war without getting hurt. You can't do that anymore than you can go into a barroom fight without getting hurt. . . . Unless the American people are willing to send their sons out to fight an aggressor, there just isn't going to be any United States. A bunch of foreign soldiers will come over and take our women and breed not only another race of people but a hardier race of people." It was a stronger version of his 1946 declaration in New Orleans: "We can lick 'em, if America gets hard. . . . Just as long as Americans have the will to fight."[4]

The blunt declarations about rugged training and a soft public were the stuff of headlines; they appeared in bold type the next day on the front pages of newspapers across the country. Editors with a proclivity for sensationalism played up the story with titles such as "Give 'Em Whiskey, Keep Girls Away." One writer even baldly acknowledged in his article that he expected it to generate controversy: "[Puller] will have a chance to put his 'tough' program in effect—despite expected howls of dismay from the WCTU [Woman's Christian Temperance Union] and other reform groups." Another paper juxtaposed a stateside photo of a beaming Chesty with that of a weary, dejected-looking soldier in the war zone. The caption implied the Marine general had not given the Army a fair evaluation: "His remarks probably didn't impress GIs like [this one] . . . rescued by a tank crew after he and six comrades had dodged ambush fire behind enemy lines in Korea for six days." (It failed to explain, of course, that the group probably had ended up in that situation when its parent outfit had bugged out—proof of Puller's point.) Some of the articles already carried quotes from people objecting to one or more of the general's remarks. The Associated Press sent out a temperate version summarizing the general's most impassioned remarks in a single sentence: "His ideas of training indicate a tough time ahead for the brigade, and a tough outfit when they have satisfied their general."[5]

Chesty spent the day flying east. The correspondents knew they had a good story and peppered him with fresh questions at each stop. Puller's answers fanned the blaze of controversy. In Chicago, he asserted there was "too damn much recreation" for troops whose only purpose was "to fight," and "they're not being taught that now." A Washington reporter played up the angle of interservice rivalry: "The general's comments—he insisted repeatedly that he was not criticizing any service—appeared meant for the Army. He pointedly told reporters at National Airport here that the Marines 'don't get ice cream.'" The same writer noted that Chesty "cut loose with some tart comments" about airpower: "He said the Air Force did not understand close air support, 'does not believe in it,' and 'has never practiced it.'" Puller also attacked the policy of joint control of air assets in Korea. By now, he was well aware that he had stirred up a hornet's nest. He told attendees at the impromptu press conference in Washington: "I didn't get shot in Korea and I hope I don't get hung here."[6]

Puller was overjoyed to finally make it home to Saluda, but the press gave him little opportunity to savor the moment. Reporters began hounding him in the village the next day, one of them accosting him as he tried to relax in civilian clothes on the front porch of the Evans home. He denied making most of the remarks attributed to him and claimed: "I have said nothing critical of the United States government or of any of its military services." He refused to be drawn into answering more questions, except to say, "Any military man knows that rigid training is necessary to ensure victory." He added: "I'd just like to get some rest, enjoy being with my family, and be left alone." By the end of the day, Chesty had drafted a formal statement repudiating the quotations attributed to him; he gave it to all newsmen who approached him for an interview.[7]

Generals at HQMC stepped into the fray in response to citizen protest letters and press queries. They answered every one with variations of a single theme—that reporters had "misinterpreted and twisted" Puller's "hurried remarks." They cited Chesty's reputation for attending religious services in the field as proof he would not have advocated use of alcohol. Lieutenant General Merwin H. Silverthorn, the assistant commandant, provided more detail in response to an inquiry from a congressman. He explained that Puller had "used 'ice cream cones' figuratively to describe what he meant by distractions from the training program." According to Silverthorn, a reporter then interjected: "I suppose you'd give them beer and whiskey." Chesty thought that was a wisecrack and quipped in return: "Might be—but what they need is pride." The assistant commandant summed up his case: "General Puller is one of the most distinguished Marines in the history of our Corps. . . . We find it easy to support him when he claims that a story-hungry reporter tried to twist a joking assent into a scandal." Headquarters was standing foursquare behind Chesty. His choice of words might not have been wise, but Marine leaders shared his opinions about tough training, the future of warfare, and the shortcomings of other services.[8]

The United Press published Puller's statement denying any critical remarks, but appended its version of the San Francisco press conference. The UP reporter claimed that Chesty's aide had asked the writers not to use any of the general's statements "that would get him in trouble." The correspondent then supposedly cleared all quotes with the junior officer. United Press was not the original source of the damaging "beer and whiskey" phrase, however; it appeared first in the *San Francisco Examiner* article. That writer had hinted in his story at the aide's after-the-fact restrictions: "Obviously, the general had much more to say, but he evidently considered it better left unsaid." In Puller's favor, the *Examiner* reporter clearly had a penchant for exaggeration, declaring in his introductory paragraphs that Peleliu was "one of the worst slaughters in history." The West Coast paper also had an anti-Marine reputation. Following the Smith-versus-Smith controversy on Saipan in 1944, it had editorialized that the Army was more cautious and competent, and thus suffered fewer casualties than the Corps.[9]

In all likelihood, Puller had said more than he was willing to admit once he realized the scale of the storm he had unleashed. The quotes in the newspaper accounts closely tracked the tone and substance of his frustrated letters to Virginia. General O. P. Smith also believed his former ADC had spoken out of turn. Smith wrote Jerry Thomas just days later: "Lewie Puller got a few things off his chest when he returned. . . . After living with Lewie for a few months, I would say that what I read in the press sounded very much like Lewie." Few Marines acquainted with the outspoken brigadier "took the denial very seriously."[10]

The controversy burned brightly, but died relatively quickly. A good portion of the public—equally dismayed at events in Korea—accepted his critique as an honest assessment of the situation. A few citizens even took pen in hand and came to his defense. One letter to a Dallas newspaper chastised the editor for printing a letter calling for the brigadier's resignation: "[The writer] should get on his knees and thank God for men like Chesty Puller, who have enabled him to enjoy the ease and comfort of life in Abilene and insured his right to worship as he pleases." One supportive editorial observed that the Marine leader "pulls no punches in talking, just as he pulls no punches in fighting." It then applauded his stance: "He is no exponent of soft and easy living for the GI, 'tis plain. But then, war isn't soft and war isn't easy—and victory goes to the side that is harder and tougher and can dish it out and take it better than the other fellow." A Richmond newspaper praised Puller as "one of the greatest fighting men the Old Dominion has produced . . . a soldier without fear, absolutely idolized by his men." *Time* magazine made no comment on the merits of Chesty's statements, but tellingly printed them next to a piece on the woes of an activated National Guard outfit labeled "the cry-baby division."[11]

The truly lamentable aspect of the episode was that Puller's valid points about tough training and the use of airpower were overwhelmed by meaningless rhetoric about whiskey and ice cream. For Chesty's part, it had been a hard lesson in how to deal with the media. *Time* noted that he "pulled his chest in, had no more to say." What he would remember most, however, was the stinging personal criticism from angry citizens. Years later he would admit: "I don't believe I was ever hurt so much as by some of those letters."[12]

☆   ☆   ☆

The people of Saluda were unfazed by the controversy and went all out to welcome their adopted son. The members of a prominent local club invited him to be the speaker at their monthly meeting, with the specific mission "to say what you wish, as you wish, on the record or off the record at your discretion, with no congressional or presidential strings attached." The group waived all other business to listen to Chesty. Immediately after, the county celebrated his return in the high school auditorium. Following a rendition of the "Marines' Hymn" by the student band, an ex-governor and the commonwealth's attorney each took a turn at introducing Puller to the exuberant crowd. Fresh from months of hard campaigning, he looked trim and fit, and every inch a hero, with rows of ribbons ascending far above the left-breast pocket of his uniform.

Chesty opened his talk by acknowledging "a certain notoriety that I've gained in the newspapers." He then spoke about Korea and gravely reiterated his belief that the nation had to take serious steps to protect itself. In an echo of the ancient English requirement that yeomen practice weekly with longbows on village greens, he suggested that "every American citizen" should own a rifle and train with it on firing ranges "at every courthouse." He claimed this would be "one of the greatest things we can do here in America as far as preparedness is concerned." He also pronounced his attachment to his wife's birthplace: "When my days of battle are over I would like to feel that Middlesex County will be my home."[13]

Chesty spent most of his remaining leave with family and friends. He delighted in taking five-year-old Lewis Jr. fishing, and doted on his two daughters. The only sour moment came when Martha had to have her tonsils out. The Pullers took her to a hospital in Richmond for the surgery. He carried her as close to the operating room as he could, then tried to turn her over to the care of an orderly. She clung tightly to him and wailed as he pried her loose. As she disappeared down the corridor, crying loudly, he remarked sorrowfully to his wife: "She will never forgive me, Virginia. This is worse than Peleliu."[14]

☆ ☆ ☆

After a month of leave, the Pullers made a "leisurely" drive to the West Coast. He reported for duty at Camp Pendleton on July 7 and rejoined old friends. General O. P. Smith commanded both the base and all troops in the region. Fellow brigadier Merrill Twining headed up the Training and Replacement Command.[15]

Puller's new outfit initially existed only on paper in midsummer

1951. The core of the 3d Brigade was the 3d Marines, an infantry regiment reactivated barely two weeks earlier and still just a skeleton. Eventually there would be artillery and tank battalions and other supporting units. When fully manned at its authorized wartime strength, Chesty's outfit would have nearly seven thousand men. In the meantime, it underwent "the normal growing pains" of starting up from scratch. Headquarters Marine Corps provided no organized cadre upon which to build. Instead, Puller would have to meld hundreds of newly transferred veteran officers and NCOs, dozens of recently commissioned lieutenants, and thousands of fresh graduates of boot camp into a smoothly functioning whole. It was a herculean task.[16]

Smith saw the primary mission of the base as readying individual replacements for Korea, but there was always the prospect that an escalation in fighting might require the deployment of the brigade. Puller was determined to be ready for anything. The beer-and-whiskey controversy did not dissuade him from his goal of stressing weapons proficiency and physical conditioning. He believed history supported his view that the Corps was only as good as the capabilities of the men who formed it: "Since the Revolutionary War, the Marine Corps has placed a great deal of importance on training the individual Marine. I plan to follow that policy." As men flooded in that summer, Chesty formed them into units and tutored them in the traditional hard school of Marine combat training, peppered now with a measure of fresh lessons from the Korean War.[17]

Despite Puller's assertion that the nature of war had not changed since the days of the Roman legions, the Marine Corps still needed to address technological advances. The preeminent concern was the atomic bomb, which could wipe out an amphibious force as it gathered offshore to conduct a concentrated assault against a defended beach. The Corps already had a theoretical answer to that problem. A 1946 board, headed by Lemuel Shepherd and including O. P. Smith and Twining, had postulated that vertical envelopment was the solution. Helicopters, flying from widely dispersed ships, would land troops behind shore defenses. Once these units attacked from the rear and cleared a portion of the coast, large seaplanes would join the helicopters in bringing in reinforcements and supplies. Thus the enemy would never have a massed target for his nuclear weapons. The difficulty in implementing the idea was the lack of suitable equipment. The helicopter had been only a marvelous toy in the immediate aftermath of World War II, but models capable of carrying a practical payload were appearing in the early 1950s. Chesty quickly found himself in the forefront of this technical and tactical revolution, since he commanded the only Marine combat force on the West Coast. It would serve as the test bed for the new ideas.[18]

Puller's education began when Shepherd (still CG of FMFPac) nominated him to attend the four-day Special Weapons Orientation Course at Sandia Base, New Mexico, in August 1951. There he received an introduction to the atomic bomb, but he was not especially impressed. He recalled his experience in World War II, where every man carried a gas mask into battle, and threw it away soon after. Both sides had possessed poison gas, but fear of retaliation prevented use of the arsenals. He anticipated that the same thing would occur with nuclear weapons now that the Soviets also had them. His opinions notwithstanding, Chesty was one of a very few Marines to participate in the training at Sandia, and he soon had occasion to use his knowledge. The brigade was preparing for Landing Exercise B-1, scheduled for February 1952. Colloquially known as LEX Baker One, it would be the largest amphibious operation on the West Coast since 1949 and a major test of the new vertical envelopment doctrine. Puller acknowledged that this emerging method of assault was "one of the most important types of training today."[19]

In the meantime, the Corps continued to grow as its supporters in Congress fought hard on its behalf. Toward the end of 1951, Truman authorized the expansion of the Marines to three divisions and three air wings. On January 7, 1952, the 3d Marine Division came back into existence and absorbed the 3d Brigade. Twining, a senior brigadier, assumed temporary command of the reactivated organization, while Puller became the assistant division commander. Chesty was not entirely happy with the change, since he felt he had put together a fine outfit: "I am sure the [brigade] could have undertaken any combat assignment with high proficiency. . . . The officers and men exhibited real ability and morale was outstanding. I hated to see the 3d Brigade broken up without being employed."[20]

LEX Baker One got underway on February 9, 1952, with Puller commanding the landing force, which consisted of the reinforced 3d Marines. The exercise opened with a period of joint training with the

Navy and culminated in a full-scale amphibious assault across the
Pendleton beaches in late February. Given the limited number (and
equally limited capacity) of helicopters available, only a portion of the
force could go ashore by air. But the aerial envelopment "was synchro-
nized perfectly" with troops flowing ashore in rubber boats and traditional landing craft. Both Chesty and his chief of staff, Colonel Ed
Snedeker, thought the operation "was quite successful." The admiral
commanding the amphibious task force was very pleased with both the
outcome and the work of the senior Marine: "BrigGen Puller's performance of duty was outstanding. Through his cooperative attitude
and that of his subordinates, and the close supervision with which he
handled his embarked troops, he instilled in all the participating forces
a great spirit of enthusiasm for the operation as a whole, and contributed greatly to its success."[21]

A few months later, Chesty's troops worked the opposite end of the
nuclear puzzle, this time practicing how to fight with the support of
atomic bombs. Elements of the 3d Marine Division deployed to Yucca
Flats, Nevada, where they observed a real blast at close range and followed it up with offensive operations. Headquarters proudly boasted
that "Marines were closer to ground zero during an atomic blast than
any other persons have been except those present at either Nagasaki or
Hiroshima." Experience in this exercise, Desert Rock IV, would serve
as the basis for the Corps' first doctrine for the employment of nuclear
weapons. Puller probably was not present in Nevada, but as one of only
three nuclear-trained officers in the division, he certainly must have
been involved in the planning for this momentous operation.[22]

The lure of technology did not distract Chesty from his emphasis
on the basics. First the brigade, then the division, experienced his ideas
of how to train for war. Observers noted that Puller's outfit "had been
honed to combat-sharpness—not by casual bivouacs or close-order
drill; but by rugged three-day marches through the scrubby boondocks
of Camp Pendleton, by night problems in surf, sand and silt, and by furious three-pronged assaults utilizing helicopters, rubber boats and
LCVPs." One unit of service troops standing inspection found that the
general overlooked no details. To the surprise and chagrin of many of
the young Marines, Puller ordered them to take off their boots and
socks and put on the spares that were supposed to be in their packs.
Many had none, because they assumed no one would ever check. The
general made sure the lesson was driven home—he ordered them to

march back to their company area wearing whatever footgear had been on their backs. It was not a long walk, even in bare feet, but word of the incident spread throughout the brigade and had the desired effect. In other instances, he had Marines stand inspection wearing only one boot, so he could check their feet, a habit he hoped to instill in younger leaders. He made no secret of his strong feelings about readiness for war: "A training officer who sends men out to the combat battalions soft of body and ignorant of their weapons ought to be court-martialed. He is guilty of manslaughter."[23]

☆ ☆ ☆

Puller continued to receive accolades for his service in Korea. The Navy Department Board of Decorations initially rejected Smith's Navy Cross recommendations for the regimental commanders at the Chosin Reservoir, in Chesty's case because he already had received the Distinguished Service Cross for part of the period covered by the new citation. Smith learned of the problem and wrote a new endorsement that lauded Puller's "vital contribution" to the defense of Koto-ri and the breakout to Hungnam. The Commandant's office "heartily concurred" and the awards board finally approved the medal for the period December 5–10, 1950.[24]

Smith presented the decoration at the 3d Marine Division's Saturday morning parade on February 2, 1952. Virginia first heard of the event when Mrs. Smith called her that morning and invited her to attend—Lewis had neglected to tell his wife about it. As the base commander bestowed the award, he jestingly whispered: "Lewie, this is your fifth Navy Cross, and they ought to do this like they do with the Air Medal . . . they ought to give you the Medal of Honor." (At that time, a fifth Air Medal brought the automatic award of the higher Distinguished Flying Cross.)[25]

Chesty already had been in a class by himself with four Navy Crosses—the only Marine ever so honored. The fifth award elevated him another notch. Around this time, he also received the Ulchi Medal, the Korean government's second highest decoration. Finally, there were three Air Medals for his numerous flights, in helicopters and observation planes, which often drew small arms fire. Now the media accurately called him "one of the Marine Corps' most highly decorated officers."[26]

There was a move to grant Puller an even higher honor. Gregory

"Pappy" Boyington, a Basic School student under Chesty, had gone on to command the famed Black Sheep Squadron in World War II and become one of the Corps' highest-scoring aces. For his daring feats in the air, he received the Medal of Honor and a Navy Cross. In February 1952, he wrote to President Truman and argued that Puller deserved the nation's highest award for valor. The former flier alleged that "because of professional jealousy in the higher echelons this truly great and courageous man has not been given his just deserts." (Pappy's motives were not entirely altruistic, since he spent most of the letter explaining that he had met a similar fate and also rated numerous awards he had never received.) The issue eventually landed in the lap of Jerry Thomas, now a lieutenant general and assistant commandant of the Marine Corps. He informed Truman's office that records at Headquarters showed that Puller "has never been recommended for the award of the Medal of Honor." Without documentation that a field commander had made such a nomination, there was no legal foundation for reviewing the record and upgrading one of the five Navy Crosses. It was a refrain HQMC would sing on many more occasions in the future.[27]

The spate of decorations also fueled fresh media interest in Puller. The *Saturday Evening Post,* a popular publication with a pro-Marine bent, printed a major piece on the feisty brigadier in March 1952. The bold title trumpeted him as the "Toughest Marine in the Corps," while large type underneath lauded him as "a real warrior general—the kind who wins the battle or dies on the field." The story opened with the beer-and-whiskey controversy, followed by a repeat of Chesty's wake-up call to the nation: "What the hell kind of people have we got in this country? . . . The trouble is, we try to kid ourselves into thinking that you can fight a war without getting hurt." He made it abundantly clear that the other services had fallen prey to that mistaken view:

> Reflecting that impossible wish, you find one branch of the service, before Korea, stressing in its recruiting such stuff as "Secure your future. Learn a trade." Another was almost guaranteeing its recruits that they wouldn't ever get shot at. The Marine Corps never tried to kid anybody. We tell our Marines that they are going to get hurt. We tell them they are going to go through hell. But we tell them, too, that whatever they are called upon to do, it will be no worse than Marines have done before. We try to teach them that

> it is a proud thing, a glorious thing, to fight as Marines have always fought, without counting the cost. And above all, we try to teach them that there are some things worse than wounds or death.[28]

The article provided Puller with a platform to sound off on the nature of military leadership and other issues. He encapsulated his ideal commander in a few sentences: "Warlike. A savagely fighting leader of combat troops. Shows positive taste for fighting, but with good common sense. Won't order his men where he won't go himself. Swears at his officers and men, but knows their names and makes them feel they are intimate with him. A driving, furious, fighting type whose men both respect and fear him." He professed that was "what I've always tried to be." He reiterated his disdain for military schools: "The best way to learn about war is in battle. You learn a hell of a lot more in one fight than you learn in a year at Staff College. Reading and studying is all right, but most officers spend too much time in schools." He did not entirely reject the idea of military education, however: "An officer never stops learning, and that one great source of knowledge is the history of men and battles of the past."

Chesty rehashed grievances against the Army and the Air Force, many of them arising out of the Korean War. There was the loss of control of Marine aviation, the absence of Marines in corps-level commands, and the sense that Marine outfits had been slighted in the award of unit decorations. He also criticized the linear defensive strategy being employed in the conflict, preferring instead to focus on the opponent's forces, not territory. His solution was to "form up the 8th Army in columns of divisions" and "keep an unrelenting pressure on the enemy until he was destroyed, no matter if we had to chase him all over Korea." Publicly, at least, Chesty no longer let these irritations over policy sour his opinion on the virtue of a military career. The article stated that he had "no intention of retiring" and that he wanted Lewis Jr. to follow in his footsteps. Puller showed only a justifiable pride in his many accomplishments: "A soldier, unless he is dishonest, can never leave his children much in the way of wealth. But he can leave them a rich heritage of courage, of loyalty, of service to his country."

Most of the article was a breezy, flattering portrait of Chesty's storied career. Typically, the writer took some liberties with the facts. Supposedly Puller had promptly left VMI and enlisted in the Corps "when

World War I broke out." There was an implication that he had been a lieutenant while the fighting was going on, but had been kept in the States because he was too good, "while less competent men went to France to lead the rifle platoons." His experience in the Banana Wars again was vastly inflated; allegedly he had participated in "forty-odd fire fights" in Haiti and "at least sixty pitched battles" in Nicaragua. As with earlier published accounts, both the real glory and the misstatements contained in this one would become part of the Puller legend.

Perhaps the only really surprising feature of the article was the emphasis on his concern that he might be forced to retire for his outspokenness. After detailing Chesty's criticism of the public, the press, and the other services, the writer strangely claimed: "Puller's present reluctance to sound off loud and clear when he thinks the Marine Corps is getting kicked around is a reflection of his desire to round out his career in battle." Referring to an expectation of a looming war with the Soviets, Chesty vowed: "I don't want anybody putting the skids under me just when a big fight is coming up. I want to be ready to go when the gong rings." There was some basis in fact for his concern, since President Truman had developed a well-earned reputation for trying to quash military opinion that differed from administration policy. But there had been no high-level backlash regarding the beer-and-whiskey episode, only strong support from Headquarters Marine Corps. Perhaps the magazine merely was seeking to elevate Puller's status in the eyes of readers by making him appear to be an earnest David under threat from some bureaucratic Goliath. Or, this simply may have been an indication that Chesty felt that some senior leaders were hostile to him. That apprehension would grow with the passage of time.[29]

As it turned out, the article generated no reaction from above and mostly praise from the public. Puller was "very pleased" that only positive mail came to Camp Pendleton: "I even received some letters of apology for letters written to me previously about my statements on returning from Korea." Chesty's strong opinions especially rang true with many of those who had suffered through the purgatory of the first months in Korea. Staff Sergeant Archie Van Winkle, a reservist who had received the Medal of Honor in the Chosin Reservoir campaign, was moved to write Puller after reading the *Saturday Evening Post*. He noted how his fellow citizen-Leathernecks in the 7th Marines had been ill prepared when war took them halfway around the world, so he applauded Chesty's emphasis on training. He also believed that Puller was the epitome of the institution: "We are proud of you, because you are not just one Marine, you are the whole Corps! You are what we think of when asked to tell of the Corps and its leaders. You are in fact, what the Marine Corps is founded on—tough fighting men." The letters "made the article worthwhile" to Chesty, but the general aspired to more: "My only hope is that we as a nation will learn from our experiences in Korea some of the things we failed to learn in the last two wars. Unfortunately, such knowledge comes only a little bit at a time."[30]

As a general and well-known hero, Puller was now in demand for public appearances. He traveled frequently and the Marine Corps even sent him back to West Point, Virginia, in April 1952 for the 250th anniversary commemoration of King William County. As the region's designated favorite son, he delivered the primary address at a ceremony honoring those who had served in wars dating back to British colonial days. With the conflict in Korea still seething, it was an unabashedly martial speech that repeated his call for a renewed national will to win. Referring with equal familiarity to the Bible and to Douglas Southall Freeman's works on the Confederacy, Chesty summoned fellow citizens to rise to the occasion: "There will always be wars and rumors of wars. Also remember that there are far worse things than death and destruction. Further remember that there is no substitute for performance of duty whether you are a statesman or a fighting man and that there must be character and integrity at all times." He closed with optimism in the ultimate outcome: "I have every confidence in our youth and under the continued blessings of the Almighty God, we will always go forward."[31]

One of the most enjoyable events for Puller had been a trip to Philadelphia for the 1st Marine Division Association's fourth annual reunion in August 1951. It was his first opportunity to attend one of the gatherings, still composed largely of World War II veterans. The long weekend of camaraderie included a parade through the city. Chesty marched at the head of the 1st Marines contingent. After he passed the reviewing stand, he led his impromptu force on an "additional foray"— to a nearby pub, where he bought drinks for all of them. That evening, after the scheduled speakers had finished their presentations at the formal dinner in the ornate hotel ballroom, many of those present started chanting: "We want Puller." They finally fell quiet when he gave the crowd a brief but rousing off-the-cuff talk. Following a memorial service for fallen comrades on the last day, the association elected new officers. Red Mike Edson, retired since 1947, took over as the president and Puller became the second vice president. The ebullient Chesty was acknowledged to be "one of the convention's outstanding personalities."[32]

☆   ☆   ☆

As Puller came up on the end of a year at Pendleton, it was time for him to move on to new duties. Lemuel Shepherd had succeeded to the commandancy in January 1952, a fact that pleased Chesty given the personal connection between the two men. The brigadier was disappointed a month later when the new Commandant informed Puller he would take over Troop Training Unit Pacific (TTUPac) during the summer. It was not the division Chesty wanted very badly, but the job at least involved preparing units for battle. He admitted as much to Shepherd in a sentence remarkably similar to one he had written in 1946: "The world does not promise peace and I feel that the training of our Marines is our most important and vital assignment." Still, he would rather be the one leading them off to war, a fact he also made plain to the Commandant: "I have been blessed with a strong and healthy body during my fifty-three years of life and I trust time is not running out before I get the opportunity for which I aspire." Shepherd definitely was not placing Puller in a backwater billet; the Commandant himself had filled the same job on the East Coast just after World War II. He also pointed out to Chesty that every brigadier who had served so far in one of the two TTUs had been promoted to major general. The godfather of Lewis Jr. even had looked out for the welfare of the Puller children, delaying Chesty's transfer so they could complete the school year at Pendleton.[33]

Puller's reputation within the Corps was continuing to grow, frequently one Marine at a time. A chief warrant officer was impressed that the general spent two hours chatting with him during his welcome-aboard meeting. A group of fighter pilots conducting escape and evasion training at Pendleton felt it was a "special treat" when the renowned infantry leader stopped to talk to them. Puller still had the right touch with units, too. Chesty's driver, Staff Sergeant Orville Jones, recalled that one of Puller's first acts as commander was to set up a beer hall to serve the men of the brigade, so they did not have to leave their own area in search of relaxation outside the barracks. The general certainly didn't coddle them, though; in addition to hard training, he maintained strict discipline. When he discovered that men were skipping morning chow and sleeping in, he ordered them marched to the mess hall each day. One of the brand-new privates in the outfit later realized that Puller's methods had taught him to be a "good Marine" and helped him "become a man."[34]

Chesty's seniors had been pleased with his performance as well. Smith praised him for demonstrating "outstanding qualities of leadership in his handling of the problems of the 3d Marine Brigade" as it grew from nothing. The general spelled out those attributes in Puller's fitness report: "A vigorous, aggressive officer who pursues his objectives without deviation. A splendid leader of men who inspires complete confidence on the part of his subordinates." Major General Robert H. Pepper, the eventual commander of the 3d Marine Division, accurately captured his ADC's strengths in a few words: "A highly qualified troop leader. General Puller is loyal, honest, and firm in his convictions."[35]

All in all, it had been a very good tour for Chesty. He had commanded a combat unit, been able to make his strongly held views known to a wide audience, avoided any unwanted controversy, and enjoyed an extended period of home life with his family. The latter undoubtedly contributed to his relatively quiet year, since Virginia was a mellowing influence on him. The chief of staff also helped in that department. When the frustrations of dealing with higher headquarters grew too great, Puller often ordered his senior assistant to draft a letter of protest. Colonel Snedeker would take his time writing a couple of versions, one of them temperate, and would place them on his commander's desk days later, after Chesty had cooled off. Invariably Puller either let the matter pass without action, or signed the more restrained document.[36]

Puller made the most of his time with his family and lavished as much attention on them as he could. He also was happy that he now was able to provide them with more of the material things he had missed when he was growing up. The Puller quarters were not elaborate, but, as a general, he did rate two enlisted men to serve as his cook and steward. He especially enjoyed giving his wife and children presents whenever there was some money beyond Virginia's strict budget. Toward the end of

1951, he and other Korean veterans finally received special combat pay for their service. Chesty kept the windfall a secret from his spouse and spent it all on Christmas gifts, including a .22 caliber rifle for Lewis Jr. There also were presents that money could not buy. One of them was the North Korean bugle Puller had sent home from the front. At Pendleton, he had his chief armorer emboss it with "Lewis B. Puller, Jr."

Chesty still left the imposition of parental punishment to Virginia, but he took a definite interest in building the character of his son and daughters. He had been impressed by the steadfastness of Catholic chaplains in combat situations and expected that nuns would bring the same sort of discipline and perseverance to their mission of educating students. He thus enrolled Virginia McC and the twins in parochial schools whenever he could. He also treated them as his mother had handled him when he was young, giving them considerable responsibility for their own decisions and actions. All three children quickly learned that his disappointment was harder to bear than any other penalty.[37]

Lewis Jr. was now old enough to absorb some of the things his father wanted to teach him, and Chesty was particularly proud that his namesake was beginning to exhibit the legendary family toughness. On one father-son hunting expedition in the Pendleton hills, the boy slipped and fell down a steep bank. Little Lewis got up dry-eyed, the rifle still firmly in his grip. The crusty brigadier later crowed to friends: "Looks like he's got the stuff in him to make a soldier."[38]

"A School Teacher's Job"
Training Other Men for War
June 1952–May 1954

Brigadier General Puller reported for duty at the Troop Training Unit Pacific on June 10, 1952. While the family moved into spacious quarters at the Marine Corps Recruit Depot in San Diego, Chesty got acquainted with his office at the Naval Amphibious Base. The installation was located on Coronado, the long, narrow peninsula of sand that forms the western shore of San Diego Bay. Normally Chesty's commute would have necessitated a costly ferry ride or a thirty-mile drive around the bay, but one of the perquisites of his rank was a Navy barge, dedicated to his use, that took him to and from work each day.[1]

Troop Training Unit Pacific had come into existence in July 1943. Its mission was to instruct individuals and units in the landing force aspects of amphibious warfare. It provided this training to all services, and was itself joint in composition, though Marines formed the bulk of its staff. It was a part of the Amphibious Training Command run by an admiral. These organizations had counterparts on the Atlantic coast. Puller's outfit was slightly different from TTULant, since he also had a hand in operating the newly created Troop Training Team (TTT). The latter group, based in Japan, performed the same function for units in the Far East. The TTT instructor force consisted of personnel provided on a six-month rotational basis from TTUPac.

Chesty's small command offered two types of training. The TTU conducted specialist courses for individuals in subjects such as em-

barkation and naval gunfire. All other instruction was for units, generally at the regimental level. Mobile training teams from TTU provided a
thirty-day package to "indoctrinate" outfits in amphibious warfare. The
early pioneers of TTU had adopted that term because they did not feel
the time allowed was sufficient to fully qualify a unit to make a combat
landing. Puller agreed "that amphibious training should be considered
in the light of post-graduate work" and that Marines should "get as
much training in amphibious warfare as possible." Without such emphasis, he thought no body of men rated "the full distinction of
Marines." It was his intention to ensure that USMC units "get all the
amphibious training which we [at TTU] are capable of giving them."[2]

The importance of the TTUs had skyrocketed after the early days of
the Korean War. In 1949, General Omar N. Bradley, the chief of staff of
the Army, had told Congress: "I am wondering whether we shall ever
have another large-scale amphibious operation. Frankly, the atomic
bomb, properly delivered, about precludes such a possibility." The 1950
landing at Inchon had proven his pronouncement premature, at best,
and Army regiments now made up the bulk of units undergoing instruction.[3]

As with many previous assignments, Puller's selection for the billet
owed much to his reputation as a trainer. But there was a great deal
more at work on this occasion. His education at Sandia (rare among
Marine officers of any rank at that point) and his leadership of the 3d
Brigade (especially in LEX Baker One) probably made him the most
experienced brigadier in the Corps when it came to "helicopter operations . . . and the effects of the atomic bomb on amphibious operations."
He thus was the perfect man to head up one of the major organizations
charged with passing such knowledge on to the operating forces. (His
cordial relationship with Navy admirals may have been an asset, too,
since TTU fell under a Navy chain of command. In spite of Puller's
usual disdain for other services, he recognized the importance of having "Marine Corps promoters" in the Navy and nurtured those who
were friendly to the Corps.) To Chesty's mind, however, it was just "a
school teacher's job," and he remained unsatisfied with the billet.[4]

Puller's narrow description of his duties did not prevent him from
trying to make a much bigger impact. His practical bent on emerging
doctrine came to the fore during a series of exercises that tested the
ability of Marine aviation to support ground forces in the vertical as-

sault. Chesty was an observer at a February 1952 operation involving the movement of troops from El Toro air station near the California coast to the Marine Corps' auxiliary landing field in the Mojave Desert. He threw a bucket of cold reality on the planners: "It was a waste of the taxpayer's money. Everything proceeded at a snail's pace, and the initial elements that were landed could have been handily wiped out before the buildup began. It was run by El Toro, and they became so involved in the techniques of flying from here to there that the tactical situation was apparently forgotten. . . . I certainly didn't learn anything that I didn't already know."[5]

That harsh judgment notwithstanding, he firmly believed in the need to formulate new methods and realistically test them. He explained to a former subordinate at HQMC: "The more I think about this matter of amphibious training the more convinced I become of the necessity of conducting amphibious exercises on a corps level in order to train our higher commanders and their staffs and to iron out the 'bugs' that develop as we evolve new amphibious doctrines. We certainly cannot do this if we continue our present stereotyped exercises over the same limited training areas which, in effect, reduce their scope to the successive landing of RCTs [regimental combat teams]. The impression that I have been gaining is that these exercises are losing their training value and are slowly degenerating into canned demonstrations."

Chesty had no grand solutions for the tactical and technical challenges, but he knew how the Marine Corps could fix the training and testing issue. He wanted to make use of the 1914 Bryan-Chamorro treaty, which gave the United States a ninety-nine-year lease on the rights to build a canal across Nicaragua. An obscure provision of the nearly forgotten agreement allowed the United States to establish a naval base on the Gulf of Fonseca. Puller reasoned that this tract on the Nicaraguan coast would give large Marine forces plenty of room to operate. He put his staff to work on the details and in April 1953 "submitted a concrete proposal to CNO [the Chief of Naval Operations] via the chain of command." He was pleased that the admiral in charge of the Amphibious Training Command "received the idea enthusiastically and indorsed my letter accordingly."[6]

When the suggestion went nowhere in Washington, Chesty broached it directly with the Commandant during the latter's June 1953 visit to Marine installations in southern California. The TTU commander brought additional arguments to bear in a subsequent letter to Shepherd: "Extensive training of Marine units in [Nicaragua] would help to keep more Marines overseas. This would be particularly important if the 1st Marine Division is released from the Far East for I firmly believe that Congress will support a large Marine Corps only so long as a large percent of it remains overseas." The Commandant showed little interest, though, and the recommendation died altogether when the CNO tabled it due to possible "adverse political inferences."[7]

Puller was certain he could have sealed the deal with the Nicaraguan leaders over a case of brandy. The American ambassador, a former Army infantryman, tended to agree after he learned the Nicaraguan minister of war had served with Chesty in the Guardia. The diplomat reported: "The other day [the minister] spent quite a lot of time telling me about you when you were in Nicaragua with the Marine Corps. He has a great admiration for you. . . . Here's the funny thing, General, in spite of you Marines being down here this is still a friendly country towards the U.S. On the slightest provocation, the Guardia Nacional Band hauls off and plays the Marine Hymn."[8]

Puller considered the lack of action on his Nicaraguan proposal symptomatic of "these politics-ridden times." He disliked having to keep a tight lid on TTU's new staff planning problem, which focused on Indochina, because it might raise the same "adverse political inferences" as his Gulf of Fonseca idea. He remained equally upset with many aspects of the ongoing Korean War, and was certain government and military leaders were keeping the public in the dark. In late 1952 he read what he considered to be one of the rare honest media reports on the struggle and immediately passed it to a friend: "Every once in a while a bit of the truth comes out, although it happens so seldom that I wonder whether they are trying to prepare the American people for another reverse." Chesty was sure the Army also was censoring the news to minimize the role of the Corps, since he saw no references to the 1st Marine Division for "months." He was not surprised when the silence was broken by a report that "our Marines had been driven back." To his delight, the alleged tactic backfired: "For the past four days, however, they have been forced to give the 1st Marine Division plenty of good publicity. It looked as if after the powers that be had permitted the name 'Marine' to appear adversely, they were forced to tell the rest of the story. It's certainly nice to see at least part of the truth come out." He still was opposed to the "defensive war with its resulting attrition" and continued to wonder "why the American people will stand for it." For the time being, however, he was circumspect about these beliefs and expressed them only in private. The *Saturday Evening Post* article had elicited no trouble, but he was not about to test the waters again anytime soon. When a writer approached him to do another story on his career, he turned her down: "I feel that there has already been too much written on my behalf and that it would be unwise to have any more publicity."⁹

There were many who thought Puller should be speaking out more rather than less. A reserve major who had gone through TTU training begged the general to address some influential organizations: "Your graduation address to the classes on August 1 is just the type of a talk that I personally would like to have our local civilians hear. The days of eloquent speeches and oratory are outmoded. What the public wants and demands today are sincere statements and facts from men who have the experience and the knowledge of what they are talking of." That same month Puller attended the 1st Marine Division Association reunion in Washington, D.C. At the formal banquet, many of his former enlisted men again shouted rowdily for Chesty to get up and talk. Puller was embarrassed, since he thought Shepherd and other senior generals sitting at the head table might have taken offense at the attention lavished on one of their juniors.¹⁰

As 1953 appeared on the horizon, career concerns reasserted themselves in Chesty's mind for the first time since the late 1940s. He made inquiries about the forced retirement of an aviation brigadier. Finding that it was due to a strict interpretation of a seldom used provision in the law, Puller exclaimed to another officer: "How legal can you get!" Shortly afterward, the Corps held another retention board for senior generals, similar to the ones that Vandegrift had pushed through in 1946. Brigadiers were not on the chopping block, but the process and its results attracted Chesty's great interest. Part of this absorption with the fate of other generals may have been the natural concern of someone who was coming up on the tail end of a long career and wondering what would come next and when. Certainly his future was on his mind when he wrote Virginia's mother and aunt in April 1953: "With the best of luck, I can only remain in the Marine Corps seven more years; the statutory retirement age is sixty-two."¹¹

Despite Puller's concerns, there appeared to be little objective reason for him to worry. His relationship with Shepherd remained cordial even after the division reunions. The Commandant paid personal calls on the Pullers during each of his subsequent visits to the West Coast, and the two generals routinely exchanged friendly correspondence. Puller only had a few close friends in the senior ranks of the Corps, such as O. P. Smith and Twining, but the widespread support he had received from HQMC during the beer-and-whiskey controversy and his selection to command the brigade and TTU indicated that he had few, if any, strong enemies there. Nevertheless, his apprehensions would only increase with the passage of time.[12]

☆   ☆   ☆

In the fall of 1952, a Marine major stationed in Taiwan suggested that TTT provide its services to the fledgling Nationalist Chinese Marine Corps. Puller liked the idea, but realized it would present challenges. He wondered if the "language barrier" could be surmounted and was unsure where the ships would come from. He was sensitive to potential diplomatic concerns, too: "I can imagine the repercussions which might result from sending an American Transdiv [transport division] to Formosa [the former name of Taiwan] and beginning the loading of Nationalist troops!" Contrary to Chesty's expectations, leaders in Washington approved the scheme, and one of his mobile training teams received the mission to conduct the instruction.[13]

Puller wanted to visit his troops on Taiwan while they were working with the Chinese, but the admiral in charge of the Amphibious Training Command prevented it. The TTU commander finally got his chance for a trip to the Far East in May, but the Navy delayed his departure for a week and forced him to miss out on a major TTT landing exercise. This period seemed full of other small, but equally irritating, difficulties with the Corps' sister service. When leaders of both the Chinese and Korean Marine Corps came to visit the San Diego area, U.S. Navy commands monopolized their schedules and left little or no time for them to see TTU. In another instance, the CNO rejected recommendations on staffing TTT without even the courtesy of an explanation. To add insult to injury, a new admiral taking over the Amphibious Training Command was junior to the Marine brigadier. In response to one of the Navy's many inexplicable actions, Chesty resignedly wrote it off as "no more than we might have expected." His exasperation showed in the closing of a letter to Brigadier General William W. Davies, the head of TTT: "Well, Bill, I suppose that this is about enough of grunts, groans, and gripes for the present time."[14]

Fellow Marines also occasionally raised Puller's ire. He did not protest Colonel Henry "Jim" Crowe's transfer from TTU to the recruit depot because he thought the legendary competitive shooter would be running the marksmanship program there, but Crowe ended up in command of the headquarters battalion. Soon after, HQMC issued orders for TTUPac's other senior colonels to move to new duty stations. Chesty was "quite a bit perturbed over losing so many experienced colonels at one time," and took up the matter with Shepherd in a long personal letter. Puller stressed the need to keep at least one of his best subordinates because it was important to have "someone who is mentally agile and quick on his feet in order to deal with the Army and Navy commands with which we work." The Commandant would not reverse the decisions of his personnel office, but he did send TTU a "very able" replacement colonel who had once been Shepherd's own chief of staff. The brigadier was only partly mollified. Noting that all of his colonels would now be new to the command, he wrote back: "I sincerely hope, for the sake of my successor on this job, that they will not all be detached at the same time."[15]

☆   ☆   ☆

Puller finally flew west across the Pacific on May 17, 1953. After working layovers in Hawaii and Japan, he arrived in Taiwan on the 26th. He already had received "glowing reports" about the great work of his Marines and was beaming with pride: "It looks like one of those rare events that pleases everyone." His visit reinforced that notion. The U.S. Army major general in charge of the military assistance effort told Chesty that the Marines "had accomplished more than all of his other advisory groups combined." Puller, in turn, was "impressed with the fine physical condition of the Chinese Marines and with their potential combat ability."[16]

Two days later, Chesty returned to Japan to tour Army outfits receiving support from TTT. (One organization was the XVI Corps headquarters. Perhaps as a nudge for his still pending Nicaragua idea, Puller wrote Shepherd: "That is the first time to my knowledge that army units have shown an interest in corps-level amphibious instruction for several years.") From there it was on to Korea for a four-day visit with the 1st Marine Division and the 1st Marine Aircraft Wing. Elements of the Korean Marine Corps put on a live-fire demonstration for him and showed how far they had come since 1950. Puller acknowledged: "The KMCs have made real progress and now seem to have a first-class fighting organization." He broached the idea of making them the second international recipient of American amphibious training. There also were meetings with the commanders of Eighth Army and the U.N. forces.[17]

The effectiveness of TTUPac should have left Chesty feeling proud. Instead, the career anxieties hinted at in early 1953 had bubbled closer to the surface. The visit to his old division in Korea may have been the cause. He found things "very different" from 1951. More important was his continuing frustration with the direction of the war in Korea and, perhaps, his unfulfilled desire to command a division in combat. (He briefly had done so, of course, in March 1951, but only in an interim role as the acting CG.) Peace talks had been going on for some time, but the negotiations were just beginning to bear fruit in the late spring of 1953. It suddenly looked like the war would soon come to an end. The 1st Marine Division also was about to receive a new commander; Ran Pate would replace Edwin A. Pollock just days after Chesty's departure. The new division CG was the complete opposite of Puller; Pate had made his reputation in World War II with "outstanding service and skill in complicated staff duties." Pollock probably rated only slightly higher on Puller's scale. The old CG had commanded 2/1 at the Battle of the Tenaru on Guadalcanal, but had spent the remainder of the war as a staff officer.[18]

It seems likely that Puller brooded on these developments during his time with the division in early June. He certainly was unhappy with the failure of the United States to win a clear-cut victory. He also may have felt a tinge of regret that another war would come to an end with him sitting on the sidelines. The selection of commanders for his beloved division could not have made him happy either—they were the epitome of the staff types he disdained. Whatever the cause, he clearly was at a low point when he spent a day on the front lines and looked down on the site of the truce negotiations from allied positions astride the Panmunjom Corridor. That evening he wrote Virginia in a somber, dejected mood: ". . . but now age has probably changed me and then too the Corps has changed, due I suppose to *man* being what he is today. I never thought this change could or would happen. You are probably right and I have been wrong from the beginning. I am confused now in not knowing what is right and what is wrong but I do know that I would not have married you if I had any idea of not making you completely happy. I am sorry, Precious, but have to admit that I am losing confidence in myself."[19]

It is impossible to tell whether Puller was unhappy due to concerns about his career or the future of the Corps or both. Or, possibly, there was some other unknown problem that was causing him consternation. In any case, he was not about to let such worries completely dominate his life: "One thing is true though and that is I love you truly and I have from the beginning and I will to the end of all time. . . . Kiss our children for me; thanks for having them for me."[20]

☆ ☆ ☆

Puller returned to "the old grind in Coronado" on the 15th of June. There was little time to relax after the long journey. There were preparations for the Commandant's visit a few days hence, arrangements to make for a trip to TTULant immediately after that, and last-minute tasks to complete before the summer crush of reserve training. There also were the usual flag officer social engagements, which were no small drain on Chesty's time, especially in a region noted for its high population of retired Marines. Toward the end of the month he wrote his counterpart at the East Coast TTU: "Please do not arrange any entertainment for me there. I have enough of it here in the San Diego area."[21]

Chesty may not have been very happy in the summer of 1953, but he felt that he was doing a good job, with his outfit "progressing very nicely." He did not hesitate to tell that to the Commandant: "With all respect and credit to [TTULant], my command has far more experience and spends far more of its time in the field training organized units other than Marine Corps units." He added in a subsequent letter: "We in TTUPac are very proud of our record of practical achievement. My one desire is to maintain and better this record." When senior officers from TTULant came out for a visit, he boasted to a friend: "We will make every attempt to indoctrinate them in the proper way of running a TTU."[22]

Puller's self-assessment was more than substantiated by senior admirals and generals. The successive heads of Amphibious Training
Command all gave him glowing fitness reports. They were impressed
by his "inspired leadership," his "integrity . . . and devotion to duty," his
knowledge of military history, and even his "administrative manage-
ment" and "pleasant personality." The Taiwanese were anxious to receive more help from Puller's mobile training teams. And Chesty's
counterpart at TTULant admitted that the West Coast outfit had "several new and very effective wrinkles in the instructional field." The
Commandant sent his own compliments to Puller: "I am pleased to
learn from many sources that you and your staff are doing a fine job at
TTUPac and take this opportunity to congratulate you on your accomplishments."[23]

Puller's standing continued to soar among Marines of all ranks. A
master sergeant who had served with him asked for assistance because
"I know that you are always mindful of the problems of enlisted men
and always a champion for their cause." A PFC with thirteen months in
the Corps also wrote for help in getting transferred to a combat unit because he had been told: "If I ever got [into a] situation that I didn't
know who to turn to, that you were the one man in the Marines I could
turn to." The respect was not limited to Leathernecks or those seeking
favors. The chief petty officers on the USS *Mount McKinley* asked the
general to autograph his photo: "With your permission we would like to
hang this picture in our Chief's Quarters."[24]

Chesty's reputation for helping out others, regardless of rank, was
still well deserved. He actively campaigned to get appropriate awards
for colonels who served with him in Korea. He also encouraged the
head of TTT to "make a few recommendations" for Marines after he
heard that an admiral was rewarding Navy personnel for planning an
amphibious demonstration off Korea. He sought the early return of a
major from the Far East due to his wife's ongoing health problems, and
tried to limit the amount of time his instructors had to spend away from
home. When he learned of a San Diego mother who had lost her son in
Korea and now did kind deeds for other Marines, he wrote her a letter
expressing his admiration and appreciation.[25]

He was still tough when the situation warranted it. After a master
sergeant was sent home from Japan "for drinking and sounding off in a
bus loaded with Army personnel," Puller promptly arranged for HQMC

to transfer the miscreant out of TTUPac. Chesty then admonished the head of TTT for not doing more on his end: "I hope that you will be able to take appropriate disciplinary action in any future cases of this nature. I dislike not being able to wash our own dirty linen." Orville Jones recalled the general's Solomon-like solution when senior NCOs complained about a new directive from Headquarters requiring everyone to display all of their uniforms for high-level inspections. Previously only junior enlisted men had done so. Puller remarked that the order said "all personnel," and then informed the officers that they would meet the requirement, too. With the example being set from above, the senior enlisted men were mollified.[26]

☆ ☆ ☆

The fighting in Korea came to an end on July 27, 1953, with the signing of a truce. This agreement to cease active combat operations did not solve underlying political differences, though, and the two sets of antagonists continued to face off on either side of a demilitarized zone. The United States also remained concerned about Soviet intentions around the world. Thus, for the first time in American history, the nation was not going to disarm itself at the end of hostilities. The Cold War was in full swing and the United States would maintain a strong national defense for the foreseeable future. The Marine Corps, cut to two skeletal divisions and wings in the late 1940s, now would remain at three full-strength air-ground teams.

For Puller and other Marines, that meant there would be no reduction in career opportunities as there had been after the two world wars. Chesty benefited almost immediately from the decision not to shrink military forces. On August 27, HQMC announced that he and eight others had been selected for permanent promotion to major general. Puller's name frequently headlined stories reporting the results of the selection board. The newspapers referred to him as a "Korean hero," "much decorated," and, not surprisingly, "outspoken."[27]

Congratulatory messages poured into his Coronado office. One Marine officer wrote: "[You] will be a bulwark of honest appraisal, a clear sighted application of principle for the sake of principle. . . . Your selection reinforces the side of professional and personal integrity." A brigadier observed: "You have done much in your time to make the Marine Corps great and by your personal courage you have set a fine example." Puller was most pleased, however, by O. P. Smith's "approval," since he looked up to his old friend with genuine "admiration."[28]

The selection seemed to blow away the funk that had gripped Chesty earlier in the summer. He admitted to friends that he was "indeed very happy" over the outcome. On the practical side, it would extend his career till the mandatory retirement age of sixty-two. Perhaps more important to him, it also could be seen as a vindication of his performance and the choices he had made in thirty-five years of service. He recently had written one young lieutenant who had been seeking advice: "I have tried to keep away from staff duty, having always felt that being a line officer was my duty as a Marine." Men such as Pate were getting ahead in the Corps, but it was clear now that there still was room at the top for someone of Puller's persuasion as well.[29]

He did not have to wait long to assume the "added responsibility" of higher rank. He underwent a physical examination on the last day of August, which found him in reasonably good health. Aside from a recent ear infection, his only apparent physical shortcomings were varicose veins in his legs, mildly high blood pressure, and arteriosclerosis. (The latter two problems had first been diagnosed in his annual physical in 1952.) In another symptom of middle age and too much time spent in an office, his weight remained a little high at 168 pounds. With the medical and administrative preliminaries completed, Puller pinned on his second star on September 28, 1953. He vowed to O. P. Smith: "It is my earnest desire to carry out the duties of a major general in a very creditable manner and thus be of greater service."[30]

The promotion meant much more than just professional satisfaction to Puller; it also ensured he could provide an improving lifestyle to his family. That was important to Chesty, who had grown up in strained economic circumstances. Taking care of his children included a good education. To ensure they received it, he had enrolled them in a Catholic academy in San Diego. He considered the cost of uniforms and tuition a small price to pay. And he was extremely proud when all three children did well. Virginia McC was his star, habitually achieving all As, but the twins were close behind. Outside the classroom, he stoked his son's interest in toy soldiers and baseball. Martha, on the other hand, proved to be more athletically inclined and showed a special flair for swimming. Chesty, perhaps recalling his own youth as a "water rat," bought the youngsters a rowboat, but Lewis Jr. was too small to row it himself. An attempt to have Jones, the driver, teach him close order drill also failed. Nevertheless, with fatherly enthusiasm, Chesty could tell the Commandant that the Puller children were "growing and developing nicely" and that Shepherd's godson had become "quite a mathematician."[31]

With the exception of occasional travel for temporary duty away from Coronado and infrequent hunting trips with friends, Puller was able to spend a fair amount of time at home. Although he was tired of the never-ending round of official social engagements, he still looked forward to an "enjoyable and relaxing evening" out on the town with Virginia. (After attending a "hilariously funny" play with his wife during one of their forays, he was moved to write the local theater company and congratulate them on their "excellent performance.") He maintained a close relationship with Virginia's family, too. He wrote occasional newsy notes to Mrs. Evans, whom he unabashedly addressed as "mother," and Virginia's aunt, who also resided in the family home at Evanslee. He promised they would always have a place to live with the Pullers, once he retired and settled back in his home state. When his brother-in-law, Bob Evans, returned from an overseas job with an airline, Chesty thought Evans's first priority should be family: "Can't he and Betty come out here [to San Diego] for a visit instead of going to Florida? I have written inviting them."[32]

☆   ☆   ☆

With the summer of 1954 approaching, Puller considered where he would go next. In mid-March, he submitted an official request for assignment as the commanding general of the 1st Marine Division. The two-sentence letter reminded HQMC he had made that his first preference for duty on all his fitness reports as a one-star general. (His second pick always had been the 2d Marine Division, until the 3d Marine Division deployed from California to Japan in 1953, at which point the latter outfit moved up in Chesty's estimation.) Headquarters answered on March 27 with an equally brief message: "It is the present intention of the Commandant of the Marine Corps to detach you from your present station on or about 1 June 1954 and assign you to duty as the Commanding General, 2d Marine Division."[33]

Although he would have preferred the 1st or 3d Marine Divisions because they were much closer geographically to likely Asian hot spots, there was considerable potential for action on the other side of the globe. Since the late 1940s, the 2d Marine Division had kept one battalion afloat almost continuously in the Mediterranean Sea. If that forward element were committed to battle, the rest of the outfit probably would not be far behind. Chesty also certainly was aware that two recent CGs of the 2d (Pollock and Pate) had both moved on to head the 1st Marine Division. As an added bonus, O. P. Smith was the commander of Fleet Marine Forces Atlantic (FMFLant) and thus would be Puller's immediate superior. But one factor undoubtedly outweighed all the others. Chesty was about to have at least part of his dream fulfilled—he would have command of a Marine division in his own right. If he needed any additional reassurance following his promotion, his transfer to this plum billet was confirmation that senior leaders in the Corps still believed he was one of the best at training Marines for war.[34]

Chesty had one last order of business at TTU, to make another grand inspection tour of his far-flung instructor detachments. His itinerary looked much like that of the previous year, with stops in Hawaii, Japan, Taiwan, Korea, and Okinawa. He departed for the Far East on March 30 and received an especially warm welcome upon his arrival in Taiwan a few days later. The new Commander in Chief of the Nationalist Chinese Army was a VMI graduate who took a personal interest in hosting a "fellow rat." Chesty was treated to the ritual inspection of highly polished troops adorned in white helmets and leggings, as well as the usual gamut of dinners and parties. What he enjoyed most was the opportunity to observe Taiwanese Marines conducting an amphibious assault. He thought the Chinese troops "looked fine, excellent" and opined that their landing "compared very favorably" with similar exercises by U.S. forces.[35]

On April 17, Puller flew on to Korea. He spoke with at least one reporter in Seoul that day and a short dispatch went out on the news wire almost immediately. Chesty had been so impressed with the Nationalist Chinese forces that he asserted they were fully ready to launch an amphibious offensive against Communist-controlled China. His only caveat was that the small Taiwanese navy would have to be "backed up by our [warships] or some other nation's." It was a theme he would repeat to other reporters two weeks later upon his return to the States.[36]

Puller's comment about possible U.S. assistance to an invasion might have created "adverse political inferences" and a national controversy at another time, but the American public was growing increasingly concerned about the threat from Communism. The Soviets apparently had caught up with U.S. hydrogen bomb technology in late 1953. The French were failing in their bid to hold on to Indochina and recently had agreed to talks with the Communist-supported rebels. In the United States itself, Senator Joseph R. McCarthy was reaching the height of his influence by denouncing alleged Communists serving in the federal government. Chesty's bellicose talk made little impression against this larger background. Puller's willingness to speak out, however, was significant. It seems likely that his selection for promotion and division command had erased the concerns he had harbored about his career since the episode with the press in mid-1951.[37]

☆ ☆ ☆

During Chesty's final, hectic days at TTU, he made a few arrangements for taking over the 2d Marine Division. His only request to the outgoing commander was that someone select an aide for him. Puller added: "My first requirement is that he be able to write a good letter." The division commander was somewhat surprised that anyone would delegate a decision of such "personal nature," so he promised instead to line up several candidates for Puller's review. The older general also jestingly despaired of finding someone to meet Chesty's only criterion: "May I say that it is often difficult to find even more senior officers who are able to write a good letter."[38]

Puller received "some of the best news I have ever had" when he learned his former chief of staff at the 3d Brigade, Ed Snedeker, would be joining him in the 2d Marine Division. Chesty informed the brigadier: "There is no one I would rather have as my ADC." Snedeker primarily had built his reputation through duty as a staff officer and was then serving as the deputy director of the Marine Corps Schools—the organization Chesty frequently disparaged. While friendship undoubtedly played a role in Puller's delight, he likely also was pleased to obtain Snedeker's expertise in planning operations and running a senior headquarters. It was another piece of evidence that Chesty seemed to be gaining some respect for the value of staff work as he moved up the chain of command. During his 1953 campaign to develop a Nicaraguan training area, he even had put forth the argument that corps-level exercises were a necessity "to train our higher commanders and their staffs." His newfound tolerance did not extend to HQMC, however, and he still could rail about someone being "just another expert from Washington; lots of theories but no concrete facts."[39]

The only ripple in Puller's new pond of contentment came in the spring of 1954 when he began to be troubled by swollen ankles. He suspected he might be suffering from gout, a debilitating disease of the joints. Instead of checking with military medical authorities, he visited his nephew, a doctor who lived in San Diego. The younger man examined his uncle and told him the problem was actually a sign of heart disease. Puller took the medication prescribed by his relative and made no mention of the problem to Navy doctors. The general was not about to let any medical issue become a stumbling block in achieving his goal.[40]

On the 1st of June, 1954, the Puller family packed up their car and drove east toward Saluda. The last three years in California had been personally and professionally rewarding to Chesty. He had every reason to expect that his next tour as commanding general of the 2d Marine Division would be equally successful.

"Go Down Slugging"
Last Days in the Corps
June 1954–October 1955

The Pullers took six days to go across the country. After spending two weeks in Saluda with Virginia's mother and aunt, the family headed south to Camp Lejeune. They arrived at the end of June 1954. There had been an undercurrent of anxiety throughout the journey. Virginia did most of the driving in deference to her husband's high blood pressure and swollen ankles. Even the children vaguely understood that his problem was serious enough to warrant concern. Puller, still seeking to minimize or cover up his medical condition, soon visited his nephew's friend, who practiced in nearby Wilmington.[1]

☆   ☆   ☆

The sprawling North Carolina base was now "a far cry from the cold and desolate tent camp back in the winter of 1941." The original temporary facility had been replaced by ninety concrete barracks and renamed Camp Geiger. It now housed mostly service and support units, while the 2d Marine Division occupied "mainside"—the sprawling cluster of red-brick buildings several miles away on the opposite shore of the New River. The division headquarters was located on prime property on the edge of the wide estuary, with the front of the structure facing down the length of Holcomb Boulevard (the main street). The base headquarters was a few blocks away, in a stately edifice across the road from the expansive grass parade deck.[2]

Family quarters had improved a great deal, too; even more so due to Chesty's increased rank. Instead of the small room in a distant fishing lodge that had sufficed in late 1944, the Pullers were now ensconced in a beautiful two-story home with a window air conditioner in the master bedroom. Located in aptly named Paradise Point, a secluded area reserved for senior officers, the house had a view of the river on one side and a golf course on the other. In accordance with Chesty's usual practice, he enrolled the twins in a Catholic school out in town, even though that necessitated a much longer ride for them each day. To better prepare teenage Virginia McC for college, he eventually sent her to live with his sister Pattie in Richmond, so his "splendid student" could attend Collegiate, an "excellent" private school.[3]

The division commander rated a staff of several enlisted Marines to care for his quarters. Orville Jones, now a gunnery sergeant, also had moved east to continue his service as Chesty's driver. The general was soon introduced to his new aide, a tall, sparely built captain fresh from a Marine detachment on a cruiser. Marc Moore's English degree had cost him a prospective assignment in charge of a rifle company, but Puller promised the aide he would get his infantry command after a year of writing good letters.[4]

Puller's tour with the 2d Marine Division began on July 1 with a formal division parade—fourteen thousand men arrayed in mass formations in the already hot morning sun. When it was time for Puller to make his remarks, habit interfered with the opening of his brief speech: "It gives me great pleasure to assume command of the 1st Marine Division." A ripple of suppressed laughter in the ranks brought him up short and he corrected his error, but no one could blame him for the slip after his long association with the 1st. Puller and the previous CG capped the ceremony by reviewing the division. Chesty would have preferred to troop the line of units on foot, but his predecessor dictated use of a specially modified jeep. As it drove slowly across the front of the division, the two generals stood in the back and held on to a highly polished brass rail. Most men got no more than a distant and fleeting glimpse of their new commander. They all knew he was a "giant" in the Corps, however, and many stood just a little taller and prouder at the sight of his ramrod posture and steadfast gaze.[5]

Chesty finally had the division command he had sought for so many years.

☆   ☆   ☆

Several newspapers hailed Puller's selection for command because of his proven leadership. One writer described him as "a warrior general, a wound-scarred professional," and a "master at the business of training men to fight." Chesty would need those skills and experience, but the job involved a lot more. The new CG began to discover that fact when he received briefs from his predecessor and the staff. One challenge was managing the transition from reliance on the draft to an all-volunteer Corps. Although Selective Service remained in place after the Korean War, the Commandant had made it his goal to maintain personnel strength without draftees. That created "many problems" for FMF units, not the least of which was achieving a high reenlistment rate. Organizational developments provided another distraction from training. Elements of the division were heavily involved in testing the proposed "quadrilateral" structure, which envisioned four infantry battalions (each with four rifle companies) in the regiment. Experimentation also continued with helicopters, seaplanes, and tactics on the nuclear battlefield. Another important but bothersome task was the campaign to raise money for the Marine Corps War Memorial—Felix de Weldon's monumental bronze statue of the Iwo Jima flag raising. When Puller took over the division, it was running far behind its counterparts in collecting contributions.[6]

Even where training seemed most important, there were administrative headaches. The 2d Marine Division's biggest event for the year would be Atlantic Fleet Exercise 1-55 (LANTFLEX). This major operation, involving two hundred ships and more than twenty thousand Marines, was scheduled for November 1954. The division and FMFLant staffs could not agree on a site aboard Camp Lejeune for the umpire headquarters, so Puller and O. P. Smith had to get involved in the decision. Another of Chesty's primary operational tasks was providing one reinforced battalion for duty with the fleet in the Mediterranean. That commitment usually left "one third of the division tied up," since one battalion landing team was overseas, another was reorganizing following its deployment, and a third was locked into preparations to go. In addition to that drain on the strength of Puller's force, the readiness of the floating battalion usually suffered due to a lack of good training opportunities. An issue of greater concern to the commander of the Sixth Fleet in the Mediterranean, however, was "proper conduct ashore by sailors and Marines on liberty." One battalion commander wrote Chesty: "The admiral has set a standard of not more than one shore patrol report for every 1,000 men on liberty." Puller might have recalled the rowdy send-off from his Horse Marines some thirty years before in Peking, but he answered diplomatically: "It is most essential that our people conduct themselves in such a way as to maintain the standards our Corps has maintained throughout the world."[7]

The new division commander had little time to master all these situations. Due to a delay in the arrival of another general, the Commandant assigned Puller to temporary additional duty as base commander for Camp Lejeune. That necessitated another change-of-command ceremony on July 11, as well as supervision of a second staff and an entirely different set of challenges. On the 14th, Chesty was off to Washington for the three-day, Corps-wide general officers conference. He flew up to FMFLant headquarters in Norfolk on July 20 for his first official visit with Smith. Two days later, Puller headed south to the Puerto Rican island of Vieques to observe his 8th Marines deployed there. He enjoyed the now rare chance to see "troops going through field problems and periods of instruction." He finally made it back to North Carolina on the 27th, but had to visit Marine Corps Air Station Cherry Point the following day.[8]

Puller was not about to miss the 1st Marine Division reunion despite his hectic schedule. He flew to New York City on August 7 (the twelfth anniversary of the Guadalcanal landings). That evening at the banquet, Chesty was seated at the head table, but Shepherd made the only formal speech. This year there were no impromptu calls for Puller to be heard, though he received a spontaneous ovation, as did Red Mike Edson and the Australian ambassador.[9]

There was no relief in sight in the dual-hatted CG's calendar. He went off to Vieques for a week-long trip in the middle of August to see the final landing exercise of the 8th Marines. Early in September, he was slated to host a visit by the quartermaster general of the Corps, the venerable Major General William P. T. "Pete" Hill. Infamous for his ability to trim supposed fat from the most frugal budgets, Hill forewarned Chesty that he had not been to Lejeune in a while and wanted "to get a good look at everything." In addition, Shepherd already had issued a set of orders for Puller to spend two weeks at HQMC starting on

September 9 to preside over a promotion board. Only then would the new base CG arrive to relieve Chesty of that burden.[10]

In addition to all this work, Puller had to participate in the many social functions required of two commanding generals. Hardly an evening went by that he was not hosting a party for a visiting dignitary or attending an event put on by a subordinate unit. On top of that, Chesty received frequent invitations to the SNCO and NCO clubs, which he accepted whenever he could. During these forays, he discovered that the clubs were not allowed to sell alcohol until after working hours. He took advantage of his temporary role as the base commander and ordered that henceforth a Marine could have a beer with noon chow if he wanted one. He also let the senior NCOs know it was up to them to make sure the privilege was not abused. His stock with the men, already high, went up another notch.[11]

The combination of a full schedule and health concerns made it difficult for Puller to demonstrate the type of leadership from the front that had helped create the Chesty legend. There was no war going on, but there was plenty of hard training, and the division commander was not out there heading up a forced march or thrashing through the dense undergrowth. Generals weren't supposed to do those sorts of things, anyway, but Puller's reputation brought the weight of unusually high expectations. One rainy day his staff car passed between the twin columns of an infantry unit slogging along both sides of the road. An understandably miserable, envious grunt called out in frustration: "Yeah, we're getting wet, Chesty, ya ol' bastard! Ya satisfied?" The implication that he was not sharing the same burdens he imposed on his troops must have stung Puller, but he merely remarked to his aide and his driver: "If it had been me out there, and the CO had come by in a staff car, I'd have said the same damned thing."[12]

No matter how heavy the workload, Puller could always make time to tangle with the bureaucracy at HQMC. Early in August, one of his captains asked to see him. The young infantry officer had served with Puller in the 1st Marines in Korea and come away with a Silver Star. Now he had orders to attend Communications Officers School, which would lead to an unwanted tour as a staff officer. Worse still, the company commander was being pulled out of his battalion just before it went overseas. Chesty sympathized with the captain's plight and immediately called the Commandant's office. He also fired off a long letter to

Ran Pate, now a three-star serving as the assistant commandant. He not only pleaded his subordinate's case, but recommended a change in policy to prevent it from happening to others who had "combat value to the Marine Corps." Pate gave Puller's arguments short shrift, replying that tours in support specialties were of "definite value to the career of the regular unrestricted officer." It was just the type of response that could make Chesty's blood boil.[13]

☆   ☆   ☆

On August 26, the division commander spent the afternoon inspecting the battalion landing team heading out to the Mediterranean a few days hence. It was a hot, humid Carolina summer day, but he stopped to check each weapon as he moved down the ranks of a thousand officers and men. That night he was out very late at a social event with the mayor of Jacksonville.

At the office the next morning, Puller seemed to be extremely tired and somewhat disoriented. He had difficulty signing papers and Captain Moore thought the general was suffering from a bad hangover. By the time Chesty broke for noon chow, he had begun "to feel badly." While making his way to the staff mess, he walked into a wall. He had little appetite, missed the ashtray when he tried to stub out a cigarette, and had trouble using his fork. Snedeker thought his boss "didn't look natural." As they enjoyed an after-lunch cigar, the ADC noticed Puller was staring vacantly. He quietly told Moore to escort the general to a nearby clinic. They barely had gotten out into the passageway when Chesty sagged against his aide and nearly blacked out. A few minutes and a wild car ride later, he was lying on an examining table in the clinic.[14]

The young Navy doctor on duty thought the general looked "acutely ill." In response to questions, Puller said he had felt "light-headed and uncoordinated" for the past half hour or so. He also mentioned he had been taking a heart medication prescribed by his nephew. His blood pressure was an extremely high 194/126 and he could not properly perform simple tests of his motor skills. The lieutenant decided his patient had suffered a mild stroke and called for an ambulance to take him to the base hospital.[15]

After his arrival at the bigger medical facility, Puller underwent another quick checkup. The doctor noted Chesty had impaired eyesight, as well as difficulty controlling his muscles. His blood pressure was still high, but now only 150/100. When the physician momentarily left the room to bring in more equipment, Puller attempted to get up. He immediately collapsed and went into convulsions. Moore called for help while Jones got the general back into bed. Medical staff rushed into the room and found Puller "thrashing wildly about." In a few moments they sedated him with an injection, which stopped the spasms, and placed him in an oxygen tent. Tests of his reflexes were symptomatic of a cerebral thrombosis, commonly known as a stroke—a noticeable deterioration of brain function due to decreased flow of blood, either from a clot obstructing an artery or from loss of blood due to a burst vessel. An electrocardiogram revealed some blockage in the arteries around his heart, as well as a pattern of strain as his heart struggled to pump blood out to his body. If the latter condition worsened, it could lead to a heart attack. Having lost awareness during this period, Puller later would recall that his only problem this day had been a slight twitching in his forearm at the infirmary.[16]

Virginia stayed with him throughout the night and the next day. The children were permitted a brief visit in the morning and Jones slipped in for a moment. Puller's blood pressure had decreased, but "his speech was irrational and somewhat thick." That evening he began to show "steady and consistent improvement." By the third day, he could sit up in bed without assistance. His condition was downgraded from critical to serious. At the end of a week, the doctors allowed him to walk a few steps and he was taken off the serious list. He already was joking about the endless tests and minimizing what had happened. The examinations showed continuing abnormalities, however. Chesty had lost some of his peripheral vision and his eyes did not properly track moving objects. Subsequent electrocardiograms were consistent with the initial observations of heart blockage and strain. A different test showed some heart enlargement, which, along with his high blood pressure, proved that his heart was working much harder than it should. The physicians confirmed the initial diagnosis of a stroke and ascribed it to a blood clot.[17]

☆　☆　☆

Puller's condition drew high-level attention. He had been whisked off to the infirmary at 1315 on August 27. Snedeker was on the phone to O. P. Smith fifteen minutes later with a report that the division commander had suffered a stroke. Shepherd was overseas, but Pate went down to Lejeune on the 29th to check on Puller. He reported to the Commandant that the patient was in "good spirits," but the long-term prognosis was not necessarily so positive: "As to prospect of return to duty, one attending doctor estimates return possible, another disagrees." Smith flew down on September 1 and was pleased to see his old friend "showing considerable improvement." Pete Hill stopped in during his inspection trip and made a similar hopeful report to the Commandant. Puller drew special encouragement from the senior quartermaster, who had survived a severe illness and managed to resume his career.[18]

The wire services beamed the incident around the nation and thereafter updated his status almost daily. The news brought thousands of cards and letters to Camp Lejeune. They came from senior officers and lieutenants, from first sergeants and brand-new privates, from veterans and civilians. All wished him a speedy recovery and praised him. Smith made sure Chesty understood what that outpouring meant: "You may not realize it, but all hands in the Marine Corps were pulling for your rapid recovery. You occupy in their affections a place which no other officer does. You have every reason to be proud and grateful for the respect and affection you have earned." Puller fully appreciated it and was "deeply moved."

Those who knew him well added entreaties that he take care of himself. Major General John Selden was direct: "Now don't be a damned fool! Pay some attention to the doctors." Shepherd was less abrupt: "My one piece of advice to you is to go slow." Smith tried to make sure that would happen and told Puller not to worry about the division until after LANTFLEX: "You now have an opportunity to catch up on your reading and enjoy your family."[19]

As September progressed, Chesty's outward symptoms slowly disappeared. The doctors let him go home on sick leave the second week of the month. Since he was feeling "no ill effects from my sickness," he was soon convinced it had been nothing more than a bit of heat prostration. The physicians admitted he was making "remarkable improvement," but that did not mean he was completely healthy. His vision and reflexes were back to normal, but his blood pressure remained high and his heart and arteries were still impaired. Chesty's only concession to his condition was to rest as ordered, cut back on cigarettes, and chew more tobacco. He told a friend that his wife was not entirely pleased with the latter change in habit: "I try to keep out of Virginia's sight, but she has suspicions, and is willing to put up with it [only] as long as I do not smoke so much."[20]

His sick leave proved much more stressful than it should have been. One morning, as the twins were getting ready for school, Lewis Jr. decided to warm himself by the gas stove. His shirttail touched a burner and quickly caught on fire. His screams brought his father racing into the kitchen and Chesty helped one of the enlisted stewards put out the spreading flames. Young Puller suffered burns that required a stay of several days in the hospital; his father's hands also had to be treated. When it was clear little Lewis would recover without significant complications, Chesty was able to joke about his medical condition being upstaged by his son's, but the emotional strain had been the last thing the general needed.[21]

☆　☆　☆

Among the letters Puller received during his convalescence was one from a retired Marine general who raised a cautionary flag: "Perhaps I shouldn't say this, but anyone who has been through what you have, will probably be threatened with retirement." The official establishment had not yet broached that subject with Chesty. Shepherd's letters to Puller spoke of the major general getting "in top shape again" and referred to an October inspection of "your division." Smith was equally upbeat and told others that his friend "is a pretty rugged character and it will take a lot to get him down." The FMFLant CG added: "The words 'failure' and 'defeat' are not a part of Gen. Puller's vocabulary."[22]

Chesty already had considered the possibility of his health bringing his career to a premature end, so he now took it very seriously in spite of the reassuring words from above. On September 14 he wrote Smith: "I was told unofficially [by the doctors] I could not be retired, and no retirement board could give me any disability at this time." Soon after, Chesty assured the Commandant he would be found "fit for duty" within days. He appended a handwritten postscript: "There was no heart attack or stroke." His responses to well-wishers repeated that claim and added: "I can't understand who gave the papers that story that was exaggerated to such an extent around the country." Puller was putting a much better face on his condition than the situation warranted. The doctors kept him on sick leave throughout October.[23]

On October 29, Chesty went before a board of medical survey at the base hospital to determine if he was fit for duty. The three physicians noted that he no longer showed residual effects of the August incident, though he still suffered from arteriosclerosis and high blood pressure. Their concluding diagnosis was that he had "hypertensive cardiovascular disease (benign)," which meant high blood pressure that was "mild in character" and "not disabling." They pronounced him fit for full duty, but also explained that the Navy's Bureau of Medicine and Surgery (BuMed) in Washington would have to review his case and make the final decision. In the meantime, he could go back to work as the commanding general of the 2d Marine Division.[24]

The new diagnosis reflected Puller's condition at the time of the board; it did not alter the belief of the physicians that their patient indeed had suffered a stroke. Chesty chose to interpret their pronouncement in a subtle but significantly different way. He was certain there had been no stroke and he wanted to believe the doctors also had changed their minds about what had happened.[25]

Puller made one other mistake in deciphering the ruling of the local doctors. He understood that "Washington" had the final say, but he was confident "the board's decision will be the determining factor" and "will be approved." He had been concerned the physicians would find he "was fit for *limited* duty only" and confided to Virginia's mother: "In this case, I would have requested retirement." He believed that threat was now over and he was jubilant: "Thank the good God!" His letters in early November all expressed the same sentiment: "I am indeed thankful for my recovery and pray that I will be fit in all respects for active duty for the next five to six years and so have the opportunity to serve the Marine Corps and my country."[26]

☆   ☆   ☆

As Chesty marked his thirty-seventh Marine Corps birthday in November, a Navy captain at BuMed reviewed the work of the Lejeune medical board. Dr. Robert Bell took a dim view of what he read, then typed a memorandum to the admiral with ultimate authority in the matter: "In my opinion this officer is not now and will not at any time in the future be physically qualified to command a combat division. I believe he should be retired at this time for physical disability. It is my understanding that the Commandant of the Marine Corps will not presume to direct the medical decision in this case. Further, that the Commandant strongly desires that no officer be retained in a duty status unless fully qualified physically to perform such duty." He added in pen: "Fit for duty means fitness to perform the job anywhere at any time." A week later, Bell made an additional report to the Navy's surgeon general on Puller's situation: "I have had extensive conversations with [the director of personnel at HQMC] who in turn has discussed it on numerous occasions with Gen Shepherd. He apparently will go along with Med. Dept. but feels that so sick a man should be retired and not carried on the active list."[27]

The chief of the bureau was Admiral Herbert L. Pugh. By chance, he and Puller had served together in the 3d Officers' Training Camp in 1919. Normally Pugh would have been responsible for the final decision on Chesty's case, but he himself was recovering from a heart attack. On November 19, BuMed placed its endorsement on the report of the Lejeune board: "It is considered desirable that this officer, for his own good as well as that of the service, receive further special study in a specially equipped and staffed center. In view of the foregoing it is recommended that he be transferred to the U.S. Naval Hospital, Bethesda, Maryland, for further study, evaluation and report." The brief ruling was signed "by direction" for Pugh by Captain Bell. That same day, HQMC sent out a letter informing Puller of the outcome and explaining that Shepherd "concurred in that recommendation." Just four days earlier, Chesty had "received word from the Commandant that I would remain as Commanding General of the 2d Marine Division." Now he was "surprised and chagrined" at this completely unexpected turn of events.[28]

On December 1, 1954, Chesty was admitted to Bethesda. For the next two weeks he underwent tests. He had very high blood pressure in the first examination and the physicians immediately put him on medication designed to lower it. His readings fluctuated wildly over subsequent days, but the average remained too high. The doctors confirmed the problems with his heart and arteries. A new test—an electroencephalogram—also revealed "minimal generalized abnormalities" in his brain that were consistent with damage inflicted by a mild stroke.[29]

Although the doctors initially indicated that Chesty was healthy enough to perform limited duty, they informed him that it was BuMed policy that anyone who had suffered a stroke could not continue on active duty. Shortly after, Puller encountered Admiral Pugh, still a patient, who confirmed the bad news. The Marine general then met with Captain Bell. He verified the bureau's policy and said it included any case of serious disease such as tuberculosis or cancer. Puller challenged that by naming previously ill generals still on duty. Bell replied that flag officers were an exception to the rule—they were retired only if the Commandant or the CNO agreed with BuMed. That possible exemption did not make Chesty optimistic, since he believed that Shepherd would have prevented the second look by Bethesda if he intended to keep the division commander on duty. Puller was convinced the decision already had been made to force him out of the Corps.

Once the doctors had observed all that they could, they allowed Puller to go home on sick leave. He would have to return in January for a medical survey board that would determine his fate. Chesty stopped in Norfolk on his way to Lejeune and told Smith the outlook was bleak, that he expected to be retired. He was in an angry, sullen mood.[30]

☆   ☆   ☆

Puller's spirits did not improve over the holidays, in part because he and Virginia disagreed. He wanted to battle to the last, but she believed he should accept whatever ruling the new board handed down. The rare discord and the prospect of early retirement left Chesty angry; Lewis Jr. would recall that his father "vented his frustration on Mother." The Camp Lejeune doctors did not help matters when they gave Chesty his annual physical examination. They noted the continuing problem with high blood pressure, but also certified that the general was "qualified for all duties of his rank at sea and in the field." Virginia stood her ground, however, and Lewis agreed to follow her advice.[31]

Just after New Year's Day, Chesty returned to Bethesda. The evening before the board, he had dinner with Homer Litzenberg (now a major general), then wrote a short note to Virginia. He told her he had met with Shepherd that day and received no encouraging words. Lewis reassured her he would accept his fate in accordance with their agreement: "Please don't worry, I won't go off half cocked. . . . I have done and will do exactly as you said but still think you should have advised me to go down slugging." He also reminded her how hard retirement would be for him: "Please take care of your dear self as I will need you more than ever now."[32]

The board of three medical officers met on January 5, 1955, and announced their decision the same day. It was their opinion that Puller had suffered a "cerebrovascular accident" in August 1954, though they hypothesized it might have been just a "transient cerebrovascular spasm." That meant either the blood clot had dissolved quickly or Puller's body had found another way to route blood to the affected area of the brain. That theory was consistent with Chesty's full recovery from the immediate symptoms of the event. The doctors acknowledged that medication was reducing his blood pressure, but it was still high and they believed the threat of a stroke or heart attack remained. They recommended that Puller "avoid excessive physical and emotional stress" and "be returned to limited duty . . . if his services with these restrictions are desired."[33]

That evening Chesty telephoned Virginia with the bad news. Since he believed the Commandant already had indicated the Corps had "no place for a limited duty officer," Puller expected to go before a retirement board within days. He told Virginia his only desire was that the process go quickly so he could get home. He was certainly unhappy, but he put up a resolute front for his wife: "Knowing that you love me is all that matters now. We will have enough to live on decently." In an echo of his poignant letters just before Inchon, he repeated a vow he had made then: "again I promise to try to make a better husband."[34]

But Puller went back on another pledge to Virginia. He enlisted the aid of Colonel Paul D. Sherman to serve as his legal counsel. The Marine lawyer was the brother of Admiral Forrest P. Sherman, CNO from 1949 until 1951. With Sherman's assistance, Chesty drafted a statement formally challenging the findings of the board. He rejected the very concept of limited duty for a general and argued he would be better off remaining a division commander: "I have competent assistants. . . . Since I am completely familiar with my daily tasks, there are no unusual stresses. . . . There will be nothing scheduled to take place before next fall which will require any activity in the field on my part. . . . The normal duties of a division commander do not require physical effort or strain." He assured higher authorities: "I shall refrain from doing things inappropriate for a man of my age and rank, such as personally inspecting all the rifles of an infantry battalion." In his initial draft statement, never submitted to the board, he had been more colloquial: "Contrary to popular opinion, the duties of a division commander do not require him to run through the woods, brandishing a sword, and yelling, 'Follow me, boys.' "[35]

His declarations appeared to mark a substantial change in his feelings about what constituted fitness for duty. As recently as 1952 he firmly had stated his belief that medical examinations were irrelevant even for generals and the only true test was performance: "Put a pack on us and send us over the hills on orders to get to a certain place at a certain time. Those that can't make it, let them retire." And he always had argued that the mark of a true leader at any level was being out front with his men. His formal description of the relatively easy life of a CG also assumed a peacetime regimen. One of the last letters he had signed before his August 1954 incident had expressed a less rosy view of the future to a fellow Guadalcanal veteran: "Rest assured that when World War III begins it would be a pleasure to have you serve with me again." Chesty's views almost certainly had not changed, but he was not about to let his strident opinions get in the way of his remaining on active duty.[36]

☆ ☆ ☆

Puller went home to Camp Lejeune on January 7 with the final decision on his future still pending. The acting chief of BuMed had approved the findings of the board; now the matter was in the lap of the Commandant. Shepherd could either provide a limited duty billet for the major general or order him to a physical evaluation board. The latter would recommend whether the Secretary of the Navy should accept the results of the medical survey board and also determine the level of disability pay Puller should receive if he were medically retired. Sherman's legal aid notwithstanding, Chesty expected to be retired in short order. He contacted a real estate agent in Richmond about renting a house there beginning in February.[37]

After conferring with senior medical officers, Shepherd issued his decision on January 26. He wrote a lengthy letter to Puller justifying the outcome and placing the entire burden on the doctors: "I wish to make it clear that neither I personally nor any officer in this Headquarters was responsible for your being brought to Bethesda for further examination. . . . I do not have the authority, nor would I care to exercise it if I did, to overrule a decision of the Bureau of Medicine and Surgery." Based on the board's conclusion, Shepherd determined: "I cannot leave you in command of the 2d Marine Division." However, he offered a surprising olive branch to Puller. The Commandant was willing to create the post of deputy base commander at Lejeune "as an assignment involving the limited type of duty specified in the recommendation of the board." Chesty could have it for five months, which would "enable the children to complete their school year and . . . you and Virginia to make plans for the future."

Shepherd tried to soften the blow with praise: "Your name is legend as a troop leader and professional soldier and will go down through generations of Marines yet to be born." He also told Puller to accept the inevitable: "I know how hard it will be for you to live any other life than that of an active Marine officer. You must realize, however, as I am beginning to do, with only eleven months more of active duty before I retire, that there comes a time when all old soldiers must pass on their swords to those we have been training to take our place. I confess it's a tough bullet to chew, but I am confident you will face it with the same courage you have demonstrated so many times on the battlefield."[38]

The Commandant's final words made a major impact on Puller, but not in the manner Shepherd desired. The letter only aroused Chesty's basic instinct to fight—it had never been in his nature to ride off graciously into the sunset. Puller penned a tough letter disagreeing with the medical board and rejecting the offer of limited duty. After some reflection, he decided to take a less confrontational approach. He undoubtedly saw the wisdom of having an additional five months to carry on the battle and to prepare for retirement if he did not win. The harsh draft letter went into the files. On February 1, Chesty sent a two-sentence note to Shepherd, accepting his offer of limited duty and thanking him for his "consideration" in making it. Orders went out immediately transferring Puller to his new billet.[39]

Chesty's carefully restrained reply to Shepherd masked the deep resentment he now held toward his superior. In the coming weeks, Puller would tell many friends the Bethesda board had been unfair, since it resulted in "my being placed twice in jeopardy." He always added: "This was the time I required help from the Commandant, but failed to receive it; others have in the past year." The assistance Puller had wanted was a decision to reject the results of the board. His anger at failing to receive it undoubtedly was fueled by a sense he had been betrayed by a longtime associate he thought he could count on: a fellow Virginian,

VMI alumnus, 1st Marine Division veteran, and the godfather of Puller's only son. Chesty's animosity would grow in the coming months and he would never forgive nor forget.[40]

Puller's ire was understandable, but unjustified. Shepherd undoubtedly had more leeway than his letter indicated, but he believed he was making the right decision for Chesty and for the Corps. Although doctors at Lejeune had declared Puller fit for duty, many (including O. P. Smith) assumed the Navy officers were doing so because they were reluctant to offend a general and national hero. The senior physicians at Bethesda, specially selected to care for flag officers and politicians, were telling Shepherd that Puller had suffered irreparable degradation from years of high blood pressure and arteriosclerosis, and was in danger of another stroke or a heart attack. The Commandant, perhaps feeling a sense of responsibility for having overloaded his subordinate with two jobs in the summer of 1954, was reluctant to ignore this expert opinion. He often had demonstrated his interest in taking care of the Puller family, and now took into account the possibility of Puller's untimely death, which would leave Virginia with three school-age children and only a half pension. (Others felt the same way. General Selden was telling Puller at this time to consider such an unhappy scenario the next time he thought about "play[ing] sergeant.") Shepherd would say repeatedly in the future: "I would not sign that man's death warrant."[41]

There were cases of ill generals who were not pushed out the door so readily. Pete Hill had stayed on after a severe medical problem, but he also had powerful connections in Congress that had allowed him to hold on to his fiefdom as Quartermaster General for more than a decade. Twining had twice undergone treatment for cancer, but was declared cured each time (and would live into his nineties). There were no such exceptional circumstances in Puller's situation—he would never be restored to full health and he had no political ties that would limit the Commandant's options. Shepherd was equally aware of numerous instances in which Marine generals had pressed on in spite of ill health and subsequently died on active duty. The Navy's Surgeon General, the Secretary of the Navy, and the Commandant definitely were concerned at this time about the effects of "prolonged stress" on flag officers. In May 1955, Shepherd would issue a directive ordering generals to reduce their levels of stress and make frequent use of leave and liberty. The Commandant's decision was not what Puller wanted, but the senior officer appears to have been motivated by genuine regard for his subordinate. Retired Colonel Justice M. Chambers, a Puller partisan who was well connected at HQMC, believed that Shepherd was "honestly and sincerely convinced" he was doing the right thing.[42]

☆   ☆   ☆

One of Puller's last acts as commanding general was hosting the celebration of the 2d Marine Division's fourteenth birthday on February 1, 1955. A few days later, he turned over the reins to Snedeker. In a sign of his tremendous frustration over this early departure, he held no ceremony and merely issued a memorandum thanking the men of the command for their "loyal support." Along with Captain Moore and Gunnery Sergeant Jones, Chesty moved into an office at the end of a passageway in the base headquarters. Camp Lejeune's commander was not comfortable with the situation. He requested "clarification" from the Commandant "as to the specific stresses or nature of duties which must be avoided" by Puller. In the end, the CG simply gave his new deputy nothing to do. That left Chesty with more time to brood over his impending fate.[43]

His mood remained "down in the dumps," at best. Aside from occasional visits from old comrades-in-arms, his few distractions in the office did not always improve his outlook. In early May he received the draft manuscript of the official history of the Inchon campaign. He was chagrined to read that the landing of the 1st Marines was characterized as disorganized and confused. He fired off a letter to the captain who had authored the account and also registered his complaint with O. P. Smith and the Commandant. He considered the description "untrue and totally uncalled for" and was upset because it "reflected unfavorably not only on me, but on the regiment as a whole." Smith backed his former subordinate because the Army and Navy were being allowed to remove negative references, which would leave a "distorted history" pointing out only Marine lapses. Chesty was ultimately successful in his campaign to get it "stricken from the official record," but the incident heightened his concern for his own place in the saga of the Corps. A few weeks later he wrote another batch of letters when he suspected his name might be left off the list of commanders of the 1st Marine Division during the Korean War.[44]

Puller's gloom was evident when a family friend sought his intervention after her son was dropped from the Basic School. Chesty looked into the situation, then rendered an unmerciful assessment: "My personal opinion in a case of this sort is that soldiers are born, not made—a young man must show a distinct aptitude to the military life. If he does not, for some reason, display these qualities for the profession of arms, it would be to his advantage to leave the service as soon as possible and seek another career." He added bitterly that he no longer had any control over his own professional life: "I regret there is nothing that I can do personally concerning your son's case, for I have no influence in the Marine Corps, and I expect to be retired this August."[45]

☆   ☆   ☆

In late February, Puller responded to a letter of commiseration from O. P. Smith. Chesty expressed his gratefulness for their "close bond of friendship" and summed up his professional life: "I've tried through the years to make an honest fight, which after all is a Marine's supreme duty. In that alone does one find satisfaction." But as he languished hour after hour, day after day in his lonely office, he increasingly grew dissatisfied with the way his career was ending. Puller decided to make at least one more "honest fight," this time to stay on active duty.[46]

Chesty's initial strategy was simple. He wanted to obtain a hearing before yet another, hopefully "impartial," board and then "point out how the policy of the Bureau of Medicine does not apply in certain cases if the Commandant does not wish it applied." That argument by itself would not alter the outcome; he must have been hoping the Secretary of the Navy would agree the situation was unjust and overrule Shepherd. Puller's vision of the possibilities began to change in early March, when he received a visit from Jimmy Hayes. The veteran of 1/7 and Guadalcanal was now a reserve lieutenant colonel, a lawyer in North Carolina, and president of the state chapter of the Reserve Officers Association (a lobbying organization with some influence in Washington). Apprised of Chesty's situation, Hayes set about plotting a more ambitious plan of attack. His ideas centered on national publicity and political connections, factors much more likely to sway the opinion of the civilian heading the Navy Department. Hayes hoped to generate this support "without involving General Puller," since he assumed Chesty would not want "to openly and publicly oppose the decision of the Commandant."[47]

Puller already was sending Hayes details of the previous medical boards and the names of three reserve officers who might help. One, Lieutenant Colonel Frank Farrell, had served at Cape Gloucester and now worked for a major New York City newspaper. Another, Colonel Henry Heming, was prominent in the 1st Marine Division Association. Although Chesty still professed his only interest was obtaining a hearing before an impartial board, he also told Hayes: "I'm sure you are on the right track." The feisty general believed he did "not have the drag or influence to fight the Washington policies," but he was fast trying to acquire some.[48]

One of Puller's strongest hopes was support from the division association. He rightfully expected that he would have the fervent backing of the members. Hayes agreed and drafted a resolution for the organization's board of directors that would "respectfully petition" the Corps "to retain General Puller on active duty for an indefinite period of time." The lawyer expected the declaration to "touch off a spontaneous reaction by Marines everywhere." Those expectations were dashed when the board tabled the resolution without action. Puller was certain he knew why: "Enough regular officers are maintained as directors to insure that the desires of Headquarters Marine Corps are carried out by the Association."[49]

Hayes brought Bob Haggerty into the informal group fighting on Puller's behalf. Haggerty was another 1/7 veteran, reserve officer, and lawyer. He also was connected to Governor Thomas Dewey, a Republican who had narrowly lost the 1948 presidential election to Truman. Although Hayes and Farrell thought they should "make a national issue of the matter," Haggerty felt it would be better "to proceed with more finesse." He believed "the approach should be essentially a political one so that face-saving retreats would be possible. Personally, I fear that Headquarters would resent a mass pressure movement to the point that the cause might be damaged beyond repair." While the small group debated tactics, Hayes informed Puller that "continued study is being given to the best method of getting the information to your men."[50]

The deliberations on the next step were short-lived. On April 4, Chesty stunned his supporters: "I have come to the decision not to press this matter any further." The only reason he provided was the lack of "backing" from HQMC. Later he would express "concern that there be no unfavorable publicity for the Marine Corps." He had known of those two factors from the start. He also clearly was not pleased with his choice: "I assure you that to come to this decision goes against my grain; for I have never been a quitter. It is particularly galling because I know I am all right physically." Perhaps Virginia's desire that he accept his fate had come to the fore again. Whatever the cause, Chesty had called off the campaign to save his career before the troops had gotten out of their assembly area. It undoubtedly had been an agonizing decision to make; now he had to live with the even more painful consequences.[51]

Hayes and Haggerty were not quite ready to quit, however, in part because they realized their former commander had reached his decision "with the greatest reluctance." They had accurately assessed Puller's conflicted state of mind. Throughout May and early June he reiterated his position that "it is useless to buck City Hall" and he searched actively for a home to rent in Richmond. But he also sent a congratulatory note to Admiral Arleigh A. Burke, the aggressive World War II destroyer commander who had just been named the new CNO. In a thinly veiled plea for intervention, Chesty spent much of the letter describing his dismay at the findings of the Bethesda medical board. He clearly remained unhappy with the decision to surrender.[52]

☆   ☆   ☆

On July 1, 1955, Puller reported to Bethesda Naval Hospital for the second time. He sought out one of the doctors who would serve on the physical evaluation board and asked what disability rating he could expect if the board found him not fit for full duty. After studying the general's medical record, the physician told Puller he would probably get at least a 40 percent rating, which would translate into physical disability pay equaling the same percentage of his active-duty pay. That figure was much less than the 75 percent retirement he already had earned based on his thirty-plus years in the Corps. The discouraging news raised Chesty's hackles. After a lifetime of service he was too sick to continue, according to the experts, but not ill enough to receive any additional retirement compensation to offset the loss of his full active-duty pay. Puller wrote Virginia in a resentful vein: "Nice people at headquarters. General Shepherd is Commandant and there is no question of his not being in on this. . . . We now know beyond a doubt what I suspected all along!" Despite his anger, he remained overtly resigned to his fate, at least for her consumption: "Please do not worry. We must take things as they come in this life. There doesn't seem to be much that we can do to change events."[53]

In succeeding days Puller underwent another battery of tests. Headquarters Marine Corps also included him in the annual general officers conference, as well as the reception at the Commandant's quarters. A photograph of Puller in his dress white uniform was featured prominently in the social pages of the Washington newspapers the next day. He sent a clipping to Virginia and proudly noted his courage was still recognized: "I am glad when they wrote of my ribbons they mentioned the five Navy Crosses."

During the conference, Chesty spoke privately about his situation with Shepherd. The senior general listened to Puller's arguments, but replied: "It is out of my hands and entirely up to the doctors." Chesty took it as one more sign that Shepherd was not being honest about the situation, which further stoked his fury. Even so, Puller held his temper in check in dealings with the Commandant. Chesty remained unfailingly correct when interacting with his superior and his letters contained the usual queries about the Shepherd family.[54]

The annual August reunion of the 1st Marine Division Association gave a welcome boost to Puller's morale. His arrival in the lobby of the hotel brought rowdy shouts and a "traffic jam" as men crowded close to talk with him. He worked his way through the press, shaking hands and greeting them all with the earnest salutation: "Good to see you, old man." The public outpouring of admiration left Chesty "choked with emotion."[55]

☆   ☆   ☆

At the beginning of August, a clinical board of three doctors (including two from the January board) met to review Puller's case. Noting that several test results "remain abnormal," they concluded that the January assessment was still valid: "This officer is not physically fit for the performance of full duty." Their work became part of the record presented to the physical evaluation board, composed of two Marine officers and a Navy doctor. The function of the latter body would be quasi-judicial in nature and it could take into account nonmedical factors.[56]

The physical evaluation board convened just after noon chow on August 10, 1955. Sherman introduced in evidence the results of the October 1954 medical board in Lejeune and called two witnesses. The first doctor admitted that the medical tests were not entirely conclusive, but he steadfastly backed up the results of the Bethesda boards. The second was a physician who had served at Lejeune. He theorized that the admitting doctors overreacted in characterizing Chesty's illness: "I think there may have been some undue emphasis placed on the severity of his condition because he was the commanding general." Puller then took the stand. He insisted he simply had suffered from the heat in August 1954. In reply to a question from Sherman, Chesty described his desires for the future: "I do not want to be retired. I still have almost six years to go until I reach the retirement age of 62. I believe that in the coming six years I'll have an opportunity to practice the knowledge that I have gained in 37 years of active duty—26 years of foreign duty—and if we do go to war during those years, I would like to take part in it instead of sitting at home twiddling my thumbs."[57]

Sherman closed with a summation worthy of a seasoned trial lawyer. He spoke for a few minutes about the medical facts, but soon got to the heart of his case: "The problem before this board is not medical, it is political. The only question is, does the Marine Corps desire his services any longer. . . . I respectfully submit that the evidence of five Navy Crosses, which you see before your eyes, should weigh just as much, if not more than the various blood pressure readings." His closing words revealed the bitterness both he and Puller felt:

> It was only five years ago that the city of Seoul was lost to the free world. At that time no one said that General Puller was a has-been. Many a younger officer wanted the job he had. None of us younger officers could have done the job better. True enough, his retirement now will hasten the day when one of the young turks will get a star. Someone will make a number when this officer, this "Marine's Marine" retires. Maybe that is good and maybe not, but gentlemen, that is precisely the situation you face. For thirty-seven years this man has held a commission on active duty. His blood has been given in the service of his country while others sat at a desk. There are younger and perhaps more brilliant planners and schemers who need promotion, but there can never be another Puller to lead and inspire the troops in carrying out these brilliant plans. Now, because he exerted himself in the August sun, must he be thrown in the discard pile?

Here, gentlemen, is the old Marine Corps, the last of those who gave to their country because of a sense of duty rather than from a keen appreciation of the finer points of public relations of the cheesecake variety. If duty requires that the old time Marine should give way to the fast talkers, then so be it. But in doing an injustice to General Puller, you would be doing a far greater injustice to the Marine Corps and our country. Yours is the decision, here and now, to decide whether or not political considerations of expediency shall outweigh loyalty to the kind of men who made the Marine Corps; our Corps which is now the tool and plaything of younger aspirants to fame. I urge you to choose to retain this officer on active duty as an example of the fidelity of the Corps to the men who have made it.[58]

The plea played upon the strong tradition of taking care of a fellow Marine. It also tarred anyone who disagreed as a political schemer looking out for himself before Corps and country.

The board deliberated for less than an hour. The two Marines voted that Puller was "fit to perform the duties of his rank." The Navy member filed a minority opinion saying that Chesty was "unfit" and that his disability should be rated at 30 percent. The decision was only a minor tactical victory for Chesty. The work of the physical evaluation board would have to be scrutinized by a physical review council. Depending on the results at that level, Puller could make a plea to an appeals board. Eventually his case would land on the desk of the Secretary of the Navy, who had the final say. There were many battles to go before the campaign would be over, but Chesty wanted to believe: "I had won my fight." Vandegrift, at Bethesda for treatment, talked to his old subordinate and came away with the impression Puller was "in the clear."[59]

Infused with fresh hope, Puller wrote Haggerty, Hayes, and Farrell and asked them to work again on his behalf: "Anything you may see fit to do to assist me in this case will be deeply appreciated." Since Chesty felt Shepherd still would play a decisive role in the outcome, he also moved on his own to counter the expected opposition. He contacted Admiral Burke and provided an update on the retirement proceedings. This time he made his object explicit: "If it is possible for you to show any friendly interest in this case, I will appreciate it."[60]

The effort to keep Puller on active duty took one step forward and two back in the next few weeks. Hayes and Haggerty contacted reporters, lobbyists, and members of Congress in an attempt to generate interest in Chesty's case. Three senators, including John F. Kennedy, passed the correspondence on to the Corps with brief form letters asking "for such favorable consideration as the communication herewith submitted warrants." Haggerty used Governor Dewey's name in a memorandum to a White House staffer in an attempt to generate presidential interest. Hayes and his compatriots kept Chesty apprised of all these activities. Arleigh Burke also told Puller he would look into the matter, though he warned: "Any action I would take would be tempered primarily by advice based on professional medical opinion." That was the same stance Shepherd had taken.[61]

The bureaucratic machine ground forward inexorably while Chesty marshaled his forces. On August 22 the physical review council announced it would "concur in the recommended findings of the minority member of the physical evaluation board." This reversal of fortunes left Puller livid and he told Sherman: "I would appreciate your fighting this thing on my behalf to the bitter end." Although the council was a Navy Department body with only one representative from the Corps in its membership, Chesty also chose to ascribe the action to the Commandant: "I cannot understand, at this stage of the game, why every effort has been made by General Shepherd to get me out of the Marine Corps. . . . I consider this less than I deserve after 37 years in the Marine Corps. I would like very much to find out what officer or group of officers has poisoned the Commandant's mind against me."[62]

The flanking attacks on the retirement process proved equally fruitless. The director of personnel for the Marine Corps fended off the halfhearted congressional inquiries with a note promising to provide full information on Puller's case once the Secretary of the Navy had completed action on the matter. Then, of course, it would be too late, but none of the senators took issue with that response. Manpower officials also refused to provide reporters with information. Sherman thought that publicity might do "some harm," so Chesty's camp refrained from giving its version of events to correspondents. Finally, the CNO declined to take action once his surgeon general rendered an internal opinion that Puller was not fit for full duty.[63]

It was like the battle for the Umurbrogol all over again. Puller and his troops were butting their heads against an implacable foe who would not be dislodged from strong defenses. Chesty was running out of options, his forces shrinking as each new attack met an unassailable cliff.

☆ ☆ ☆

The appeals board convened on September 2, with Sherman again pleading his client's case. General Litzenberg headed this group, composed of two other Marines and two Navy doctors. Since the board had the dual role of making a recommendation on Puller's duty status and on his disability rating, Sherman was placed in the unenviable situation of trying to prove two contradictory propositions. He had to argue that Chesty was fit for service and also insist the general was sick enough to rate much higher disability pay if he was retired. The lawyer recurred to the same themes used before the physical evaluation board, though he refrained this time from disparaging characterizations of those who disagreed. His praise for Chesty moved beyond mere mention of awards: "General Puller is practically the 1st Marine Division, altogether in one man. . . . Of the Marines today, General Puller is probably the most famous on active duty, and will go down in the annals of the Marine Corps as probably the number one Marine the Corps has ever had." Sherman reiterated his paradoxical themes in his final remarks: "If you can't find it in your hearts, if you can't find it in your minds, to say that General Puller is a good Marine still, then for heaven's sake say that he is so sick that he warrants the maximum disability."[64]

Hayes and Puller both thought Sherman's work was "masterful," but the appeals board provided no relief to Chesty. It found him unfit for duty and only raised his disability rating to 40 percent. The outcome "greatly surprised" Puller, since he had expected a friendly hearing from the head of the board. Chesty believed Litzenberg should have been "deeply in debt to me," since he felt he had aided the former CO of the 7th Marines during their service together in the Korean War. "I am confident that if it had not been for this help I extended Litzenberg, he would never have made brigadier general, much less major general, in the Corps." Litzenberg did have high regard for Puller, but apparently believed that Chesty was minimizing his physical problems.[65]

The matter was now up to the Secretary of the Navy. Sherman's part in the process was over and he counseled Puller to seek political help. That avenue already had been exhausted, however, and Chesty's partisans were either unable or still unwilling to mount a media campaign. Like the Commandant and the CNO, the Secretary was reluctant to override the firm opinion of the medical experts. He might have authorized continued limited duty, but that was an unlikely option. O. P. Smith thought the Corps "would have greatly benefitted" by placing Puller in a billet, such as command of a recruit depot, where he could continue to inspire Marines. Chesty had vowed repeatedly that he would not serve in a restricted status, though, and had taken the brief stint in the base headquarters solely to have the chance to fight for a return to full duty. Shepherd also believed, with some justification, that Chesty could never sit idly back in a purely ceremonial role. The Commandant told his son-in-law: "If General Puller stayed on active duty, he would kill himself." Smith had the same apprehension and qualified his recommendation for a recruit depot with the caveat, "if health permits."[66]

On October 6, the Secretary informed Puller that he would be retired at the end of the month. Chesty had expected it, but it nevertheless was "a great disappointment and a stunning blow." He still felt he had been treated unfairly and his career had been cut unjustifiably short. And he held the Commandant and HQMC entirely responsible: "There is no bitterness in my heart against the Marine Corps, but there is plenty against certain individuals. Why certain individuals have had it in for me I don't know. I did not think I had made enemies among the high echelons of the Corps, but apparently I have. It is my opinion that it is not among the 'young turks,' but among my contemporaries and seniors that amenity is lacking."[67]

The campaign, indeed, had turned out like Peleliu. In both cases, Puller still thought he had plenty of fight left in him, but higher authorities were convinced otherwise and ordered him off the field of battle, his objective still not secured. Now there would be no additional five years of duty, no fresh opportunities to campaign on behalf of Corps and country, no more whirring shrapnel or cracking bullets, no more husky commands or the heavy tread of marching feet, no more morning colors or twilight taps. But there was, and always would be, thirty-seven years of glory unparalleled in the history of the Corps.

25

"Never Forget the Battles of the Past"
The Golden Years
1955–1960

On October 10, 1955, the Marine Corps announced Puller's pending retirement. The news sparked a nationwide spate of stories recounting the highlights of his service and the swaggering yarns his career had inspired. The articles extolled both his martial prowess and the leadership that had earned him "the affection of thousands of Marines." The superlatives heaped upon him were richly deserved. "Perhaps no Marine of modern times better exemplified the vaunted spirit of the Corps." "One of the legendary Marine heroes of all time." "One of the toughest and most colorful Leathernecks of them all." "Wherever Marines gather and talk of past battles, the name of Maj. Gen. Puller must figure largely in their conversation." A newspaper editorial marking the near simultaneous retirements of Puller, O. P. Smith, and a celebrated Army general noted that Chesty was "tough, cocky, profane, and uncouth." But the writer believed that the memory of each man "will gleam brightly . . . for each is of heroic mold and rich in those qualities of understanding and leadership that sparked in the men under them the best that their men could give, in darkling decades when the best was what their country had to have." A columnist in North Carolina punctuated the unique place of the legendary Leatherneck in the annals of his service: "The Marine Corps has developed many fine officers, but even the Marines have been able to come up with but one Chesty Puller."[1]

Along with Puller's retirement orders, Shepherd sent a personal note to mark the occasion. He praised Chesty for his "superlative caliber of leadership," his "tenacious fighting spirit and indomitable courage," and his "burning devotion to duty." The Commandant declared: "The glorious history of our Corps has been forever illuminated by your illustrious achievement." In a sign that he did not yet realize the depth of enmity created by the forced retirement, he added: "Your friendship I shall always cherish."[2]

There were letters from many others of every rank. Vandegrift wrote: "The Corps will miss you, Lewis, for by your unselfish service, integrity, and courage under difficult circumstances you have set a high example. . . . Your name is now a legend in the Corps and all fighting men salute you." A former corpsman in 1/7 assured his old commander: "The Marines who served under you loved and respected you. . . . As a citizen of this country I say thanks to you for your great part in preserving the freedom and liberties which we enjoy." Puller may have appreciated most the simple tribute from his steadfast friend O. P. Smith: "My association with you has meant much to me over the years. Your example of devotion to duty is legend in the Marine Corps. Your methods have always been honest, direct and forthright. There is no indirection or deviousness in your character. You have acted with singleness of purpose guided by your highest sense of right. These are the traits of character I have admired."[3]

☆   ☆   ☆

Puller was in no mood for an elaborate ceremony to mark his retirement; it was a day to be dreaded, not celebrated. It made no difference that he would receive the rank of lieutenant general for "having been specially commended for performance of duty in actual combat." Virginia and the children remained at the quarters; he did not want them to attend the event. Chesty simply walked down the passageway to the roomier office of the base commander and borrowed it for a few minutes. The only attendees were two correspondents, Captain Moore, Gunnery Sergeant Jones, and Sergeant Major Robert L. Norrish (who had served as a private in Puller's trophy-winning drill platoon in 1926). Chesty asked the sergeant major to do the honors of pinning on the new stars. Puller stood ramrod straight and stone-faced in front of the crossed flags of the nation and the Corps as Norrish added the final tribute of a grateful country to the shoulder straps of the general's beribboned service blouse.[4]

At the completion of the brief formalities, Puller gave a terse but heartfelt statement to the reporters. He explained his rationale for choosing Norrish for the duty: "I wanted to show my great admiration and appreciation to the enlisted men in the Marine Corps and the junior officers." He added that without their assistance "I would never have risen to my position of lieutenant general" and his units "would never have gone forward and achieved their objectives, regardless of almost certain death." He expressed only one regret after thirty-seven years, two months, and twenty-nine days of duty: "I won't be present for the next war." The low-key ceremony produced high emotion as a legendary career came to an end. The few men present struggled to keep their composure as their eyes misted over. A reporter provided a welcome distraction when he asked the general and the other three Marines to pose for a picture. As the shutter snapped, Chesty growled out his last official words: "I hate like hell to go."[5]

☆　☆　☆

Puller often had professed an intention to retire to Saluda, his wife's hometown, but he had not expected to do so until he was sixty-two. In 1954, when he first had faced the prospect of leaving the Corps early, he had decided to move the family to Richmond. He wanted to provide his children with the amenities of a large city, especially good private schools, such as Collegiate, where Virginia McC already was enrolled. Possibly his choice was influenced by opportunities for a second career as well, since there was little prospect of suitable employment for a general in the sleepy hamlets of the Tidewater. His sister Pattie lived in the capital, too.

By the fall of 1955, this initial plan had fallen by the wayside and the Pullers were headed to Saluda after all. One factor was Virginia's mother, who was recovering from injuries suffered in a traffic accident. She let her son-in-law know she would be "happy at the thought of having you and yours in Saluda" and that her grandchildren were "a constant joy to me." Chesty had a strong sense of family and always had been "tender and kind" to Mrs. Evans, whom he treated like his own parent. He also considered Saluda a natural home in any case. West Point was only a dozen miles away, several generations of Pullers had lived in adjacent Gloucester County, Major John W. Puller's name was engraved on the monument to Confederate war dead at a nearby courthouse, and another ancestor had donated the land for the local Episcopal church.[6]

Residing in a village of two hundred souls in rural Virginia practically guaranteed Puller would not work. His opportunities were circumscribed not only by his location, but also by ethics rules that forbade his involvement in any defense-related industry for two years. His own scruples ruled out any offer that appeared designed to use his name to boost business with fellow Marines. There was a lead about a well-paid position as a consultant to the Senate Armed Services Committee, but it required lots of travel and long hours. That did not suit his blood pressure condition or his desire to spend more time with his family. Virginia may have considered his enforced idleness an added bonus of moving to Saluda, since she was anxious about his health. The Bethesda doctors had given Chesty an encouraging prognosis—under the right circumstances: "If I take care of myself and get plenty of rest, I can expect to live to reach an old age." His wife was doing all in her power to make him follow that advice. (A few years later, when friends put forward Puller's name for chief of police of Richmond, he squelched the idea with the half-joking reaction: "If I take the position, she will divorce me.") Lewis Jr. would recall about his father: "There was an unstated premise that he was unable to do any strenuous work."[7]

Although Chesty assured his wife they would "have enough to live on decently," he felt his financial situation was constrained at best. Having lost his battle for a higher disability rating, he had elected to draw his normal retirement compensation, which amounted to 75 percent of his active-duty salary. In addition to that one-fourth reduction from his previous earnings, he also no longer received tax-free housing and food allowances. Finally, there was a deduction of nearly 20 percent to provide a survivor benefit for Virginia if he died. For typical retired couples, the resulting amount would have been enough, but he still had three children to raise and put through college. Moreover, as Mrs. Evans knew, "he adores them & wants them to have every advantage." Chesty placed great store in providing his family with private schooling, domestic help, and other hallmarks of a refined lifestyle. Money thus was no small concern to him.[8]

Virginia had shrewdly managed their finances from the beginning, however, and her husband was surprised to find in October 1955 that she had amassed enough in savings bonds to pay for a house. At an auction in the middle of the month, the Pullers bought a small home in the heart of Saluda. It had stood empty for some time, required repairs, and was not "pretentious" (Chesty called it "the cottage"), but it suited the family's needs. The one-and-a-half-story house was surrounded by shade trees, hedges, and grass. It was architecturally pleasing, with matching wings, dormers, and an entry porch topped by a white wooden railing. There was sufficient space for the antiques and heirlooms the Pullers had acquired over the years, as well as room for his books and memorabilia. Most important of all, there was a fireplace on each side of the house. Virginia had never ceased reminding Lewis of her dream every time they had driven by a place with that architectural feature—now they finally had a house with two chimneys to call home.[9]

☆　☆　☆

Virginia's mother was concerned about her son-in-law's disposition in the aftermath of his bitter retirement. In late October she had written him a long letter full of counsel:

> I know it is hard to take—this blow from a friend or I should say one who was supposed to be. . . . But again that was his fault, not yours and you must not think your life is finished by any means. Since you can look any man in the eye, you must feel that this chapter of your life is closed, but there will be many other broad avenues opening up for you and yours. You owe it to your wife and children to show interest in everything around you—your home, your church, your community and all the things that go to make up life. . . . Since you have no real hobby, try to develop a love for the yard and vegetable gardens. . . . Think of our wonderful Virginia, she must be made to know that you are happy with her and the children, for that is the only way for her to be happy and her happiness means much to you and me. . . . That is what I expect of you and I know you will not fail me.[10]

Mrs. Evans did not have to worry—Chesty was not about to spend his retired years sulking. His mother-in-law may have thought he had no outside interests (and he once had written that the military was his only hobby), but he had more than enough pastimes to keep himself busy. He informed a reporter on his first day in Saluda that he wanted to teach his son how to shoot, go "hunting and fishing," and "catch up on reading military history." The living room had built-in bookcases in one corner; Virginia placed a comfortable chair and lamp right there. It became his habit to spend "long hours here reading and rereading his books." The family would soon joke that he knew Douglas Southall Freeman's three-volume *Lee's Lieutenants* "by heart." He also had time for another passion—bridge—and a frequently used card table occupied the center of the cozy den. He reveled in the chance to spend time with his children as well, but it was not all play. He took a keen interest in helping them with homework and told another correspondent: "My main mission in life now is the education of my children." He had promised Virginia: "I will live only for you and our precious children and my requirements will be your great love, a little food, and a daily can of tobacco." He would never admit it to Shepherd, but Chesty followed the Commandant's final advice to "enjoy the relaxation you have so deservingly earned."[11]

Puller looked forward to an easygoing retirement, but he was not about to moderate his convictions or his willingness to express them. An interviewer asking about the general's plans also received an earful on the future of conflict and the country. Chesty repeated his long-held assertion that "push-button warfare is a thousand years away." He also introduced a new theme about the quality of the nation's youth: "They're as good as their fathers and grandfathers were—I fought with all three generations. If Americans have the proper leadership on high levels, we'll never have anything to fear." In a relatively short time, the strong opinions of a retired Tidewater general would have more impact than anyone could imagine.[12]

☆   ☆   ☆

On Sunday, April 8, 1956, Staff Sergeant Matthew McKeon, a drill instructor at Parris Island, took his platoon of seventy-five recruits on a night march into a small, swampy tidal estuary on the base. During the course of the frustrating day with his subpar unit, he had drunk some alcohol and then decided that a dose of cold water and mud might improve discipline. Instead, panic ensued when the rear of the loose column drifted into deep, swift water. McKeon and some of his stronger swimmers attempted to save those in trouble, but when the last wet, shivering, dazed recruit stumbled onto dry land, a head count revealed only sixty-nine men. It would take more than twenty-four hours to recover the six bodies from the muck at the bottom of Ribbon Creek. The Marine Corps suddenly was faced with a public scandal that could shatter its very foundation—the tough basic training that had molded generations of men into the victors of Belleau Wood, Guadalcanal, the Chosin Reservoir, and dozens of other desperate battles.

The new Commandant, General Pate, did some things well and others poorly in his response to the crisis. Skilled in bureaucratic machinations, he wisely informed key supporters in Congress of the problem before he broke the news to the media. He promised and delivered a quick investigation, made the results public as soon as possible, and put in place vigorous new leadership to implement needed reforms of the recruit-training system. The latter included steps to reduce stress on DIs and to limit the potential for maltreatment of privates. Those actions staved off a formal congressional inquiry and gave the Corps a chance to clean its own house. On the negative side, before Pate knew the full story he condemned McKeon. That not only created problems of fairness in the pending legal proceedings, it also left DIs feeling that one of their own was being made the scapegoat for the entire chain of command. The Commandant's subsequent statement that "the Marine Corps is on trial for the tragedy of Ribbon Creek just as surely as is Sergeant McKeon" went too far in the other direction and gave the press and public unnecessary cause to question the Corps.[13]

A well-known trial lawyer from New York City offered to join the defense team. Emile Zola Berman was the son of immigrant Russians who had a taste for "revolutionary socialism." He inherited his parents' activism, and also served as an officer in the Army Air Forces in World War II, earning the Distinguished Flying Cross in the process. Before the court-martial began in July 1956, he used the threat of a wide-ranging indictment of the Corps' training practices to win concessions from the institution. In return for Pate's agreement to serve as witness for the defense, Berman vowed to use the Corps' reputation for uncompromising training as a positive part of his case. Instead of accusing the service of allowing rampant abuse of recruits, the defense team would argue that their client merely had been employing time-honored and necessary toughness to mold his charges into effective fighters.

Berman's strategy would strengthen the position of the Corps with the public rather than denigrate it.[14]

Given intense media interest in the case, the auditorium in the base school was turned into a makeshift courtroom to accommodate dozens of reporters. There was no air-conditioning and few windows, which made things exceedingly uncomfortable in the midsummer heat and humidity. The Secretary of the Navy named seven officers to the court (the equivalent of a civilian jury). In addition to one Navy doctor, there were six Marines, three of whom had started their careers as enlisted men at Parris Island. A Navy captain with little experience in criminal cases served as the law officer (essentially a judge). The charges against McKeon involved drinking on duty, culpable negligence in the six deaths, and oppression. The latter was an ill-defined offense involving maltreatment of subordinates.[15]

During the course of the two weeks it took the prosecution to present its case, Berman twice asked for extended weekend recesses "to undertake a mission which I regard as of the highest importance connected with this case." The court granted both requests. One of these periods likely was used to meet with the Commandant and review his possible testimony. The other almost certainly entailed a visit to Saluda. Soon after, the defense announced its list of witnesses. Prominent among them was Puller. On July 22, two days before the prosecution received those names, a national weekly journal published an interview with Chesty titled "Is Toughness Necessary?" Several of the questions and answers would parallel exactly what would transpire in court a few days hence. The article simply may have arisen from interest in the trial, but it more likely was a part of the media campaign Berman had orchestrated from the time he took over the case. He was counting on the retired general as one of his two star witnesses.[16]

The other major witness was Pate. He apparently was ill at ease during his appearance and tried to cover it with humor that seemed out of place under the circumstances. His wearing of sunglasses while he sat on the stand testifying under oath further detracted from his already damaged prestige. In response to questions from Berman, the Commandant completely reversed his earlier public position endorsing McKeon's court-martial and calling for the strongest possible punishment. Now he expressed the opinion that the DI should lose one rank for drinking in front of a recruit. As for the other charges, the Commandant thought the staff sergeant rated, at most, transfer away from his duties "for lack of judgment." Pate's about-face came too late to alter the opinion of DIs, who thought he had thrown them all to the wolves.[17]

The contrast with Puller could not have been more stark. Chesty arrived on the base the same day the Commandant gave his testimony. That evening, the retired general visited the SNCO club and was greeted with "a window-shaking ovation." The enthusiastic reception brought an unusually broad smile to his poker face. A newsman who was there accurately observed that Puller "is probably more universally respected in the Corps than any other living Marine." Pate went to the NCO club that same evening, but "it didn't go too well there."

The next day, August 2, Chesty walked into the packed auditorium. As the general strode purposefully up the aisle, the president of the court stood and called the large room to attention—a sign of respect not accorded Pate the day before. The standing-room-only crowd was the largest yet for the trial and all felt an air of drama. Puller wasted no time in establishing his dominance of this unaccustomed arena. He sat confidently in the witness stand, legs crossed and one arm crooked over the back of the chair, eight rows of ribbons covering his entire left breast, apparently cool in his uniform jacket and tie despite the sweltering conditions. With his trademark stentorian voice reverberating off the walls, he nodded toward the rear: "Now, if I don't talk loud, somebody back there sound off and I'll talk louder." Everyone laughed.[18]

Berman opened by having Puller describe his career, as if that recitation were needed to impress the members of the court. The lawyer next asked about Chesty's training as a recruit in 1918. The witness emphasized one principle: "The main thing . . . that I have remembered all my life . . . is that esprit de corps means love for one's own military legion; in my case, the United States Marine Corps. It means more than self-preservation, religion, or patriotism." In an echo of his tutelage under Vandegrift and others in Haiti, Puller added: "I've also learned that this loyalty to one's corps travels both ways, up and down." The court was on notice that he intended to look out for both the institution and McKeon.

In response to Berman's next two questions, Chesty referred to history as a guide. He cited Von Steuben, George Washington's German drill master in the Revolutionary War, as the authority on the mission of any military force—"success in battle." Then he quoted another military genius: "Napoleon stated that the most important thing in military training was discipline. Without discipline an army becomes a mob." Subsequent queries brought forth Puller's ideas about training recruits. He thought DIs should have "broad discretion" in developing discipline and esprit de corps, and felt books and classrooms were not the best way to teach those subjects: "The training of a basic Marine is confined almost entirely to outside in the field, on the drill ground, on the rifle range."

The lawyer launched into two long questions in the form of hypothetical situations, both closely based on the facts in McKeon's case. In response to the first example, Chesty stated he did not believe that marching troops into a swamp constituted oppression. The second hypothetical asked for a simple judgment whether the night march for the purpose of instilling discipline was "good military practice." The general was not about to pass up a chance to emphasize an issue he considered important: "In my opinion, the reason American soldiers made out so poorly in the Korean War was mostly due to the lack of night training. And if we are going to win the next war I say that from now on fifty percent of the training time should be devoted to night training."

It was now the prosecution's turn. The two Marine officers (both of them mustangs) found the general a hostile witness. He interjected his own query in the middle of one question, refused to agree with a simple assumption at the heart of another, and went off on an unrelated issue about night training in response to a third. When the senior prosecutor, a major, pointed out that Puller must have misunderstood the last question, Chesty baldly admitted: "I know. I just wanted to get that into the record." Asked about the existence of limitations on DIs, Puller answered: "When I was on Parris Island as a recruit and drill instructor . . . the drill instructors had practically unlimited authority." Challenged about the wisdom of night training for new recruits, the general argued that training regulations were not a complete guide: "I know that in anything I ever commanded I get most of the glory and all of the blame and I have willingly taken the blame and I would train my troops as I know they should be trained regardless of a directive."

The prosecutor asked his own hypotheticals, emphasizing McKeon's failure to reconnoiter the waters, his loss of control over the formation, and his neglect of potential problems for nonswimmers. Puller gave his opponents their only point when he agreed that was "not good leadership," but he raised his voice and emphasized: "I would say that this night march was or is a deplorable accident." Pressed on the issue, Chesty sided with the Commandant: "I think I read in the papers yesterday in the testimony of General Randolph 'Mac' Pate before this court that he agrees and regrets that this man was ever ordered tried by general court martial." The government lawyers ended their frustrating cross-examination and excused the witness. He had been on the stand for forty-seven minutes. After a half-hour recess, Berman decided not to call other witnesses and announced he had completed his case. In a final testimony to Puller's preeminence in the court, the defense asked for a delay the next day, so everyone could attend Puller's review of the morning parade. The president of the court readily assented.[19]

That evening, Chesty attended a "hastily organized" party at the NCO club. The defense, the DIs, and most correspondents were so certain the official influence of the Commandant and the personal prestige of Puller would carry the day that the "occasion had every earmark of a victory gathering." The facility was "jammed as it never has been before," but the crowd went silent and the Marines snapped to crisp attention as the retired general entered. Someone led him to a microphone and he boomed out an impromptu speech: "I have talked enough for today. This will be my last request. I want you to do your duty and this Marine Corps will be as great as it has been for another thousand years. Do your duty and have no fear and no one will attempt to destroy the Marine Corps for another thousand years." When he fell silent, the throng erupted in a "vast thunder of applause."[20]

The following morning, Puller presided over the parade and handed out awards to drill instructors. The trial resumed with closing arguments by the lawyers. Just after noontime, the court began its deliberations. Contrary to speculation about the importance of the two senior witnesses, the members of the court discussed the generals and agreed to disregard their testimony. The seven jurors all felt McKeon's actions had been fundamentally wrong. After several hours of debate, the court convicted him on one of two alcohol-related charges and also found him guilty of negligently causing the deaths of the six recruits. They decided he was innocent of the more serious accusation of oppression. The court's decision on punishment was even more astonishing to those who had assumed the staff sergeant was off the hook after Pate and Puller testified in the DI's favor. The defendant and his lawyers "were taken aback" when the court sentenced McKeon to a reduction in rank to private, nine months of hard labor, loss of most of his pay, and a bad conduct discharge. Ultimately the Secretary of the Navy would decrease the punishment, but McKeon's career was ruined.[21]

Puller's testimony had not played an important part in the outcome, but his appearance made banner headlines in newspapers. And, in contrast to the beer-and-whiskey episode, this time his comments on military readiness received positive attention in the media. At a time when President Dwight D. Eisenhower was emphasizing a strategy of reliance on nuclear weapons and cutting funds for conventional forces, Chesty's stance added fuel to a backlash in certain sectors of the armed forces. The Army was instituting changes to toughen recruit training, enhance the role of NCOs, and reinvigorate professionalism in the ranks. Pate also assigned strong personalities to oversee the reform of Marine recruit depots. Major General David M. Shoup and Brigadier General Wallace M. Greene, Jr., would do outstanding jobs and go on to become the next two commandants after Pate. They ensured that the type of strenuous training advocated by Puller remained the hallmark of the Corps.[22]

☆　☆　☆

The few days of active duty had tremendous personal ramifications for Puller. For the first time since his unwilling retirement, he was back in the national spotlight. The media had not only trumpeted his message, it had sung his praises, too. One newspaper represented his testimony as "one of the most dramatic courtroom appearances in military history." Correspondents vied to produce the most vivid descriptions of the general and his place in the Corps. "Chewing his words as if they were a quid of tobacco and spitting them out with enough force to carry above a full gale at sea." "A wide mouth that looks as if it would be ideal for chewing cactus." "The jut-jawed general is the very model of an old-fashioned fighting Marine." "The blunt, wondrously profane, barrel-chested little man is recognized as the toughest, and among the bravest, of all Marines." "The idol of every noncom and drill instructor." "Almost as much revered as the 'Halls of Montezuma.' " "When a genius for leadership, a keen intelligence, devotion to duty and indomitable will to win are electrified by rare bravery. . . . '*There* is a man!' " The reporters also repeated many elements of the Puller legend and, typically, twisted the facts.[23]

Chesty thoroughly enjoyed his reputation as "a man who says what he thinks," and the McKeon trial gave him his first opportunity as a retiree to reach a national audience. It also provided him with the chance to tell his version of the events that had caused his retirement. One newspaper reported: "Gen. Puller's contention is that some violent statements attributed to him about the namby-pamby softness of the American people resulted in his getting his walking papers." The writer added: "The 'milk-vs-whiskey' crack attributed to him cast Gen. Puller into near-oblivion for a while. But by early 1952 he was in command of troop training for the Pacific at Coronado." Leadership of the 3d Brigade was far from "near-oblivion," of course, and the 1951 controversy was an unlikely reason for his retirement in 1955 (given his intervening selection for promotion and division command). Chesty had made up his mind long ago, however, that he had been forced out of the Corps for outspokenness. He would repeat the refrain for the remainder of his days.[24]

Now that correspondents realized he was still good copy even in retirement, they beat a path to his door whenever they needed a pithy quote on military matters. The well-known national magazine *Esquire* utilized Puller to skewer Pate in January 1958. The piece, titled "Waste of an Old Warhorse," justifiably wondered about the "vacillation of the Corps command at its highest levels" and juxtaposed that weakness with "the kind of spirit personified" by the retired general from Saluda. In a none too subtle jab at Pate's background as a staff officer, the writer quoted Puller: "There is no substitute for battlefield experience. . . . A top officer must have command *in* combat. . . . I not only thought you had to get all the active duty possible, but also had to distinguish yourself, not through words, but in action and deeds accomplished." The article indirectly supported Chesty's contention that he had been unjustly forced off active duty: "His adherents believe [he] was eased into retirement because his bluff ways would prove too much for the drawing rooms of political Washington. . . . High blood pressure is not necessarily incapacitating—Puller continues to lead an active outdoor life—but it offers a traditionally convenient reason for retirement." The conclusion noted that "Puller yearns mightily to be in uniform again" and "there are Marines everywhere, in uniform and out, who wish that Chesty Puller were back."[25]

Several months later, a Richmond newspaper devoted an entire page to a feature article on the Virginia hero. The writer had captured his material as Puller paced back and forth across his Saluda living room, holding forth on his career and national defense. Nearly seven years after the fighting withdrawal from the Chosin Reservoir, his attitudes about weapons, training, and history had not changed: "I believe in the future, atomic bombs and all the rest of it, but you can't forget the past. Korea proved we are making a great mistake in depending too much on advanced weapons and neglecting to prepare our troops sufficiently in the fundamentals of warfare. We didn't use the bomb. We had to fall back and fight the war just as Jackson did at Chancellorsville. We can never forget the battles of the past in preparing for the future. We lost Korea and unless a change of thinking takes place we've won our last war." He also had strong views about issues outside the military field. He took on foreign aid and education priorities in one fell swoop, arguing that reliance on "two-bit interpreters" overseas resulted in a waste of American largesse: "We have people over there who can't even talk to anybody. It's just as important to train our youth to speak foreign languages as it is to teach them science."

The article contained the now obligatory implication that his retirement was improper. Citing a "feeling throughout the Corps" that Puller's health problems were "not serious," the reporter noted: "Marines wonder if in peacetime their most decorated leader may have been considered 'too much Marine' for Washington teas and intrigues." The bittersweet ending of the piece undoubtedly reflected Chesty's growing sadness at his isolation from the Corps he loved so dearly: "The sign that he is restless is most apparent when the compact, vital man grows silent, abstract. His wife, catching him in that mood the other evening, asked him if he wished anything. 'Yes,' he said, in a growl so low it was almost a whisper. 'I'd like to see once again all the Marines who ever served with me.' "[26]

The Virginia department of the American Legion invited Puller to speak at its July 1959 convention. His talk covered a wide range of national issues, only one of them directly related to the military. Citing a recent news report, he noted the commander of North Atlantic Treaty Organization forces had admitted a Soviet invasion would reach West European ports in ten days. Chesty growled: "The way things are governed it will take ten days [for us] to drop the atomic bomb. By that time the Russian troops would not be in Russia but in Geneva, Paris, Rome—in all those cities. Now where will we drop the bomb? On those cities? Why can't NATO stop the Russians? I'll tell you, NATO hasn't got the armies and the soldiers are armed with carbines—an abortion that has largely supplanted the old-fashioned American rifle. If an American soldier can't carry a 10-pound rifle, what hope have we got?"

He touched on foreign aid and languages again, this time adding: "I don't believe in letting people starve but you don't have to give them everything in the world. Men with self-respect won't starve." He stood aghast at the national debt of $280 billion: "More than all debts of all countries in the world combined. The government can never repay it . . . we have no intention of repaying it. We are practically bankrupt." Having seen monetary inflation at work in war-ravaged nations, he was very concerned about that threat in the United States. He had no solution and worried "there may be a time when today's $10,000 insurance policy may not be enough to buy a ham sandwich." He repeated his theme about the quality of American youth serving in the armed forces, but cautioned "you can't spread us out too thin." A newspaper covering the story reminded readers that during Puller's military career, he "was frequently in trouble with superiors because of his straight-from-the-chest remarks."[27]

Chesty was just as quick to speak out about local issues in the Tidewater. In 1958, he and Virginia attended a panel discussion on teen behavior hosted by the Parent-Teacher Association. When the experts had talked themselves out, the moderator asked if anyone in the audience wished to add anything. Puller jumped to his feet: "I certainly do." As he launched into a favorite topic, he began walking up and down the aisle, his drill field voice holding everyone's attention. "I keep hearing and reading about the terrible teenagers of today. Leave them alone. They don't need to be downed or upheld. I am tired of hearing all this ballyhoo. Every newspaper and magazine you pick up is full of it. Just don't worry about the young boys of today. They don't need to be coddled and they don't deserve to be condemned." After repeating his view that the young Marines at the Chosin Reservoir were at least the equal of the Revolutionary War soldiers at Valley Forge, he concluded: "Leave your sons alone and let them grow up to be *men*." The last word boomed off the walls like a cannon shot. He sat down and his hundred or so fellow citizens cheered and applauded.[28]

Puller also had pointed out to his listeners that his comments were primarily about boys: "I know the girls have to have a certain amount of supervision." He informed a reporter later just how great he thought the differences were between the genders: "I can talk to men. I wouldn't even attempt to talk to women. They don't even think like we do." He had no trouble relating to his daughters, though. A visitor to the Puller home overheard Chesty asking Martha how she had fared in making a speech to a school assembly. The thirteen-year-old replied that she had done well, till two boys in the front row had made faces and caused her to giggle. Putting on an especially stern look, her father growled: "Nobody could make me laugh, if I didn't want to." He got the desired result—she screwed up her small face and he broke down in laughter.[29]

Chesty loved his daughters, but he could not help but take a special interest in the son who would "carry on the Puller name." Lewis Jr. was his constant companion in the mostly male activities that dominated the retired general's life. There were frequent father-son hunting and fishing expeditions, during which Chesty schooled his heir in marksmanship, sportsmanship, and the finer points of Southern courtesy and honor. The boy was not very successful in athletic endeavors, but he managed to kill his first deer at the age of eleven. The older Puller was ecstatic at the rite of passage and bragged to everyone that his son had managed the feat much earlier in life than he had. Chesty was equally ready to avenge any slight against his children. Lewis Jr. would recall many years later what transpired when he was scolded by a store clerk for reading a magazine without buying it. Puller immediately had confronted the burly man and snarled into his face: "Leave the boy alone, or you and I can go outside and settle this." Chesty was, in the eyes of his children, "a good father."[30]

☆   ☆   ☆

Puller had been placed on the temporary disability retired list in 1955. Theoretically he could regain his active status if he fully recovered, but his condition was not one that could be cured. Regulations required a final disposition of his case at the end of five years. In September 1960, HQMC transferred him to the retired list. The formality meant little; he was now sixty-two, the legal maximum age for service. The last shred of possibility of returning to duty was gone.[31]

With the exception of the McKeon trial, Chesty had not had any significant official contact with the Corps since the bitter separation of 1955. The finality of his new status in 1960 might have deepened that divide. Instead, circumstances conspired to bring the institution and its greatest hero together again. By late 1959, the Eisenhower administration had lost patience with long-standing Marine opposition to plans to centralize control of military affairs in the Joint Chiefs of Staff and the Department of Defense. Lieutenant General Twining, a prime candidate to replace Pate as Commandant, had been a leading opponent of unification since the 1940s. In an effort to bring Leathernecks into line, the civilian chain of command reached well past Twining and other senior Marines to select Shoup to be the next head of the Corps. The competent and courageous major general (awarded the Medal of Honor for his role at Tarawa) was well qualified for the job, but his civilian superiors valued him most for his lack of "extreme service partisanship." Following Shoup's anointment as Commandant in January 1960, all the lieutenant generals in the Corps retired. That chain of events almost certainly instigated the Secretary of the Navy's June 1960 request for Puller to serve as president of that summer's major general selection board. Chesty had no connection to the recent turmoil in senior Marine ranks and, perhaps more important, had no known history of participation in anti-unification efforts.[32]

At the same time, Colonel Ray Davis contacted his former commander with another proposal: "General Snedeker has suggested to me that you would make the ideal president for the 1st Marine Division Association during the next year." The choice was driven in part by waning interest in the organization, which traditionally had been run by retired senior officers. Davis was honest about their plight: "As you well know, we cannot continue to grow or even survive unless we have strong personal ties between enlisted and officers. . . . Because you epitomize for all of us the virtues and greatness of 'FIGHTING MARINES' more so than any other living man, we now are turning to you in hopes that you will accept the nomination."[33]

Puller wanted to be on active duty for more than the couple of weeks offered by the secretary. He also was just then being permanently retired by the Corps. The refusal of the Navy Department and the division association to help him in his hour of need in 1955 still "made him sore." But he had been away too long from an organization he loved and he craved the comradeship of Marines. He assented to serve on the board and be president of the association.[34]

The 1st Marine Division Association held its 1960 reunion in

Washington in late June. Puller was the first to register on the opening evening of the event. On the 25th he was unanimously voted into office. That night at the formal banquet, Julian Smith acted as the master of ceremonies and introduced the generals at the head table. The crowd of two thousand gave a warm welcome to the dignitaries as a spotlight fell on each one in turn. Smith saved Puller, the president-elect, for last: "I now give you Chesty—" The final words were drowned out by the din of roaring voices, clapping hands, and stomping feet.

The thunder continued as Puller made his way from the far end of the head table to the microphone. When he finally quieted the crowd, he boomed out a salutation—"Marines!"—and the walls reverberated again with a cacophonous response. After a pause to let the noise die down, he announced his goal of rejuvenating the association and asked everyone to help him in "recruiting new blood." Observing briefly that the country always would come out on top "so long as we've got the 1st Marine Division," he closed: "One of the greatest men I ever heard of was a flatfoot—Commodore Steven Decatur. And he said: 'My country, may she always be right—but my country, right or wrong.' Conduct yourselves accordingly and we won't have a damned thing to fear from anybody." That brought the ballroom to pandemonium yet another time as he moved back to his seat.

For the next few hours, Chesty held court at the end of the head table as a long line of Marines waited to have a few words with their former commander or get his autograph on anything they had handy. They had missed him in his five years of absence. And he had missed them. It was, perhaps, the finest and most memorable moment of his retirement years.[35]

26

"Return with Your Shield or on It"
The Twilight Years
1960–1971

Puller's career was the stuff of legend and many people in and out of the media industry believed the public would relish his fascinating story. A retired Marine general had written Chesty with just that idea in 1954, encouraging him to put together his memoirs. Puller was not interested: "I am no author, and no one else will write my biography if I can help it." A year later, Chesty was inclined to think about recording his experiences, but only after "he tired of higher-priority projects carried out with rod and gun." There were plenty of writers, though, who were willing to earn what they could from his name whether he went along or not. In January 1957, a men's magazine called *Real Adventure* had printed "Toughest S.O.B. in the Marines." The article followed the broad outlines of Chesty's life, but contained almost as much exotic fiction as fact. A similar journal, *Lancer,* published an equally lurid piece in November 1960.[1]

The financial straitjacket of retirement already had changed Chesty's mind long before those stories appeared. Following the Ribbon Creek tragedy, attorney Berman had brokered a book and movie deal between his star witness and Jim Bishop, a well-known author and correspondent. But Bishop never got around to writing the book. In late 1959, a newspaper reporter and part-time author with six books to his credit became interested in Puller's story. Burke Davis, then living in North Carolina, specialized in Revolutionary War and Civil War heroes, but the accounts of Chesty's courage intrigued him. As it happened, the writer was getting ready to send his son to Christchurch School (an Episcopal boarding school near Puller's home), which Lewis Jr. already attended. Chesty also recently had received a gift from his old 3d OTC compatriot Tom Pullen. It was one of Davis's well-regarded biographies of a Confederate general. When the author wrote Puller with the idea of doing a book, Davis found an eager reception. His stock only increased in Chesty's eyes when the retired general found a reference to Major John W. Puller in Davis's volume on Jeb Stuart.[2]

The idea received a mixed response in the publishing world. Davis was certain his "far-famed narrative style," coupled with Puller's "controversial [remarks] about so many fairly important people," would "take fire." An editor at Putnam's, which had just published Pappy Boyington's pugnacious autobiography, *Baa Baa Black Sheep,* thought "an *unvarnished* book" on Chesty would be "one hell of a book . . . a very big book." His emphasis indicated he hoped for a feisty tale similar to Boyington's. Davis's agent was not so enthusiastic in light of the glut of post–World War II memoirs: "I cannot get over asking myself whether the public, in any considerable number, would go for the story of another general." One publishing house agreed and also thought Puller's bellicose statements would make him look like an unappealing "blood drinker."[3]

Little, Brown & Company, an "aggressively gambling" Boston firm, was just then trying to win Davis away from his present publisher and was willing to offer a deal, no matter what the topic. The package of incentives included a $20,000 advance against future royalties. The biographer and his potential subject already had reached an agreement to take an equal share in any proceeds. Chesty's prospective half, $10,000, would exceed his annual retirement income and help put his children through college. Davis cautioned his partner "it is not sure-fire that much money will pour upon us," but the writer also passed along the news that the movie rights to Boyington's book had brought "around a quarter million dollars." Chesty confided to Davis: "I would certainly like a bit of change for my family in my old age." The bargain was clinched when the author satisfied Mrs. Puller that the contract "gives the General final approval of the script" and "leaves you control of the image of the General presented in the book." The collaborators signed the agreement in November 1960, but they already had been hard at work.[4]

In the summer of 1960, Davis had taken a new job as a historical writer for Colonial Williamsburg, forty miles down the road from Saluda. On weekends he either would drive to visit the general or would meet him in between at the naval weapons station in Yorktown. At each session, Chesty paced up and down, puffed on a pipe, and pontificated, while the author scribbled furiously. Davis would admiringly tell reviewers a few months later: "Puller is so full of stories. He'd just spill out a story when something would occur to him—and it would be a different one and a good one every time." Davis's only complaint was his subject's inability to express deep feelings. Asked what it was like when he was wounded at Koli Point, Chesty replied: "Well, hell, it felt as if I'd been shot." Anxious to present Puller in the best light, the writer pumped him for "any gossip, criticism, scandal, near-scandal, any incidents which brought you enemies . . . [so] we can defend ourselves in advance." Puller asked HQMC to open its official records, but the Korean documents were still classified and the rest were only available for inspection in Washington. Davis ended up relying mainly on excerpts from Chesty's personnel file.[5]

In the space of a few weeks that winter, writing practically nonstop in every spare moment, Davis strung the anecdotes together and churned out a polished manuscript. The fast-paced story painted a vivid portrait of Puller and the events in which he had played such a large part. But the author was having second thoughts about the process. He confided to his editor: "This is more memoir than biography. There is also a problem of the *other* sides of some stories which are not included, at Puller's insistence." Davis had tried to "protect General Puller from his own slips of recollection" by having O. P. Smith, Johnny Selden, and a few other trusted Marine friends look over the more controversial portions of the manuscript. They found significant problems. Smith told Davis: "Lewie's recollections are rather surprising, and do not conform with my recollections, and, in some cases, are at variance with recorded history." Smith and Selden had the same explanation for this apparent disconnect: "Lewie, over the years, has reviewed in his mind the Peleliu operation and, with the benefit of hindsight, has thought of things he might have said or done. Gradually, these things . . . have become facts to him." The contract gave Davis no opportunity to change things, but he sought to protect his own reputation with a special author's note highlighting that the book "does not pretend to be an objective history."[6]

Marine! appeared in print in February 1962. It received wide, generally favorable, recognition in the press. Many reviewers gave it high praise, but a few were less enthusiastic. *Time* magazine called it a "gaudy, bloody, gung-ho account . . . one unabashed gush of hero worship." The well-regarded weekly news journal admitted "there is plenty of hero to worship," but it questioned the accuracy of some passages. A newspaper declared: "It is an admiring book—perhaps too admiring."[7]

General S.L.A. Marshall, probably the premier popular historian of the Army at that time, slammed the biography in a long review in the *Detroit News*. He dubbed it a "mean book . . . heavily laden with raw meat and contempt," and maintained "its carelessness about historic fact . . . is monumental." His concern, of course, was the negative portrayal of the U.S. Army, particularly in the opening months of the Korean War. Puller justifiably questioned his critic's self-described credentials: "I got quite a kick out of Marshall being referred to and claiming to be a veteran soldier. . . . He certainly has never commanded anything in combat." Chesty made his own literary review of a recent Marshall publication: "I read about a third of *Night Drop,* went to sleep several times and have now quit trying to finish the book."[8]

The publisher found the *Time* and Marshall reviews "annoying," but felt "the book is off to a good start." Puller wanted to help publicize the biography, but events intervened to stop him.

☆   ☆   ☆

Two nights before *Marine!* was due to appear on store shelves, Chesty woke up in severe pain. The family physician came to the house and determined the problem was an enlarged prostate. An ambulance took him to the Portsmouth naval hospital, where doctors decided the gland had to be removed. The operation nearly did what numerous battlefield enemies and tropic diseases could not do. Although the basic procedure appeared to go well, he began to bleed in the recovery ward. Attempts to stop the hemorrhaging failed and he was rushed back into surgery that evening. Throughout the long day and night he received nine blood transfusions. The emergency repairs finally slowed the bleeding to a minimal level, but it did not stop altogether until four days later. The loss of blood hindered his recuperation, then an infection created additional problems. It would be several weeks before Chesty fully recovered. The surgeons had one good piece of news; there had been no cancer involved.[9]

The close brush with mortality brought Chesty and his son closer together. During Puller's long stay in the hospital, he had needed sedatives to dull the pain so he could sleep. For a time after his return home, he was awake late each night, unable to fall asleep without the aid of the drug. Lewis Jr. was up into the wee hours as well, studying hard to maintain his reputation as a good scholar at Christchurch School. The outspoken Marine had never revealed much of himself to his son, but now confided that he feared the slow deterioration of his body and dreaded the prospect of becoming a burden to his family. He also articulated his pride in having a son to carry on the Puller bloodline. The conversations caused the high school junior to reflect on his own future and he began to realize that somewhere, somehow, family tradition would draw him into the service of his country.[10]

☆ ☆ ☆

The fanfare generated by Puller's biography touched off a move by admirers to obtain the Medal of Honor for their hero. That was not a new idea. In 1952 Boyington had made such a plea to President Truman. Clifton B. Cates, commander of the 1st Marines on Guadalcanal and Vandegrift's successor as Commandant, had told an interviewer in the 1950s that someone with five Navy Crosses "in my opinion should have the Medal of Honor." General O. P. Smith had made a similar comment, albeit in a humorous vein, when he had presented the fifth award of the Navy Cross to his friend.[11]

This time the proposal was both serious and well supported. It began with a March 1962 editorial in a Richmond newspaper. The piece cited the words of Boyington and Smith in *Marine!,* as well as the accounts of Chesty's heroics described therein. It concluded: "The Medal of Honor is long past due for this fabulously brave combat soldier and front-line fighter." A retired Marine, serving as president of the VMI alumni association, quickly took up the cause. He contacted Vandegrift, O. P. Smith, and other luminaries of the Corps for assistance, and argued that Puller's ongoing hospitalization added urgency to the quest.[12]

Smith pointed out "there can be no duplication of awards." If one of Chesty's Navy Crosses was upgraded, he then would have only four of them, so Smith suggested "special legislation might be the answer." Representative Thomas N. Downing already had asked President John F. Kennedy to consider recommending Puller for the nation's highest military honor. The request went to HQMC, which provided the same answer it had given to Boyington's proposal a decade before: "In the absence of a recommendation and in view of the expiration of the time limit, consideration of the Medal of Honor in General Puller's case is precluded by law." Downing was not deterred. He and another representative sponsored a bill to award the medal to Chesty "in recognition of his long and distinguished career during which on numerous occasions . . . he distinguished himself conspicuously by gallantry and intrepidity at the risk of his life above and beyond the call of duty." The proposed legislation ended up dying in committee when the congressional session came to a close that fall. Puller's supporters had not succeeded in their goal, but they had let their hero know just how much they revered him.[13]

☆   ☆   ☆

The Puller offspring were now making their way out into the world. Virginia had graduated from Smith College in 1961 and married Lieutenant William H. Dabney that fall. Chesty considered his son-in-law a welcome addition to the family. Dabney had earned his degree from VMI in 1960, but, more important in the general's eyes, had risen to the rank of sergeant in the Corps before that. Martha and Lewis Jr. both went off to college in the fall of 1963. She initially attended Stratford College in Danville, while he began at Washington and Lee University, adjacent to VMI. Chesty had hoped his son would go to the storied military school, but did not pressure the young man and readily accepted his decision.[14]

With two tuition bills to handle at the same time, the Pullers were counting on *Marine!* and its offshoots. Prospects initially seemed good. The book was hardly in print when Davis began to talk about a second that would focus on Chesty's experience in Nicaragua. There were telephone calls, too, from Hollywood producers interested in making a movie. The most intriguing offer asked Puller to serve as a technical adviser during filming at the substantial salary of $500 per week. Chesty thought his biography could serve as the basis for "several pictures."[15]

These high hopes did not entirely pan out. Sales of *Marine!* dwindled rather quickly to a steady dribble and most movie producers lost their enthusiasm. Davis and Puller agreed to the one remaining movie deal, which eventually netted the Pullers an advance of $10,000. There was big talk thereafter from the producer that James Cagney, Charlton Heston, Paul Newman, Kirk Douglas, or Eddie Albert would star as Chesty, but no real activity. At least the initial payment for movie rights was enough to "solve the entire problem of getting the twins through college." Chesty regretted receiving it in a lump sum, though, due to the tax consequences: "I hate to give Uncle Sam 37% of my hard earned little bit of money and for him to then give it to the welfare of this old senseless world." He also reconciled himself to the fact that his life story was not going to reap any more substantial sums to provide the better life he wanted for his family: "I have come to the decision that our present cottage will have to suffice for Virginia and me."[16]

☆   ☆   ☆

As time passed, the slow routine of retirement began to weigh heavily on Chesty. Just prior to his 1962 surgery, he told a Marine correspondent: "Never leave the Corps until you are absolutely unable to continue. It's the greatest life there is. I miss it terribly." It was not just an idle statement; a Saluda resident previously had told the same writer: "He misses the Marine Corps. I don't believe he's completely happy in retirement." Several months later, pacing in his hotel room during a division reunion, Puller made almost the same remark to a civilian reporter: "The truth is, I haven't been happy since they retired me in 1955. I'd go back in as a squad leader tomorrow." One of the things he yearned for most was the camaraderie. During a speech at a January 1963 change-of-command ceremony for a reserve unit, the general lamented: "I am dreadfully lonesome. Come and see me some time." It was not his only public request to Marines to "please pay a visit." When the twins went off to school, Chesty felt even more isolated: "Our house now seems empty and quite lonely."[17]

Many people did call on him. Some were old companions from as far back as World War I. Others were brand-new privates, drawn to the Puller legend and awed that he would invite them in for a long chat. There were civilians and men from other services, too. It made no difference how inconvenient the timing might be, the general "graciously welcomed" them all. His family occasionally chafed at interruptions of meals and other private events, and Virginia frequently had to suggest diplomatically to guests that it was time to leave. Nevertheless, she and the children also realized he "needed his loyal following." One Marine who interrupted a birthday party wrote afterward to apologize, but also noted: "Unfortunately you belong to history."[18]

Puller's separation from the Corps hit home with special force in the late fall of 1962, when the Cuban Missile Crisis erupted. On October 22, 1962, President Kennedy announced a quarantine of Cuba to prevent the shipment of nuclear-tipped missiles. For a time it appeared the United States was on the brink of war with the Soviet Union. The retired general lamented his status as others deployed for possible battle: "My son-in-law has shoved off and it seems strange that I am not with the out-going Marines." He remained supremely confident, however, in the abilities of himself and the Corps. He told Burke Davis: "I really think I am qualified to take our three Marine divisions ashore there, march to Havana, hang Castro, and wind up the affair in several weeks." A few days later, after diplomacy backed by the threat of force achieved a temporary resolution, Chesty publicly announced: "If we had sent in the two Marine divisions that were available, this whole damn mess would be over now."[19]

☆   ☆   ☆

Chesty continued to speak out on issues large and small. At a late 1962 public hearing on dredging the James River, he supported the local oystermen, who opposed the plan. He strongly disagreed with the purpose of the project: "What is this nonsense of trying to make Richmond a seaport? If God Almighty had meant Richmond to be a seaport, he would have put it down by the sea." He also seemed ahead of his time in voicing a wider concern. Citing the pulp mill that had employed him as a youngster, he complained about the effect on the environment: "A damn tree won't even grow in that polluted air. . . . To hell with industry. To industrialize God's green earth is to ruin it."[20]

Puller was the guest speaker for a graduating class of Virginia state troopers in November 1963. He used the opportunity to criticize judges who were too easy on criminals, then turned it into a lesson in professionalism for the new policemen: "I'm telling you young men what you are up against, but I'm also telling you that it is none of your business. . . . We all must take orders. Just remember, improve yourself and one day you will be at the top and you can give orders."[21]

Three weeks later, President Kennedy was assassinated. The tragedy caused some federal and state legislators to initiate bills placing tighter controls on firearms. Puller publicly cautioned against the danger of basing laws on emotional reactions: "Many will be written in such a way that they could disarm America. We must be careful." He argued: "This great country of ours never would have won the West if our civilians had not exercised the right to carry arms. . . . It is important that we have a right to own rifles and shot guns." When the Virginia Senate entertained restrictive legislation soon after, Chesty went to Richmond and lobbied against it.[22]

As always, he reserved his most pungent critiques for military issues. He vigorously opposed a 1963 plan to reorganize the National Guard, and ventured that Secretary of Defense Robert S. McNamara would not have put forward such an ill-considered plan if the former businessman "had seen a little service." Chesty frequently returned to the theme that the services had to place much more stress on night training: "In future wars all combat operations will be carried off under cover of darkness. God gave us the best camouflage in the world— darkness—so why spend billions of dollars to buy it?" He also wondered if the Corps was making a mistake in placing too much emphasis on the vertical assault. Helicopters were fine for moving troops, he believed, but could not handle the heavy equipment and supplies needed to support a large force.[23]

Puller's concern over military preparedness heightened in 1964 as the United States became increasingly involved in Indochina, where a North Vietnamese–inspired Communist insurgency was threatening the governments of Laos and South Vietnam. There were no American ground units deployed as yet, but Marine advisers and helicopter squadrons (and their Army counterparts) were assisting the South Vietnamese forces.

Chesty voiced his first thoughts on the conflict during that summer's division reunion in San Francisco. It was not an auspicious setting, as he himself reminded reporters. Recalling the beer-and-whiskey episode, he said he initially had vowed he "didn't want to see any newsmen" on this trip to the Bay Area. Minutes later, he "startled" the correspondents with a shocking proposal to win the war in Vietnam. "If I had the authority, I'd order back to active duty 10,000 non-commissioned officers who left the Marine Corps after putting in 20 years. I'd give every one of them a Browning Automatic Rifle—the best weapon ever made. I'd stop by Formosa for the loan of 100,000 Nationalist Chinese troops. I'd put the 10,000 NCOs among them, one to every squad. And with them I'd clean out Vietnam inside of six weeks." Puller brushed aside questions about the willingness of the Vietnamese to allow their ancient enemies into the country or the practicality of Americans leading Chinese troops. (As head of TTUPac in 1952, he himself had wondered how a handful of instructors would communicate with the Chinese; now the language barrier seemed irrelevant for thousands of squad leaders.)

One reporter commented in print the next day: "It was this simplicity that had kept him from rising above division commander. He seemed unable to recognize—even yesterday—that life is sometimes complex." The observation was less than accurate, of course, since Chesty had retired for medical reasons before there was an opportunity for higher command. The correspondent's shallow analysis also overlooked the subtlety of Puller's personality, which was fully displayed during the press conference. In response to a question about the wisdom of invading North Vietnam, the retired general said he would not recommend it. The same reporter noted that Chesty then grinned, "aware his answer had caused surprise." Coming on the heels of his stated disdain for the San Francisco press, Puller's Vietnam idea may have been nothing more than an example of his penchant for saying the unexpected in order to rattle anyone who approached him with a smug attitude. Chesty was certainly serious about one comment, however. Asked if he had learned anything in Korea that would help in Vietnam, he replied: "The lesson is to keep from getting licked again."[24]

There was another possible explanation for Puller's remarks. The accumulating deterioration of his health definitely was beginning to impact his mental faculties, though signs of such problems so far had been rare and relatively minor. Those who talked with him noticed that he sometimes would "ramble at great length" or "wander somewhat afield" from the topic of conversation. His line of reasoning also occasionally seemed incongruous. During the debate about dredging the James River, for instance, he had questioned the decision-making ability of the Army Corps of Engineers on the grounds that "they never heard a shot fired in anger." On most occasions he was still sharp, but time was beginning to take its toll.[25]

☆   ☆   ☆

Puller's fondness for speaking without regard for the consequences finally brought him real trouble. In the fall of 1964, a Marine who had served in 1/7 on Guadalcanal filed a legal challenge against *Marine!* He had been identified in the book as the man who had thrown away his mortar rounds prior to a critical engagement along the Matanikau. Now he was "a substantial Philadelphia businessman" and was suing the publisher, the author, and Chesty for libel. Puller expressed confidence about the outcome to Davis: "I don't believe we should be unduly worried. . . . I remember everything about the incident and you stated it truly in *Marine!*" Truth was a defense against the charge, but the defendants would have to depend on twenty-year-old memories to make their case. The plaintiff's primary evidence consisted of a Silver Star he had received for actions during the Battle for Henderson Field, his proof that he had been a good Marine.[26]

Jimmy Hayes, the 1/7 veteran and lawyer who had helped Puller in 1955, told his former commander to settle the suit, since the medal had not been mentioned in the book: "It has been said that a half-truth is worse than a lie. The thought has just struck me that we may be in that half-truth category." Eventually the publisher followed that path, primarily to avoid the expense of finding witnesses and going to trial. Chesty was not pleased that "our side surrendered with little or no fight." He was more incensed when Little, Brown exercised its right under the contract and asked him and Davis to reimburse the company for the $30,000 settlement. The two men soon learned that the publisher would not press the issue, but instead would withhold future royalty payments until earnings on the book recouped the legal costs. Since it would take many years for sales to generate that much revenue, the outcome was a final blow to the hope of the Pullers that *Marine!* would bolster their retirement income.[27]

Another strain on Chesty in 1964 was his son's surprising failure at Washington and Lee. The excellent student at Christchurch School did not focus on his studies when faced with the freedom of college life; he left under an academic cloud after one semester. Typical of Puller's approach to parenting, he did not criticize his son and concentrated instead on finding a university where the young man could finish his education. When that proved difficult at first, Chesty wrote Davis: "I am up against a brick wall. He (Lewis) has done nothing dishonorable and I fail to see how a lot of college professors have the field tied up as they do." The bad news was offset by the simultaneous arrival of Virginia Puller Dabney's first child; Chesty was elated to have a grandson. Martha was doing well in school, too, and would go on to graduate from Mary Washington.[28]

Puller had made good on his 1955 promise to his wife to "live only for you and our precious children." The years of enforced separation were done with and he strove mightily to be the consummate family man. During those rare occasions in retirement when the couple were apart, his letters to her showed the same tenderness he had exhibited when overseas. One note followed close on the heels of Virginia's departure on a trip: "I have missed you ever since you drove away to Kentucky and hope I will get a card from you tomorrow telling me that you love me. I know you do, Sweetheart—I just am missing and longing for you. Please have a wonderful time and come back when you can arrange to and keep on loving me." Virginia still hated to see the constant media hype "about Lewis being so hard and tough and mean and all." In her world, he was always "just the sweetest thing."[29]

☆　☆　☆

Puller's retirement vow notwithstanding, he still had the desire to fulfill another pledge he had made before their marriage, to answer "the beat of the drum" whenever the guns sounded. The Corps had been his first priority for most of his adult life and that remained his reflexive response. During a 1964 visit to the hospital for a checkup, Puller ran into an old acquaintance who was about to retire. The colonel remarked: "I feel sort of like a man who is about to be divorced by a gal he still loves after being married to her for 30 years." Chesty replied immediately: "Yes, but there are a lot of gals and there's only one Marine Corps."[30]

Puller heard the siren song of his first love in early 1965. In response to guerrilla attacks on American military advisers in South Vietnam, President Lyndon Johnson authorized air strikes against the North. He next ordered a brigade of Marines to go ashore at Da Nang in the South on March 8. Their mission was to defend a major airfield, but many observers knew that offensive combat was sure to follow. This escalation in American participation in the war was barely underway when action exploded on the other side of the globe, close to U.S. shores. Johnson ordered Marines into the Dominican Republic on April 28, to evacuate American citizens from the midst of a civil war and then restore order to the Caribbean nation.

With Leathernecks embroiled in two major contingencies, Chesty could stand it no more. On May 14 he fired off a short letter to the Commandant, General Greene. Puller got right to the point in his opening sentence: "It is earnestly requested that I be ordered to active duty and assigned to a combat command." He went on to explain: "I am physically fit, young enough in years, and qualified by experience for further service." He described his service in Haiti and Nicaragua to prove he was "quite informed and qualified for service in Latin America." To establish his credentials for Vietnam, he noted: "I have served for over sixteen years in Asia and its islands and have fought the Japanese, the North Koreans, and the Communist Chinese." He concluded: "I am tired and ashamed to look the tax payers of the United States in the face."[31]

Greene responded with a polite but firm refusal. Puller was not about to let the matter end there. He invited a reporter to his home, provided copies of the letters to and from the Commandant, and then lambasted American policy and tactics in both theaters. Chesty thought U.S. forces in the Dominican Republic had made a serious error by limiting their involvement to street patrols and not going after arms depots at the outset: "This means we'll be faced with the possibility of guerrilla warfare there for many years to come." He was more concerned about Vietnam, where "many things are wrong." He disapproved of the Corps' defensive role: "Why should Marines have to waste their time guarding air bases? Doesn't the Air Force have night watchmen?" He further disputed the decision of senior Marines in Vietnam to adopt a "spreading ink-blot strategy," which concentrated on control of the population. Instead, Puller advocated offensive operations: "The first principle of warfare is to concentrate more of our people against the enemy's. . . . To win we must form our people in columns and head for the Communists and destroy them." He also advocated an air campaign against North Vietnamese cities, a naval blockade, and amphibious assaults. He derided helicopters as "sitting ducks" useful only for "evacuating wounded and bringing in small supplies." And he argued for a unified command of all allied forces under an American. As always, Puller emphasized the importance of "military history," citing Caesar and the more modern example of the French failure in Indochina: "We haven't learned a thing from the French defeat; in fact, we seem to be copying much of the bad tactics of the French." Chesty closed with an acknowledgment of the quality of the opponent, North Vietnam's

leader, Ho Chi Minh: "He is backed by years of guerrilla warfare experience, and a man successful in that type of war can be successful in any
type of war."[32]

The wide-ranging indictment received extensive play in the national media. It also inspired numerous letters to the President, the Secretary of Defense, and the Commandant, all advocating Puller's return
to duty. One group of North Carolina veterans wrote their congressman: "Only a Marine who has served under Puller can know what it
would mean to have the 'Old Man' reading the maps, directing the strategy, and usually cruising somewhere in the vicinity of the fire-fights." A
newspaper editorial also supported Chesty's "bold, blunt, and vigorous"
plan. Even General Greene privately agreed with Puller's position on
blockades, amphibious operations, and heavier air strikes against North
Vietnam.[33]

The retired general had raised many valid questions about U.S. policy and he would continue to be a harsh critic of the war, but during the
1960s he frequently and substantially changed his opinions on the conflict. In an interview with Davis a few years before, Puller had recognized just how tough it would be to defeat the North Vietnamese and
their Viet Cong allies in the South. He had told his biographer that conventional outfits always came out badly in campaigns against irregular
forces. In his opinion, the Communists had melded popular political
backing and guerrilla operations to develop a new form of warfare that
could only be foiled by a similar style of infiltration tactics. In Korea,
he had derided the value of airpower for any purpose other than close
support of ground troops. His 1965 comments, on the other hand, called
for a strategic air campaign and division-sized conventional combat on
the ground. Just a few weeks later, he would remark that defense spending was mismanaged because "we can't lick ragamuffins in Southeast
Asia." That disparagement of the enemy seemed completely at odds
with his previous caution that Ho Chi Minh and the Communists were
tough foes. Chesty's outspoken denunciations would grow more extreme and intemperate as time passed, but they bore one common, accurate thread—that the United States was failing to effectively prosecute
the war.[34]

Puller's widely divergent views on Vietnam undoubtedly were the
first significant evidence of his deteriorating intellect. In the years since
his retirement, he had not moderated his eating or smoking habits in

any substantial way, so his arteriosclerosis and blood pressure were worsening. He had not yet suffered any documented recurrence of his 1955 cerebral trouble, but his daughters later suspected that his occasional bouts of dizziness during this period may actually have been small seizures. By 1968 he was showing visible symptoms in the form of aphasia, a neurological condition that affected his ability to remember and properly use words.[35]

☆　☆　☆

Puller was not allowed to march to the sound of the guns, but his son could. Lewis Jr. had graduated from William and Mary in 1967. By his own admission, he had eked his way through school with a "lack of meaningful direction." Chesty had never pressed his namesake to join the Corps, but often had proclaimed publicly: "I'd be proud for my son to become a Marine." Now, with a half million Americans fighting in Indochina (among them Captain Bill Dabney, Virginia's husband, and Captain Michael P. Downs, Martha's fiancé), it seemed natural for the young man to follow in his father's footsteps. Lewis Jr. required a waiver for his eyesight, but it would be the only favor granted to the son of the most famous Marine. If anything, during his subsequent ten weeks at Officer Candidate School in Quantico, his status brought unwanted scrutiny that made the challenging course even tougher than normal. Young Puller proved his mettle in that crucible and pinned on the gold bars of a second lieutenant on February 1, 1968.[36]

Whether it was an auspicious time to begin a military career depended on one's point of view. If Lewis Jr. agreed with his father's pre-Inchon statement that a military professional was lucky to have a war, then the new lieutenant was indeed fortunate. On the other hand, U.S. policy and strategy were not working well in this conflict. American forces also were just then undergoing their greatest trial in Indochina. The Communists had launched their Tet Offensive on the last day of January and the situation looked bleak. A few weeks hence U.S. leaders would proclaim tactical victory in this phase of the war, but the enemy had scored a strategic coup that undercut American public support for the war effort. To young Puller's credit, he did not let the ballooning casualty lists dissuade him from his chosen course of becoming an infantry officer.[37]

In the midst of his five-month stint at the Basic School, Lewis Jr.

found out that his girlfriend, Linda Todd, was pregnant. His mother and Toddy's parents were upset by the revelation, but Lewis was relieved that "my father accepted our situation with love and understanding." The young couple were married a few days later.[38]

Chesty's calm response was based in part on a long-expressed wish that his son produce "at least two grandsons" to carry on the Puller line. The older man's delight at having the process underway a little sooner than expected may have derived in part from his health, which was now deteriorating at a pronounced rate. On May 2, 1968, he was admitted for a brief period to the Portsmouth naval hospital following a stroke. (His sister Pattie had died unexpectedly in Richmond only a week before.) As recently as December 1967 he had insisted publicly that he was "fit for duty," but he undoubtedly was beginning to realize his time was running short. Others were noticing, too. Correspondents always had found Puller hale in appearance, but a newspaper report about the August 1968 division reunion referred to his physical state as "failing." Bill Dabney, upon his return from Vietnam in October 1968, was shocked by "the startling difference" in his father-in-law's condition.[39]

Lieutenant Puller completed his training in July and went on a month of leave prior to his departure for Vietnam. When that all-too-brief period came to a close, Chesty pulled his son aside in the front yard of their Saluda home and began to repeat a story Lewis Jr. had heard countless times since he was a boy. It was the lesson of the stoic Spartan mothers, who told their male offspring prior to battle: "Return with your shield or on it." Chesty broke down before he could finish and the moment ended in a tight embrace. The young man, wiping tears away from his own face, later recalled that it was the first time he had ever seen his father cry. A few days later, a fellow retired Marine told Puller that he had a grandson in Vietnam. Chesty replied: "Tell him to pray that he gets a good platoon sergeant." General Puller almost certainly was entreating the Almighty for a similar favor for Lewis Jr.[40]

☆   ☆   ☆

In August 1968, Lieutenant Puller reported for duty with Company G, 2d Battalion, 1st Marines in Vietnam. He took over a rifle platoon and soon experienced many aspects of a typical tour in the bush—booby traps, snipers, ambushes, night probes of the perimeter, helo assaults, helo medevacs. He had missed out on the urban warfare of Hue City and the intense defensive battle of Khe Sanh, but he faced plenty of small-scale action that could be just as deadly. In his first two months of combat he earned a Purple Heart for a slight wound from a booby trap explosion.

On October 11 Puller and Golf Company helicoptered into a clearing near a village that was the object of that day's cordon-and-search mission. As the Marines fanned out to form a noose around the hamlet, a squad of Communist soldiers emerged and headed straight for Puller's position. He attempted to fire at them, but his rifle jammed, so he took off running for the nearby company command group. He had taken only a few steps when he set off a land mine rigged from a dud 105mm artillery round. The explosion blew away both his legs, sheared off parts of both hands, and inflicted other injuries. As he lay on the ground, semiconscious and bordering on shock, he was not yet aware of the extent of the damage and did not understand why his radio operator repeatedly screamed: "Pray, Lieutenant, for God's sake, pray."[41]

Heroic efforts on the part of the platoon corpsman prevented Puller from dying on the spot from loss of blood or shock. As the lieutenant drifted in and out of consciousness, he turned over control of his unit to his senior NCO and ordered those around him not to tell his wife before she had her baby. A helicopter took him to the base hospital at Da Nang, where surgery stabilized his condition. General Lew Walt, the assistant commandant, personally called Saluda and told Chesty what had happened. Lewis's wounding made national news. One story noted that his platoon sergeant, a corporal, praised his commander as "a good man . . . cool and calm." Those few words from an NCO were a fitting tribute for the son of Chesty Puller.[42]

The commander of 2/1 "did not think Puller had a chance." The doctors were skeptical about his odds, too. On October 16 he was flown out of the war zone to better medical facilities in Japan. Informed of that move and the grave prognosis, Chesty announced he would fly there to see his son. There was intense concern on the part of Mrs. Puller and HQMC that the long trip would be too much for the general, especially in light of the added stress of what he would find at the other end. Despite medical advice that young Puller could not be transported safely, the Marine Corps ordered him brought home. The transfer was delayed a few days while he underwent surgery for a stress ulcer brought on by the shock of his wounds. Contrary to the expectations of the physicians, the lieutenant survived the operation that removed two thirds of his stomach. On October 23 he was flown to Andrews Air Force Base outside Washington.[43]

Owing to young Puller's tenuous hold on life, only one member of his family was allowed to see him at a time. Chesty was the first. Lewis Jr. recalled the "wrenching" episode years later:

> He stood quietly at the foot of my bed for a few moments, surveyed the wreckage of his only son, and then, unable to maintain his stoic demeanor, began weeping silently. He moved to my side and grasped my shoulder as if that simple act of communion would stay the convulsions that now racked his stooped frame, and I in my helpless state was unable to reach out or otherwise console him. It was only the second time in my life that I had seen my father cry, and as the nurse led him from my room, I felt an aching in my heart that all but eclipsed the physical pain from my wounds.[44]

The tears did not begin to convey just how greatly affected Chesty was by his son's dismemberment. The hard-bitten leader had been able to accept the death of his brother and so many others in combat, but this was almost more than he could bear. It would be years before Lewis Jr. learned from others "how utterly shaken he was by what happened to me, and how utterly just torn apart." Most of the time, though, Chesty showed a stolid, resolute face to the world. Doctors were surprised when he spoke to them about artificial limbs and rehabilitation at a point when they doubted their patient would survive. On other occasions, his aphasia worsened into more serious lapses of memory and he forgot that his son had even been wounded.[45]

☆   ☆   ☆

In a short combat career of two months, the son had not been able to duplicate his father's extraordinary exploits. In the aftermath of his near-mortal wound, however, Lewis Jr. more than lived up to the Puller reputation for toughness. His survival itself was a miracle, but he then faced incredible physical and emotional challenges as he sought to reconcile himself to life with a broken body. In the difficult times to come, moments of happiness were few and far between. One of them was the birth of Lewis and Toddy's first child in November 1968. Without hesitation, they named their son Lewis Burwell Puller III. The arrival of new life gave a much needed boost to the hospitalized father, who finally was making the first steps along the road to improvement. The moment was one of unalloyed joy for Chesty. He gleefully repeated a sentiment he had expressed earlier about the Dabney children: "That's immortality!"[46]

In February 1969, Martha and Mike Downs got married. It was a military wedding, of course, and Chesty wore his dress blues. He relished the role of escorting his daughter down the aisle and, perhaps in a playful reprise of his own wedding, mixed a little humor with familial love. Before the two started the short walk, he told her if she wanted to change her mind, he could quickly turn the event into a cocktail party. A month later, Lewis Jr. and Toddy were able to move into an apartment at the Philadelphia naval base, where he was undergoing physical rehabilitation. The first visit of Lewis and Virginia took the older couple back in time—it was the same small quarters they had occupied after their marriage in 1937.[47]

As Lewis Jr. struggled to rebuild his shattered life, his father's vitality continued to slip away. A series of strokes gradually sapped Chesty's mental and physical strength. A massive seizure on October 8, 1970, left him hospitalized for months. By the summer of 1971, he was no longer able to live at home and was confined to a long-term-care facility. At the end of September, pneumonia and a kidney infection attacked his frail body. The end came the evening of October 11, 1971. Virginia could not bear to see his final moments and her daughters escorted her back to Saluda. Lewis Jr. kept watch as his father struggled for a last few breaths and then succumbed. It was three years to the day after the son's grievous wounding in Vietnam. It was, in the precision Chesty liked to use about the length of his career, exactly fifty-three years, two months, and sixteen days since he had walked into a recruiting office in Richmond and taken the first step toward leaving his indelible mark on the Corps.[48]

☆ ☆ ☆

General Puller was laid to rest on October 14, 1971, in the small cemetery adjacent to Christ Church near Saluda. Befitting Chesty's simple approach to life, the ceremonies were modest. There was no funeral procession with marching troops, a caisson, and the traditional riderless horse with boots facing backward in the stirrups. There were no eulogies either. Following a brief service in the church, six Marines carried the casket outside and through the short rows of headstones, many of them marking the resting places of Virginia's ancestors. The minister raised a few final prayers to heaven, a squad fired three rifle volleys, a bugler played the solemn notes of taps, General Leonard F. Chapman (the Commandant) reverently handed a folded flag to Virginia Puller, and it was over. Dozens of active and retired generals, a congressman, and hundreds of friends and fellow Marines had shown up to pay their respects, but the heart of everyone connected to the Corps was there in the tree-shaded churchyard.

Chesty, the man, was gone, but his legend was destined to live on forever.

Epilogue

In the days after Puller's death, newspapers around the nation carried long obituaries filled with glowing tributes. Nearly every article described him as "the most decorated Marine in the history of the Corps." Some writers encapsulated his career in his awards, as if his medals and his courage told the entire story of his life and his place in the Corps. One reporter trotted out the quote attributed to General Cates in the early 1950s: "He's about the only man in the Corps who really loves to fight. I'll go further; he's the only man in any of our services who loves fighting." Even Admiral Arleigh Burke, another renowned hero, had once written: "Men fought under Chesty Puller and they fought magnificently because he knew how to fight."[1]

In recognizing Chesty's valor, many seemed to miss the true essence of Puller. He was indeed a courageous warrior, but that was not the source of his legendary status. What endeared him to his fellow Marines was his leadership. His decorations themselves reinforce the point. His five Navy Crosses were not for individual bravery—instead they recognized his critical role in each instance in leading his unit to victory.

The rare quality of outstanding leadership can come in many forms. Some inspire their followers with lofty words. Others command respect due to their unrivaled competence. Puller's ability to motivate men came from a simpler source. His Marines knew that he would ask no more of them than he was willing to put forth himself, and that was everything he had. They knew that when they were putting their lives on the line, he would be right out front with them. They knew that he would zealously look out for their welfare and shield them as much as possible from both the daunting hardships and the petty troubles of a tough profession. They knew that he understood what they were going through and saw things from their point of view. He was, in their eyes, a lofty figure who was right at home among the lowliest of them. Few men can rise to greatness and still genuinely retain the common touch. Medals and rank never changed Puller; he possessed the heart of a private throughout his long career and his men idolized him for that simplicity. One editorial mourning his passing captured the result: "There were few Marines who would not have tried to establish a beachhead in hell at a nod from Chesty Puller."[2]

Not everyone loved Puller. Like most famous combat leaders, he inspired equally strong passions on both sides. Like any man, he had flaws and made mistakes. Over the years, those shortcomings have been distorted and magnified along with the rest of his legend. Sometimes he had only himself to blame, since he often cultivated an image at odds with his true beliefs and actions. He enjoyed the reputation of taking on every challenge with a frontal assault, even if he operated in most situations with a great deal more subtlety. He wanted to be remembered solely for his abilities as a commander, so he pointedly ignored those many occasions when he had performed well as a staff officer. He wanted to be known as a modest man from the countryside, even though he knew a lot more about history, warfare, and the nature of people than many of his contemporaries. He was a complex man who somehow seemed to live life effortlessly and simply.

Despite shortcomings real and imaginary, his preeminent standing in the Corps has stood the test of time precisely because his renown was never based on flawless tactics, stirring speeches, or a chestful of medals. While other heroes have lost some of their luster with the passage of time, his approach to the challenge of commanding men has endured as a paramount touchstone in an institution that prizes leadership above all other qualities. Chesty is certainly not the only great leader in the long history of the Corps, but he remains the best known and most revered of all Marines, officer and enlisted. Generations of Marine NCOs and officers have been raised to follow, as best they can, in the huge footprints he left behind. And as long as there is a Corps, Chesty Puller will continue to inspire Marines to look out for their subordinates, give their utmost, and lead from the front.

No Marine could ask for a greater legacy.

Note on Sources

To compress the extensive endnotes, I have employed several shortcuts. All books are cited in the notes simply by the author's last name and a shortened title. Articles from periodicals are cited in full in the notes (and not included in the Bibliography), unless they appear in more than one chapter, in which case they follow the convention used for books. All personal papers and oral histories are cited in short form in the notes and fully described in the Bibliography.

Primary documents held by the National Archives are cited in the following format: box number, series number, and record group. Primary documents still owned by the Marine Corps and stored at the Washington National Records Center in Suitland, Maryland, are cited by box number and series number. Where applicable, box numbers are provided for collections in other archives.

Where two or more sources in a given endnote are from the same series or collection, I have omitted duplicate identifying information from the initial citations. Finally, the following key provides abbreviations for many frequently used sources:

AAVP	Alexander A. Vandegrift Papers
BDP	Burke Davis Papers
DANFS	*Dictionary of American Naval Fighting Ships*
HP	Eric Hammel Papers
HSTL	Harry S. Truman Library
JCSP	Julian C. Smith Papers
MAEP	Merritt A. Edson Papers
MCG	*Marine Corps Gazette*

MCHC	Marine Corps Historical Center, Washington, D.C.
MCRC	Marine Corps Research Center, Quantico, Virginia
MR	Puller's Medical Record
NHC	Naval Historical Center, Washington, D.C.
OPSP	O. P. Smith Papers
PBF	Puller Biography File, MCHC
PP	Puller Papers (located at MCRC)
PR	Puller's Personnel Record
RG	Record Group
SP	Simmons Papers
VMI	Virginia Military Institute
WNRC	Washington National Records Center

Source Notes

Preface

1. Robert Asprey, a Marine author who helped General Alexander A. Vandegrift write his memoirs, cited *Marine!* as an example of a common defect to avoid in such books: "Once, just once, in 37 years Chesty must have been wrong . . . but you would never find such an admission." Davis to Mrs. Puller, 30 Jun 1960, BDP; *Marine!,* p. ix; Asprey to Vandegrift, 23 Jan 1962, Box 13, AAVP.
2. Heinl OH, p. 100; Davis, *Chesty Puller's Rules,* p. 23.
3. General Simmons uttered this fascinating quote to another Marine officer in Vietnam, who recalled it for the author. The general adapted it from the more mundane original contained in Sir Ian Hamilton's 1907 book, *A Staff Officer's Scrap-book During the Russo-Japanese War.* Hamilton's version: "On the actual day of battle truths may be picked up for the asking; by the following morning they have already begun to get into their uniforms." Moore to author, 5 Jul 1999; Simmons to author, 12 Oct 1999.
4. For an example of an attempt to draw lessons from *Marine!,* see Macak, LtCol Richard J., Jr., "Lessons from Yesterday's Operations Short of War," *MCG,* Nov 1996, p. 56.

Chapter 1: "Making a Man and a Soldier": Genesis of a Marine, 1898–1919

1. News clipping, Pullen Papers.
2. News clippings, 30 Jul 1946 and 28 Sep 1950, PP; BGen Edwin H. Simmons speech, 9 Nov 1978, SP.
3. I am deeply indebted to both Robert K. Krick and his son, Robert E. L. Krick, who generously provided considerable information from their own research in primary and secondary sources on Puller's nineteenth-century ancestors. The details of the Puller family in the 1800s are almost entirely based on their efforts. News clipping, 25 Jan 1984, PP; family tree, possession of Virginia Puller Dabney; Wayland, *History of Shenandoah County,* pp. 659–60; Brown and Brown, *Carter Hall,* pp. 1, 15.
4. Maas, "Old Warhorse"; Fridell, "Chesty"; Puller to Virginia, 16 Jun 1964, PP; Gloucester County Census, 1850 and 1860, and Marriage and Birth Records, Virginia State Library (courtesy of Robert E. L. Krick); Driver, *5th Cavalry,*

p. 245; R. K. Krick to author, 8 May 1998; R. G. Dun Collection, Virginia Vol. 16, p. 373E, Baker Library, Harvard University.

5.   Driver, *5th Cavalry,* pp. 22–49.

6.   Driver, *5th Cavalry,* pp. 48, 245; Smith, *Reminiscences,* pp. 54–55; Haden, *Stuart's Cavalry,* p. 10; Cincinnatus Ware letter, 2 Aug 1863, graciously provided by Michael Silverman.

7.   Martin to Stewart [*sic*], 10 Nov 1862, J.E.B. Stuart Papers, Huntington Library; Driver, *5th Cavalry,* pp. 31–32, 46.

8.   Freeman, *Lee's Lieutenants,* Vol. 2, pp. 457–64; Gilmor, *Four Years,* pp. 65–70; McClellan, *Stuart,* p. 211; Smith, *Reminiscences,* p. 55; Ware, *Kelly's Ford,* pp. 6–7.

9.   Ware, *Kelly's Ford,* p. 7; Scott, *Rebellion,* pp. 58–65.

10. Wiatt, *Confederate Chaplain,* pp. 40–41.

11. The family connection between Patton and Puller was a very distant one. Lewis's great-great-great-grandfather William Williams was also the great-great-great-great-grandfather of Patton. Krick, *Lee's Colonels,* p. 400; Wayland, *Shenandoah County,* pp. 658–60; *Confederate Military History,* p. 1270; Durkin, *Dooley,* pp. 108–9; Blackford, *Letters,* p. 169; D'Este, *Patton,* p. 14; Krick to author, 5 Apr and 19 May 1999.

12. Lewis Puller believed that a Major Stubbs, who served with John Puller, had taken in the Puller orphans. However, there was no Stubbs, officer or enlisted, in the 5th Cavalry. The most likely candidate was Captain Lawrence S. Stubbs, a militia officer from Gloucester Courthouse. The 1870 census, however, shows no young Pullers living with Stubbs, so he must have provided only a short-term refuge if he was the Good Samaritan. Puller interview notes, BDP; 1870 Gloucester Census and 1885 Gloucester Death Records (courtesy R.E.L. Krick), Virginia State Library; R. L. Krick to author, 8 May 1998; Montague, *Gloucester County,* p. v; Martin, "Toughest Marine."

13. Puller interview notes; Puller to Virginia, 15 Oct 1950, BDP; VMI Biography, 1 Nov 1918, VMI Archives.

14. Puller interview notes, BDP; Foyle interview with author, 24 Jan 1996; Fridell, "Chesty."

15. O. P. Smith OH, p. 333; Erskine OH, p. 103.

16. News clipping, 10 Oct 1950, PP; news release, 7 Feb 1962, PBF; Puller/Lee OH, p. 7.

17. News clippings, 10 Oct 1950 and 22 Mar [?], PP; certificate from secondary school, VMI; excerpts from West Point Yearbook, 1916, BDP; Fridell, "Chesty."

18. O. P. Smith OH, p. 333.

19. Eastwood's correct name and the nature of his service come from Driver, *5th Cavalry,* p. 204. *Marine!,* p. 16; speech for King William County Anniversary, Apr 1952, BDP.

20. Mrs. Puller's views on the education of her sons are inferred from two letters written in January 1919. One expressed her regret that Lewis had chosen the Marines over VMI. The other described her attempts to use the influence of her state senator and an administrator at VMI to gain a scholarship there for Sam. Mrs. Puller to Anderson, 10 and 14 Jan 1919, VMI Archives; draft manuscript and Puller interview notes, BDP; news clippings, "West Point High Reunion" and "John Marsh Jr. to Dedicate Plaque," PP.

21. *The Bomb,* 1918 VMI Yearbook, p. 8, and Puller's matriculation form, VMI; VMI archivist to author, 25 Mar 1996.

22. News clipping, 1 Nov 1955, PP.

23. R. W. Jeffrey to Davis, 26 Nov 1960, VMI Archives; news clipping, 13 May 1962, PP; D'Este, *Patton,* p. 64.

24. News clipping, [1918], VMI Archives; VMI archivist to author, 25 Mar 1996.

25. The only record of the reason for Puller's choice is in a 1952 magazine article, which stated that Puller enlisted in the Corps "because as a Marine he could get a commission at the age of twenty." *Officer Procurement,* p. 5; Puller to R. W. Jeffrey, 21 Nov 1960, VMI Archives; Puller to MGC, 1 Dec 1919, PR; Martin, "Toughest Marine"; Maas, "Old Warhorse."

26. Pullen to Davis, 1 Jun 1960, BDP; Millett, *Semper Fidelis,* p. 305.

27. Enlistment papers, 25 Jul 1918, and Puller to CMC, 21 Apr 1947, PR; Mrs. M. M. Puller to Gen Nichols, 29 Jul 1918, and Nichols to Puller, 30 Jul 1918, VMI Archives.

28. Maj R. W. Coyle, "Parris Island in the War," *MCG,* Dec 1925, p. 187; Farrell OH.

29. *Marine!* (pp. 21–22) cites the recollections of a Corporal John DeSparre regarding Puller's demonstrated abilities. DeSparre supposedly was Puller's DI, but the muster rolls do not show him associated with Puller's recruit battalion. He would get to know Puller in 1921 as a fellow student in Candidates School. Shoemaker to Davis, 16 Nov 1960, BDP; Muster Rolls, Parris Island, Aug–Sep 1918, MCHC; Marine Barracks DC to MGC, 26 Aug 1921, Box 234, 18, RG 127.

30. Small Arms Record, PR.

31. Pullen to Davis, 1 Jun 1960, BDP; Conduct Record, 1 Oct 1918, PR; Company F Muster Rolls, Aug 1918, MCHC.

32. *Marine!,* p. 22; Chronological Record, PR; Shoemaker to Davis, 16 Nov 1960; Landrath to Davis, 1 Mar 1962, BDP; *Camp Lejeune Globe,* 10 Jun 1955; NCO School Muster Rolls, Sep 1918, MCHC.

33. Hoffman, *Legend,* p. 22.

34. PR; Pullen to Davis, 1 Jun 1960, BDP.

35. Coyle, "Parris Island in the War."

36. Pullen to Davis, BDP; PR; Mrs. Puller to Anderson, 10 Jan 1919, VMI Archives; Millett, *Semper Fidelis,* p. 200.

37. Farrell OH, p. 249; OIC, OTC to MGC, 4 Jun 1919, PR; Pullen to Davis, 1 Jun 1960 and 15 Jul 1960; Landreth to Davis, 1 Mar 1962, BDP.

38. Moskin, *Marine Corps,* p. 207; Puller to Pullen, 2 May 1920; Shoemaker to Davis, 16 Nov 1960, BDP; news clipping, Pullen Papers, MCHC; MGC to Puller, 19 Jun 1919, PR.

39. Pullen to Mrs. Puller, 27 Oct 1971, PP.

40. Puller to MGC, and MGC to Recruiting OIC, 27 Jun 1919, and Puller to MGC, 1 Dec 1919, PR; Rupertus Bio File, MCHC.

Chapter 2: "The Great Lessons of Warfare": Haiti, 1919–1921

1. Millett, *Strife,* p. 76.

2. Constabulary to Brigade, 4 Aug 1920, Box 11; Brigade to MGC, 13 Dec 1920, Box 81, Haiti Series, RG 127; "The Haitian Gendarmerie," *MCG,* June 1926, p. 73; Col Frank E. Evans, "Salient Haitian Facts," *MCG,* Feb 1931, p. 14.

3. "The Haitian Gendarmerie," p. 78; Constabulary Det, Report of Activities, 15 Jul 1921, Box 11, Haiti Series, RG 127; Silverthorn OH.

4. Millett, *Semper Fidelis,* p. 199; Haiti Casualties, 1915–1934, Box 31, 8166, WNRC; Chief of Gend. to Secretary of State, 28 Jan 1919, Box 13, Haiti Series, RG 127.

5. Puller's recollection of his encounter with the district commander sets the date for his first operation, since the officer mentioned in his interview with Davis did not take command of the district until August 6, 1919. Puller's oral history indicates the patrol occurred after "several days" in Haiti. A report of a large bandit group "discovered along Mirebalais–Las Cahobas road" on August 7 very likely came from Puller's pack train. Daily Diary Report, Box 30, 8166, WNRC; Puller/Lee OH, p. 6, MCHC.

6. Puller/Lee OH, pp. 6–11; Instructions for Patrol Officers, 24 May 1923, Box 1, 39, RG 127; "Care and Feeding of Native Animals," *MCG,* Dec 1929, p. 298.

7. Daily Diary Report, 13 Jun and 14 Jul 1919, Box 30, 8166, WNRC.

8. Although Puller recalled that Napoleon Lyautey was a lieutenant recently promoted from the rank of sergeant major, that name does not appear in the Gendarmerie records. The likeliest possibility is a Lieutenant Charles Liauteaud. He was not commissioned until 1922, but may have risen from the ranks and been with Puller in 1919 as an NCO. Clairmont probably was Henri L. Clermont, since the latter was commissioned from the ranks, and someone of the caliber described in *Marine!* (p. 31) would have been a likely candidate to become a lieutenant in the fledgling Gendarmerie. Clermont was known as "one of the real tough Haitians," and he would become one of Calixte's senior colonels. *Gendarmerie HQ News,* 1 Sep 1922, Library, MCHC; Precedence Tables of Officers of the Gendarmerie, 25 Nov 1919, and Gend. to Brigade, 1 Mar 1921, Box 81, Haiti Series, and Hill to Gend., 26 Mar 1919, Box 1, 173, RG 127; Calixte to Smith, 1 Jun 1929, Box 62, OPSP; Thompson to Davis, 11 Sep 1964, BDP; "The Gendarmerie d'Haiti," *MCG,* Nov 1962, p. 41; Puller/Lee OH, p. 13; Haitian Lineal List, circa 1934, Haiti Reference File, MCHC; Calixte, *Haiti.*

9. Brigade documents note on August 6, 1919, that "Mirebalais reports sending out night patrols to investigate reports as to new bandit camps." Daily Diary Report, 6 Aug 1919, Box 30, 8166, WNRC; Farrell OH, p. 309, MCHC; *Marine!,* p. 32.

10. There is no identifiable record of this action in the official reports, but they are incomplete and sketchy for this period. The district did score a number of victories during the late summer and fall of 1919 and a September 9 action at Bois Pain sounds somewhat similar to the results obtained in Puller's account. That action does not appear in the list of "principal engagements" of the Gendarmerie that year, though, and it might have been fought by a Marine unit. I have adopted Puller's version as he related it to Burke Davis. Constabulary to Brigade, 4 Aug 1920, Box 11, Haiti Series, RG 127; Daily Diary Report, Aug and Sep 1919, Box 30, 8166, WNRC; *Marine!,* p. 33.

11. The story of the horse and rider might seem apocryphal, except that Brunot would come to a bad end. In 1924 he would be convicted at a general court-martial and stripped of his rank. He also was punished in December 1919, just days after Puller's departure from Company A, for "neglect of duty." Diary of Company A, 31 Dec 1919, Box 25; List of Haitian Officers Whose Connection

with the Garde Were Severed Under Unfavorable Circumstances, Jan 1930, Box 23, 8166, WNRC; *Marine!*, p. 36; Puller interview, BDP.

12. The quote is underlined in the Jackson biography owned by Puller. Although that book was published in 1937, the original two-volume version appeared in 1898. Even if Puller had not read the words by 1919, he certainly was aware of the nature of Confederate leadership from his previous studies. Henderson, *Jackson,* p. 616.

13. Vandegrift, *Once a Marine,* p. 55; Daily Diary Report, 9 Oct 1919, Box 30, 8166, WNRC.

14. The accounts of the Georges engagement conflict in several details, but I generally have followed Brunot's report, written by a participant near the time the events occurred. *Marine!,* pp. 37–39; Martin, "Toughest Marine"; Maas, "Old Warhorse"; Brunot, Patrol Diary, 30 Nov 1919, Box 25, and Mirebalais to Gend., Oct and Nov 1919, Box 31, 8166, WNRC; Annual Report of the Constabulary, Jul 1919 to Jun 1920, Box 11, Haiti Series, RG 127; Citation for Médaille Militaire, PR.

15. The words Puller recalled forty years later echoed a phrase underlined in his favorite book: "The grand principle of concentration at the decisive point." *Marine!*, p. 39; Moskin, *Marine Corps Story,* p. 126; Henderson, *Stonewall,* p. 647.

16. *Marine!* (p. 41) credited Puller with initiating the creation of all the airfields outside Port-au-Prince, to include one at Mirebalais. A July 25, 1919, entry in the brigade commander's journal shows that he inspected the "aviation field" at Mirebalais, then flew on to the "aviation field" at Hinche. This was a week before Puller arrived in the country. Puller/Lee OH, pp. 55–60; Daily Diary Report, 23 Jul and 13 Aug 1919, Box 30, 8166, WNRC.

17. Daily Diary Report, 14 Nov 1919, Box 30, 8166, WNRC.

18. Hanneken to Puller, 15 Jan 1937, PP.

19. Raymond to Gend., 27 Nov 1919, and Brunot to Gend., 30 Nov 1919, Box 25, 8166, WNRC; Constabulary Summary, 1919–1920, 4 Aug 1920, Box 11, Haiti Series, RG 127.

20. Puller to Gend., 1 Jan 1920, Box 5, and Raymond to Gend., 27 Nov and 1 Dec 1919, Box 25, 8166, WNRC.

21. Brigade to MGC, 13 Dec 1920, Box 81, Haiti Series, RG 127.

22. QM Clerk John D. Brady, "Haiti," *MCG,* Jun 1924, p. 149; Intelligence Report on Aux Cayes, 9 May 1921, Box 4, 165, RG 127; Silverthorn OH, pp. 144–52, MCHC.

23. Puller to Gend., 1 Jan and 1 Feb 1920, Box 5, 8166, WNRC; Port-à-Piment Intelligence Report, 15 Jun 1921, Box 4, 165, and Monthly Report, Aux Cayes, 1 Aug and 31 Dec 1919, Box 1, 176, RG 127; Commission, PR.

24. In one of the many instances where *Marine!* (p. 46) tried to demonstrate Puller's willingness to buck the system, the book claimed that the injections were against established policy, but that was a standard treatment in use by Navy doctors at the time. This treatment also was used for severe malaria cases during World War II. Puller to Pullen, 5 May 1920, BDP; Millett, *Strife,* p. 81; Medical Annex, Phase V, Guadalcanal Report, Box 4, 63A-2534, RG 127.

25. Puller to Pullen, 5 May 1920, BDP; Maj Earl H. Ellis, "Bush Brigades," *MCG,* Mar 1921, p. 1.

26. Maj Franklin A. Hart, "The History of the Garde d'Haiti," 1934, pp. 82, 97,

MCRC; Puller to Pullen, 5 May 1920, BDP; Fitness Reports, Jan, Feb–Mar, Apr–Jul 1920, PR; Silverthorn OH, p. 152, MCHC.

27. Brigade to All Officers, 14 Jun 1919, Box 23, and MGC to Brigade, 27 Sep 1919, Box 30, 8166, WNRC.

28. MGC to SecNav, 12 Oct 1920, Haiti Geo File, MCHC; Lejeune, *Reminiscences,* p. 466; Millett, *Semper Fidelis,* pp. 199, 203; "Senate Inquiry into Occupation and Administration of Haiti and the Dominican Republic," 20 Apr 1922, Box 20, OPSP.

29. Callwell, *Small Wars: Their Principles and Practice,* pp. 72, 78; U.S. Marine Corps, *Small Wars Manual;* Hoffman, "Small Wars" and "Small Wars Manual," *The War of 1898,* pp. 511–16.

30. HQMC memo, 1 Sep 1922, Hanneken Bio File, MCHC.

31. Patton's biographer has provided a good synopsis on racial views in the officer corps of the U.S. armed forces in the early twentieth century. Puller never recorded his views on race, but he clearly believed by the end of his career that merit was more important than color, as evidenced by the glowing endorsement for warrant officer that he submitted for Master Sergeant Edgar R. Huff, then one of the senior black staff NCOs in the Corps. Interview notes, and Puller to Pullen, 5 May 1920, BDP; Puller/Lee OH, 1961, p. 43, MCHC; Mixson to MGC, 25 Oct 1922, and Rossell to MGC, 12 Oct 1922, PR; Christian to Gend., 1 Jan 1921, Box 1, 176, RG 127; Vandegrift to Lyman, 14 Jan 1936, Box 1, AAVP; Puller to Huff, 18 Aug 1955, PP; D'Este, *Patton,* p. 171.

32. As testimony to early inflation in fitness reports or the hazards of memory, years later Rossell would say that Puller was "just ordinary" during his time in Haiti. Rossell OH, p. 16, MCHC; Monthly Report, Aux Cayes, 31 Jan, 29 Feb, and 30 Apr 1920, Box 1, 176, RG 127; Fitness Reports, Jan, Feb–Mar, Apr–Jun 1920, PR.

33. Puller told Davis that he was a subdistrict commander at Verrettes and this could have been the only time he filled that billet. However, there are also indications he may have been at Mirebalais. Interview notes, BDP; Curtis to MGC, 7 Oct 1922, PR; *Marine!,* p. 44; Daily Diary Report, 19 May and 19 Jun 1920, Box 30, 8166, WNRC.

34. Gend. to Brigade, 15 Jul 1921, Box 11, Haiti Series, RG 127.

35. Puller to Pullen, 2 May 1920, BDP; Daily Diary Report, 4 Apr 1920, Box 30, 8166, WNRC.

36. Haiti Casualties, Box 31, 8166, WNRC; McCrocklin, *Garde,* p. 124; Millett, *Semper Fidelis,* p. 199.

37. "History of Gendarmerie d'Haiti," [circa 1925], Box 26, 8166, WNRC; Gendarmerie to Brigade, 15 Jul 1921, Box 11, Haiti Series, RG 127.

38. Although *Marine!* (p. 45) paints Puller as driving the prisoners like slaves, that was undoubtedly an exaggeration given the intense scrutiny from the ongoing investigations of the *corvée* and atrocities. The story is also reminiscent of another apocryphal account (*Marine!,* p. 200) about the bayoneting of wounded prisoners on Cape Gloucester. Dept. of the South, Patrol Reports, Oct 1920, Box 2, 165, and Neuhaus to Gend., 1 Oct 1920, Box 1, 176, RG 127; "Petite-Rivière," 9 April 1921, Box 25, 8166, WNRC; Silverthorn OH, p. 151, MCHC.

39. Neuhaus to Gend., 1 Dec 1920, and Christian to Gend., 1 Jan and 1 Feb 1921, Box 1, 176, RG 127; Fitness Reports, Jul–Dec 1921, PR.

40. Intelligence Report, St. Marc, 12 May 1921, Box 4, 165, and Puller to Gend., 8 Mar and 9 Apr 1921, Box 1, 176, RG 127.

41. Promotion Warrant, 7 Apr 1921, and Good Conduct Medal Certificate, 28 Apr 1921, PR; Gend. to MGC, 11 Apr 1921, Box 81, Haiti Series, RG 127.

Chapter 3: "I Have Some Perseverance": A Junior Officer in Peacetime, 1921–1928

1. Puller to MGC, 1 Dec 1919, and MGC to Puller, 3 Jan and 13 Apr 1920, and Mrs. Puller to MGC, 21 Apr and 9 Jun 1920, PR; Puller to Pullen, 2 May 1920, BDP; "The March of Events," *MCG,* Dec 1921, p. 446.

2. Heinl, *Soldiers of the Sea,* p. 228; Millett, *Strife,* p. 81; Hoffman, *Legend,* p. 27; Gend. to MGC, 26 Jul 1920, and MGC to Gend., 13 Aug and 7 Sep 1920, PR.

3. Of the three men in Haiti selected, Gunnery Sergeant John F. Connaughton had eight years' prior service, Sergeant David Kipness had sixteen years' prior service, and Sergeant John A. Bemis had enlisted in 1917 and graduated from 3d OTC with Puller. Both Kipness and Bemis had served with the AEF in France. A sergeant major and a corporal with time in the AEF and temporary commissions dating from 1918 did not make it. MGC to Puller, 26 Mar 1921; MGC to Brigade, 7 Sep 1920; Puller to CMC, 7 Mar 1946, PR; Gend. to MGC, 8 Nov 1921, Box 80, Haiti Series RG 127; *Navy Register,* 1919, 1920, 1922, 1924, NHC; Bemis Bio File, MCHC.

4. "Status of Commissioned Personnel," *MCG,* Jun 1921, p. 231; Nalty, *Officer Procurement,* p. 6; Gend. to Brigade, 7 Jun 1921, Box 81, Haiti Series, and MGC to All Commanders, 10 Jan 1922, Box 234, 18, RG 127; MGC to Brigade, 11 Jun 1921, and Brigade to MGC, 20 Jun 1921, PR.

5. Vogel, Memorandums, 8 and 27 Jun 1921, Box 234, 18, RG 127; "NCO Candidates for Commissions," *MCG,* Mar 1922, p. 78; Nalty, *Officer Procurement,* p. 6; *Annual Report of the Navy Department for 1924,* p. 665, MCRC.

6. Summary Court Memorandum, 14 Nov 1921; Rockey to MGC, 24 Sep 1921, PR; Putnam to MGC, 12 Dec 1921; Buckley to MGC, 18 Jan 1921, Box 234, 18, RG 127.

7. *Marine!* (p. 46) would claim that Puller had failed, along with 90 percent of his class, because someone had changed the rules at the last minute and would not allow the students to refer to their trigonometry texts during the test. Vandegrift was under the impression that Puller had become upset with his trigonometry instructor and failed when he turned in a blank paper in protest on an exam. Vandegrift, *Once a Marine,* p. 59; MGC to SecNav, 12 Dec 1921, and Examining Board to SecNav, 8 Feb 1922, Box 234, 18, RG 127; "The March of Events," *MCG,* Mar 1922, p. 106; Linsert and Megee Bio Files, MCHC.

8. Marine Barracks Washington to MGC, 20 Feb 1922, and SecNav to SecState, 28 Jul 1922, and Circular of Information for Applicants, undated [circa 1921], Box 81, Haiti Series, RG 127; HQMC to Gend., 23 Feb 1922, PR.

9. Vandegrift, *Once a Marine,* p. 59; Brady, "Haiti," *MCG,* Jun 1924, p. 149; Puller to Wise, 18 Mar 1955, PP; Vandegrift to MGC, 9 Feb 1923, PR.

10. Heinl OH, p. 220; "Correspondence," *MCG,* Dec 1927, p. 243.

11. Brigade to MGC, 25 Mar 1921, Box 81, Haiti Series, and Report of Strength, 31 May 1922 and 1 Feb 1923, Box 1, 167, RG 127; Fitness Reports, Jul 1922–Jul 1923, PR; "Correspondence," *MCG,* Dec 1927, p. 243.

12. *Gendarmerie News,* Jun 1922, MCHC Library; Gend. to Brigade, 15 Jul 1921, Box 11, Haiti Series, RG 127.

13. Capt M. B. Curtis, Maj J. A. Rossell, Maj A. A. Vandegrift, 1stlt J. A. Mixson, Capt J. L. Perkins, and Capt H. L. Smith recommendations, Oct and Nov 1922, PR; Puller draft manuscript, p. 249, BDP.

14. Vandegrift to MGC, 9 Feb 1923, and MGC to Commissioner, 5 Apr 1923, PR; MGC to Marine Barracks Washington, 7 Apr 1923, Box 234, 18, RG 127; Vandegrift, *Once a Marine,* p. 59; Vandegrift to Leroy, 4 Oct 1938, Box 1, AAVP.

15. Enlistment Papers, 30 Jun 1923, and Gend. to Brigade, 29 Jun 1923, and Gend. to HQMC, 26 Jun 1923, PR.

16. Subsequent accounts credited Puller with having fought forty "actions" in Haiti and Davis referred to him as "one of the most seasoned combat officers in the Corps." The number is certainly far lower than forty. He was in the combat zone for only four months, August through November 1919. During the first half of August he was on supply train duty and had, by his own recollection, only one minor contact. His activities are well documented from late October through the end of November. During that period he had four battles. The annual report of the Gendarmerie lists all "principal engagements," to include three of those four, but no others involving Puller. The Marine Corps official report on Haiti described all of the major engagements with *cacos,* but Puller did not figure in any of them. Major Ostermann, a senior officer in Mirebalais during Puller's time there, referred in December 1919 to Puller's participation "in several skirmishes." The number of forty contacts apparently was first broached in a 1952 article based on an interview with Puller. In that same piece, the writer referred to Puller's sixty "pitched battles" in Nicaragua, where conclusive records show only twenty-two contacts. With regard to comparisons with the experience of other officers, dozens of Marine leaders had spent much more time battling the *cacos* and hundreds had fought much larger and much deadlier battles in France. *Marine!,* p. 46; Henderson, *Stonewall,* p. 36; Ostermann to MGC, 18 December 1919, PR; Martin, "Toughest Marine"; Book of Contacts, Box 20, 38, RG 127; Constabulary Summary, 1919–1920, 4 Aug 1920, Box 11, Haiti Series, RG 127; Hart, "The History of the Garde d'Haiti," 1934, MCRC; Puller/Lee OH, p. 18.

17. "Medical Abstract," MR; Grades of Candidates for Commission, Box 234, 18, RG 127.

18. MGC to Ostermann, 17 Dec 1923, and Rossell to MGC, 29 Jan 1924, Box 234, 18, RG 127; MGC to Candidates, 11 Jan 1924, PR; Rossell OH, p. 15.

19. PR; *Annual Report of the Navy Department for 1924,* p. 665, MCRC; *Marine!,* p. 46; Vandegrift, *Once a Marine,* p. 59; Vandegrift OH, p. 261, MCHC.

20. Shulimson, *Mission,* p. 103; MGC to Puller, 6 Mar 1924, PR; Lejeune to Personnel Section, 7 Nov 1921, and "Memo for Gen. Feland," 29 May 1924, Box 117, 18, RG 127.

21. Cooley OH, p. 5, MCHC; Davis to MGC, 23 Dec 1924 and 22 Jan 1925, Box 117, 18, RG 127; Fitness Reports, Mar 1924–Jan 1925, PR; interview notes, BDP.

22. General Regulations and Routine, 2 Feb 1925, and Henley to MGC, 31 Dec 1924, Box 117, 18, RG 127; Jordahl OH, p. 11.

23. Henley to MGC, 31 Dec 1924 and 7 Jan 1925, Box 117, 18, RG 127; Basic School Diploma, 27 Jun 1925, PR; Hart OH, pp. 12–16.

24. Basic Class Standings, 27 Jun 1925, Box 117, 18, RG 127; Chronological Record, PR.

25. Jordahl OH, p. 13; Puller to MGC, 18 May 1925, and MGC to Puller, 20 Jun 1925, PR.

26. Millett, *Semper Fidelis*, p. 324.

27. *Marine!* (p. 50) had Puller reporting aboard on a Friday, the battery commander leaving that day, and the shoot occurring just a few days later with Puller in command. The records show that Puller was with the unit for thirteen days prior to his taking over as the acting commander for the next eighteen days. During that era Quantico was much smaller than it is today and the artillery did not fire there. Thus the shoot he recalled almost certainly was the regimental exercise conducted at Camp Meade the following month. (Puller also misremembered his mentor as a Bernoski.) In this case, Puller likely was following his penchant for fleshing out the bare bones of his memories into a story that made what he considered to be an important point. Chronological Record, PR; interview notes, BDP; Muster Rolls, Jul–Sep 1925, MCHC; Buckner, *10th Marines,* pp. 32–33.

28. Puller to MGC, 10 Sep 1925, and Chronological Record, PR.

29. Quantico to MGC, 9 Dec 1925; 1st District to Quantico, 4 Dec 1925; MGC to Puller, 4 Dec and 19 Dec 1925; Fitness Report, Nov–Dec 1925, PR; Norrish interview, BDP; *Camp Lejeune Globe,* 17 Jun 1955, p. 4; Muster Rolls, Sep 1918, MCHC.

30. MGC to Puller, 12 Oct 1925; Puller to MGC, 26 Jun and 16 Nov 1925, PR.

31. Chronological Record; Fitness Report, Jan 1926, PR; Mersky, *Aviation,* p. 19.

32. Although Puller recalled that the first meeting with Virginia occurred in the spring of 1926, the records indicate that he did not take leave during that time frame. Also, he and Virginia remembered that she was "about seventeen." She was born February 19, 1908, which would suggest a 1925 meeting, though they might have been mistaken about her age. She attended Saint Mary's from 1924 through 1927. Sam Puller Bio File, MCHC; Pullen to Davis, 1 Jun 1960, BDP; Muster Rolls, Sep 1925, MCHC; Chronological Record, PR; Sally Wooten (Saint Mary's Alumnae Office) interview, 8 Jun 1999; Virginia Dabney interview, 14 Oct 1998; *Marine!,* p. 53.

33. Mersky, *Aviation,* pp. 21–22; "Memo for Major Fegan," 27 Mar 1934, Box 1, 93-0051, WNRC; Woods OH, p. 25.

34. Hoffman, *Legend,* p. 37.

35. Advisory Board Proceedings, 5 May 1925; Puller to MGC, 1 Sep 1928, PR.

36. Merrill Twining and Evans Carlson also failed flight school. Merritt Edson had his wings revoked after several crashes revealed a problem with depth perception.

37. Puller to MGC, 6 May 1926; HQMC to Puller, 14 May 1926, PR.

38. *Marine!,* p. 53.

39. Twining, *No Bended Knee,* p. 133; Twining interview with author, Jan 1996.

40. Puller/Lee OH, pp. 107–12; Moskin, *Marine Corps Story,* p. 92; Shulimson, *Mission,* p. 159; Twining interview with author, Jan 1996; Fitness Report, Oct 1926–Mar 1927, PR.

41. *Marine!,* p. 55; Chronological Record, PR.

42. Puller to MGC, 10 Feb and 1 Sep 1928; King to MGC, 11 Sep 1928, PR.

43. MGC to Dept. of the Pacific, 29 Mar 1928, PR.

44.   Medical Abstract, MR; Hospital Discharge; Chronological Record; Fitness Reports, Jun–Nov 1928, PR.
45.   Moskin, *Marine Corps Story,* pp. 212, 164.
46.   Capt O. P. Smith, "In the Wake of the Expeditions," *MCG,* Sep 1927, p. 146.
47.   Puller to MGC, 4 May and 16 Oct 1928, PR.

Chapter 4: "Days of Hard Marching": First Tour in Nicaragua, 1928–1930

1.   COMSPERON to MGC, 1 Dec 1927, Box 83; Guardia to MGC, 21 Oct 1928; MGC to Guardia, 29 Oct 1928, Box 85, Nicaragua Series, RG 127.
2.   Brigade to COMSPERON, 27 Oct 1931; CO, 3/5 to CO, 5th Regt, 3 Dec 1929, Box 1, 76-30, WNRC.
3.   Memorandum for MGC re Guardia Agreement, 1 Aug 1927; Sellers to CNO, 22 Sep 1928; Little to MGC, 19 Oct 1928; Barber to Brigade, 14 Feb 1929, Box 83; MGC to Manlove, 18 May 1927, Box 85, Nicaragua Series, RG 127.
4.   Guardia Annual Report, 8 Nov 1928; Extra Compensation Memorandum, 2 Apr 1930; Strength and Distribution, Oct 1927–Oct 1928, Box 82; Jefe to Brigade, 29 Jul 1929, Box 83, Nicaragua Series; GN-3 to Jefe, 29 Nov 1929, Box 33, 43A; Guardia Det Orders #7 and 8, 5 Sep and 15 Oct 1928, Box 1, 214, RG 127; Roster of Officers Detached, 8 May 1930, Vogel Papers, MCRC; LtGen Vernon E. Megee, "U.S. Military Intervention in Nicaragua, 1909–1932," unpub. MA thesis, U. of Texas, 1963, p. 125; Erskine OH, p. 101; Craig OH, p. 69; Hogaboom OH, pp. 62, 70; Good OH, p. 65.
5.   Brigade Memorandum, 16 Jul 1928; Guardia General Order 109-1929, 10 Sep 1929, Box 1, 222, RG 127.
6.   Fitness Reports, Dec 1928–May 1929; Beadle to Puller, 9 Mar 1929, PR.
7.   According to *Marine!* (p. 58), Puller went to Corinto to replace a Lieutenant Stevens who had been shot by a mob with his own pistol. The detailed records of the Guardia contain no documentation of a mob incident or the wounding of an officer. Corporal Ward M. Stevens, a Guardia cadet, transferred out of Corinto the day before Puller's arrival, but the muster rolls report no injury and he soon was on duty with the field forces in Jinotega. Fitness Report, 1 Apr–6 May 1929; Chronological Record; MGC to Puller, 5 Feb and 26 Jul 1929; Guardia Commission, 1 May 1929, PR; GN Order #17-1929, Box 25, 38, RG 127; Puller interview notes, BDP; Muster Rolls, GN Detachment, Mar and Apr 1929, MCHC; Smith, *Guardia.*
8.   Description of Jinotega, 1920, Box 20, 38; Political Division, Box 29, 43A; GN-3 to B-3, 29 Aug 1929, Box 1, 222, RG 127.
9.   Schroeder, *Defend,* pp. 202, 348–54, 368, 508, 522; Smith, *Guardia,* pp. 69–70.
10.   Brigade to MGC, 25 Mar 1921, Box 81; Guardia to MGC, 29 Nov 1927, Box 83; Guardia Annual Report, Oct 1928–Sep 1929, Box 82, Nicaragua Series; Dunlap to Floyd, 28 Jun 1928, Box 1, 221; Davis to Area Commander, 16 Jul 1928, Box 3, 204; McCoy to Brigade, 21 Oct 1928, Box 1, 39; Brigade to CO, Matagalpa, 22 Oct 1928, Box 1, 221, RG 127.
11.   GN Special Order #26, 23 Mar 1929; GN Special Order #57, 1 Aug 1929, Box 25, 38; Jefe to Officers, 27 Mar 1929, Box 2, 198; 1st Bn Order #2, 27 Apr 1929; GN to Brigade, 3 Aug 1929, Box 1, 222; 1st Bn to GN, 14 May 1929, Box 9, 202, RG 127; GN to Central Area, undated, Box 7, JCSP.
12.   GN Special Order #52, Box 25, 38; GN to Officers, 27 Mar 1929, Box 2, 198,

RG 127; Fitness Reports, Apr 1929–Mar 1930, PR; Erskine OH, p. 103; Craig OH, p. 68; Craig to Davis, 22 Nov 1960, BDP.

13. Central Area to Erskine, 8 Nov 1929, Box 36, 43A, RG 127.

14. Puller to Battalion, 17 Jul 1929, Box 1, 200; Central Area Ops Reports, Aug–Dec 1929, Box 5; Hanneken to Central Area, 29 Oct 1929, Box 13, 202, RG 127; Erskine OH, p. 100; Craig to Davis, 22 Nov 1960, BDP; Fitness Report, Oct 1929–Mar 1930, PR.

15. Central Area Ops Reports, Jan 1930, Box 6, 202; Book of Contacts, Box 20; USMC Casualties in Nicaragua, Box 19, 38; Guardia Annual Report, Oct 1928–Sep 1929, Box 82, Nicaragua Series, RG 127.

16. *Marine!* (p. 60) mistakenly describes the capture and death of Altamirano during this operation. There was no such action that day and Altamirano survived until after the Marines left Nicaragua. In fact, Puller reported in 1932 that his unit was attacked by Altamirano. Macaulay to Davis, BDP; Puller to Jefe Director, 3 Oct 1932, Box 1, 200; Puller to Central Area, Contact Report and Endorsement, 22 Feb 1930, Box 11; Puller to Central Area, Patrol Report, 22 Feb 1930, Box 13, 202; 1st Battalion Order #2, 27 Apr 1929, Box 1, 222, RG 127.

17. Central Area Ops Reports, Jan–May 1930, Box 6, 202, RG 127.

18. The timing of Puller and Lee joining Company M is a good example of the danger of relying on memories long after the fact. In a 1995 interview Lee recalled that he had formed Company M (not true) and was there before Puller (true). Puller believed that he had joined before Lee and selected him to be his second in command (not true). *Marine!,* pp. 60–61; Cpl Shanze Lee, "War in Nicaragua," *Quantico Sentry,* 31 Mar 1995; Elizabeth P. Donovan, "Marine 'Ironman' Still Tough as Nails," *Navy Times,* 2 Oct 1989, p. 6; Guardia Annual Report, Oct 1929–Sep 1930, Box 82, Nicaragua Series; Lee, Patrol Report, Feb 1929, Box 24, 43A; Central Area Ops Report, 12 Mar 1930, Box 6, 202, RG 127; Puller to GN, 1 Jun 1931, Box 1, 193, RG 127.

19. GN to Central Area, 17 May 1930, Box 9; Central Area to GN, 7 Jun 1930; Puller to Central Area, 8 Jun 1930, Box 11, 202, RG 127.

20. Puller to Central Area, 8 Jun 1930, Box 10; Central Area to GN, 7 Jun 1930, Box 17; Central Area Monthly Record, 7 Jul 1930, Box 2, 202, RG 127; Puller/Lee OH, p. 51.

21. Webb to Central Area, 23 Jun 1930, Box 13, 202, RG 127.

22. In an interview at Guadalcanal in 1942, Puller would recall his emphasis on officers' mounts slowing down patrols, but he would place it incorrectly in Haiti. His emphasis in Nicaragua on rapid movement by lightly burdened infantry borrowed a page, perhaps unconsciously, from his hero Jackson. During the 1862 campaign in the Shenandoah Valley, Stonewall's troops had covered an amazing amount of ground and fought several battles, thereby confounding Union generals and forcing them to focus on defending Washington. The Confederate soldiers grew exhausted and footsore, but gloried in their reputation as Jackson's "foot cavalry." Puller to Central Area, 17 Jul 1930, Box 13, 202, RG 127; Reeder, *Fighting,* p. 34; McPherson, *Battle Cry,* p. 457.

23. Puller to Central Area, 17 Jul 1930, Box 13; Central Area to GN, 4 Mar 1931, Box 9, 202, RG 127; Diary of a Guardia Officer, Denig Papers.

24. Brigade to MGC, 28 Feb 1928, Box 30, 38; 1st Bn Order #2, 27 Apr 1929, Box 1, 222, RG 127.

25. Hoffman, *Legend,* pp. 58, 62; Diary of a Guardia Officer, p. 151; Good OH, p. 57.
26. Julian Smith, quoted in Fridell, "Chesty."
27. MR; Puller to Central Area, 28 Jul 1930, Box 10, 202, RG 127.
28. Puller to Central Area, 28 Jul 1930, Box 10; Central Area Ops Report, 28 Jul 1930, Box 6, 202, RG 127.
29. In Puller's memory, it took twenty days to track down this group and he did so only by ignoring an order to go to their last reported location. He claimed he had caught up by cutting across their roundabout route, but was reprimanded by Webb for disobeying orders. The text follows Puller's official report, which paints a much different picture. Puller interview notes, BDP.
30. Puller to Central Area, 22 Aug 1930, Box 10, 202, RG 127; GN News #7; GN to President, 2 Sep 1930, Box 6, JCSP; diary, Denig Papers.
31. GN Order #57, 3 Sep 1930, Box 31, 43A; GN News #9, Box 1, 205, RG 127.
32. Central Area Ops Reports, Aug–Sep 1930, Box 6, 202, RG 127; GN News #12, JCSP.
33. Puller to Central Area, 16 Sep 1930, Box 10, 202, RG 127.
34. Central Area Monthly Record, 14 Oct 1930, Box 2; Central Area Ops Reports, Box 6; Central Area to GN, 27 Nov 1930, Box 9, 202, RG 127; GN News #18; 1st Bn Order #7, 7 Nov 1930; Automatic Weapons in Central Area, Box 7, JCSP.
35. GN News #20, 21, and 22, JCSP; Central Area Monthly Record, 15 Dec 1930, Box 2; Central Area Ops Reports, Nov 1930, Box 6; Puller to Central Area, 20 Nov 1930, Box 10, 202, RG 127.
36. Diary, p. 153, Denig Papers; Julian Smith OH, p. 127; Ltr to Julian Smith, 11 Dec 1930, Box 6, JCSP.
37. Puller to Central Area, 30 Nov 1930, Box 10, 202, RG 127.
38. During the small wars of the 1920s and 1930s the Navy Cross was given out routinely for acts that would seem to pale in comparison with deeds of bravery receiving the same award in later and bigger conventional conflicts. But at the time it was the lowest award for combat valor among the few naval service medals in existence. In any case, the Marines of this period earned their Navy Crosses by operating in small groups far from any support—they had no one to turn to for reinforcements, resupply, or medical aid. It took a different sort of courage to fight these lonely wars and Marines such as Puller and Lee demonstrated it time and again. Chronological Record; Navy Cross Citation, PR; Lee interview notes, BDP; Central Area Ops Reports, Dec 1930, Box 6; Smith to Jefe, 3 Dec 1930, Box 10, 202, RG 127.
39. Lee to Central Area, 21 Dec 1930, Box 10, 202, RG 127; GN News #25 and 26, JCSP.
40. GN News #28, JCSP; Central Area Ops Report, 12 Jan 1931, Box 6, 202; Book of Contacts, Box 20, 38; Guardia Annual Reports, 1 Dec 1930 and 1931, Box 82, Nicaragua Series, RG 127.
41. Central Area Monthly Record, 17 Mar and 8 Apr 1931, Box 2; Central Area Ops Reports, Jan–May 1931, Box 6, 202; Central Area Journal, Box 2, 198, RG 127; GN News #31, 34, 37, 42, 45, JCSP; Treatment Record, Feb–Mar 1931, MR; Lee interview notes, BDP.
42. Red Cross to MGC, 7 May 1931, PR; GN News #41 and 50, JCSP; Central Area Ops Reports, Apr 1931, Box 6, 202, RG 127; "The Managua Disaster," *MCG,* Aug 1931, p. 12.

43. Puller to Central Area, 15 May 1931, Box 11; Puller to Central Area, 15 May 1931, Box 14, 202, RG 127.

44. Puller to MGC, 27 Jan 1931; MGC to Guardia Det, 1 Jun 1931, PR; GN News #50 and 51, JCSP; Puller to GN, 1 Jun 1931, Box 1, 193; Ops Report, 2 Jun 1931, Box 6, 202, RG 127; MGC to All Officers, 11 Sep 1930, Vogel Papers.

45. Citation for Medal of Merit; Citizens to Smith, 2 Jun 1931; Fitness Reports, Apr 1930–Jun 1931, PR; news clipping, "Nicaragua Guardia Has Difficult Task," Box 7, JCSP.

Chapter 5: "The Toughest Proposition": Fort Benning and Nicaragua, 1931–1932

1. Merritt to Smith, 4 May 1931; Smith to Williams, 30 Dec 1931; Smith to Ben, 26 Dec 1932, Box 62, OPSP; Jordahl OH, pp. 43–45.

2. Smith to Kennedy, 4 Dec 1931; Smith to Dutch, 13 Feb 1932, Box 62, OPSP; O. P. Smith OH, p. 47; Cray, *General,* pp. 104–6; Perret, *War to Be Won,* pp. 10–18; Millett, *Strife,* p. 106; Bradley, *Soldier's Story,* pp. 15–16.

3. Millett, *Strife,* p. 106.

4. Infantry School to MGC, 6 Jun 1932, Box 110, 18, RG 127; Bowser OH, p. 36; Maj Michael Shisler, "General Oliver P. Smith," *MCG,* Nov 1978, pp. 42–47; Brown Bio File, MCHC; Millett, *Strife,* pp. 58, 104.

5. Thomas OH, p. 103; Smith to Charlie, 16 Jan 1932, Box 62, OPSP; Infantry School Certificate of Completion, 1 Jun 1932, PR; Millett, *Strife,* pp. 106–7.

6. Smith to Dutch, 13 Feb 1932; Merritt to Smith, 4 May 1931, Box 62, OPSP.

7. Puller interview notes; Mead to Davis, 31 Oct 1960, BDP; Smith to Davis, 29 Jun 1960, Box 19, OPSP; O. P. Smith OH, pp. 44–45.

8. Puller to MGC, Report of Record Practice, 19 May 1932, PR; Smith to Dutch, 13 Feb 1932, Box 62; Smith to Davis, 29 Jun 1960, Box 19, OPSP; O. P. Smith OH, p. 46.

9. Smith to Dutch, 13 Feb 1932, Box 62, OPSP; *Marine!,* p. 70.

10. Thomas to Wife, 28 May 1932, Thomas Papers; Vandegrift to Hunt, 4 Oct 1938, Box 1, AAVP.

11. Puller's disdain for military education seems to have been a later phenomenon, since no expressions on that point appeared till the middle of World War II. *Marine!,* p. 75; Jordahl OH, p. 44; Thomas OH, p. 103; O. P. Smith OH, p. 44; Puller to Grady, 25 Feb 1955, PP.

12. There is no direct evidence that Puller contacted the *jefe director* and asked for his intervention, but it seems likely that is what happened. The *jefe* understood the assignment process and would not have waited till the last minute to make his wishes known. Moreover, he had not included Puller's name in a December 1931 list of officers desired for constabulary duty. Eligible List, 22 Dec 1931, Box 85, Nicaragua Series, RG 127; Puller to MGC, 21 Dec 1931; MGC to Puller, 26 Apr 1932; GN to MGC, 2 May 1932, PR.

13. Musicant, *Banana Wars,* p. 353; MGC to CNO, 29 Jul 1932, Box 82, Nicaragua Series; GN to American Minister to Nicaragua, 8 Aug 1932, Box 33, 43A, RG 127.

14. GN-2 Reports, Jul 1931 and Apr and Sep 1932; B-2 Report, May 1932, JCSP; Central Area Record of Events, 16 Aug 1932, Box 1, 39, RG 127.

15. Chronological Record; Fitness Report, Jul 1932, PR; news clipping, BDP.

16. Central Area Ops Report, Jul and Aug 1932, Box 7, 202; Distribution of Troops,

11 Apr 1932, Box 82, Nicaragua Series; Puller to GN, 18 Sep and 3 Oct 1932, Box 1, 200, RG 127.

17. Puller/Lee OH, p. 115; Puller to GN and Endorsement, 21 Aug 1932, Box 1, 200, RG 127; GN-2 Report, Aug 1932, JCSP.

18. Puller to GN, 18 Sep 1932, Box 1, 200, RG 127.

19. Central Area Ops Report, Sep 1932, Box 7, 202, RG 127.

20. Puller/Lee OH, pp. 30–32, 46–47; Lee interview, BDP; Central Area to GN, 20 Sep 1932, Box 1, 202; Puller to GN, 3 Oct 1932, Box 1, 200, RG 127; GN to SecNav, 10 Nov 1932, PR; Heinl, *Soldiers,* pp. 284–86, 631.

21. Heinl, *Soldiers,* p. 286.

22. Puller to GN, 3 Oct 1932, Box 1, 200; Central Area to GN, 20 Sep 1932, Box 1, 202, RG 127; Hogaboom OH, p. 65; GN to SecNav, 10 Nov 1932, PR.

23. Puller's emphasis on the necessity of fire support is especially interesting in light of later critiques of his leadership at Peleliu. Puller to GN, 5 Nov 1932, Box 14; Central Area Record of Events, Oct 1932, Box 2, 202, RG 127; GN-2 Report, Oct 1932; GN News #125, JCSP.

24. Smith to Central Area, 19 Nov 1932, Box 1, 37; Central Area Ops Report, Nov and Dec 1932, Box 7, 202, RG 127.

25. Brigade to COMSPERON, 12 Nov 1932, Box 1, 76-30, WNRC.

26. Puller to GN, 31 Dec 1932, Box 1, 39, RG 127; Carlson, "One Year Ago Today"; Lee interview notes; Puller interview notes; Linsert to Davis, 17 Nov 1960, BDP; Puller/Lee OH, pp. 149–52; Constabulary Commission, PR.

27. GN News #127, Box 85, Nicaragua Series, RG 127; Macaulay to Davis, 3 Apr 1962, BDP; Smith, *Guardia Nacional,* pp. 130, 151.

28. Puller had fought in twenty-two of the Guardia's 510 contacts (4.5 percent), and had accounted for seventy-seven of the confirmed 1,115 Sandinista dead (6.9 percent). Fitness Report, Aug–Sep 1932, PR; Book of Contacts.

29. Interestingly enough, Lee would be the one enshrined in Sandinista mythology as the quintessential Yankee invader, perhaps because he spent more time with Company M than Puller did. Schroeder, *Defend,* pp. 429–34; Camp Lejeune public affairs release, 1945, PBF, MCHC; "Col Lewis Puller," news clipping, 1 Aug 1945, PP; "Lewis B. Puller," *Proud Tradition: Marine Corps League News,* Mar 1982, p. 37.

Chapter 6: "An Exceptionally Confident Officer": On the China Station, 1933–1936

1. Puller to MGC, 18 Sep 1932; MGC to Puller, 27 Sep 1932, PR; "USMC Operating Plan," *MCG,* Aug 1932, p. 50.

2. News clipping, PBF; Puller to MGC, 7 Mar 1941, PR; Lee obituary, *Leatherneck,* Mar 1999, p. 61; *Leatherneck,* Nov 1954, p. 29.

3. The Navy Department Board of Awards had upgraded the *jefe director's* recommendation for a Distinguished Service Medal. Citation, PR.

4. Strength Report of Guard Detachments, Nov 1933, Box 5, 152, RG 127; *American Legation Guard Annual* 1933, Russell Papers.

5. Vandegrift to Potts, 27 Sep 1935 and 26 Feb 1936, Box 1, AAVP; Turner, *Thomason,* p. 237.

6. Various files, Box 5; Strength Report, 31 Dec 1934; Rifle Range Report, 1934, Box 7, 152, RG 127; Vandegrift to Lyman, 14 Jan 1936, Box 1, AAVP.

7. Rifle Range file, Box 7; Match correspondence, Jul 1934, Box 6, 152, RG 127.

8. The injury appears in his medical record only in the form of the recollections of him and his doctor as they account for the deformity in a 1940 physical. Capt Pedro A. del Valle, "On Polo," *MCG,* Jun 1927, p. 96; Physical Exam Record, 2 May 1940, MR; interview notes, BDP; *Annual,* 1933, p. 141; Guard CO to All Officers, 17 Mar 1933, Box 4, 152, RG 127.

9. Puller to Guard CO, 26 May 1933, Box 4; Post Order, 15 Mar 1934, Box 6, 152, RG 127.

10. "The Pay Situation," *MCG,* Feb 1934, p. 30; "Living Conditions in the Marine Corps," *MCG,* Jun 1927, p. 110; "Living Conditions in China," *MCG,* Mar 1928, p. 67; *The 4th Marines,* p. 10.

11. "The Sino-Japanese Situation," *MCG,* May 1932, p. 49, and Aug 1932, p. 56; Turner, *Thomason,* p. 248.

12. *Annual,* 1933, pp. 67–69.

13. Box 5; Puller to Guard CO, 28 Mar 1934, Box 7, 152, RG 127.

14. *Legation Guard News,* 5 Dec 1933, BDP; Chronological Record, PR.

15. Millett, *Semper Fidelis,* p. 229; "The Mounted Detachment in 1934," *American Legation Guard Annual,* 1934, Russell Papers; Vandegrift OH, p. 386; Fitness Report, Oct 1933–Mar 1934, PR.

16. Fitness Report, Mar–Aug 1933, PR; *Marine!,* pp. 87–89; letter to editor clipping, *Shipmate,* PP; Vandegrift to Lyman, 14 Jan 1936, Box 1, AAVP.

17. Asiatic Fleet to Puller, 17 Aug 1934; Fitness Report, Apr–Sep 1934, PR; Berkeley interview notes; Waters to Davis, 3 Oct 1960, BDP; Moncure OH, p. 25; Deck Logs, 1933–34, RG 24.

18. Puller to MGC, 8 Sep 1934 and 3 Apr 1935; MGC to Puller, 30 Apr 1935, PR; Vandegrift to Smith, 10 Jan 1936, Box 1, AAVP; MGC to All Officers, 14 Jun 1934, Sims Papers.

19. "USMC Operating Plan for FY 1933," *MCG,* Aug 1932, p. 50.

20. *DANFS,* Vol. I, p. 74; Roskill, *Naval Policy,* Vol. I, pp. 581–82, Vol. II, p. 159.

21. Except where otherwise noted, the details of events on board *Augusta* are taken from her deck logs, RG 24, NA; Fitness Report, Oct 1934–Apr 1935, PR; Mustin OH, p. 72; Leverton OH, p. 53, NHC; Les Kimble, "Chesty," [1962], PP.

22. "King Neptune's Day," *MCG,* Nov 1937, p. 20; Hayney to Davis, 21 Jun 1960, BDP.

23. Potter, *Nimitz,* p. 160; Nimitz to Davis, 6 Feb 1961; Waters to Davis, 3 Oct 1960; Hayney to Davis, 21 Jun 1960, BDP; Fitness Reports, Sep 1934 and Oct 1934–Apr 1935, PR; Mustin OH, p. 56; Moncure OH, pp. 2, 18, 25.

24. Potter, *Nimitz,* p. 160; Waters to Davis and interview notes, BDP; Augusta to Puller, 12 Nov 1934, PP.

25. RAdm Joseph C. Wylie, Jr., "My Shipmate, Chesty Puller," *USNIP,* Dec 1985, p. 85.

26. Leverton, OH, p. 8.

27. Waters to Davis, 3 Oct 1960, BDP; *Augusta* to Puller, 31 Mar 1936; CINCAF to *Augusta,* 30 Apr 1936; MGC to Puller, 6 Apr 1936, PR; Heinl OH, p. 119.

28. MGC to Puller, 19 Sep 1935; Acceptance of Commission, 7 Feb 1936, PR; Deck Log, 9 Nov 1935, RG 24; Worton OH, p. 34; O. P. Smith OH, p. 13; Vandegrift OH, p. 425.

29. Thomason to Puller, 6 Feb 1935 [probably 1936], PP.

30. Fitness Reports, Jul–Sep 1935 and Apr–May 1936, PR.

Chapter 7: "So Very Happy and Contented": Basic School and China Again, 1936–1941

1. Puller to MGC, 15 Jan 1936; MGC to Dept of the Pacific, 13 May and 1 Jun 1936, PR.
2. 2dLt J. D. Hittle, "The Basic School Completes Another Year," *MCG,* Jun 1938, p. 26; Masters OH, pp. 8–11; Daily Schedules, 1938–39, Box 517, RG 127.
3. "Officer Procurement," *MCG,* Feb 1936, p. 18; "Procurement Program for Second Lieutenants," *MCG,* Mar 1938, p. 26; Basic School to MGC, 20 Sep 1939, Box 517, RG 127; Heinl OH, pp. 12, 16, 80, 227–28; Hittle OH, p. 6; Robertson OH, pp. 75–76; Kyle OH, p. 8; Nickerson OH, pp. 123–26; Jordahl OH, p. 57; Davis interview, 15 Nov 1995.
4. News clipping, 13 Aug 1936, BDP.
5. Hoffman, *Legend,* pp. 97–100; Basic School to MGC, 17 Jan 1936, Box 517, RG 127; Hanneken to Puller, 15 Jan 1937, PP; Heinl OH, pp. 64, 1278; Stewart OH, p. 4; Robertson OH, pp. 81, 84; Jordahl OH, p. 60; Puller/Lee OH, p. 3; R. Davis OH, pp. 58, 107–8; Davis interview, 15 Nov 1995.
6. Basic School to MGC, 17 Jan 1939, Box 517, RG 127; Honsowetz to author, 29 Mar 1996; Walt, "Comments About Chesty Puller," 28 Dec 1982, copy in possession of author.
7. 1stLt Wayne M. Brown, "Basic School with 'Capting' Puller," *Shipmate,* Nov 1987, p. 15; Honsowetz to author, 29 Mar 1996; Galer interview with author, 18 Jun 1996; Robertson OH, pp. 83–84; Stewart OH, p. 4; Kyle OH, p. 11; Hittle OH, pp. 8–9.
8. Hittle, "Basic School Completes Another Year"; Walt to Puller, 28 Jul 1960; Walt interview notes, BDP; Jordahl OH, p. 58; Basic School to MGC, 9 Nov 1937, Box 61, 18, RG 127.
9. "The Major General Commandant's Speech to the Graduating Class, Basic School, 1937," *MCG,* May 1937, p. 41.
10. 1927 Yearbook, p. 49, Saint Mary's Archives; Robert Evans interview, 22 Sep 1998.
11. Puller to Virginia Puller, 16 Aug 1937, PP.
12. Hanneken to Puller, 15 Jan 1937, PP; *Marine!,* p. 99; interview notes, BDP; Tom Bartlett, "Living with a Legend," *Leatherneck,* Jun 1985, p. 18; Leave Papers, May 1937, PR.
13. I am indebted to Robert K. Krick for providing most of the information on Virginia Evans's forebears. Cox, *Old Houses,* pp. 22–23; Brock, *Virginia,* pp. 687–88; Krick, *Lee's Colonels,* p. 275; Col E. B. Montague biographical summary; news clipping, 2 Jul 1919, VMI Archives; Yearbook, 1927, pp. 37, 48, 52, 54; Saint Mary's Archives; Robert Evans interview, 22 Sep 1998.
14. *Marine!,* p. 100.
15. Puller interview; Pullen to Davis, 1 Jun 1960; E. L. Smith to Davis, 5 Nov 1960, BDP; Bartlett, "Legend"; news clippings, 17 Nov 1937; Presten to Puller, 16 Mar 1964, PP; Heinl OH, pp. 98–101; Leonard OH, p. 137; Brown, "Basic School with 'Capting' Puller"; news release, 7 Feb 1962, PBF; Frank, "A Giant Passes."
16. Virginia Dabney interview, 14 Oct 1998.
17. Puller to MGC, 9 Mar and 23 Jul 1937 and 19 Sep 1938; MGC to Puller, 22 Apr

1939, PR; Vandegrift to Puller, 22 Sep 1938; Vandegrift to Hunt, 4 Oct 1938, Box 1, AAVP.

18. Puller to CMC, 8 Mar 1946, PR.
19. Fitness Report, Apr 1939; Basic School Rosters, Aug 1936, Apr and Sep 1937, PR; Basic School Roster, Aug 1938, Box 61, 18, RG 127.
20. Asiatic Fleet to *Henderson,* 31 May 1939, PR; William to Hammel, 26 Feb 1979, HP.
21. Hunt to Williams, 28 Aug 1939, Sims Papers, MCHC.
22. Brandt to author, 30 Jun 1998; Albers to author, 14 Jul 1999.
23. Deck Logs, RG 24; Lewis to Virginia, 28 Mar 1940, PP; Brandt to author, Aug 1998; Albers to author, 14 Jul 1999.
24. Authorized Strength, Box 10, 65A-5188, WNRC; *MCG,* Mar 1938, p. 28, Mar 1939, p. 34, and Nov 1939, p. 36; *Navy Register,* 1 Jul 1939 and 1 Jul 1940; news clipping, 23 Dec 1939, PP.
25. Asiatic Fleet to MGC, 26 May 1939 and 13 May 1940, Box 863, RG 127; Harrison interviews with Collier and Peck; Price to Vandegrift, 10 Dec 1936, Box 1, AAVP; Honsowetz OH, pp. 224–25; Koch Papers.
26. Buster OH; 4th Marines phone book, Sep 1940, VMI.
27. Col R. D. Camp, manuscript on China Marines, p. 54.
28. Chronological Record, PR; Asiatic Fleet to MGC, 11 Sep 1941, Box 1672, RG 127.
29. Puller to MGC, 14 Apr 1941, PR; notes on Lewis to Virginia, 8 Nov 1940; Lewis to Virginia, 14 Jan 1941, BDP; Puller to Mother [Evans], 1 Sep 1940, Virginia Dabney's possession; Virginia Dabney to author, Apr 2000.
30. Dupuy and Dupuy, *Encyclopedia,* pp. 1125–56; Morison, *Operations,* Vol. III, pp. 62–63; Asiatic Fleet to MGC, 26 May 1939, Box 863; Asiatic Fleet to MGC, 11 Sep 1941, Box 1672, RG 127.
31. Lewis to Virginia, 17, 20, and 31 Jan 1941, BDP.
32. Lewis to Virginia, 9 and 12 Jan 1941, BDP.
33. *Marine!* (p. 105) claimed that Puller was more than five months past the end of his tour when his transfer orders finally came in October. In fact, he arrived on the China station on July 9, 1939, and departed on August 14, 1941, barely a month over the standard two-year tour. A letter to his wife makes it clear that his normal tour was supposed to end in the summer of 1941. Puller's boast about *his* battalion is likely apocryphal, since he was only in command for a month. Lewis to Virginia, 5, 17, 27, and 29 Jan 1941; interview notes, BDP; Puller/Lee OH, p. 77; news clipping, 28 Sep 1950, PP; Curtis OH, p. 34.
34. Lewis to Virginia, 26 Jan 1941, BDP; Asiatic Fleet to MGC, 11 Sep 1941, Box 1672, RG 127.
35. This story has many variations depending on the source. The annual report of the fleet lists each incident in the period up to June 30, 1941, and this is the only one that roughly fits with the facts as described by Puller and Honsowetz. It is possible that their incident took place in July or early August 1941, but Puller specifically mentions that Curtis was his battalion commander at the time; Curtis relinquished that billet on April 14. Asiatic Fleet to MGC, 11 Sep 1941, Box 1672, RG 127; Puller/Lee OH, pp. 78–80; Honsowetz OH, pp. 50–52; Koch Papers; Martin, "Toughest Marine."
36. Lewis to Virginia, 5 and 6 Feb 1941, BDP; Virginia Puller Dabney and Martha Puller Downs interviews with author.

37.   Puller to MGC, 4 Jan 1941; 4th Marines to Dept of Pacific, 16 Aug 1941, PR;
       Puller to Pullen, 25 Oct 1943, BDP; Condit, *Ground Training,* p. 93.

Chapter 8: "The Enemy Are on the Hill": New River and Samoa, September 1941–August 1942

1.   Authorized Strength, Box 10, 65A-5188, WNRC.
2.   Edson diary, 3 and 20 Sep 1941, Box 3, MAEP; Chronological Record; MGC to
       Puller, 5 Aug 1941, PR.
3.   Webb and Sims Bio Files, MCHC; GN News #41, JCSP; Watson to Hammel,
       8 Sep 1980, HP; Wismer OH, p. 15; Day to author, 16 Nov 1995.
4.   Smith, *Coral and Brass;* Craig OH, p. 25; Heinl OH, pp. 142–44.
5.   Sheppard to Davis, 17 Jun 1960, BDP; Pullen to Mrs. Puller, 27 Oct 1971, PP;
       Kelly to Hammel, 30 Mar 1980, HP.
6.   1stMarDiv Special Order #154-41, 27 Sep 1941, HP; 1stMarDiv Special Order
       #600, 28 Sep 1941, PR; Dr. E. L. Smith, excerpts from letters home, BDP;
       Markowski to Puller, 30 Oct 1955, PP; Mike Capraro, "General Chesty Puller."
7.   Twining, *No Bended Knee,* p. 9; Smith excerpts, 13 Mar 1942; Smith, "Fore-
       sight," 29 Nov 1943; Puller and Cox interviews; Smith, "Still Bravely Singing,"
       Hospital Corps Quarterly, Jan 1944; Briggs to Davis, BDP.
8.   *Marine!* (p. 112) implies that this story came from Lieutenants Willie Dumas
       and David Condon of 1/7. The muster rolls show a Second Lieutenant William J.
       Dumas with 1/7 in December 1941, but he had left the battalion prior to March
       1942. I found no record of a Lieutenant Condon and he definitely did not accom-
       pany the 7th Marines to Samoa. At least one officer does not recall either of
       them. 1/7 Muster Rolls, Dec 1941 and Mar 1942; Roster of 3d Marine Brigade
       Officers, 27 Jul 1942, HP; Parish to author, 22 May 1998.
9.   One underlined quote in *Stonewall* is especially apt: " 'You are right,' says Lee
       on August 4, 'in not attacking them in their strong and chosen position. They
       ought always to be turned as you propose, and thus force them on to more favor-
       able ground.' " *Stonewall,* p. 400, PP; Cox interview notes; White to Davis,
       [circa 1960], BDP.
10.   Smith excerpts, 7 Nov 1942, BDP.
11.   Smith excerpts, 17 Mar 1942; Smith to Davis, 5 Nov 1960; White to Davis,
       7 Dec 1960; Briggs to Davis, undated, BDP.
12.   Smith excerpts, 13 Mar 1942; Briggs to Davis, undated, BDP; Thomas OH
       (1973), p. 229.
13.   Thomas OH (1973), p. 235; Smith excerpts, 13 Dec 1941.
14.   Ashurst to Edson, 28 Mar 1940 and 11 May 1941, MAEP; Hoffman, *Legend,* pp.
       127, 319; Smith excerpts, 14 and 17 Mar 1942; Cox to Davis, 1 Sep 1960, BDP.
15.   5th Marines Order #7-41, 6 Oct 1941; "By Regimental Order," Box 6, HP; Smith
       excerpts, 7 Nov 1941; news clipping, 13 May 1962, PP.
16.   Vandegrift OH, pp. 526–28; Thomas OH (1973), p. 228; Twining to Millett,
       13 Jul 89, in possession of Millett; Smith excerpts, 8 Jan 1942.
17.   Smith excerpts, 18 Jan and 17 Mar 1942; Puller interview notes; Cox to Davis,
       1 Sep 1960; White to Davis, 5 Feb 1962, BDP; Tulloch to author, 4 Dec 1995;
       Thomas OH (1973), p. 227; Martin, "Toughest Marine."
18.   CMC to AFAF, 12 Mar 1942; 1stMarDiv to 7th Marines, 14 Mar 1942, Box 45,
       65A-5188, WNRC; Smith excerpts, 20 Mar 1942.

19. Puller told Davis that he also had confidence because all but one of his officers in 1/7 had come up from the ranks. Of five officers for whom biographical information is readily available, only one had prior enlisted service. Puller interview notes, BDP; Thomas OH (1981), p. 34; taped 25th anniversary interviews on Guadalcanal of Puller et al., OH Section, MCHC.

20. Lewis to Virginia, 28 Mar 1942, PP; *Marine!,* p. 116; Cox interview notes, BDP.

21. Samoa Defense Force to CMC, 14 May 1942, Box 46, 65A-5188; Memo for Record, 10 Apr 1950, Box 2, 14051, WNRC; Smith excerpts, 28 Jan 1943, BDP.

22. Griffith diary, Apr 1942, Griffith Papers; Smith excerpts, Apr 1942; LtCol Charles J. Beasley, "The End Is in Sight," HP; Beck to author, 15 Mar 1996.

23. Notes on Lewis to Virginia, 7 May 1942, BDP.

24. Bales to 2d Brigade, 8 Feb 1942, Box 43; 3d Bde Op Plan #2-42, 18 Apr 1942, Box 45, 65A-5188, WNRC; Smith excerpts, May 1942; Griffith diary, May 1942.

25. Griffith diary, 2 Jun 1942; Gerald White diary, 30 May 1942, BDP; Bde Special Order #77-42, 26 May 1942, Box 45, 65A-5188, WNRC; Puller to CMC, 22 May 1942, PR.

26. 3d Brigade Memo, 11 Apr 1942, Box 43, 65A-5188, WNRC.

27. White diary, 13 Jun 1942; Griffith diary, 23 Jun 1942; 3d Bde Unit Report, 20 Jun 1942, Box 43, 65A-5188, WNRC.

28. 3d Bde Unit Reports, 18 and 30 May and 10 Jun 1942; King to Holcomb, 20 Mar 1942, Box 45, 65A-5188, WNRC.

29. Griffith diary, 23 Jun 1942; White diary, 13 Jun–3 Jul 1942; Smith excerpts, 6 Jul and 1 Aug 1942; Hayes interview notes, BDP; 3d Bde Annual Report, 6 Sep 1942; An Informal History of the 2nd Marine Brigade, Box 43, 65A-5188, WNRC.

30. 3d Bde Unit Reports 5 and 6, 20 Jul and 23 Aug 1942; 3d Bde Record of Events, 25 Jul 1942, Box 43, 65A-5188, WNRC; White diary, 9 Jul–10 Aug 1942.

31. Smith to Virginia Puller, 27 Jan 1951, PP; White diary, 17 Jun 1942; Griffith diary, 28 Jun 1942; Hayes interview notes, BDP.

32. Wismer OH, pp. 14–15; White diary, 9 and 14 Aug 1942; Griffith diary, 4 and 17 Jul 1942; Smith diary, 22 Aug 1942; 7th Marines Op Order #5-42, 13 Aug 1942, Box 45, 65A-5188, WNRC; *Marine!,* p. 117; Day to author, 26 Jan 1999.

33. LeFevre to Hammel, 19 Jul 1980, HP; Hayes interview notes; Smith to Davis, 5 Nov 1960, BDP.

34. White to Davis, 7 Dec 1960 and 5 Feb 1962, Box 29; Smith excerpts, 13 Dec 1942, BDP; Drew Pearson and Robert S. Allen, "Washington Merry-Go-Round," 30 May 1942, PP.

35. Henderson, *Stonewall,* pp. 616, 623.

36. Davis got the saluting story from a Marine who said he had only heard about it secondhand. Captain Zach D. Cox's account of how officers in 1/7 learned about Puller's chow line policy was eerily similar to Lee's recollections: "Puller never told us not to eat until the men had been fed, but he saw to it that we never did. He was always at the end of the chow line, so we caught on." White to Davis, 18 Nov and 7 Dec 1960; Cox interview, BDP; Puller/Lee OH, p. 132.

37. Griffith diary, 2 Aug 1942; news clipping, 10 Oct 1955, PP.

38. Griffith diary, 2, 6, 23, and 28 Jun, 15 Jul, and 21 Aug 1942; Watson to Hammel, 8 Sep 1980, HP.

39. Price to Barrett, 16 Jul 1942, Box 8, 127-6587; 3d Bde Op Plan #7-42, 22 Jul 1942; 7th Marines Op Order #5-42, 13 Aug 1942, Box 45, 65A-5188, WNRC; Smith to Virginia Puller, 27 Jan 1951, PP; White diary, 17 Aug 1942; Griffith diary, 16 Aug 1942; Hayes interview, BDP; Kelly to Hammel, 11 Sep 1980; Watson to Hammel, 8 Sep 1980, HP.

40. 7th Marines Op Orders, 16 and 17 Aug 1942; 3d Bde to Samoa Defense Force, 19 Jul 1942, Box 45, 65A-5188, WNRC; Mahood to Hammel, 29 Oct 1963, HP; Griffith diary, 17 and 25 Aug 1942; White diary, 22 Jul and 17 and 19 Aug 1942; Smith excerpts, 25 Aug 1942; Briggs to Davis, undated, BDP.

41. 3d Bde to 7th Marines, 21 Aug 1942, Box 45, 65A-5188, WNRC; Smith excerpts, 22 Aug 1942; Smith manuscript, undated; Smith to Davis, 27 Feb 1962, BDP; news clipping, *Philadelphia Inquirer,* 22 Aug 1942, Pierce Papers.

42. *Marine!,* p. 120.

43. Samoa Defense Force Unit Report #4, Sep 1942; 3d Bde Unit Report #6, 23 Aug 1942, Box 43, 65A-5188, WNRC; Griffith diary, 17, 19, and 29 Aug 1942; White diary, 27 Aug 1942; Kelly to Hammel, 11 Sep 1980, HP; Puller to Dr. Smith, 24 Oct and 17 Dec 1943, BDP.

44. Rogers Bio File, MCHC; Beasley, "The End"; Kelly to Hammel, 9 Mar 1980, HP; Haggerty to Smith, [1943], BDP; Rogers to Bastedo, 12 Aug 1942, Stanley Jersey personal collection.

45. White diary, 28 Aug–12 Sep 1942; Mahood to Hammel, 29 Oct 1963, HP; Turner to SouthPac, 27 Sep 1942, Box 4, 63A-2534, WNRC.

Chapter 9: "You're Not Going to Throw These Men Away": The First Weeks on Guadalcanal, September–October 1942

1. Turner to SouthPac, 27 Sep 1942, Box 4, 63A-2534, WNRC; Griffith diary, 9–18 Sep 1942; Mahood to Hammel, 29 Oct 1963, HP; White diary, 15–18 Sep 1942; Smith manuscript.

2. *Marine!,* p. 122; Thomas OH (1981), p. 34; Mahood to Hammel, 29 Oct 1963, HP; Parry, *Three-War,* p. 69.

3. Puller interview notes; Hayes interview notes; news clipping, "Cries of Wounded in Jungle Recalled by Navy Surgeon," Sep 1942, BDP; Smith manuscript; Griffith diary, 18 Sep 1942; 1/7 Unit Report, 18 Sep 1942, Box 6; Div Report, Phase V, Annex P, Box 4, 63A-2534; Puller to Division, 30 Sep 1942, Box 2, 92-0010, WNRC; Markowski to Puller, 30 Oct 1955; Roster of Casualties, PP; Frank, *Guadalcanal,* p. 252; Watson to Hammel, 8 Sep 1980, HP.

4. Vandegrift to Turner, 24 Sep 1942, Box 2, AAVP; Thomas OH (1973), p. 227; Twining OH, p. 183; Frisbie Bio File, MCHC; Millett, *Strife,* p. 192.

5. Twining interview with author, 23 Jan 1996; Watson to Hammel, 26 Sep 1980, HP; Twining OH (1973), pp. 182–83; Day to author, 16 Nov 1995; Streit interview with author, 11 Sep 1994; Moore to author, 10 Oct 1999.

6. Div Report, Phase V.

7. The division commander thought officers in the States should be studying the lessons of Rogers's Rangers from the colonial era as preparation for the Pacific. D-Series Tables of Organization, 1 Jul 1942; Olliff to Smith, 8 Dec 1943, HP; Vandegrift to Holcomb, 15 and 20 Sep 1942, Holcomb Papers; 1/7 Unit Report, 18 Sep 1942, Box 6, 63A-2534, WNRC.

8. Vandegrift to Turner, 24 Sep 1942, Box 2, AAVP.

9. *Marine!* (p. 127) made it look as if Puller had been in front of the point squad and crossed the river well before his battalion. Actually the squad came from the last unit in the column, Company A, which had become separated. Haggerty to Smith, [1943]; Cameron to Puller, 23 Mar 1943, BDP; Watson to Hammel, 8 Sep 1980, HP; Wismer OH, p. 10; Puller to Division, 30 Sep 1942, Box 2, 92-0010, WNRC.

10. *Marine!* (p. 128) recounts that Puller saved the officer's life by pinning his tongue to his collar to prevent him from suffocating on it. Others on the patrol interviewed later insisted that did not occur. 1/7 Unit Report, 19–20 Sep 1942, Box 6; Div Report, Phase V, Annex R, Box 4, 63A-2534; Puller's Patrol, Box 2, 92-0010, WNRC; Griffith diary, 19–20 Sep 1942; White diary, 20–21 Sep 1942; Hayes interview notes; news clipping, "Cries of Wounded in Jungle," Sep 1942, BDP; news clipping, "How Yanks Fight in Guadalcanal Jungles," 12 Oct 1942, Box 35, EP; Watson to Hammel, 8 Sep 1980, HP.

11. Conoley to CO, 2/7, 23 Sep 1942, Box 2, 92-0010; Clemens to Millett, 21 May 1989, copy in possession of author; Clemens manuscript, p. 181, Clemens Papers; Smith manuscript; Hayes interview notes; Tregaskis to Davis, 19 Jul 1960, BDP; Curtis diary, 21 Sep 1942; Streit interview, 11 Sep 1994.

12. Div Report, Phase V, Box 4, 63A-2534, WNRC; Vandegrift to Turner, 24 Sep 1942, Box 2, AAVP; Thomas OH (1973), p. 390; Vandegrift, *Once a Marine,* p. 166.

13. Frank, *Guadalcanal,* p. 269.

14. Mehrlust to Hammel, 22 Jun 1980, HP; Clemens manuscript, p. 182, Clemens Papers; Puller's Patrol, Box 2, 92-0010; 1/7 Unit Report, 24 Sep 1942, Box 6, 63A-2534, WNRC.

15. Smith manuscript; Fuller interview notes; Olliff to Smith, 8 Dec 1943; Puller to Dr. Smith, 17 Dec 1943, BDP; Mehrlust to Hammel, 22 Jun 1980, HP; Kelly to Historical Division, 16 May 1944, Box 6, 63A-2534; Puller Patrol, Box 2, 92-0010, WNRC.

16. Haggerty to Smith, [1943]; Briggs to Davis, undated; Pennington interview notes, BDP; Puller's Patrol; Puller to Division, 30 Sep 1942, Box 33, 46B, RG 127; Griffith diary, 23 Sep 1942; Watson to Hammel, 26 Sep 1980, HP; Artillery Annex, Phase V, 1stMarDiv After-Action Report, Box 4, 63A-2534, WNRC.

17. Puller provided accurate casualty figures in a September 30, 1942, report. Griffith diary, 23 Sep 1942; White to Davis, 24 Jan 1960; Briggs to Davis, BDP; 1/7 to Div, D-3 Journal, Box 3, 63A-2534, WNRC; Puller to Division, 30 Sep 1942, Box 33, 46B, RG 127; 1/7 Roster of Casualties, PP; Zimmerman, *Guadalcanal,* p. 97; Bergerud, *Touched,* pp. 433–34.

18. There has been confusion over the years regarding the identity of the CO of 2/5. The official campaign history mentions Lieutenant Colonel Walker Reaves in the text, but lists Captain Joseph J. Dudkowski in the appendix. The battalion after-action report bears the typed name of Reaves, but no signature. Griffith's book on the campaign mentions Dudkowski and I have followed his lead. CG to Puller, D-3 Journal, Box 3; 2/5 to CG, 28 Sep 1942, Box 7, 63A-2534, WNRC; Zimmerman, *Guadalcanal,* pp. 97, 183; Griffith, *Guadalcanal,* p. 135.

19. Attached overlay, Puller to Division, 30 Sep 1942, Box 33, 46B, RG 127.

20. Twining, *No Bended Knee,* p. 109.

21. Moore, *Presences,* p. 71; Smith, manuscript, p. 18, BDP.

22.   D-3 Journal, 25–26 Sep 1942, Box 3; Div Report, Phase V, Annex P, Box 4, 63A-
       2534, WNRC; Puller to Division, 30 Sep 1942, Box 33, 46B, RG 127; Connor to
       Hammel, Sep 1963, HP; Puller to 1stMarDiv, 19 Jul 1943, Smolka Papers; Van-
       degrift to Turner, 28 Sep 1942, Box 2, AAVP; Smolka to author, 18 Jul 1996;
       Monssen War Diary, 26 Sep 1942, NHC.
23.   The records provide no clear statement as to when the amphibious assault be-
       came part of the plan. Most accounts assume that Edson ordered the operation
       only after the raiders engaged the enemy on the 27th and 2/5's attack was re-
       pulsed. However, Kelly recalled that 1/7 received the orders from division
       around 1000, before either of those events, and he believed that they had been
       part of the previous evening's plan. Puller told Davis that he had proposed the
       crossing upriver or the landing as alternatives on the evening of the 26th. Kelly
       to Historical Division, 16 May 1944, Box 6, 63A-2534, WNRC; Puller interview
       notes; Kelly to Smith, BDP.
24.   1st Raiders to CG, 3 Oct 1942, Reynolds Papers; 2/5 to CG, 28 Sep 1942, Box 7;
       Div Report, Phase V, Box 4, 63A-2534, WNRC.
25.   Marine records routinely cited *Ballard* as the ship assisting throughout the
       Matanikau operation of September 26–27. However, it definitely was *Monssen*
       that fired in support of Puller on the 26th and again late in the afternoon of the
       27th. *Monssen*'s logs also show a shore bombardment mission "in support of
       Marine operations on Matanikau River" at 1245 on the 27th, followed by antiair-
       craft fire against Japanese planes at 1353. In all probability, division had
       arranged for support from *Monssen,* not *Ballard,* but in the absence of conclusive
       proof, I have followed the previously accepted version of events surrounding the
       landing of 1/7. *Monssen* War Diary, 27 Sep 1942, NHC; Kelly to Hammel, 14 Jul
       1980; Moore to Hammel, 21 Jun 1963, HP.
26.   Puller interview notes, BDP; *Marine!,* p. 135.
27.   2/5 to CG, 28 Sep 1942, Box 7; Kelly to Historical Division, 16 May 1944, Box 6;
       Div Report, Phase V, Box 4, 63A-2534; Puller Patrol, Box 2, 92-0010, WNRC;
       Haggerty to Smith, [1943]; Puller interview notes; Kelly to Smith, 1943; Kelly
       to Davis, 22 Jan 1961; news clipping, "Cries of Wounded in Jungle Recalled by
       Navy Surgeon," Sep 1942, BDP; Kelly to Hammel, 17 and 30 Mar 1980; Connor
       to Hammel, Sep 1963, HP; Smoot OH, pp. 101–2; *Monssen* War Diary, 27 Sep
       1942, NHC.
28.   Friendly casualty figures in the division report are inaccurate, but have been re-
       peated in both the official history and Richard Frank's fine work. 1/7's daily re-
       ports listed twenty-five killed in action by name, though one of these men also
       showed up on the muster rolls as wounded. Likely the latter is more accurate. 1/7
       Unit Reports, 29 and 30 Sep 1942, Box 6, 63A-2534; Puller to Division, 30 Sep
       1942, Box 2, 92-0010, WNRC; 2/5 Muster Rolls; 1st Raiders to CG, 3 Oct 1942,
       Reynolds Papers; Puller Summary of Operations, [1942], Box 33, 46B, RG 127;
       1/7 Roster of Casualties, PP; 1st Raiders Roster of Casualties, Box 24, MAEP.
29.   Vandegrift to Turner, 28 Sep 1942, Box 2, AAVP; Fuller interview notes; Puller
       interview notes, BDP.
30.   There seems to be no common name for the series of battles along the banks of
       this river; often they are referred to merely by their dates. Some authors and par-
       ticipants have called this the First Matanikau, but 1/5 fought a battle there on Au-
       gust 27–28 that probably rates that title. In addition, many Marine leaders at the

time used the designations I now employ. Edson referred to the late September action as Second Matanikau and the 7th Marines Record of Events named the early October battle Third Matanikau. Twining to Millett, 16 Jun 1989, copy in author's possession; Kelly to Smith, 15 Dec 1943, BDP.

31. Griffith diary, 26 Sep 1942; Kelly to Smith, 15 Dec 1943, BDP; Thomas OH, p. 392; Puller to Division, 30 Sep 1942, Box 33, 46B, RG 127.

32. Fuller interview notes; Kelly to Smith, 1943, Box 27; Puller to Dr. Smith, 17 Dec 1943, BDP; *Marine!,* p. 140; Day to author, 16 Nov 1995; Puller to CMC, 19 Oct 1942, Box 2, 92-0010, WNRC; 1/7 Unit Report, 14 Dec 1942, Box 30, 46B, RG 127; Griffith diary, 27 Sep 1942; Moore to Hammel, 21 Jun 1963; Kelly to Hammel, 14 Jul 1980, HP; Fridell, "Chesty."

33. Watson to Hammel, 8 Sep and 23 Oct 1980, HP; Tulloch to author, 4 Dec 1995; Smith manuscript, p. 23; Puller interview, BDP; 1/7 Unit Report, 29 Sep 1942, Box 6, 63A-2534; 7th Marines Patrol Reports, Box 2, 92-0100, WNRC; 3/7 overlay, 23 Nov 1942, Box 29, 46B, RG 127.

34. Nimitz to Davis, 6 Feb 1961, BDP; Vandegrift, *Once a Marine,* p. 171.

35. CO to 7th Marines, [Oct 1942], Box 2, 92-0010; Medical Annex, Div Report, Box 4, 63A-2534, WNRC; Smith diary, 3–4 Oct 1942; White diary, 3 Oct 1942, BDP; Griffith diary, 28 Sep 1942.

36. Fuller interview; Smith manuscript, pp. 22–23; Smith diary, 3–4 Oct 1942 and 21 Jan 1943; White diary, 2–3 Oct 1942, BDP; Beasley, "The End," HP; Griffith diary, 28 Sep–5 Oct 1942.

37. Although Puller probably wrote home on a regular basis from Guadalcanal (as he did in all other campaigns), no letters survive now in either the Burke Davis Papers or the Puller Papers. This excerpt is taken from *Marine!* (p. 142).

38. Unless otherwise noted, details of this operation are taken from the following sources: Operation Plan #2-42, 6 Oct 1942, Box 7; Div Report, Phase V, Box 4; 1/7 to 1stMarDiv, 10 Oct 1942, Box 6, 63A-2534; 7th Marines Record of Events, 7–9 Oct 1942; 2/7 to 7th Marines, 10 Oct 1942, Box 2, 92-0100, WNRC; Griffith diary, 6–7 Oct 1942; White diary, 11 Oct 1942.

39. The division after-action report said that division maintained control, but the actual operations order made no clear statement on this question. The official history follows the division report, but both Thomas and Griffith indicated that Edson was in charge. Edson would later say that Third Matanikau was "under my immediate command." Zimmerman, *Guadalcanal,* p. 101; Frank, *Guadalcanal,* p. 284; Griffith, *Guadalcanal,* p. 142; Merillat, *Guadalcanal Remembered,* p. 172; *Fighting on Guadalcanal,* p. 29; Thomas OH, p. 401; Col Houston Stiff, "That So and So Grin," copy in possession of author; 1stMarDiv Report, Phase V, p. 10; Wismer OH, pp. 13, 17; James Smith to author, 2 Apr 1999.

40. John Hersey, "The Battle of the River," *Life,* 23 Nov 1942, pp. 99, 101.

41. Hersey, p. 104; Watson to Hammel, 23 Oct 1980; Smith excerpts, 21 Jan 1943.

42. White diary; 2/7 Report; Whaling to CMC, 26 Jan 1949, Box 2, 14051, WNRC; Kelly to Hammel, 10 Jun 1980, HP.

43. Twining interview, 23 Jan 1996; Vandegrift OH, p. 821.

44. 2/7 Report; 1/7 Report.

45. Many years after the fact, Fuller and Kelly said that Puller was talking directly to Sims. Puller's report written just two days after the event quotes the order (as I

have done in the text), then goes on to describe the orders he issued to his companies, after which he spoke to Sims and convinced him to rescind the contents of the initial message. Only Kelly provides his basis for believing it was Sims on the other end during the first call, saying that a communicator called Puller to the phone by saying it was the regimental commander. Kelly also went on to say that Puller cut the phone lines immediately after the call, which would be entirely inconsistent with Puller's report that he made a call later to get the order revoked. It is likely that the communicator said simply that it was regiment on the line or that Kelly rolled forty-year-old memories of both calls into one. The recollections of Puller's strong reaction are undoubtedly correct, but he likely did not give vent to his anger directly to the colonel. 1/7 Report; Fuller interview, BDP; Kelly to Hammel, 10 June 1980; Watson to Hammel, 23 Oct 1980, HP.

46. 1/7 Report; Puller to Div, Recommendation for Awards, 15 Oct 1942, Box 2, 92-0010, WNRC; White diary; Griffith diary; Haggerty to Smith, undated, BDP; Thomas OH, p. 403.

47. Griffith diary; 1/7 Roster of Casualties; 1stMarDiv Report, Phase V, p. 14; Intelligence Annex, Box 4, 63A-2534; 1/7 Unit Report, 10 Oct 1942, Box 6, 63A-2534, WNRC; Puller, Summary of Operations, [1942], Box 33, 46B, RG 127; Vandegrift to Rupertus, 10 Oct 1942, Box 2, AAVP.

48. White diary; Kelly to Hammel, 10 Jun 1980; Moore to Hammel, 21 Jun 1963, HP.

49. Twining, *No Bended Knee*, pp. 116, 142; Twining interview with author, 23 Jan 1996; Comments by General Thomas on Personnel and Plans on Guadalcanal, 1 May 1947; Vandegrift Conference, 1 Feb 1943, Guadalcanal Records, MCHC; Vandegrift OH, p. 893; Thomas OH, p. 447; Snedeker OH, p. 55; Hawkins to Hammel, 28 May 1963; Watson to Hammel, 23 Oct 1980, HP.

Chapter 10: "You've Got Bayonets, Haven't You?": The Battle for Henderson Field, October 1942

1. History of the 164th Infantry, 8 Oct 1942–30 Jun 1943, Box 5626, RG 407; Stannard, *Coffin Corner*, p. 5.

2. Griffith diary; White diary; 1/7 Roster of Casualties; 1/7 Unit Reports, 14 and 15 Oct 1942; Vandegrift to Dewitt, 17 Oct 1942, Box 6, Guadalcanal Records, MCHC; Frank, *Guadalcanal*, pp. 319, 322, 326; Millett, *Strife*, p. 201; Lefevre to Hammel, 17 Dec 1980; Kelly to Hammel, 25 Aug and 11 Sep 1980, HP; Puller to Pullen, 25 Oct 1943, BDP.

3. Frank, *Guadalcanal*, pp. 330, 337–41.

4. Translations of Captured Documents, 12 Dec 1942, Box 45, 65A-5188; Intelligence Annex, p. 20, Box 4, 63A-2534, WNRC.

5. Griffith diary, 15 Oct 1942; 1stMarDiv Report, Phase V, p. 21.

6. Haggerty to Smith, BDP; Smith manuscript, p. 27; Millett, *Strife*, p. 497; Frank, *Guadalcanal*, pp. 330–33; Puller to Lane, 17 Oct 1942, VMI.

7. Puller to Div, Recommendation for Awards, 15 Oct 1942, Box 2, 92-0010, WNRC.

8. Hayes interview; Hayes to Davis, 25 Sep 1965; Runzer to Davison, 18 Oct 1965, BDP; 1/7 Muster Rolls, Aug 1942.

9. 1/7 Unit Report, 20 Oct 1942; Tables of Organization for Infantry Battalion and Regiment, 1 Jul 1942, MCHC; 3d Marine Brigade Table of Organization, 21 Mar 1942, Box 43; CMC, "Defense of Western Samoa," p. 6, Box 45, 65A-5188,

WNRC; 1stMarDiv Report, Phase V, p. 4; Medical Annex, Phase V, pp. 4–5; Lawrence OH, p. 13; Tulloch to author, 4 Dec 1995; Graham to author, 26 Sep 1995; Eisenhower to author, 8 Nov 1995; McGillivray interview with author, 10 Oct 1995; Wismer to Hammel, 24 Jun 1980; Kelly to Hammel, 25 Aug 1980; Watson to Hammel, 8 Sep 1980, HP; Puller interview, BDP; Vandegrift, *Once a Marine*, p. 186; Stannard, *Coffin Corner*, p. 49; Vandegrift to Turner, 24 Sep 1942, Box 2, AAVP.

10. There was some dispute over who decided to establish the outpost. Twining's memoir seems to provide the most plausible story and is supported by Stannard's and Watson's recollections of Seabees building an airstrip in the Bowling Alley. 1/7 Unit Report, 21 Oct 1942, Box 6, 63A-2534; 7th Marines Patrol Reports, 22–23 Oct 1942, Box 2, 92-0010, WNRC; 1/7 Record of Events, 21 Oct 1942, Box 30, 46B, RG 127; Davis to Sheppard, 26 Jun 1960, BDP; Beasley, "The End"; Watson to Hammel, 8 Sep and 23 Oct 1980, HP; Thomas OH (1973), p. 432; Twining, *No Bended Knee*, p. 122; Stannard, *Coffin Corner*, p. 30.

11. 1stMarDiv Report, Phase V, pp. 21–23; Twining, *No Bended Knee*, pp. 131–32; Thomas OH (1973), pp. 431, 405.

12. Puller and Fuller interviews, BDP; Watson to Hammel, 8 Sep and 23 Oct 1980; Kelly to Hammel, 25 Aug 1980, HP; Griffith diary; 3/7 overlay, 23 Nov 1942, Box 29, 46B, RG 127.

13. Major sources used throughout this section include 1/7 Summary of Ops, 27 Oct 1942, Box 6, 63A-2534; 164th Report of Battle for Henderson Field, 28 Jun 1943; Box 5628, RG 407; Stannard, *Coffin Corner;* Frank, *Guadalcanal*, p. 342; Translation of Captured Japanese Documents, 9 Dec 1942, Box 45, 65A-5188, WNRC.

14. Chihaya, *Fading Victory*, p. 245.

15. Stannard, *Coffin Corner*, p. 58; 1stMarDiv Report, Phase V, p. 23; Beasley, "The End"; Watson to Hammel, 8 Sep 1980; Kelly to Hammel, 25 Aug 1980, HP; Sheppard to Davis, 1 Aug 1960; Briggs to Davis, undated; Puller interview, BDP.

16. Briggs to Davis, undated; Berry to Smith, [1943], BDP.

17. 1stMarDiv Report, Phase V, Annex R; Beasley, "The End"; Diary of Lt Miyazawa, Oct 1942, PP.

18. Stannard, *Coffin Corner*, p. 62.

19. All participants seem to agree that platoons were dropped off as they proceeded along the trail; that would not have occurred if the head of the battalion had reached Puller's CP first. In all probability, Hall reported initially to Frisbie's CP (on the road to Edson's Ridge) and conferred with Puller via telephone while he waited for his battalion to come up. Or Hall may have gotten to the 1/7 CP well before his battalion made it to the communications trail. Twining claimed credit in his memoirs for the decision to "immediately" throw in 3/164 as soon as the firing started. That does not accord with other sources, but it seems likely that he was the one who started the movement of 2/164's reserves to 1/7. Puller interview; Smith manuscript, p. 35; Watson to Hammel, 23 Oct 1980; Kelly to Hammel, 25 Aug 1980, HP; Sheppard to Davis, 1 Aug 1960, BDP; Beasley, "The End"; Baglien, "Account"; Baglien, "Second Battle"; Thomas OH (1973), p. 433; Twining, *No Bended Knee*, p. 133.

20. Kelly to Hammel, 25 Aug 1980; Robert Cromie, "2,300 Japs Die," *Washington Times-Herald*, 10 Nov 1942.

21. Puller, Award Recommendation for Basilone, 31 Oct 1942; Baglien, "Second Battle."

22. *Marine!* (p. 157) describes a phone conversation between Puller and Sims, with the senior officer portrayed in a poor light. There would not have been such a call, since Sims and the main regimental CP were in charge of the Matanikau front at the time. Puller interview; Fuller interview; Smith manuscript, p. 34; Sheppard to Davis, 1 Aug 1960, BDP; Mather, "Puller Memories," BDP; Cromie, "2,300 Japs Die"; Twining, *No Bended Knee,* p. 133.

23. Stannard, *Coffin Corner,* pp. 65, 70; Fuller interview.

24. 1/7 Report; Cromie, "2,300 Japs Die"; Translation of Captured Japanese Documents, 9 Dec 1942, Box 45, 65A-5188, WNRC.

25. 1/7 Unit Report, 25 Oct 1942, Box 6, 63A-2534, WNRC; Cromie, "2,300 Japs Die"; Stannard, *Coffin Corner,* pp. 74–75; Briggs to Davis, undated, BDP; Beasley, "The End."

26. Briggs to Davis, undated, BDP.

27. Translation of Captured Japanese Documents, 9 Dec 1942, Box 45, 65A-5188, WNRC; Miyazawa diary; Miller, *Guadalcanal,* p. 164.

28. 1/7 Unit Report, 26 Oct 1942.

29. Contrary to the story in *Marine!* (p. 162) that Puller had been forced to cajole division into burying the dead, that process was taken care of by the 164th and nearly completed by the time Chesty supposedly was initiating his complaints. 1/7 Unit Report, 27 Oct 1942; Puller, Summary of Operations, [1942], Box 33, 46B, RG 127; 164th Infantry, "Report of Battle for Henderson Field," 28 Jun 1943; Baglien, "Report," p. 8; Frank, *Guadalcanal,* p. 364; Miyazawa diary.

30. Army casualty figures are much less precise and may have been lower than the figure I have taken from the June 1943 report. Baglien lists twenty-four killed by name. Summary of Operations, 27 Oct 1942; 164th Infantry, "Report of Battle for Henderson Field," 28 Jun 1943; 1/7 Roster of Casualties, PP; Frank, *Guadalcanal,* p. 364; Miller, *Guadalcanal,* p. 166; Baglien, "Report," p. 7.

31. Stannard, *Coffin Corner,* pp. 60, 68; Miyazawa diary; Puller to Twining, 28 Oct 1942, Box 6, 63A-2534, WNRC; Translation of Captured Japanese Documents, 9 Dec 1942; Chihaya, *Fading Victory,* pp. 258–59; 1stMarDiv Report, Phase V, p. 26; Fridell, "Chesty."

32. 1/7 Summary of Operations, 27 Oct 1942; Cromie, "2,300 Japs Die"; Division Bulletins 63a-42 and 64a-42, 29 Oct 1942, Box 2, AAVP; MacGillivray to author, 26 Jun 1996; news clipping, [1943], courtesy MacGillivray.

33. The story of the Medal of Honor recommendation comes solely from Day. Although no award documents exist to directly support his recollection, one unrelated source buttresses his version. An Army officer interviewing Marines in November 1942 for a lessons-learned pamphlet on Guadalcanal noted that Puller "is being recommended by General Vandegrift for the Medal of Honor for leading his battalion, with 7 holes in him, continually for 24 hours." While the reference is obviously to the Koli Point action (described in Chapter 11) rather than the Battle for Henderson Field, it nevertheless indicates that Puller or someone in the senior echelons of the 7th Marines believed that Chesty had been recommended for the award. Puller's fitness report for the period says that he was recommended for the Navy Cross, but since it was written months after the battle, it may merely have reflected the action eventually taken by division. Day to author,

16 Nov 1995; Twining interview, 23 Jan 1996; Awards Branch Review of Records, 9 Mar 1998; Vandegrift to Hagan, 15 Mar 1962, BDP; Fitness Report, 20 Sep 1942–31 Mar 1943, PR; Reeder, *Fighting on Guadalcanal,* p. 32.

34.   Navy Cross Citation, PP.

Chapter 11: "Evacuate Me, Hell!": Final Days on Guadalcanal, October–December 1942

1.   Within a few months, Puller would claim credit for his battalion and supporting arms for killing 1,462 Japanese on October 24–25, as "counted after the battle." No records made in late October support that figure, however. Puller to Twining, 28 Oct 1942, Box 6, 63A-2534, WNRC; Puller to 1stMarDiv, 26 Aug 1943, Box 30; Puller, Summary of Operations, [1942], Box 33, 46B, RG 127; Baglien, "Report," p. 7; Smith manuscript, p. 37.

2.   The incident with the Japanese warrant officer is corroborated by both Puller and a sergeant who witnessed it. The subsequent death of the warrant officer comes from a letter written a year or so after the event. The writer, Captain Haggerty, refers to 1/7 killing three Japanese and wounding two others that night. He then related that the warrant officer "died when he reached the CP for questioning." From his version, which makes no reference to Puller or any ill treatment, it is clear that the officer was already in a bad way at the time of his capture. 1/7's daily report for October 28 mentions the one enemy, a "superior private," captured by the battalion during this period, and lists enemy casualties as one officer and three men killed, lending credence to Haggerty's recollection. 1/7 Unit Reports, 28–29 Oct 1942, Box 6, 63A-2534; Puller to Division, 29 Oct 1942, Box 2, 92-0010, WNRC; Guadalcanal 25th anniversary interview with Puller, OH, MCHC; Griffith diary, 27 Oct 1942; Puller interview notes; Haggerty to Smith, undated, BDP; Reeder, *Fighting on Guadalcanal,* p. 47.

3.   Many of the basic details of the Koli Point action are drawn from 7th Marines Narrative, Box 2, 92-0010; and 164th Infantry, "Report of Battle for Koli Point," 28 Jun 1943, Box 5628, RG 407. Wismer OH, p. 10; Thomas OH (1973), p. 447.

4.   Zimmerman, *Guadalcanal,* p. 136; 164th Infantry, "Report of Battle for Koli Point," 28 Jun 1943, Box 5628, RG 407.

5.   Kelly to Hammel, 20 Sep 1980, HP; Puller to Division, 9 Nov 1942, Box 6, 63A-2534, WNRC; 7th Marines R-3 Report, 4 Nov 1942, Box 29, 46B, RG 127; Wismer OH, p. 10; Griffith diary, 8 Nov 1942.

6.   When Puller read months later in the regimental after-action report that he supposedly had sent Company A to "wipe out the enemy," he protested to division that he had done no such thing precisely because Rupertus had prohibited any action. It remains unclear who did give the order, but it may have been the 7th Marines operations officer, based on the language in his daily report. Puller to 1stMarDiv, 26 Aug 1943, Box 30; R-3 Report, 4 Nov 1942, Box 29, 46B, RG 127; Haggerty to Smith, undated, BDP; 1/7 Roster of Casualties, PP; notes in flyleaf (re casualties), *Stonewall,* PP; Griffith diary, 9 Nov 1942; Sasser to Smith, 28 Jan 1944, BDP; 164th Infantry, "Report of Battle for Koli Point."

7.   Parry, *Three-War Marine,* p. 77.

8.   Griffith, *Guadalcanal,* p. 187; Comments by Gen Thomas on Personnel and Plans on Guadalcanal, 1 May 1947, Box 6, Guadalcanal Records, MCHC.

9.   Of the four sources who report that Puller had exposed his command group on

the beach, only one appears to have been a direct witness. However, the casualties for the day strongly indicate the story is true, since the vast majority of the dead and wounded were from the battalion headquarters. Kelly to Hammel, 20 Sep 1980; Watson to Hammel, 8 Sep and 23 Oct 1980, HP; Haggerty to Smith, undated, BDP; Wismer OH, p. 11; 1/7 Roster of Casualties, PP; Kelly to CMC, 2 Jun 1950, Box 2, 14051, WNRC; 1/7 Record of Events, 8 Nov 1942, Box 30, 46B, RG 127.

10. Puller to Sims, 2 Apr 1945, Sims Papers; Puller to Division, 9 Nov 1942, Box 6, 63A-2534; 7th Marines Narrative, Box 2, 92-0010, WNRC; Kelly to Hammel, 20 Sep 1980, HP; Sheppard to Davis, 17 Sep 1960, BDP.

11. Sgt Leopold Jupiter, news release, Jan 1943, BDP; Puller to Sims, 2 Apr 1945, Sims Papers; Puller to Board of Review for Decorations, 2 Mar 1946; Sims to COMSOPAC, 1 Feb 1944, PR; Weber to CMC, 11 Jan 1949; Kelly to CMC, 2 Jun 1950, Box 2, 14051, WNRC; Puller to 1stMarDiv, 26 Aug 1943, Box 30, 46B, RG 127; Sheppard to Davis, 17 Sep 1960, BDP.

12. There is no authoritative description of Puller's wounds. He referred to them variously as coming from machine gun fire, sniper rounds, and shrapnel. Three witnesses ascribed them to artillery. The battalion's roster of casualties provides a major clue. Of the twenty-six men wounded on November 7–8, all of the seventeen headquarters personnel are listed as having shrapnel wounds (Puller being one of several men with multiple injuries). Of the nine men from line companies listed, eight had gunshot wounds (all but one of those a single wound) and the other was a concussion. It seems probable from this document that the command group was hit solely by artillery fire. If Puller was hit in the explosion of the very first shell, it is possible he temporarily was knocked unconscious or suffered from shock and really did not know what had struck him. 1/7 Roster of Casualties, PP; Medical Abstract, 3 Oct 1944; Blakeney Memorandum, 4 Aug 1955, MR; Chronological Record, 8 Nov 1942, PR; Puller to 1stMarDiv, 26 Aug 1943, Box 30, 46B, RG 127; LeFevre to Hammel, 19 Jul 1980; Moore to Hammel 21 Jun 1963, HP; Sheppard to Davis, 17 Sep 1960; Puller interview notes; Smith manuscript, p. 38, BDP; Martin, "Toughest Marine."

13. 1stMarDiv Report, Phase V, p. 30.

14. Puller to Division, 9 Nov 1942, Box 6, 63A-2534, WNRC; Sheppard to Davis, 17 Sep 1960, BDP.

15. Harlan Curtis diary, Nov 1942, author's copy; Griffith diary, 7–18 Nov 1942; 1stMarDiv Phase V Report, Medical Annex; Smith manuscript, pp. 21, 38–39; Fuller interview notes; Haggerty to Smith, undated, BDP; Kelly to Hammel, 27 Jul 1980; Moore to Hammel, 21 Jun 1963, HP; 1/7 Record of Events, 18 Nov 1942; 1/7 Unit Report, 4 Dec 1942, Box 30, 46B, RG 127.

16. Curtis diary, Nov 1942.

17. News clipping, 22 Jan 1943, VMI Archives; Clinical Record, 11 Apr 1943, MR; Zimmerman, *Guadalcanal,* footnote, p. 153.

18. Griffith diary, 19 Nov 1942; Smith diary, 15 Nov 1942; Lewis to Virginia, 12 Aug 1944; Smith manuscript, p. 38, BDP.

19. Smith diary, 15 Nov 1942 and Jan 21 1943; Shantz to General Smith, 27 Nov 1943; Paul Curtis interview; Fuller interview, BDP; sample casualty letter, 20 Oct 1942, PBF; Roberts article, PP.

20. Weber to Division, 16 Nov 1942; 7th Marines Narrative, Box 2, 92-0010,

WNRC; Chronological Record, PR; 1/7 Unit Reports, 11, 13, 19–22 Nov 1942, Box 29, 46B, RG 127.

21. Haggerty to Smith, undated; Smith manuscript, pp. 38, 41; Griffith diary, Nov–Dec 1942, BDP; Watson to Hammel, 8 Sep 1980, HP; Curtis diary, 1 Dec 1942; 1stMarDiv Phase V Report, Medical Annex; Div Circular #27a-42, 7 Nov 1942; *8th Marines Report on Guadalcanal,* Vol. I, MCRC.

22. Fuller interview; Snedeker interview; Smith excerpts, 7 Dec 1942; Smith to Davis, 5 Nov 1960, BDP; Kelly to Hammel, 30 Mar 1980; LeFevre to Hammel, 17 Dec 1980, HP; Smith, "Marine, You Die!" *Harper's,* Sep 1943, p. 317; Medical Examination, 30 Nov 1953, MR; Hayes to Mrs. Puller, 25 Sep 1950, PP.

23. Tulloch to author, 5 Jan 1996; White to Davis, circa 1960; Briggs to Davis, circa 1960; Cameron to Puller, 23 Mar 1943; Sheppard to Davis, 17 Jun 1960; Smith excerpts, 15 Nov 1942; Moore to Smith, 20 Mar 1944; Puller to Smith, 24 Oct 1943, BDP; Moore to Hammel, 21 Jun 1963; Beasley, "The End," p. 6, HP.

24. Wismer OH, p. 9; Kelly to Hammel, 30 Mar 1980, HP; Vandegrift to Davis, 25 Nov 1960, BDP.

25. 7th Marines Narrative, Box 2, 92-0100, WNRC; Wismer OH, p. 20; Mehrlust to Hammel, 22 Jun 1980, HP; Twining, *No Bended Knee,* p. 174.

26. The number of medals was not necessarily an accurate representation of relative achievement, especially in this case, since Puller was much more inclined to submit nominations than his fellow commanders in the 7th Marines. Both Hanneken and Williams were considered stingy with awards. 1/7 Roster of Casualties, PP; Puller to Smith, 24 Oct 1943, BDP; Day to author, 8 May 1999.

27. 25th anniversary interviews, OH Section, MCHC; Vandegrift memo, 5 Dec 1947, Box 2, 14051, WNRC.

28. Briggs to Davis, circa 1960, BDP.

Chapter 12: "A Great Deal of Hard Work Ahead": Interlude in the Rear, January–December 1943

1. ADC to Puller and endorsements thereon, 31 Dec 1942, PR; *Marine!,* p. 173.

2. Endorsement, 9 and 11 Jan 1943, PR; news clipping, [Jan 1943], PP; Virginia Puller to Smith, 7 Jan 1944, BDP; *Marine!,* p. 174.

3. Reeder, *Fighting on Guadalcanal,* pp. iii, 26–35, 45; Pogue, *Marshall,* p. 75.

4. Puller/Lee OH, p. 98; Virginia Puller to Smith, 7 Jan 1944, BDP; Memo for Chief of Staff re Puller, 1 Feb 1943, PR; Cray, *General of the Army,* pp. 106, 356, 368; Perret, *There's a War,* p. 26, footnote 3; Pogue, *Marshall,* pp. 36, 75.

5. *Marine!* (p. 176) asserts that Puller considered the carbine "no good" when he saw it at Aberdeen. However, he recommended it highly in recorded remarks to Headquarters just days later. His poor opinion of the carbine would develop only later. Bone, Memorandum for Division of Personnel, 19 Jan 1943, PR; Notes on Discussion with LtCol Puller, 28 Jan 1943, Vandegrift File, Guadalcanal Records, MCHC.

6. Sgt Leopold Jupiter, press release, 17 Jan 1943, BDP.

7. "Marine Officer Back from Guadalcanal," 22 Jan 1943, VMI Archives; "Driving Japs off Guadalcanal Just 10-Day Task," [23 Jan 1943]; *Newsweek,* 1 Feb 1943, p. 24, PP; "Guadalcanal Hero Foresees Complete Jap Defeat There," 23 Jan 1943, PBF.

8. Puller/Lee OH, p. 100; Notes on Discussion with LtCol Puller; E Series Tables

of Organization, 15 Apr 1943, and F Series Tables of Organization, 27 Mar 1944, MCHC; Edson to CMC, 27 Jan 1944, Box 14, 63A-2535, WNRC.

9. Rockey, Memo and Responses Thereto, 2 Mar 1943, Vandegrift Conference File, Guadalcanal Records, MCHC.

10. CMC to Puller, 3 Feb 1943, PR; Puller to Smith, 24 Oct 1943, BDP; Puller/Lee OH, p. 99.

11. Twining, *No Bended Knee,* p. 164; speech, 9 Nov 1978, SP; Vandegrift to Rupertus, 10 Oct 1942, Box 2, AAVP.

12. Puller interview notes, BDP; Marshall to Puller, 20 Mar 1943; Marshall to Holcomb, 20 Mar 1943, PR.

13. CMC to Puller, 16 and 23 Mar 1943; Record of Leave, PR; Puller/Lee OH, p. 98; Puller interview notes; Puller to Smith, 24 Oct 1943, BDP.

14. Puller to Smith, 24 Oct 1943; Mrs. Puller to Smith, 7 Jan 1944; Puller to Pullen, 25 Oct 1943, BDP.

15. Vandegrift to Holcomb, 26 Dec 1942, Box 6, Guadalcanal Records, MCHC.

16. Diary, 7th Marines R-2 File, Box 13, 65A-5188, WNRC.

17. Chronological Record, PR; 1stMarDiv SAR Cape Gloucester, Phase I, p. 2, Box 10, 65A-5188, WNRC.

18. Test Results, 15 Feb 1943; Clinical Record, 11 Apr 1943, MR; Rogers to author, 2 Jan 1996.

19. Chronological Record, PR; 1stMarDiv SAR, p. 2; 1/7 Record of Events, May–Dec 1943, Box 13, 65A-5188, WNRC; Puller to Smith, 24 Oct and 17 Dec 1943, BDP.

20. Day to author, 16 Nov 1995; Streit interview with author, 11 Sep 1994; Fitness Report, 1 Apr–21 Jun 1943, PR.

21. Rupertus Bio File, MCHC; Heinl OH, pp. 287–88; Vandegrift to Lyman, 14 Jan 1936, Box 1; Vandegrift to Holcomb, 7 Apr 1945, Box 9, AAVP.

22. Diary, 7th Marine R-2 File, Box 13, 65A-5188; Major Frederic Peachy letter, 25 Mar 1952, Box 4, 14051, WNRC; Leonard OH, p. 62; Day to author, 16 Nov 1995; Streit interview with author; *Marine!,* pp. 185, 188.

23. Shepherd Bio File, MCHC; "The New Commandant," *Leatherneck,* Jan 1952, p. 14.

24. Jeremiah O'Leary, "Chesty Puller Was a Marine's Marine," *Old Breed News,* Apr 1990; Maj Robert L. Gibson to author, 8 Mar 1996; Maj C. H. Godfrey to author, 14 Feb 1996; Sasser to Smith, 28 Jan 1944, BDP; *Marine!,* pp. 185–86.

25. COMSOPAC to Puller, 17 Jun 1943, PP; Puller to CMC, 19 Nov 1942 and 18 Apr 1944, PR; Puller to 1stMarDiv, 19 Jul 1943, Smolka Papers; Sasser to Smith, 28 Jan 1944, BDP; Puller to 1stMarDiv, 26 Aug 1943, Box 30, 46B, RG 127.

26. News clippings, Oct 1943, PP; Smith, "Marine, You Die!" *Harper's,* Sep 1943.

27. Day to author, 16 Nov 1995; Puller to Lottie, 2 Jul 1943, in possession of Virginia Dabney Puller; Puller to Pullen, 25 Oct 1943, BDP; Hoffman, *Legend,* p. 240.

28. The primary sources for division's period in New Guinea are 1stMarDiv SAR Cape Gloucester, Phase I, Box 10; 1/7 Record of Events, May–Dec 1943; 7th Marines R-1 Journal, Oct–Dec 1943, Box 13, 65A-5188; 1stMarDiv War Diaries, Oct and Nov 1943; Combat Team C War Diary, Oct 1943, Box 18; 7th Marines War Diary, Dec 1943, Box 104, 65A-5099, WNRC. Shaw, *Isolation of Rabaul,* pp. 309–12, provides a useful overview. The quotes are found in 1st

Marines History, Dec 1942–Apr 1944, Box 40, 65A-5099, and Diary, 7th Marines, R-2 File, Box 13, 65A-5188, WNRC.

29. Chronological Record, Sep 1943, PP; *Victory in Papua,* pp. 125–26; 1stMarDiv SAR, Phase I.

30. 7th Marines War Diary, Dec 1943, Box 104, 65A-5099; 7th Marines Operation Order #3-43, 26 Nov 1943, Box 13, 65A-5188, WNRC; Streit interview with author.

31. Fields OH, p. 95.

32. Davis OH, p. 109.

33. Puller to Mrs. Puller, 2 Dec 1943; Puller to Pullen, 25 Oct 1943, BDP.

Chapter 13: "Directing the Attack from Forward": Cape Gloucester, December 1943–February 1944

1. D-3 Journal, 28 Dec 1943, Box 12; Rupertus to Krueger, 6 Jan 1944, Box 11, 65A-5188, WNRC; Kenney, *Reports,* pp. 329, 334. Except as otherwise noted, the details for the Cape Gloucester campaign are taken from the 1st Marine Division Special Action Report (SAR), Boxes 10 and 11, and the 7th Marines R-1 and R-2 Journals, Box 13, Series 65A-5188, WNRC.

2. Shaw, *Isolation,* pp. 352, 357; SAR, Phase I, Intelligence Annex.

3. 7th Marines R-1 Journal, 26 Dec 1943, Box 13, 65A-5188, WNRC.

4. Rupertus to Krueger, 6 Jan 1944; *Marine!,* p. 190.

5. LtCol William J. Dickinson letter, circa 1952, Box 4, 14051, WNRC.

6. Shaw, *Isolation,* p. 360; 7th Marines R-1 Journal, 30 Dec 1943; 7th Marines R-2 Journal, Box 13; 2/7 Journal, Box 12, 65A-5188, WNRC.

7. D-3 Journal, 31 Dec 1943; Division SAR, Phase II, Part I.

8. 7th Marines R-1 Journal, 2 Jan 1944; 1stMarDiv War Diary, 2 Jan 1944, Box 18, 65A-5099, WNRC.

9. 7th Marines R-1 Journal, 3 Jan 1944.

10. 7th Marines, R-1 and R-2 Journals, 3 Jan 1944.

11. Col J. F. Bird, "Report on BACKHANDER Operation," 9 Jan 1944, Box 13, 65A-5188, WNRC.

12. The recollections of the coffee incident are backed up by the message in the R-1 Journal. John Nelson to author, 21 Dec 1994; 7th Marines R-1 Journal, 4 Jan 1944; Puller interview notes, BDP; *Marine!,* pp. 192–93.

13. Peachy letter, 25 March 1952, Box 4, 14051, WNRC; Author interview with LtCol Victor H. Streit, 11 Sep 1994; Sasser to E. L. Smith, 28 Jan 1944, BDP; Col John S. Day to author, 16 Nov 1995; Thomas OH, p. 227a.

14. Oswald W. Marrin, Jr., to author, 7 Feb 1996.

15. Joseph S. Skoczylas letter, circa 1952, Box 4, 14051, WNRC; 7th Marines R-1 and R-2 Journals, 7 Jan 1944; Draft of 7 Jan 1944 War Diary, Sims Papers.

16. ADC Group Op Order #12-44, 9 Jan 1944, Box 13, 65A-5188, WNRC; 7th Marines R-1 Journal, 8 Jan 1944; Walt, "Comments About Puller," 28 Dec 1982, copy in possession of author.

17. McMillan, *Old Breed,* p. 213; Dick Rowland to Davis, BDP

18. 7th Marines R-1 Journal, 11 Jan 1944.

19. 1st Marine Division SAR, Phase III, p. 16; D-2 Record of Events for 31 Jan 1944; 7th Marines R-2 Journal, 20 Jan 1944; diary, author unknown, 7th Marines R-2 Files, Box 13, 65A-5188, WNRC.

20. *Marine!,* p. 196; Mrs. Puller to Smith, 7 Jan 1944, BDP.

21. CO, 7th Marines to CG, Sixth Army, 22 Jan 1944, PR.

22. Masters OH, p. 121; Col Waite W. Worden to author, 7 Feb 1996.

23. Many other well-respected officers thought of casualty levels in the same way. In 1945 O. P. Smith applied that analysis to Peleliu: "This is just a personal opinion. I do not have the figures, but I am sure that a study of the Army casualties on Peleliu as compared to ours will indicate who did the aggressive fighting. I know up to the time I left (1 November) the Army casualties were minor." Smith to Metcalf, 29 Oct 1945, Box 22, OPSP; LtCol John D. Crowley to author, 9 Feb 1995; Smith, *U.S. Marine Corps,* pp. 297–98.

24. MacArthur later agreed to Krueger's request to expand the scope of the operation. Rupertus to Krueger, 6 Jan 1944, Box 11, 65A-5188, WNRC; Rupertus to Vandegrift, 18 Feb 1944, Box 10, AAVP; "Personal Narrative: New Britain and Peleliu," pp. 7, 12, Box 22, OPSP.

25. Op Order 2-44, 21 Jan 1944, in Phase IV, 1st Marine Division SAR.

26. "Personal Narrative," p. 6, OPSP. Many of the details for the work of the Gilnit Group are drawn from the D-3 Journal and 7th Marines Patrol Journal, Box 12; D-2 Record of Events, Box 11, 65A-5188, WNRC; Puller's 20 Feb 1944 Patrol Report attached to Part IV of the 1st Marine Division SAR; and the draft article "Patrol in New Britain," Evans Papers. Burke Davis's account of the operation, based almost entirely on a breezy summation in *The Old Breed,* seriously distorts the timing of events and inaccurately portrays Puller dragooning stray individuals and units into his outfit as he moved toward Agulupella.

27. O. P. Smith would later write, probably tongue-in-cheek, that the chair was "the only loot of consequence" brought back by Puller. 7th Marines Patrol Journal, 2 Feb 1944; Smith narrative, p. 7; news clipping, undated, BDP.

28. Evans draft article.

29. The mercy killing of dying Japanese is an example of Puller's tendency during his interviews with Burke Davis to inflate incidents in a manner he perhaps thought would make good copy. He told Davis that in his report on the patrol, he described the bayoneting of the Japanese and concluded "The pig sticking was fine." In reality, neither the incident nor any such comment appeared in his patrol report. Interview notes, BDP; *Marine!,* p. 200; D-3 Journal, 3 Feb 1944; Day to author, 21 Feb 1998.

30. D-3 Journal, 4 Feb 1944.

31. LtCol Ralph M. Wismer to Historical Division, 7 Mar 1952; LtCol John Day to Historical Division, 7 Mar 1952, Box 4, 14051, WNRC; D-3 Journal, 3 Feb 1944.

32. Rowland to Davis, 11 Dec 1960; Mather to Davis, [1960], BDP; BGen Gordon Gayle to author, 15 Aug 1994; Col Nikolai Stevenson interview with author, 14 Nov 1995; Preston Parish to author, 22 May 1998; Evans draft article; 3/1 War Diary, 11 Feb 1944, Box 47, 65A-5099, WNRC.

33. D-3 Journal, 8 Feb 1944.

34. D-3 Journal, 12–13 Feb 1944; Miller, *Cartwheel,* pp. 283–84, 288; Hough, *New Britain,* p. 137.

35. D-3 Journal, 14 Feb 1944.

36. The Rupertus message took up more than two pages in the log, an unprecedented length. D-3 Journal, 15 Feb 1944.

37. Mather to Davis, [1960], BDP.

38. Puller Report, 20 Feb 1944; Puller/Lee OH, p. 52; Division SAR, Phase III, p. 11.

Chapter 14: "Until the Downfall of the Japanese Empire": Cape Gloucester and Pavuvu, February–August 1944

1. Harry Horsman to author, 20 Aug 1994; Peter Abdella to Mrs. Puller, 14 Oct 1971, PP; Stevenson interview with author; Puller to Commandant, 21 Feb 1944, PR; BGen James F. Lawrence to author, 31 Jan 1995, and OH, p. 35; Rev. James M. Rogers to author, 2 Jan 1996.

2. Col Houston Stiff to author, 22 Jul 1994; Col Bernard T. Kelly to author, 14 Oct 1994.

3. BGen Gordon D. Gayle to author, 15 Aug 1994.

4. 1stMarDiv War Diary, Mar 1944, Box 18; History of 1st Marines, 31 Jul 1944, Box 40, 65A-5099, WNRC; 7th Marines Training Directive, 3 Feb 1944, Box 31, 46B, RG 127.

5. History of 1/1, p. 18, 7 Jun 1944, Box 40, 65A-5099, WNRC; Pope OH.

6. 1/1 War Journal, Feb–Mar 1944, Box 40, 65A-5099, WNRC; History of 1/1, p. 26; Smith narrative, p. 47.

7. News clippings, PP; Sims to COMSOPAC, 1 Feb 1944; Puller to CMC, 18 Apr 1944, PR; Sims to Metcalf, 14 May 1945, Sims Papers; Harrison to Smith, 3 Feb 1947, Box 37, OPSP; O. P. Smith OH, p. 122.

8. History of 1/1, p. 26; 1/1 War Journal, 27 Apr 1944; Shaw, *Isolation of Rabaul*, p. 429.

9. Smith narrative, p. 12.

10. LtCol Henry J. Adams, Jr., to Historical Division, circa 1952; Maj Frederick Peachy to Historical Division, 15 May 1952, Box 4, 14051; D-2 Record of Events, 17 Feb 1944, Box 11, 65A-5188; interview with Gen Julian Smith, 27 Jun 1966, Box 1, 74-12, WNRC; news clipping, BDP; Henderson OH, p. 490; Negri OH, p. 37; Masters OH, pp. 130–31; Wismer OH, p. 25.

11. Rupertus to Vandegrift, 13 Jul 1944, Box 3, AAVP; History of 2/1, 8 Jun 1944; History of Regimental Weapons Company, 10 Jun 1944, Box 40, 65A-5099, WNRC; Smith narrative, pp. 52–53, 57.

12. One corps staff officer developed a "very low opinion of Rupertus" in part due to his emphasis on personal comfort: "That was a disgrace to the Marine Corps the way the division lived. Everybody except him. He lived like a king. The division lived in squalor." Nor was this the first time Rupertus had exhibited such behavior. While CO of the Marine Barracks in Cuba just prior to World War II, he had diverted much of the heavy equipment of a defense battalion to assist in building his quarters, which one officer described as "manorial in their dimensions . . . some of the finest large quarters . . . the Marine Corps has ever built." Henderson OH, p. 367; Heinl OH, pp. 289–90; Smith narrative, pp. 51, 55, 61; Rupertus to Vandegrift, 2 Jun 1944, Box 2, AAVP; 1stMarDiv War Diary, Jun 1944, Box 18, 65A-5099, WNRC.

13. Enlisted personnel to Commandant, 3 Jun 1944; Selden, Memo for CG, 12 Jul 1944; Vandegrift to Rupertus, 24 Jul 1944, Box 3, AAVP; 1stMarDiv War Diary, Jul 1944, Box 18, 65A-5099, WNRC.

14. 1/1 War Journal, 28 Apr–24 Aug 1944, Box 40, 65A-5099, WNRC; John Loomis to Davis, 28 Oct 1960, BDP; Col Bernard T. Kelly to author, 14 Oct 1994; MGen

Jonas M. Platt to author, 24 Aug 1994; Col John S. Day to author, 17 Dec 1995; Del Stelck to author, Jul 1999; O'Leary, "Chesty Puller"; Smith, *Marine,* p. 3; McMillan, *Old Breed,* p. 213.

15. Rev. James M. Rogers to author, 2 Jan 1996; Stevenson interview; BGen Gordon Gayle to author, 15 Aug 1994; Streit interview with author, 11 Sep 1994.

16. Loomis to Davis; Puller to Virginia, 3 Aug 1944, BDP; Streit interview with author; Capt John Todd interview with author, 7 Feb 1996; Aubuchon interview with author, 11 Mar 1996; Gayle to author; Platt to author; Leonard OH, p. 57; Platt OH, p. 70.

17. Puller to Virginia, 20 and 21 Jun 1944; Puller to Virginia excerpts, 1 and 3 Aug 1944; Mrs. Puller to Cdr Smith, 20 Oct 1944, BDP; Puller to Virginia, 5 and 7 Aug 1944, PP; *Marine!,* p. 207.

18. Puller to Virginia, 7 and 8 Aug 1944, PP; Puller to Virginia excerpts, 2 Aug 1944, BDP; Kelly to author, 14 Oct 1994; Smith OH, p. 333; Honsowetz OH, p. 136; Henderson, *Stonewall,* p. 639.

19. According to Lieutenant William Moody, who was there, Sam Puller had washed a shirt and was hanging it out to dry on a hedge surrounding the CP site when he was hit. General Shepherd, the brigade commander, also indicated that Sam was killed in the CP, not while walking the front lines as recorded in the official campaign history. Shaw, *Central Pacific,* p. 521; Honsowetz OH, p. 262; Col R. L. Smith interview notes; Selden to Davis, 6 May 1962, BDP; Puller to Mother [Mrs. Evans], 14 Aug 1944; Puller to Anderson, 18 Oct 1944; Shepherd to Fishburn, 15 Aug 1944; Moody to Puller, 5 Apr 1948, PP.

20. D-3 Journal, Box 12, 65A-5188, WNRC; Rupertus to Vandegrift, 2 Jun 1944.

21. Rupertus to Vandegrift, 13 Jul 1944, Box 3, AAVP.

22. In fairness to the 1st Marine Division, HQMC had not yet devised a mechanism to ensure that lessons learned in each new operation were fully disseminated. Rupertus to Vandegrift, 2 Jun and 13 Jul 1944; R to V, 7 Sep 1944, Box 9, AAVP; Millett, *Strife,* p. 228.

23. Rupertus to Vandegrift, 13 Jul 1944; Rupertus to Vandegrift, 9 Aug 1944, Box 10, AAVP; Smith OH, pp. 333–34; Smith narrative, pp. 59, 76; Smith to Davis, 29 Jun 1960, OPSP; Puller interview, BDP.

24. Kelly to author, 14 Oct 1994.

25. Puller interview notes, BDP; Davis OH, pp. 129–30; Davis, *Ray Davis;* Pope OH; Kelly letter; Smith narrative, p. 77; Rogers letter; Stevenson letter.

26. "History of 1st Marine Regiment: 26 Aug–10 Oct 1944," Box 1, 74-93; LtCol Lewis J. Fields to Historical Division, 17 Mar 1950, Box 2, 14051, WNRC; O. P. Smith Memorandum, 4 Feb 1947; news clipping, 1 Aug 1946, PP.

27. LtCol Jonas M. Platt to Historical Division, 7 Feb 1950; Col R. P. Ross to Historical Division, 7 Nov 1949; Fields to HD, Box 2, 14051, WNRC.

28. There are widely varying recollections regarding whether there was a regimental gathering and what Puller might have said. Although I could find no corroboration for the event taking place in the contemporary records, the number of people clearly recalling it makes it likely it did occur. Rogers letter; Day letter; Kelly letter; Stevenson letter; Bluff to Stevenson, 27 Apr 1997; Gilliland, *Peleliu,* p. 13.

29. 1stMarDiv War Diary, Aug 1944, Box 18, 65A-5099; Capt William B. Newton, Jr., to Historical Division, 11 Mar 1950, Box 2, 14051, WNRC; Col Lloyd S. Partridge, "Observer's Report on Palau Operation," 6 Oct 1944, Box 24641, RG

407; Smith narrative, p. 83; Hough, *Peleliu,* p. 35; Platt OH, p. 69; Smith OH, p. 149; Rogers to author, 2 Jan 1996.

Chapter 15: "If There Is Such a Thing as Glory in War": Peleliu, September 1944

1. Adm Oldendorf to BGen Jerome, 25 Mar 1950, Box 2, 14051; TF32, "Report on Peleliu," 16 Oct 1944; 1/1 History, 23 Nov 1944, Box 1, 74-93; "Peleliu: Its Terrain and Defense," Oct 1944, Box 40, 65A-5188, WNRC; 1stMarDiv SAR, Annex K, Naval Gunfire, p. 8.
2. Pratt, *Marines' War,* p. 337; Smith narrative, p. 26; Hunt, *Coral,* p. 35.
3. Unless otherwise noted, details of the battle are drawn from 1stMarDiv Special Action Report, 1944; History of the 1st Marine Regiment; LT 3/1 Record of Events, Box 1, 74-93; 1/1 History; and D-2 Journal, Box 39; 1stMarDiv Operation Plan 1-44, 15 Aug 1944, Box 40, 65A-5188, WNRC.
4. Division Intelligence Section, UDT Report, 13 Sep 1944, Box 40, 65A-5188, WNRC; LT 3/1 Record of Events; Hunt, *Coral,* p. 68.
5. Smith narrative, pp. 17, 22; 2/1 Record of Events, 15 Sep 1944, copy provided by J. Nicholas Russo.
6. Platt OH, p. 74.
7. Selden to HD, 26 Oct 1949, Box 2, 14051, WNRC.
8. D-2 Journal, 15 Sep 1944.
9. D-2 Journal, 15 Sep 1944; Platt OH, p. 74; 2/1 Record of Events, 15 Sep 1944.
10. 1/1 History, pp. 9, 11; 2/1 Record of Events, 15 Sep 1944.
11. Leckie, *Strong Men,* p. 392.
12. D-2 Journal, 16 Sep 1944.
13. D-2 Journal, 16 Sep 1944.
14. LtCol Jonas M. Platt to HD, 7 Feb 1950, Box 2, 14051, WNRC.
15. History of 1st Marines, p. 11; 1/1 History, p. 17; Col R. P. Ross, Jr., to HD, 7 Nov 1949, Box 2, 14051, WNRC.
16. History of 1st Marines, p. 11.
17. LtCol Ray Davis to HD, 7 Mar 1950, Box 2, 14051; 2/1 Record of Events, 17 Sep 1944; 2/7 War Diary, 17 Sep 1944, Box 2, 74-93, WNRC; D-2 Journal, 18 Sep 1944.
18. BGen Spencer S. Berger, USMC(Ret), "Recollections," Peleliu Symposium, Las Cruces, NM, 4 Nov 1989 (copy of remarks provided by J. Nicholas Russo).
19. Watkins, *Brothers in Battle;* Honsowetz interview with Russo; Shults reminiscences, "Peleliu—The Unknown Battle," p. 43.
20. 2/7 War Diary; LtCol Berger to HD, 19 Mar 1950, Box 2, 14051, WNRC.
21. 1st Marines History, p. 13; LtCol Elbert D. Graves to HD, 14 Mar 1950, Box 2, 14051, WNRC.
22. 1/1 History, pp. 21, 27; 2/1 Record of Events, 18 Sep 1944.
23. Pope would receive the Medal of Honor and four of his officers and men would be awarded the Navy Cross for this engagement. 1st Marines History, p. 14; 1/1 History, p. 25; 2/1 Record of Events, 20 Sep 1944; Maj Pope to HD, 8 Mar 1950; Lt Robert J. Powell to HD, undated, Box 2, 14051, WNRC; Pope to author, 15 Feb and 16 Mar 1998.
24. Maj Charles H. Brush to HD, circa 1950, Box 2, 14051, WRNC; 2/1 Record of Events, 18 Sep 1944.
25. "Man of War," *Time,* 9 Oct 1944, p. 66; news clipping, 21 Sep 1944, PP;

"Marines Win Bloody Hill," *Detroit Free Press,* 20 Sep 1944; LtCol Victor H. Streit, "On the Right Flank with 3/7 at Peleliu," *Old Breed News,* Oct 1994; Berger recollections, transcript of Peleliu Symposium, 4 Nov 1989.

26. Smith would later say that visits to a Puller CP were "always an adventure." 2/7 War Diary, pp. 7–8; Smith to Davis, 29 Jun 1960; Kelly letter, 29 Oct 1994; *Time,* 9 Oct 1944, p. 66; Honsowetz OH, p. 10; Smith narrative, p. 61.

27. Puller interview notes, BDP.

28. Watkins, *Brothers in Battle.*

29. 2/1 Record of Events, 20 Sep 1944.

30. Pope to author, 16 Mar 1998; Brush letter; John Loomis to Davis, 28 Oct 1960, BDP.

31. 2/1 Record of Events, 21–23 Sep 1944; 1/1 History, p. 32; Rogers to author, Oct 1998.

32. Coleman thought the date might have been the 20th, but a journal entry shows a visit to the 1st Marines CP on the 21st and that would accord with the timing of the subsequent change in division orders. 3/7 R-2 Journal, 21 Sep 1944, Box 2, 74-93; Deakin OH, pp. 54–55; Col William F. Coleman to HD, [1950], Box 2, 14051, WNRC; Rosenthal OH, pp. 30–31.

33. Contrary to other Puller campaigns, there are no stories from Peleliu about his appearance in the front lines with the troops and no interviewees for this chapter could remember seeing him outside his CP at any time. General Ray Davis recalled that during the latter stages of the battle Puller was on a stretcher and Chesty's inability to move about probably saved his life. While his analysis is almost certainly correct, his memory about the stretcher is not supported by any of the many other participants who saw Puller during this time. Davis OH, p. 132; Rogers letter, 2 Jan 1996; Kelly letter, 29 Oct 1994; Watkins, *Brothers in Battle.*

34. 1stMarDiv Field Order #2, 21 Sep 1944, and #3, 22 Sep 1944; Silverthorn OH, p. 325; Henderson OH, p. 364; Hough, *Peleliu,* p. 104; Selden to Davis, 12 Oct 1960, BDP; Field OH, p. 125; O. P. Smith OH, p. 139; Smith narrative, p. 81; BGen Walter A. Wachtler to HD, 1 Mar 1950; Coleman to HD, [1950], Box 2, 14051, WNRC.

35. Kelly letter, 14 Oct 1994; Smith to Davis, 29 Jun 1960; Honsowetz OH, p. 14; Day to author, 17 Dec 1995; D-2 Journal, 23 Sep 1944.

36. 3/1 Record of Events, p. 23; D-2 Journal, 23 Sep 1944; Smith to Davis, 29 Jun 1960, Box 19, OPSP.

37. Puller to Virginia excerpts, 24 and 29 Sep 1944, BDP.

38. Day to author, 9 Jan 1996; Mrs. Puller to Smith excerpts, 20 Oct 1944, BDP; clippings of photos of memorial service; news clipping, 7 Sep 1946, PP.

39. Puller to Mrs. Evans, 29 Sep 1944, PP; Puller to Smith, 10 Oct 1944, BDP.

40. Movement Order #3-44, 28 Sep 1944, in 1stMarDiv War Diary, Sep 1944; Rupertus to Vandegrift, 18 Oct 1944, Box 10, AAVP.

41. If one adds the number of troops departing Peleliu to the number of casualties, the total exceeds the number who came to the island on September 15. While there may be errors in one or more of these sets of figures, the difference is likely accounted for by lightly wounded who remained in action with the regiment and by replacements received during the operation. The debate about casualty percentages will never be settled to any degree of certainty. Although figures for losses sustained are accurate and readily available, there are no comparable published statistics on the number of replacements fed into regiments during the

course of a battle and thus no way to compute true percentages. Moreover, the length of time in the front lines also should factor into any comparison. However, it is a fact that the losses of the 1st Marines at Peleliu were lower in absolute terms than all but two regiments at Iwo Jima and Okinawa. The highest figure for Iwo Jima was the 26th Marines, with 2,675 casualties. The 4th Marines led the list on Okinawa with a total of 2,947. Garand, *Western Pacific Operations,* p. 797; Hough, *Peleliu,* p. 183; Bartley, *Iwo Jima,* pp. 218–20; Nichols, *Okinawa,* pp. 305–7; 1stMarDiv SAR, Annex G, p. 2; C-1 Report, IIIAC, 16 Oct 1944, Box 39, 65A-5188, WNRC. The "butcher" quotation can be found in the remarks of the interviewers in R. G. Davis OH, p. 133, and Honsowetz OH, p. 9. Examples of the assertion that the 1st Marines' casualties were "the heaviest losses ever suffered by a regiment in Marine Corps history" are in Ross, *Peleliu,* p. 275, and Gailey, *Peleliu,* p. 134.

42. Deakin OH, p. 56; Henderson OH, p. 363; Henderson to author, 26 Sep 1993; BGen Gordon Gayle, presentation on Peleliu, World War II in the Pacific Conference, Aug 1994.

43. The list of naval gunfire missions on Peleliu in the TF 32 report does not appear to accord with the number of missions actually fired. For example, 1/1's War Diary said the battalion called in twenty-seven missions on September 20; the TF report recorded only nine total that day from throughout the division. Possibly the TF records covered only requests for fire from general support ships and not direct support ships. In any case, the list does provide some indication of relative use. Day, Smith's operations officer, thought Puller called on supporting arms "when he could use them." TF 32 report on Peleliu and Angaur, 16 Oct 1944, Box 1, 74-93, WNRC; D-2 Journal, 16 Sep 1944; 1/7 Summary of Operations, [1942], Box 33, 46B, RG 127; Day letter, 16 Nov 1995.

44. LtCol Edwin A. Law to HD, 10 Mar 1950, Box 2, 14051, WNRC; Day letter.

45. Hough, *Peleliu,* pp. 98–99; Maj John R. Chaisson to HD, 8 Mar 1950, Box 2, 14051; Partridge, "Observer's Report"; 2/11 SAR, Box 2, 74-93, WNRC.

46. In the eleven days from D+3 through D+13, Navy fliers dropped a total of twenty-four 1,000-pound bombs; for the period D-Day through D+13, eighty-seven napalm tanks. On September 30 alone, for instance, Marine fliers dropped twenty 1,000-pound bombs and on October 8 they employed thirty-five of the blockbusters just in the morning pre-assault bombardment. TF 32, Report on Peleliu and Angaur; D-3 Periodic Report, 8 Oct 1944, Box 39, 65A-5188; 1/1 History, p. 30; 1stMarDiv War Diary, Sep 1944, Box 18, 65A-5099, WNRC; Fridell, "Chesty."

47. Even an officer who wondered whether "ten times the gunfire would have helped" did believe that it would have made a difference in the case of Hunt's Point. 1stMarDiv SAR, p. 27, and Annex K, p. 1, and Annex L, p. 6; 3/1 Operations Report, p. 14, Box 39, 65A-5188; Col William H. Harrison to HD, circa 1950, Box 2, 14051, WNRC.

48. George McMillan to Davis, 17 Oct 1960, BDP; Pope OH; Stevenson interview with author, 14 Nov 1995; Stevenson interview notes, BDP.

49. Hoffman, *Once a Legend,* pp. 244–45, 291; draft speech, circa Jul 1944, Box 3, AAVP.

50. Smith OH, p. 141; news clipping, "3 Virginians Play Big Role in Seoul Drive," circa Sep 1950, PP; D'Este, *Patton,* p. 554.

51. One writer later reported that both Rupertus and Puller "had shrugged off a sug-

gestion" to view the Umurbrogol from the air after the artillery observation planes came ashore on September 19. Such a trip had revealed to Bucky Harris the opportunity for flanking the ridgeline via the coastal route. In Chesty's case, there would have been little point in his taking a flight at that time to confirm the soundness of that tactical option, since he did not have the resources to implement it. Gayle, *Bloody Beaches,* p. 25; LtGen Raymond G. Davis to author, 17 Oct 1994.

52.   Record of interview with LtGen Julian Smith, 27 Jun 1966, Box 1, 74-12, WNRC; J. Smith OH, p. 328; Puller interview notes, BDP.

53.   Col H. D. Harris interview notes, 28–31 Oct 1949; Maj Donald A. Peppard to HD, 7 Mar 1950, Box 2, 14051, WNRC; Partridge, "Observer's Report"; LtCol Arthur M. Parker, Jr., to author, 31 May 1994; Day to author, 16 Sep 1996.

54.   Puller interview notes; Smith to Davis, 29 Jun 1960, BDP.

55.   The description of Jackson was underlined in Puller's copy of *Stonewall* (p. 664). Davis letter, 17 Oct 1994; O. P. Smith OH, p. 145.

56.   One is reminded of Fitzhugh Lee's analysis of the lessons of Kelly's Ford: "A determined rush upon the foe is the part of sound policy as it is the part of true courage." Jim Butterfield interview with author, 1995; Lewis E. Douglas to author, 5 Dec 1995; O. P. Smith OH, p. 141.

Chapter 16: "Nobody's Got Use for a Combat Man": A Hero Without a War, October 1944–June 1950

1.   Virginia Puller to Smith, 20 Oct 1944, BDP; Entries, 2–9 Oct 1944, MR; Shaw to Puller, 8 Nov 1955, PP; Snedeker OH, p. 71.

2.   "Man of War," *Time,* 9 Oct 1944, p. 66; Virginia to Hart, 7 Oct 1944; Hart to Virginia, 10 Oct 1944, BDP.

3.   1stMarDiv War Diary, Oct 1944, Box 18, 65A-5099, WNRC; Rupertus to Vandegrift, 23 Oct 1944, Box 3, AAVP; CG to Puller, 3 Nov 1944, PR.

4.   CG, 1stMarDiv to CG, FMFPac, 2 Nov 1944, PR; Puller to Sims, 2 Apr 1945, Sims Papers; Puller to Anderson, 18 Oct 1944, PP; Puller to Smith, 10 Oct 1944, BDP; Hoffman, *Once a Legend,* p. 282.

5.   Fitness Report, 1 Apr–2 Nov 1944; Recommendation for Legion of Merit, 3 Oct 1944, PR.

6.   Virginia to Smith, 20 Oct 1944; Christmas card, Dec 1944; Puller interview notes, BDP; Puller to CMC, 4 Dec 1944; Officer's Leave Record, PR.

7.   Honsowetz OH, p. 58; *Marine!,* p. 232; Training Command Special Order 13-45, 13 Jan 1945; Fitness Report, 15 Jan–1 Feb 1945, PR; Christmas card, Dec 1944, BDP. Edson to Thomas, 26 Jan 1944, Box 5, MAEP; Condit, *Ground Training,* pp. 176–203; Hanneken Bio File, MCHC.

8.   Condit, *Ground Training,* p. 194.

9.   *Camp Lejeune Globe,* 24 Jan, 7 Feb, 4 Jul, and 14 Jul 1945; news clipping, "Colorful Marine Hero at Lejeune," 21 Feb 1945, PBF.

10.   Entries, 4–11 Jul 1945, MR; CMC to Puller, 31 Jul 1945, PR; *Camp Lejeune Globe,* 22 Aug 1945.

11.   Vandegrift to H. M. Smith, 17 Aug 1945, Box 3, AAVP; *Camp Lejeune Globe,* 19 Sep 1945; MTC Special Order #177-45; Recommended Citation for Award, 16 May 1946; Fitness Reports, 1 Feb–31 Mar and 1 Apr–30 Sep 1945, PR.

12.   There are a number of indications that Puller had hopes of commanding a divi-

sion or thought his promotions came too slowly. The major one was his March 1946 letter to HQMC (covered more fully later in this chapter) complaining about his relative seniority and the "extent" of his "services" during the war. Another was a comment by his wife to the former surgeon of 1/7, made just after Peleliu: "Someday I am sure my husband would love [to have] a division. . . . We'd like so much to have you take care of the medical end." While that was possibly just idle chat on her part, it seems more likely that she got the idea from Puller. Puller also told Burke Davis that Rupertus had said, "Lewie, you should make general on Peleliu." One can surmise that his relating of that incident to Davis signaled that he believed he should have been promoted. Virginia to Smith, 20 Oct 1944; Puller interview notes, BDP; Puller to O. P. Smith, 12 Sep and 13 Nov 1945, Box 62, OPSP; Puller to CMC, 8 Mar 1946, PR; news clipping, Sep 1950, PP; *Marine!*, p. 233.

13. For examples of the myth of Puller's slow promotion, see *Marine!*, p. 233, Leckie, *Strong Men Armed*, p. 77, Bergerud, *Fire*, p. 159; "They Were All Chesty Puller's True Sons," *Washington Evening Star*, 20 Oct 1971, Puller Papers, MCHC. Puller would be promoted to brigadier general in early 1951 with six others, all seven bearing dates of rank as colonels within the same two-week period in late 1942. (During the war, dates of rank were frequently backdated to well before the day on which an officer actually received his promotion.) *Combined Lineal List*, 1 Jan 1954, MCHC.

14. Puller had been moving ahead of other officers. In January 1943, as a lieutenant colonel, he was thirty-six places behind Twining on the seniority list. In July 1945, as a colonel, he was only nineteen places back. Hoffman, *Once a Legend*, p. 261; Holcomb to Vandegrift, 19 Oct 1943, Box 2, AAVP; *Combined Lineal List*, 1 Jan 1943 and 1 Jul 1945, MCHC.

15. Vandegrift to Holcomb, 25 Oct 1945, Box 3, AAVP; CMC to Puller, 7 Mar 1946, PR.

16. Puller likely examined his records and obtained details on the pending board during a period of temporary duty at Headquarters in mid-February 1946. In the introduction to *Stonewall* (pp. vii–viii), Viscount Wolseley described Jackson as one of those best "fitted by natural instincts, by education, by study, and self-discipline to become leaders of men." Wolseley, a field marshal, also wrote that Jackson had "trained himself mentally, morally, and physically for the position to which he aspired." Puller to CMC, 8 Mar 1946; HQMC to Camp Lejeune, 8 Feb 1946, PR.

17. While Puller did have four months of combat service in Haiti, he overlooked several considerations that likely gave the other Marines there an edge before the Neville Board. His five competitors had considerably more experience as NCOs (in one case, sixteen years), all had been commissioned originally in 1918 (well before Puller), and three had seen service with the AEF in France. Thus, even if Puller had been a corporal, he might still have come up short in comparison. MGC to 1st Brigade, 7 Sep 1920, PR; *Navy Registers*, 1919, 1920, 1924, NHC.

18. *Marine!*, p. 237; Puller/Lee OH, p. 93.

19. Puller to CMC, 8 Mar 1946, PR; Roberts, "Chesty."

20. Burke Davis wrongly places the receipt of the Bronze Star on Pavuvu, and the words ascribed to Puller at that time obviously reflected his postwar sentiments. They first appeared in print in a 1952 magazine article and I have quoted that

version. Puller to Sims, 2 Apr 1945; Metcalf to Sims, 23 May 1945, Sims Papers; Blakeney Memo for Honsowetz, 24 Jan 1951, PP; Honsowetz OH, p. 12; *MCG,* Feb 1944, p. 56; Martin, "Toughest Marine"; *Marine!,* p. 205.

21. Puller to Smith, 12 Sep 1945; Smith to Puller, 13 Sep 1945; O. P. Smith to Julian Smith, 20 Jul 1945, Box 62, OPSP.

22. Virginia Puller, note on family Christmas card, 1945, VMI Archives; Streit interview with author, Sep 1994.

23. *Camp Lejeune Globe,* 3 Oct and 20 Dec 1945, 16 Jan and 20 Mar 1946; *Marine!,* pp. 234–35.

24. Marston to Vandegrift, 19 Dec 1945, Box 3, AAVP.

25. HQMC to Camp Lejeune, 20 Jun 1946, PR; *Marine!,* p. 236.

26. Although Puller and Shepherd were not close, they had served together at Cape Gloucester and Shepherd had been Sam's brigade commander on Guam. The general also was a Virginian, a VMI man, an Episcopalian, and a leader who looked out for his troops. Mrs. Shepherd was a friend of Puller's sister Emily, too. With that background, he made an excellent choice to be Lewis Jr.'s godfather. "Marine Corps Reserve," Box 10, AAVP; "CMC Directs Support of the Reserve," *Reserve Bulletin,* Feb 1947, Box 1145, 18A, RG127; Virginia Dabney to author, Apr 2000.

27. News clippings, 1 Aug 1946, PP.

28. CMC to Puller, 2 Jul 1946; Memo to the Director of Personnel, 19 Sep 1946; Pate to Puller, 5 Sep 1946, PR.

29. SgtMaj W. X. Durkee to *MCG,* 7 Jun 1998; Durkee to author, 18 Jun and 6 Jul 1998.

30. News clipping, 7 Sep 1946, PP; *Reserve Bulletin,* Feb 1947; Sgt Edward J. Evans, "Reserve Power," *Leatherneck,* Oct 1947, p. 3.

31. "Organization of Marine Post-War Reserve Units Revealed," *Camp Lejeune Globe,* 13 Feb 1946; *Reserve Bulletin,* Feb 1947; Smith to Geer, 28 Jul 1951, Box 10, 14051, WNRC; news clipping, 7 Sep 1946, PP.

32. Frost, "His Beat"; news clipping, 7 Sep 1946, PP.

33. Frost, "His Beat"; Roberts, "Chesty."

34. Pate to Puller, 5 Sep and 31 Oct 1946; Vardy to Puller, 5 Feb 1947; Board of Levee Commissioners to Puller, 26 Sep 1947, PR; 10th Battalion I-I to Division of Reserve, 7 Jan 1947; Thomas Memo on Summer Training, 2 Dec 1946, Box 1145; Roll to Puller, 18 Dec 1947, Box 861, 18A, RG 127.

35. *Reserve Bulletin,* Feb 1947; Thomas Memo on Summer Training, 2 Dec 1946; Robinson Memo on Inspections, 21 Oct 1947, and Shelburne Memo on Inspections, 9 Oct 1947, Box 828; Puller to Roll, 5 and 27 Apr 1948, and Roll to Puller, 9 and 30 Apr 1948, Box 861, 18A, RG127.

36. Clement Memo on Reserve Coordinators, 19 Feb 1948, Box 1142, 18A, RG 127; Muster Rolls, 8th Marine Corps Reserve District, Jan 1948, MCHC.

37. Puller to CMC, 5 Jan 1948, PR.

38. CMC to Puller, 23 Mar 1948; Puller to CMC, 21 Apr 1947, PR; *Marine!,* p. 239.

39. News clipping, circa Apr 1948, BDP; Fitness Report, 1 Apr–9 Jun 1948, PR.

40. Erskine OH, p. 104.

41. IG to CMC, 26 Jun 1947; "Report of Inspection," 7 Mar 1947, Box 853, 18A, RG 127.

42. Pepper Memo, 24 Nov 1948; Coleman Memo, 23 Jul 1948; IG to Plans & Poli-

cies, 27 Jul 1948; CMC to CG, FMFPac and FMFLant, 6 Aug 1948, Box 828, 18A, RG 127.

43. Jacques, *Sergeant Major,* pp. 53–66.

44. Fitness Reports, 10 Jun–30 Sep 1948 and 1 Oct 1948–31 Mar 1949; Report of Inspection, 25 Feb 1949, PR; Easter Roster, 1949, PP; Puller interview notes, BDP; Jacques, *Sergeant Major,* p. 63.

45. Bauernschmidt OH, p. 223.

46. Virginia Puller interview notes, BDP; Jacques, *Sergeant Major,* p. 62; Puller to Evans, 20 Sep 1948, PP.

47. Medical History, 28 Apr 1948; Physical Examination, 4 Nov 1950, MR.

48. Puller to CMC, 1 Feb 1950, PR.

49. Civilian Background, 1950, PR; Puller/Lee OH, p. 84.

50. Giusti, *Mobilization,* p. 5; "Col Krulak Receives Honors; LtCol Murray Now CO Fifth," *Pendleton Scout,* 16 Jun 1950.

51. Smith to Erskine, 7 Apr 1950, Box 56, OPSP.

Chapter 17: "A Chance to Excel": The Inchon Landing, June–September 1950

1. *Pendleton Scout,* 9 and 23 Jun 1950; *MCG,* Feb 1944, p. 55; Giusti, *Mobilization,* p. 34; Norman Polmar, "Historic Aircraft," *Naval History,* Jun 1998, p. 53.

2. Puller would later portray the ROK army as being armed solely with carbines, evidence in his mind of typical mismanagement by politicians and staff officers. While the South's army was not as heavily equipped as the NKPA, its early defeats also must be ascribed to shortfalls in training, tactics, experience, and leadership. Puller/Lee OH, pp. 92–93; Puller interview notes, BDP; *Marine!,* p. 241; Montross and Canzona, *Pusan Perimeter,* pp. 33–34.

3. Walker to Eighth Army, 3 Aug 1950, Box 6, 65A–5196, WNRC.

4. Puller to CMC, 3 Jul 1950, PR; Carlon to Hammel, 22 Feb 1980, HP; Puller/Lee OH, p. 84; Puller to Smith, 5 Jul 1950; Smith to Puller, 5 Jul 1950, Box 56, OPSP.

5. Smith to Liversedge, circa 12 Jul 1950, Box 56, OPSP; CG, FMFPac to Puller, 14 Jul 1950, PR; *Marine!,* p. 242; Geer, *New Breed,* pp. 2, 107; Virginia Dabney to author, Apr 2000.

6. Smith, "Notes on Service at Camp Pendleton," Box 19, OPSP; Bowser OH, p. 182.

7. Smith OH, p. 194; A Report of the Activities of FMFPac from 25 Jun 1950 to the Amphibious Assault at Inchon, Box 5, 77-0039, WNRC.

8. Smith OH, p. 196.

9. In 1999, the site of Tent Camp 2 was known as the 52 Area and was home to the School of Infantry. Map of the base, 1945, Base History Office, Camp Pendleton, CA.

10. The unknown story in the creation of the 1st Marines is why the CO of the 2d Marines did not simply transfer with his regiment and become the new CO of the 1st. The CO of the 6th was supposed to assume that role for the 7th Marines, but had a heart attack and the job fell to Colonel Homer L. Litzenberg. Dowsett interview, 2 Nov 1954, Box 5, 77-0039, WNRC; Report of Activities; Giusti, *Mobilization;* Smith, "Aide-Mémoire," p. 10, Box 34; Location by Battalions and Squadrons of the FMF, 1 Jul 1950; Status of FMF, 31 May 1950, Box 39, OPSP; Smith journal, 8 Feb 1951.

11. Puller, Unit Report for Aug 1950, 7 Sep 1950, Box 80, 61A-2265, WNRC; Smith, "Aide-Mémoire," p. 17; Smith journal, 4, 12, and 13 Aug 1950, Box 47, OPSP.

12. Puller interview notes, BDP; Capt George C. Westover interview, 21 Dec 1950, p. 7; Capt J. F. McInteer interview, 30 Nov 1950, p. 5, Box 4, 77-0039, WNRC; Gen Robert H. Barrow, "A Company in Korea, 15 Sep–11 Dec 1950," HP.

13. Smith journal, 14 Aug 1950; Bowser OH, p. 189.

14. Capt Robert H. Barrow interview, 8 Oct 1951, Box 5, 77-0039, WNRC; Carlon to Hammel, 22 Feb 1980; Barrow, "A Company," HP.

15. Biographies of Rickert and Ridge, Box 9, 61A-2265, WNRC; *Camp Lejeune Globe,* 9 Sep 1954; Sutter Bio File, MCHC.

16. Barrow was among those who gave Puller's reputation little thought, though he did know others who were concerned about it. Barrow OH, pp. 179–80; Thompson to author, 9 Dec 1996; William B. Hopkins interview; Blazer to Davis, 11 Aug 1960, BDP; Keaney to Virginia Puller, 11 Oct 1972, PP; speech, 10 Mar 1988, SP; Jones OH, pp. 164, 166.

17. Owens interview; Stiles interview, BDP; LtCol William F. Koehnlein to author, 12 Jan 1996.

18. Chambers interview; Devine interview, BDP; BGen Ernest R. Reid, Jr., interview with author, 5 Dec 1995; Boley interview, 25 Oct 1999; Thompson to author, 26 Nov 1995; Greenwood, *Lifetime;* Frank Elliott, "Chesty's Driver," *Leatherneck,* Nov 1982, p. 33.

19. Col Carl L. Sitter, speech at VMI, 18 Apr 1998; interview with author, 1 Oct 1998; Jones OH, pp. 167–69.

20. Barrow interview with author, 23 Jan 1997; Keaney to Virginia Puller, 11 Oct 1972; Ross Valentine, "It Takes All Kinds of Courage," undated news clipping, PP; Maj W. C. Reeves interview, BDP; Jones OH, pp. 163, 178.

21. Smith to West, 13 Aug 1962, Box 19, OPSP.

22. McInteer interview, p. 16; Westover interview, p. 13; 1st Marines Historical Diary, Sep 1950, Box 80, 61A-2265; 2/1 SAR, 29 Aug–7 Oct 1950; 3/1 SAR, 28 Aug–7 Oct 1950, Box 6, 65A-5196, WNRC; Sitter interview.

23. Bowser OH, p. 202; Bowser to author, 21 Nov 1995; Reid interview; 2/1 and 3/1 SARs; Montross and Canzona, *Inchon-Seoul,* p. 55.

24. Jones interview; Puller to Virginia, 9–15 Sep 1950, BDP.

25. Bowser OH, p. 220; Smith Briefing for Correspondents, 13 Sep 1950, Box 32, OPSP.

26. Craig, "Field Notes," p. 35.

27. Heinl, *Victory,* p. 43; Cray, *General,* p. 691; 2/1 SAR.

28. Puller's talk to his officers is rendered in slightly different words and set in several different scenes, depending on the source. Since he sailed on an LST, it is certain that he did not give it on the way to the objective, since he would have reached barely more than his immediate staff and a handful of other officers. 3/1's SAR mentions two briefs by the regiment for "unit commanders" on the *Noble* prior to sailing, which is undoubtedly when and where he made this speech, though he may have given a similar version in other meetings with small groups in the final days before they shoved off. One officer recalled that Puller's speech was broadcast over the ship's loudspeaker. Heinl, *Victory,* p. 77; Col Robert A. Foyle interview with author, 24 Jan 1996; Boely interview, 25 Oct

1999; 3/1 SAR; Landing Force Call Signs, Inchon Op Order, Box 6, 65A-5196, WNRC; Maj Lyle H. Worster interview; Puller to Virginia, 9–15 Sep 1950, BDP.

29. Puller to Virginia, 9–15 Sep 1950, BDP.

30. Montross and Canzona, *Inchon-Seoul,* p. 94.

31. Unless otherwise noted, operational details are taken from Montross and Canzona, *Inchon-Seoul,* the SARs of the 1st Marines, 2/1, and 3/1, and the 1st Marines Unit Reports for this period. Puller was incensed after the war when the Marine Corps' official historian placed "entirely uncalled-for emphasis on the disorganization and confusion." His pressure resulted in changes in the final manuscript, but not to the original facts. All of the many interviews recorded by the Historical Division attested to the chaos in the later assault waves. Draft news release, 18 Aug [Sep] 1950, Box 9; 1st Marines Unit Report, 15–18 Sep 1950, Box 80, 61A-2265, WNRC; Puller interview notes; Jones interview, BDP; Draft news release, undated, PBF; news clipping, circa Sep 1950, PP; Puller to Canzona, 11 May 1955; Sutter to Puller, 19 May 1955, Box 19, OPSP.

32. Barrow, "A Company."

33. Craig to Davis, 22 Nov 1960, BDP; Craig OH, p. 186; Craig, "Field Notes," p. 37.

34. The meeting with MacArthur is one of those events that have become encrusted with legend. The earliest account is contained in a newspaper article by a reporter who witnessed it. The conversation used here is what he recorded, with the exception of the CP discussion, which came from Wright. The reporter actually placed the visit to Puller after the one to Murray, whereas Smith's account, contained in his journal, places Puller first. Burke Davis further confused the story by combining events that took place at a later MacArthur visit with this first one. News clipping, 17 Sep 1950; Wood to Davis, 17 Aug 1960, BDP; Wright to Davis, 13 Jul 1960, PP; Smith journal, 17 Sep 1950.

35. Wray to author, 30 Nov 1995; Jones interview; Westover interview, p. 99.

36. Smith journal, 18 Sep 1950.

37. G-3 Journal, 19 Sep 1950, Box 6, 61A-2265, WNRC; Smith to Montross, 28 Jun 1955, Box 19, OPSP.

38. Barrow OH, pp. 188–91.

39. 1st Marines SAR, 19 Sep 1950; news clipping, 19 Sep 1950, BDP.

Chapter 18: "You'll Take a Lot Fewer Casualties": The Seizure of Seoul, September 1950

1. Draft news release, 21 Sep 1950, Box 9, 61A-2265, WNRC.

2. *Leatherneck,* Oct 1951, p. 51; Hawkins to author, 4 May 1998; Nickerson OH, p. 191; Hawkins, Comments on Close Air Support in Korea, 8 Jan 1951, Box 5, 77-0039, WNRC.

3. 1st Marines Unit Report, 18–24 Sep 1950, Box 80, 61A-2265; Capt Bruce F. Cunliffe interview, 24 Aug 1954, Box 5, 77-0039, WNRC.

4. In talking directly to Almond, Puller unwittingly contributed to a festering dispute between Smith and the corps commander. A few days later Smith would confront Almond over his practice of issuing orders directly to the regimental commanders. 1st Marines Ops Report, 20 Sep 1950, Box 81; G-3 Journal, 21 Sep 1950, Box 6, 61A-2265, WNRC; Heinl, *High Tide,* p. 168; O. P. Smith to A. C. Smith, 25 Feb 1954, Box 18, OPSP; Smith journal, 24 Sep 1950.

5. News clipping, circa Sep 1950, PP; Korea Medal of Honor Winners, Box 32, OPSP.

6. Smith to Geer, 28 Jul 1951, Box 10, 14051, WNRC; Barrow OH, p. 213.

7. Williams to Hammel, 26 Feb 1979, HP; Jimmy Cannon, "The Best Marine of Them All," PBF.

8. Westover interview, p. 53; Smith journal, 21 Sep 1950.

9. Westover interview, pp. 55–59; G-3 Journal, 21 Sep 1950.

10. Westover interview, p. 53; Barrow interview, 8 Oct 1951, Box 5, 77-0039, WNRC.

11. Heinl to Smith, 28 Sep 1966, Box 19, OPSP; Heinl, *High Tide,* p. 177.

12. Barrow OH, p. 204.

13. Hawkins, CAS in Korea; 2/1 and 3/1 SARs; 1st Marines Unit Report, 24 Sep–1 Oct 1950, Box 80, 61A-2265, WNRC.

14. Craig to Canzona, 25 Aug 1954, Box 5, 77-0039, WNRC; 1st Marines Unit Report, 24 Sep–1 Oct 1950; 1st Marines SAR, 23 Sep 1950; Smith journal, 23 Sep 1950.

15. Barrow OH, pp. 210–12; Barrow interview, 8 Oct 1951, p. 96; Maj David W. Bridges interview, 18 Oct 1954, Box 5, 77-0039, WNRC.

16. Barrow interview, 8 Oct 1951, p. 101; Barrow OH, p. 211; G-3 Journal, 24 Sep 1950; Smith journal, 24 Sep 1950; Geer, *New Breed,* p. 175.

17. Friddell, "Chesty"; McInteer interview, 30 Nov 1950.

18. Puller to Smith, 6 Oct 1950, Box 56, OPSP.

19. Puller to Smith, 6 Oct 1950; Smith, "Aide-Mémoire," p. 201–2; Lowe to Davis, 30 Jan 1961, BDP.

20. Lowe interview, 8 Dec 1950, Box 2, 77-0039, WNRC; Puller to Smith, 6 Oct 1950; Lucas draft article, 26 Jan 1952, BDP.

21. Murray OH, p. 204.

22. News clipping, 6 Oct 1950, BDP.

23. Westover interview, 21 Dec 1950, p. 69; 1st Marines Unit Report, 24 Sep–1 Oct 1950.

24. The "punch in the nose" quote comes from Sexton, but Smith reviewed and made comments on the interview and did not challenge that assessment. News clipping, 6 Oct 1950, BDP; Barrow interview with author; Murray OH, p. 206; McInteer interview, pp. 71–72; Maj Martin J. Sexton interview, 16 May 1951, Box 4, 77-0039; Smith to Geer, 28 Jul 1951, Box 10, 14051, WNRC.

25. The tardiness of the tanks may have reminded Chesty of a Jackson tale set during the Seven Days' Battle. When a regimental commander arriving late on the scene tried to explain the cause, Stonewall cut him off: "But, Colonel, I ordered you to be here at sunup." Capt Bryan J. Cummings interview, 12 Oct 1954; LtCol Reginald R. Myers interview, 1 Feb 1955, Box 5, 77-0039, WNRC; Henderson, *Stonewall,* p. 376.

26. Westover interview, 21 Dec 1950, p. 79; Barrow OH, p. 219; Barrow interview, 8 Oct 1951, p. 142; Ridge interview, 18 Oct 1954.

27. Howe, *Tales,* p. 11; News clipping, 25 Sep 1950; Fisher interview, BDP; Simmons in Barrow OH, p. 221; Foyle interview with author, 24 Jan 1996; Puller to Miller, 2 Jul 1952, PP; Degernes interview with author, 22 Sep 1999; Boley interview with author, 25 Oct 1999.

28. Wray to author, 30 Nov 1995.

29. Barrow called the night attack "one of the most stupid decisions ever made."

Smith journal, 25 Sep 1950; Fisher interview, 18 Feb 1951, Box 2, 77-0039, WNRC; Barrow to author, 30 Jun 1998.

30. The official history, based largely on the regimental and division SARs, provides a very different account. I have based my account on the 3/1 SAR, an after-action report done on September 26, 1950, by Major Simmons, and interviews with other participants recorded in the early 1950s. All of these sources came from much closer to the action than regiment or division. G-3 Journal, 26 Sep 1950; Simmons to CO, 3/1, 26 Sep 1950, Box 81, 61A-2265; 3/1 SAR; Westover interview, pp. 86–89; McInteer interview, p. 76; Ferguson interview, undated, Box 5, 77-0039, WNRC; Smith journal, 25 Sep 1950; news clipping, 26 Sep 1950, PP; 1st Marines SAR, 25 Sep 1950; Simmons interview with author, 2 Apr 1998; Hawkins to author, 4 May 1998.

31. 1st Marines Unit Report, 24 Sep–1 Oct 1950; news clipping, 26 Sep 1950, PP; Geer, *New Breed,* p. 170; Lowe to Davis, 30 Jan 1961; Puller to Smith, 6 Oct 1950, Box 56, OPSP.

32. Murray OH, p. 205; news clipping, 26 Sep 1950; Kelley to Puller, 6 Jul 1956, PP; Craig, "Field Notes," p. 39.

33. News clippings, "Puller Directs Fighting from Right out in Front," "Chesty Puller—Fightingest Marine," "Col Puller, Virginian, Among Top Fighting Men on Korean Battlefront," "The Best Marine of Them All," "Col Lewis Puller: A Perfect Leatherneck," "3 Virginians Play Big Roles in Seoul Drive," PP, PBF, and BDP.

34. Geer, *New Breed,* p. 171; Lowe to Davis, 30 Jan 1961, BDP; Westover interview, p. 116; 1st Marines Unit Report, 24 Sep–1 Oct 1950; G-3 Journal, 26 Sep 1950.

35. Devine interview; Jones interview, BDP; Leon Utter, "YEMS, YAMS, PG, E3, and YOU," *MCG,* Jul 1960, p. 19.

36. Smith journal, 28 Sep 1950; Puller interview, BDP.

37. 1st Marines Unit Report, 24 Sep–1 Oct 1950.

38. Puller interview notes; Craig to Davis, 22 Nov 1960, BDP; Craig OH, p. 190; news clipping, Robert P. Martin, "Col Lewis Puller: A Perfect Leatherneck," 4 Nov 1950, PBF; Craig, "Field Notes," p. 39.

39. 1st Marines Unit Report, 24 Sep–1 Oct 1950; 1st Marines SAR; Sexton interview, 16 May 1951; Smith to Davis, 29 Jun 1960, Box 19, OPSP.

Chapter 19: "Not My Way of Fighting a Battle": On to North Korea, October–November 1950

1. Smith journal, 1 Oct 1950; 1st Marines Messages, 5 Oct 1950, Box 81, 61A-2265, WNRC; Puller to Smith, 6 Oct 1950, Box 56, OPSP; Puller to Virginia, 5 Oct 1950, BDP.

2. Smith journal, 30 Sep 1950; Puller to Virginia, 4 Oct 1950, BDP.

3. Puller to Virginia, 4, 5, 9, and 10 Oct 1950, BDP; Mrs. Puller to relative, 11 Oct 1950; news clippings, "Still the Same Boy" and "Col Puller, Virginian," PP; *Marine!,* p. 103.

4. Puller to Virginia, 5 Oct 1950, BDP.

5. Puller to Virginia, 6 and 9 Oct 1950, BDP.

6. Puller to Virginia, 11 Oct 1950, BDP; Smith journal, 9 Oct 1950; news clipping, "A Perfect Leatherneck," 4 Nov 1950, PBF.

7. Puller to Virginia, 11 Oct and 30 Dec 1950, BDP; Westover interview, p. 97.

8. Puller to Virginia, 12, 13, and 15 Oct 1950, BDP; Craig, "Field Notes," p. 41.

9.   Division Messages, 2 Oct 1950, Box 22, 65A-5099, WNRC.

10. Basic details are taken from the appropriate SARs and historical diaries and from the official history. 1st Marines Historical Diary for Oct 1950, 8 Nov 1950, Box 80, 61A-2265; 1st Marines SAR for 7 Oct–15 Dec 1950, 15 Jan 1951, Box 2, 77-0039; 2/1 SAR for 8 Oct–15 Dec 1950; 3/1 SAR for 7 Oct–25 Nov 1950, 1 Jan 1951, Box 6, 65A-5196, WNRC; Montross and Canzona, *Chosin;* Smith journal, 21 Oct 1950.

11. Montross and Canzona, *Chosin,* p. 35; Smith journal, 25 Oct 1950.

12. Reid interview; Montross and Canzona, *Chosin,* p. 39; *Marine!,* p. 291; Honsowetz OH, p. 138; Fitness Report, Jul–Sep 1950, PR; Selden to Davis, 12 Oct 1960, BDP; news clipping, 25 Oct 1950, PP.

13. Bridges interview, 7 Jul 1951, Box 5, WNRC.

14. 1/1 to 1st Marines, 28 Oct 1950, Box 81, 61A-2265, WNRC; Barrow OH, p. 232; Montross and Canzona, *Chosin,* pp. 54–55.

15. Hawkins to author, 4 May 1998; Smith journal, 28 Oct 1950; Puller to Virginia, 8 Nov 1950, BDP; 1st Marines Operations Report, 30 Oct 1950, Box 81, 61A-2265, WNRC; Barrow OH, p. 236; Hawkins, "Comments on Close Air Support in Korea"; Hopkins interview, BDP.

16. Puller felt very strongly about the POW issue. He described his thoughts in an interview with Davis and later wrote the author insisting that they be included in the biography. In addition to his concerns about the effectiveness of former POWs, Puller resented the fact that they "were rewarded by being paid double (twice as much as men who did their duty)." Interestingly enough, Bill "Iron Man" Lee had spent all of World War II as a prisoner of the Japanese. Chesty never mentioned whether that had affected his view of his old friend from Company M. Like some of Puller's other opinions expressed in later life, it is conceivable that his thoughts about POWs were formed well after the fact and did not affect his actions in the early 1950s. However, there is no evidence either to support or debunk that conjecture. Puller interview; Puller to Davis, 23 May 1961; Chambers interview, BDP; Hawkins to author, 4 May 1998.

17. Hawkins's personal awards in World War II included a Distinguished Service Cross and a Bronze Star with Combat V. The chaplain for 1/1 thought Hawkins was "a very cool customer and a very fine officer." Hawkins later was promoted to colonel and served in other important billets until his retirement in 1965. Reeves interview, BDP; Barrow OH, p. 268; Barrow, "A Company"; Paradis to Hammel, 13 Jul 1979, HP; Schmuck Bio File, MCHC; Jones OH, p. 175.

18. Puller to Virginia, 4 Nov 1950, BDP.

19. Puller to Virginia, 6, 9, 10, 12, and 21 Nov 1950; Puller to Virginia McC, 4 Nov 1950, BDP; Pay Chart, Jul 1946, Box 10, AAVP.

20. Puller to Virginia, 15 and 20 Nov 1950, BDP.

21. Puller to Virginia, 8 Nov 1950, BDP.

22. Cowart, *Miracle,* p. 105.

23. News clipping, "Marine Battalion Kills 800," BDP; Lt C. R. Stiles, "The Dead End of Ambush Valley," Box 3, 77-0039, WNRC.

24. Puller interview, BDP; 1st Marine Division Op Order #19-50, 5 Nov 1950, Box 22, 65A-5099; 1st Marines Unit Report, 5–12 Nov 1950, Box 80, 61A-2265, WNRC.

25. Stanton, *Tenth Legion,* pp. ix, 287; Roe, *Dragon,* p. 94; Yu, "What China

Learned," p. 6; 1st Marine Division SOP 3-11, Local Defense, 8 Nov 1950, Box 22, 65A-5099, WNRC.

26. Barrow OH, pp. 245–46; Barrow, "A Company"; Stiles, "The Dead End of Ambush Valley."

27. Barrow OH, p. 251; 2/1 SAR, 7 Nov 1950.

28. Craig to Hammel, 23 Feb 1979, HP.

29. Smith to Cates, 15 Nov 1950, Box 19, OPSP; Yu, "What China Learned," p. 13.

30. Reeves interview; Puller to Virginia, 10 and 12 Nov 1950, BDP; photo captions, 10 Nov 1950, Box 80, 61A-2265, WNRC.

31. News release, 1 Dec 1950, Box 9, 61A-2265, WNRC; Koehnlein to author, 12 Jan 1996; 2/1 SAR, 6 and 22 Nov 1950; Owens interview; Puller to Virginia, 8 Nov 1950, BDP; Medal of Honor Winners—Korea, Box 32, OPSP.

32. Puller to Virginia, 8, 10, and 18 Nov 1950, BDP.

33. The division order contained no such provision for the other regiments. 1stMarDiv Op Order #22-50, 17 Nov 1950, Box 22, 65A-5099, WNRC; Smith journal, 18 Nov 1950; Puller to Virginia, 18 Nov 1950, BDP.

34. SSgt Mike Shutak, news release, circa Nov 1950, Box 9, 61A-2265; J. A. Smith interview, 15 Feb 1951, Box 2, 77-0039, WNRC.

35. In a letter to the Commandant, Smith had noted that nearly all the "serious contacts" after the Wonsan landing had been made by the 1st Marines. Williams to Hammel, 16 Jan 1979, HP; Smith to Cates, 17 Dec 1950, Box 2; Bowser interview, 2 Jan 1951, Box 5, 77-0039; 1st Marines Op Order #15-50, 27 Nov 1950, Box 80, 61A-2265, WNRC; Smith to Cates, 15 Nov 1950, Box 19, OPSP; Bowser to author, 21 Nov 1994; Ray Davis interview with author, 15 Nov 1995.

36. Marine Corps Technical Bulletin #2-49, Cold Weather Clothing and Related Equipment, 18 Feb 1949, Box 22, 65A-5099, WNRC.

37. Friddell, "Chesty"; 1st Marines SAR, S-4 Annex; Geer, *New Breed,* p. 266; Gibson to Hammel, 3 Aug 1979; Tighe to Hammel, 28 Mar 1979, HP; Annex B (Intel) to X Corps Op Order #7, 24 Nov 1950, Box 22, 65A-5099, WNRC.

38. Puller to Virginia, 12 and 23 Nov 1950, BDP; 2/1 SAR, 23 Nov 1950.

39. Puller to Virginia, 23 and 27 Nov 1950, BDP.

40. Puller to Virginia, 18 and 27 Nov 1950, BDP.

41. Recent sources indicate there may have been as many as 150,000 PLA soldiers in the X Corps zone, a number far higher than previously accepted estimates. X Corps to 1st Marine Division, 26 Nov 1950, Box 22, 65A-5099, WNRC; Yu, "What China Learned," p. 9; Roe, *Dragon,* pp. 205, 233–34.

Chapter 20: "Not All the Chinese in Hell": The Chosin Reservoir, November–December 1950

1. Smith to Cates, 15 Nov 1950, Box 19, OPSP.

2. Fehrenbach, *This Kind of War,* p. 246; Smith to Cates, 17 Dec 1950, Box 2, 77-0039, WNRC; Smith journal, 28 Nov 1950.

3. SSgt Mike Shutak, news release, circa Nov 1950, Box 9, 61A-2265, WNRC; 1st Marines SAR, 28 Nov 1950.

4. Forney Report, circa Jan 1951, Box 2, 77-0039; Smith journal, 29 Nov 1950; Drysdale to CG, 1st Marine Division, 30 Nov 1950, Box 81, 61A-2265, WNRC; Sitter to author, 1 May 1999.

5. Smith to Leckie, 5 Jul 1962, Box 19, OPSP; Capraro interview, 12 Feb 1951, Box 4, 77-0039, WNRC.

6. 2/1 SAR, 29 Nov 1950; 1st Marines SAR, 29 Nov 1950.

7. 2/1 SAR, 29 Nov 1950.

8. Montross and Canzona, *Chosin,* p. 234.

9. Barrow OH, p. 270.

10. 1st Marines Intelligence Summary, 28 Nov 1950, Box 81, 61A-2265, WNRC; 1st Marines SAR, p. 28; Puller interview, BDP; Barrow, "A Company."

11. Smith to Wornham, 14 Nov 1953, Box 32, OPSP.

12. McLaughlin OH, p. 93; Dickerson interview, 25 Jul 1951, Box 3, 77-0039, WNRC.

13. 1st Marines Unit Report, 26 Nov–17 Dec 1950, Box 81, 61A-2265; Lorigan to HD, 7 Dec 1955, Box 6, 65A-5196, WNRC.

14. Another factor in the decision to form Task Force Drysdale may have been Ridge's insistence to the division operations officer that George Company "be expedited in its movement with any other tactical units deemed possible." 1st Marines to 1st Marine Division, 28 Nov 1950, Box 81, 61A-2265; Smith journal, 28 and 29 Nov 1950; Smith to Cates, 17 Dec 1950, Box 2, 77-0039; Ridge to Montross, 1955, Box 6, 65A-5196, WNRC; Smith to Heinl, 19 Aug 1960, Box 19, OPSP.

15. *Time,* 18 Dec 1950, p. 26; Goldman to Smith, 12 May 1956, Box 19; Smith interview, Jan 1951, Box 32, OPSP.

16. Appleman, *East of Chosin,* p. 305.

17. Owens, *Colder Than Hell,* p. 302; Geer, *New Breed,* p. 332.

18. The first mention of the famous "surrounded" quote is in Geer's *New Breed,* p. 311. Geer says that Puller said it to reporters, but evidence suggests none were in Koto-ri at the time he supposedly said it. Capraro, the assistant division public information officer, would have been around during briefings to correspondents, but he never heard it and suspects "it is more myth than reality." I have found no newspaper articles containing the quote, a juicy line that would surely have made it into print. Another version had it that Puller simply radioed Schmuck: "We have contact on four sides." Smith journal, 1 Dec 1950; Smith to Leckie, 15 Nov 1959; Smith to Davis, 29 Jun 1960; Wray to *Life,* 20 Dec 1972, Box 19, OPSP; Greenwood, *Lifetime,* p. 78; Martin, "Toughest Marine"; Maj Mike Capraro, "General Chesty Puller: The Man and the Myths," news clipping, PP; Hopkins interview; Cornely interview, BDP; Glodowski interview with author, 11 Dec 1995; Buck interview with author, Oct 1999.

19. Puller to Virginia, 30 Nov and 1 Dec 1950, BDP.

20. Puller to Virginia, 1, 2, and 3 Dec 1950, BDP.

21. Puller wrote Virginia only that there was "quite a story connected with its delivery." He did not tell her about the ambushed convoy until much later. Puller to Virginia, 1 and 2 Dec 1950 and 18 Jan 1951, BDP.

22. The story of Puller threatening the Army sounds like an apocryphal tale, but Puller would tell his aide in 1955 that it was true. The lieutenant in the operations section also verified it in an interview with Davis in 1960. 1st Marines Unit Report, 26 Nov–17 Dec 1950; Worster interview, BDP; Moore to author, 9 Oct 1999; Martin, "Toughest Marine."

23. 2/1 SAR, 1–6 Dec 1950; 1st Marines Unit Report, 26 Nov–17 Dec 1950; 1st

Marines SAR, p. 30; 1st Marines to 1stMarDiv, 3 Dec 1950, Box 81, 61A-2265, WNRC; Puller Recommendation for Lt Mallone, 29 Dec 1951, PP.

24. Puller to Virginia, 9 Oct and 2 Dec 1950 and 10 Jan 1951; Jones interview; Reeves interview, BDP; Williams to Hammel, 16 Jan 1979, HP; Martin, "Toughest Marine"; Virginia Dabney interview.

25. Smith journal, 2 Dec 1950; Montross and Canzona, *Chosin,* p. 303.

26. X Corps General Orders #66, 15 Dec 1950, PP; 1st Marines Personnel Report, 24 Dec 1950, Box 81, 61A-2265; Capt Roscoe L. Barrett to Montross, 9 Aug 1955, Box 6, 65A-5196, WNRC; 1st Marines SAR, 7 Dec 1950; 1st Marines Unit Report, 26 Nov–17 Dec 1950; Puller to Virginia, 4 and 5 Dec 1950; Reeves interview, BDP; Bowser to author, 21 Nov 1995; Carmin to author, 13 Oct 1994. Stanton, *Tenth Legion,* p. 313.

27. Puller to Virginia, 1 and 4 Dec 1950, BDP.

28. Puller to Virginia, 5 and 7 Dec 1950, BDP.

29. Capraro, "Chesty Puller"; *Time,* 18 Dec 1950, p. 26; Fridell, "Chesty"; speech, 9 Nov 1978, SP.

30. Smith journal, 7 and 9 Dec 1950; Shepherd OH, p. 462.

31. Smith journal, 8 Dec 1950; news clipping, *Honolulu Advertiser,* 2 Sep 1954, PP; photo supplement, 1st Marine Division SAR, Dec 1950, Box 22, 65A-5099, WNRC.

32. 1st Marines SAR, 8 Dec 1950.

33. Barrow, "A Company."

34. 2/1 and 1st Marines SARs, 9 Dec 1950.

35. Speech, 9 Nov 1978, SP; Jones interview, BDP.

36. There is very little information about Puller's activities during this night. The only piece of contemporary evidence is a message from the traffic control point at Sudong saying that he had passed through before 0830 on December 11, well before either the tanks or 1/1. 1st Marine Division Messages, 11 Dec 1950, Box 26, 61A-2265, WNRC; Appleman, *Escaping,* p. 314.

37. Considerable confusion surrounds these events. Puller's written order was issued on December 7 and it called for the tanks to intersperse with the regimental vehicle train. Smith's orders on the 9th made it obsolete, but Puller's staff produced no new written directive. Memories and official reports differ on what happened that night. 1st Marines Op Order 16-50, 7 Dec 1950, Box 80, 61A-2265; 2/1 SAR, 10 Dec 1950; 1st Marines SAR, 10 Dec 1950; Schmuck interview, 8 Aug 1956; Gall interview, 18 Dec 1953, Box 6, 65A-5196; Gall interview, 11 Feb 1951, Box 2, 77-0039, WNRC; Hargett to Hammel, 26 Mar 1980, HP; Montross and Canzona, *Chosin,* pp. 328–29.

38. Speech, 9 Nov 1978, SP; 2/1 SAR, 11–12 Dec 1950; Carlon to Hammel, 22 Feb 1980, HP.

39. 1st Marines SAR, 10–11 Dec 1950; Smith OH, p. 256; Hargett to Hammel, 26 Mar 1980, HP; *Marine!,* p. 319; Smith OH, pp. 253–54; 1stMarDiv Messages, 10 Dec 1950, Box 26, 61A-2265, WNRC.

40. Puller to Virginia, 13 Dec 1950, BDP; Barrow, "A Company."

41. Puller's odd decision was akin to Stonewall Jackson's rare failure of aggressiveness in the Seven Days' Battles, ascribed to "stress fatigue" by one historian. McPherson, *Battle Cry,* p. 471.

42. 1stMarDiv SAR, 9 Dec 1950; "Extracts from Chinese Documents Dealing with

Chosin Reservoir Operation," Box 32, OPSP; 1st Marines SAR, p. 29; Smith journal, 11 Dec 1950; Geer, *New Breed,* p. 368.

43. Smith thought that there "would have been no point in holding Hungnam." Murray OH, p. 249; Krulak to Hammel, 14 May 1979; Craig to Hammel, 23 Feb 1979; Shepherd journal, 7 Dec 1950, HP; Puller interview; Puller to Virginia, 14 Dec 1950, BDP; Smith interview, Jan 1951, Box 32, OPSP.

44. Puller to Virginia, 13 and 14 Dec 1950, BDP; Smith journal, 11 Dec 1950; 1st Marines SAR, p. 29.

45. *Time,* 18 Dec 1950, pp. 26–27; news clipping, 12 Dec 1950; Lowe to Davis, 30 Jan 1961, BDP; Division Memorandum 238-50, 19 Dec 1950, PP.

Chapter 21: "Befuddled and Disgusted": Central Korea, December 1950–May 1951

1. 2/1 SAR, 14 Dec 1950; Stiles interview, BDP; Puller to Virginia, 15, 18, and 20 Dec 1950 and 30 Jan 1951, BDP; Simmons, "Why You Should Study Military History," *Fortitudine,* Fall 1995, p. 7; Wray to author, 30 Nov 1995; Degernes interview with author, 22 Sep 1999.

2. Smith journal, 17 Dec 1950; Smith, "Aide-Mémoire," p. 1239; Craig OH, p. 193; Craig, "Incidents of Service," p. 46; 1st Marines Historical Diary, Dec 1950, and 1st Marines Unit Report, 17–24 Dec 1950, Box 80, 61A-2265; 1st Marine Division Messages, 29 Dec 1950, Box 22, 65A-5099, WNRC; Murray OH, p. 249.

3. Smith, "Aide-Mémoire," p. 1246; 1stMarDiv Messages, 21 Dec 1950; 2/1 Historical Diary, 24–29 Dec 1950, Box 6, 65A-5196, WNRC; Andow diary, 20 and 27 Dec 1950, Andow Papers; Sexton interview, 16 May 1951, pp. 100–102.

4. Puller to Virginia, 16, 19, and 29 Dec 1950 and 3 Jan 1951, BDP; Puller to Virginia McC, 1 Jan 1951, PP.

5. Puller to Virginia, 24 and 25 Dec 1950; Puller interview, BDP.

6. *Time,* 18 Dec 1950, p. 17, and 25 Dec 1950, p. 19; news clipping, 3 Nov 1950, Box 32, OPSP; Puller to Virginia, 27 Dec 1950, BDP.

7. Ridgway's recollection of how Puller appeared in 1951 was probably based more on his desire to pay a compliment to a fellow veteran than it was on actual memory. In Ridgway's own memoirs (*Soldier,* pp. 38–39), he pays tribute to Puller and other Marines he met in Nicaragua who later served with him in Korea. In fact, the Army leader left Nicaragua by the time Puller arrived there, so the supposed 1928 meeting was apocryphal. In the same fashion, *Marine!* (p. 326) says that Puller "took an instant liking" to Ridgway, a recollection controverted by Puller's letters home. Montross, Kuokka, and Hicks, *East-Central Front,* pp. 9–10; Ridgway interview, 19 Oct 1969, pp. 14, 18, Box 19, OPSP; Ridgway to Davis, 27 May 1960; Smith, "Aide-Mémoire," p. 1279; Puller to Virginia, 17 Jan 1951, BDP; Murray OH, p. 250.

8. Puller to Virginia, 21, 24, 28, and 29 Dec 1950 and 2, 4, and 18 Jan 1951, BDP; Quirk to Wife, 2 Apr 1951, Quirk Papers.

9. Puller to Virginia, 21 Dec 1950 and 18 Jan 1951, BDP; Craig OH, p. 196; Craig, "Incidents of Service," pp. 48, 54.

10. Puller to Virginia, 22, 26, and 27 Dec 1950 and 3 and 10 Jan 1951, BDP.

11. Marshall, "He's a Model Lt. General with Feet of Clay," *Detroit News,* 11 Feb 1962, p. 3E.

12. Koehnlein to author, 8 Dec 1995 and 12 Jan 1996; Barrow OH, p. 297; Wray to author, 30 Nov 1995.

13. Kenneth A. Aubin, "A Puller Vignette," *MCG,* Nov 1995, p. 32; Andow diary, 26 Jan 1951; Smith, "Aide-Mémoire," p. 1380.

14. Craig interview, 8 May 1951, Box 4, 77-0039; 1st Marines Unit Report, 7–14 Jan 1951, Box 81, 61A-2265, WNRC; Smith journal, 17 Jan 1951; Puller interview, BDP.

15. Smith, "Aide-Mémoire," pp. 1320, 1350, 1407; Smith journal, 18 Jan 1951.

16. Smith, "Aide-Mémoire," pp. 1351, 1354; Smith journal, 19–21 Jan 1951.

17. Barrow OH, p. 299; Barrow interview, 23 Jan 1997.

18. Smith, "Aide-Mémoire," p. 1360; Smith journal, 24–27 Jan 1951; Smith to Silverthorn, 28 Jan 1951, Box 58, OPSP; Craig to Davis, 22 Nov 1960; Jones interview, BDP; Craig OH, p. 195.

19. Smith, "Aide-Mémoire," p. 1357; Smith journal, 28 Jan 1951; Smith OH, p. 29; 1st Marines Unit Report Outline, Box 81, 61A-2265, WNRC; Fitness Report, Jul–Sep 1950, PR; Bowser to author, 15 Jun 1998.

20. Puller to Virginia, 25 Jan and 9 Feb 1951, BDP.

21. Puller to Virginia, 31 Jan 1951, BDP; Perret, *Old Soldiers,* pp. 565–66.

22. 2/1 Historical Diary, 1 Feb 1951, Box 6, 65A-5196; 1st Marines Unit Report, 28 Jan–4 Feb 1951, Box 80, 61A-2265, WNRC; news clippings, PP and PR; Jones interview; Puller interview, BDP; "Three Gunnys," *Leatherneck,* May 1951, p. 28.

23. Task Force Puller Memorandum #1-51, 1 Feb 1951, PP.

24. Puller to Virginia, 9 Feb 1951, BDP; Merritt Edson, letter of 22 Jan 1944, quoted in Censor to 2d Marine Division, undated, Box 9, MAEP; Smith to Kendall, 15 Jun 1954, Box 57; Smith, "Personal Narrative: New Britain to Peleliu," p. 59, Box 22, OPSP.

25. Smith OH, p. 255; Bowser to author, 21 Nov 1995; Craig to Canzona, 4 Mar 1954, Box 5; Craig interview, 8 May 1951, Box 4, 77-0039; Appendix 1, 1stMarDiv Historical Diary, Mar 1951, Box 15, 61A-2265, WNRC; Smith to Davis, 11 Jun 1960; Puller interview, BDP.

26. Puller to Virginia, 4–6 Feb 1951, BDP.

27. Puller to Virginia, 4 and 9 Feb 1951, BDP; General Puller's Log, 2–10 Feb 1951, PP.

28. Puller to Virginia, 8 Feb 1951, BDP; Smith journal, 1 Feb 1951.

29. Montross, Kuokka, and Hicks, *East-Central Front,* p. 58; Smith journal, 14 Feb 1951.

30. Montross, Kuokka, and Hicks, *East-Central Front,* p. 67; 1stMarDiv Historical Diary, Feb 1951, p. 20, Box 23, 65A-5099.

31. Smith, "Aide-Mémoire," p. 1403; Smith journal, 20 Feb 1951; Smith to Montross, 28 Jul 1953; Smith to Montross, 13 Oct 1957, Box 19, OPSP; Perret, *Old Soldiers,* p. 568.

32. Smith to Montross, 28 Jul 1953; Smith to Warner, 5 Sep 1971, Box 19, OPSP; Puller to Virginia, 24 Feb 1951, BDP.

33. Puller to Virginia, 24 Feb 1951, and partial letter circa late Feb 1951; news clipping, 24 Feb 1951, BDP; Smith journal, 28 Feb 1951.

34. In Smith's one formal operations order as head of IX Corps, he repeated his practice of limiting Puller's ability to commit his reserve. No other division in

the corps was regulated in that fashion and the corps reserve consisted of an Army regiment, so it clearly was directed solely at Puller. 1stMarDiv Op Order #7-51, 27 Feb 1951, Box 23; 1stMarDiv G-3 Journal, 28 Feb 1951, Box 35, 61A-2265; 1stMarDiv Historical Diary, Mar 1951, pp. 2, 7, Box 40, 65A-5099, WNRC; IX Corps Op Order 14, 2 Mar 1951, Box 32, OPSP.

35.   Puller interview; "Controversial Material," BDP; FMFPac to CMC, 1 Mar 1951, G-3 Journal, Box 35, 61A-2265, WNRC.

36.   *Marine!* (p. 338) recounts Puller's meeting with the Air Force commander in Korea regarding the JOC. Logs meticulously recording the arrival and departure of senior officers indicate no such visit occurred while Puller was the CG, though messages from the division fully substantiate the gist of the story— that Puller was incensed with the Air Force's failure to provide adequate support. General Puller's Log, 1 Mar and 18 Apr 1951, PP; Div Air Officer to CG, FMFPac, 1 Mar 1951, and 1stMarDiv to IX Corps, 3 Mar 1951, G-3 Journal, Box 35, 61A-2265; 1stMarDiv Historical Diary, Mar 1951, Box 23, 65A-5099, WNRC; Puller interview, BDP; Montross, Kuokka, and Hicks, *East-Central Front*, p. 78; Smith OH, p. 285.

37.   Smith to Montross, 13 Oct 1957, Box 19, OPSP; news release, 4 Mar 1951, Box 22, 61A-2265, WNRC; *Marine!*, p. 337; Puller to Virginia, 30 Dec 1950, BDP; 1stMarDiv Historical Diary, Mar 1951.

38.   General Puller's Log, 1–4 Mar 1951, PP; Puller to Virginia, 17 Mar 1951, BDP.

39.   Smith OH, p. 265; Puller to Virginia, 5 and 6 Mar 1951, BDP; Fridell, "Chesty."

40.   Puller to Virginia, 5 and 6 Mar 1951, BDP; Smith journal, 28 Feb 1951; Cates to Mrs. Smith, 14 Mar 1951, Box 58, OPSP.

41.   Board of Awards to CG, 1stMarDiv, 26 Mar 1951, and 12th endorsement thereon, 4 Oct 1951, PR; Bowser to author, 21 Nov 1995.

42.   The evidence pointing to a significant illness comes primarily from his driver, Jones, who told Davis that Puller suffered from pneumonia while he was ADC and had to take daily shots to recover from it. If so, it must have been at this point, since this was the only time Puller appeared to curtail his activities. Although there are no entries in his medical record during this period, those records were kept at the division rear echelon in Masan. An evaluation of a chest X ray in 1953 did note that there were marks on his lungs, "probably due" to a former case of pneumonia. Smith OH, p. 264; General Puller's Log, PP; Annual Physical, 14 Dec 1953, MR; Jones interview, BDP; Jeremiah O'Leary, "Chesty Puller Was a Marine's Marine," *Old Breed News,* Apr 1990.

43.   Montross, Kuokka, and Hicks, *East-Central Front,* p. 86.

44.   Puller to Virginia, 17 Mar 1951, BDP; Smith journal, 27 Mar 1951.

45.   "The Shame and the Glory of Korea," *Fortnight,* 19 Feb 1951, p. 16 (copy in Forney Papers); Smith journal, 29–30 Mar and 2–6 Apr 1951; Smith OH, pp. 266–69; Silverthorn to Smith, 30 Mar 1951, McQueen Papers; Department of the Army to CINCFE, 1 Apr 1951, Box 32, OPSP; General Puller's Log, 4 Apr 1951, PP; news clipping, "War Film Stirs Service Squabble," 22 Mar [195?], BDP.

46.   Perret, *Old Soldiers,* pp. 566–71; Puller interview, BDP.

47.   Smith journal, 15 Apr 1951; Smith OH, p. 271.

48.   Burke Davis gave Puller credit for inspiring the Army artillery battalion that fought well, but that hardly seems possible, since Puller's log indicates he was setting up a new CP for the division at the time. Moreover, the battalion had been

well led from the first in Korea and needed no outside motivation. 1stMarDiv Historical Diary, pp. 50, 52, Apr 1951, Box 24, 65A-5099, WNRC; Montross, Kuokka, and Hicks, *East-Central Front,* pp. 109, 115; *Marine!,* p. 339.

49. SSgt Don Fergusson, "Humor in Uniform," *Reader's Digest,* Sep 1960, p. 27.

50. General Puller's Log, 25–26 Apr 1951, PP; Millett, *Strife,* pp. 291–92; Thomas OH, p. 733; news clipping, 15 Mar 1951, PBF.

51. Smith to Montross, 19 Aug 1956, Box 19, OPSP; Smith to Geer, 28 Jul 1951, Box 10, 14051, WNRC; Fitness Report, 1 Oct 1950–26 Apr 1951, PR.

Chapter 22: "I Hope I Don't Get Hung": Training and Experimenting, May 1951–June 1952

1. Millett, *Semper Fidelis,* p. 496; "Puller to Command New Marine Brigade," *Washington Star,* 15 Mar 1951, PBF; "Puller to Use Battle Experience in Forming New Marine Outfit," news clipping, 12 Apr 1951, BDP.

2. News clipping, "Puller Leaves Korea to Join Va. Family," [May 1951], PP; Silverthorn to Battle, 8 Jun 1951, PR.

3. Endorsements on CG 1stMarDiv to Puller, 8 May 1951, PP; news clipping, "General Says Reds Lack Follow-Through," 23 May 1951, BDP.

4. Yu, "What China Learned," p. 10; news clippings, 29 Oct 1950 and 23/24 May 1951, in PBF, PP, PR, and VMI Archives.

5. News clippings, 24 May 1951, PR and PBF.

6. "Puller Shifts His Fire from Ice Cream to Air Force," *Washington Post,* 25 May 1951, p. 2.

7. News clippings, 25 and 26 May 1951, PP and PBF.

8. An official Marine Corps speakers guide for Armed Forces Day 1953 emphasized tough training and the importance of ground forces even in the atomic age. Silverthorn to Battle, 8 Jun 1951; McQueen to Christenson and McQueen to Massey, 18 Jun 1951, PR; Armed Forces Day Speakers Guide, 1953, PP.

9. "Korea Marine General Denies Criticizing GIs," *New York World Telegraph,* 26 May 1951, PBF; "General Brings Bitter Lesson from Korea," *San Francisco Examiner,* 24 May 1951, p. 1, BDP; *Time,* 12 Mar 1945.

10. Smith to Thomas, 12 Jun 1951, Box 56, OPSP; news clipping, "General Puller, of Marines, Will Retire," 10 Oct 1955, PP.

11. Hayes to Puller, 4 Jun 1951; Hargrave to *Dallas Morning News,* 27 May 1951, PP; news clipping, "Chesty Puller Pulls No Punches," 25 May 1951, VMI Archives; "General Puller, a First Class Fighting Man," *Richmond Times-Dispatch,* 26 May 1951, PBF; "Off the Chest," *Time,* 4 Jun 1951, p. 24.

12. "Off the Chest," *Time,* 4 Jun 1951, p. 24; Maas, "Old Warhorse."

13. "Puller Wants Every Boy a Dan'l Boone," *Richmond Times-Dispatch,* 6 Jun 1951, VMI Archives.

14. News clippings, *Richmond News Leader,* 24 May and 13 Jun 1951, PP; Puller interview notes, BDP.

15. "Puller, Home at Saluda," *Richmond Times-Dispatch,* 25 May 1951; news clipping, "Pullers in Camp Pendleton Quarters," [Jun 1951]; "Simultaneous Duty of Four Generals," *San Diego Evening Tribune,* 11 Aug 1951, PP; Puller to HQMC, 17 Jul 1951, PR.

16. CMC to FMFPac, 20 Mar 1951, Box 2, 76-94, WRNC; Snedeker OH, p. 111; "The Third Division," *Leatherneck,* Mar 1953, pp. 25–26.

17. "A Salute to a Marine," *Tell-N-It to the Marines,* Sep 1951, BDP; Smith OH,

p. 304; Smith, "Notes on Service at Camp Pendleton," p. 3, OPSP; news clippings, [Jul 1951], PP.

18. Millett, *Semper Fidelis,* pp. 454, 510.

19. Shepherd to CMC, 8 Aug 1951; Sandia graduation certificate, 24 Aug 1951; Bowser to FMFPac, 29 Mar 1952, PR; Puller interview notes, BDP; Puller to McInerney, 18 Jun 1952, PP.

20. Millett, *Semper Fidelis,* pp. 508–10; news clipping, 9 Jan 1952; Puller to Shepherd, 8 Mar 1952, PP.

21. "The Third Division," pp. 25–27; Snedeker OH, p. 111; McInerney to FMFPac, 28 Mar 1952, PR.

22. Millett, *Semper Fidelis,* p. 509; "The Third Division," p. 27; news item, *Leatherneck,* Jul 1952, p. 35; Armed Forces Day Speakers Guide, 1953, PP.

23. "The Third Division," p. 27; Sliwinski interview, BDP; Harold H. Martin, "Toughest Marine in the Corps," *Saturday Evening Post,* 22 Mar 1952, pp. 41, 108; photo album, 3 Jun 1952, PP; Coughlin interview with author, 28 Jun 1999.

24. Smith to SecNav, 4 Apr 1951, and endorsements thereon, PR; Smith to Blakeney, 21 Sep 1951, Box 37, OPSP.

25. Smith later surmised that Puller had taken the joke seriously and instigated a move to get the Medal of Honor. Although there would be many such attempts, there is no indication that Chesty ever started any of them. "5th Navy Cross to Marine Hero," 5 Feb 1952, PP; *Marine!,* p. 355; Smith OH, p. 307; Smith to Davis, 11 Jun 1960; Smith to Hagan, 17 Mar 1962, BDP.

26. The fifth Navy Cross matched him with Commander Roy M. Davenport, USN, for the most ever given to any member of the naval services. Puller mistakenly was claiming a few extra awards, believing he rated a Purple Heart with six stars—one award for each piece of metal he had taken at Koli Point. He merited only the basic medal and would not discover his error till much later. Thomas to SecNav, 14 and 19 May and 24 Aug 1951, PR; Citations for Air Medals; Fischer to Virginia Puller, 22 Aug 1978; news clippings, [Jul 1951] and 11 Aug 1951, PP; Puller to CMC, 14 Sep 1953, PBF; Davenport Bio File, NHC.

27. Sherrod, *Marine Corps Aviation,* p. 431; Boyington to Truman, 28 Feb 1952; Thomas to President's Naval Aide, 4 Apr 1952, PR.

28. Hoffman, *Once a Legend,* pp. 390, 394; *Saturday Evening Post* to Puller, 18 Sep 1951, PP; "Toughest Marine in the Corps."

29. "Toughest Marine in the Corps"; Hoffman, *Once a Legend,* pp. 336–37, 346, 360, 367, 392.

30. Van Winkle to Puller, 19 Mar 1952; Hayes to Puller, 21 Apr 1952; Puller to Martin, 22 Jul 1952, PP.

31. News clipping, "Cartoonist Gets Honor Medal," 5 Sep 1951; Puller to Smith, 29 Oct 1951; Pepper to Puller, 9 May 1952; CMC to Puller, 7 Apr 1952; program of King William County 250th Anniversary, Apr 1952, PP; Marine Corps League to CMC, Jul 1952, PR; speech for King William County Anniversary, Apr 1952, BDP.

32. TSgt Robert W. Tallent, "Division Reunion," *Leatherneck,* Oct 1951, pp. 27–29; Smith to Puller, 2 Aug 1951, PP; Ray Davis to Puller, 1 Jun 1960; Schlemmer letter, *Old Breed News* [195?], BDP; Rogers to author, 2 Jan 1996.

33. Fitness Report, 15 Feb–10 Jun 1952, PR; Shepherd to Smith, 18 Feb 1952, Box 59, OPSP; Puller to Shepherd, 8 Mar 1952; Mrs. Shepherd to Mrs. Puller, 19 Oct

1971, PP; Jones interview notes, BDP; "The New Commandant," *Leatherneck,*
Jan 1952, p. 14; Bo Shepherd Memorandum, 30 Oct 1993, PP; Virginia Dabney
interview with author.

34. Horn to Puller, 12 Nov 1968; Gaeddert to Puller, 26 Aug 1964; Johnson to
Puller, 22 Sep 1953, PP; Puller and Jones interview notes, BDP; Peterson, *Short
Straw,* p. 33.

35. Fitness Reports, 20 May 1951–10 Jun 1952, PR.

36. Snedeker interview notes, BDP; Coughlin interview with author, 28 Jun 1999.

37. Virginia Dabney interview.

38. Puller interview notes, BDP; Horn to Puller, 12 Nov 1968, PP; Puller, *Fortunate
Son,* pp. 4–5; Martin, "Toughest Marine."

Chapter 23: "A School Teacher's Job": Training Other Men for War, June 1952–May 1954

1. Amphibious Training Command Pacific Fleet to Puller, 11 Jun 1952; Puller to
CMC, 23 Jul 1953, PR; Pepper to CMC, 30 Apr 1952; Puller to Walker, 23 Jun
1953; Puller to Cresswell, 26 Jun 1953, PP; Coughlin interview, 28 Jun 1999.

2. Puller, "The Troop Training Unit in Amphibious Operations," [1953]; Puller to
Davies, 18 Sep 1952 and 12 May 1953; Puller to Shepherd, 19 Jun 1953; Puller
to Pollock, 12 May 1953, PP; MSgt R. T. Fugate, "Troop Training Team," *Leatherneck,* Jun 1953, pp. 22–27; TTUPac, Briefing for CMC, 22 Jun 1953, Box 138,
65A-5099, WNRC.

3. Heinl, *Soldiers of the Sea,* p. 1.

4. In 1953, Puller wrote to a fellow Marine general and asked him to assist an admiral transferring into his area: "Admiral McInerney is not only a good friend of
mine but is one of the best Marine Corps promoters we have in the Navy. He has
put in good word for us many times and is usually ready to champion our cause."
Puller to Marsh, 25 Nov 1952; Puller to Davies, 1 Apr 1953; Puller to Ames,
27 Feb 1953, PP; Fitness Report, 11 Jun–31 Aug 1952, PR.

5. TTU to Puller, 18 Sep 1952 and 10 Feb 1953; Puller to Davies, 24 Mar 1953, PP.

6. Puller to Stewart, 22 Apr 1953; *Encyclopedia of American History,* p. 361.

7. Puller to Shepherd, 17 Jul 1953; Shepherd to Puller, 21 Jul 1953; Puller to
Davies, 3 Dec 1953, PP; Miller interview notes, BDP.

8. Whelan to Puller, 1 Sep 1952; Gaitan to Bledsoe, 12 Jul 1952, PP.

9. Puller to Davies, 3 Dec 1953; Puller to Christian, 21 Oct 1952; Puller to Cantrell,
21 Nov 1952; Puller to Sabin, 26 Nov 1952; Puller to Selden, 16 Aug 1952;
Puller to Kelley, 6 Jan 1953, PP.

10. Tuban to Puller, 20 Aug 1952; TTU to Puller, 4 Aug 1952, PP.

11. Puller to Davies, 27 Jan and 24 Mar 1953; Puller to Snedeker, 1 Apr 1953; Puller
to Mother [Mrs. Evans] and Nannie, 1 Apr 1953, PP.

12. *Marine!* (p. 360) paints this period as "the beginning of the end" for Puller in the
Marine Corps. Among other causes, Davis alleged that senior leaders had put an
end to Chesty's Nicaraguan proposal because they were humiliated that they had
not come up with the idea: "They just couldn't admit to Congress and the public
that we'd wasted all that money on inadequate [stateside] training bases." Davis
mistakenly placed the Nicaraguan event in mid-1954, after Chesty's promotion
to major general, but it took place well before that. Puller interview, BDP; Puller
to Shepherd, 28 Oct and 28 Nov 1952 and 17 Mar 1953; Shepherd to Puller,
25 Mar and 7 Jul and 21 Jul 1953, PP; final Puller corrections, p. 442, BDP.

13. Davies to Puller, 15 Oct 1952; Puller to Davies, 28 Oct 1952; Puller to Shepherd, 7 Feb 1953, PP.

14. Puller to Davies, 21 Aug and 28 Oct 1952 and 24 Mar, 7 Apr, and 15 May 1953; Puller to Shepherd, 7 Feb and 17 Mar 1953, PP.

15. Puller to Shepherd, 17 Mar and 13 Apr 1953; Shepherd to Puller, 25 Mar 1953; Puller to Davies, 7 Apr 1953, PP.

16. Davies to Puller, 17 Mar 1953; Puller to Davies, 15 May 1953; Puller to Shepherd, 19 Jun 1953; TTU to Puller, 13 May 1953, PP; Puller interview, BDP.

17. Puller to Shepherd, 19 Jun 1953; Puller itinerary, May–Jun 1953, PP.

18. Puller to Carney, 24 Jun 1953, PP; Meid, *West Korea,* pp. 313–14, 336–37; Pate and Pollock Bio Files, MCHC.

19. *Marine!* (p. 345) mistakenly places this letter toward the end of Puller's 1950–1951 tour in Korea. However, Chesty's reference to the "peace conference" and "fighting" place it with absolute certainty in June 1953, the only time he was in Korea while both those events were taking place. The more intriguing and frustrating feature of the document is the absence of the first page, which would provide not only the exact date, but the reason for Puller's dejected mood. The quote used here begins with the very first word of the existing second page (conveniently numbered by Puller). Puller to Virginia, [Jun 1953], BDP.

20. Puller to Virginia, [Jun 1953], PP.

21. Puller to Carney, 24 Jun 1953; Puller to Cresswell, 26 Jun 1953, PP; TTUPac, Brief for CMC, 22 Jun 1953, Box 138, 65A-5099, WNRC.

22. Puller to Shepherd, 28 Oct 1952 and 7 Feb and 17 Mar 1953; Puller to Davies, 15 May 1953, PP.

23. Fitness Reports, 11 Jun 1952–1 Jun 1954, PR; Chase to Puller, 29 Jul 1953; Cresswell to Puller, 30 Apr 1953; de'Flamini to Puller, 9 Dec 1952; Shepherd to Puller, 25 Mar 1953, PP.

24. Jaklewicz to Puller, 24 Aug 1952; Biggers to Puller, 8 Dec 1952; Reynolds to Puller, 1 Dec 1952, PP.

25. Puller to Snedeker, 15 Sep 1952; Puller to Murray and Litzenberg, 20 Nov 1952; Puller to Davies, 18 Sep and 28 Oct 1952 and 15 May 1953; Puller to Schick, 9 Dec 1952, PP.

26. Puller to Davies, 14 Aug 1953, PP; Jones interview notes, BDP.

27. News clippings, 27 Aug 1953, PP and PBF.

28. Puller's expression of admiration for Smith was genuine, for no other letters responding to congratulations from generals or admirals mentioned such a sentiment. He would repeat it on several future occasions. Hayward to Puller, 9 Sep 1953; Wornham to Puller, 1 Sep 1953; Puller to Smith, 13 Sep 1953 and 29 Aug 1955, PP.

29. Puller to Wornham, 10 Sep 1953; Puller to Van Winkle, 5 May 1953, PP; Virginia Dabney interview.

30. Puller to Smith, 13 Sep 1953; Report of Physical Evaluation Board, 10 Aug 1955, p. 13, PP; CMC to Puller, 27 Aug 1953; Puller endorsement on appointment, 28 Sep 1953; Report of Medical Survey, 1 Nov 1954, PR; Report of Medical Examination, 12 Nov 1952; Chronological Record of Medical Care, 31 Aug 1953, MR.

31. Puller to Bruck-Curtis Co., 21 Oct 1952; Puller to Shepherd, 7 Feb 1953; Puller to Mother [Mrs. Evans], 1 Apr 1953, PP; Puller, *Fortunate Son,* pp. 7–10.

32. Puller to Moody, 2 Mar 1954; Puller to Mother, 1 Apr 1953; Puller to Adams, 11 Oct 1954; Garces to Adams, 29 Jul 1952, PP.

33. Puller to CMC, 17 Mar 1954; Fitness Reports, 1951–1954; CMC to Puller, 27 Mar 1954, PR; Puller to Davies, 23 Mar 1954, PP.

34. Puller would list the 1st Marine Division as his first choice of duty on his initial fitness report as CG of the 2d Marine Division. Meid, *West Korea,* p. 336; news clipping, [May 1954], PP; Fitness Report, Jun–Aug 1954, PR.

35. TTU to Puller, 22 Mar 1954; Puller to Hart, 26 Mar 1954; Sun Li-Jen to Puller, 19 May 1954; news clipping, 17 Apr 1954, PP.

36. News clippings, Apr 1954, PP.

37. News clipping, *Charleston Evening Post,* 5 May 1954; Puller to Wornham, 10 Sep 1953, PP; Puller, *Fortunate Son,* p. 10.

38. News clipping, 9 May 1954; Puller to Good, 25 May 1954; Good to Puller, 2 Jun 1954, PP.

39. Snedeker had received a Navy Cross for commanding the 7th Marines on Okinawa, but all his other combat tours involved staff duty. Puller to Snedeker, 24 May 1954; Puller to Stewart, 22 Apr 1953; Puller to Davies, 27 Jan 1953, PP; *Camp Lejeune Globe,* 8 Jul 1954, p. 12.

40. Report of Physical Evaluation Board, 10 Aug 1955, pp. 13, 21.

Chapter 24: "Go Down Slugging": Last Days in the Corps, June 1954–October 1955

1. Virginia Dabney interview; Moore to author, 31 Aug 1999; Puller, *Fortunate Son,* pp. 10–11.

2. Leave Record, Jun 1954, PR; Hayes to Puller, 2 Jul 1954, PP; *Leatherneck,* Apr 1952, p. 49.

3. Puller, *Fortunate Son,* p. 11; Puller to Smith, 26 Feb 1955, PP.

4. Elliott, "Chesty's Driver"; Moore to author, 25 Aug 1999.

5. *Camp Lejeune Globe,* 1 and 8 Jul 1954; news clipping, 1 Jul 1954, VMI Archives; Schlegel interview, BDP; Carmin to author, 13 Oct 1994; Moore to author, 26 Aug 1999.

6. News clipping, 27 Jun 1954; Address by the Commandant to Principal Staff Officers HQMC, 2 Jan 1953; Good to Puller, 19 May and 2 Jun 1954, PP; Smith to Banks, 17 Nov 1953, OPSP; Puller to CMC, 7 Feb 1955 and Snedeker to CMC, 8 Feb 1955, Box 70, 65A-5099, WNRC; Millett, *Semper Fidelis,* p. 525; *Camp Lejeune Globe,* 8 Jul 1954.

7. Puller to Smith, 28 Jul 1954; Smith to Puller, 4 Aug 1954, Box 57, OPSP; Snedeker OH, p. 113; Mandeville to Puller, 21 Jul 1954; Puller to Mandeville, 3 Aug 1954, PP.

8. CMC to Puller, 8 Jun 1954, PR; CMC to Puller, 6 Jul 1954; Puller to Lamson-Scribner, 12 Jul 1954; Puller to Vandegrift, 2 Aug 1954; Puller to Berger, 2 Aug 1954, PP; *Camp Lejeune Globe,* 8, 15, and 29 Jul 1954; Smith personal log, 20 Jul 1954, Box 47, OPSP.

9. Pollock to Puller, 21 Jul 1954, PP; Puller to Smith, 2 Aug 1954, Box 57; Smith personal log, 7–8 Aug 1954, Box 47, OPSP.

10. CMC to Puller, 6 Aug 1954; CG to Puller, 16 Aug 1954; Hill to Puller, 20 Aug 1954, PP.

11. Moore to author, 26 Aug 1999.

12. Jones interview, BDP; Moore interview, 15 Oct 1999.
13. Puller to Pate, 14 Aug 1954; Pate to Puller, 18 Aug 1954, PP; Degernes interview with author, 22 Sep 1999.
14. There are conflicting accounts about the morning of August 27. Puller would tell his August 1955 retirement board he had spent the first half of the day inspecting gear in warehouses. His aide recalled the time was spent in the office on paperwork. Given Puller's physical state that day and his inability to remember what happened at the clinic and hospital, it is likely he also was mistaken about his schedule that morning. That conclusion is supported by his statement at his January 1955 board, where he described the August 26 inspection of the battalion, but made no mention of any warehouse inspection the next day. In subsequent years, he also referred only to the inspection of the battalion. Report of Physical Evaluation Board [hereinafter PEB Report], 10 Aug 1955, p. 20, PP; Report of Board of Medical Survey [hereinafter November Report], 1 Nov 1954, PR; Puller Statement, 5 Jan 1955, MR; Smith OH, p. 325; Snedeker interview, BDP; Moore to author, 31 Aug 1999; *Marine!,* p. 362; Fridell, "Chesty."
15. Chronological Record of Medical Care, 27 Aug 1954, MR.
16. My interpretation of Puller's medical records is indebted to Dr. Mark Reardon, who patiently explained the meaning of numerous medical terms and indicated their possible significance. PEB Report, p. 20; November Report; Moore to author, 31 Aug 1999.
17. November Report; Puller, *Fortunate Son,* p. 12; *Camp Lejeune Globe,* 2 Sep 1954; Puller to Fenton, 27 Oct 1954, PP.
18. Smith, personal log, 27–28 Aug and 1 Sep 1954, Box 47, OPSP; HQMC to Snedeker, 27 Aug 1954; Pate to CMC, 29 Aug 1954, PR; Shepherd to Puller, 20 Sep 1954; Puller to Hill, 15 Nov 1954, PP.
19. News clippings, 28–30 Aug 1954, VMI Archives and PBF; Shepherd to Puller, 13 Sep 1954; Smith to Puller, 17 Sep 1954; Selden to Puller, 5 Oct 1954, PP; Smith to Woodbury, 15 Sep 1954, Box 57, OPSP; Puller, *Fortunate Son,* p. 14.
20. Puller to Smith, 14 Sep 1954, Box 57, OPSP; Puller to Jerome, 20 Sep 1954; Puller to Anderton, 9 Oct 1954, PP; *Camp Lejeune Globe,* 23 Sep 1954; November Report.
21. Puller, *Fortunate Son,* pp. 13–14.
22. The original letter cautioning Puller about retirement is no longer present in either the Puller or Davis papers and is quoted from *Marine!,* p. 365. Shepherd to Puller, 13 and 20 Sep 1954; Hayes to Farrell, 15 Mar 1955, PP; Smith to Woodbury, 15 Sep 1954, Box 57, OPSP; Fitness Report, Sep 1954–Feb 1955, PR.
23. Puller to Jerome, 20 Sep 1954; Puller to Shepherd, 24 Sep 1954, PP; Puller to Smith, 14 Sep 1954, Box 57, OPSP.
24. November Report; Hospital to Puller, 1 Nov 1954, PP; 2dMarDiv to FMFLant, 1 Nov 1954, PR.
25. The November Report made three separate references to "his thrombosis." Puller to Shepherd, 5 Nov 1954, PP.
26. Puller to Fenton, 27 Oct 1954; Puller to Selden, 2 Nov 1954; Puller to Shepherd, 5 Nov 1954, PP.
27. Bell, BuMed memo, 9 Nov 1954, MR.
28. Pugh was a Marine corporal, but he had left the service before the completion of 3d OTC to resume his college education. He went on to medical school and a

Navy commission. 19 Nov 1954 endorsement on November Report; Ridgely to Puller, 19 Nov 1954, PP; PEB Report, p. 19; Puller to Lowe, 15 Nov 1954; Draft Statement, [Jan 1955], PP; Statement Concerning the Finding of the Board of Medical Survey, 5 Jan 1955, MR; Pugh Bio File, NHC.

29. FMFLant to Puller, 25 Nov 1954; Marine Casual Det to 2dMarDiv, 3 Dec 1954; Report of Board of Medical Survey [hereinafter January Board], 5 Jan 1955, PP; Hogan to Burke, 2 Sep 1955, MR.

30. Smith, personal log, 17 Dec 1954, Box 47, OPSP; PEB Report, pp. 19–20; Draft Statement, [Jan 1955]; Puller to Livingston, 18 Feb 1955, PP.

31. Puller to Virginia, 4 Jan 1955; Report of Medical Examination, 23 Dec 1954, PP; *Camp Lejeune Globe,* 16 Dec 1954; Puller, *Fortunate Son,* p. 14.

32. Puller to Virginia, 4 Jan 1955, PP.

33. At that time it was BuMed policy that anyone showing consistent diastolic blood pressure readings over 100 would fail his physical examination. One senior doctor would tell a later board that a result over 100 "means he is going to have trouble pretty soon." Puller's average diastolic readings during his stay at Bethesda were 100. Report of Board of Medical Survey, 5 Jan 1955; PEB Report, p. 6, PP; Reardon interview with author, 1998.

34. Puller to Virginia, 5 Jan 1955, PP.

35. Puller to Sherman, 24 Jan 1955; Draft Statement, [5 Jan 1955], PP; Statement to Board, 5 Jan 1955, MR.

36. Martin, "Toughest Marine"; Puller to Williams, 27 Aug 1954, PP.

37. Puller to Marsteller, 19 Jan 1955, PP.

38. Shepherd to Puller, 26 Jan 1955, PR.

39. Puller to Shepherd, 31 Jan and 1 Feb 1955; Puller to Livingston, 18 Feb 1955, PP; CMC to Puller, 1 Feb 1955, PR.

40. Puller to Farrell, 10 Feb 1955, PP; Moore to author, 5 Sep 1999; Selden to Davis, 5 Nov 1960; final Puller corrections, p. 442, BDP; Smith OH, p. 325.

41. There are no documents from that time revealing what doctors told Shepherd, but those opinions are inferred from information the physicians provided later in the year to other authorities. Shepherd also would tell his son that the head of BuMed had stated that Puller "would not survive" if he stayed on active duty. Smith OH, p. 325; L. C. Shepherd III Memorandum, 30 Oct 1993, Puller Papers, MCHC; Hogan Memorandum, 19 Aug 1955; Hogan to Burke, 2 Sep 1955, MR; Moore to author, 5 Sep 1999; Election of Retirement Options, 15 Mar 1954, PP; Selden to Davis, 5 Nov 1960, BDP.

42. The deaths on active duty included Rupertus in 1945 and General Roy S. Geiger in 1947. Rupertus had died of a heart attack while eating dinner at the 8th and I Marine barracks. Chesty's eldest daughter later would agree that her father's bitterness had been misdirected at Shepherd. Millett, *Strife,* pp. 230, 322–23; Shepherd to General Officers, 21 May 1955; Hayes to Haggerty, 2 Jun 1955, PP; Rupertus Bio File, MCHC; Virginia Dabney interview.

43. Noble to CMC, 3 Feb 1955, PR; Smith to Puller, 4 Feb 1955, PP; *Camp Lejeune Globe,* 27 Jan and 3 and 10 Feb 1955.

44. Norrish to Davis, 15 Jul 1960, BDP; Puller to Canzona, 11 May 1955; Puller to Smith, 12 May 1955; Smith to Puller, 18 May 1955, Box 19, OPSP; Puller to Shepherd, 12 May 1955; Puller to Canzona, [Jul 1955], PP; *Camp Lejeune Globe,* 10 Jun 1955.

45. Puller to Shannon, 25 May 1955, PP.
46. Puller to Smith, 26 Feb 1955, PP.
47. Puller to Farrell, 10 Feb 1955; Hayes to Mrs. Puller, 3 Mar 1955; Puller to Hayes, 14 and 15 Mar 1955, PP.
48. Puller to Hayes, 4 Mar 1955; Puller to Bryan, 16 Mar 1955, PP.
49. Hayes to Farrell, 15 Mar 1955; Puller to Weiner and Clarke, 16 Mar 1955; Hayes to Haggerty, 18 Mar 1955; Puller to Hayes, 22 Mar 1955, PP.
50. Hayes to Farrell, 11 and 15 Mar 1955; Hayes to Puller, 25 Mar and 2 Jun 1955; Haggerty to Hayes, 16 Mar 1955, PP.
51. Puller to Hayes, 22 Mar and 4 Apr 1955; Haggerty to Hayes, 1 Jun 1955; Puller to Sherman, 15 Jun 1955, PP.
52. Puller to Upshur, 3 May 1955; Puller to Marston, 23 May 1955; Haggerty to Hayes, 1 Jun 1955; Hayes to Haggerty, 2 Jun 1955; Haggerty to Puller, 2 Jun 1955; Puller to Burke, 1 Jun 1955; Puller to Hayes and Haggerty, 7 Jun 1955; Puller to Sherman, 15 Jun 1955, PP.
53. PEB Report, p. 8; Puller to Virginia letters of 4 and 6 Jul 1955, quoted on p. 236 of a draft manuscript, BDP.
54. Puller to Virginia, 19 Jul 1955; CMC to Puller, 7 Jun 1955; Puller to Shepherd, 12 May 1955; news clipping, 13 Jul 1955, PP; Smith, personal log, 12 Jul 1955, Box 47, OPSP; Puller to Virginia letter circa mid-Jul 1955, quoted on p. 236 of a draft manuscript, BDP.
55. News clipping, 10 Oct 1955, PBF.
56. Clinical Board Report, 8 Aug 1955, PP.
57. PEB Report, pp. 10–17 and 20, PP.
58. PEB Report, pp. 23–24, PP.
59. Case Work Sheet, PEB Report; Puller to Brown, 7 Oct 1955; Vandegrift to Puller, 29 Oct 1955, PP.
60. Puller to Hayes and Haggerty, 16 Aug 1955; Puller to Farrell, 19 Aug 1955, PP; Puller to Burke, 15 Aug 1955, MR.
61. Hayes to Puller, 22 Aug 1955; Haggerty to Puller, 21 Aug and 8 Sep 1955; Puller to Sherman, 25 Aug 1955; Neville to Sen. Bible, 29 Aug 1955, PP; Lehman to CNO, 29 Aug 1955; Kennedy to Dornin, 31 Aug 1955; Bare to Lehman and Kennedy, 6 Sep 1955, PR; Burke to Puller, 25 Aug 1955, MR.
62. PRC to PEB, 22 Aug 1955; Puller to Hayes, 24 Aug 1955; Puller to Sherman, 25 Aug 1955, PP.
63. Bare to Bible, 6 Sep 1955; Puller to Sherman, 25 Aug and 16 Sep 1955; Puller to Brown, 7 Oct 1955; Puller to Vandegrift, 24 Oct 1955, PP; Bare to Kennedy and Lehman, 6 Sep 1955, PR; Hogan Memorandum, 19 Aug 1955; Hogan to Burke, 2 Sep 1955, MR.
64. Physical Disability Appeal Board Record, 2 Sep 1955, MR; Sherman to Puller, 16 Sep 1955, PP.
65. Puller's aide recalled that Chesty was referring to Litzenberg's desire for an early transfer home in April 1951. As Chesty remembered it, he had talked the regimental commander out of filing a formal request that might have ruined his career. General O. P. Smith had a different recollection—that he had restrained his ADC from giving the colonel a full dressing-down. Both versions could be accurate. Hayes to Puller, 2 Sep 1955; Sherman to Puller, 16 Sep 1955; Puller to Sherman, 22 Sep 1955; Almond to Puller, 17 Nov 1955, PP; Moore interview, 15 Oct 1999.

66. Puller had listed the recruit depots as his top two choices on his final fitness report as division commander, an indication that he and Smith had talked about that option. Sherman to Puller, 16 Sep 1955, PP; Smith to Davis, 11 Jun 1960, BDP; *Marine!,* p. 372; Shepherd Memorandum, 30 Oct 1993, Puller Papers, MCHC; Fitness Report, Sep 1954–Feb 1955, PR.
67. Puller to Brown, 7 Oct 1955; Puller to Sherman, 22 Sep 1955, PP.

Chapter 25: "Never Forget the Battles of the Past": The Golden Years, 1955–1960

1. News clippings, 10–18 Oct 1955, PBF; news clipping, 4 Nov 1955, PP.
2. CMC to Puller, 7 Oct 1955, MR; Shepherd to Puller, 10 Oct 1955, PR.
3. Vandegrift to Puller, 29 Oct 1955; Blackwell to Puller, 6 Nov 1955, PP; *Marine!,* p. 372.
4. Puller was not the only famous Marine general to leave the Corps unhappily and without ceremony. Red Mike Edson had done the same when he retired in protest against unification in 1947. CMC to Puller, 7 Oct 1955, MR; news clippings, 1 Nov 1955, PP; *Camp Lejeune Globe,* 17 Jun 1955; Smith OH, p. 326; Hoffman, *Once a Legend,* p. 380.
5. News clippings, 1 Nov 1955, PP; Moore interview, 15 Oct 1999.
6. Mother [Mrs. Evans] to Lewis, 26 Oct 1955; Puller to Mrs. Puller, 16 Jun 1964, PP; news clipping, 22 Oct 1955, PBF; Evans to Davis, 29 Jan 1962, BDP; interviews with Virginia Dabney and Martha Downs, 11 Oct 1999.
7. Certificate Required of Officers upon Retirement, [Oct 1955]; Perkins to Puller, 30 Oct 1955, PP; news clipping, 23 Nov 1960; Puller to Davis, 1 Dec 1960; excerpt of Aug 1955 letter, Puller to Mrs. Puller, draft manuscript, p. 237, BDP; Puller, *Fortunate Son,* p. 17.
8. His emphasis on providing for his family was most strongly expressed during his time in Korea. He wrote Virginia: "I haven't accomplished very much, not as much as I thought I would when you consented to marry me, or at least I have not given you the many things that I thought I would be able to." Further evidence of his feelings of financial constraints came when he was looking for a house in Richmond. He explained to one real estate agent: "Being a retired Marine officer, the price consideration must be taken into serious account." Puller would not rate full Social Security retirement benefits for another eight years, and then would receive only $65 per month. Puller to Marston, 23 May 1955; Computation and Election of Monthly Retired Pay, 7 Oct 1955; pay stub, Feb 1970; Puller to Mrs. Puller, 12 Nov 1950, PP; CMC to Puller, 15 Jul 1960, PR; Evans to Davis, 29 Jan 1962, BDP.
9. Virginia Dabney interview, 14 Oct 1998 and 11 Oct 1999; news clippings, 22 Oct 1955 and Oct [1965], PP; Puller, *Fortunate Son,* p. 17.
10. Mother to Lewis, 26 Oct 1955, PP.
11. News clippings, 1 Nov 1955 and Oct 1965; Puller to Marlboro Books, 17 Oct 1955; Shepherd to Puller, 10 Oct 1955, PP; excerpt of Aug 1955 letter, Puller to Mrs. Puller, draft manuscript, p. 237, BDP; Puller, *Fortunate Son,* p. 18; Maas, "Old Warhorse."
12. News clipping, 1 Nov 1955, PP.
13. For an excellent account of the Ribbon Creek incident and the trial, see Stevens's *Court-Martial at Parris Island.* Despite occasional small flaws (such as a reference to Puller as "just retired to his farm"), it is a thorough narrative of all that happened. Pate's quote is on page 60.

14. Stevens, *Court-Martial,* pp. 67–70.

15. Stevens, *Court-Martial,* pp. 57, 71.

16. It is certain that the defense did not select Puller to appear in court without de-
     tailed discussions beforehand to ascertain his stance. That must have entailed a
     face-to-face meeting in or near Saluda, since the New York attorney would make
     reference in court to a meeting with Mrs. Puller. According to all three Puller
     children, she remained in Saluda when Chesty went to the recruit depot. News
     clippings, 27 Jul and 13 Sep 1956, PP; *Marine!,* p. 380; Stevens, *Court-Martial,*
     pp. 92, 102, 111, 137, 140; Puller, *Fortunate Son,* p. 20; Virginia Dabney and
     Martha Downs interviews, 11 Oct 1999.

17. Stevens, *Court-Martial,* pp. 129–33.

18. News clipping, 1 Aug 1956, PP; Shaw OH, p. 316.

19. News clippings, 2–3 Aug 1956, PP; Stevens, *Court-Martial,* pp. 138–41.

20. News clippings, 3 Aug 1956, PP; *Newsweek,* 13 Aug 1956, BDP.

21. The court acted correctly in ignoring the testimony of the generals. The law offi-
     cer had mistakenly overruled the proper objections lodged by the prosecution.
     News clippings, 3–4 Aug 1956, PP; *U.S. News & World Report,* 17 Aug 1956,
     p. 8; Stevens, *Court-Martial,* pp. 132, 149–51.

22. Shaw OH, p. 315; Bem Price, "Army Eyes Tougher Training," *Wisconsin State
     Journal,* 22 Aug 195[?], clipping in PP; Simmons, *The Marines,* pp. 280–82.

23. Among the errors was a statement that Puller had landed on Guadalcanal on Au-
     gust 7, 1942. Another implied that he had enlisted in 1917 "because he was in a
     hurry to go to war." Ross Valentine, "It Takes All Kinds of Courage," [1956];
     news clippings, Jul–Aug 1956, PP.

24. News clipping, 27 Jul 1956, PP.

25. *Esquire* did only slightly better in checking its facts, although its mistakes tended
     to be less outrageous than those contained in the tabloid magazines. Maas, "Old
     Warhorse."

26. Fridell, "Chesty."

27. News clippings, 24–25 Jul 1959, PP and VMI Archives.

28. News clipping, 5 Mar 1958, VMI Archives.

29. News clipping, 5 Mar 1958, VMI Archives; Fridell, "Chesty."

30. Puller, *Fortunate Son,* pp. 22–26; Slavin, "Separate Peace."

31. CMC to PEB, 30 Nov 1959; CMC to Puller, 29 Sep 1960, PR; CMC to Puller,
     18 Jul 1960; PEB Summary, 10 Aug 1960; Judge Advocate General Memoran-
     dum, 7 Sep 1960, MR.

32. Millett, *Semper Fidelis,* pp. 543–44; Simmons, *The Marines,* p. 281; SecNav to
     Puller, 2 Jun 1960, PR.

33. Davis to Puller, 1 Jun 1960, BDP; Malley to Puller, 16 May 1960, PP.

34. Puller interview notes, BDP.

35. Davis to Pennington, 27 Jun 1960; news clipping, 23 Jun 1960; *Old Breed News,*
     Jul 1960, BDP; *Marine!,* pp. 391–93.

Chapter 26: "Return with Your Shield or on It": The Twilight Years, 1960–1971

1.   An example of the fiction in "Toughest" was that Puller was "commander of the
     4th Regiment, the famous Horse Marines, stationed in Shanghai." Scheyer to
     Puller, 20 Oct 1954; news clipping, 1 Nov 1955, PP; Frank Dunne, "Toughest
     S.O.B. in the Marines," *Real Adventure,* Jan 1957, PBF; Andersen Williams,
     "Chesty Puller: The Marine the Japs Couldn't Kill!," *Lancer,* Nov 1960, BDP.

2. Horton to Davis, 18 Apr 1961; Puller to Cushman, 1 Feb 1962; Puller to Davis, 27 Jan and 17 Mar 1960; Davis to Pullen, 16 May 1960; Smith to Davis, 25 Oct 1960; news clipping, 11 Feb 1962; "Books," Oct 1962, BDP; Stevens, *Court-Martial,* p. 75.

3. Collins to Davis, 16 Feb 1960; Davis to Jean, 27 Jul 1960; Minton to Davis, 15 Aug 1960; Davis to Barnes, 29 Sep 1960; Loomis to Davis, 7 Oct 1960, BDP; Israel to Puller, 26 Apr 1960, PP.

4. Collins to Davis, 16 Feb 1960; Collins to Puller, 5 May 1960; Davis to Spiller, 28 Jun 1960; Davis to Mrs. Puller, 30 Jun 1960; Minton to Davis, 26 Aug 1960; Little, Brown to Davis, 2 Sep 1960; Davis to Puller, 8 Sep 1960; Cushman to Puller, 18 Nov 1960; Puller to Davis, 30 Nov 1961, BDP; news clipping, 13 May 1962, PP.

5. Puller to CMC, 13 Jul 1960; CMC to Puller, 8 Aug 1960, PR; Davis to Spiller, 28 Jun 1960; Davis to Puller, 22 Jul 1960, BDP; Puller to Jeffrey, 21 Nov 1960, VMI Archives; Heinl OH, p. 100.

6. "Books," Oct 1962; Davis to Puller, 15 Nov 1960; Davis to Cushman, 8 Apr 1961, BDP; Smith to Selden, 23 Oct 1960; Selden to Smith, 5 Nov 1960, Box 19, OPSP; *Marine!,* p. ix.

7. Curtis Brown Ltd to Davis, 19 Jul 1961; Jim McAllister, "Paperbacks," [undated]; Robert Mason, "Puller: Great Fighter, Field Leader," [undated], BDP; news clippings, 18 and 24 Feb, 18 Mar, 8 Apr, 13 May, and 16 Sep 1962, PP; "The Fabulous General Chesty," *Time,* 2 Mar 1962, p. 79.

8. Marshall had based his reputation for historical accuracy on his habit of interviewing troops fresh from battle. Controversy enveloped his acknowledged prestige in the 1990s when it was revealed that he had made up some of his "facts." Marshall, "He's a Model Lt. General with Feet of Clay," *Detroit News,* 11 Feb 1962; "Slander on GIs Attacked," *Norfolk Pilot,* 16 May 1962; Puller to Davis, 7 Apr 1962, BDP; Frederic Smoler, "The Secret of the Soldiers Who Didn't Shoot," *American Heritage,* Mar 1989, p. 37.

9. Cushman to Davis, 19 Feb 1962; Hagan to Davis, 19 Feb 1962; Puller to Davis, 31 Mar 1962; news clipping, 14 Mar 1962, BDP; news clipping, 16 Feb 1962, VMI Archives; Record of Medical Care, 1 Feb 1962, MR.

10. Puller, *Fortunate Son,* pp. 28–29.

11. Fridell, "Chesty."

12. News clipping, 6 Mar 1962, PP; Hagan to Vandegrift, 7 Mar 1962, Box 6, AAVP; Puller to CMC, 21 Mar 1962, PR.

13. Smith to Hagan, 17 Mar 1962, BDP; Downing to President, 27 Mar 1962; CMC to Downing, [undated draft]; Shoup to Lann, 26 Apr 1962; CMC to Middlesex County Ruritan Club, 25 Apr 1962, PR; Downing to Puller, 10 May 1962; Hagan to Vinson, 3 Mar 1963; "2 Bills Seek Honor Medal for Puller," [May 1962]; news clipping, 15 May 1962, PP.

14. Virginia Dabney interview; Puller, *Fortunate Son,* p. 33.

15. Puller to Davis, 30 Nov 1961; Davis to Cushman, 1 Feb 1962; Ellsworth to Puller, 1 Feb 1962, BDP.

16. Davis to Puller, 27 Mar 1962; Puller to Davis, 30 Mar, 30 Apr, 30 May, 24 Jul, 3 Oct 1962 and 8 Aug and 22 Sep 1963; Collins to Davis, 10 Jul 1962; Davis to Collins, 4 Aug 1964, BDP; news clippings, 10 May 1962 and 11 May 1963, VMI Archives; news clippings, 17–18 Dec 1968, PP; news clipping, 30 May 1980, PBF.

17. News release, 7 Feb 1962; news clipping, 11 Aug 1962, PBF; news clipping, 14 Mar 1962; Puller to Davis, 22 Sep 1963, BDP; news clipping, 20 Jan 1963, VMI Archives.

18. News clipping, Oct 1965; Williams to Puller, 26 Jun 1967, PP; Godfrey to author, 14 Feb 1996; Puller, *Fortunate Son,* p. 19.

19. MacDonald to author, 20 Jan 1997; Puller to Davis, 26 Oct 1962, BDP; news clipping, 1 Nov 1962, VMI Archives.

20. News clipping, 1 Nov 1962, VMI Archives; news clipping, 2 Nov 1962, BDP.

21. News clipping, 2 Nov 1963, VMI Archives.

22. News clipping, 1 Dec 1963; Smith to Puller, 11 Feb 1964, PP.

23. News clipping, 20 Jan 1963, VMI Archives; news clipping, 11 Aug 1962, PBF.

24. News clippings, 31 Jul and 1 Aug 1964, PBF.

25. Runzer to Davison, 18 Oct 1965; news clipping, 2 Nov 1962, BDP; news clipping, 1 Nov 1962, VMI Archives.

26. No one recalled the man's punishment for absence from duty on Samoa, written evidence that would have supported Puller's version. Davis to Puller, 22 and 26 Oct 1964; Puller to Davis, 28 Oct 1964; Lawyers to Davis, 9 Sep 1965, BDP.

27. Puller suffered the added indignity of being caricatured in a Korean War novel as a bloodthirsty commander named "Guts Pusher." Hayes to Puller, 28 Sep 1965; Puller to Davis, 3 Dec 1966; Collins to Davis, 28 Oct 1964 and 14 Dec 1965; Davis to Powell, 22 Dec 1966; Plonlan to Davis, 26 May 1962, BDP; Coughlin to Puller, 13 Jan 1967, PP; Smith to West, 13 Aug 1962, Box 19, OPSP.

28. Virginia Dabney interview; Puller to Davis, 3 and 11 Feb 1964, BDP.

29. Puller to Mrs. Puller, 16 Jun 1964, PP; news clipping, *Reader's Digest,* [circa 1972].

30. Robertson to Puller, 20 May 1964, PP.

31. Puller to CMC, 14 May 1965, PR.

32. Greene to Puller, 27 May 1965, PR; news clippings, 9 Jul 1965, PP.

33. News clipping, 12 Jul 1965, PBF; letters, Jul 1965, PR.

34. Puller's most radical comments began to appear in 1966. In one interview, he castigated American forces as "barracks troops . . . who haven't fought a war in 12 years. I'd burn down every barracks and military schoolhouse in the U.S. and make them live constantly in the field." Two months later, he disparaged the enemy as a marginal opponent: "These little Viet Cong are about that high [gesturing below his shoulders] and weigh about 98 pounds. A good Marine can lick a dozen of them." In early 1968, he traced U.S. failures to the fact that none of the senior Army leaders had ever been in combat. The men in question had, in fact, distinguished themselves in heavy fighting in World War II and Korea. Simmons, *The Marines,* p. 283; Puller interview notes, BDP; news clippings, 26 Jul 1965 and 7 Jan 1968, PP; news clippings, 23 Sep, 12 Oct, and 13 Nov 1966, VMI Archives.

35. Virginia Dabney interview.

36. Puller, *Fortunate Son,* pp. 30–40; Biographical Summary, Puller Jr. Bio File, MCHC; Mitchell, "Is Toughness Necessary?"

37. Lewis Jr. would mistakenly recall that the Tet Offensive began several weeks after he started Basic School. His official records place the completion of his OCS stint and the beginning of TBS on February 1, 1968. Puller, *Fortunate Son,* pp. 45, 47.

38. Puller, *Fortunate Son,* p. 53.

39. Puller, *Fortunate Son,* p. 55; Admission Report, 2 May 1968, MR; Wilson to Puller, 14 Dec 1967, PP; news clippings, 10 May and 15 Aug 1968, VMI Archives; Virginia Dabney interview.

40. In a 1956 interview, Puller mentioned that he was raising his ten-year-old son on the Spartan parable. Puller, *Fortunate Son,* p. 59; news clipping, 15 Aug 1968, VMI Archives; Mitchell, "Is Toughness Necessary?"

41. *Fortunate Son,* pp. 125, 156–57.

42. The dramatic story of the severe wounding of a hero's son would attract considerable media attention. In at least one case, it brought forth pure fiction. A week after the event, a nationally syndicated story described the writer's alleged meeting with Chesty in 1945. Among the inventions was the touching tale of Major General Puller heading home to see his son for the first time, since the boy had been born while he was off fighting in the Pacific. Silver Star citation; news clippings, 16 Oct 1968, Puller Jr. Bio File; *Fortunate Son,* p. 159; news clipping, [Oct 1968], VMI Archives.

43. News clippings, 16 Oct 1968; Memos for the Record, 16 and 18 Oct 1968; Biographical Data, Puller Jr. Bio File; Puller, *Fortunate Son,* p. 161.

44. Puller, *Fortunate Son,* p. 162.

45. Virginia Dabney and Martha Downs interviews, 11 Oct 1999; Slavin, "A Separate Peace"; Puller, *Fortunate Son,* p. 239.

46. Virginia Dabney interview; Puller, *Fortunate Son,* p. 175.

47. Puller, *Fortunate Son,* pp. 196, 202.

48. News clippings, 14 Oct 1970, VMI Archives; Medical Status Report, 29 Sep 1971; Report of Death, 15 Oct 1971, PR; Puller, *Fortunate Son,* pp. 239–41, 256–57, 268–69.

Epilogue

1. Among the common errors in the obituaries were statements that Puller saved the two women in Australia in the 1930s even though "he couldn't swim a stroke"; that he had received a dozen wounds in his career; that he had led the 1st Marines out of the Chosin Reservoir "trailed by the shattered remnants of less-favored regiments." One error would have upset Chesty the most—the oft-repeated assertion that he had never commanded a division in combat. A writer with no apparent knowledge of history stated that Puller's idol was Andrew Jackson! As for the title of "most decorated," comparisons of decorations are misleading because there is no way to weight the value of different medals. A number of Marines have more awards than Puller, particularly in the aviation field due to the Air Medal. Others have one or more Medals of Honor in addition to the Navy Cross. Chesty remains, however, the only Marine ever to receive five Navy Crosses. News clippings, letter, and telegrams, PBF and PP; Burchard, "Marine Gen. 'Chesty' Puller," *Washington Post,* 12 Oct 1971; Burke to Davis, 21 Nov 1971, BDP.

2. "Chesty's Last Beachhead," *Washington Evening Star,* 13 Oct 1971, PBF.

Bibliography

Books

Alexander, Joseph H., and Merrill L. Bartlett. *Sea Soldiers in the Cold War.* Annapolis: Naval Institute, 1995.

Appleman, LtCol Roy E., AUS(Ret). *East of Chosin.* College Station: Texas A&M University Press, 1991.

————. *Escaping the Trap.* College Station: Texas A&M University Press, 1990.

Bartley, LtCol Whitman S. *Iwo Jima: Amphibious Epic.* Washington: USMC, 1961.

Bergerud, Eric. *Touched with Fire.* New York: Viking, 1996.

Blackford, Susan Leigh, comp. *Letters from Lee's Army.* New York: Scribner's, 1947.

Bradley, Gen Omar N. *A Soldier's Story.* New York: Henry Holt, 1951.

Brock, Dr. R. A. *Virginia and Virginians.* Vol. II. Spartanburg, SC: The Reprint Company, 1973.

Brown, Stuart E., Jr., and Anne Barton Brown. *Carter Hall.* Berryville, VA: Virginia Book Co., 1978.

Buckner, Maj David N. *A Brief History of the 10th Marines.* Washington: USMC, 1981.

Calixte, Col Demosthenes P. *Haiti: The Calvary of a Soldier.* New York: Negro University Press, 1969.

Callwell, Col C. E. *Small Wars: Their Principles and Practice.* London: Harrison and Sons, 1906.

Chihaya, Masataka, trans. *Fading Victory: The Diary of Admiral Matome Ugaki.* Pittsburgh: University of Pittsburgh Press, 1991.

Condit, Kenneth W., Gerald Diamond, and Edwin T. Turnbladh. *Marine Corps Ground Training in World War II.* Washington: USMC, 1956. Manuscript version in MCHC Library.

Confederate Military History: Extended Edition. Vol. IV, *Virginia.* Wilmington, NC: Broadfoot Publishing, 1987.

Cooling, Benjamin F., ed. *Case Studies in the Development of Close Air Support.* Washington: U.S. Air Force, 1990.

Cowart, Glenn C. *Miracle in Korea.* Columbia, SC: University of South Carolina Press, 1992.

Cox, Virginia D., and Willie T. Weathers. *Old Houses of King and Queen County.* Walkerton, VA: King and Queen County Historical Society, 1973.

Cray, Ed. *General of the Army: George C. Marshall.* New York: Norton, 1990.

Davis, Burke. *Marine!* Boston: Little, Brown, 1962.

Davis, Gen Ray, and Col William J. Davis. *The Story of Ray Davis: MOH.* Fuquay-Varina, NC: Research Triangle Publishing, 1995.

Davis, Col William J. *Chesty Puller's Rules of Success.* San Diego: Marine Books, 1995.

D'Este, Carlo. *Patton: A Genius for War.* New York: HarperCollins, 1995.

Driver, Robert J., Jr. *5th Virginia Cavalry.* Lynchburg, VA: H. E. Howard, 1997.

Dupuy, R. Ernest, and Trevor N. Dupuy. *The Encyclopedia of Military History.* New York: Harper & Row, 1986.

Durkin, Joseph T., ed. *John Dooley, Confederate Soldier: His War Journal.* Washington: Georgetown, 1945.

Fehrenbach, T. R. *This Kind of War.* Washington: Brassey's, 1994.

The 4th Marines and Soochow Creek. Bennington, VT: Intl Graphics, 1980.

Frank, Richard B. *Guadalcanal.* New York: Random House, 1990.

Freeman, Douglas Southall. *Lee's Lieutenants.* New York: Scribner's, 1943.

Gailey, Harry A. *Peleliu: 1944.* Annapolis: Nautical & Aviation Publishing, 1983.

Garand, George W., and Truman R. Strobridge. *Western Pacific Operations.* Washington: USMC, 1971.

Gayle, BGen Gordon D. *Bloody Beaches: The Marines at Peleliu.* Washington: USMC, 1996.

Geer, Andrew. *The New Breed: The Story of the U.S. Marines in Korea.* New York: Harper & Brothers, 1952.

Gilliland, Ann Owens. *Peleliu Remembered.* Fort Worth, TX: Booker Publications, 1994.

Gilmor, Harry. *Four Years in the Saddle.* New York: Harper's, 1866.

Giusti, Ernest H. *Mobilization of the Marine Corps Reserve in the Korean Conflict, 1950–1951.* Washington: USMC, 1951.

Greenwood, C. I. *Once Upon a Lifetime.* Springfield, IL: Tomahawk Publishing, 1989.

Griffith, BGen Samuel B., II. *The Battle for Guadalcanal.* Annapolis: Nautical & Aviation Publishing, 1979.

Haden, B. J. *J.E.B. Stuart's Cavalry.* Charlottesville, VA: News Printing, 1900s.

Heinl, Robert Debs, Jr. *Soldiers of the Sea.* Annapolis: Naval Institute, 1962.

———. *Victory at High Tide.* Philadelphia: Lippincott, 1968.

Henderson, Col G.F.R. *Stonewall Jackson and the American Civil War.* New York: Longman's Green, 1937.

Hoffman, Jon T. *Once a Legend: "Red Mike" Edson of the Marine Raiders.* Novato, CA: Presidio Press, 1994.

Hough, Maj Frank O. *The Assault on Peleliu.* Washington: USMC, 1950.

Hough, LtCol Frank O., and Maj John A. Crown. *The Campaign on New Britain.* Washington: USMC, 1952.

Howe, George W., comp. and ed. *Tales By "a few good" Marines,* Fredericksburg, VA: American History Company, 1992.

Hunt, Capt George P. *Coral Comes High.* New York: Harper & Brothers, 1946.

Jacques, SgtMaj Maurice J., and Maj Bruce H. Norton. *Sergeant Major, USMC.* New York: Ivy Books, 1995.

Kenney, Gen George C. *General Kenney Reports.* Washington: U.S. Air Force, 1987.

Krick, Robert K. *Lee's Colonels.* Dayton, OH: Morningside, 1991.

Leckie, Robert. *Strong Men Armed.* New York: Random House, 1962.

Lejeune, MajGen John A. *The Reminiscences of a Marine.* Philadelphia: Dorrance, 1930.

McClellan, H. B. *The Life and Campaigns of Major General J.E.B. Stuart,* Boston: Houghton Mifflin, 1885.

McCrocklin, James H. *Garde d'Haiti.* Annapolis: Naval Institute, 1955.

McMillan, George. *The Old Breed.* Washington: Infantry Journal Press, 1949.

McPherson, James M. *Battle Cry of Freedom.* New York: Oxford University Press, 1988.

Meid, LtCol Pat, and Maj James M. Yingling. *U.S. Marine Corps Operations in Korea: Operations in West Korea.* Washington: USMC, 1972.

Merillat, Herbert C. *Guadalcanal Remembered.* New York: Dodd, Mead, 1982.

Mersky, Peter B. *U.S. Marine Corps Aviation: 1912 to the Present.* Baltimore: Nautical & Aviation Publishing, 1983.

Miller, John, Jr. *Cartwheel: The Reduction of Rabaul.* Washington: U.S. Army, 1959.

———. *Guadalcanal.* Washington: U.S. Army, 1989.

Millett, Allan R. *In Many a Strife.* Annapolis: Naval Institute, 1993.

———. *Semper Fidelis: The History of the United States Marine Corps.* New York: The Free Press, 1982.

Montague, Ludwell L. *Gloucester County in the Civil War.* Gloucester, VA: deHardit Press, 1965.

Montross, Lynn, and Capt Nicholas A. Canzona. *U.S. Marine Corps Operations in Korea: The Chosin Reservoir Campaign.* Washington: USMC, 1957.

———. *U.S. Marine Corps Operation in Korea: The Inchon-Seoul Operation.* Washington: USMC, 1955.

———. *U.S. Marine Corps Operations in Korea: The Pusan Perimeter.* Washington: USMC, 1954.

Montross, Lynn, Maj Hubard D. Kuokka, and Maj Norman W. Hicks. *U.S. Marine Corps Operations in Korea: The East-Central Front.* Washington: USMC, 1962.

Moore, Bishop Paul. *Presences.* New York: Farrar, Straus & Giroux, 1997.

Morison, Samuel E. *History of United States Naval Operations in World War II.* Vol. III. Boston: Little, Brown, 1988.

Morris, Richard B., ed. *Encyclopedia of American History.* New York: Harper & Row, 1976.

Moskin, J. Robert. *The U.S. Marine Corps Story.* New York: McGraw-Hill, 1982.

Musicant, Ivan. *The Banana Wars.* New York: Macmillan, 1990.

Nalty, Bernard C. *A Brief History of U.S. Marine Corps Officer Procurement.* Washington: USMC, 1970.

———. *The Right to Fight: African-American Marines in World War II.* Washington: USMC, 1995.

Nichols, Maj Charles S., Jr., and Henry I. Shaw, Jr. *Okinawa: Victory in the Pacific.* Washington: USMC, 1955.

Owen, Joseph R. *Colder Than Hell: A Marine Rifle Company at Chosin Reservoir.* Annapolis: Naval Institute, 1996.

Parry, Col Francis F. *Three-War Marine.* Pacific, CA: Pacifica Press, 1987.

Perret, Geoffrey. *Old Soldiers Never Die.* New York: Random House, 1996.

———. *There's a War to Be Won.* New York: Random House, 1991.

Peterson, Capt Bernard W., USMCR(Ret). *Short Straw: Memoirs of Korea.* Scottsdale, AZ: Chuckwalla, 1996.

Pogue, Forrest C. *George C. Marshall: Organizer of Victory.* New York: Viking, 1973.

Potter, E. B. *Nimitz.* Annapolis: Naval Institute, 1976.

Pratt, Fletcher. *The Marines' War.* New York: William Sloane, 1948.

Pugh, Adm Herbert Lamont. *Navy Surgeon.* Philadelphia: Lippincott, 1959.

Puller, Lewis B., Jr. *Fortunate Son.* New York: Grove Weidenfeld, 1991.

Reeder, LtCol Russell P., Jr. *Fighting on Guadalcanal.* Washington: GPO, 1943.

Ridgway, Gen Matthew B. *Soldier: The Memoirs of Matthew B. Ridgway.* New York: Harper & Brothers, 1956.

Roe, Patrick C. *The Dragon Strikes: China and the Korean War.* Novato, CA: Presidio Press, 2000.

Roskill, Stephen. *Naval Policy Between the Wars.* London: Collins, 1976.

Ross, Bill D. *Peleliu: Tragic Triumph.* New York: Random House, 1991.

Schroeder, Michael J. *"To Defend Our Nation's Honor": Toward a Social and Cultural History of the Sandino Rebellion in Nicaragua, 1927–1934.* Ann Arbor, MI: University Microfilms International, 1997.

Scott, Robert N. *The War of the Rebellion: A Compilation of the Official Records of the Union and Confederate Armies.* Series I, Vol. XXV, Part I. Washington: GPO, 1889.

Shaw, Henry I., Jr. *Central Pacific Drive.* Washington: USMC, 1966.

Shaw, Henry I., Jr., and Maj Douglas T. Kane. *Isolation of Rabaul.* Washington: USMC, 1963.

Sherrod, Robert. *History of Marine Corps Aviation in World War II.* Washington: Combat Forces Press, 1952.

Shulimson, Jack. *The Marine Corps' Search for a Mission.* Lawrence, KS: University Press of Kansas, 1993.

Simmons, Edwin H., and J. Robert Moskin, ed. *The Marines.* Quantico, VA: Marine Corps Heritage Foundation, 1998.

Smith, Gen Holland M. *Coral and Brass.* New York: Scribner's, 1949.

Smith, Maj Julian C. *A Review of the Organization and Operations of the Guardia Nacional de Nicaragua.* Washington: USMC, circa 1937.

Smith, Nellie S., comp. *Reminiscences, Confederate Soldiers of Gloucester County, Virginia.* Gloucester, VA: UDC, 1998.

Smith, Robert E. *A Marine in World War II.* Davenport, IA: Stevens Publishing, 1993.

Smith, S. E., ed. *The U.S. Marine Corps in World War II.* New York: Random House, 1969.

Stannard, BGen John E. *The Battle of Coffin Corner.* Self-published.

Stanton, Shelby. *America's Tenth Legion.* Novato, CA: Presidio Press, 1989.

Stavisky, Samuel E. *Marine Combat Correspondent.* New York: Ivy Books, 1999.

Stevens, John C., III. *Court-Martial at Parris Island.* Annapolis: Naval Institute, 1999.

Turner, Martha. *The World of Col. John W. Thomason.* Austin, TX: Eakin Press, 1984.

Twining, Gen Merrill B. *No Bended Knee.* Novato, CA: Presidio Press, 1996.

U.S. Marine Corps. *Small Wars Manual.* Washington: USMC, 1940.

Vandegrift, Gen Alexander A. *Once a Marine.* New York: W.W. Norton, 1964.

Ware, W. H. *The Battle of Kelly's Ford.* Newport News, VA: Warwick, 1922.

Watkins, R. Bruce. *Brothers in Battle.* Excerpted on the World Wide Web.

Wayland, John W. *A History of Shenandoah County, Virginia.* Strasburg, VA: Shenandoah Publishing, 1927.

Wiatt, Alex L. *Confederate Chaplain, William Edward Wiatt: An Annotated Diary.* Lynchburg, VA: Howard, 1994.

Zimmerman, Maj John L. *The Guadalcanal Campaign.* Washington: USMC, 1949.

Periodicals

Bartlett, Tom. "Living with a Legend." *Leatherneck,* Jun 1985, p. 18.

Craig, Edward A. "Field Notes" and "Incidents of Service." *Military History Journal of the Pacific,* Winter 1997–1998, p. 3.

Elliott, Frank. "Chesty's Driver." *Leatherneck,* Nov 1982, p. 34.

Fridell, Guy. "Gen. 'Chesty' Puller." *Richmond News Leader,* 12 Nov 1958.

Frost, O. "His Beat Is the World." *New Orleans Times-Picayune,* 10 Nov 1946. Copy in BDP.

Maas, Peter. "Waste of an Old Warhorse." *Esquire,* Jan 1958.

Martin, Harold H. "Toughest Marine in the Corps." *Saturday Evening Post,* 22 Mar 1952.

O'Leary, J. A., Jr. "Chesty Puller." *Washington Star,* 10 Oct 1955.

Roberts, Sgt Nolle T. "Chesty Puller." *Leatherneck,* Jun 1948, p. 10.

Yu, Bin. "What China Learned from Its 'Forgotten War' in Korea." *Strategic Review,* Summer 1998, p. 4.

Personal Papers

Andow, A. Andy, MCRC.

Clemens, Martin, MCHC.

Davis, Burke, University of North Carolina at Chapel Hill (BDP).

Denig, BGen Robert L., MCHC.

Edson, MajGen Merritt A., Library of Congress (MAEP).

Evans, BGen R. A., MCHC.

Forney, E. H., MCHC.

Griffith, Capt Robert H., MCHC.

Hammel, Eric, MCHC (HP).

Koch, Capt William C., MCHC.

McQueen, John C., MCHC.

Pierce, Bill, MCHC.

Pullen, Thomas G., MCHC.

Puller, Lewis B., MCRC (PP) and MCHC.

Quirk, James T., HSTL.

Reynolds, Irv, MCHC.

Russell, Clem, MCRC.

Simmons, BGen Edwin H., MCHC (SP).

Sims, Amor L., MCHC.

Smith, Gen Julian C., MCHC (JCSP).

Smith, Gen Oliver P., MCRC (OPSP).

Smolka, John J., MCHC.

Thomas, Gen Gerald C., possession of Col Gerald C. Thomas, Jr.

Vogel, Clayton B., MCHC.

Oral Histories

Bauernschmidt, RAdm George W., 1970, NHC.

Bowser, LtGen Alpha L., 1970, MCHC.

Buster, Ivan L., 1992, MCHC.

Cooley, LtGen Albert D., 1967, MCHC.

Craig, LtGen Edward A., 1968, MCHC.

Davis, Gen Raymond G., 1978, MCHC.

Deakin, BGen Harold O., 1973, MCHC.

Erskine, Gen Graves B., 1975, MCHC.

Farrell, MajGen Walter G., 1967, MCHC.

Fields, LtGen Lewis J., 1976, MCHC.

Good, LtGen George F., 1974, MCHC.

Hart, MajGen John N., 1970, MCHC.

Heinl, Col Robert D., Jr., 1972, MCHC.

Henderson, BGen Frederick P., 1976, MCHC.

Hittle, BGen James D., 1970, MCHC.

Hogaboom, Gen Robert E., 1972, MCHC.

Honsowetz, Col Russell, circa 1972, MCHC.

Honsowetz, Col Russell, taped interview by J. Nicholas Russo, 1995.

Jones, Capt Glyn, 1977, NHC.

Jordahl, BGen Russell N., 1973, MCHC.

Kyle, MajGen Wood B., 1977, MCHC.

Lawrence, BGen James F., 1978, MCHC.

Leonard, Col John P., Jr., 1983, MCHC.

Leverton, RAdm J. Wilson, Jr., 1969, NHC.

Masters, LtGen James M., 1981, MCHC.

McLaughlin, LtGen John N., 1980, MCHC.

Merrill, Dr. John E., 1979, MCHC.

Moncure, Capt Sam P., 1969, NHC.

Mustin, VAdm Lloyd M., 1970, NHC.

Negri, Col Peter J., 1974, MCHC.

Nickerson, LtGen Herman, Jr., 1980, MCHC.

Pope, Maj Everett P. (untranscribed), 1996, MCHC.

Robertson, LtGen Donn J., 1978, MCHC.

Rosenthal, Joe S., 1975, MCHC.

Rossell, Col Joseph A., 1967, MCHC.

Silverthorn, LtGen Merwin H., 1973, MCHC.

Smith, LtGen Julian, 1973, MCHC.

Smith, Gen Oliver P., 1973, MCHC.

Smoot, VAdm Roland N., 1972, NHC.

Snedeker, LtGen Edward W., 1973, MCHC.

Stewart, BGen Joseph L., 1973, MCHC.

Thomas, Gen Gerald C., 1973, MCHC.

Twining, Gen Merrill B., 1975, MCHC.

Vandegrift, Gen Alexander A., 1962, MCHC.

Wismer, Col Ralph M., 1979, MCHC.

Woods, LtGen Louis E., 1968, MCHC.

Worton, MajGen W. A., 1969, MCHC.

Other Material

"Peleliu—The Unknown Battle," unpublished transcript of historical symposium conducted by Marine Corps League detachment, Las Cruces, New Mexico, 4 Nov 1989. Copy in possession of author.

Index

Within entries for Marine Corps units,
unit designations are indicated in **bold.**

A

Aberdeen Proving Ground, 215
Adams, Maj Henry J., Jr., 258
Air Medal, 449
Almond, MajGen Edward M.:
    Inchon-Seoul, 329–330, 349, 354,
        359, 361–362, 416, 433
    Chosin, 370, 375, 377–378, 386,
        388–389, 396, 402
Altamirano, Pedro, 65–66, 69, 72,
    76, 79, 93
Aogiri Ridge battle, 240–242, 244
    see also Walt's Ridge
Associated Press, 442
Atlantic Fleet Exercise 1-55, *see*
    LANTFLEX
Aubuchon, Lt John J., 261
Augusta (CA-31), 108–113, 122,
    123–124, 165, 169
Australian–New Guinea
    Administrative Unit, 246
Aux Cayes, Haiti, 33–33, 35–36, 38

B

Bailey, Maj Kenneth D., 163
Baldwin, Hanson W., 415
Ballard (AVD-10), 164

Barba, Maj William H., 246
Barber, Capt William, 397
Barnett, MajGen George, 3–4
Barrow, Capt Robert H., 331, 342,
    346, 350, 352–354, 360
    Majon-ni, 378–379
    Chosin, 380, 394, 409
    guerrilla hunt, 418, 421
Basic School:
    Puller as student, 49–51
    Puller as instructor, 114–122
    later connection with, 222, 229,
        241, 253, 322, 331, 450, 490
    Lewis Jr. as student, 531
Basilone, Sgt John, 189, 194
Batraville, Benoit, 27, 33, 39
Beall, LtCol Olin L., 397, 402
Beasley, Capt Charles J., 182, 208
Bell, Dr. Robert, 482–484
Berger, LtCol Spencer S., 277,
    281–284, 286
Berman, Emile Zola, 505–507, 509,
    517
Bethesda Naval Hospital, 483–484,
    486–487, 492, 494–495, 502
Bishop, Jim, 517
Bland, Capt Richard F., 351–352
Blake, Col Robert, 137
Bodey, Sgt Jan, 335
Both (USAT), 226

N

Q

R

About the Author

LtCol Jon T. Hoffman, USMCR, has spent his entire career as an infantry officer and military historian. He is presently serving as the deputy director of the Marine Corps History and Museums Division. He has a bachelor's degree from Miami University (Ohio), a law degree from Duke University, and a master's degree in military history from Ohio State University. Hoffman's previous book, *Once a Legend: "Red Mike" Edson of the Marine Raiders,* received the Marine Corps Heritage Foundation's 1994 Greene Award. His numerous articles in professional military journals have earned him a variety of other writing honors. A native of Fremont, Ohio, he now resides in northern Virginia.

About the Type

This book was set in Times New Roman, designed by Stanley Morison specifically for *The Times* of London. The typeface was introduced in the newspaper in 1932. Times New Roman has had its greatest success in the United States as a book and commercial typeface rather than one used in newspapers.